JEWISH
HOLIDAY COOKING

A FOOD LOVER'S TREASURY OF CLASSICS *and* IMPROVISATIONS

JEWISH
HOLIDAY COOKING

Jayne Cohen

WILEY

JOHN WILEY AND SONS, INC.

Published by John Wiley & Sons, Inc., Hoboken, New Jersey
Published simultaneously in Canada

Cover photography by Ben Fink
Cover prop styling by Mary-Ellen Weinrib
Cover food styling by Alison Attenborough

The following recipes have been adapted from recipes previously published by the author in *Bon Appetit,*
April 2002: Smoked Whitefish Gefilte Fish with Lemon-Horseradish Sauce, Moroccan-Flavored Brisket
with Dried Apricots and Prunes, Salad of Bitter Herbs and Oranges, and Potato-Leek Matzoh Balls; in
Bon Appetit, December 2001: Mediterranean Chickpea Latkes, Herbed Spinach Latkes with Feta-Yogurt
Sauce, and Walnut-Cherry-Cheese Latkes with Chunky Cherry Applesauce; in *Food and Wine,* April
2000: Tangy Haroset Bites, Artichoke Soup with Light Herbed Matzoh Balls, Slow-Braised Brisket with
Rosemary, Shallots, and Red Wine; and in *Gourmet,* September 1993: Leek Croquettes from Rhodes,
Egyptian Ground Fish Balls with Tomato and Cumin, Pumpkin and Sweet Potato Soup with Sweet
Potato Knaidlach, Syrian Apricot-Stuffed Meat Rolls with Tart-Sweet Cherry Sauce, Egyptian Black-
Eyed Peas with Cilantro, and Hungarian Plum Tart.

For general information on our other products and services or for technical support, please contact our
Customer Care Department within the United States at (800) 762-2974, outside the United States at
(317) 572-3993 or fax (317) 572-4002.

Wiley also publishes its books in a variety of electronic formats. Some content that appears in print may
not be available in electronic books. For more information about Wiley products, visit our web site at
www.wiley.com.

LIBRARY OF CONGRESS CATALOGING-IN-PUBLICATION DATA

Cohen, Jayne.
  Jewish holiday cooking : a food lover's classics and improvisations / Jayne Cohen.
    p. cm.
  Includes bibliographical references.
  ISBN: 978-0-471-76387-1 (cloth)
   1. Cookery, Jewish.   2. Fasts and feasts—Judaism.   3. Holiday cookery.   I. Title.
  TX724.C546 2007
  641.5'676--dc22

                              2006027612

PRINTED IN THE UNITED STATES OF AMERICA

10 9 8 7 6 5 4 3 2 1

Once again, to the memory of my parents,
Joan and Max Cohen, who taught me how
to celebrate at the banquet of life

And to

Howie and Alex, for celebrating joyously there with me

ACKNOWLEDGMENTS

I am privileged to have extraordinary agents and generous friends, Elise and Arnold Goodman. They have been there for me from day one, fifteen years ago, when Elise first contacted me after reading a Rosh Hashanah article that I wrote for *Gourmet*, saying she was sure I was nursing "an idea for a book." Simply stated, without them, this book would not be. I cherish their affection, unwavering support, and faith in me and aspire to always live up to their high standards.

From the first day we met, my editor, Pam Chirls, had a keen, clear-eyed vision that would shape the work into the beautiful cookbook it was meant to be. Many thanks also to the rest of the talented group at Wiley who helped make the book come to life: Natalie Chapman, publisher; and Pam's hard-working team, Christine DiComo, assistant editor, and Christina Solazzo, senior editorial assistant. I am very grateful to production manager Leslie Anglin, who started the project, and to production editor Amy Zarkos, who completed it with such skillful attention to detail; to copyeditor Suzanne Fass and North Market Street Graphics for all their careful work; and to proofreader Elizabeth Marotta. Special thanks to the gifted Alison Lew of Vertigo Design for her splendid interior designs and layouts and for gracefully incorporating my treasured family photographs. Heartfelt gratitude to publicist

Gypsy Lovett for always working so hard and so cheerfully to get the word out.

Deepest appreciation to cookbook author and food photographer extraordinaire, James Peterson, who, ably assisted by Alice Piacenza, passionately translated my food into superb photos for the cover. I owe a special debt of gratitude to dear friend, Claudia Sidoti, who prepared and styled mouthwatering photo recipes with that extra ingredient—love. And many, many thanks to Suzanne Sunwoo for creating a cover that is a thing of beauty.

Jewish Holiday Cooking had its genesis in my first book, *The Gefilte Variations*, and I owe a great deal to Maria Guarnaschelli and all the others who made that work possible and taught me so much. And I'd particularly like to thank the readers of that book who shared my passion and inspired me to begin this project and see it through, even when I thought I could not swallow one more matzoh ball.

I turned to many people while working—and eating—my way through this book. To paraphrase Ecclesiastes, there are no new recipes under the sun. The infinite world of Jewish cuisine and traditions from which I borrowed freely has been over five thousand years in the making, and I owe an enormous debt to those who have shared their heirloom recipes and brought their traditions alive as well as those who opened the doors and orchestrated meetings with them. In addition to the people I mention in the text, I would particularly like to thank Anna (Kuki) Ben-David, Romiel Daniel, Jessica Dell'Era, Honorable Sukru Elekdag, Farhad Eshaghpour, Arnold Kaye, Larry Kaye, Tammy Koppel, Georgie London, Moris Roso, Amiel Rossabi, Leyla Schick, my cousin Jackie, the Honorable Jacqueline Silbermann, and Julie Visnogradsky and family. In Italy, Lia Hassan, Tina Ottolenghi, Ester Silvana Israel, and Rafi D'Angeli and in Paris, Arlette and Claude Lustyk generously shared glimpses of their Jewish worlds. Many thanks to Giorgio Scattolin, Segretario Generale della Biblioteca Internazionale "La Vigna" in Vicenza, Italy, for all his help poring through books on Italian-Jewish cooking. And I am immensely grateful to the hundreds of Jewish cookbook writers who have preceded me. I list just a small sample in the bibliography.

My profound thanks to Rabbi Yoel Schonfeld and Rabbi Chaim Wakslak and his wife, Rivka Wakslak, who provided invaluable information on kashrut.

Eleanor Yadin was always so helpful to my research during the innumerable hours I spent at the Dorot Jewish Division at the New York Public Library.

In the food world, warmest thanks to Grace Young and Damon Fowler for their support, advice, and friendship. And I want to specially thank Kristine Kidd, of *Bon Appetit* magazine, and Ronnie Friedland, of Interfaithfamily.com, for always encouraging my work.

A thousand thanks to the incomparable farmers of the Union Square Greenmarket for providing me with such fabulous ingredients to start with.

Dear friends generously volunteered to test recipes for me: Vivian Ellner, Jesse Theobald-Ellner, and Suzan Zoukis, and especially Dr. Mary McLarnon, who worked patiently and graciously until she had perfected all the challahs, and Maria Springer, for taking time to answer every question and shepherding me through the Passover fruit tortes.

I am grateful as always to the indefatigable Mary Koneval. Warm thanks for the special efforts of Erika Jakubovits, Tony Kaufmann, and Dr. Lucille A. Roussin. Profound gratitude to Patti Burris who made that memorable visit to the synagogue in Casale Monferrato happen, and to Don Burris, for working as my personal Los Angeles public relations firm when he isn't practicing law. And I cannot forget Chris Wong, for his endearingly gentle criticism and spirited enthusiasm, whether tasting yet another dish or cheerfully offering to clean up afterward.

I am blessed with wonderful friends: Lilyan Aloma, who photographed me for the book jacket, and Ed Kabak, Susan Dwyer Metzger, and Christina Sidoti, who have enriched this book with their imagination and professional expertise. My adored niece and nephew, Arielle and Jake Schindelheim, always offered wise counsel and support.

Among the most precious gifts my parents gave us was a close and loving bond to family. Throughout the inevitable childhood sibling bickering, I remember my mother and father always working to patch things up and settle our differences. It paid off: my sister and brother continue to be such an integral part of my life. Sami Schindelheim has not only been my sounding board and enthusiastic cheerleader, but she has also tirelessly sought out recipes and information for me through her exceptional network of family and friends in the Orthodox community. Steven Cohen always had a ready ear for my kvetching, an appetite for my latest experiment, and willing hands to scrub the pots.

Husband, best friend, soulmate—no words adequately describe Howard Spiegler. Despite the demands of his hectic law practice, he always found time to hear a new paragraph, taste one more bite of brisket, or trumpet my latest article or book in an email to every member of his firm. Warmed by his love, it is easy for me to celebrate and share delicious memories around our table with family and friends.

Alex, my darling daughter, my spiritual muse, inspired me to revisit worlds I had left behind and explore new ones to create vivid new traditions to nourish her. Born with an eager but exacting palate, wise judgment, ferocious energy, and a generous heart, she has been invaluable to me during the many years this project has taken. *Jewish Holiday Cooking* is for her—and for all those who, like her, will be celebrating with friends and family all the holidays to come.

And many thanks to my cherished in-laws, the whole Stein family; my treasured Schindelheim family; all my wonderful cousins: Adrienne Suffin, the Robinsons, the Paloffs, the Bennetts, the Bernsteins, the Cohens, and the Kaufmans; close friends, Lilyan Aloma and Philip Meskin, David Cabassa, Anna Teresa and the late Harold Callen, D'ror Chankin-Gould, Arnie Kaye, Emily Kaye, Trudy Smoke and Alan Robbins, Carole Sorell and Richard Altman, and the Compton/Lee, Delson/Ginsburg, Metzger, Sidoti/Einhorn, Brown, and Warrington families, and all my other beloved, intrepid tasters.

Pantry and Procedures

Sabbath

Rosh Hashanah

Breaking the Yom Kippur Fast

Sukkot

Hanukkah

Purim

Passover

Shavuot

INTRODUCTION

y father put two freshly roasted ducks on the table and poured a soft red wine.

My sister and I, twentysomethings at the time, had come home for Passover, but this was not our seder. It was a midnight "snack" to sustain us as we cooked late into the night. We were trying to create the taste of Passover without my grandmother, who had died that winter.

We were a family who cooked together, much as other families ski or play football. Even when we couldn't agree on anything else, everyone—mother, father, sister, brother, and I—performed in balletic synchronicity in the kitchen and later at the table.

But we prepared splendid Italian suppers, lavish seafood feasts, not the Ashkenazi cooking of my grandmothers. Except for my mother's briskets and the occasional chicken soup she fussed over during *Late, Late Show* commercials while awaiting my father's return from a gin game, we usually ate hard-core Jewish food only when my maternal grandmother stayed at our house for the holidays.

Grandma's rustic chopped liver, matzoh balls, and especially the chopped hard-boiled eggs she mixed with sautéed and raw onions (my family's customary stand-in for the traditional hard-boiled eggs dipped in salt water that begins most Ashkenazi seder meals) were part of the timeless holiday ritual. We had never thought to copy down her recipes. Doesn't timeless mean forever?

That first Passover without my grandmother we shared a secret suspicion that allowing her foods to vanish from our table meant losing something much greater and more vital. And we could not bear another loss.

We could not imitate her cooking. In my family, we like to *potchkeh* or play with our recipes. We read cookbooks for inspiration, not instruction. And wasn't Jewish food meant to be potchkehed with? Jews are constantly encouraged to question and reinterpret the accepted, as no one who has read the Passover Haggadah can forget. There, the learned rabbis argue over the number of plagues God visited on the Egyptians. Not just ten, but ten times ten—the number of fingers on God's hands. No, argues another sage, that number to the tenth power. Among Jews there is always yet another way to see things.

So we decided to make foods familiar enough to taste like Passover, yet still be fresh and inventive. Dishes reimagined so that they reflected our changing palates and insatiable culinary curiosity.

Just as my father brought to life the story of the Hebrews' liberation from slavery and exodus from Egypt with modern parallels of oppression, we updated and renewed the wonderful Passover foods so they remained vivid and meaningful, the ritual never stale.

That night, when we divided the foods to be cooked among us, I volunteered for the matzoh balls. While TV grandmothers pop fresh chocolate chip cookies into the oven, my little grandma had always whipped up an extra batch of golf ball–sized matzoh balls for me to nibble as I readied the plate of special ceremonial foods used in telling the Passover story.

I read the recipe on the matzoh meal box and experimented with a few variations, perfuming the dumplings with wild onions and sassy spring herbs. And kept on experimenting.

Every year since then, the special festival dishes have become more important to me. Cuisine connects us to our past, and encoded in our recipes are our family stories and history, a reminder of those whom we have lost and traditions that remain fragile. Rereading this book, I am struck by how many holiday foods are linked to family and friends now gone and how these recipes have kept them alive for me. For food is a metaphor for all that is delicious in life, for everything that we share with those we love.

Jewish cooking is above all *bubbe* (grandmother) cuisine, and through the meals that we share with our children, it is also our link to the future. But unless you continue to update the recipes and create new food traditions, grandmother cuisine will die out when the grandmothers die, when no younger generations are eager to learn to prepare these foods. Many baby boomers are already totally dependent on their parents when it comes to Jewish recipes. They are unable to cook these foods for their own children, much less pass recipes down to them.

Our gastronomical selves evolve, new ingredients and cooking methods become available, and for a cuisine, like a culture, to survive, it cannot remain static. The story of Yiddish should prove a cautionary tale. Yiddish would forever remain a linguistic dinosaur without the new conversational classes that have sprung up and the new dictionaries that create needed words and phrases for modern speech, infusing the language with fresh, new life. And this same ferment, taking place in so much of contemporary Jewish culture, was the impetus for my cookbooks.

When I first began writing about food, my primary language was not my culinary mother tongue—Jewish. Jewish food was what we ate on holidays. I loved it at home, with a private passion.

Partly, of course, this was a telling commentary on the deteriorated state of Jewish cooking in the United States: careless cooking methods and overreliance on convenience foods. But more to the point, I think, is what it reveals about the stereotyped perception of Jewishness.

This is the question of beauty—what I think of as the aesthetics of Jewishness. Can you be too Jewish to be beautiful? In her provocative silkscreen *Four Barbras* from *The Jackie Series*, Deborah Kass answers the question even as she asks it. Kass's work, part of the controversial exhibit "Too Jewish? Challenging Traditional Identities," at The Jewish Museum in New York ten years ago, proudly celebrated Barbra Streisand's frankly ethnic face as a transcendent cultural icon, akin to Jacqueline Kennedy Onassis, in the format the artist borrowed from Andy Warhol's famous series.

But it was rare until recently for artists to celebrate their Jewishness in their work. In aesthetics, Jews like Mark Rothko and Barnett Newman, led by Jewish art critics like Clement Greenberg, strove for the universal. They rose to international prominence creating abstract art that declared itself "universalist"—art with nothing overtly (or even symbolically) Jewish. Of course, there were exceptions like Ben Shahn, whose work dealt with explicitly Jewish themes. But by and large, Jewish beauty was assimilationist. To a child growing up in the 1950s and 1960s, "Oh, you don't look Jewish" was a compliment more often than not, whether delivered by Jews or non-Jews: it meant you were pretty. And by inference, looking Jewish meant you were not.

The same aesthetics applied to food. My mother, a superb, imaginative cook, could not help but leave her imprint on the Jewish food she prepared for us. But her real flights of fancy were reserved for the Italian meals she whipped up for company or other special occasions. Jewish food was, well, too *Jewish* to be beautiful.

Like many American Jews who came of age while actively involved in the civil rights movement, I began to appreciate my own roots as I explored other minority cultures. Not only were these diverse ethnic groups beautiful, but so was mine: we too were a vivid patch in the exciting crazy quilt of multiculturalism.

I was not alone. Today Jewish chefs around the country express their Jewishness in their dishes, challenging the marginalized, exclusionary concept of Jewish food as nongourmet: dreary and unrefined.

The culture serves as inspiration, however, not imprisonment. For only by rethinking, questioning, and reinventing—in the best midrashic tradition—can we guarantee it will remain meaningful to us.

Jews have always believed, in a very real sense, that you are what you eat: foods remain forever in our bodies, transformed into blood, brains, heart, and even soul. More than mere corporal nourishment, the proper food keeps both body and soul healthy. The physical becomes the spiritual, as we approach God through eating, worshiping at this unique altar, the table.

For food is truly magical. Through the simple act of eating, Jews partake of a mystical but very real communion with their families, their traditions, and the world itself. In improvising in this culinary universe, I have varied the ingredients and experimented with different styles, but always the essential—the magic—endures.

I hope that *Jewish Holiday Cooking* will rekindle old food memories and create indelible new ones, linking celebrants with my grandmothers and all the grandparents before and after them. Those accustomed to preparing the cuisine and those just starting out will find both excellent renditions of well-loved classics and a wealth of imaginative improvisations for each holiday. While much of the material is drawn from my first book, *The Gefilte Variations: 200 Inspired Re-creations of Classics from the Jewish Kitchen*, there are more than a hundred brand-new recipes and tips, many as quick and simple as they are dressy and delicious.

But Jewish holidays are about more than food, and this book is about more than cooking—it's about celebrating with family and friends. By inviting others to share in our holiday meals, we connect them to our people, and even more, to the warm embrace of our family.

There is a broad range of ways contemporary Jews observe the holidays. Today's celebrants include not just traditional Jews and those rediscovering their roots, but the newly Jewish and innumerable interfaith families as well. Many need basic information on how to celebrate the holidays; others are looking for new customs to incorporate into their lives and creative ways to keep the traditions vital.

WHAT IS JEWISH FOOD?

Can the food of a people dispersed all over the world centuries ago, cooking the many disparate foods of their adopted homelands, be described as a cuisine? A cuisine that would find common elements in a beef kibbe, tart-sweet with apricots and tamarind, and a tender brisket, heady with onion gravy? Or delicate gefilte fish and *bellahat*, Egyptian spicy ground fish balls?

There *is* a Jewish cuisine. But it cannot be defined as simply any food cooked by Jews. By that logic, pasta primavera and Mexican salsa, now made with kosher ingredients by Jewish cooks, are Jewish foods.

Nor are the only true Jewish foods matzoh, *haroset* (the Passover fruit-nut paste that commemorates the mortar the Jews used in ancient Egypt), and long-simmering Sabbath dishes like *hamin* and *cholent*. We cannot deny chopped liver or *huevos haminados* (oniony hard-cooked eggs) because they are not eaten by all Jews. Jewish cooking is perhaps the original regional cuisine, with a purview that nearly spans the globe.

Blintzes may first have been prepared in a Russian kitchen as pancakes meant to evoke the winter sun at Shrovetide. But haven't Jews, who welcome summer with them at Shavuot, adapted and adopted them long enough to call them their own? When does an immigrant food become naturalized? Surely baked beans are solid New England fare, though many food historians believe the Pilgrims borrowed their overnight Sabbath stews from Jewish versions during their sojourn in Holland, or that seafaring captains brought the Jewish dish back from North Africa.

THE VARIED WORLD OF JEWISH CUISINE

Comprising the largest segment of world Jewry, the Ashkenazim (from *Ashkenaz*, the Hebrew word for Germany) are descended from the Jews who originally settled in France and Germany, later emigrating east and north to Poland, Russia, the Baltic, and Central Europe. While their cuisine was far from homogeneous—contrast Hungarian stews spicy with paprika and hot peppers with sweet Polish dishes like raisin-studded stuffed cabbage or honey-sweet tsimmes—there is a recognizable commonality. Most Ashkenazim came from cool climates and worked with similar ingredients: beets, carrots, cabbage, potatoes. Few had access to the sea, so they developed a love for freshwater fish. Their shared food traditions were also a by-product of the interaction among the various Ashkenazi communities through trade, marriage, and the constant migrations resulting from persecution and expulsion (an integration made easier because they spoke the same language, Yiddish). Later the cuisine became further standardized in the apogee of such intermingling, the American melting pot.

Sephardim (from the Hebrew *Sepharad*, meaning Spain) refers technically to those Jews and their descendants expelled from the Iberian peninsula beginning in 1492, but it also has come to mean all the Jews from the diverse communities of the Balkans, the eastern Mediterranean, North Africa, the Middle East, and parts of Asia. There had been a Jewish presence in all these lands for centuries: Jews have made Morocco home at least since Roman times, and the Jewish community in Iraq dates back to antiquity when King Nebuchadnezzar brought Jews to Babylonia as captives after he destroyed the First Temple in 586 BCE.

Many of these Muslim areas welcomed the Spanish and Portuguese Jews—indeed, the Ottoman Sultan Bayazid II invited them, avowing, "[Ferdinand] is impoverishing his country and enriching my kingdom"—and they brought with them not only their language, Ladino, but their foods and cooking techniques as well. These, in turn influenced and were influenced by all the different culinary traditions of the new lands they settled.

Sephardi cooking then is really a constellation of disparate cuisines, revolving to some extent around similar ingredients like sun-soaked vegetables and fruits, lamb, saltwater fish, oils, herbs, and aromatic spices. While the boundaries are permeable, at least four very general types of cooking styles can be distinguished: the cuisines of the eastern Mediterranean Jews (Greece, Turkey, and the Balkans), where the cooking of the Iberian Jews had the greatest influence; the Maghreb (North Africa)

Jews; and the two major Jewish communities of the Middle East: Egypt and the Levant; and Iran and Iraq.

Although it is often classified as Sephardi by Ashkenazi Jews, Italian cuisine is quite distinct. Jews have lived in Rome continuously for twenty-one centuries: *La cucina ebraica* is an amalgam of the foods of the ancient Jewish communities, the Sephardi and Ashkenazi émigrés, and their Italian-Christian neighbors.

The third largest group of Jewry, the Yemenite Jews, trace their ancestry to the celebrated union of Solomon and Sheba in the ninth century BCE. Because they were fairly isolated from other Jews, not only their customs but also their fiery hot cuisine developed differently.

Separate mention should also be made of the Asian Jewish communities. Many Jews who settled in the stops along the Silk Route—the fabled names out of Coleridge like Samarkand, Bukhara, and Tashkent—originally came from Iran. Cut off from their forebears, they developed a rich, festive cuisine greatly influenced by their Central Asian and Russian neighbors. The cuisines of two of the three far-flung Jewish settlements in India—the Bene Israel of the Konkan Coast and, later, Bombay, and the Cochini Jews from the Malabar Coast—bear strong resemblance to the Hindu and Muslim cooking there. The Baghdadis, who make up the third community, centered in Bombay and Calcutta, were Iraqi and Syrian Jews. Their unique foods blend elements of the Jewish Middle East with Indian and, to a lesser extent, British cookery.

Some time ago I was in the New York home of a Jewish woman originally from Pune, on the western coast of India. Accustomed to celebrating Rosh Hashanah at the end of the furious monsoon season, she prepared the same traditional foods with which she welcomed the New Year back home. The apartment was filled with the aromas of chicken curry simmering on the stove and platters of *halwah*, sweet puddings enriched with coconut milk (in avoidance of the dairy that would contravene kosher law), cooling on the dining table.

Such strong smells are intensely evocative. And I was indeed transported—but not to a place of pink palaces, gold-caparisoned elephants, and silk saris in rainbow colors. Instead, I was back in my Polish grandmother's apartment on Davidson Avenue in the Bronx, inhaling the same warm, homey smells of sizzling onions, sweet cinnamon, and toasted poppy seeds from her Rosh Hashanah brisket, tsimmes, and honey cookies she used to cook in the old white Formica kitchen.

Was the food the same, or the grandmothers? Probably a little of both. The most festive—and delicious—Jewish cooking is centered around home celebrations, whether with the immediate family at quiet Sabbath dinners or the whole raucous extended *mishpocheh* at the Passover seder. And table ceremonies like dipping challah and apples in honey to ensure a sweet new year appear invented to engage the family and delight the children.

There are no trained chefs, educated on elegant, codified recipes, who prepare Jewish banquet dishes in royal kitchens or luxe restaurants. The best Jewish restaurants mimic fine Jewish home cooking—not the other way around. This homeyness that informs every aspect of the cuisine, from the favored ingredients to the cooking techniques to the family-centered style of eating, is born of an ancient religion, deeply rooted in ritual and the rhythms of the natural world.

Take brisket and beef kibbe, for example. They are both carefully braised over gentle fires—one of the long, slow meat-cooking methods like stewing and oven- or pan-roasting that have for centuries warmed Jewish kitchens from Beirut to Bialystok and the Bronx.

Such cooking methods are no accident. Jewish dietary laws require that meat be soaked and salted to remove the blood so it no longer resembles the flesh of a live animal. By tradition, it is usually cooked well-done enough that no trace of blood remains visible. For the blood of any being is sacred to God: "Ye shall eat the blood of no matter of flesh" (Leviticus 17:14).

Kashrut, the dietary laws, also proscribe eating—in addition to pork, rabbit, and any other animal that does not chew its cud and have split hooves—many of the tender cuts of kosher animals. Because Jacob injured his thigh during his fight with the angel (Genesis 32:33), meat from the hindquarters, like filet mignon, sirloin, and leg of lamb, is taboo, unless the sciatic nerve is removed first—a difficult and expensive process. (Some non-Western Jews do remove the sciatic nerve from animals: in Kaifeng, China, where a flourishing community of Jews settled in the tenth century, Jews were called *Tiao Kia Kisou* [sect which extracts the sinews].) So long, patient simmering is also necessary to tenderize the tougher cuts that are permissible.

And the word "gefilte" may belong to Eastern European Jews, but the process of separating fish from its bones and grinding it up is common to much of Jewry. On Sabbath and religious holidays, Jews are not permitted to work. For some, meticulously removing the flesh from tiny fish bones was a labor that swallowed up some of the joy of the holy day. And yet, one is encouraged to eat fish on these days as it is a symbol of fruitfulness and a mystical means to taste a bit of Paradise and ward off the evil eye. The solution: ground fish balls, which also stretch the supply of fish and can be prepared in advance.

Foods that can be readied ahead characterize much of Jewish cookery. Since Jews are not permitted to kindle fires on the Sabbath but are exhorted to feast then, foods like kugels, *tagines* (Moroccan stew-like dishes), and, yes, curries, are fixed in advance and then simply heated through, or like cholents and *dafinas,* are slow-cooked overnight on previously lit fires. And from diverse Jewish communities come imaginative cold dishes, especially well-seasoned fish, developed with the injunction against Sabbath cooking in mind. Because no last-minute cooking is permitted, the whole family can sit down together to eat.

An ancient people, Jews have a taste for ancient foods. The onions and garlic that nourished the Hebrew slaves in Egypt are relished today by Jews everywhere. Those well-done meat dishes would lie leaden on the tongue without garlic, roasted or sautéed, and crisply browned or gently stewed onions to provide the requisite aromatic lift.

The pomegranates that quenched the thirst of the Israelites as they wandered forty years in the desert are still sought out by Jews regardless of how difficult they are to find in their new homelands, especially for the fall holidays when the fruit is at its peak. And biblical ingredients like lamb, figs, dates, barley, lentils, almonds, and pistachios still locate a dish as Jewish for many.

Dairy- and grain-intensive foods are central to the Jewish culinary universe. Dairy or vegetarian meals assume more significance when obtaining meat slaughtered according to kashrut has proven difficult. The legendary beauty Queen Esther, wife of the Persian King Ahasuerus, relied on legumes like chickpeas and lentils for sustenance, since no kosher meat was available at the court where the wicked Haman held sway. And during the Inquisition, when it would have been perilous for them to kosher their meat, many "secret" Jews depended on eggs and dairy for protein.

The biblical injunction "a kid must not be seethed in its mother's milk" means that meat and dairy (any food containing milk or milk products, including butter and cheese) may never be eaten at the same meal—and observant Jews wait one, three, or six hours (depending on local custom) after eating any meat before swallowing a dairy product. (There is no waiting period, however, between eating dairy—except for hard cheeses—and, subsequently, eating meat. One must simply cleanse the palate with a drink or a piece of bread.) When dairy foods are eaten—like blintzes slicked with rich sour cream, cheesy *fritadas*, and creamy puddings—they become the focus of the meal, rather than flavoring adjuncts to the meat dishes.

Although many dishes derived from humble foods like kasha and lentils, even the poorest Jewish kitchens had exotic sweet-smelling spices available—usually cinnamon, cloves, and nutmeg at least—because they were integral to the Saturday night Havdalah ceremony, evoking the fragrance of the hereafter as Queen Sabbath is escorted out. (The need for special spices, fruits, and nuts for ceremonial use like Havdalah, Passover haroset, and the Sukkot bouquet is one reason Jews became important international traders in such foodstuffs.) Cinnamon and other aromatic spices are frequently called for in both Ashkenazi and Sephardi savory and sweet recipes.

The spice of Sabbath became a metaphor for its unique flavor, and preparing especially fragrant and sapid foods was a means of honoring the festive days. Glistening fresh fish and vegetables just plucked from the garden need little adornment, but foods prepared ahead for a holiday and either kept heated or eaten chilled require exuberant seasoning to make them sparkle. Some Jews added sweetening, some spicy or savory flavoring. And many, in disparate communities from Morocco and Italy to Germany and Poland, added both. After all, the taste for sweet-and-sour or sweet and savory has potent resonance for a people whose every joy is tinged with bittersweet: whose wedding laughter is momentarily shattered by the traditional breaking glass, who punctuate their most joyous festivals with poignant allusions to their enemies' sorrows, and their own.

The Jewish kitchen revolves around the Sabbath and the seasonal cycle of holidays. Though the specifics of a dish may differ according to local availability of ingredients, cooking traditions, and customs, all foods prepared for holidays and other life-cycle events speak to the same ritual and symbolic concerns. Ashkenazi Jews may fry latkes, and Israelis their *sufganiyot* (jelly doughnuts), but both foods are inspirited with the miracle of the oil that burned in the holy lamp for eight days at Hanukkah. Although the permissible foods vary from community to community, all Jews have a unique Passover cuisine rooted in the absence of leavening to commemorate the unleavened bread the Hebrews ate during their hasty exodus from Egypt.

Everyday fare too resonates with that abiding Jewish love for symbolism. "Soul food" in its most basic sense, Jewish dishes are routinely used to explain and reinforce the mysteries of life. Returning from the cemetery, most Jews in mourning commonly eat round foods, such as eggs, bagels, and lentils, which reflect the eternal cycle of life. Symbolic of abundance, stuffed dishes—whether made from grape leaves or cabbage—are especially enjoyed at harvest time.

We turn to foods inspired by our heritage at life-cycle events, like the *brit milah* or the festive Kiddush collation served after a bnai mitzvah service. Illness too is part of the life cycle—whether one is felled by the newest flu or the Serious Blues, ancient as Ecclesiastes. Foods invested with tradition taste richer and more comforting. I hope you will enjoy many of these Jewish dishes not just on the holidays, but year round.

HOW TO PLAN A JEWISH HOLIDAY MEAL

Does preparing a Jewish holiday celebration—whether for a small family or a large, extended one—differ from making any large meal? It does in several ways.

Jewish holiday foods not only speak to special ceremonies and traditions, but they are also usually richer, more complex, and often more work. It's not that we are commanded to seek out early spring asparagus for the seder, prepare a Shavuot cheesecake from an heirloom recipe or Hanukkah latkes with sublime crunch. But these extra touches or grace notes, the *hiddur mitzvah* so intrinsic to Judaism, enhance our enjoyment of the holidays, making them more meaningful to us.

For holidays like Passover and Rosh Hashanah, hosts may need to select special foods that will remain moist and flavorful through a predinner service so that everyone can sit down together at the table.

The menus may have been set in stone years ago: in some families, introducing new foods or experimenting with different recipes at the holiday table is tantamount to serving lamb chops on Thanksgiving. Creative cooks may be met with pleas for the old way or the way Grandma, Uncle Jesse, or my mother made it—even when the object of such Proustian fixation is nearly inedible, indigestible, or just plain same-old.

While this is not the case with my daughter (who after all grew up tasting buckwheat polenta and goat cheese wonton-ravioli for her mother's articles from the time she was five), it is often so with my sister's family, with whom we spend so many holidays. If this describes your home too, here is what I've learned.

- Include children—and whenever possible, spouses—in both planning and preparing the meal. It sounds like a cliché, but they really are much more likely to try something they've had a hand in putting on the table.

- Don't plan an entire menu of all new foods; introduce just a few at a time. If you offer a choice of two main courses at your seders, experiment on only one. Offer one novel side dish at a time. If you want to try a delicious new haroset, serve it alongside your familiar one.

- Many Jewish holidays run more than one day (not to mention Shabbat, which comes fifty-two times each year). If you start out with potato pancakes on the first day of Hanukkah, that still leaves plenty of holiday time to enjoy Mediterranean Chickpea Latkes or Italian Apple Fritters. Families who sit down to two holiday dinners on Rosh Hashanah and Passover are likely to find new foods welcome on the second night. And those who celebrate only one seder can try more inventive Passover cuisine during the remainder of the holiday. Then, no longer unfamiliar, these new dishes may well find a place on your holiday table next time.

Much of Jewish cooking is rather filling for contemporary tastes, and the special occasion foods are even more so. Many Ashkenazi dishes are based on dairy (sour cream, butter, and cream cheese), heavy starches, and rich meats. Sephardi food, while lighter in general, relies on generous quantities of oil. And both cuisines make lavish use of eggs.

I have reduced unnecessary amounts of oil in recipes, I trim off the meat fat, and thoroughly skim soups and gravies (detailed instructions for removing fat from gravies is given in The Jewish Kitchen: Removing Fats on page 21). But many recipes frequently call for real butter, real sour cream, whole milk, and other rich foodstuffs—not substitutions.

Blintzes and brisket are celebration foods—certainly, you are not going to eat them every day. And when you do serve them, round out the meal with fresh salads, seasonal vegetables, and fruit (either a light compote or beautiful uncooked fruit, artfully arranged on dessert plates). For centuries, Jews ate their Saturday lunch cholent (a heavy, meat-and-starch meal-in-a-pot) accompanied by a starchy kugel, or pudding. They probably had no choice, given the paucity of other foods, especially vegetables. But we do. To best enjoy a rich cholent or dafina (the Sephardi equivalent), eat it with a salad of fresh-tasting tart and bitter greens. (The suggested menus for each holiday will further assist you in planning meals.)

Cooking and hosting a Jewish holiday meal that tastes of love and tradition—especially for a table full of invited family and friends—is a lot of work. But much of the preparation can be done ahead; in fact, many foods, like brisket, stews, and soups, are best when made in advance. You'll find lots of time-saving hints and shortcuts in each chapter, including quick fixes for a fuss-free seder (see Tips for Planning a Seder Menu: Time Out, page 365).

And consider sharing some of the preparation and cooking chores: potluck meals are a wonderful way to encourage guests' participation in the celebration. Think beyond potluck break-the-fasts on Yom Kippur to potluck Hanukkahs, where everyone brings another latke, or a potluck return-to-hametz after Passover, each guest bringing a different pasta or pastry.

By the way, if a guest asks you what to bring to your holiday celebration, suggest dessert—unless you've prepared it beforehand—because your own oven is likely to be occupied most of the time with savory foods.

NOTES TO THE COOK

Good cooks are good eaters. Excited by delicious food, they keep sampling and adjusting their work until that charmed moment when flavors, texture, temperature, and appearance coalesce and, as the girl with the golden tresses said, "it tastes just right."

Throughout this book I give approximate cooking times for various stages in a recipe. But ultimately, these are only guidelines. The exact time it will take you to caramelize onions, for instance, will depend on many factors: the onions themselves (how much moisture and natural sugar they contain, how finely you have cut them), the type and size of the pan, the degree and kind of heat you are using, other ingredients like salt that you may have added, as well as your own personal preferences. In the end you decide whether the onions are sweetly browned enough.

By all means, adjust the seasonings to suit your ingredients and your tastebuds. Once I prepared Honeyed Quince-Apple Blintzes, using fruit from the fragrant centerpiece that had graced my table for a couple of weeks. The fruit looked ripe and fresh and bore no telltale signs of discoloration. Yet it tasted singularly dull and lackluster with the seasoning called for in the recipe, quantities that, the six or seven times I had previously made the blintzes, had always produced beautifully flavored fruit. Perhaps I had let the quinces and apples languish too long, unchilled, in my steam-heated apartment. Perhaps they were insipid to begin with. I should have tasted the raw fruit first. Luckily, I did sample the cooked fruit before I filled the blintzes, and by adding another quarter teaspoon or so of cinnamon and vanilla, an extra teaspoon or two of honey, and a squeeze of lemon, I was able to revive the tired flavor.

Use these recipes as departure points for your own explorations, either changing flavorings or making other substitutions as your tastes and the seasons dictate. Often suggestions for variations are given in the Cook's Note at the end of a recipe. If a dish is not in your food memory—if you are not sure what it is supposed to taste like—use the descriptions and your mind's tongue to determine what you want it to taste like when you begin experimenting.

It's always nice to "lighten up" in the kitchen, even with special occasion food. Here are some ideas:

• Fresh fruit, barely cooked and sweetened, adds a flavorful burst as a top to rich noodle puddings; roasted fruit makes a fine filling for blintzes. Fresh fruit sauces, such as Fresh Raspberry Applesauce or Fresh Persimmon Sauce, or the Orange, Onion, and Date Salad provide a lighthearted but full-flavored counterpoint to fried latkes, blintzes, and brisket.

• Dried fruit, such as tart apricots, dates, and especially prunes, round out flavors in recipes and contribute body to a variety of foods, including soups and sauces.

• Intense fat-free fruit concentrates (such as pomegranate molasses and *temerhindi* [tamarind]) and full-bodied fruit juices, like apple-cranberry and prune, reduced over high heat to deepen their flavors, add clean-tasting zest and decrease reliance on added sugars. Reduced carrot juice makes Rosh Hashanah Sweet Carrots with Fennel Salt taste more carroty and sugary, with no added sweetening.

• Fruits and vegetables, soft-cooked or pureed, can fill out soups, gravies, and sauces. And they can be used to replace butter and eggs, lightening and enriching pâtés and grains. I substitute some pureed caramelized onion for part of the hard-boiled egg in a chopped liver variation, and use meltingly tender cubes of eggplant instead of gobs of butter to moisten kasha.

- Reduce, reduce, reduce soups, sauces, and gravies to concentrate flavors and thicken them.

- Vary the textures in a dish to create the impression of lightness. For example, I combine both sautéed and crisp raw onions in the chopped chicken liver recipes and Chopped Eggs and Onions. To make latkes, I grate most of the potatoes coarsely, ensuring a crunchy crust; I puree the remainder for a creamy interior.

HOW TO USE THIS BOOK

In addition to the new takes on holiday standards, classic, and international Jewish dishes in each holiday chapter, you'll find a list of recipes from other chapters that would enhance your celebration, too.

I've devised a variety of suggested menus for every holiday (including several nonmeat meals). Arranging these foods (many of them quite rich and filling) into appealing, well-balanced meals requires a graceful tango between, on the one hand, the exigencies of Jewish traditions, and, on the other, contemporary demands for lighter, fresher tastes. To round out these menus, I have added some simple dishes for which no recipe is given. These straightforward foods—mostly salads and vegetables—are in the repertoire of most home cooks or easily prepared from the descriptions given. Feel free to supplement the menus with your own favorite dishes. And after you become familiar with the recipes, you will find it easy to compose delectable menus of your own.

Because the dietary laws proscribe eating foods containing meat or meat products with foods containing milk or its derivatives, I have designated recipes as meat, dairy, or pareve. (Pareve foods, considered "neutral," contain neither meat nor dairy and so may be eaten with either, and are suitable for vegetarian diets. However, though dairy-free, many pareve recipes contain eggs, so vegans will need to check the ingredients list.) If a recipe may be categorized in more than one way, depending on your choice of ingredients (for example, butter instead of margarine, chicken versus vegetable broth), it bears all possible labels.

"We remember the fish which we
did eat freely of in Egypt . . ."

—NUMBERS 11:5

THE JEWISH KITCHEN

FISH

And in Rome, Poland, and New York, too. Throughout the Diaspora and in Israel, fish has been a cardinal fixture of Jewish cuisine.

Fat golden carp, set thrashing in bathtubs on Thursday, metamorphosed into savory gefilte fish come Friday morning. Gleaming red and gray mullet and sweet-fleshed sole were fried and marinated for elegant cold Sabbath lunches. Stewed or roasted, sauced with fresh green plums or spicy gingersnaps, the choicest fresh fish graced the festive meals.

And during the workaday week, there was preserved fish: smoked, salt-crusted, or brined—herring, mostly, and anchovies. Later there was salmon in all its permutations, including canned, which in America was quickly adopted for the ubiquitous dairy meal, salmon croquettes.

Not all fish are kosher. Permissible fish must have fins, and scales that are visible to the naked eye, overlap, and can be detached from the skin. So not only are all shellfish, like shrimp, lobster, clams, and oysters forbidden but also swordfish, catfish, skate, and shark, among others, because they lack true scales. Rabbis have debated for centuries whether the scales of the sturgeon conform to the strict laws of kashrut; today most observant Jews refrain from eating it.

But fish that are kosher require no special treatment in the Jewish kitchen. They are free from the stringent laws of slaughter and preparation that govern meat and poultry. Anyone—fishmonger or home cook—can kill a permissible fish, and it needs no soaking and salting to ritually purify it. And fish are considered pareve; like vegetables and grains, they may be eaten at meat or dairy meals and cooked and served in either meat or dairy pots and dishes. (However, observant Jews refrain from eating fish and meat together in the same dish, like veal seasoned with anchovies, or gefilte fish poached in chicken broth. Traditionally, after a fish appetizer, they will cleanse their palates with a bit of bread, a sip of wine or whiskey, or, in more luxurious surroundings, even a tart sorbet, before tucking into a meat course.)

According to Jewish mystical tradition, eating fish is not merely practical—it is fraught with magical optimism. Ever since the biblical blessings in Genesis to "be fruitful and multiply" and "fill the waters of the sea," fish have symbolized fertility and immortality, abundance, and prosperity.

"... the feast was worthy of a king. There was fish that brought to mind the biblical verse about the great whales."

—CHAIM N. BIALIK, *The Short Friday*

Dining on fish brings a taste of Paradise, a mystical means to preview the exquisite serenity of the Messianic Age. For according to the legend in the Book of Job, the Leviathan, a monstrous fish embodying evil, will be defeated when the Messiah arrives, and the righteous will feast upon its flesh.

MEATS AND POULTRY

A BRIEF DISCUSSION OF KOSHER MEAT AND POULTRY

Just like humankind, animals too are sacred to God, and while permission to partake of their flesh was finally granted to Noah (Genesis 9:3), there has always been a pervasive sense among Jews that meat is at once imbued with God's holiness and tainted by the profanity of blood.

A precious gift, meat is so highly esteemed that it will grace the Sabbath and holiday feasts that honor God. It is a food so special it should be eaten only if it is craved. But before it can be savored, meat—more God's food than any other—must be strictly regulated more than any

> "There is no joy without meat and wine."
>
> —BABYLONIAN TALMUD: PESACHIM 109A

> "The best of milky foods is a meat dish."
>
> —SHOLEM ALEICHEM

other food. These regulations are kashrut, the Jewish dietary laws that determine what is kosher, or fit to eat.

Many reasons have been suggested for the specifics of kashrut—why certain animals are permitted and not others, why meat and milk may not be eaten together, and so on. A few of these explanations are economic and environmental (the pig would not flourish in the arid Middle East; the pig is more likely to transmit trichinosis in warm climates, etc.); some are cultural (the Jews wanted to differentiate themselves from the surrounding people and their pagan practices). Some or all of this may be valid. But I believe the initial restrictions derived from the simultaneous sense of wonder and revulsion at consuming flesh and the concomitant need to reconcile meat-eating with God's universe by subjecting it to God's laws.

Kashrut determines not only what meats—indeed, even what *cuts* of permissible meats—may be eaten, but also, to some extent, how they are to be prepared. So to fully understand Jewish cuisine, it is worthwhile briefly examining these dietary regulations.

The permitted mammals include only those that have split hooves and chew their cud: cattle, sheep, goat, deer, antelope, gazelle, and buffalo. Prohibited are the pig, horse, hare, rabbit, and camel, among others. Of poultry, no birds of prey may be eaten.

These permitted animals must be healthy; the *shochet* (ritual slaughterer) checks before and after slaughter to make sure there are no signs of sickness or damage. If, for example, it is found after slaughtering an animal that it had lesions on its lungs, the animal would be considered *treyf* (unfit to eat).

The strict procedure for ritually slaughtering meat and poultry was designed to be less painful to the animal. An extremely sharp, smooth knife is drawn across the throat. Poultry, of course, is easier to slaughter this way than mammals. It is joked that the giraffe, a kosher animal, has never been eaten by Jews because it is impossible to determine where to draw the knife on the throat. Because all animals must be slaughtered according to kosher ritual, hunting is forbidden: deer, buffalo, quail, and pheasant must be farm raised. (The Israelites used nets to catch the large flocks of quail that fell, exhausted by their long, migratory flight, near the camp in the wilderness.)

While all parts of poultry may be eaten, only certain parts of mammals are allowed. The sciatic nerve, located in the thigh area, must be removed—a very difficult and costly process that would necessitate hacking up the tenderest, most expensive cuts, rendering them impossible to sell as prime meat. So Ashkenazi and most Sephardi butchers do not sell the meat from the hindquarters; instead, it is sold to nonkosher butchers. Tender cuts like leg of lamb, porterhouse, and sirloin steaks, which come from the hindquarters, are proscribed.

Animal blood is strictly prohibited ("No soul of you shall eat blood." Leviticus 17:12). To purge meat and poultry of blood, they must be soaked in cold water for thirty minutes and covered with coarse salt for one hour (a process usually carried out today by kosher butchers). Instead of being soaked, the liver, an extremely bloody organ, must be sprinkled with salt and broiled until it changes color before it is eaten or cooked further in a recipe. (These processes will draw out most of the blood; the residue of blood in the tissues will provide moisture to the meat.) The brief salting extracts impurities; like brining, it imbues kosher meat with an appealing, lightly seasoned taste and concentrates the meat flavor. Kosher chickens produce clearer soup and they are consistent prizewinners in taste tests.

Kosher meats are sold very fresh: the koshering process is performed no longer than seventy-two hours after slaughtering. Unlike nonkosher meats, they do not develop the full-bodied flavor and tenderness that comes with aging.

COOKING JEWISH MEATS

The Jewish cook, faced with the least tender cuts of meat, made tougher still from lack of aging, often gravitated to parts with lots of connective tissue that would soften with slow braising, like brisket and flanken. Long, gentle cooking produced meats that were completely cooked through, with no trace of blood. If meats were roasted, broiled, or sautéed, they were usually served well-done, not rare. (Kashrut does *not* require that meats be cooked until well-done. After the meat has been properly soaked, salted, and rinsed, it may be cooked any way—or not at all. Served in fine kosher steakhouses, like Le Marais in Manhattan, steak tartare, chopped raw beefsteak, is perfectly permissible. But, perhaps because of the strong taboos against consuming blood, most traditional Ashkenazi Jews have refrained from eating rare meat.)

Sometimes ornery cuts of meat were minced, then combined with sautéed fennel, eggplant, masses of shimmery onions, or other imaginative ingredients to make them tender and tasty.

Jewish cooks concocted beautifully flavored sauces, savory with garlic, onions, and leeks, or sweet and sweet-sour from fragrant spices, such as cinnamon, ginger, and cloves, and exotic, fleshy fruits like prunes, pomegranates, and quinces. They coaxed the tough and dry to aromatic succulence.

THE GRAVY BOAT

Flavorful sauces remain to this day an integral part of Jewish meat cooking; brisket and similar cuts want a mantle of gravy to keep them moist and tasty. These are simple pan sauces, developed organically in the course of slow-cooking the ingredients together. I reduce the pan liquids to concentrate the flavors. Then I add body by pureeing some of the aromatic vegetables, like carrots and onions, and the sweet, mellow chestnuts or other special ingredients braised with the meat. You'll find delicious flour-free pan sauces here, derived, for example, from the whole garlic cloves, tomatoes, and honey used in preparing the meat.

I find that slow-cooking sometimes flattens the flavor of a sauce. So just before serving, I rejuvenate the sauce by stirring in more of the fresh herbs starring in the dish, or chopped parsley or chives, some grated lemon zest or a drop of juice, a bit of raw garlic puree, a tart-sweet jolt of pomegranate molasses, even a generous grind of fresh pepper. Reheat just to combine flavors. To add silkiness, try a little artichoke puree (available jarred).

To reheat meats, bring the sauce to a simmer, add the meat slices, and warm slowly until the meat is heated through. If you have only a small amount of sauce, reserve it for serving, and heat the meat in a little simmering broth.

REMOVING FATS

Many Jewish cuts contain a fair amount of fat. And slow, moist cooking methods like braising draw out the fats in the meat and distribute them in the pan sauce.

To defat this sauce, take the meat out of the pan and keep it warm. Strain the cooking liquids from the solids, like carrots, garlic, and other aromatics. If the liquid looks fatty, you might want to line the strainer first with a few sheets of paper towels (this will also blot up some of the grease from the cooked vegetable solids with which you will be thickening the gravy).

If you have the time, you can cool this liquid, then refrigerate it or pop it into the freezer for a while, until the fat solidifies—then you can scrape off the fat.

In the real world—mine at least, of last-minute everything—that is rarely practical. So pour the strained liquid into a tall glass or two or a special gravy skimmer, if you have one. Allow it to rest a moment, and you'll notice most of the clear, light fat rising to the top. Carefully dip a small ladle or large spoon into the layer of clear fat to remove it and discard. Continue until you have spooned out as much of the fat as possible. (Or pour out the fat through the top spout of your gravy skimmer.)

If you accidentally stir the top layer of grease down into the gravy, let stand briefly until separated again, then continue removing the remaining fat. Should the gravy still be fatty, strain it again through a couple of thicknesses of paper towels. For desperate degreasing measures, fill the strainer with ice (you'll want whole cubes here, which will melt less, not ice pieces). Quickly pour the cooled gravy through—the fat should be trapped on the ice.

Nothing beats a warm brisket sandwich on sour rye, savored in a quiet, clean kitchen after the maelstrom has been set to rights. So always remember to put aside enough gravy and meat for late-night noshing.

PANTRY AND PROCEDURES

MATZOH

(For a fuller discussion of matzoh, other varieties around the world and more ways to use it, including as a flavored, toasted flatbread, see Matzohs, page 378, Toasted Za'atar Matzohs, page 220, and Toasted Sesame-Cumin Matzohs, page 298).

The regular matzoh that Jews are commanded to eat on Passover instead of bread is a thin, crisp cracker made simply of wheat flour (there are special ritually prepared oat and spelt varieties for those who are wheat intolerant) and water—no yeast or other leavening and no salt. To prevent fermentation, the entire preparation, from mixing flour and water to baking the matzoh, should take no more than eighteen minutes. According to Eve Jochnowitz, a culinary historian who has done extensive research on the subject, matzoh is currently sold in many supermarkets in Poland—despite the fact that few Jews have remained there since the Holocaust. The Jewish cracker is marketed there as a pure and wholesome health and diet food for everyone.

Plain matzoh *is* pure and elemental, wheaty-tasting without the spongy, yeasty quality of bread or the flavorings or additives of crackers, and is an ideal substitute for these starches in recipes. I use matzoh not only in Passover recipes, but also year-round, for matzoh brie, in some stuffings and kugels, and to make home-ground matzoh crumbs for crunchy coatings.

Why grind your own matzoh when perfectly acceptable matzoh meal is available in most supermarkets? Packaged matzoh meal is very finely ground, perfect for fluffy matzoh balls, meat loaf, latkes, and most kugels. But if you want a coarse, crumbly topping, particularly one combined with butter or oil and toasted until golden and crunchy, you need to grind your own. And for crumb coatings, I find the texture and flavor are superior when the crumbs are not ground uniformly. Also, there are times when fresh matzoh meal is not available, when you know that matzoh meal has been sitting on the grocer's shelf—or yours—for far too long.

Then there are the flavored matzoh, especially egg matzoh: terrific, but unavailable ground unless you do it yourself.

TO MAKE MATZOH CRUMBS AND HOMEMADE MATZOH MEAL: Whirl small pieces of matzoh in a blender or food processor using the pulse motion until the desired texture is achieved. Or place in a resealable plastic bag and use a rolling pin or your hands to crush the matzoh. A medium grind with a slightly uneven texture is best for crumb coatings. Blend to the texture of sand for matzoh meal with a powdery consistency (and, if necessary, rub the fine crumbs through a fine-mesh sieve to remove any remaining coarse pieces).

TO TOAST MATZOH CRUMBS OR MATZOH MEAL: Preheat the oven to 350°F. In a baking pan, melt some butter, warm a little olive oil, or use a combination of both. Add matzoh crumbs or meal, season to taste with salt and pepper, toss to combine, and spread out in an even layer. Toast in the oven until fragrant and golden, 15 to 20 minutes, stirring every once in a while to redistribute the oil and prevent burning. Stir in other seasonings, if you'd like: spices and herbs (such as paprika, cumin, rosemary, or thyme), minced garlic, and grated cheese (2 to 3 tablespoons of Parmesan, hard Cheddar, or other well-flavored variety for every cup of matzoh crumbs or meal).

FLAVORED MATZOH (INCLUDING EGG, WHOLE-WHEAT, AND EGG AND ONION, ETC.): Check the ingredients on the package. Some contain zesty seasonings like onion or garlic and are excellent served as crackers or used in cooking as flavorful crumbs or savory stuffing. Whole-wheat matzoh is wonderful in Toasted Sesame-Cumin Matzohs (page 298). Egg matzoh, made simply of flour, egg yolks, and apple cider, is superb as a cracker (divine with cream cheese) or in matzoh brie. And it makes delicious crumbs—the slight sweetness from the cider provides an almost caramelized edge to the crumbs when they are toasted or fried.

But other flavored matzohs contain positively bizarre or inappropriate ingredients, like malt, rye, white and brown sugar, as well as additives and preservatives. So read the labels carefully.

AVAILABILITY AND STORAGE: Plain and several flavored kinds are available year-round in most supermarkets. (Although during Passover many Jews enjoy flavored matzoh, like the egg and whole-wheat varieties, which have been produced under stringent rabbinic supervision; strictly Orthodox Ashkenazi Jews eat only plain matzoh on Passover, reserving the flavored kinds for the rest of the year.)

Egg matzoh can usually be found for only a couple of months close to Passover. It sells out quickly and manufacturers often don't make more until the next season. I buy several extra boxes when I find them and store them for later use.

Matzoh meal can usually be purchased year-round. In January or February, freshly produced matzoh meal for Passover makes its appearance in supermarkets. But if you find a box in December stamped for Passover use, it's probably almost a year old and you might consider grinding your own from fresh matzoh.

Although matzoh and matzoh meal are generally not made with added oil (some flavored varieties might be), there is, of course, oil in the flour itself, which can turn rancid and musty after prolonged exposure to air. And moisture can make matzoh soggy. As with preservative-free crackers and bread crumbs, both matzoh and matzoh meal must be well wrapped to keep them from going stale. Unless you will be using up an opened box of matzoh within three or four days (fewer in very humid areas), it's a good idea to store the matzoh in an airtight plastic container or resealable plastic bag instead of the cardboard box it comes in. Don't leave a box of matzoh meal in the pantry, its perforation seal pushed open and left yawning. Keep it tightly closed in an airtight glass jar or plastic container, or purchase matzoh meal in the recently available special cylinders with a resealable plastic top. Store in the refrigerator, especially if it is not used on a regular basis. And if you trot out that same box of meal for two or three short appearances a year, consider keeping it in the freezer.

Let your nose be your guide in determining freshness: like crackers, matzoh and matzoh meal should smell fresh and wheaty. Discard any that smell musty or stale. If matzohs have become soggy, you can recrisp them in the oven at 350°F for a few minutes. And read the Passover section about toasting matzoh for superb, fresh-from-the-oven flavor.

SCHMALTZ, OLIVE OIL, BUTTER, AND OTHER FATS

More, perhaps, than they longed for the pomegranates, the dates, and the figs, the Jews of Central and Eastern Europe missed the olives and the rich, green-gold oil made from them in *eretz* Israel. In Europe, olive oil was expensive to import; when the Jews could buy it, they reserved it for ritual lamps or medicinal purposes.

For their daily cooking needs, they adopted the butter of their Gentile neighbors for dairy meals, and they turned to schmaltz, fat rendered from geese or chickens and flavored with onions, for meat meals.

My grandmother served schmaltz often when I was little—sometimes spread thick as butter on corn-rye bread with *griebenes* (the bits of crackling skin and onions formed in rendering the fat) and coarse salt. But as she grew older and more concerned with cholesterol counts, she substituted corn oil, often disguised with onion flavoring to better resemble the golden schmaltz she adored. I find corn oil a rather dowdy replacement for schmaltz. I prefer the lush yet grassy-clean taste of intensely aromatic extra virgin olive oil. *Plus ça change . . .*

There are, however, certain foods in the Ashkenazi kitchen that were really developed for schmaltz, that rely on it not just for its rich flavor, redolent of onions and poultry, but for its texture as well: solid when chilled, semisolid at room temperature. Because it is never completely liquid like oil, unless it is warmed, schmaltz—like butter—combines differently with foods. Matzoh meal mixed with schmaltz forms clumps, while matzoh meal and oil crumble together. A batter made with schmaltz produces fluffier and more tender matzoh balls than one made with oil. (Butter too makes a wonderful matzoh ball, scrumptious in dairy or pareve soups—see Fresh Borscht with Dilled Onion-Butter Matzoh Balls, page 499).

"This part of Fifth Avenue always seemed fat to him, fat and prosperous: like chicken *schmaltz*."

—HENRY ROTH, *Mercy of a Rude Stream*

So I make a flavorful fat with some texture that I usually use to prepare matzoh balls and other dumplings, and often to enrich chopped liver, chopped eggs and onions, grated black radish, and grains like kasha. Do *not* use it for sautéing foods; this schmaltz contains too much water because of the pureed onions.

OLIVE OIL SCHMALTZ

yield: ABOUT ⅔ CUP

2 cups finely chopped onions

¾ teaspoon salt

¼ cup olive oil

IN a strainer, toss the onions with the salt. Cover them with a paper towel and weight down with a bowl or plate topped with a heavy object like a large can of tomatoes. Let the onions drain for at least 30 minutes, tossing them occasionally. Place the onions in fresh paper toweling or a clean kitchen towel, and squeeze out as much liquid as possible.

WARM the oil in a 8- or 9-inch heavy skillet. Add the onions and cook, uncovered, over the very lowest heat. As their moisture evaporates, the onions will shrink considerably and the ever-deepening gold oil will appear to increase. Stir occasionally, spreading the onions out in the skillet and making sure that they do not stick or color past gold. After cooking for 60 to 75 minutes, they should be very soft and have exuded most of their liquid. Let the mixture cool slightly, then scrape all the onions and oil into a blender (a food processor won't work well here).

BLEND to emulsify the ingredients, stopping to scrape down the contents when necessary. Continue blending until you have a smooth, rich puree.

STORE tightly covered in the refrigerator. It will thicken and become more schmaltz-like when chilled. It will keep for at least 3 to 5 days.

Maybe it was the way that Grandma's chicken schmaltz spread on coarse bread—cold, thick, and congealed—coated my teeth like melted Chapstick the last time I ate it. At any rate, I never cared to cook with it in my own kitchen and tossed out buckets of fat from Hanukkah geese and innumerable chickens and ducks.

But I came back to the fat of my birthright in, of all places, Paris, where we celebrated Passover during my daughter's college junior year abroad. We'd spent two days shopping not only for foodstuffs but also little necessities missing from our rented apartment kitchen, like a stockpot. By the time I picked up the brisket I had ordered in the Jewish neighborhood, I knew I wasn't going to make my Olive Oil Schmaltz—and besides, I didn't have an extra pan to do it. I asked for chicken fat at the kosher mart, and the *patronne* reminded me they used goose fat instead. *Tant mieux!* It produced the finest matzoh balls I ever made.

Unlike the Olive Oil Schmaltz that I can enjoy whenever I want, it's still an indulgence. But for special occasions, homemade Poultry Schmaltz has become a real treat at our house.

Now I know why schmaltz with *griebenes* is also known as schmaltz *mit neshamas*: "fat with souls."

POULTRY SCHMALTZ

yield: **ABOUT 1 CUP**

SAVE bits of fat and skin from chickens, ducks, and geese in the freezer until you have about 2 cups fat and a little skin. Trim away any poultry meat clinging to the fat or skin. Cut into small pieces and place in a heavy saucepan. Add about ½ cup water, turn heat to the lowest simmer, and cook slowly, uncovered, until the fat melts and the water is evaporated, 30 to 40 minutes. Add about ½ cup finely chopped yellow onion and continue cooking, stirring every once in a while, until the onion and poultry skin (*griebenes*) have become crisp and golden brown (do not let them get too dark or they will taste burnt and bitter). This can take up to 2 hours or more of unattended time, so you might want to double the recipe when you prepare it. (I usually do it when I am performing other slow-moving kitchen chores like making soup or baking.) Strain the fat through a fine-mesh sieve into a glass jar, tamping down on the *griebenes* to extract all the flavorful fat. Store the schmaltz and *griebenes* separately, tightly covered, in the refrigerator.

ADD the *griebenes* to chopped liver, chopped eggs and onions, and all potato dishes: kugels, blintzes, latkes, potato matzoh balls, or mashed potatoes. They would make a glorious substitute for bacon in a kosher BLT.

For frying foods well seasoned with onions, garlic, or herbs, such as potato latkes, I use olive oil. It doesn't taste like the traditional schmaltz, but like schmaltz, it does have a rich, flavorful taste that enhances foods. And, after all, it was olive oil that burned in the lamp for eight days in the Temple—not chicken fat. In dishes where the taste of olive oil is important, as in the Green Olive Sauce (page 305), I use an excellent quality extra virgin oil.

I often turn to canola oil for its high smoke point and mild taste, especially for high-temperature frying, particularly when it comes to moist foods like New Mexican Sweet Potato Latkes (page 273) or Italian Apple Fritters (page 282).

I also use other fine vegetable and nut oils: the toasty, popcorn flavor of unrefined corn oil for a more nuanced *mamaliga* (Romanian corn meal mush), also marvelous for American corn bread and muffins; a delicate sunflower or sesame oil when a light touch is required in a nondairy dish; or even better, avocado oil, which imparts a wonderful buttery taste to food and is excellent for frying. To prevent butter from burning at high temperatures, I often combine it with a little avocado oil. (Most people think the cholesterol content of avocado oil is astronomical. They are wrong: its cholesterol content is zero. Its price, however, can be astronomical.) Another option for frying dairy foods is ghee, the Indian equivalent of clarified butter, available commercially in many specialty stores with kosher certification. Melted ghee is also excellent for brushing phyllo sheets.

Pricey—but worth it—fragrant nut oils, such as walnut or hazelnut, make stellar salad dressings and are particularly appealing in baking with nondairy ingredients, when using butter would render the dish inappropriate for a meat meal.

Because I don't use these delicate oils as frequently as I do olive oil, after opening I store them tightly sealed in the refrigerator, where they will keep for months. Any cloudiness or congealing disappears when the oil returns to room temperature. These oils are available in health food and specialty shops, as well as many well-stocked supermarkets.

For dairy dishes, I always use sweet (unsalted) butter. Despite the ads, no margarine will ever taste as good as pure butter. Besides, margarine contains as many calories as butter, and processing techniques and preservatives render any benefits garnered from the reduced cholesterol levels questionable at best.

SOUR CREAM, YOGURT CREAM, AND *LABNEH*

Slathered on blintzes and onion-laced herring, spooned over strawberries, whisked into fruit soup, Jewish food can be extravagant with thick, luscious sour cream.

Delicious? Yes. Fattening? Absolutely. But real sour cream is a sensational splurge.

And there are alternatives.

You *can* substitute reduced-fat sour cream. But personally, I tend to stay away from most such products—either the taste itself is strange or the ingredients list contains too many weird, unwholesome additives. I'd rather eat the real stuff, just less frequently. And between times, I use the Sephardi counterpart made of drained yogurt, sometimes referred to as yogurt cheese, here called yogurt cream.

> "And her face always looked strained and worried, as if her shipload of sour cream had just sunk."
>
> —I. L. PERETZ, "IN THE MAIL COACH"

Many cookbooks claim plain yogurt is a good alternative to sour cream. It is not: it's watery and flat-tasting. But when most of the liquid whey is removed, the sweet, tangy flavors become more concentrated and the yogurt develops more body. Then even plain low-fat and nonfat yogurts can taste rather creamy and make a perfectly acceptable substitute for sour cream where fat is not essential to the dish. And sometimes the tart clean taste of yogurt cream actually works better than sour cream in a dish such as Sautéed Chive Mamaliga with Feta-Scallion Sauce (page 524).

Labneh, Middle Eastern drained yogurt, usually made from whole milk or cream, is a sensuous treat. The most delicious *labneh* I ever tasted was made by a Palestinian New Yorker, who used equal parts of half-and-half (or light cream) and whole milk. Eating it was bliss. Prepared *labneh* can be bought in Middle Eastern markets, many specialty stores and supermarkets. Substitute it for either sour cream or yogurt cream in any recipe.

For a rich-tasting yogurt cream, use whole-milk yogurt. Or for the best of the Ashkenazi and Sephardi worlds, stir a spoonful or two of sour cream into thick yogurt cream made from whole or low-fat milk.

TO PREPARE YOGURT CREAM: Line a strainer or colander with uncolored paper towels or a double thickness of cheesecloth. Or place a coffee filter in the drip funnel of a coffeemaker like Melitta or Chemex. Spoon in whole-milk, low-fat, or nonfat yogurt. Set strainer, colander, or funnel over a bowl or cup to catch the liquid whey, and let drain in a cool place until the yogurt is as thick and creamy as desired, from 30 minutes to 2 hours or more. (One quart, 4 cups yogurt, will yield about 2 cups yogurt cream.)

Tangy yogurt cream lends itself to many seasonings: honey or maple syrup and finely chopped dates, vanilla, or fragrant spices for a sweet taste; garlic mashed to a paste with salt, dried mint, fresh dill, etc., for a fresh, savory flavor.

If you allow the yogurt to continue to drain for about 24 hours, it becomes a wonderful soft yogurt cheese. Season the cheese with a few drops of extra virgin olive oil, salt, and either garlic or fresh herbs or both.

Store covered in the refrigerator for up to 1 week.

BEEF STOCK

yield: 2½ TO 3 QUARTS

*B*y setting aside a cup or two of clear chicken soup for the freezer every time I make it (see page 62), I usually have enough available for most cooking needs. And when I don't, I doctor purchased broth for an excellent Almost Homemade (page 70). Using good homemade chicken broth does beef recipes no injustice, in most cases. But there are times when only a full-bodied beef stock will do—for simmering Flanken (page 87) or adding dimension to Tangy Russian Cabbage Soup (page 223), for instance.

These dishes call for deep, rich flavors, so first I caramelize the meat, bones, and aromatics. Because I have a very wide, heavy pot (an 8-quart Dutch oven), I can do everything—browning and simmering—in one pot, on top of the stove. A regular stockpot is neither wide nor heavy enough to brown the ingredients well. If you don't have a large enough saucepan or Dutch oven, use a 5- to 6-quart pot for browning, then transfer everything to a stockpot. Either way is simpler and less messy than caramelizing the ingredients by oven-roasting them.

About the bones: while marrow bones are often suggested, I find they can give the stock a slightly greasy quality that can be quite unpleasant in many dishes. Many butchers will not charge for soup bones—knuckle, shank, shoulder, and neck are good choices—if you request them when placing a large meat order. If you buy meat infrequently, request bones whenever you do and store them in the freezer until you are ready to prepare the stock.

1 to 2 tablespoons mild olive or vegetable oil

3 pounds lean stewing beef, such as chuck or neck meat, trimmed and cut into 3-inch pieces

2 pounds knuckle, shank, shoulder, or neck bones (if bones are very meaty, you can reduce the amount of beef to 2 pounds), trimmed of as much fat as possible

½ pound onions, cut into coarse chunks (2 cups)

IN an 8- to 10-quart Dutch oven or heavy saucepan with a lid, heat 1 tablespoon oil over moderately high heat. Working in batches so you don't crowd the pan, lightly brown the meat (don't let it get too crusty), and transfer it to a platter. In the same pan, brown the bones on all sides, then transfer them to the platter. Add another tablespoon of oil, if necessary, and the onions, carrots, parsnip, and garlic. Brown them in the dark meat residue, stirring and scraping them with a wooden spoon as they begin to bronze around the edges, about 10 minutes. Add the wine and stir constantly to scrape up the browned bits. Add 1 quart of the water and boil for 3 minutes, stirring, to pick up any remaining meat and vegetable bits. (If using a smaller pan, transfer everything now to a stockpot.)

ADD the meat, bones, remaining 3 quarts water, peppercorns, and salt. Turn the heat to medium and bring to a slow bubble, skimming any

½ pound carrots, scraped and cut into coarse chunks (1½ cups)

1 parsnip, peeled and cut into coarse chunks

3 large garlic cloves, peeled

½ cup dry red or white wine

4 quarts cold water (quality is important here, so if you use bottled water for coffee or tea, use it here)

20 peppercorns, crushed

1 teaspoon salt

1 small rutabaga or white turnip, peeled and cut into chunks

3 celery stalks, including leaves if available, coarsely chopped

1 cup loosely packed fresh flat-leaf parsley sprigs

froth and scum that rise to the surface. When the soup begins to "smile" (tiny bubbles break along the edge of the pot), turn the heat down to very low. Let the soup simmer for about 30 minutes, skimming frequently. Add the rutabaga or turnip, celery, and parsley, and raise the heat slightly to bring it back to a simmer. Let it bubble for a few minutes, then turn the heat down as low as possible, put the lid on, leaving it slightly askew, and continue skimming occasionally. Simmer the soup for at least 2 or 2½ hours longer—3 to 5 is even better. Do *not* let the soup boil. If necessary, use a flame tamer or *blech*, or put it on top of two burner grates stacked together. (Make sure the soup is bubbling, though ever so gently. If there is no movement at all on the surface, the soup will spoil.) Add more salt if you want, but remember this is a stock: the other dishes in which you will use it may be salty enough, and besides, the stock's flavors will become more concentrated when you boil it down.

LET the soup cool to room temperature in the pot, *uncovered*. (Hot soup in a covered pot may turn sour.)

STRAIN the cooled soup through a wire-mesh sieve pressing down on all the meat, bones, and vegetables to extract as much of their flavorful juices as you can, then discard the solids. (If desired, you can save the meat and the carrots and dice them finely to serve in the stock. However, most of the flavor will have been extracted from them already.)

REFRIGERATE the soup, covered, overnight, or until all the fat has congealed on top. Carefully scrape off the fat and discard it. If the soup still seems fatty, line a wire-mesh sieve with a layer of paper towels and pour the soup through into a clean bowl or pot. (If the soup has jelled from chilling, bring it to room temperature first.) If the paper towels become thickly coated with fat, change them once or twice during the process.

STORE the stock in the refrigerator up to 1 week or freeze for up to 3 months.

VEGETABLE STOCK

yield: ABOUT 6 CUPS

*B*ecause vegetable stock is pareve or neutral (that is, it contains neither meat nor dairy), according to the dietary laws, it may be eaten with either. But meat dishes generally rely on meat stocks; in Jewish cooking, it is foods glossed with butter or topped with cream that give vegetable stock its reason for being. Only vegetable stock can jazz up a plain pilaf destined to partner a butter-gilded fish. It is the sole stock base for a soup that will be enriched with sour cream or yogurt. And kasha, often insipid when prepared with plain water, turns inspired with a stock that permits generous lacings of genuine sweet butter instead of margarine.

You can purchase acceptable ready-made versions of chicken and beef stock that will do nicely in a pinch for sauces, stews, and so on, but good-quality vegetable stocks are harder to find. Fortunately, they are much quicker to make than the meat-based kind (in fact, lengthy cooking will ruin, not improve, a vegetable stock).

This is one of those recipes for which I am reluctant to provide exact ingredients and measures because it can be varied endlessly according to availability of produce and how the stock will ultimately be used. So think of this recipe as a guide.

Some of the optional ingredients here will give you bigger flavors. Use them when you desire a stronger, darker stock. Tomatoes make everything sing, but with a rather full-throated voice. Soy sauce and the liquid from soaking dried mushrooms can be insistent, too. You may want to start with smaller quantities of these ingredients, and keep tasting as you go along, adding more as necessary. If you have the corncobs left over after scraping the kernels for another use, they will provide an earthy sweetness.

And by all means, add other vegetables: anything in the onion family, a little sweet red pepper, more fresh mushrooms (parings are fine), fennel, pea pods, a small potato, celery root, fresh herbs. Aim for balance and complexity—no one ingredient should overwhelm the others. And avoid strong or bitter-tasting vegetables, like broccoli, members of the cabbage family, eggplant, and pungent greens.

1 tomato (optional)

2 tablespoons olive oil or unsalted butter or 1 tablespoon of each

2 large onions, 1 coarsely chopped, 1 thinly sliced

2 medium carrots, scraped and diced

2 celery stalks, coarsely chopped

1 small parsnip, peeled and coarsely chopped

1 small turnip, scraped or if waxed or thick-skinned, peeled, coarsely chopped

IF you are using the tomato, char it to give it some character and to remove the peel easily: rinse and pat it dry. Spear it through the stem

½ pound fresh cultivated regular or shiitake mushrooms, wiped clean (pieces and stems are fine)

6 to 8 garlic cloves, peeled and smashed

About 1 teaspoon soy sauce (optional)

4 to 6 sprigs fresh thyme or ¼ teaspoon dried leaves

5 peppercorns, crushed

1 teaspoon salt

10 fresh flat-leaf parsley sprigs

1 Turkish bay leaf

¼ cup celery leaves or 1 teaspoon celery seed, crushed lightly

OPTIONAL ADDITIONS

Up to 1 cup zucchini or summer squash chunks, strips of mild lettuce or green Swiss chard leaves, or coarsely chopped chard stalks

2 corncobs

Up to ¼ ounce dried mushrooms, soaked in 2 cups hot water for 30 minutes, or until soft, then rinsed for grit and finely chopped

Some liquid from soaking the dried mushrooms (or leftover mushroom liquid from another recipe), strained through a sieve lined with a paper towel or a coffee filter to remove any remaining grit

2 quarts cold water (quality is important here, so if you use bottled water for coffee or tea, use it here)

end with a long-handled fork and lightly blacken the skin on all sides over a gas burner, as you would roast a pepper. Let it cool until you can handle it, then pull off the peel with your fingers. Cut the tomato in half, scoop out and discard the seeds and core. Chop the pulp coarsely and set it aside.

IN a 6-quart Dutch oven or very wide heavy saucepan, heat the oil and/or butter over moderately high heat until sizzling. Add all of the onions and sauté for about 15 minutes, frequently lifting and scraping the pieces from the bottom of the pan as the onions caramelize to a deep golden bronze.

ADD the carrots, celery, parsnip, and turnip, and cook until the edges of the vegetables are tinged with brown. Add the fresh mushrooms and garlic, and cook until the mushrooms give up their liquid. Sprinkle with the soy sauce, if using, and the thyme, peppercorns, and salt. Add the tomato, if using, and sauté for 5 minutes. Add the parsley, bay leaf, celery leaves or seeds, the zucchini, squash, and/or chard, if using, and sauté for 1 to 2 minutes. Add the corncobs, soaked dried mushrooms, and/or the mushroom soaking liquid, if using. Add the water. Bring to a gentle boil, so the bubbles just begin to break along the edges, then reduce to a simmer. Cook for 45 to 60 minutes, partially covered, until the vegetables are very soft.

STRAIN immediately through a wire-mesh sieve or a colander fitted with paper towels, pressing hard against the solids with the back of a wooden spoon to extract all of the flavorful liquids. Taste and adjust the seasonings. If the stock lacks character, concentrate the flavors by reducing the liquid slightly. (Don't reduce this stock too much—it will turn bitter.)

LET cool completely, *uncovered*, then cover and refrigerate. The stock will keep up to 5 days refrigerated, or up to 3 months frozen.

BLINTZES

yield: 16 TO 18 BLINTZ LEAVES

Blintzes may seem complicated, but they are as easy to prepare as crepes. Easier, in fact, since they are cooked on one side only. They are the ideal pastry for the rolling pin-challenged.

Like strawberry shortcake and Wallis Simpson, they were meant to be rich. On the other hand, such hefty doses of butter, cream, and cheese are best enjoyed in the company of more pristine flavors, like gently treated fresh or dried fruit.

Devise your own combinations for fillings from the liveliest fruits at the market, and feel free to potchkeh with the more detailed recipes throughout the book. Cooking the fruit just long enough to bring out its natural sugars (or macerating delicate raw fruits like blueberries in hot liquids, such as reduced fruit juice) and avoiding fillers like cornstarch will keep the flavors brisk and fresh-tasting. If you find that your fruit is too wet for a filling, stir in a few tablespoons of ground blanched almonds or cream cheese to soak up the juices.

BLINTZ LEAVES (THE BASIC CRÊPE)

1 to 1¼ cups milk, preferably whole

3 large eggs

¾ cup unbleached all-purpose flour

¼ teaspoon salt

2 tablespoons unsalted butter, melted and cooled

Additional unsalted butter, ghee, or, less preferably, a mild, flavorless oil (such as avocado), or a combination of butter and oil, for frying

IN a blender, mix 1 cup of the milk, the eggs, flour, salt, and butter until smooth. Transfer the batter to a bowl. (To prepare batter by hand, beat the eggs and butter together in a bowl; mix in ½ cup of the milk; gradually add the flour and salt, whisking until smooth, then add another ½ cup of milk; whisk until well blended.)

LET the batter rest for at least 30 minutes or up to 2 hours at room temperature. If refrigerated, the batter should rest for at least 2 hours or up to 12 hours (overnight is fine).

STIR the batter well (don't rebeat it because you want to avoid foamy bubbles). It should have the consistency of light cream. If necessary, thin it with some of the remaining milk. You may have to add more milk if the batter thickens as it stands.

HEAT a very lightly buttered 6- or 7-inch skillet or crêpe pan over moderately high heat until sizzling. (A nonstick pan works particularly well, but I find you do have to butter the pan, at least for the first blintz, to avoid a slightly rubbery texture.) Pour about 2 tablespoons of batter into the hot pan (a coffee measure is good for this), and immediately tilt the pan from side to side to distribute the batter evenly over the bottom. You may find it easier both to add the batter and swirl while holding the pan off the heat. Don't allow the batter to extend up the sides of the pan when tilting or the blintz edges will become too thin and crackly.

COOK just until the top of the blintz is slightly dry and the edges start to curl. The bottom should be pale gold, not brown. Do *not* cook the other side. Loosen the blintz with a spatula and turn it out onto wax paper or a large platter, fried side up. Repeat until all the batter is used up. Pile the finished blintz leaves on a platter, separating each with sheets of wax paper or a clean kitchen cloth, and keep the exposed leaves covered to prevent them from drying out. Brush the pan with additional butter or oil only if necessary, and remember to stir the batter periodically. To avoid tears, let the freshly prepared blintz leaves cool to room temperature before filling. (And the wax paper is easier to remove when the blintz leaves are cool.)

BLINTZ leaves may be prepared ahead. Let them cool to room temperature, keeping them separated by wax paper, then wrap well with foil. Refrigerate for up to 3 days, or freeze them for up to 1 month, separated by the wax paper and well wrapped with heavy-duty foil or in a freezer-proof container. Bring them to room temperature before filling to prevent tearing them.

COOK'S NOTE: Add very little butter or oil to the pan when preparing the leaves. The batter already contains butter, so if you use a nonstick pan, you may not need to add any, after the first blintz. To grease the pan, dip a paper towel *very* lightly in melted butter or oil and quickly film the pan. If you put too much in or if the butter burns as you fry the leaves, wipe the pan clean with a paper towel so as not to transfer any burned butter taste.

Work quickly greasing the pan, adding the batter, and turning out the finished leaf. The pan should always be hot before you add the batter.

Allow the batter to rest, and stir, don't beat, to eliminate most of the bubbles. Occasionally, bubbles will form on top of a cooking blintz leaf, and generally they are superficial and will cause no damage. But if a bubble looks like it will create a real hole through the finished leaf, I immediately smooth over it with some of the still wet batter from another part of the blintz, or I dab on a smidgen of fresh batter to cover it, letting the leaf continue cooking until it seems dry. (Because the leaves are very thin, cooked only on one side, and most fillings are rather wet, even fairly small holes could mean fillings oozing out while blintzes are frying.)

FILLING THE BLINTZES

SPREAD 1 heaping tablespoon of the filling across the middle of the cooked side of each blintz. (Tempting as it may be to use up that extra bit of filling, do not overfill blintzes or they might explode.) Fold in the sides, then fold the bottom of the blintz over the filling, and roll up, jelly-roll fashion, pulling the top over tightly. You should have a neat package. Place filled blintzes seam side down, so they don't open up.

AT this point, you can refrigerate the blintzes for a couple of days or freeze them for up to 1 month, if you want to, and fry them just before serving. Don't bother to thaw frozen blintzes, but adjust cooking time accordingly.

COOK'S NOTE: Fillings should always be cooled at least to room temperature. I find it is often easier to work with chilled fillings: they are firmer and less runny.

COOKING THE FILLED BLINTZES

TO fry the blintzes, heat butter, a mild oil, or a combination, in a heavy skillet over medium heat until sizzling. (The best medium for frying blintzes is probably clarified butter, since its higher smoke point means it won't easily burn; yet, it will still imbue the blintzes with that pure butter taste. While I almost never take the time to prepare clarified butter, I sometimes use ghee, the Indian equivalent, available commercially in many specialty stores with kosher certification.) Add the blintzes seam side down, without crowding the pan. Cook, turning once, until golden brown on both sides, 2 to 3 minutes per side. Adjust the heat, if necessary, and watch that the butter does not scorch.

OR you can bake them, for a slightly lighter taste. Preheat the oven to 450°F. Melt a generous quantity of butter or butter mixed with a little oil on a rimmed baking sheet or in a shallow baking pan. Add the blintzes and turn to coat well on all sides. Arrange the blintzes (seam side down) on the sheet so their sides are not touching. Bake for 10 to 15 minutes, until crisp and golden brown on both sides. I usually find it is not necessary to turn them; if they seem slow to brown on top, however, I flip them over for a few minutes. When preparing a large number of blintzes for company, it is usually easiest to bake them.

WONTON WRAPPERS

When I first began buying wonton wrappers in New York City's Chinatown, I noticed a kosher seal on several brands. Apparently, using paper-thin wonton wrappers to make kreplach was not a novel idea.

But it is a delicious one, an elegant, easy, inexpensive timesaver. And even if I had time enough to make my own dough, I doubt it would turn out as delicate and thin as these egg-enriched little pasta squares.

If you can't find wonton wrappers in Asian stores, look for them in health-food and specialty stores and most supermarkets (often they are kept in the refrigerated section of the produce department). The non-Asian ones may be somewhat thicker and less delicate, but they too will work well as kreplach wrappers.

TO PREPARE WONTON KREPLACH: Thaw wonton wrappers, if frozen, and bring to room temperature. These fragile little squares dry out easily, so keep them covered with plastic wrap or a slightly dampened kitchen towel. Remove wrappers as needed, leaving the rest covered to prevent cracking and drying.

Prepare an egg wash: in a small bowl, beat an egg with 1 teaspoon water. (You can use plain water to seal the kreplach, but the egg creates a more permanent "glue.")

Put a wrapper on a lightly floured surface. Mound 1 heaping teaspoon of filling in the center of the wrapper. Dip your finger in the egg wash and "paint" the edges all around the filling. Or use a small pastry brush to paint. Fold the *krepl* (singular of kreplach) into a triangle by pulling one corner of the square over to the opposite corner. Carefully press down all around the filling to force out all the air and seal the edges firmly. It's important to push out the air, otherwise the krepl may fill up with water as it is being poached. Trim away any excess dough around the filling with a sharp knife, or curl the two opposite corners together, dab with egg wash, and pinch tightly closed.

You can also make larger kreplach, as called for in Poached Prune Kreplach with Honeyed Cream and Pecans (page 328). Place 1 heaping tablespoon of filling in the center of a wrapper, paint the edges with egg wash, and cover with a second wrapper. Press out air, seal, and trim. Or trim off the excess dough using cookie cutters in fanciful shapes—great fun to do with children.

Place filled kreplach on a dry kitchen towel and cover with plastic wrap. Let them rest for 15 to 20 minutes so the egg wash seal can dry (turn them occasionally).

To poach, bring a large, wide pot of salted water to a gentle boil. Add the kreplach, in batches as necessary, and cook for 3 to 7 minutes, depending on the brand of wrapper you are using, until they float to the surface and are tender. Never let the kreplach boil rapidly: they will fill with water or explode, or both! And don't try to save time by cooking the kreplach in broth—inevitably one will rupture and ruin your broth.

Use a skimmer to transfer the kreplach as they are done to a dry kitchen towel or paper towels to drain briefly. They are too fragile to be dumped into a colander. If you aren't serving them soon, moisten them with a little broth, sauce, butter, or oil, and keep them warm until needed.

After they are poached, kreplach can be served in soup, or sautéed or baked with butter or oil. For an unusual preparation, make them pot sticker–style. (Follow the instructions for Potato-Onion Kreplach, Pot Sticker–Style on page 518.)

I find it easier to stuff kreplach with a filling that has been chilled: it is firmer and less runny. Use the fillings in this book to start, then improvise some of your own. Try the cheese blintz filling and its savory variation—or any of the fruit blintz fillings. Ground liver works well as does mashed chickpeas or pumpkin sauced with yogurt cream, crushed garlic, mint, and olive oil. And don't forget your refrigerator full of leftovers.

STORING THE WRAPPERS: Fresh wonton wrappers tend to dry out quickly after only a few days in the refrigerator, so make sure they are very well sealed. Wonton wrappers can be frozen in airtight packages for two to three months (after that, they tend to dry out); don't refreeze them.

POMEGRANATE MOLASSES AND *TEMERHINDI* OR *OURT*

I am crazy about pomegranate molasses (sometimes called pomegranate concentrate or syrup), the thick, tangy-sweet concentrate of reduced tart pomegranate juice and often sugar and lemon juice. It has myriad uses in the kitchen, from barbeque sauces, marinades, and gravies to flavoring dips like hummus and even guacamole. I call for it in several recipes. You'll find it in Middle Eastern markets, specialty stores, and many supermarkets. Once opened, it should be tightly stored in the refrigerator, where it will keep almost indefinitely. (For more on pomegranate molasses, see Spiced Pomegranate Molasses Applesauce on page 295). *Temerhindi*, also known as *ourt*, and a concentrate of tamarind, lemon juice, and sugar, is usually prepared at home by Middle Eastern Jews in a rather time-consuming process. It is available ready-made at Middle Eastern Jewish groceries. *Temerhindi* is delectably tart and sweet, like pomegranate molasses, which makes a good substitute for it. If neither is available, a fair stand-in can be made by boiling together a mixture of one part prune butter (lekvar), one part sugar, and two parts lemon juice until it has the consistency of thick tomato sauce. In a pinch, mix equal parts of lekvar and apricot butter with a bit of lemon juice, and simmer together for a few minutes until well combined.

SALT

For very special seasoning, I sprinkle either fine *fleur de sel* (French sea salt) or English Maldon sea salt on such indulgences as Rosh Hashanah challah smeared with a sublime honey. I sometimes use regular table salt for baking—for example, in some breads.

But for regular purposes, I nearly always use kosher salt for cooking and at table. I prefer its pure, clean flavor and coarse texture. Because of its large crystals, it doesn't melt into foods and is essential for certain recipes like curing Pastrami-Style Salmon (page 197) or salting eggplant. When a recipe calls for coarse salt, choose either the coarsest grind of kosher salt available or a coarse sea salt.

When no type is specified in a recipe, feel free to substitute your own favorite salt, bearing in mind that kosher salt is somewhat milder than most other kinds. Figure that 1 teaspoon of regular table salt is approximately equivalent to 2 teaspoons of Diamond Crystal Kosher Salt (the brand I have used in these recipes) and about 1¼ teaspoons of Morton's Kosher Salt.

A NOTE ON SALTING: I usually add salt at several stages in a recipe. I find it flavors the food better than when added all at once at the conclusion of the cooking. And I usually wind up adding less salt in all.

"It was the darkness and emptiness of the streets I liked most about Friday evening, as if in preparation for that day of rest and worship which the Jews greet 'as a bride'. . . . I waited for the streets to go dark on Friday evening as other children waited for Christmas lights."

—ALFRED KAZIN, *A Walker in the City*

Sabbath

No wonder the Sabbath is frequently personified as a beautiful queen, princess, or bride: traditional Jewish families eagerly begin feverish preparations for its arrival as if for a royal visit.

Cooks seek out the best foods and wines in the markets, and often put aside especially choice or exotic fruits found during the week to be savored when the Sabbath comes. Most of the finest Jewish recipes derive from the Sabbath kitchen: for many poor Jews, it was the one day of the week that they would taste meat, chicken, or wine.

The freshly scrubbed house percolates with the sounds and smells of Sabbath cooking. A sniff of tsimmes, puckery-sweet with rhubarb and prunes, tantalizes the nose. And the crisp skin of lemon-roasted chicken and puffy little matzoh balls, waiting for soup, invite filching by hungry children just home from school.

For the most observant, everything must be readied before the Queen's arrival, not only the Friday evening meal but Saturday's hot lunch as well. Kindling fires and cooking are among the thirty-nine activities classified as work, and therefore are prohibited while the Sabbath is in progress. In addition to festive foods like challah, chicken soup, chopped chicken livers, and gefilte fish, Jews have created a whole set of special dishes to accommodate the special Sabbath restrictions:

cholents, hamins, and dafinas—lusty one-pot meals made beforehand then left to cook overnight in the slowest ovens, savory kugels and *fritadas* (frittatas) warmed up on hot trays, and spicy fresh fish dishes from Jewish kitchens all over the globe, prepared ahead and served cold.

As night falls on Friday, the hustle and bustle cease and a hush falls over the house. The table, cleared of mail, keys, and other weekday detritus, has been transformed: now it is an elegant altar of spotless linen, gleaming silver, and china set to honor the Sabbath.

As Jews light the candles and recite the Kiddush blessing over the wine to usher in the Sabbath, the parents bless the children. The joyous family meal is especially delicious and savored leisurely.

The following day, the Queen's presence is still felt, as the family continues to move in step with her unique rhythm. Since the most ancient times (it is the only holiday mentioned in the Ten Commandments), even those whose six-day work week revolved around mindless drudgery and endless toil could look forward to an evening, then an entire day—the Sabbath—devoted to resting their bodies, renewing their spirits, and strengthening the bonds with those they loved.

The numerical value of the letters in the word *dag* (Hebrew for fish) adds up to seven, and Sabbath is the seventh day of the week. And so whoever ate *dag* on the Sabbath was thought to be safe from the judgment of *Gehenna*, the hellish afterlife for the damned.

Although prepared differently in the myriad kitchens of the Diaspora, a special fish dish usually appears at one or more meals on every Jewish Sabbath: Friday night, the hearty Saturday lunch, or the light meal at Sabbath's close. In fact, two widely divergent chopped fish recipes, gefilte fish and Middle Eastern ground fish balls like Egyptian *bellahat*, may both owe their origins to the injunction against Sabbath work, which includes *borer* (picking over bones). Removing the bones from the fish and chopping it up in advance afforded Jews from Eastern Europe and North Africa a delicious, pleasurable way to enjoy their Sabbath fish.

In Talmudic times (70 to 500 CE) a hot meal was not an everyday occurrence. To honor the Sabbath, it became a *mitzvah* (good deed), to serve hot food at the Saturday midday meal. Here we dish up robust,

"Wherewith does one show delight in the Sabbath . . . with beets, a large fish, and garlic."

—BABYLONIAN TALMUD: SHABBAT 118B

"A Jew without hot food on the Sabbath is like a king without a state."

—JEWISH PROVERB

slow-cooked Duck and White Bean Cholent or a dafina combining falling-off-the-bone lamb with little boats of stuffed eggplant, accompanied by tart, crisp green salads. In warm weather, there is *desayuno* (a Sephardi-style brunch), featuring Spinach Cheese Squares, roasted eggs, and perhaps an Ashkenazi Sorrel-Onion Noodle Kugel.

Saturday night, when it is time to bid farewell to the Sabbath, she is escorted off in the enchanting Havdalah ceremony. Jews burn a braided candle, pour a full cup of wine, and breathe in fragrant spices, reminding them of the special Sabbath sweetness they have tasted. This sweetness will fortify them as they return to the routine world. Just until Wednesday, when they begin anticipating the beautiful Sabbath to come.

Many American Jews, even if they are not Orthodox, still find some way to mark the Sabbath as sacred and separate it from the workaday week. For some, this is the special Friday night dinner—perhaps the only time during a busy week when the family sits down together—or the quiet Saturday spent with loved ones. For others, it is the unique aura of *shalom beit* (peace in the house) that settles over the family: the commandment in Exodus 35:3 ("Ye shall kindle no fire throughout your habitation upon the Sabbath day") may also refer to flaring tempers and simmering anger.

For me, as a child, it was the Kiddush, the blessing chanted before the Friday evening meal to usher in the Sabbath. Never bound by custom, my father always let me, his daughter, "make" the Kiddush—though traditionally the benediction is recited by men—because I, a passionate eight-year-old who had just begun Hebrew school lessons, was burning to take over the ceremony.

And so it became my job as much as setting the table every evening. I chanted the prayers and sipped the sweet, syrupy wine from my father's worn Kiddush cup, shined so often and so hard that no inscriptions were any longer visible. Then I'd pass the cup around so everyone could drink in the Sabbath's sweetness—mother, father, sister, brother, grandfather, usually a guest or two, and back to me. A circle that was a warm embrace and inviolate family nexus.

There were times, of course, that I absented myself, when I was a guest at a friend's, or later a boyfriend's, home. And I can still hear the note of disappointment—and chastening—in my father's voice when I told him I wouldn't be home for dinner: "Do you know it's Friday night?" he'd ask.

But next Friday, I'd be back. No Kiddush wine ever tasted so sweet as at my father's table.

In homes in which the Sabbath is not observed in the traditional way, the routine demands of contemporary life can make even simple Sabbath observance seem difficult. A Friday night dinner when your daughter regularly performs in the school plays and her older brother wants to grab a pizza and hang out with friends on weekends? Saturdays that begin with carpool for the soccer team?

But the ancient wisdom of setting aside one day of the week and noting it as special still applies today. Shabbat not only rests our bodies and renews our spirits but also nourishes our families.

Many families decide to begin celebrating Shabbat when their children are small. For others, Friday evening seems the perfect time for their grown children (and their families or significant others) to come home for dinner. And, for some, Shabbat becomes the night to break bread with their family of friends.

Here are just some of the ways to bring Shabbat traditions into nontraditional families.

- Before the Sabbath starts, it is customary to put aside money for *tzedakah* (charity) and special tzedakah boxes—beautiful heirlooms or colorful ones made by the kids—are familiar fixtures in Jewish homes. Put money in the box every Friday, and make the decision of where to donate the money a family one. Encourage your children to contribute some of their own money to the collection, or to a different cause that is important to them.

- If a family member is away—a child at school or camp, a parent traveling on business, grandparents who live out-of-town—this is a wonderful time to call, wish him or her a good week, and say I love you.

- Families traditionally usher in Shabbat by lighting candles: usually two, though some light an extra candle for each child or even each member of the household. While candlelighting was a woman's job in the past, there is no reason why the father or all the family members can't take part. Kindling the flames focuses attention on the moment, announcing the commencement of the Sabbath, and the soft lights emanate a protective glow over the house. If your children arrive home later in the evening, well past candlelighting, consider giving them their own candles to light at that time.

- Filled now with a sense of our blessings, we are aware of the gifts our children are to us. For a parent, this may be the most beautiful part of Shabbat—the time to bless your children using the traditional blessing from a prayerbook or one you create in your own words. If you incorporate just one Shabbat tradition into your life, let it be this one. If you have been arguing all week, take a break, bless and kiss your child. If your children go out on Friday night, bless them when they come home or the following day.

Many parents "store up" their blessings for the day their child becomes bar or bat mitzvah or marries. You'll find that weekly Shabbat blessings connect you intimately to your child, and eventually prepare a meaningful foundation for your blessings at these special milestones.

This is also a perfect time for all members of the family to bless each other.

Before dinner is served, chant the Kiddush. *L'chaim!* To life! The celebrated toast reminds us that from the beginning of Jewish time, wine has embodied both life's blessings and its blessedness. Kiddush, the prayer over wine, means "sanctification," and the Friday night benediction, completed by the requisite drink of wine, symbolically consecrates the family and the dinner that follows. Pass the cup around the table so that everyone can share the taste of life's joys.

Ashkenazi and Sephardi literature abounds with descriptions of memorable Shabbat dinners, of foods imbued with the unique spice of Sabbath itself. A luscious home-cooked meal served on your best china would be fabulous, but there are simpler ways to make the dinner special: fill a vase with fragrant lilacs; offer a dessert too rich for your weekday table; splurge on red meat like Easy Onion-Braised Brisket or a beautiful, high-carb Onion Challah or other bread you try to avoid during the week. Sit down together at the same time and eat leisurely. If you have young children, read a story or sing family songs to encourage them to stay at the table.

If at all possible, try to have your kids bring their friends home rather than go out, or arrange to serve dinner early, before they leave for the evening. If they do miss dinner, consider deferring Shabbat dessert—or just plain milk and cookies—until they return home. And bless them then.

"When I marched in Selma," the eminent theologian Abraham Joshua Heschel said, "my feet were praying;" some families regularly pray with their hands on Shabbat instead of attending worship services. At the Village Temple in New York City, every Saturday while services are taking place downstairs in the sanctuary, volunteers—young children to ninetysomethings—work in the soup kitchen upstairs preparing a hearty lunch for homeless guests. If your family prefers to pray with their hands on Friday night or Saturday, and local synagogues do not have a similar program (in Orthodox and most Conservative congregations, traditionally such work would not be permitted in the synagogue on the Sabbath), consider other opportunities in your area for which you might regularly volunteer, like Friday night or Saturday morning read-alouds in the children's or geriatric section of your hospital.

- Shabbat has always been a time for visiting extended family and close friends, a time to strengthen bonds with those we love. Gathering around the table—whether for a special meal like Shabbat lunch or just pie and ice cream on September afternoons on the screened porch—invites conversation. And without baseball blaring from the TV, Grandpa may share a family memory; leaving video games or the laptop at home will encourage children to actively participate with stories of their own.

- Or revive a long-lost family tradition: the Cousins Club. When all their parents had passed away, my mother's cousins realized that with the older generation gone, it was up to them to stay in touch with each other. They decided to get together once a month for a potluck Shabbat dinner. The vibrant meal they share reflects the rich tapestry of cultures the family now comprises.

- And for many families, spending time together outdoors on Shabbat brings a heightened sense of our place in the universe. Visiting a botanical garden or nearby hiking trail as the seasons unfold, taking a leisurely family walk every Saturday afternoon, watching the sun set or the constellations appear in the Friday night sky—all connect us to the rhythms of the natural world and to one another.

SABBATH
menu suggestions

SPRING AND SUMMER

FRIDAY EVENING DINNERS

*Mary's Onion Challah

*Gefilte Fish Quickly Steamed Between Cabbage Leaves

*Classic Chicken Soup with *Matzoh Balls

*Lemon-Roasted Chicken, *Rhubarb-Prune Tsimmes, and *Jeweled Brown Rice

or

*Grilled Bass with Pomegranate-Mint Vinaigrette and *Fresh Corn Kugel

Tender green beans

Summer tomato platter: red, yellow, and orange tomatoes sprinkled with fresh herbs

Fresh peaches and toasted almonds or bowl of sweet red and yellow cherries

*Classic Challah

*Egyptian Ground Fish Balls with Tomato and Cumin (*Bellahat*)

or

*Chopped Eggs and Onions with black olives, garlic dill pickles, and pickled tomatoes

*Chicken with Olives and Preserved Lemon; couscous or

*See index for page numbers

*Syrian Pilaf

or

*Provençal Roasted Garlic–Braised Breast of Veal with Springtime Stuffing

Roasted asparagus

Fresh seasonal berries with *Hazelnut Macaroons

SATURDAY LUNCHEONS

*Chilled Minted Cucumber Soup

or

*Celery *Avgolemono* (Greek Egg Lemon Soup; served tepid, if desired, and without Chicken Matzoh Balls)

*Italian-Jewish Marinated Fried Fish (*Pesce en Saor*)

*Roasted Red Peppers or salad of mixed greens

*Rich Noodle Pudding Baked with Fresh Plums and Nectarines or *Peach Buttermilk Kugel or *Roseberry-Rhubarb Gelato

*Grandmother's Cold Fruit Soup

*Huevos Haminados

*Sorrel-Onion Noodle Kugel or *Spinach Cheese Squares

*Israeli Salad

Fresh nectarines or melon wedges with *Caramel Rugelach

or

*Old-Fashioned Rice Pudding or *Poppy Seed Butter Cake (Mohn Cake)

*See index for page numbers

FALL AND WINTER

FRIDAY EVENING DINNERS

*Classic Challah

*Chopped Chicken Liver from the Rue des Rosiers,
*Grated Black Radish and Endive Salad in Shallot
Vinaigrette

or

*Pastrami-Style Salmon with chopped onion, capers,
and lemon slices

*Moroccan Fish with Chickpeas and Saffron-Lime Aioli

or

*Coffee-Spiced Pot Roast with Kasha Kreplach and
Toasted Garlic Challah Crumbs

or

*Chicken Paprikash with *Nockerl* (Dumplings)

Fresh steamed spinach dressed with extra virgin olive oil
and lemon juice

*Moroccan-Flavored Carrot Kugel

Ripe Comice or Bartlett pears with toasted walnuts

or

*Jewish Sautéed Apple Cake or *Dried Fruit Compote
with Fresh Pineapple, Pistachios, and Mint

* Classic Challah

*Almost-Homemade Soup (from *Cheater's Chicken in the
Pot) with *Fried Onion and Chicken Kreplach

*See index for page numbers

or

*Rich Beef Broth (from *Flanken recipe) with *Mishmash Kreplach (Beef, Potato, and Fried Onion Kreplach)

*Classic Sweet-and-Sour Stuffed Cabbage or *Cabbage Stuffed with Mushrooms and Meat or *Easy Onion-Braised Brisket

*Onion-Crusted Light Potato Kugel

or

*Crackletop Potato Kugel

Salad of fresh tart greens

*Roasted Apple-Walnut Noodle Kugel

or

Fresh citrus platter: blood or navel orange slices dusted with cinnamon; clementines

SATURDAY LUNCHEONS

Ruby red grapefruit halves

*Duck and White Bean Cholent

or

*Garlicky Lamb and Lima Hamin with Little Eggplant Boats

or

*Herbed Beef Cholent with Onion Gonifs

Watercress and orange salad with cumin vinaigrette

Seasonal selection of fresh and dried fruits: red grapes, apples, Medjool dates, and toasted walnuts

*See index for page numbers

Fresh papaya halves with lime

*Kasha Varnishkes with Fried Eggplant, Mushrooms, and Onion Marmalade

or

*Zucchini Fritada

Arugula and endive salad

*Hungarian Chocolate-Walnut Torte with fresh whipped cream or vanilla ice cream

or

*Upside-Down Caramel-Cranberry-Pecan Noodle Kugel

or

*Turkish Silken Ground-Rice Pudding (*Sutlaj*) with *Fresh Persimmon Sauce

CLASSIC CHALLAH

yields: 2 MEDIUM LOAVES

*B*read has always been the heart of the Jewish meal. When the benediction over the bread is made, it is unnecessary to recite prayers over any of the other foods eaten.

The exception is the Kiddush, the blessing chanted over wine that introduces every Sabbath and important holiday. At these times the challah is covered with a white cloth, some say to protect it from embarrassment at seeing the wine blessed first. The two uncut loaves of challah on the Sabbath table echo the double portion of manna God provided to the wandering Israelites before each weekly Sabbath. The seeds usually sprinkled on the braided breads before baking symbolize the manna enveloped with dew to keep it fresh-tasting for the following day.

After the motzi (bread blessing) is recited, some families slice the challah and others quite literally "break bread"—tearing off knobs of the twisted bread with their fingers, rather than cutting it with a knife. They remember the verse in Exodus 20:22 comparing a metal knife to an instrument of war and don't wish to profane the newly blessed loaf.

Then everyone eats a piece of the egg-rich bread and the Sabbath dinner begins.

2 envelopes (¼ ounce each) active dry yeast

¼ cup plus 1 teaspoon sugar

¼ cup mild olive, avocado, or other favorite mild oil, plus additional for greasing the bowl, plastic wrap, and baking sheet

2 large eggs

2 teaspoons table salt (not coarse salt)

4 to 5 cups bread flour, plus additional for dusting the work surface, kneading, and shaping the dough

FOR THE TOPPING

HAVE all ingredients, except topping, at room temperature.

POUR 1 cup warm water (100 to 110°F) into a food processor fitted with a steel blade. Sprinkle the yeast over the water and add 1 teaspoon of the sugar. Allow the mixture to dissolve and proof, 5 to 10 minutes.

ADD the remaining ¼ cup sugar, the oil, eggs, and salt to the yeast mixture. Pulse for a few moments to combine. Add the flour, 1 cup at a time, pulsing briefly after each addition. After you've added 4 cups, process briefly until the dough forms a ball around the blade. (If the dough seems too moist, add additional flour in small increments through the feed tube until the sides of the processor bowl are clean but the dough still appears to be a little sticky.) Continue processing for 2 to 3 more minutes to knead the dough until it is smooth and elastic.

FORM the dough into a ball and place it in a greased bowl. Cover with greased plastic wrap. Allow the dough to rise in a warm, draft-free place until double in bulk, 2 to 3 hours. (Or start the bread the day before you plan to bake it, and let the dough rise slowly overnight in the refrigerator. Allow it to come back to room temperature before proceeding.) To

1 large egg lightly beaten with 1 teaspoon water

Poppy or sesame seeds (optional)

test whether the bread has fully risen, gently press it with a fingertip. If the indentation remains, the dough has risen sufficiently.

PUNCH the dough down, then let it rise a second time until double in bulk, about 2 hours.

PUNCH the dough down again and divide it into six equal pieces. Using your palms, roll the pieces into identical ropes about 10 inches long. Braid the ropes into two loaves, using three ropes for each loaf. An easy way to do this evenly is to start the braid in the middle, braid to one end, then turn the loaf upside down and braid to the other end. Turn the ends under and press down to keep them joined together.

TRANSFER to a greased baking sheet. Apply the first coat of egg wash (reserve the rest), brushing it all over. Cover with greased plastic wrap and allow to rise for a third time until double in bulk, about 1 hour.

PREHEAT the oven to 350°F. Mix about 2 tablespoons of poppy or sesame seeds, if using, into the remaining egg wash. (If omitting seeds, apply the plain second egg wash glaze.) When the loaves have risen, brush the glaze over the top. Bake about 35 minutes on the middle rack, until the loaves are golden brown and sound hollow when tapped on the bottom. Transfer to a rack and let cool, or remove from the baking sheet and place directly on the oven rack to cool in the oven with the door left ajar.

COOK'S NOTE: You can flavor the bread with ground spices, such as cinnamon or cardamom (about 2 teaspoons); fresh herbs, such as chopped dill (up to ¼ cup) or rosemary (no more than 3 tablespoons); or a hint of tarragon paired, perhaps, with aniseed or fennel seeds sprinkled on top instead of poppy seeds. Add the spices or herbs when you add the oil, etc., to the yeast. Another tasty variation: sprinkle lightly with coarse salt instead of, or in addition to, the seeds.

"When you bake your own *hallahs* for the Sabbath, they have a different taste entirely. Your heart rises as you watch the loaves rise in the pan."

—CHAIM GRADE, *My Mother's Sabbath Days*

MARY'S ONION CHALLAH

yield: 2 MEDIUM LOAVES

Though he lived to be 94, my grandfather never tasted an ice cream that could match the ones he remembered buying from the old Turkish vendor back in Minsk or Smolensk before he arrived in New York at age 12.

He taught me a valuable food lesson: our most cherished food memories inevitably lead to disappointment. Perhaps that is because our culinary selves are constantly evolving—we taste the world with a different tongue at various times in our lives. Or maybe no real food could ever live up to one garnished with the patina of memory, burnished with age.

For me, with Ratner's oniony egg rolls, it was a little of both. In the years since the demise of the beloved dairy restaurant on Delancey Street on the Lower East Side, I've tasted many versions of the rolls, some purportedly made exactly according to the recipe published in The World-Famous Ratner's Meatless Cookbook. *None excited the way the oniony little breads, smeared with cold sweet butter, did.*

To paraphrase, the fault was not with the rolls, but with me that they were underlings. What I was after was far more oniony and buttery-tasting than the rolls had ever been.

My good friend Dr. Mary McLarnon, a consummate baker, had never tasted Ratner's onion rolls, but as I explained the taste memories that I wanted this book's challah to channel (challah and Jewish egg rolls are often made from the same rich dough), her blue eyes lit up. Since the bread had to be pareve, we talked about doing a triple rise to achieve the butteriness. A few days later, Mary dropped off two fragrant loaves for us to taste.

Not satisfied, Mary kept working on ways to boost the onion flavor until it tasted as incredibly aromatic as it smelled. The touch of cumin, reminiscent of Alsatian-Jewish bakeries, somehow made it more buttery.

Finally Mary brought two more loaves when Alex was home for Thanksgiving vacation. There were five of us that night—Alex, her boyfriend, my brother, my husband, and me—and we polished off every crumb.

It wasn't Ratner's onion roll. It was better.

2 large yellow onions, peeled and cut into coarse chunks (about 1 ½ pounds)

3 large garlic cloves, peeled and quartered

HAVE all ingredients, except glaze, at room temperature.

IN a food processor, pulse the onions and garlic until finely chopped but not pureed. Drape a damp, thin kitchen towel or double thickness of cheesecloth over a strainer set in a bowl. Scrape the onion-garlic

1 cup onion-garlic liquid (reserved from recipe)

2 envelopes (¼ ounce each) active dry yeast

1 teaspoon plus ¼ cup sugar

¼ cup plus 2 tablespoons mild olive oil

2 large eggs

Table salt

2 teaspoons ground cumin, preferably freshly toasted

4 to 5 cups plus 1 tablespoon bread flour, plus additional for dusting the work surface, kneading, and shaping the dough

Coarse salt

Oil for greasing the bowl, plastic wrap, and baking sheet

1 large egg lightly beaten with 1 teaspoon water, for glaze

mixture onto the cloth, gather the ends of the cloth together, and twist and wring until you have squeezed as much liquid as possible into the bowl, reserving it. Set aside the onion-garlic mixture. Don't bother to wash out the food processor.

MEASURE the reserved onion-garlic liquid, adding enough plain water, if necessary, so that you have 1 cup. Warm the liquid to 100 to 110°F, and add it to the food processor. Sprinkle the yeast over the liquid, add 1 teaspoon of sugar, and allow the mixture to dissolve and proof, 5 to 10 minutes.

ADD ¼ cup oil, the remaining ¼ cup sugar, the eggs, 2 teaspoons table salt, and cumin. Pulse for a few moments to combine. Add the flour, 1 cup at a time, pulsing briefly after each addition. After you've added 4 cups, process briefly until the dough forms a ball around the blade. (If the dough seems too moist, add additional flour in small increments through the feed tube until the sides of the processor bowl are clean but the dough still appears to be a little sticky.) Continue processing for 2 to 3 more minutes to knead the dough until smooth and elastic.

SHAPE the dough into a ball and place it in a greased bowl. Cover with greased plastic wrap. Allow the dough to rise in a warm draft-free place until double in bulk, 2 to 3 hours. (You can begin the bread the day before you plan to bake it, and let the dough rise slowly overnight in the refrigerator. Bring the dough back to room temperature before continuing.) To test whether the bread has fully risen, gently press it with a fingertip. If the dent remains, the dough is ready.

WHILE the bread is rising, warm the remaining 2 tablespoons oil in a large heavy skillet over medium heat. Add the reserved chopped onion and garlic, salt lightly, and cook uncovered over low heat, stirring occasionally, until very soft, up to 40 minutes. Raise the heat to medium, and continue cooking, lifting and turning, until golden and caramelized and all pan liquid has been absorbed. If necessary, turn the heat up to high for a few moments and cook, stirring, just until the pan liquid disappears. Cool the mixture to room temperature.

PUNCH the dough down. Now, using your hands or a floured rolling pin, gently flatten the dough and shape it into a circle about ¾-inch thick. In a small bowl, mix about three-quarters of the caramelized onion mixture with 1 tablespoon flour, and spread it over the dough, leaving a 1-inch margin. Sprinkle lightly with the coarse salt. Fold in the edges and reform the dough into a ball. Sprinkling with more flour as necessary, knead for 1 to 2 minutes to lightly incorporate the onions into the dough. Let the dough rise a second time until double in bulk, about 2 hours.

PUNCH the dough down and divide it into six equal pieces. Using your palms, roll the pieces into identical ropes about 10 inches long. Braid the ropes into two loaves, using three ropes for each loaf. An easy way to do this evenly is to start the braid in the middle, braid to one end, then turn the loaf upside down and braid to the other end. Turn the ends under and press down to keep them joined together.

IF you find the dough is difficult to work because the onions push through to the surface, you can shape it into two turbans instead: divide the dough into two pieces. With your palms, roll each piece into a long rope, thicker at one end. Holding the thicker end on the work surface with one hand, with the other hand spiral the rope around the thick end, forming a turban. Tuck the end of the rope under the edge to hold in place.

TRANSFER to a greased baking sheet. Apply the first coat of egg wash (reserve the rest), brushing it all over. Cover with greased plastic wrap and allow to rise for a third time until double in bulk, about 1 hour. Meanwhile, preheat the oven to 350°F.

MIX the remaining caramelized onions into the remaining egg wash. When the loaves have risen, brush the egg wash–onion mixture over the top. Just before placing in the oven, sprinkle lightly with coarse salt. Bake for about 35 minutes on the middle rack, until the loaves are golden brown and sound hollow when tapped on the bottom. Transfer to a rack and let cool, or remove from the baking sheet and place directly on the oven rack to cool with the oven door left ajar.

COOK'S NOTE: For a subtly spicier flavor, season the caramelized onion liberally with freshly ground black pepper.

Make sure the cloth you use to strain the onions has been washed only in unscented detergent. I use inexpensive men's cotton handkerchiefs—they're great for this and similar kitchen chores.

Not through Proust or Camus, Colette, or Chanel. Not even through French food. I became a Francophile early by way of Toni Home Permanents.

On Sunday nights in the days before cream rinse, my mother attempted to distract me as she wielded her comb through the chewing gum, wisteria blossoms, and web-like tangles that inhabited my hair. And she had to find a way to keep me cooperative through the longer process of applying vile-smelling lotion to my unfashionably straight locks, then rolling them up in the doll-size pink rubber curlers that left me with hair like stiff radish sprouts. So she taught me French.

And I loved it. I loved the way the words sounded. I loved her accent. Later on, I learned she mispronounced half the words, her definitions were off, her accent execrable. No matter. I loved her, and because of her, I loved everything French.

I didn't get to France until I finished college, but after that I returned as frequently as my finances would allow. One of my favorite areas was the former Jewish ghetto around the rue des Rosiers, now the site of some very *à la mode* designer boutiques and a number of stores still selling Judaica as well as Ashkenazi and Sephardi foods.

On one visit, I took my daughter to Sacha Finkelstajn, an Eastern European delicatessen with a refined Gallic touch. As in the *cave* of a *grand chateau de vins*, the *vendeuses* ply you with generous samples until you finally decide what to purchase. The spicy golden onion rolls are ethereal, and the chopped herring is whipped to a mousse-like froth and garnished with delicate lingonberries. But to Alexandra, my husband, and me, the silken chopped liver is the finest of the treasures.

Unfortunately, Blueberry, our little Yorkie-poodle, devoured the sandwiches in the car while we were out touring Monet's gardens at Giverny. We returned to Paris the next Passover and this time we left Blueberry home. I had written to the *patronne* at Finkelstajn's for the recipe but received no response. Now I pleaded with her but *non*, she never gave it out. "Just one ingredient. What makes it so airy, what packs that subtle bite?" I persisted. Little by little, she told me things. There was no secret ingredient. It was simply a matter of proportion. Then she drew me a diagram: equal amounts of liver, egg, and onion, plus sufficient oil to make it creamy. And another diagram of the onions: two-thirds sautéed lightly, one-third raw. Simple Cartesian logic.

Haunted by the taste memory, I weighed it out at home and came up with this recipe, much eggier than more familiar versions. For all of us, it has become an edible souvenir of our beloved Paris.

CHOPPED CHICKEN LIVER FROM THE RUE DES ROSIERS

yield: 6 TO 9 GENEROUS APPETIZER SERVINGS

This luscious chopped liver relies on perfectly cooked hard-boiled eggs: tender and moist, without chalky greenish yolks or tough, rubbery whites. For a foolproof method for preparing them: place the eggs in a heavy saucepan large enough to accommodate them in a single layer. Add ½ teaspoon salt (to prevent cracking) and enough cold water to cover them by at least 2 inches. Partially cover the pan and bring the water to a full boil over medium heat. Immediately turn off the heat. Then cover the pan, remove it from the heat, and allow the eggs to stand for 15 minutes. Pour off the water and cover the eggs with fresh, cold water, to prevent further cooking, until they are cool. To remove the shells easily, peel the eggs under cold running water or submerge in a bowl of very cold water.

7 large eggs

Approximately 6 tablespoons olive oil or 3 tablespoons olive oil plus approximately 3 tablespoons Olive Oil Schmaltz (page 27) or Poultry Schmaltz (page 28)

1 pound onions, diced (about 4 cups)

Coarse salt

1 pound fresh (not previously frozen) chicken livers, rinsed, fat and any green spots removed

Freshly ground black pepper

PREHEAT the broiler.

HARD-BOIL the eggs, cool, and peel them. Cut the eggs into eighths.

IN a 10-inch heavy skillet, heat 3 tablespoons oil over medium heat. Add 2⅔ cups of the onions, sprinkle lightly with salt, and cook, stirring from time to time, until soft and rich gold, about 15 minutes. Do not let the onions brown or they will make the texture chewy.

MEANWHILE, prepare the liver: line the broiler rack with either heavy brown paper sprinkled with water or foil. Pat the livers dry with paper towels, and spread them out on the broiler rack. Sprinkle them lightly with salt and broil about 4 inches from the flame until lightly browned on top, 3 to 4 minutes. Turn, sprinkle the other side with salt, and broil for another 3 to 4 minutes. Add the broiled livers to the onions in the skillet, season generously with salt and pepper to taste, and sauté for about 1 minute, tossing and turning the ingredients. Let cool slightly.

TRANSFER the contents of the skillet to a food processor and pulse on and off to chop coarsely. Add the eggs and 1 tablespoon of oil or schmaltz. Pulse. Add the remaining 1⅓ cups raw onion and pulse on and off a few more times until the desired texture is achieved. I prefer it slightly coarse—a rustic rather than a fine-textured pâté, but some like a smooth spread. (Alternatively, you can chop all the ingredients by hand in a wooden bowl with a hand chopper. Chop the liver and sautéed onions first, then add eggs and additional oil or schmaltz. Finally, add the raw onions and chop again.)

SCRAPE the mixture into a large bowl. Adjust the seasoning and add 1 to 2 tablespoons (or to taste) more oil or schmaltz as needed to make it moist and rich. Mix again so the ingredients are well combined. Refrigerate covered until thoroughly chilled.

SERVE cold, on lettuce, radicchio, or alternating green and red Belgian endive leaves for an elegant presentation. Or pack the chopped liver into small custard cups or cleaned tuna cans and invert onto frilly greens. Accompany the liver with the suggested vegetables and breads. It is terrific served with a condiment of grated black radish. Or stir crunchy chopped red radish into the liver just before serving.

GRATED BLACK RADISH AND ENDIVE SALAD IN SHALLOT VINAIGRETTE

yield: ABOUT 6 SERVINGS

½ pound black radish (available at many greengrocers, specialty and ethnic markets, and some well-stocked supermarkets)

Coarse kosher salt

⅓ cup finely chopped shallots

About 1 tablespoon plus 2 teaspoons fresh lemon juice

¼ teaspoon grated lemon zest

About 4 tablespoons best-quality extra virgin olive oil, Olive Oil Schmaltz (page 27), or Poultry Schmaltz (page 28)

Freshly ground black pepper

2 small Belgian endives

2 tablespoons chopped fresh parsley, preferably flat-leaf

PEEL the radish and grate it coarsely in a food processor or use the large holes of a hand grater. Place in a colander or strainer, sprinkle with about 1 tablespoon salt, and mix well. Weight the radish down with a plate and heavy object like a can of tomatoes, and allow to drain for about 1 hour, stirring it around every 15 to 20 minutes. Squeeze all moisture from the radish, rinse with fresh water, and squeeze thoroughly dry again. (It's easiest to do this using your hands.)

MEANWHILE, in a small bowl, combine the shallots, lemon juice, zest, and olive oil or schmaltz; season well with salt and pepper. Stir in the grated radish and allow the flavors to unfold and mingle for at least 20 minutes.

CUT the endives into fine shreds, then toss with the grated radish and shallot mixture. Taste and adjust seasonings (it takes quite a bit of salt), adding more oil or schmaltz and lemon juice as needed. Sprinkle with the parsley. Serve with Chopped Chicken Liver (pages 59 and 300) or Chopped Eggs and Onions (page 388).

"For the Sabbath, I have to prepare a radish with chicken fat for my husband. If I don't, as far as he's concerned, the Sabbath just isn't the Sabbath."

—CHAIM GRADE, *My Mother's Sabbath Days*

CLASSIC CHICKEN SOUP

yield: 2½ TO 3 QUARTS

One 5- to 6-pound fowl or stewing hen (not a roaster) and its giblets (reserve the liver for another use)

2 chicken feet or 1 pound chicken wings

4 quarts cold water (quality is important here so if you use bottled water to make coffee or tea, use it here)

Salt

2 large onions, 1 peeled and quartered, 1 washed and roots trimmed but left unpeeled, and quartered

2 parsnips, scraped and cut into chunks

3 celery stalks, cut into large chunks

½ cup celery leaves

5 large carrots, scraped and halved

2 or 3 garlic cloves, peeled

6 fresh parsley sprigs, preferably flat-leaf

1 parsley root (*petrouchka*), peeled and cut into chunks, optional (often found in greenmarkets and specialty stores, as well as supermarkets with well-stocked produce departments)

2 large leeks, trimmed (reserve long green leaves), washed of all traces of sand and cut into large pieces, or 1 sweet red onion, peeled and quartered

PREPARE the chicken: I find it easier to work with the chicken when it is cut up, so I divide it roughly into quarters. Remove all visible fat from the chicken and giblets. Remove the skin from the neck and the neck and tail openings. Wash all the pieces thoroughly, including feet or wings, and place in your largest stockpot, which should be tall and straight-sided. Add the water and about 1½ teaspoons of salt to begin with.

TURN the heat to medium and bring to a simmer. As the soup cooks, keep skimming off any scum and fat that rise to the surface. When the soup begins to "smile," that is, tiny bubbles open and close along the edge of the pot, turn the heat down to very low. Skim the soup constantly; at this point, you really need to fret over it. When the soup is just about clear, add the onions, parsnips, celery stalks and leaves, carrots, garlic, parsley sprigs, parsley root, leeks, peppercorns, and bay leaf, and raise the heat slightly to bring it back to a simmer. Continue skimming any froth or scum.

WHEN the soup is again clear, turn the heat down as low as possible. Cover the surface of the soup with the leek greens or lettuce leaves, and put the pot lid on, leaving it slightly askew. Simmer the soup for at least 2½ to 4 hours longer—overnight is better still. (Some cooks simmer their soup in a 200°F oven overnight.) Never let the soup boil; if necessary, use a *blech* (flame tamer), or put it on top of two burner grates stacked together. (But do make sure the bubbles are breaking very gently on the surface. If there is no surface movement at all, the soup might spoil.)

ADJUST the seasonings. Using a slotted spoon, remove the chicken and carrots and set aside. Let the soup cool to room temperature in the pot, *uncovered*. (Hot soup in a covered pot may turn sour.)

WHILE the soup is cooling, pick over the reserved chicken and discard the bones, skin, and other inedible parts. Reserve the chicken for another use or refrigerate along with the carrots to serve in the soup.

STRAIN the cooled soup through a fine-mesh sieve, pressing down on all the vegetables to extract as much of their juices as you can, then discard the vegetables.

10 to 12 peppercorns, lightly crushed

1 Turkish bay leaf

Several leaves of mild-flavored lettuce such as Boston or iceberg, if no leek greens are available

About ½ cup snipped fresh dill

Accompaniments: kreplach, matzoh balls, cooked fine egg noodles, rice, or kasha

REFRIGERATE the soup covered overnight, or until all the remaining fat has congealed on the top. Carefully scrape off the fat and discard it. If the soup still seems fatty, line the sieve with a layer of paper towels and pour the soup through it into a clean bowl or pot (if the soup has jelled from chilling, bring it to room temperature first). If the paper towels become thickly coated with fat, you might want to change them once or twice during the process.

BEFORE serving, reheat the soup. Taste for salt and pepper and add lots of fresh snipped dill. If you feel the soup is not strong enough, reduce it over high heat to concentrate the flavors. Serve the soup very hot, with additional fresh dill, the reserved carrots, and, if desired, shreds of the soup chicken. It is delicious with kreplach, matzoh balls, egg noodles, rice, kasha, or just plain.

From Maimonides on, much has been made of the curative powers of Jewish chicken soup—"Jewish penicillin," "the doctor that makes house calls," and so on. Now, it seems, the doctor often needs "doctoring"—and not just in America. A friend in Verona, Italy, confessed that Italian Jews at times enhance their homemade soups with imported Israeli bouillon cubes for a needed jolt of flavor.

Broth is no more than the simmered essence of its ingredients, and the problem here, of course, is the weakened flavor of the chicken itself. Traditional Jewish chicken soup was always made from a tough old hen with plenty of character. Today's battery-feeding produces picture-pretty birds with lots of fat and little flavor. And those "yellow rings" extolled in Antin's story from 1911 (see page 64) have lost their appeal now—to us they taste merely of grease, not of chicken. So how do you coax out enough flavor from a lackluster bird to make a splendid soup?

Over the years I've gleaned some *trucs* for preparing excellent Jewish chicken soup.

1. Start with the best-quality fowl you can find; kosher chickens make especially clear, flavorful soup, and organic kosher chickens are now available. If at all possible, buy feet, or at least some extra wings, to give the soup extra body. I find that although chicken backs are fine for making chicken stock, they are too fatty and lack the requisite clarity of flavor for a soup meant to be served solo. It may seem

extravagant to use a large hen for soup—after all, the cooked chicken cannot be served later as an entree (you've already extracted all the flavor from it). However, the meat is perfectly good for chicken salad, sandwiches, Fried Onion and Chicken Kreplach (page 68), and Dayenu (page 67), or served cut up in soup. Or prepare Chicken Latkes: combine coarsely shredded or chopped chicken with sautéed onions (garlic and mushrooms too, if desired), eggs, fresh herbs, and matzoh meal or soaked and drained challah. Season well, form into little cakes or drop by heaping tablespoons into hot oil. Fry over medium-high heat until golden-brown on both sides.

2. To compensate for the often anemic taste of today's chickens, I add lots and lots of earthy, aromatic vegetables to provide the soup with strength and character.

3. It's a struggle, but I resist the temptation to use a lot of water. And if the soup tastes too watery when I'm finished, I reduce it as much as necessary, even though it pains me to see the fruits of all my labor just boiling away.

4. Long, slow cooking will extract every bit of flavor from both chicken and vegetables. Using a huge stockpot—a 20- or even 24-quart size, far larger than the contents would warrant—and a tiny flame, so there is no danger of the soup boiling, I cook it for at least four hours, and more often overnight.

5. To prepare the chicken, I remove every bit of fat and some of the excess skin, since they don't add any flavor and later I'll just have to discard the grease they produce.

6. Skim, skim, skim. Froth and scum taste bitter and look terrible.

7. To prevent the precious flavors from evaporating, after I have finished skimming the soup, I cover the surface with a layer of the green part of the leeks used in the soup. If I have no leeks, I use the outer leaves of a mild lettuce.

8. And lastly, I *never* bring the soup to a boil. That roiling bubble action traps fat and scum beneath the surface, bonding them to the liquid, so that the soup becomes clouded, murky, and impossible to clarify. Instead, I let it simmer gently for the entire cooking period, "smiling," as the French say of the tiny bubbles that open and close along the edge of the pot. (Boiling the finished soup—strained and defatted—to reduce it is, of course, another matter.)

"Do you think there will be *any* yellow rings on the soup? I saw the chicken soup the women from the sick-visiting society brought old Rachel when she was sick, and it was all yellow on top—*fat!*—and smelt so good!"

—MARY ANTIN, "MALINKE'S ATONEMENT"

TWO CLASSIC MATZOH BALL RECIPES

yield: 6 TO 8 SERVINGS

Featherweight matzoh balls so delicate they quiver when you sigh—these are not the stuff our dreams are made on. My family prefers matzoh balls with a rich flavor you can really taste, buttery and light-textured, but not so fluffy you might as well be eating scrambled eggs. I've experimented with many slight variations, including my grandmother's addition of club soda, and for years relied on the standard, back-of-the-matzoh-meal-box recipe that called for a few tablespoons of broth stirred into the batter. This recipe, using slightly more of the flavorful fat and no liquid at all, is our hands-down favorite. On the very rare occasions when we have any left over, we enjoy them heated up with a bit of broth or sautéed (chill them before frying so they don't fall apart) and served as a side dish, with or without gravy.

4 large eggs

1 recipe Olive Oil Schmaltz (page 27; see Cook's Note) or 6 tablespoons Poultry Schmaltz (page 28) or, less desirably, 6 tablespoons mild olive or avocado oil (the fat should be at room temperature)

4 teaspoons grated onion

1 cup matzoh meal (you can substitute up to ¼ cup finely ground skinned almonds for an equal quantity of the matzoh meal)

1 teaspoon baking powder (optional; see Cook's Note)

Kosher salt

Freshly ground black pepper

Up to 4 tablespoons finely minced fresh herbs (dill, chives, parsley, or a combination) and/or 2 pinches of ground ginger (optional)

IN a large bowl, beat the eggs and schmaltz or oil until well blended and thick. Whisk in the onions. Mix together the matzoh meal, baking powder, if using, salt (figure about 1½ teaspoons), and pepper to taste, and stir into the egg mixture. Stir in the optional seasonings, if using. Cover the mixture and refrigerate for at least 2 hours or up to 24 hours, so the matzoh meal can fully absorb the liquids and seasoning.

BRING 4 quarts water and 1½ tablespoons salt to a boil in a large, wide pot with a lid.

THE balls formed from the soft batter may not hold their shape well, especially those made without baking powder. Not to worry: they will be very tender. Shape the batter into walnut- or olive-size balls, and place on a platter. When the water comes to a rapid boil, reduce the heat a bit. Carefully slide the balls in one at a time. Or you can form the balls using two spoons and drop them right into the water. Don't crowd the pot—if necessary, prepare the matzoh balls in two batches or use two pots. When the water returns to a gentle boil, immediately cover the pot tightly and lower the heat to a simmer. Cook for 35 to 45 minutes, without removing the lid. (They will cook by direct heat as well as by steam, which makes them swell up—lifting the lid will reduce some of that steam.) Test for doneness: remove a matzoh ball and cut it in half. It should be tender, fluffy, and completely cooked through. If it isn't, continue cooking for a few more minutes.

REMOVE the matzoh balls gently with a skimmer or a large slotted spoon—they are too fragile to pour into a colander. To serve, heat the chicken soup, add the matzoh balls, and simmer until they are heated through. (Don't eliminate this vital step: matzoh balls cooked in water need to absorb some of the soup's flavor—see Cook's Note.) Ladle into warmed shallow bowls and serve immediately. Or cover the drained matzoh balls with some broth and set aside for a few hours until you are ready to heat them.

COOK'S NOTE: Olive Oil Schmaltz, a puree of oil-stewed onions, provides not only flavor but also a texture approximating a semisolid fat, which makes the matzoh balls fluffy and light. If you want a tasty substitute other than poultry fat, similar aromatic blends such as purees of roasted garlic or mushrooms sautéed or braised until soft, combined with some oil (add a chopped fresh herb, for extra flavor, if you'd like) also work well. And I've made exquisite matzoh balls using the above recipe but substituting ⅓ cup jarred artichoke puree mixed with 2 tablespoons olive oil for the schmaltz. For another delicious variation, see the Roasted Fennel Matzoh Balls (page 389).

For an acceptable Poultry Schmaltz substitute, some cooks reserve the congealed fat scraped from the top of chilled chicken soup and supplement it with oil, if needed.

I make this recipe without baking powder on Passover. I think of it here as insurance—with it, you are much less likely to experience serious Knaidlach Failure: matzoh balls that fall apart, that won't swell up, that are too tight or too tough. When carefully prepared, however, these matzoh balls made without baking powder will be tender and buttery tasting, too. To keep them light and fluffy, remember not to lift the lid at all until you suspect they are ready, that is, not before at least 35 minutes have elapsed.

Though cooking the matzoh balls in broth would make them very flavorful, it would also cloud the broth. So I cook them in well-salted water, then let them simmer in broth for a while, drinking in its rich taste.

A very close runner up, this matzoh ball—eggier and a little more delicate in flavor and texture—calls for separating the eggs. Have all ingredients at room temperature.

4 large eggs, separated
Kosher salt

IN a large bowl, beat the egg whites with a pinch of salt until they hold peaks that are stiff but not dry. In another bowl, beat the yolks with

¼ cup Olive Oil Schmaltz (page 27) or 3 tablespoons Poultry Schmaltz (page 28) or, less desirably, 3 tablespoons mild olive or avocado oil

Freshly ground black pepper

4 teaspoons grated onion

Up to 4 tablespoons finely minced fresh herbs (dill, chives, parsley, or a combination) and/or 2 pinches of ground ginger (optional)

1 cup matzoh meal

the fat, about 1½ teaspoons salt, or to taste, and a little pepper, until thick and creamy. Whisk in the onion and seasonings, if using. Fold the whites into the yolk mixture until just combined. Slowly and gently fold in the matzoh meal. Cover the mixture and refrigerate for at least 2 hours or up to 24 hours, so the matzoh meal can fully absorb the liquids and seasoning.

FOLLOW the directions above for poaching, draining, and serving the matzoh balls.

I was stumped by the name *Dayenu* that Ester Silvana Israel, avid cook and secretary of the Jewish community of Verona, Italy, used for matzoh balls—either traditional Ashkenazi knaidlach or more uniquely Italian kinds, incorporating bits of chicken or other meats.

I questioned her as we walked through the pink marble columns of her exquisite synagogue. Smiling, she wondered whether I remembered the song from the Passover service?

"Of course," I replied. "Each miracle God performed would have been *dayenu* (enough); each would have sufficed to show God's love. Nothing else was necessary."

"Well, so too with the matzoh balls," she explained. "Each one is so filling it would be enough; each could suffice for the entire meal. But there is always more and still more yet to come."

I've given two recipes for matzoh balls here. To make Dayenu, matzoh balls Italian-style, add up to three-quarters cup cooked chicken, finely shredded and then cut into bits, to these recipes. For additional matzoh ball recipes, including ground chicken matzoh balls, dumplings made of whole matzoh instead of matzoh meal, and a wonderful herbed matzoh ball made with no fat other than what's in the egg yolks, see the index.

FRIED ONION AND CHICKEN KREPLACH

yield: ABOUT 30 KREPLACH

*T*hroughout this book, onions are cooked in many ways, depending on the texture and taste desired—soft and sweet, rich and caramelized, golden and crispy. In this recipe, they are salted first to draw out the moisture and then fried. If you are pressed for time or don't want to bother, omit the soaking and fry the onions a little longer over medium heat.

Using a high proportion of savory fried onion to the chicken ensures that the filling for the kreplach won't be dry—even if the chicken left its flavor in the soup pot.

2 large onions, very thinly sliced (about 4 cups)

Coarse kosher salt

1 cup cooked chicken (use light and dark meat; leftover from preparing chicken soup is fine)

A few tablespoons of chicken broth

2 tablespoons mild olive or canola oil

1 large garlic clove, minced

1 large egg, lightly beaten

1 tablespoon finely chopped fresh dill

Freshly ground black pepper

About 30 wonton wrappers (see page 39; have some extra in case of tearing)

Egg wash (1 to 2 large eggs, as needed, each beaten with 1 teaspoon water)

SEPARATE the onions into rings. To draw out the moisture, toss in a bowl with 1½ teaspoons salt. Set aside for about 20 minutes, stirring from time to time. Then place the onions between sheets of paper towels, pressing down to soak up as much onion water as possible.

MEANWHILE, prepare the chicken: roughly shred it (preferably using your fingers, so you can easily find any little bits of gristle or bone) and place in a bowl. If the chicken is very dry—usually the case if you are using chicken left over from making soup—spoon some broth over it, mix well, and let it drink in the liquid for at least 15 minutes.

HEAT the oil in a large heavy skillet over medium-high heat. Add the onions, and keep tossing with a spatula as they soften and begin to turn golden, about 10 minutes. Stir in the garlic and continue cooking and turning, until the mixture is a deep caramel color, but before it turns crispy, about 5 minutes.

STIR the onions into the chicken and let cool slightly. Add the egg, dill, and salt and pepper to taste. Refrigerate the mixture, covered, for at least 1 hour.

FILL and trim the kreplach (see page 39), using about 1 heaping teaspoon of filling per krepl, folding into a tight triangle, and sealing with the egg wash.

POACH the kreplach. In a large, very wide pot, bring at least 5 quarts of lightly salted water to a boil. Slip in the kreplach, one by one, being careful not to overcrowd the pot (if necessary, cook them in batches or use two pots). Lower the temperature slightly (the kreplach might

Accompaniments: Classic Chicken Soup (page 62), gravy, fried onions, or mushrooms from Mishmash Kreplach (page 330)

explode if the water is boiling furiously) and poach until tender, 3 to 6 minutes (exact time will depend on the brand of wonton wrapper used). Lift out the kreplach, a few at a time, with a large skimmer, gently shaking the skimmer so the water drains back into the pot (they are too fragile to pour into a colander).

SERVE the kreplach in soup. Or serve poached or sautéed kreplach with gravy, fried onions, or fried mushrooms as a side dish or appetizer.

"What should I be doing? Eating kreplach?"

—ISAAC BASHEVIS SINGER, "GIMPEL THE FOOL"

CHEATER'S CHICKEN IN THE POT AND ALMOST-HOMEMADE SOUP

yield: 6 TO 8 SERVINGS

When I want chicken broth that tastes homemade, but haven't time enough to prepare it, I turn to this recipe. It produces a broth fine enough for a festive dinner or soothing elixir and excellent, silky poached chicken.

Serve the soup and chicken together plain, or for a substantial chicken-in-the-pot, embellish with matzoh balls, cooked rice, or other starches.

You can also present the tender chicken as a separate course, moistened with a little broth and accompanied by coarse salt, horseradish, and pickles. Or reserve it for chicken salad or other dishes that call for poached chicken.

8 cups good-quality, low-sodium purchased chicken broth

6 sprigs fresh flat-leaf parsley and/or a few celery leaves

1 small onion, peeled and sliced

1 medium carrot, scraped and coarsely chopped, plus 1½ cups scraped carrots cut into bite-size chunks or 2-inch lengths

Salt and freshly ground black pepper

2 pounds boneless, skinless chicken breasts, well trimmed of fat and sinews

1 cup peeled young turnips and/or 1 cup peeled parsnips, diced or cut into bite-size chunks

2 tablespoons chopped fresh dill, plus additional for garnish

Optional accompaniments: for the soup, matzoh balls; cooked egg noodles, rice, kasha, kreplach; or red new potatoes, boiled until tender; for the chicken, coarse salt, horseradish, sour pickles

CHOOSE a lidded, deep skillet large enough to accommodate all the chicken in one layer. Add about 5 cups of the broth, the parsley and/or celery leaves, onion, and chopped carrot and bring to a boil. Adjust the heat and simmer for 5 to 10 minutes to blend the flavors. Season to taste with salt and pepper.

ARRANGE the chicken in a single layer in the broth; if necessary, add more broth so that the chicken is completely immersed. Simmer gently, covered, for about 5 minutes. Turn off the flame, but don't remove the lid or move the pot. Let the chicken rest for about 15 minutes, then check to see that it is just cooked through. If not, leave the chicken in the pot for a few more minutes, covered, without the heat on.

TRANSFER the chicken breasts to a deep dish, spoon some of the broth over to keep them moist, and tent with foil.

STRAIN the poaching liquid into a large saucepan and add the remaining broth. Bring to a boil, then stir in the remaining carrots, turnips, and parsnips, if using. Reduce the heat and cook until the vegetables are tender.

CUT the chicken into bite-size pieces and add to the soup, together with the dill and any starchy accompaniments you choose to serve, and warm until everything is heated through. Serve the soup in warmed bowls, sprinkled with more dill.

OR present the chicken separately, either as another course, along with coarse salt, horseradish, and pickles, if using, or at another meal.

CHILLED MINTED CUCUMBER SOUP

yield: ABOUT 8 SERVINGS

*U*tterly refreshing on a hot day or sultry evening, this gorgeous celadon soup makes a fine starter, or when served in attractive mugs or glasses, an unusual accompaniment to a summer Shabbat dinner or lunch or to a Shavuot meal. Or offer it in demitasse cups, a family collection of china teacups, or oversized shotglasses for a stunning break-the-fast drink on Yom Kippur.

The only cooking here is boiling water for the mint tea which, along with the yogurt, provides the structure of the soup and subtly underscores the fresh mint and dill flavoring. To make the soup richer, you can use all or some *labneh* or a combination of yogurt and sour cream as a substitute for the yogurt.

For a delicate garlic flavor without the back-of-the-throat harshness of the raw cloves, the garlic infuses the soup as it chills but is plucked out just before pureeing. To find the garlic easily, spear the cloves with toothpicks before you add them to the soup.

4 cups peeled, seeded, chopped cucumbers (scoop out the seeds with a spoon)

Coarse kosher salt and freshly ground black pepper

4 garlic cloves, peeled and crushed

1 quart plain yogurt or *labneh* (4 cups), or a combination of *labneh* or sour cream and yogurt

3 cups freshly brewed mint tea (use caffeine-free herbal mint tea), cooled

1/3 cup fresh mint leaves, tightly packed, plus additional for garnish

1/4 cup fresh dill leaves

Best-quality extra virgin olive oil or a fine walnut or other nut oil (optional)

IN a large bowl, stir together the cucumbers, about 1½ teaspoons salt and a few grindings of pepper. Add the garlic, then beat in the yogurt or *labneh* and tea. Cover and refrigerate for at least 4 hours.

SCOOP out the garlic and discard it. Stir in the mint and dill. Puree the soup in the blender in batches. (A food processor will not produce the same smooth texture). This soup tastes best a little salty, so adjust the seasoning.

IF serving the soup as a first course, ladle it into bowls and, if you like, dribble a bit of fine oil on top. To serve as a beverage accompaniment to a meal, spoon the soup into tall glasses or cups. Garnish with fresh mint leaves.

COOK'S NOTE: The soup can be prepared a day ahead. Puree, then return it to the refrigerator until ready to serve.

GEFILTE FISH QUICKLY STEAMED BETWEEN CABBAGE LEAVES

yield: ABOUT 8 SERVINGS

Inspired by the Chinese method for preparing tender, soft dumplings, I cushion these wonderfully delicate fish balls between cabbage leaves for a gentle twenty-minute steam bath. The wet vapor helps preserve all the subtle flavors of the fish while the nutty-sweet cabbage wrapper keeps it moist as it steams, and later as it chills without broth in the refrigerator.

The fish mixture here is particularly delicious. Extra egg yolks and a little pureed carrot and parsnip bring added flavor and a lush softness. No fish broth, but a bit of the liquid from cooking the sweet vegetables moistens the matzoh meal filler.

The result is gefilte fish brimful of flavor yet light and fresh tasting. To complement it, mellow the horseradish's fire with some mayonnaise seasoned with fresh dill.

FOR THE FISH BALLS

⅓ cup diced, scraped carrots

⅓ cup diced, peeled parsnips

3 tablespoons matzoh meal

2 tablespoons mild olive or canola oil

1½ cups coarsely chopped onion

Salt and freshly ground black pepper

1 tablespoon chopped shallots

2 tablespoons chopped fresh dill, plus 16 additional sprigs

2 pounds fish fillets, skin and any bones removed and discarded, rinsed to remove any scales, patted dry, and cut into 1-inch pieces; or 2 pounds fish ground by your fishmonger (see Cook's Note)

2 large eggs

PREPARE the fish balls: in a small saucepan, bring 1 cup lightly salted water to a boil. Add the carrots and parsnips, and simmer until the vegetables are very tender. Drain, reserving the cooking water, and transfer the vegetables to a food processor. Put the matzoh meal in a small bowl and stir in ⅓ cup of the reserved cooking water. Let this mixture sit so that the matzoh meal can soften as it soaks in the liquid.

WARM the oil in an 8-inch skillet. Add the onions, sprinkle lightly with salt and pepper, and sauté, stirring, over medium heat until soft, shiny, and just beginning to color palest gold, 8 to 9 minutes. Don't let them brown. Transfer the onions and any oil remaining in the skillet to the food processor. Add the shallots and the chopped dill to the food processor and puree until fairly smooth. Transfer the mixture to a large wooden chopping bowl or a wooden chopping board. (Don't wash out the food processor if you are grinding your own fish.) If your fish is not ground, put it, about 2 teaspoons salt, and ⅛ teaspoon pepper in the food processor and pulse just until the mixture is chopped fine, but not pasty. Add the fish to the wooden bowl or board. (If you are using preground fish, add it now, seasoned with salt and pepper.) Add the matzoh meal mixture. Beat the eggs and yolks in a bowl until thick and lemon-colored. Using a hand chopper or cleaver, work the eggs and lemon juice into the fish mixture, a little at a time. (Hand-chopping at this point incorporates air into the mixture, making it lighter and fluffier than pulsing in the food processor.)

TEST for seasoning. Poach a teaspoon of the fish mixture in lightly salted boiling water for a few minutes. Taste and, if needed, add additional salt

2 large egg yolks

2 tablespoons fresh lemon juice

FOR THE DILL-HORSERADISH MAYONNAISE

1 cup mayonnaise

⅓ cup finely minced dill

⅓ cup plus 1 tablespoon prepared white horseradish, drained

About 12 large cabbage leaves, washed (you can use slightly imperfect or dark green outer leaves)

Soft lettuce leaves, endive, or radicchio, for lining plates

and pepper. Chill the fish mixture, covered, for at least 1 hour or up to 4 hours. It will be easier to mold and the fish balls will be fluffier.

WHILE the fish is chilling, combine the ingredients for the dill-horseradish mayonnaise. Cover and refrigerate.

STEAM the fish balls: you'll need a large, wide pot such as a 5- to 6-quart Dutch oven or heavy casserole with a tight-fitting lid, and a rack that stands at least 2 inches high. (A simple round cake rack works well. If it is not high enough, set it over 2 custard cups or empty tuna cans in the pot.) Fill the pot with water to a depth of 1 inch.

LINE the rack with a layer of cabbage leaves. Form the fish mixture into 16 ovals, using a scant ¼ cup for each, wetting your hands with cold water, if needed to work the sticky mixture. Depending on the variety of fish used, the mixture may be very soft but will firm up as it cooks and, later, as it chills. Bring the water in the pot to a boil. Gently put as many ovals on top of the cabbage leaves as will fit comfortably in a single layer without touching. Place a sprig of dill on each fish oval. Top the fish with another layer of cabbage leaves and cover the pot tightly. Turn the heat down to medium and steam for 20 to 25 minutes, until the ovals are completely cooked through at the center. (When steamed in raw cabbage leaves, the fish will probably take closer to 25 minutes; when steaming the second batch in the now-cooked cabbage leaves, it will probably take about 20 minutes.) Line a platter with some of the cooked cabbage leaves and carefully put the cooked fish on top of them. Using additional cabbage leaves as needed, cook any remaining fish ovals in the same way, transferring the fish as it is done to the cabbage-lined platter. Remove and discard the dill sprigs from all the ovals, and cover with a layer of cooked cabbage leaves to keep them moist. Let everything cool to room temperature. Wrap the platter with plastic wrap and chill the fish until cold.

FOR best flavor, serve the fish chilled but not icy cold. Remove the fish from the cabbage leaves and arrange attractively on platters or individual plates lined with lettuce, endive, or radicchio, and accompany with the dill-horseradish mayonnaise.

COOK'S NOTE: I like a combination of half salmon and half red snapper or lemon or grey sole. And I've made a terrific, plush-tasting gefilte fish with half Chilean sea bass and half flounder. Or use your own or your fishmonger's favorite mixture. Avoid very strong-flavored fish like bluefish or mackerel. Be sure to use a combination of fat and lean fish. (See the chart on page 149 for some fat and lean fish options.)

MOROCCAN FISH WITH CHICKPEAS AND SAFFRON-LIME AIOLI

yield: 4 TO 6 SERVINGS

When I first tried this dish, I loved the classic Moroccan flavors, but somehow it seemed as if I were tasting each one separately: chickpeas, fish, and heady spices, disparate notes that didn't quite harmonize for me. Then I whipped up a batch of Cheater's Aioli—jarred mayonnaise flavored with saffron and lime—folded it into the pan juices, and a lovely melody was born.

3 cups freshly cooked chickpeas (see page 326; reserve about ½ cup of cooking liquid) or two 15-ounce cans chickpeas, rinsed and drained

8 large garlic cloves, sliced

1 to 2 teaspoons hot red pepper flakes or 4 to 6 dried red chile peppers, or to taste

4 to 5 tablespoons extra virgin olive oil

½ teaspoon ground coriander

Salt and freshly ground black pepper

2 pounds fish fillets, 1 inch thick (bass, snapper, cod, haddock, or other firm-fleshed white fish)

2 tablespoons fresh lemon or lime juice

1 teaspoon cumin seeds, lightly toasted and freshly ground

¼ cup chopped fresh cilantro

1 teaspoon grated lime or lemon zest

YOU can prepare the whole dish in one pan: a deep 12-inch wide oven-proof sauté pan or cast-iron skillet. Combine the chickpeas, reserved cooking liquid, if using freshly cooked, or ½ cup water if using canned, garlic, pepper flakes or hot peppers, 2 tablespoons of the olive oil, the coriander, and salt and pepper to taste. (Alternatively, if you don't have a similar pan, combine the ingredients in a regular skillet or saucepan—you may need a little more liquid.) Simmer the chickpeas over low heat, covered, for 30 minutes, to marry the flavors.

PREHEAT the oven to 350°F.

WHILE the chickpeas are cooking, prepare the Saffron-Lime Aioli: crush a pinch of saffron threads into a small bowl. Add 1 tablespoon hot water, stir, then let the saffron soak for about 10 minutes. Press the threads with the back of a spoon to release more color and flavor. Stir in the mayonnaise, lime juice, olive oil, garlic, cumin, and salt and pepper to taste. Let the flavors unfold while you make the fish.

PICK out and discard the hot peppers, if used, from the chickpeas. Scoop out about half the chickpeas from the skillet and set them aside in a bowl. Arrange the remaining chickpeas evenly in the pan (or if you used a small pan, arrange half of the the chickpeas in a baking pan just large enough to accommodate the fish), and place the fish over the chickpeas in the pan. Sprinkle the fish with lemon or lime juice, cumin, and salt and pepper to taste. Top with 2 tablespoons of the chopped cilantro. Spoon the remaining chickpeas over the fish. Drizzle everything with 2 to 3 tablespoons of olive oil. Cover the pan (or use heavy-duty foil), and bake for 25 to 30 minutes, or until the fish is just cooked through; the exact time will depend on the variety and thickness of the fish. To

Optional garnish: cilantro sprigs

Saffron threads

1/2 cup mayonnaise, good-quality jarred such as Hellmann's, or even better, homemade

2 tablespoons fresh lime juice

1 tablespoon best-quality extra virgin olive oil

1 garlic clove, finely minced

3/4 teaspoon cumin seeds, lightly toasted and freshly ground

Salt and freshly ground black pepper

Liquid from baking the fish (optional)

test the fish for doneness, insert a thin-bladed knife in the thickest part. The fish should be opaque or show a slight bit of translucence, according to your preference.

CHECK the aioli for seasoning. If desired, thin it out with a tablespoon or so of the cooking liquid from the fish.

SCATTER the remaining 2 tablespoons of cilantro, the lime or lemon zest, and, if you'd like, some more hot pepper flakes over the fish. I like to stir some of the aioli into the chickpeas and pan liquid, dollop a little atop the fish, and pass the rest separately in a sauce boat. But if you prefer, serve all the aioli on the side. Garnish the platter with cilantro sprigs.

ITALIAN-JEWISH MARINATED FRIED FISH (*PESCE EN SAOR*)

yield: 6 TO 8 SERVINGS

bove the night music, the Venetian skies boom and burst into explosive colors, sending showers of rainbow meteors skittering across the heavens, their shimmering reflections dancing in the inky canals.

It is the Festa del Redentore *(Feast of the Redeemer), celebrated every July 19th since 1576 to commemorate the end of a plague that had devastated the city. Among the traditional ritual of foods eaten before the blaze of spectacular fireworks is an ancient Venetian-Jewish dish, sole in a sweet-and-sour sauce of onions, raisins, and pine nuts, served cold.*

Unlike some Italian-Jewish foods whose name betrays their provenance—artichokes alla giudia and several others with a "Sara" or "Rebecca" appended to the title come readily to mind—the Jewish origins of Pesce en Saor *are not always acknowledged. But culinary historians, both those with an Italian focus and those with a Jewish one, trace the dish to the traditional methods Jews devised to preserve fish for the Sabbath. In Italy, Jewish cooks doused fried fish with hot vinegar, then to counteract the acidic taste, added sweet fried onions, raisins, and sugar. (This pattern—using vinegar or lemon as a preservative, then sweetening to eradicate the resulting sour taste—may explain why so many vastly different Jewish communities throughout the world developed their own sweet-and-sour fish dishes.) A fondness for raisins and pine nuts was acquired in Sicily, where Jews had dwelled from ancient times until they were expelled at the end of the fifteenth century.*

The result is a well-flavored, make-ahead fish excellent for holidays and company buffets. I round out the flavors by caramelizing the onions and bedding the fried fish on fresh sliced oranges—their sweetness, and the concentrated sugars in the soaked raisins, obviate the need for any added sugar. This dish is especially good accompanied by a salad of marinated roasted red peppers (see page 240).

2 pounds lemon sole, grouper, red snapper, perch, or similar nonoily, fairly firm-fleshed fish fillets (choose fillets no more than ½-inch thick)

About 1 cup unbleached all-purpose flour

CUT the fillets in half lengthwise and, if necessary, remove the thin bony strip that runs through the middle of many fillets. Cut the pieces into 4-inch lengths. If time permits, soak the fish in a pan of cold, lightly salted water for about 20 minutes. (This centuries-old technique not only seasons the fish but also helps it to stay firm when fried.)

Salt and freshly ground black pepper

Olive oil, for frying, plus 2 tablespoons

1 large, juicy unpeeled orange, preferably thin-skinned, very thinly sliced

1½ pounds onions, very thinly sliced (6 cups)

¼ cup pine nuts

¼ cup raisins

½ cup moderately priced balsamic vinegar or mild red wine vinegar

2 anchovies, finely chopped (optional)

1 cup fresh orange juice

1 Turkish bay leaf

Optional garnish: bright green leaves of parsley, curly endive, frisée, or other greens

PAT the fish dry with paper towels. Spread flour on a sheet of wax paper or a platter and season with salt and pepper. Dredge the fish pieces thoroughly in the seasoned flour, then shake lightly to remove all excess. Heat ¼ inch of oil in a large heavy skillet until hot but not smoking. Fry the fish in batches until nicely golden on both sides. Drain well on paper towels.

CHOOSE a casserole or nonreactive baking dish just large enough to accommodate the fish in one layer and line it with the orange slices. Place the fish on top, overlapping the pieces slightly, if necessary.

PREHEAT oven to 350°F. Wipe out all the oil in the skillet, then warm 2 tablespoons fresh oil in it. Add the onions and toss until completely coated with the oil. Salt and pepper lightly, cover the pan, and cook slowly over very low heat for 35 to 40 minutes, until the onions are meltingly tender. Stir from time to time to make sure onions don't burn.

WHILE the onions are simmering, toast the pine nuts on a baking sheet in the oven for about 7 minutes, until fragrant and lightly golden. Shake the baking sheet from time to time to ensure even toasting. Set the toasted nuts aside to cool. Soak the raisins in the vinegar.

WHEN the onions are very tender, stir in the anchovies, if using (they add an elusive, subtle depth), and cook for 2 minutes, stirring to dissolve them. Add the raisins and vinegar, orange juice, and bay leaf. Turn the heat up to high, and cook, uncovered, until the liquid is reduced by half and the onions are caramelized and richly colored, 15 to 20 minutes. Be sure to stir frequently to redistribute the syrupy juices and, if necessary, turn the heat down a bit to prevent the onions from sticking and burning. Season generously with salt and pepper and remove the bay leaf.

SPREAD the caramelized onion mixture evenly over the fish. Scatter the toasted pine nuts on top. Wrap well with plastic and refrigerate for at least 6 hours or overnight (even better when served after 48 hours). It will keep very well for at least 4 days.

THE fish is best at room temperature, so remove it from the refrigerator at least 1 hour before serving. Brighten the dish with a garnish of greens, if desired.

LEMON-ROASTED CHICKEN

yield: 3 TO 4 SERVINGS

For maximum flavor, I rub the marinade right into the chicken flesh beneath the skin and then I roast it on a layer of lemons. Butterflying the chicken enables you to spread the marinade on more of the meat under the skin and to remove more of the fat trapped there, especially between the joints. Because so much fat is removed with this method, the skin never becomes soggy, and a final sizzle under the broiler crisps it up delectably.

One 3½- to 4½-pound frying or roasting chicken (preferably fresh, not previously frozen), butterflied down the backbone and pounded gently so it lies flat easily

1½ tablespoons coarsely chopped garlic

2 tablespoons chopped fresh thyme or 4 teaspoons dried

3 tablespoons fresh lemon juice

Salt and freshly ground black pepper

Olive oil

2 lemons

½ teaspoon packed light brown sugar

RINSE the chicken and pat dry. Remove all visible fat. Starting at the neck end, gently loosen the skin by sliding your hand underneath the breast and carefully working your way back to the legs. Remove as much fat as possible beneath the skin, paying particular attention to the fat deposits around the thighs.

IN a food processor or blender, puree the garlic, half of the thyme, the lemon juice, ½ teaspoon salt and ¼ teaspoon pepper. Lift up the skin and spread about half the mixture all over the breast and down to the drumsticks. Rub the remaining mixture all over the outside of the chicken. Cover loosely with plastic wrap and refrigerate for at least 4 hours, but preferably overnight.

ABOUT 30 minutes before you are ready to begin cooking the chicken, remove it from the refrigerator to bring it to room temperature. Preheat oven to 350°F.

CHOOSE a heavy ovenproof skillet (12-inch cast-iron is ideal) large enough to accommodate the chicken. Rub it lightly with oil. Thinly slice the lemons, discarding the pits, and arrange them evenly over the bottom of the skillet. Sprinkle the lemons with the brown sugar. Turn the heat to moderately high and cook for 5 minutes. Add the chicken, skin side down, and continue cooking for about 10 minutes. Occasionally slide a wooden spoon under the chicken to prevent the skin from sticking to the lemons. Peek underneath—the skin should be coloring a rich gold in spots.

SPRINKLE the top with the remaining thyme and salt and pepper to taste, and place the skillet, chicken still skin side down, in the oven. Roast for 30 minutes. Leaving the layer of lemons on the bottom of the pan, turn the chicken skin side up. Season it all over with salt and pepper and continue roasting for 30 to 55 minutes longer, until the juices run clear when the thigh is pierced with a skewer or a thermometer inserted into the thickest part of the leg or thigh reads 170°F.

GIVE the chicken skin a final crisping by running the chicken under the broiler for a few minutes, moving the pan as necessary so both the front and back are evenly browned and crackly.

LET the chicken rest for about 10 minutes before carving.

CHICKEN PAPRIKASH WITH *NOCKERL* (DUMPLINGS)

yield: **4 TO 6 SERVINGS**

*E*rica Vinik's kitchens—whether in Budapest, Israel, Canada, or Long Beach, New York—have always been filled with Hungarian aromas: "paprika, fresh vegetables, onions, a lot of garlic, more garlic, and then some more garlic."

As a little girl, Erica trailed her mother around the stove but wasn't allowed to touch anything. "My mother was not only very quick but ambidextrous, too. She would beat the yolks with one hand and the whites with the other. She was very precise and didn't want me to mess anything."

Even copying down her mother's recipes proved daunting: yahrzeit glasses might stand in for traditional measuring cups and tablespoons, based on the family's heavy, oversized pewter cutlery, were the equivalent of ladles.

To recreate Hungarian favorites like chicken paprikash and noodles laced with sautéed cabbage slivers, Erica relied on her flavor memory. "The taste was in my mouth, and so I just kept working until I'd achieve it."

In this recipe, fragrant vegetables and paprika imbue not just the chicken, but the delicious nockerl as well, which are not boiled first, as in typical fashion, but cooked entirely in the luscious sauce.

FOR THE CHICKEN

4 to 5 pounds bone-in, skinless chicken thighs

2 tablespoons olive oil

Salt and freshly ground black pepper

1 large onion, chopped (2 cups)

About 2 cups sweet red and yellow peppers, chopped and seeded

1½ tablespoons finely chopped garlic

1 large, fresh plum tomato, chopped

1 cup chicken broth, preferably homemade (see pages 62 and 70) or good quality, low-sodium purchased

PREHEAT oven to 350°F.

WASH the chicken and pat thoroughly dry with paper towels. In a heavy, deep ovenproof skillet (plain or enameled cast-iron is ideal) large enough to accommodate all of the chicken in a single layer, heat the oil over medium-high heat until shimmering. Sauté the chicken, in batches if necessary to avoid crowding the pan, until golden on both sides. Transfer the chicken to a platter and season with salt and pepper.

HEAT the remaining oil in the skillet then add the onions. Salt and pepper lightly, and cook over medium heat, scraping up the browned bits with a wooden spoon, lifting and tossing until the onions are softened and translucent. Stir in the peppers, increase the heat slightly, and sauté until the peppers begin to caramelize around the edges. Add the garlic and cook for 2 to 3 minutes, stirring. Stir in the tomato and adjust the heat to high. Add the broth, the paprikas (more or less, according to taste), and salt and pepper to taste, and bring to a boil.

About ¾ teaspoon hot paprika (see Cook's Note)

About ¼ teaspoon mild paprika

FOR THE NOCKERL

⅔ cup unbleached all-purpose flour

3 large eggs, beaten to blend

Salt

RETURN the chicken pieces to the pan and spoon some of the vegetables and cooking sauce over them. Cover the pan first with foil and then with the lid. Put the pan in the oven and cook for about 30 minutes, until cooked through, turning the chicken pieces around in the sauce two or three times. Transfer the chicken to a platter and tent with foil to keep warm.

MAKE the dumplings: in a medium bowl, mix the flour, eggs, and a generous pinch of salt to a smooth batter. Bring the sauce to a boil in the skillet. Place the bowl of batter next to the skillet. Scoop out a scant teaspoon of the batter and drop it into the sauce, using a second teaspoon to push the batter off the spoon. Continue making dumplings, dropping them evenly around the pan so each one can swell up flavored with the sauce. Cook the dumplings over medium-high heat, uncovered, for about 6 minutes, until plump and firm but not hard. (This will be another few minutes after they solidify.)

TO serve, arrange the chicken on a platter. Surround with the dumplings and nap everything with the pan sauce.

COOK'S NOTE: Much of the success of this dish rides on fresh, aromatic paprikas, a combination of sweet and hot spices. If your paprikas no longer have real fragrance, invest in new ones. Find a brand you like: good paprika should add more than orange color to foods. I often prepare this dish with smoked paprikas.

During my father's last summer, I took the Long Island Railroad to his apartment, spending days with him while Alex was in day camp.

*H*e had always been a master storyteller who "owned" every story he ever told, from folktales like "Why the Sea is Salty" to sagas of the Lower East Side peopled with petty thieves named Cheesecake and Second Story. It wasn't until months after I had discovered Charles Lamb that I conceded to my friends my dad hadn't made up "A Dissertation on Roast Pig"—though he certainly told it better.

In the beginning, when he could still sit upright, cradled in pillows, he told me stories again, new ones I had never heard before, and "Matzoh Ball" stories, those I knew well and was always hungry for: how his family of nine had just one electric light bulb, hung over the kitchen table where everyone ate, talked, and did their homework; how he met my mother.

But as the days passed and his appetite diminished, we knew the chemotherapy wasn't working. So I took over. Yet since he now, as the Psalmist says, "walked through the valley of the Shadow . . . ." I found that everything I spoke of from our world rang hollow and trivial.

Except one: recipes. The less he was able to eat, the more he wanted me to tell him recipes: how my mother used to prepare canned salmon, including the exact amount of white vinegar and onions she added, mush (pronounced "moosh") steak from the old French Roumanian restaurant, fried with gobs of onions in chicken schmaltz. He listened, rapt, correcting me every time I omitted some petty ingredient, forgot the garlic, or a squeeze of lemon. It was as if I were telling spellbinding family stories, and he wanted to make sure I had every detail right.

And then I realized that our recipes *were* our family stories; they nourished us with all that is delicious in life.

I didn't just feed him with recipes: the recipes stimulated his appetite, at least for a while. I would prepare the foods we talked about, and he would eat as much as his shrinking body permitted. We spent a lot of time on his mother's tongue with raisin sauce, and we distilled a recipe for sweet-and-sour stuffed cabbage that reflected both my grandmothers' kitchens, sans the gingersnaps— "excessive," we both agreed.

The tongue was first, so I overcame my longstanding disgust at handling the organ, bought the ingredients for preparing the dish, and went to his apartment to cook it. He wasn't there.

My brother called from the hospital where he was waiting with my father's nurse. "Dad's in the ER, but we're bringing him home. Make the tongue," he urged, "maybe he'll eat it."

He did come home, not that day, but the next. By then, he wasn't eating anything but sips of water.

My brother ate the tongue. And I never made the sweet-and-sour stuffed cabbage.

One day, when I told my daughter the story of the stuffed cabbage, she asked me to tell her the recipe. Then I made it for her.

CLASSIC SWEET-AND-SOUR STUFFED CABBAGE

yield: ABOUT 8 SERVINGS

My father and I decided to add a little tomato puree to the meat and bit of rice, ensuring that the filling would remain tender and succulent in these subtly sweet-and-sour cabbage rolls.

FOR THE CABBAGE ROLLS

¼ cup long-grain rice

1 large head green cabbage or 2 smaller heads

2 pounds lean ground beef (ground turkey—dark meat from the thigh, especially—works well here, too)

2 large eggs, beaten

½ cup canned tomato puree

Salt and freshly ground black pepper

3 tablespoons light olive or other mild oil

4 cups finely chopped onion

2 tablespoons chopped garlic

2 tablespoons brown sugar

START the cabbage rolls: in a small bowl, soak the rice with a little warm water to cover. Using a sharp knife, carefully cut away the large outer leaves of the cabbage from the core end. Rinse, then blanch them in a large pot of boiling salted water, 4 or 5 at a time, until just soft enough to bend and fold without breaking. Drain and pat dry as they are done, and set them aside to cool. Coarsely chop the inner leaves too small to roll, and set aside; use no more than 2 cups of them for the sauce (any remainder can be discarded or saved for another purpose).

IN a large bowl, combine the meat, eggs, tomato puree, salt (figure about 2 teaspoons kosher salt), and pepper to taste. Add the rice, drained, and mix well. Set the filling aside while you sauté onions and garlic.

IN a very large (7- to 8-quart) Dutch oven or heavy ovenproof casserole, warm the oil over medium heat until it shimmers. Add the onions, salt and pepper them lightly, and sauté, lifting and turning occasionally, until softened and pale gold. Add the garlic and continue cooking for 5 more minutes. Scoop out about half of this mixture, put it in a small bowl to cool slightly, then add it to the filling and mix well.

ADD the reserved chopped cabbage to the onion-garlic mixture remaining in the pot, sprinkle with salt, and stir well. Cover the pot and cook over medium heat until the cabbage is lightly steamed and greatly reduced in volume. Uncover the pot, strew with the brown sugar, and sauté over moderately high heat, lifting and turning the vegetables so they don't scorch, until the cabbage is softened and very lightly bronzed in parts. Turn off the heat.

PREHEAT the oven to 325°F.

STUFF the cabbage leaves: place them on a work surface, curled edges up, like an open palm. Cut out the hard little triangle at the base of each stem. Put about ⅓ cup of filling (depending on the size of the leaf) in

One 28-ounce can Italian plum tomatoes, coarsely chopped, with their juice

1 cup canned tomato puree

1 cup chicken broth, preferably homemade (see pages 62 and 70) or good-quality low-sodium purchased

1 cup chopped onion

3 tablespoons fresh lemon juice

2 tablespoons brown sugar

2 teaspoons minced candied ginger

2 teaspoons cider vinegar

Salt and freshly ground black pepper

1 Turkish bay leaf

½ cup golden raisins

the center. Fold the stem end of the leaf over the filling, then tuck in the two sides. Pull the top over these folds to enclose the roll. They should be compact and rounded, but remember, the rice will drink in the puree and the meat juices and expand somewhat, so leave a little extra room. Place the finished rolls seam side down as you work.

PREPARE the sauce: in a food processor fitted with the steel blade, combine all the sauce ingredients except the bay leaf and process until smooth.

PLACE the cabbage rolls seam side down on top of the sautéed vegetables. Pack them together closely, making multiple layers as necessary. Pour the sauce evenly over them, bury the bay leaf deep amidst the rolls, cover the pot tightly and bring to a boil. Transfer to the oven and bake for 2 hours, stirring in the raisins after the first hour. If necessary, bake an additional 30 minutes to 1 hour, uncovered, until the cabbage is very tender.

SERVE the cabbage rolls with lots of challah or other good bread or mashed potatoes because you'll want to sop up all of the wonderful sauce. Excellent reheated and even better the second day.

EASY ONION-BRAISED BRISKET

yield: ABOUT 8 SERVINGS

A featured player in countless holiday productions throughout the Diaspora, sautéed onion takes on multiple roles here, providing not only the wonderfully savory flavor but also all the aromatic moisture in which the brisket gently braises, and even the body for the simple, flour-free gravy.

5 tablespoons mild olive oil

A first- or second-cut beef brisket (about 5 pounds), trimmed of excess fat, wiped with a damp paper towel, and patted dry

6 large garlic cloves, peeled and crushed

Salt and freshly ground black pepper

2 pounds onions, thinly sliced (about 8 cups)

¼ cup mild vinegar (moderately priced sherry or balsamic are good choices)

HEAT 3 tablespoons of the oil over medium-high heat in a large Dutch oven or heavy flameproof casserole large enough to accommodate the meat in one layer (see Cook's Note). Add the brisket, and brown it well to caramelize the meat on all sides, about 10 minutes in all. Don't allow it to develop a hard, dark crust, which would make the meat tough or bitter. Transfer the brisket to a platter, fat-side down.

SPRINKLE the garlic cloves with enough salt and pepper to season the brisket, then mash the seasoned garlic to a paste. Spread half of the garlic paste over the top (nonfat side) of the brisket, and set the meat aside.

PREHEAT the oven to 300°F.

POUR off all the remaining fat in the pan, and add the remaining 2 tablespoons fresh oil. Add about half the onions, salt and pepper them generously, and sauté over medium-high heat, lifting and tossing them occasionally, until they have greatly reduced in volume and turned light golden. Stir in the remaining onions. After all the onions have softened, stir less frequently so they can build up the lovely dark *fond* that helps them brown more quickly. When all the onions are burnished a rich gold, add 3½ tablespoons vinegar. Increase the heat to high, and cook, scraping up all the caramelized brown bits from the bottom of the pan with a wooden spoon, for 3 to 4 minutes, until all the liquid is evaporated.

PLACE the brisket on the bed of onions, fat side up. Spread the remaining garlic paste over the top (fat side) of the brisket.

SPOON about half of the onions all over the top and sides of the brisket, so that the meat is sandwiched between layers of onion. Cover tightly first with foil, then with the lid.

BRAISE the brisket in the oven, basting with the pan juices and turning the meat every 30 minutes or so (be sure to recover the pan tightly), until the meat is fork tender, 3½ to 4 hours. Let the meat rest in the pan sauce for at least 1 hour, but preferably overnight, covered, in the refrigerator.

WHEN you are ready to serve the brisket, scrape off any congealed fat from the surface, if you have refrigerated the dish. Transfer the cold meat to a cutting board, and slice the meat thinly across the grain at a slight diagonal.

PREPARE the gravy: strain the braising mixture, reserving the onion-garlic mixture. Skim and discard as much fat as possible from the liquid. Puree the defatted liquid, together with about half the reserved onion-garlic mixture and the remaining ½ tablespoon vinegar, in a food processor or blender. Transfer the pureed mixture to the cleaned pan. Add the remaining onion-garlic mixture and boil over high heat for about 5 minutes to concentrate the gravy and marry the flavors. Reduce the heat, add the meat, and reheat it slowly in the gravy until piping hot. Taste and adjust seasoning.

ARRANGE the sliced brisket on a serving platter. Spoon some of the hot sauce all over the meat and pass the rest in a separate sauce boat.

COOK'S NOTE: If you don't have a pan large enough, you can cut the brisket in two and sauté it in batches. (The meat will shrink as it cooks, so that you will be able to fit it in one layer later.) Or sear the meat under the broiler: cover the broiler pan with foil to minimize cleanup. Place brisket, fat-side up, under a preheated broiler, and broil for 5 to 6 minutes on each side, or until nicely browned. Move the meat around as needed, so that it sears evenly.

FLANKEN WITH TART GREENS

yield: 4 TO 5 SERVINGS

This dish is commonly translated as "boiled beef," but it is actually beef long-simmered in water with aromatic vegetables. My grandmother's method uses a full-bodied beef or chicken broth instead as the cooking medium, along with plenty of earthy vegetables, producing succulent meat as well as a lusty-flavored soup. Though eight cups of broth may seem extravagant, in effect you are borrowing it and returning it deepened by the vibrant flavors of the meat and vegetables, as a husky soup that really sings, ready to be served at another meal. To garnish it, use the leftover flanken to make the Mishmash Kreplach on page 330. Or ladle the soup over egg noodles and sprinkle with lots of chopped fresh dill. Offered solo, the broth is wonderfully restorative on frosty days, and it makes a refined opener to a rich meat dinner.

Flanken is a bony Jewish cut of beef made by cutting short ribs across the bone. It is available in kosher butcher shops and from many nonkosher butchers in areas with large Jewish populations. If unavailable, you can substitute chuck short ribs.

Horseradish, the traditional accompaniment to flanken, can overpower the almost-sweet meat. I prefer broccoli rabe, whose gentle bitterness plays well against the richness of the beef. But I have both horseradish and mustard available for guests who insist.

4 pounds lean beef flanken

8 cups Beef Stock (page 32); chicken broth, preferably homemade (see pages 62 and 70), or good-quality, low-sodium purchased

1 large onion, thickly sliced

3 large garlic cloves, peeled and crushed

2 carrots, scraped and quartered

1 parsnip, peeled and quartered

1 parsley root, peeled (optional)

PUT the beef and stock in a 6-quart Dutch oven or wide heavy saucepan, partially cover, and bring to a bare simmer: the liquid shivering, occasional bubbles breaking gently and noiselessly on the surface. Don't allow the liquid to come to a boil; that will make the broth cloudy and the meat tough. Regulate the heat as necessary. Use a skimmer to remove as much foam and scum as possible as they rise to the surface.

AFTER the flanken has simmered for about 30 minutes, add the onion, garlic, carrots, parsnip, parsley root, if using, celery, and bay leaf. Season to taste with salt and pepper, bearing in mind that if you started with a salted broth, it will get saltier as it cooks down. Place the lid slightly askew and continue cooking over very low heat for 2½ to 3 hours, or until the meat is fork-tender. Let the flanken rest in the broth for about 15 minutes, then take it out and arrange it on a serving platter. Spoon a little of the broth over the meat to keep it moist. (If you need to reheat the flanken, simmer it in enough broth to cover.)

2 celery stalks, including leaves if available, quartered

1 bay leaf, preferably Turkish

Salt and freshly ground black pepper

FOR THE GREENS

1 pound broccoli rabe, cleaned, stems trimmed and cut into bite-size pieces, leaves and florets coarsely chopped, or an equal amount of trimmed, roughly chopped kale, mustard or turnip greens

1 tablespoon chopped garlic

2 tablespoons olive oil

1/8 teaspoon hot red pepper flakes (optional)

Salt

About 3 tablespoons broth from the flanken

Accompaniments: kosher sour dill pickles, coarse salt, grated horseradish, and sharp mustard (for traditional tastes, if desired)

STRAIN the soup, discarding or reserving the cooked vegetables according to preference (they will be quite soft; I usually discard all but the carrot and sometimes the parsnip and parsley root). Remove as much fat as possible from the broth by refrigerating it thoroughly until the fat solidifies, then just lifting it off. (You can deal with the soup at your leisure, of course, if you are in a hurry to get the flanken on the table.) Reserve 3 tablespoons of the broth for the greens.

ABOUT 30 minutes before you are ready to serve the flanken, prepare the greens: bring a large pot of well-salted water to a boil. Add the broccoli rabe or other greens, cover, and cook, stirring occasionally, until tender but not mushy, about 4 minutes. Drain thoroughly.

IN a large heavy skillet, sauté the garlic in the oil over medium-low heat, stirring, for 1 minute, until pale golden (do *not* let it brown). Add cooked greens, raise the heat to medium, and sauté for about 3 minutes, stirring occasionally. Add the reserved flanken broth, the pepper flakes, if using, and salt to taste, and continue cooking for another 3 minutes, lifting and tossing the greens, to meld the flavors.

SLICE the flanken across the grain. Serve each guest a portion of broccoli rabe topped with slices of flanken. If desired, ladle a little hot broth over the meat to moisten it. Pass the pickles and coarse salt, and for the tradition-bound, horseradish and mustard.

My grandmother had flanken.

I don't mean she consumed prodigious amounts of it, or that she served up her superb version often, though both are true.

I refer, instead, to her arms.

Her dark olive skin was perfectly smooth and taut across her elegant face. But the soft flesh from her gently sloping shoulders to her wide, tired feet hung in rounded folds like an old shower curtain.

When she left the house, every bit of that loose flesh was constrained: in a heavy pink satin brassiere and matching girdle, strong support hose, and then, beautifully tailored clothes with long or three-quarter-length sleeves.

But not when she was cooking. At her apartment in the Bronx or at our house, preparing the delicacies that marked our holiday feasts, my tiny grandmother permitted herself to wear a sleeveless housedress with extra-large armholes to accommodate her upper arms.

One such morning, my brother, my sister, and I sat eating the lumpy but delicious farina she had made, our sleepy eyes hypnotically fixed on the huge pleats of flesh flapping rhythmically, the identical color of the boiled beef she was cutting up.

"Flanken," my brother whispered. "Look at Grandma's flanken. She has flanken on her arms."

But she got the last laugh.

Now that my sister and I are in our fifties, we know just how hard it is to keep arms free of flanken.

COFFEE-SPICED POT ROAST WITH KASHA KREPLACH AND TOASTED GARLIC CHALLAH CRUMBS

yield: ABOUT 8 SERVINGS

Growing up in a large, traditional Jewish family, my father never cooked anything until he met my mother. He learned by watching her prepare latkes and lasagne, bistecca alla pizzaiola and brisket in the kitchen of their chartreuse and shocking pink apartment: grist for the endless dinner parties Mom's cousins remember vividly today, though they took place more than sixty years ago.

Constitutionally incapable of following a written recipe, my parents expanded their culinary repertoires in different ways. Besides the cookbooks my mother used as departure points, there were the late night radio shows that inspired creative pancake-making forays at 3AM or escarole baked with meat, raisins, and pine nuts at our next big dinner.

My father, on the other hand, was smitten with a number of food crushes. Black bean soup, after he had tasted it at the Coach House restaurant, lasted a few years. There were on and off trashy flirtations with onion soup mix and the like. But coffee added to pot roast or a stew—an idea he had gleaned from a newspaper years ago—remained a longtime companion.

I remembered the coffee recently and relied on its slightly bitter acidity to bring just the right balance to the barbeque spice flavors in this meltingly tender pot roast. To partner the meat, kasha kreplach, topped with garlicky crumbs for crunch, make a delectable, if unusual, side dish. For years I have been serving kreplach and ravioli made with wonton wrappers as accompaniments to stews and saucy meats: when stuffing is not on the menu, I sometimes prepare pureed chestnut-and-shallot–filled wontons alongside the Thanksgiving turkey, napping both with good gravy.

This is one dish I like to plate in the kitchen, instead of serving family-style. That way, I don't have to explain how to layer the ingredients, then watch the delicate kreplach turn cold and adhere to one another while waiting for diners to serve themselves the meat first.

FOR THE FLAVOR PASTE

8 large garlic cloves, coarsely chopped

2 tablespoons dark brown sugar

1 tablespoon kosher salt

1 tablespoon ground cumin, preferably freshly toasted and ground

COMBINE all the flavor paste ingredients in a food processor and process to a coarse puree. Pat the paste all over the meat and let it drink in the seasonings for at least 2 hours or up to 24, wrapped in plastic or a resealable plastic bag and refrigerated.

REMOVE the meat from the refrigerator and let it come to room temperature. Preheat the oven to 300°F.

1 teaspoon cracked black peppercorns

½ teaspoon ground cinnamon

FOR THE POT ROAST

A 4- to 5-pound boneless chuck eye roast (I've found that this produces the most succulent pot roast, but if unavailable, chuck shoulder or other boneless chuck roast will yield a very fine dish too), trimmed of excess fat, wiped with a damp paper towel and patted dry

4 tablespoons olive oil

2 cups chopped onion

2 cups scraped carrots, coarsely chopped

2 teaspoons smoked or fragrant sweet paprika

2 to 3 cups chicken broth, preferably homemade (see pages 62 and 70), or good-quality, low-sodium purchased

1 cup strong brewed coffee

⅓ cup cider vinegar

Kasha Kreplach with Toasted Garlic Challah Crumbs (recipe follows)

SCRAPE the flavor paste off the meat (otherwise, it may burn during the initial browning) and reserve it. Pat the meat dry. In a large Dutch oven or other lidded flameproof casserole big enough to accommodate the meat, heat 2 tablespoons of the oil over medium-high heat until it is hot but not smoking. Add the meat and brown it on all sides, about 10 minutes. Transfer to a platter and set aside.

WIPE out all the oil from the pan, add the remaining 2 tablespoons oil, and heat until shimmering. Add the onions, salt and pepper lightly, and cook over medium heat until softened, about 5 minutes. Stir in the carrots and continue cooking, turning occasionally, for 5 more minutes. Add the reserved flavor paste and the paprika, cooking and stirring until fragrant, about 1 minute. Add 2 cups of the broth, the coffee, and the vinegar, and bring to a boil, using a wooden spoon to scrape up any delicious browned bits clinging to the bottom of the pan.

REDUCE the heat to a simmer. Place the meat and any juices it has thrown off into the pan; if needed, add more broth so that the liquid comes half way up to the sides of the meat. Arrange a sheet of foil over the meat, then cover tightly with the pan lid.

OVEN-BRAISE the meat, turning and basting it with the pan liquid every half-hour until the meat is very tender, 3½ to 4 hours.

WHILE the meat is cooking, prepare the kasha kreplach.

TRANSFER the meat to a carving board; keep it warm beneath a foil tent. Skim as much fat as possible from the pan sauce. If necessary, strain the pan liquid (reserving the solids—most of the aromatic vegetables will have melted into the sauce) into a large glass, wait for it to settle, then spoon off the clear fat that has risen to the top (see page 21).

IN a large skillet, boil the defatted pan juices and reserved solids, reducing until nicely thickened and glossy. Taste and correct seasoning.

I like to serve this already plated for guests. Slice the pot roast and arrange on individual plates. Top with some kreplach, then a generous shower of pan gravy. Scatter the challah crumbs over all.

KASHA KREPLACH WITH TOASTED GARLIC CHALLAH CRUMBS

yield: ABOUT 50 KREPLACH

This will probably make more kreplach than you need for this dinner, but it is difficult to prepare less than one cup of kasha (since it is mixed with a whole egg). And leftover kreplach (uncooked) can be frozen. Arrange them, unwrapped, in a single layer on a baking sheet, place in the freezer until solidly frozen, then wrap in freezer packaging. You can also use the filling to make "lazy kreplach:" boil the wonton wrappers as you would pasta squares and drain them. Grease a rimmed baking sheet or pan and on it place one or two wrappers for each guest, in a single layer, sides not touching. Spread some of the filling on each wrapper and cover with another wrapper. Continue adding a few layers of filling and wrappers to each with the remaining filling and wrappers, creating a stack or two of kreplach for each guest. Add some broth to the bottom of the pan, and drizzle each stack with gravy and a bit more broth. Bake at 325°F until everything is heated through. Serve guests the stacks of lazy kreplach, topped with the challah crumbs.

FOR THE KASHA KREPLACH

1 large egg plus 2 large egg yolks

1 cup kasha

2 cups chicken broth, preferably homemade (see pages 62 and 70), or Vegetable Stock (page 34)

Salt and freshly ground black pepper

3 tablespoons olive oil

2 cups finely chopped onion (about ½ pound)

1 cup mashed potatoes (leftover is fine)

About 100 wonton wrappers (see page 39; it's a good idea to have extra in case of tearing)

Egg wash (1 or 2 large eggs as needed, each beaten with 1 teaspoon water)

PREPARE the kasha: in a medium bowl, beat the egg with a fork. Stir in the kasha and mix until each grain is thoroughly coated with egg. Bring the broth to a simmer. In a heavy medium skillet with high sides or a wide heavy saucepan, toast the kasha over medium heat, turning and breaking up the kasha constantly until the egg begins to dry and the grains separate, about 3 minutes. Add the simmering broth and salt and pepper to taste, then cover and cook over very low heat until tender and all the liquid is absorbed, about 10 minutes. Transfer to a large bowl and let cool.

IN a medium skillet, heat the oil until shimmering. Add the onions and sauté, stirring occasionally, until speckled with deep bronze. Add the onions to the kasha. Stir in the mashed potato, and combine well. Taste

**2 slices challah, about
³/₄ inch thick**

**2¹/₂ tablespoons extra
virgin olive oil**

**2 teaspoons minced fresh
garlic**

**Salt and freshly ground
black pepper**

**1 to 2 tablespoons
chopped flat-leaf parsley
(optional)**

and adjust seasonings: it should be well salted and peppery. Add the egg yolks and mix thoroughly. Refrigerate until cold.

MAKE the challah crumbs: preheat the oven to 325°F. Arrange the challah on a rimmed baking sheet and toast on both sides until dry and crisp. Or toast lightly in a toaster oven. Let cool, then tear into pieces and pulse in a food processor until coarsely ground. Measure out 1 cup; use any extra for another purpose. In a medium skillet, warm the oil over medium heat. Add the garlic and crumbs, and cook, stirring, until golden brown. Season well with salt and pepper. Stir in the parsley, if using.

FILL and trim the kreplach (see page 39), using 1 tablespoon of filling and 2 wonton wrappers for each krepl and sealing them with the egg wash.

POACH the kreplach: in a large, very wide pot, bring at least 5 quarts of lightly salted water to a boil. Slip in the kreplach, one by one, being careful not to overcrowd the pot (if necessary, cook them in batches, or use two pots). Lower the temperature slightly (the kreplach might explode if the water is boiling furiously) and poach until tender, 3 to 6 minutes (exact time will depend on the brand of wonton wrapper used). Lift the kreplach out, a few at a time, with a large skimmer, gently shaking the skimmer so the water drains back into the pot (the kreplach are too fragile to pour into a colander).

THE kreplach are now ready to be sauced.

SEPHARDI-STYLE STUFFED MEATBALLS WITH CELERY ROOT AND CARROTS

yield: ABOUT 4 SERVINGS

*I*n both Sephardi and Italian-Jewish cooking, there is a wealth of recipes for ground meat or poultry cooked with vegetables. Most familiar, of course, are meat-stuffed vegetables, baked or braised; meat is also mounded between vegetable slices, then breaded and fried, or prepared as in this recipe, combined with chopped vegetables, formed into meatballs, fried, and then braised.

I've cooked these meatballs over braised celery root and carrots, a favorite Sephardi combination. If you can't find celery root—or if the knotted bulb appears too daunting—substitute fennel or celery, perhaps intensifying their flavors with a generous pinch of crushed fennel or celery seeds.

And instead of the green olives or roasted red peppers I've combined with the meat here, you can experiment with other cooked vegetables as well, such as chopped spinach, fried eggplant, or braised fennel. Adding vegetables to the meatballs both flavors and lightens them, making this method a particularly good choice when you are using ground chicken or turkey.

1 thick slice challah (about 1 inch) or good-quality white bread, crusts removed

2½ cups chicken broth, preferably homemade (see pages 62 and 70), or good-quality, low-sodium purchased

1 tablespoon chopped garlic, plus 2 teaspoons minced

5 tablespoons chopped fresh parsley

1 large egg

1 pound ground chicken, turkey, or beef

1 cup pitted green olives, chopped (use good-quality brine- or oil-cured), or ½ cup minced roasted red pepper (see page 240)

TEAR the bread into 2-inch pieces and put it into a small saucepan. Add ½ cup of the broth and cook over medium heat until the bread has absorbed all the liquid. Transfer the mixture to a food processor, together with the chopped garlic, 2 tablespoons of the parsley, and the egg and then process until well combined. Put the meat in a large bowl and add the pureed bread mixture, the olives or red peppers, and salt and pepper to taste. Knead with your hands until the ingredients are thoroughly amalgamated. If you have time, refrigerate for at least 30 minutes to let the flavors blend.

PREPARE the vegetables: peel and trim the celery root and cut it into large cubes—you'll have 3½ to 4 cups. (To facilitate the peeling, cut it into large pieces first, then trim and peel.) Cut the carrots into pieces roughly, the same size as the celery root—you'll have about 2 cups.

WETTING your hands as needed, form the meat into walnut-size balls. Heat about ¼ inch of oil in a large, heavy, deep-sided skillet or sauté pan until hot but not smoking. Add the meatballs and sauté in batches until

Salt and freshly ground black pepper

1½ pounds celery root (also called celeriac)

1 pound carrots, scraped

Olive oil, for frying

Juice of 2 lemons

1 teaspoon grated lemon zest

lightly browned on all sides but not cooked through. (This is the one-pot method. If time is a problem or you don't have a deep-sided sauté pan, fry the meatballs in a regular skillet and braise the vegetables at the same time in a Dutch oven or heavy casserole.) Transfer the meatballs to a platter as they are done.

WIPE out the skillet, add 3 tablespoons fresh oil, and heat until hot. Add the celery root and carrots and sauté over medium-high heat, in batches if necessary, until the vegetables turn golden brown at the edges. Keep lifting and turning with a spatula so the vegetables color on all sides. If you worked in batches, return all vegetables to the skillet. Add the lemon juice, remaining 2 cups broth, 2 teaspoons minced garlic, and salt and pepper to taste. Stir well, then simmer over low heat, covered, for about 10 minutes. The vegetables should be almost tender at this point.

ADD the meatballs to the pan, and spoon the pan liquid and vegetables over them. Cover and simmer gently for 10 minutes, or until the vegetables are very tender and the meatballs are cooked through. Adjust the salt and pepper and stir in the lemon zest and the remaining 3 tablespoons parsley.

TRANSFER the meat and vegetables to a serving platter, and ladle some of the pan juices over them. Pass the remaining pan sauce separately. (If you want a more concentrated pan sauce, reduce it for a few minutes over high heat after you have removed the meatballs and vegetables.)

CHOLENT

Call it *cholent, shalet, dafina, hamin, s'keena, tabit*: nearly every Jewish community in the Diaspora has come up with a version, or several, of this quintessential Jewish dish. It is a one-pot hot meal—meats, vegetables, legumes, and/or grains are all cooked together in a casserole—traditionally prepared on Friday afternoon and left to simmer very slowly in the oven until the Saturday midday meal.

These casseroles were created to solve a singularly Jewish problem: how to honor the Sabbath lunch with hot foods when no fires may be kindled—or ovens lit—after sundown on Friday. (The Jewish Sabbath, like all Jewish days, begins with sunset and ends the following evening. "And there was evening and there was morning: the first day," says Genesis 1:5.)

Because the Sabbath laws prohibit the act of cooking as well as lighting fires, observant Jews do not stir the dish, add additional ingredients or seasonings, or degrease the cholent while the Sabbath is in progress. Cooks trim as much fat as possible before cooking, or they can prepare the cholent well in advance, refrigerate it, and remove the fat before reheating. (Warming up cooked food on a previously lit fire—a stove burner or oven kept on overnight—is permissible.) Guests may season the food at the table.

But you need not restrict the cholent of Sabbath to the traditional Saturday lunch. Robust and aromatic, it is ideal cold weather comfort food. Prepare it on a blustery January or February morning when rattling winds make you long for richly caramelized, slow-cooked flavors, and let it stew all day in a gentle oven or Crockpot, steaming up the windows. You'll come home to an ineffably tantalizing fragrance and a deeply soul-satisfying meal.

Ah, the aroma. Too often it is more glorious than the taste. Because the ingredients can be rather heavy (when meats were scarce, cooks often took the kitchen sink approach, tossing in virtually everything but to fill out their cholents) and are cooked so long, traditional cholents, especially to the uninitiated, can be unpleasantly thick and tired-tasting.

SOME GUIDELINES: DELICIOUS CHOLENTS FOR CONTEMPORARY TASTES

- Today there is no reason not to limit the amount and number of starches used. Beans, with rice, perhaps, or a dumpling, along with some white potatoes, is usually the most I include in a Sabbath stew.

- Barley, simmered for very long periods, tends to swell up enormously, drinking up a great deal of the cooking liquid, and can become rather mushy. If you include it, go easy, adding just enough to lend a creaminess to the cholent. Or try soaking it overnight in cold water ($1/2$ cup barley to 2 cups water) when you soak the beans, for fluffier barley.

- If you are cutting down on meat, include more sturdy vegetables along with the beans. Carrots, celery root, fennel, parsley root, parsnips, and rutabagas are all good choices. They will impart their earthy, herbal flavor and, in turn, beautifully absorb the aromatic cooking juices. Roasted shallots make a wonderful addition.

- Because the lengthy cooking flattens out the flavors, eliminating the complex high notes, before serving, introduce some fresh, vivacious tastes. Shower the cholent lavishly with fresh herbs or rouse it with a jolt of freshly ground black pepper or finely minced fresh garlic. Something citrusy—the finely grated peel or a splash of juice—will also enliven the cholent and pull the flavors into balance, while mitigating its richness.

- Yes, it is a *rich* dish. If health reasons do not permit you to indulge in a regular portion, enjoy it as an appetizer. Round out the rest of the meal with a big, tart salad and whole-grain bread like a sour rye. Chilled Crenshaw melon or other seasonal fresh fruit makes the best finish.

- Cholents freeze beautifully and reheat well. Leftovers become perfect make-ahead meals. And it's easy to remove the fat from cholents prepared in advance. Remember to add a dash of fresh flavoring just before serving.

DUCK AND WHITE BEAN CHOLENT

yield: **4 TO 6 SERVINGS**

This spoon-tender duck and creamy bean casserole is reminiscent of a fine cassoulet, to which it is no doubt related. European Jews wealthy enough to enrich their cholents—the stew that for many was the taste of Sabbath itself—with duck and goose found the lush flesh would remain succulent and tender even after the prolonged cooking from Friday afternoon to midday Saturday. Today, kosher confit d'oie (long-simmered preserved goose) is still sold in Jewish delicatessens in France for creating lavish Alsatian-style cholents.

But the lengthy, gentle braising that renders such incomparably supple meat and enchants the house with a heavenly perfume will also fade the pungent seasonings. They will need some brightening up. So just before serving, I send in a fresh infusion of flavors: brisk minced garlic, rosemary, and snappy lemon zest.

1½ cups dried white beans (about 12 ounces) such as cannellini or great Northern, washed, picked over, soaked overnight in cold water to cover by at least 2 inches, and drained

One 4 ½- to 5 ½-pound fresh duck (or, if unavailable, thawed frozen), cut into eighths, wingtips, tailbone, and neck removed

1 tablespoon olive oil

Salt and freshly ground black pepper

1 cup chopped shallots

8 large garlic cloves, coarsely chopped

1 cup dry red wine

10 to 12 pitted prunes, quartered

4 large waxy potatoes, peeled and cut into quarters, or 6 medium, halved

PLACE the beans in a very large (7- to 8-quart) Dutch oven or heavy flameproof casserole in which you will be cooking the cholent.

RESERVE the duck liver and giblets for another use. Pull off and discard as much excess fat as possible (or save for rendering—see page 28). Rinse the duck pieces and thoroughly dry with paper towels.

HEAT the oil in a 10- to 12-inch heavy skillet (cast-iron is ideal), until very hot but not smoking. Working in batches, add the duck and brown on both sides over medium-high heat, beginning skin side down. Transfer the duck as it is browned to the Dutch oven or casserole. Let the browned duck rest until cool enough to handle, then remove the skin from each piece. If your cholesterol permits, return the skin to the skillet and fry over moderately high heat until crisp on both sides, to render out as much fat as possible (it will be a delicious flavoring for the cholent). Cut the skin into small bits and add to the Dutch oven or casserole. Sprinkle the skin and the duck pieces all over with salt and pepper. (If you choose not to crisp the skin, simply discard it.)

REMOVE all but 1 tablespoon of the fat remaining in the skillet and discard or reserve it for another use. Add the shallots and sauté over medium heat until softened, about 5 minutes. Add the garlic and continue cooking for 3 minutes, or until golden. Transfer the mixture to the Dutch oven.

2 tablespoons chopped fresh rosemary leaves

1 tablespoon chopped fresh sage

2 teaspoons grated orange zest

About 6 cups chicken broth, preferably homemade (see pages 62 and 70), or good-quality, low-sodium purchased

FOR THE LEMON-GARLIC GARNISH

2 to 3 teaspoons grated lemon zest

2 teaspoons minced or pressed garlic

1 tablespoon finely chopped fresh rosemary leaves

2 tablespoons finely chopped fresh parsley, preferably flat-leaf

$\frac{1}{2}$ teaspoon salt

ADD the wine and prunes to the skillet and turn the heat up to high, scraping up all the browned bits with a wooden spoon. Cook until the liquid is reduced by half, then transfer the mixture to the Dutch oven.

PREHEAT the oven to 200°F. Add the potatoes to the Dutch oven, sprinkle the herbs, orange zest, and salt and pepper to taste over all, and combine well. Add 6 cups broth—it should just cover all of the ingredients; if necessary, add a bit more. Bring to a gentle boil and then simmer for 10 minutes. Cover very tightly with foil and the lid. Transfer to the oven and bake undisturbed for at least 8 hours, or overnight.

PREPARE the lemon-garlic garnish: combine all the ingredients in a small bowl, cover, and refrigerate until ready to serve.

JUST before serving the cholent, stir in lemon-garlic garnish.

HERBED BEEF CHOLENT WITH ONION GONIFS

yield: 6 TO 8 SERVINGS

"Gonif," she called, trailing me into the kitchen. Other children stole from the cookie jar. But what cookie could compare with my grandmother's huge, cold matzoh balls, satin-sleek with fat, gleaming like golden goose eggs in the moonlight?

"Stop! There won't be any left for tomorrow. You little gonif, you thief."

But she was laughing. She always made extra. It was the one food she knew I'd always eat, and she was engaged in a constant struggle to put more weight on me, which would no doubt cure me of the twin maladies, anemia and straight hair.

Reading through a pile of Jewish cookbooks in a secondhand store years later, I was intrigued to learn about a matzoh-ball-type dumpling cooked in a cholent, ironically called a gonif. It seems the dumpling, placed on top of all the savory ingredients, steals their flavors and becomes enriched by them.

In the following cholent, the slow-cooking herbed flanken or short ribs make these oniony gonifs quite rich indeed. I usually include poultry so those who want to cut down on some of the red meat in this very filling dish can do so.

FOR THE ONION GONIFS

4 tablespoons olive oil

1 cup finely chopped onion

Salt and freshly ground black pepper

5 large eggs

1 cup matzoh meal

3 tablespoons finely chopped fresh parsley, preferably flat-leaf

2 teaspoons grated lemon zest

1½ teaspoons baking powder

⅓ cup chicken broth

START the gonifs: heat 1 tablespoon of the oil in a 7- to 8-inch skillet, add the onions, and sauté over moderate heat until softened and pale gold, about 5 minutes. Add salt and pepper to taste, and set the skillet aside to cool.

IN a large bowl, beat the eggs until thick and light. Add the remaining 3 tablespoons oil and beat until smooth. Fold in the matzoh meal, parsley, lemon zest, baking powder, about 1½ teaspoons salt (or to taste), and a generous amount of pepper. When the onions have cooled to room temperature, stir them in, along with the broth. Mix very well, cover the bowl, and refrigerate for at least 1 hour or up to 12 hours.

PREPARE the beans: put them in a large saucepan together with the carrots, bay leaf, thyme, rosemary, onion, and garlic. Add enough cold water to cover the ingredients by 2 inches. Bring to a gentle boil over medium heat, skimming off the froth as it rises to the top. As soon as it

2 cups cannellini or great Northern beans (1 pound), or a combination of either with cranberry or kidney beans, washed, picked over, soaked overnight in cold water to cover by at least 2 inches, and drained

3 large carrots, scraped and quartered

1 Turkish bay leaf

1 fresh thyme sprig

1 fresh rosemary sprig

$\frac{1}{2}$ small onion, peeled

2 large garlic cloves, peeled and smashed

FOR THE HERB PASTE

2 tablespoons coarsely chopped onion

1 tablespoon coarsely chopped garlic

1 tablespoon minced lemon zest

2 tablespoons fresh lemon juice

1 tablespoon chopped fresh rosemary leaves

2 teaspoons minced fresh thyme

2 teaspoons salt

5 peppercorns, crushed

Olive oil

$3\frac{1}{2}$ to $4\frac{1}{2}$ pounds flanken or short ribs, cut in pieces

$1\frac{1}{2}$ to $2\frac{1}{2}$ pounds turkey thighs or legs (optional)

begins to boil, reduce the heat to a simmer, partially cover the saucepan, and cook for about 40 minutes, until the beans are almost tender. Drain the beans. Pick out and discard the herbs, onion, and garlic, but reserve the carrots. Transfer the beans and carrots to a 7- to 8-quart Dutch oven or flameproof casserole.

WHILE the beans are cooking, prepare the herb paste: in a blender or mini food processor, combine the onions, garlic, lemon zest, lemon juice, rosemary, thyme, salt, and peppercorns. Puree, stopping to scrape down the container as necessary, until the mixture is well combined and fairly smooth. Scrape the mixture into a 13 by 9-inch glass baking dish.

TRIM as much fat as possible from the meat and pat it dry. (You really can't skim the fat from the cooked cholent, unless it is prepared well in advance and refrigerated.) Lightly grease a deep 10- to 12-inch heavy skillet and heat it over medium-high heat until it is hot, but not smoking. Add the flanken or short ribs, in batches, if necessary, so you don't overcrowd the pan, and brown lightly on all sides over medium-high heat. Transfer the meat to the baking dish and smear the herb paste all over. If using the turkey, heat the skillet again (if needed, film it with oil again) over moderately high heat. Add the turkey and lightly brown it on all sides, then transfer it to the baking dish and rub all over with the herb paste.

PREHEAT the oven to 200°F.

ASSEMBLE the cholent ingredients: discard any fat in the skillet and heat the 2 tablespoons oil. Add the onions and sauté over moderately high heat until softened and lightly speckled with brown, about 5 minutes. Add the parsnips and garlic, and continue sautéing until dotted bronze around the edges. Add the wine, bring to a boil, and cook, scraping up all the browned bits, for 2 minutes. Stir in the tomatoes and their juices, the rosemary, thyme, and salt and pepper to taste, and bring to a simmer. Cook, stirring, for 2 to 3 minutes, to mingle the flavors. Stir the mixture into the beans in the Dutch oven.

SALT and pepper the bean mixture to taste, taking into account the saltiness of the broth you are using in the recipe. Add the beef, turkey, if using, and potatoes, burying them in the beans. Add the broth and bring to a slow boil.

2 tablespoons olive oil

1½ cups chopped onion

**2 parsnips, peeled and
quartered**

**3 tablespoons coarsely
chopped garlic**

½ cup dry red wine

**One 16-ounce can Italian
plum tomatoes, chopped,
and their juices**

**2 tablespoons chopped
fresh rosemary leaves**

**1 tablespoon chopped
fresh thyme**

**Salt and freshly ground
black pepper**

**6 to 8 small waxy or
all-purpose potatoes
(about 2 pounds), such
as red new potatoes or
Yukon gold (if you have
access to heirloom
varieties: Caribe, Russian
Banana, or Yellow Finn
would be particularly
delicious), scrubbed,
unpeeled (unless the peel
is thick or unpleasant),
and halved**

**4 cups chicken broth,
preferably homemade
(see pages 62 and 70),
Beef Stock (page 32), or
good-quality, low-sodium
purchased**

**Chopped fresh flat-leaf
parsley and fresh minced
chives, for garnish**

LIGHTLY form the gonif batter into dumplings the size of golf balls. (Don't compress the batter too much or the gonifs will be dense and hard. If you prefer, you can make the gonifs smaller, about the size of walnuts.) When the broth is gently boiling, slide in the gonifs, one at a time. Cover the pot tightly with foil and the lid and transfer it to the oven. Let the cholent cook undisturbed for 8 hours, or overnight.

TO serve, place two gonifs, two potato halves, beans, and slices of meat and/or poultry in shallow soup bowls. Ladle in some broth. Sprinkle generously with the parsley and chives to freshen the flavors.

GARLICKY LAMB AND LIMA HAMIN WITH LITTLE EGGPLANT BOATS

yield: 6 TO 7 SERVINGS

This Sabbath stew celebrates timeless Sephardi tastes. Nestled on top of limas and rice, garlic-suffused lamb simmers slowly overnight to melt-in-the-mouth tenderness. For added dimension, I cook little meat-stuffed eggplants along with the stew. Sephardim frequently include stuffed zucchinis or other vegetables in their hamins; they are analogues of the gonifs, the starchy dumplings Ashkenazim add to their cholents. Like a gonif, these eggplant boats seem to pilfer the fragrant aromas from the stew as they cook to creamy succulence.

The idea for these eggplant boats came from Oded Schwartz's In Search of Plenty. *For a simpler, but still memorable preparation, make the hamin without them.*

3 small-medium eggplants (6 to 8 ounces each)

Coarse salt

2 cups dried large lima beans (about 1 pound), washed, picked over, soaked overnight in cold water to cover by at least 2 inches, and drained

1½ cups long-grain rice, rinsed and drained

6 to 8 small lamb shanks (5 to 6 pounds total)

6 tablespoons olive oil

3 cups chopped onion plus ½ cup chopped shallots, or 4 cups chopped onion

Freshly ground black pepper

1 whole head of garlic, separated into cloves and peeled

1½ cups chopped plum tomatoes (about three-quarters of a 28-ounce can, drained, or 1 pound fresh)

CUT a large, thin lengthwise slice from each eggplant. These will be the lids for the eggplant boats, so reserve them. Scoop out as much eggplant flesh as possible without damaging the peel. (Many people use spoons, melon ballers, or apple corers, but I find they are not sharp enough. A small paring knife is easier to manipulate without tearing the peel.) Put the eggplant flesh in a colander, toss with 2 teaspoons coarse salt, and weight it down with a plate or bowl topped with a heavy object like a can of tomatoes. Let the eggplant drain for about 30 minutes while you prepare everything else.

PLACE the limas and rice on the bottom of a very large, heavy, flame-proof casserole or Dutch oven (7- to 8-quart capacity).

TRIM the lamb of as much visible fat as possible. Wipe with damp paper towels and pat thoroughly dry. In a 10- to 12-inch heavy skillet, heat 2 tablespoons of the oil until hot, but not smoking. Sear the lamb over medium-high heat, in batches, if necessary, to avoid crowding the pan, until evenly browned on all sides. Transfer the meat to a platter and set aside.

WIPE out the fat from the skillet and heat 2 tablespoons fresh oil. Add the onions and sauté over medium-high heat, lifting and turning them until golden brown, about 15 minutes. Salt and pepper well and stir into the limas and rice. (Don't wash out the skillet yet.) Salt and pepper the lamb

Grated zest and juice of 1 lemon

2 teaspoons fresh thyme leaves or ¾ teaspoon dried, crumbled

½ pound lean ground beef

6 cups chicken broth, preferably homemade (see pages 62 and 70); Beef Stock (page 32); or use good-quality, low-sodium purchased

all over and arrange on top of the onions, limas, and rice. Strew the garlic cloves over the lamb.

IN a small bowl, stir together 1 cup of the tomatoes, the lemon zest and juice, thyme, and salt and pepper to taste, and pour over the garlic layer.

PREHEAT the oven to 200°F.

FINISH the eggplant boats: rinse the eggplant flesh under cool, running water and then squeeze it dry with your hands, extracting as much of the bitter juices as possible. Pat dry with paper towels. Heat the remaining 2 tablespoons oil in the skillet, add shallots (or alternative onions), and sauté until softened, about 5 minutes. Add the eggplant flesh and cook over medium-high heat, stirring, until tender, 2 to 3 minutes per side. Stir in the ground beef and sauté until the meat loses its red color. Stir in the remaining ½ cup tomatoes, and salt and pepper to taste. Cook, stirring, for 2 minutes. Stuff the eggplant shells with the meat mixture and cover with the reserved eggplant lids. Arrange these eggplant boats on top of everything in the casserole.

POUR in the broth. Bring to a gentle boil on top of the stove and simmer 10 minutes. Cover the casserole tightly with foil and the lid, place in the oven, and cook for 8 hours, or overnight.

TO serve, cut the eggplants in half or thirds. The lamb will be meltingly tender and falling off the bone, so you need not serve each guest an entire shank. Instead, dish out some lamb pieces, accompanied by limas, rice, and a piece of the velvet-soft stuffed eggplant.

ISRAELI SALAD

yield: 6 TO 8 SERVINGS

A breakfast staple on Israeli kibbutz tables for many years, this salad has become wildly popular in Jewish communities worldwide. The refreshing mix of juicy vegetables and herbs is especially good served alongside unsauced roasted or grilled foods.

The salad is endlessly variable. For extra crunch and color, you can include slices or cubes of carrot and radish. Other delicious additions: tiny pieces of peeled lemon flesh (especially mild Meyer lemon), bite-size pieces of toasted pita bread or Za'atar Matzohs (page 220), olives, or for dairy meals, crumbled feta or goat cheese. Or sprinkle with a little oregano in place of the za'atar.

The moist vegetables that make the salad so refreshing can also render it watery and dilute the dressing. Salting then draining the cucumber and tomatoes helps eliminate some of their juices. Cutting the vegetables into tiny cubes, though very attractive, produces a lot more vegetable water, so I prefer pieces cut all the same size, but not too fine. If the salad does become watery despite all precautions (it naturally exudes juices as it sits), serve it with a large slotted spoon and pass some extra dressing at the table.

3 cucumbers, peeled if waxed or if peel is bitter-tasting or thick, seeded, and cubed

Coarse kosher salt

5 or 6 tomatoes, cored, seeded, and cut into small pieces

3 large sweet red peppers (I also like to add a couple of fresh, mildly hot red peppers, like smoky aji dulce or Hungarian wax peppers), seeds and membranes removed, flesh cut into cubes

1 cup thinly sliced scallions (about 5), white and light green parts only

LINE a colander or wire-mesh sieve with a double thickness of paper towels. Add the cucumbers and toss them with 2 teaspoons salt. Cover with more paper towels and weight the cucumbers down with a heavy object like a can of tomatoes. Set the colander over a bowl, and let drain in the refrigerator for 1 hour.

IN a large serving bowl, toss the tomatoes with ½ teaspoon salt, and set aside until the tomatoes throw off a small pool of juice.

PREPARE the dressing: combine the ingredients in a jar and shake to blend well. Taste and adjust seasonings; it should be deeply flavored, as the juices exuded by the vegetables will continue to dilute it.

WHEN you are ready to serve the salad, discard the juice the tomatoes have released, and pat them dry. Rinse the cucumbers lightly, squeeze to rid them of as much water as possible, and pat them dry. Add the

1 cup chopped flat-leaf parsley

½ cup mixed fresh herbs (preferably at least 2 of the following: dill, mint, cilantro)

FOR THE DRESSING

About ¼ cup best-quality extra virgin olive oil

About 3 tablespoons fresh lemon juice

1 large garlic clove, minced

About ¾ teaspoon ground cumin, preferably freshly toasted and ground

Salt and freshly ground black pepper

About 1 teaspoon smoked paprika (optional)

About 1 teaspoon grated lemon zest (optional)

Optional garnish: za'atar

cucumbers and the remaining salad ingredients to the bowl, and toss with enough dressing to moisten all ingredients thoroughly. Taste and adjust seasoning. If desired, finish with a liberal dusting of za'atar (1 tablespoon or more, to taste). Pass any remaining dressing separately.

"In summer Father chopped a fine salad of tomatoes, cucumbers, green peppers, spring onions, and parsley, gleaming with olive oil."

—AMOZ OZ, *A Tale of Love and Darkness*

RHUBARB-PRUNE TSIMMES

yield: ABOUT 4 SERVINGS

When it comes to combining foods, I'm not one for hard and fast rules. I've been seduced by cheese cake made supernal with a zap of ground chiles, and I adore savory meats, poultry, and even fish perfumed and mellowed by fruits. But unmitigated sugariness makes my mouth say dessert; fruits must have a spicy or tart accompaniment to segue gracefully into a main course. To me, a tsimmes (sweetened, festive fruit and vegetable stew, with or without meat) of sweet fruits is one-dimensional without some tang or heat.

To provide well-nuanced character here, I add the sprightly bloom of fresh rhubarb to sweet-and-sour prunes and fragrant honey for a meatless tsimmes irresistible as a side dish or condiment for poultry or meat. Make this tsimmes in spring or early summer with big-flavored field rhubarb or year-round with the milder lipstick-pink hothouse variety.

2 cups chopped onion

2 tablespoons mild olive or canola oil

2 garlic cloves, finely chopped (2 teaspoons)

Salt and freshly ground black pepper

¼ cup fragrant honey (floral like lime or orange blossom, or herbal like lavender or thyme, would be perfect)

¼ teaspoon ground cinnamon

1½ cups carrots, scrubbed (and scraped if desired), cut into 1-inch chunks

1 cup prune juice

1 pound rhubarb, ends trimmed (discard leaves— they can be toxic), tough strings removed with a vegetable peeler, and stalks cut into 1-inch pieces (4 cups)

1½ cups pitted prunes, halved, or quartered if large

IN a 10-inch, heavy skillet, sauté the onion in the oil over medium heat until wilted, about 5 minutes. Stir in the garlic and cook for a minute or two. Sprinkle generously with salt and pepper to taste, turn the heat down to medium-low, cover, and sweat the mixture slowly, stirring occasionally, until the onions are quite soft but still pale-colored, 10 to 15 minutes.

ADD the honey and cinnamon, and mix until well distributed. Add the carrots and cook, stirring, for about 5 minutes.

ADD the prune juice and bring the mixture to a boil. Add the rhubarb and the prunes and simmer over moderate heat, stirring every once in a while, until the rhubarb is soft and the carrots are tender but not falling apart, 12 to 18 minutes.

TURN the heat up to high and boil the mixture, uncovered, until the liquid in the pan is thick and syrupy. Taste and adjust seasoning.

SPINACH CHEESE SQUARES

yield: 6 TO 8 SERVINGS

Mediterranean Jews so adore fresh spinach that little mountains of the leftover emerald "tails" are a hallmark of their holiday cooking. Called ravikos *by Sephardim and* testine di spinaci *by Italian Jews, these stems are slow-braised until they turn almost red. They are usually served Thursday nights, when it is customary to eat lightly in preparation for the next day's feasting, and a large stockpile of them has accumulated from the Sabbath preparations.*

The leaves often end up in light, eggy vegetable gratins, a Sephardi specialty, especially popular at the desayuno, *a festive brunch served after morning services on Sabbath and holidays.*

Notwithstanding spinach's bad rap, even kids seem to love these crustless, cheesy squares, here freshened up with plenty of green herbs. Good hot, warm, or at room temperature, they make a fine lunch, brunch, or light supper. Or cut them into bite-size pieces for a marvelous hors d'oeuvre. They freeze beautifully.

2 pounds fresh spinach or two 10-ounce packages frozen leaf spinach, thawed

3 tablespoons unsalted butter, plus additional butter (or oil) for greasing the pan

1/2 cup chopped shallots or 1 cup chopped onion

Salt and freshly ground black pepper

4 ounces cream cheese (1/2 cup), softened

4 ounces of crumbled feta (1 cup; break it up well using your fingers)

1/2 pound farmer cheese (7.5 ounce package is fine)

4 large eggs

2 teaspoons dried oregano or mint

IF using fresh spinach, wash it thoroughly to remove all traces of sand. Cut off any tough stems and discard them. Place the spinach with just the water that clings to its leaves in a large saucepan. Cover and cook over medium heat, stirring occasionally, until wilted, about 8 minutes.

PLACE the cooked fresh or the thawed frozen spinach in a colander and, with your hands or the back of a spoon, press out as much liquid as possible. It should be rather dry. Chop the spinach fine.

MELT the butter in a large skillet. Add the shallots or onion and sauté until softened, 5 to 7 minutes. Add the spinach and cook, stirring, until the spinach is tender and the butter is absorbed, 3 to 5 minutes. Season with salt (just a bit—remember that the cheeses can be rather salty) and pepper. Set aside to cool.

PREHEAT the oven to 350°F.

COMBINE the cream cheese, feta, and farmer cheese in a food processor and blend well. Break the eggs into a glass measuring cup with a pouring spout. With the machine running, add the eggs, one at a time, through the feed tube, and process until smooth. Crumble in the oregano or mint. Add the spinach mixture, dill, and parsley, and pulse about 15 seconds to combine well; do not puree.

¾ cup finely chopped
fresh dill

½ cup finely chopped
fresh flat-leaf parsley

3 tablespoons matzoh
meal

3 tablespoons shredded
Cheddar or grated
Parmesan cheese

3 to 4 tablespoons pine
nuts, lightly toasted
(optional)

GREASE a 13 by 9-inch baking pan and sprinkle the bottom and sides with the matzoh meal. Pour the spinach batter into the pan and smooth the top. Sprinkle with the Cheddar or Parmesan, scatter the pine nuts over evenly, if using, and bake for about 40 minutes, until lightly golden and the edges start to pull away from the sides of the pan. It should feel slightly firm, but it will not set until it has cooled for at least 20 minutes. Serve warm (reheat if necessary) or at room temperature, cut into squares.

COOK'S NOTE: Beautifully fresh Swiss chard is increasingly available in markets these days. It is much easier to clean than spinach, and I find its sweet yet distinctively earthy green leaves make an excellent substitute in this recipe.

I also vary the cheeses; experiment with some of your favorites, using a mixture of mild (Jarlsberg, Gruyère, Muenster, cottage cheese) and sharp (Kasseri, kashkaval, Cheddar, Parmesan).

"Any city where there are no green vegetables—a sage may not dwell therein."

—BABYLONIAN TALMUD: ERUVIN 55B

KASHA VARNISHKES WITH FRIED EGGPLANT, MUSHROOMS, AND ONION MARMALADE

yield: 6 TO 8 SERVINGS

*P*roperly cooked so it remains dry and fluffy, kasha, when mixed with noodles, could swallow up butter or chicken fat by the cupful. I remove the temptation to slather on lots of fat by moistening this hearty grain with plenty of caramelized onions and mushrooms. I also add sautéed eggplant for the same reason: fried cubes of it, like mushrooms, bring a melting butteriness to foods.

Though most American recipes for kasha varnishkes *call for bow tie noodles, I find them too thick and starchy here, requiring, like the kasha, a lot of additional moisture. I break wide noodles in half to resemble the square noodles originally used—and best suited—for this dish.*

The eggplant, mushrooms, and onions enrich and lighten the kasha varnishkes at the same time. You don't really need all three (and if pressed for time, you could eliminate either the mushrooms or the eggplant—or the noodles), but cooked together this is a very satisfying dish, substantial enough to serve as centerpiece for a delicious vegetarian meal (or near-vegetarian, if using chicken broth). To simplify preparations, make it in advance, up to the point of heating the ingredients in the oven. And you need to use only one skillet for all the vegetables.

1 large eggplant (1 to 1¼ pounds), peeled and cut into 1-inch cubes

Coarse kosher salt

About ½ cup olive oil

1½ pounds onions, coarsely chopped (6 cups)

Freshly ground black pepper

1 to 2 tablespoons fresh thyme or marjoram leaves

About ½ pound mushrooms, wiped clean, trimmed, and sliced (2 cups)

PUT the eggplant in a colander, and sprinkle evenly with 2 teaspoons salt. Weight the eggplant down (I use a plate or bowl with a large can of tomatoes on top), and let drain for about 1 hour, stirring the pieces around after 30 minutes. Rinse the eggplant and press it very dry with paper towels.

WHILE the eggplant is draining, heat 3 tablespoons oil in a 10- to 12-inch heavy skillet over medium heat. Add the onions and salt and pepper them lightly. Cook for 2 minutes, stirring so they are thoroughly coated with oil. Cover, turn the heat down to the lowest simmer, and cook slowly until the onions are meltingly tender, 35 to 40 minutes. Stir from time to time to make sure the onions don't burn. When they are very soft, remove the lid, raise the heat to high, and brown them to a rich caramel gold. Stir frequently with a wooden spoon to redistribute the syrupy juices. If necessary, turn the heat down a bit to prevent the onions

1 tablespoon chopped garlic

1 large egg

1 cup kasha, preferably coarse-grind

2 cups chicken broth, preferably homemade (see pages 62 and 70), Vegetable Stock (page 34), or good-quality, low-sodium purchased

4 ounces broad (wide) egg noodles (broken in half, if desired)

Olive Oil Schmaltz (page 27), Poultry Schmaltz (page 28), margarine, or if using vegetable broth, butter (optional)

¼ cup finely minced scallions or 3 to 4 tablespoons chopped fresh chives, for garnish

2 tablespoons chopped fresh parsley, for garnish

from sticking and burning. When the onions are thick and jam-like, stir in the thyme or marjoram. Adjust the seasoning and transfer the mixture to a very large bowl.

LIGHTLY rinse out the skillet and dry it. Add 2 tablespoons fresh oil and turn the heat to high. Add the mushrooms and cook, stirring frequently, until they release some juice, about 5 minutes. Sprinkle with salt and pepper, add the garlic, and continue sautéing, lifting and turning often until all the liquid has evaporated and the mushrooms are golden brown, about 7 minutes. Add the mushrooms to the onions.

WIPE out the skillet and in it heat the remaining 3 tablespoons oil over medium-high heat until hot, but not smoking. Add the eggplant in batches, if necessary, and fry until tender and lightly browned on both sides. Add more oil to the skillet, if needed, but always make sure the oil is very hot before adding the eggplant—this will prevent the eggplant from absorbing too much oil. Transfer the eggplant to the onions and mushrooms in the bowl.

PREHEAT the oven to 350°F.

PREPARE the kasha: in a medium bowl, beat the egg with a fork. Stir in the kasha and mix until each grain is thoroughly coated with egg. Heat the broth to simmering. In a heavy medium skillet with high sides or a wide heavy saucepan, toast the kasha over medium heat, turning and breaking up the kasha constantly until the egg begins to dry and the grains separate,

"But Ephraim and Izzy, given their secret horde of Jewish soul food, were not as infected as the rest of the company . . . [The] ever-resourceful Izzy . . . was able to leaven their intake of poisonous meat with delicacies that Izzy had shrewdly held back. So one Friday night they might gorge themselves on kasha fried in chicken fat and the next on rice prepared in a similar fashion."

—MORDECAI RICHLER, *Solomon Gursky Was Here*

about 3 minutes. Add the hot broth and salt and pepper to taste, then cover and simmer over very low heat until tender and all the liquid is absorbed, about 10 minutes.

MEANWHILE, bring 2 quarts water and 1½ teaspoons salt to a rolling boil. Add the noodles, and cook until tender but still firm to the bite. Drain and stir into the vegetables.

IN a lightly greased 3-quart shallow casserole, combine the kasha with the other ingredients. Adjust the seasoning to taste. If the mixture seems dry, add schmaltz or dot with margarine or butter as needed. Bake just until heated through. Sprinkle with the scallions or chives and the parsley and serve hot.

ONION-CRUSTED LIGHT POTATO KUGEL

yield: 8 TO 10 SERVINGS

Some people tear off long ribbons of crisp skin from freshly roasted birds. Others will pick off the nuts or steal the chocolate curls from picture-perfect cakes.

This kugel is made for the onion snatchers: a lavish, meltingly tender layer of sweet, bronze-edged onions, aromatic with rosemary, beckons from atop the crisp crust. I add mashed potatoes to the grated raw ones for an especially light and creamy interior.

1½ pounds onions, very thinly sliced (6 cups)

Kosher salt

6 tablespoons olive oil

1 teaspoon minced garlic

Freshly ground black pepper

6 large or 8 medium russet (baking) potatoes, peeled

4 large eggs

1 teaspoon baking powder

1 to 2 tablespoons chopped fresh rosemary leaves

Best-quality extra virgin oil, for drizzling

SEPARATE the onion into rings. To extract moisture, toss in a large bowl with 2 teaspoons salt and set aside for about 20 minutes. Stir the onions around from time to time. Dry the onions between sheets of paper towels or cotton kitchen towels, pressing down to soak up as much of the exuded liquid as you can.

IN a 10- to 12-inch heavy skillet, heat 3 tablespoons oil over medium-high heat. Add the onions and garlic, and cook, lifting and tossing with a spatula as they soften and become golden brown, 15 to 20 minutes. The mixture should be well salted and peppery, so season accordingly. Set aside to cool.

DICE 2 (if large) or 3 (if medium) of the potatoes and place in a saucepan of salted water. Bring to a boil, then simmer until the potatoes are tender. Mash the potatoes, using a ricer, food mill, or masher, until smooth, and place in a very large bowl. Stir in about half of the fried onions, setting the rest aside.

PREHEAT the oven to 400°F.

GRATE the remaining potatoes using the medium shredding disk in a food processor or over the large holes of a hand grater. Place the grated potatoes in a colander or large strainer and rinse well under cold water to remove most of the starch. Squeeze out as much liquid as possible, then add them to the mashed potatoes. Beat the eggs in another bowl until thick and light. Whisk in the baking powder. Combine the eggs with the potatoes and season generously with salt and pepper.

POUR 3 tablespoons oil into a large, shallow baking pan (13 by 9-inch or similar size, preferably enameled cast-iron or metal, not glass). Thoroughly rub the oil around the bottom and sides of the pan and place in the oven until sizzling hot. Transfer the potatoes to the pan and spread with a spatula; top with the remaining fried onions. Sprinkle with the rosemary. Drizzle with the extra virgin oil. If you love salty crusts, you may want to sprinkle a bit more coarse salt and some pepper over the top.

BAKE for about 30 minutes on the uppermost shelf of the oven, then turn the temperature down to 350°F. Continue baking for 25 to 40 minutes longer, until the kugel is firm, the top is golden, and the onions are crispy.

LET the kugel cool until set. If necessary, reheat before serving.

FRESH CORN KUGEL

yield: **6 TO 8 SERVINGS**

*T*hickened only by creamy pureed corn kernels and scented with flowery dill, this summery kugel depends for sweetness on truly fresh corn, whose sugars have not yet begun the descent into starch. Pale white corn will produce an exquisitely subtle kugel; more robust yellow kernels make for a richer pudding with a decidedly corny taste.

½ cup chopped onion

1 tablespoon mild olive, canola, or avocado oil, plus additional for greasing the pan

Salt and freshly ground black pepper

3½ cups fresh corn kernels, cut from 3 to 7 ears of sweet corn (the number of ears will depend on whether you use the slim, silvery white–kernel corn or thicker, butter-yellow varieties)

1 cup chicken broth, preferably homemade (see pages 62 and 70) or good-quality, low-sodium purchased

4 large eggs

2 tablespoons chopped fresh dill

2 tablespoons toasted matzoh crumbs (egg matzohs are especially nice) or toasted matzoh meal (see page 24)

PREHEAT the oven to 325°F.

IN a 7- or 8-inch skillet, sauté the onions in the oil over moderate heat, stirring, until very soft, 7 to 8 minutes. The onions should remain tender and sweet, so don't allow them to color past gold. Season with salt and pepper, and set aside to cool.

PUT 2 cups of the corn in a food processor or blender. Add ½ cup of the broth and puree the mixture until smooth, scraping down the bowl when necessary. Add the remaining ½ cup broth, salt and pepper to taste, and pulse to combine well.

LIGHTLY grease the bottom and sides of a 12-inch gratin dish or shallow 3-quart baking pan.

IN a large bowl, beat the eggs until thick and light. Stir in the dill, the cooled onion, the pureed corn, and the remaining 1½ cups whole corn kernels. Transfer the mixture to the prepared dish.

SEASON the matzoh crumbs with salt and pepper, and sprinkle over the top of the kugel.

PLACE the gratin dish inside a larger baking pan and pour enough boiling or scalding-hot tap water to come two-thirds of the way up the sides of the gratin dish. Bake the kugel for about 1 hour and 10 minutes, until the golden brown top is puffed slightly and a toothpick inserted in the middle comes out clean.

LET the kugel cool for at least 25 minutes, until set, before cutting into wedges to serve. Reheat if necessary.

SAUTÉED CABBAGE AND GARLIC NOODLE KUGEL

yield: 6 TO 8 SERVINGS

*L*ike potatoes, beets, and carrots, protean cabbage turned up on Ashkenazi tables in many forms, from tart sauerkraut to a sugared filling for delicate strudel dough, not to mention lusty cabbage soup and meat-stuffed cabbage rolls. A favorite among Central European Jews was an irresistible tangle of sautéed cabbage ribbons and golden egg noodles, lavishly sprinkled with poppy or caraway seeds.

First parboiled, the cabbage is then lightly browned, intensifying its flavors to a nutty sweetness, which is heightened by the poppy seeds. Garlic cloves—lots of them—are my addition. They're very slowly sautéed until the olive oil is deeply flavored and the garlic is soft and mellow.

I've also added eggs and broth, and made the recipe a kugel, or baked pudding. Sturdy, economical dishes that can be cooked ahead and reheated for holiday meals, kugels were originally starchy puddings baked along with the Sabbath cholent. Eventually, they became very popular and Jewish cooks began baking them in separate pans, binding the ingredients—savory or sweet—with eggs and thickening them with various starches. They remain well-liked today, especially potato and noodle puddings, for preparing a kugel is an excellent way to avoid last-minute preparation and give "staying power" to a side dish or vegetable.

This kugel complements any grilled or roasted meat or chicken.

---

2 tablespoons toasted matzoh meal (see page 24) or toasted bread crumbs

One medium-to-large head of green cabbage (1½ to 2 pounds)

Salt

8 ounces medium flat egg noodles (not the twisted spiral kind, which won't absorb as much of the flavoring)

5 tablespoons extra virgin olive oil, plus additional for greasing the pan

PREPARE a 13 by 9-inch baking pan: grease it well and sprinkle the bottom with the matzoh meal, shaking out any excess.

START the cabbage: discard any bruised or tough outer leaves, then cut the head into six wedges. Trim away the hard center core. In a large pot or Dutch oven, bring 4 to 5 quarts cold water and 1 tablespoon salt to a rolling boil. Add the cabbage, and cook, uncovered, for 8 to 10 minutes, until the cabbage is just tender. Reserving the cooking water in the pot, scoop out the cabbage with a slotted spoon and transfer it to a colander to drain.

BRING the reserved cabbage cooking water back to a boil in the pot and in it cook the noodles until they are just tender. Drain them well, then transfer to a large bowl and toss them with 1 tablespoon of the oil.

¼ cup garlic cloves, coarsely chopped

3 tablespoons poppy seeds

Freshly ground black pepper

6 large eggs

2 cups chicken broth, preferably homemade (see pages 62 and 70), Vegetable Stock (page 34), or good-quality, low-sodium purchased

IN a 10- to 12-inch heavy skillet, warm the remaining 4 tablespoons oil over very gentle heat. Add the garlic and cook slowly, stirring occasionally, until the garlic turns palest blond, 8 to 10 minutes. Scoop out the garlic with a slotted spoon and set it aside in a small bowl. Reserve the oil, now deliciously infused with garlic, in the skillet.

PREHEAT the oven to 350°F.

USING your hands, squeeze out as much liquid as possible from the cabbage. (Alternatively, you can press down on the cabbage with the back of a spoon, if you are reluctant to use your hands, although I find this method less efficient.) Lay the cabbage between layers of paper towels and press to remove surface moisture. Slice the cabbage into coarse shreds, then cut the shreds into bite-size pieces.

HEAT the reserved garlic oil in the skillet over moderately high heat. Toss in the cabbage and sauté, lifting and turning over high heat, until it is flecked here and there with a nutty brown, about 10 minutes. Add the reserved garlic and the poppy seeds, season generously with salt and pepper, and cook, stirring for 2 to 3 minutes to marry the flavors. Remove the pan from the heat and let it cool slightly.

ASSEMBLE the kugel: in a large bowl, whisk together the eggs and broth until smooth. Stir in the noodles and the cabbage, and combine thoroughly. Spoon the mixture evenly into the prepared baking dish and bake for 50 minutes, or until the kugel feels firm, its lightly browned edges are pulling away from the sides, and a knife inserted in the center comes out clean.

ALLOW the kugel to set for at least 25 minutes before cutting into squares to serve. Reheat if necessary.

JEWELED BROWN RICE

yield: 7 TO 8 SERVINGS

y family loves rice with gems of tangy dried fruit, pistachios, and almonds. Eager to include more whole grains at our table, I prepare this version using brown rice.

Brown rice suffers undeserved bad press, most likely because its nutty goodness is so often marred by a soggy, sticky texture. To keep the grains separate and fluffy, I bake the rice spread out in a shallow pan and hold off adding the fruit and other embellishments until the rice is fully cooked.

2 cups brown basmati rice

4 cups chicken broth, preferably homemade (see pages 62 and 70), Vegetable Stock (page 34), or good-quality, low-sodium purchased

Salt

1½ cups dried fruit, pitted and coarsely chopped (aim for the tart/sweet balance you prefer, choosing sour or sweet varieties of at least two of the following: cherries, apricots, cranberries, dates, and prunes)

6 tablespoons mild olive, canola, or avocado oil

Saffron threads, 2 pinches

3 cups chopped onion

¼ teaspoon ground cinnamon

¾ cup pistachios, lightly toasted and coarsely chopped

PREHEAT the oven to 375°F.

RINSE the rice well in cold water, drain it, and combine with the stock and 1 tablespoon salt (less if your stock is salty) in a 13 by 9-inch baking dish. Spread the ingredients evenly in the pan, cover tightly with foil, and bake for 1 hour.

MEANWHILE, put the dried fruit in a bowl, cover with warm water, and let soak. Crush saffron into a small bowl. Warm 3 tablespoons oil in a small saucepan, then whisk it into the saffron. Set aside to infuse.

IN a large heavy skillet, heat the remaining 3 tablespoons oil over medium-high heat. Add the onions, sprinkle lightly with salt, and sauté, lifting and tossing occasionally, until the onions are tender and colored a rich gold. Don't let them get crisp or brown. Stir in the cinnamon and cook for 2 minutes over medium heat, stirring. Drain the fruit (discarding the liquid) and add it to the onions. Cook for a few minutes, stirring, to blend the flavors. Remove the skillet from the heat and set aside until the rice is cooked.

WHEN the rice is done, turn the oven down to 350°F. Sprinkle the saffron oil over the rice and toss gently to coat the grains evenly. Add the onion-fruit mixture and combine well. Cover the pan with the foil and bake for 10 minutes. Taste and adjust salt.

FLUFF the rice with a fork, scatter the pistachios over the top, and serve.

COOK'S NOTE: This is usually given a little orange flavor with candied orange peel or a couple of drops of orange extract (a flavoring extract like vanilla). We prefer it without any orange, but you may enjoy it that way.

DRIED FRUIT COMPOTE WITH FRESH PINEAPPLE, PISTACHIOS, AND MINT

yield: 8 TO 10 GENEROUS SERVINGS

When the chill weather comes, old-fashioned dried fruit compotes are the classic finish to simple Sabbath dinners. Light and wholesome, they taste of deep flavors and contain no milk products to compromise the dietary laws.

But there's the rub. Without the tart dairy tang of sour cream, crème fraîche, or yogurt as complement, the meltingly silky fruit turns cloyingly sugary after just a few bites. A sweet compote needs a bright acidic sparkle to pull its flavors into balance.

Fresh ripe pineapple is the answer. Its brash tart-sweetness is not overwhelmed by the dark-winy dried fruit. Simmered in tea that's been infused with orange and spices, the dried fruit matures in the refrigerator for a day or two—three or four is even better (the compote will keep for up to two weeks in the refrigerator). Just before serving, I stir in chunks of sassy-sweet, beautifully perfumed pineapple, a crunch of pistachios or almonds, and chopped fresh mint.

If avoiding dairy is not a concern, serve the compote—with or without the pineapple—with sour cream, crème fraîche, yogurt cream, or labneh, for dessert or a delightful breakfast. The compote also makes a wonderful companion to cheese blintzes.

2 bags fragrant black tea, such as Earl Grey, English Breakfast, Assam, or Darjeeling

One 2-inch piece vanilla bean, split

1 cinnamon stick

2 or 3 cardamom pods, crushed

3 whole cloves

½ cup sugar minus 1 tablespoon; if not using dates, use ½ cup sugar

Pinch of salt

½ fresh orange

IN a 4- to 5-quart heavy saucepan, combine 3 cups water, the tea bags, vanilla bean, cinnamon, cardamom, cloves, sugar, salt, and a wide strip of zest (with no white pith) cut from the orange (reserve the rest of the orange). Bring to a boil, then reduce the heat and simmer, stirring occasionally, for 10 minutes. Remove the tea bags, cinnamon, cardamom, and cloves, and discard them, leaving the vanilla bean and orange zest in the pan.

ADD the dried fruit to the pan, stir well, cover, and simmer gently for 30 to 35 minutes, until the fruit is very tender. Lift out the orange zest and discard it. Find the vanilla bean and either discard it or rinse it so it can be reused. Stir in the juice from the reserved ½ orange and the lemon juice.

COOL the compote to room temperature, then cover it tightly. Refrigerate for at least 6 hours. But the compote tastes best if prepared a day or two before you plan to serve it, so the flavors can fully unfold, mingle, and mature.

1 pound pitted prunes
(about 2½ cups)

½ cup dried apricots,
halved, or quartered if
large

¼ cup dates, pitted and
chopped (optional)

1 tablespoon fresh lemon
juice

1 perfectly ripe fresh
pineapple, peeled, cored
and cut into bite-size
chunks (see Cook's Note)

Chopped toasted
pistachios, or sliced
blanched almonds, for
garnish

Chopped fresh mint, for
garnish

JUST before serving, gently toss the pineapple with the compote and spoon the mixture into pretty glass bowls or large stemmed glasses. (If you don't plan to serve all of the compote at one meal, toss only part of the pineapple with the compote in the serving bowls, reserving the remaining pineapple to be added just before serving the rest of the compote). Top with pistachios or almonds and a sprinkle of fresh mint.

COOK'S NOTE: Other spice combinations work well here: try vanilla with black peppercorns or a Turkish bay leaf, or experiment with some of your own favorites. Or eliminate the spices and add amaretto or Frangelico. Replace the sugar with orange blossom honey or with half sugar and half raspberry preserves.

Both the new, super-sweet variety of fresh pineapple and canned pineapple lack the requisite tang essential for this recipe. If you can't find a fresh, tart-sweet pineapple, substitute navel or blood oranges, peeled and sliced.

JEWISH SAUTÉED APPLE CAKE

yield: 10 TO 12 SERVINGS

o, it doesn't look Jewish, and no, it's not the apples or the batter. It's the oil that identifies this old-fashioned cake as Jewish in both synagogue and church cookbooks alike. Dairy-free, the cake could grace a meat meal, and its easy simplicity made it ubiquitous on Ashkenazi Shabbat and holiday tables.

But truth to tell, the cake is not really about oil at all: it's all about the apples. And the more apples you can fit into the cake, the better the flavor. So I take the extra step of sautéing them, which greatly reduces them in volume and, at the same time, brings out all the caramelly goodness of the fruit's sugars.

Using insipid apples—especially since so many of them are called for here—will just produce a big "is that it?" So choose a balance of sweet and tangy kinds or a single well-flavored variety full of complex tastes. Forget Red Delicious and go for big flavor and the freshest fruit you can find.

This is a great make-ahead dessert: the flavors deepen, and the taste actually improves the next day.

FOR THE APPLES

2 to 3 tablespoons avocado, canola, or other mild oil, plus additional for greasing pan

8 cups tart and sweet apples, peeled and sliced ½-inch thick

½ cup packed brown sugar

½ teaspoon salt

1 tablespoon fresh lemon juice

2 teaspoons ground cinnamon

GENEROUSLY grease a 10-inch springform pan.

PREPARE the apples: heat the oil over medium-high heat in a very large, heavy skillet with steep sides (avoid nonstick here; it won't caramelize the apples well) until it is hot, but not smoking. Sauté the apples in batches over medium-high heat until they are golden brown on both sides, transferring them to a large platter as they are done. When you have finished sautéing the apples, put them all back into the pan, sprinkle with the brown sugar and salt, and cook, lifting and turning them, until the sugar dissolves and the apples are very tender and lightly caramelized. Sprinkle with the lemon juice and cinnamon, and cook for about 3 more minutes to mingle the flavors and evaporate any pan liquid. Set the apples aside to cool.

PREHEAT the oven to 350°F.

MAKE the batter: stir together the flour, baking powder, cinnamon, salt, and nutmeg in a large bowl.

FOR THE BATTER

2½ cups unbleached all-purpose flour

2 teaspoons baking powder

1 teaspoon ground cinnamon

¼ teaspoon salt

⅛ teaspoon freshly grated nutmeg

3 large eggs

1¼ cups sugar

¾ cup avocado, canola, sunflower, or other mild oil

½ cup unsweetened applesauce

2 teaspoons vanilla extract

IN another large bowl, using an electric mixer, beat the eggs with the sugar until pale and thick, about 5 minutes. Beat in the oil, applesauce, and vanilla.

WITH the mixer on low speed, gradually beat in the dry ingredients. Continue beating until the batter is smooth.

POUR half the batter into the prepared pan. Cover with half the apples. Spoon the remaining batter over the apples and arrange the rest of the apples on top. Bake until a toothpick inserted in the center comes out clean; begin checking at 1½ hours, but because of the moist apple layer in the middle, the cake can take up to 2 hours or more.

LET the cake cool on a rack before you remove the sides.

COOK'S NOTE: The cake will take considerably less time to bake if prepared in a 13 by 9-inch pan, with a single layer of batter, topped by a single layer of apples, though the presentation will not be quite as attractive.

> ". . . and the taste of manna was like the taste of cakes baked with oil."
>
> —NUMBERS 11:7

ROASTED APPLE–WALNUT NOODLE KUGEL

yield: 6 TO 8 SERVINGS

ere apples combine with walnuts and prunes to work an alchemy of golden autumn tastes. For a tempting dairy version, see the variation that follows.

Walnut, avocado, canola or your favorite oil, for greasing the pans

6 large or 8 to 10 medium sweet, flavorful apples (such as Royal Gala, Golden Delicious, or Braeburn; about 3 pounds), peeled, cored, and quartered, or cut into sixths if large

1/3 cup packed brown sugar

2 tablespoons fresh lemon juice

2 cups unsweetened apple juice

1/2 cup granulated sugar

1/3 cup pitted prunes, quartered

1 1/2 teaspoons vanilla extract

Salt

4 ounces medium flat egg noodles (not the twisted spiral kind, which won't absorb as much of the liquids and flavoring)

1/2 cup walnuts, lightly toasted and coarsely chopped

1 teaspoon ground cinnamon

1/8 teaspoon nutmeg, preferably freshly grated, or mace

4 large eggs, separated

1/3 cup graham cracker crumbs (optional)

PREHEAT the oven to 400°F. Line a large baking sheet or very shallow roasting pan with lightly greased foil and on it spread out the apples in a single layer, rounded sides down (so that most of the sugar will be trapped and melted in the curve, rather than sliding off onto the pan). Sprinkle with the brown sugar and lemon juice and roast in the middle of the oven until lightly browned and just tender, 25 to 35 minutes, depending on the variety of apples. Turn the apples over halfway through the cooking process, and spoon the accumulated syrupy juices over them. Remove the apples from the oven and reduce the oven temperature to 350°F. When the apples are cool enough to handle, cut into large chunks.

GREASE an 8- or 9-inch square baking pan (or other shallow 8- to 10-cup baking pan) thoroughly.

IN a wide, heavy medium saucepan, combine the apple juice, granulated sugar, prunes, vanilla, and a pinch of salt. Bring to a boil and continue cooking over high heat, stirring occasionally, until reduced by about half. Remove from the heat and cool slightly.

BRING 2 quarts cold water and 1 teaspoon salt to a rapid boil in a large saucepan. Add the noodles and cook until tender. Drain well. In a large bowl, combine the noodles, prune mixture, roasted apples, walnuts, cinnamon, and nutmeg. In a separate bowl, beat the egg yolks well until thick and light, and stir into the mixture. In a clean bowl, beat the whites until stiff but not dry. Gently fold about one third of the whites into the batter, then fold in the rest.

TURN the batter into the prepared pan and smooth the top. If desired, sprinkle with graham cracker crumbs.

BAKE the kugel for about 45 minutes, or until it feels firm, the sides pull away slightly, and the top is lightly browned. Let cool completely to set. You can eat it at room temperature, but to really savor the toasty apple flavors, warm the kugel until heated through. It may not cut neatly, and perhaps it will appear somewhat messy on the plate, but it will taste divine.

COOK'S NOTE: This is also lovely flavored with a little crystallized ginger.

Dairy Version

Follow the above recipe, up through combining noodles, prune mixture, roasted apples, walnuts, and spices. In a separate bowl, use an electric mixer on low speed to beat 8 ounces cream cheese (softened and cut into bits) with 1 cup evaporated milk until smooth and fluffy. Beat in the yolks. Combine this with the noodle-prune-apple mixture, then fold in the beaten whites, as above. Pour into a slightly larger pan (at least 9 inches square) that has been well greased. Sprinkle top with ½ cup graham cracker crumbs mixed with 3 tablespoons melted butter. Bake for 45 to 50 minutes at 350°F, following the directions for cooking and serving above.

"Beauty diffuses itself in the world as an apple."   —THE ZOHAR

UPSIDE-DOWN CARAMEL-CRANBERRY-PECAN NOODLE KUGEL

yield: ABOUT 12 SERVINGS

I don't like complicated desserts. Those that do require a bit more fuss must still retain their innocence—which is why many of my favorites are as likely to show up on the breakfast table as at teatime or dinner's end.

I'm particularly fond of noodle pudding, or kugel, whose lush, melting texture is forgiving enough even for the most pastry-shy and invites lots of homey experimentation. I always prepare it in large quantities because leftovers make such wonderful brunches and snacks.

This kugel, blanketed with warm, gooey caramel zapped with tart cranberries, is lovely on a crisp, autumn Shabbat afternoon—or morning.

FOR THE TOPPING

10 tablespoons (1¼ sticks) unsalted butter, plus additional for greasing the pan

2½ cups cranberries, washed, picked over, and patted dry

1 cup lightly toasted pecans, coarsely chopped

1⅓ cups packed dark brown sugar

¼ teaspoon salt

FOR THE KUGEL

Salt

12 ounces wide, flat egg noodles (not the twisted spiral kind, which won't absorb as much of the liquids and flavoring)

4 tablespoons (½ stick) unsalted butter, melted

½ cup dried cranberries (if very dry, plump them

MAKE the topping: generously butter the bottom and sides of a 13 by 9-inch glass baking dish and scatter the cranberries and pecans evenly on the bottom.

IN a heavy medium saucepan, combine the brown sugar, butter, and salt. Cook over medium heat, stirring, until the mixture comes to a boil. Pour this caramel evenly over the cranberries and pecans in the pan.

FOR the kugel, bring 5 quarts of cold water and 1½ teaspoons salt to a rapid boil in a large pot. Add the noodles and cook until just tender. Drain the noodles and return them to the pot. Stir the butter in until melted and let cool.

MIX the dried cranberries into the noodles (I like to use my fingers to toss them together, breaking up any clumps of dried fruit).

IN a very large bowl, beat the cream cheese on low speed until smooth and fluffy. Gradually beat in each of the following, one by one, until well blended: the cottage cheese, sour cream, eggs, vanilla, maple syrup or sugar, and a generous pinch of salt. Add the noodles and toss until thoroughly combined. Spoon the cheese-noodle mixture evenly over the prepared cranberry-pecan topping in the pan. Smooth the top, then cover the pan with foil and refrigerate for at least 4 hours or, preferably, overnight.

in very hot tap water for 20 minutes and drain before using)

8 ounces cream cheese, softened and cut into bits

1 cup small-curd creamed cottage cheese (see Cook's Note)

1 cup sour cream

5 large eggs

1 teaspoon vanilla extract

½ cup pure maple syrup or granulated sugar

PREHEAT the oven to 350°F.

BRING the kugel to room temperature. The baking pan will be quite full, so set it on a cookie sheet lined with foil, in case the bubbling caramel causes spillover. Uncover the pan and bake for about 1 hour, or until the top is golden-brown and feels firm, a knife inserted in the center comes out clean, and the sides of the kugel pull away from the pan slightly.

LET the kugel cool on a rack until set. The kugel is best warm (reheat if necessary) but also tasty at room temperature. Don't serve it refrigerator-cold.

TO serve, run a thin-bladed knife around the edges to loosen the kugel, then place a large platter or cutting board over the baking pan. Holding the platter and baking pan together tightly with both hands, invert the baking pan over the platter. Remove the baking pan and replace any fruit or nuts remaining in the pan on top of the kugel. Or cut and serve the kugel directly from the pan, inverting the spatula as you place the kugel on individual dessert plates.

COOK'S NOTE: For a less rustic, more cheesecake-like texture, pass the cottage cheese through a fine-mesh strainer before combining it with the other ingredients.

CLASSIC NOODLE KUGEL

yield: 12 TO 16 SERVINGS

*M*y cousins Sheila and Sheldon Lebowitz's delectable classic noodle kugel is crunchy with a cinnamon-sugared cornflake crust. It's a surefire crowd-pleaser with all generations.

FOR THE KUGEL

1 pound medium or wide flat egg noodles (not the twisted spiral kind, which won't absorb as much of the liquids and flavoring)

Salt

8 tablespoons (1 stick) unsalted butter, melted, plus additional for greasing the pan

8 ounces cream cheese, cut into bits and softened

1½ cups sugar

5 large eggs

2 cups sour cream

1½ cups milk

1 pound small-curd creamed cottage cheese (2 cups)

1 tablespoon vanilla extract

FOR THE TOPPING

2 cups cornflakes

¼ cup packed brown sugar

1½ to 2 teaspoons ground cinnamon

PREHEAT the oven to 450°F.

IN a large pot, cook the noodles in 6 quarts lightly salted boiling water until just tender. Drain, return to the pot, and toss with about 4 tablespoons of the butter.

IN a very large bowl, combine the cream cheese, sugar, and the remaining butter. Beat on low speed until smooth. Beat in the eggs, one at a time, the sour cream, milk, cottage cheese, vanilla, and a generous pinch of salt. Fold in the noodles and combine well.

GENEROUSLY butter the bottom and sides of a 14 by 11-inch baking pan. Turn the noodle mixture into the pan and smooth it evenly.

MAKE the topping: Put the cornflakes in a large bowl and crush them coarsely using your fingers (or place them in a heavy plastic bag and crush with a rolling pin). Stir in the brown sugar and cinnamon to taste and combine well. Strew the crumbs evenly over the kugel.

BAKE the kugel for 5 minutes, then reduce the oven temperature to 350°F and continue baking for 1 hour, or until it feels firm, a knife inserted in the center comes out clean, and the sides of the kugel pull away from the pan slightly.

LET the kugel cool on a rack until set. It is best served warm (reheat if necessary) and also good at room temperature; don't present it refrigerator-cold.

COOK'S NOTE: Sheila and Shelly often add an additional 8 ounces of noodles (a total of two 12-ounce packages) for a more substantial kugel.

Any—or all—of the following make delicious embellishments: 1 cup dried fruit (such as black or golden raisins, tart dried cherries or cranberries; if the fruit is very dry, plump first in hot tap water, then drain), 1 cup pecans, lightly toasted and coarsely chopped, or 2 cups apple or pear chunks, sautéed with brown sugar and cinnamon until tender.

OTHER SUGGESTIONS FOR SABBATH

FOR FRIDAY NIGHT DINNER

*Chopped Chicken Liver with Caramelized Onions

*Egyptian Ground Fish Balls with Tomato and Cumin (*Bellahat*)

Any of the other *Gefilte Fish recipes

*Esau's Pottage (Red Lentil Soup)

*Kreplach or *Matzoh Ball recipes for *Classic Chicken Soup

*Celery *Avgolemono* (Greek Egg Lemon Soup) with Chicken Matzoh Balls

*Chicken with Olives and Preserved Lemon

Fesenjan Redux (Roast Duck Breasts with Quince, Pomegranate, and Walnut Sauce)

*Apricot- and Orange-Scented Goose with Roasted Garlic

Any of the *Brisket recipes

*Meat Tsimmes with Prunes and Carrots

*Slow-Braised Lemon Veal with Leeks

*Wild Mushroom–Potato Kugel or *Crackletop Potato Kugel

*North African Cooked Carrot Salad

*Moroccan-Flavored Carrot Kugel

*Caramelized Onion and Carrot Tsimmes with Candied Ginger

*Cider-Baked Apples Stuffed with Halvah

*See index for page numbers

Any of the *Fruit Compote recipes

*Hungarian Chocolate-Walnut Torte

FOR SATURDAY LUNCH

*Huevos Haminados

*Sorrel-Flavored Mushroom Barley Soup

*Sorrel-Onion Noodle Kugel

*Zucchini Fritada

Any of the *Sweet Noodle Kugel recipes

Any of the *Cheese Cake recipes

Any of the *Rugelach or *Hamantaschen recipes

*Turkish Silken Ground-Rice Pudding or *Old-Fashioned Rice Pudding

*See index for page numbers

"The pineapple groans under her sharp knife like a live fish. Its juice, like white blood, trickles onto my fingers. I lick them. It is a tart-sweet taste. Is this the taste of the New Year?"

—BELLA CHAGALL, *Burning Lights*

Rosh Hashanah

1 AND 2 TISHRI (SEPTEMBER OR OCTOBER)

Rosh Hashanah celebrates both the New Year and a birthday—humankind's. But in place of revelry, there is reflection; instead of joyful music, the shrill wail of the shofar summons us to cleanse our souls and our hearts.

"Some of the townspeople stood on the wooden bridge reciting the 'tashlikh'; others lined the river banks. Young women took out their handkerchiefs and shook out their sins. Boys playfully emptied their pockets to be sure no transgressions remained."

—ISAAC BASHEVIS SINGER, "TASHLIKH"

For Rosh Hashanah is the Day of Judgment, when God inscribes our fate for the coming year in the Book of Life. The decree, however, is not final: the book is shut, the judgment sealed on Yom Kippur. So we can change our destiny during the next ten days, the Days of Awe, with prayer, charity, and reparation of the wrongdoings we have committed against others.

Judaism teaches that God created the world, but left it not quite finished, so that we could become the Maker's partners in the creative process by completing the work. This process is called *tikkun olam* (literally, the repair of the world), and it is by bettering ourselves

130

and restoring what is damaged and imperfect in life that we honor and celebrate the birth of Creation.

The holiday is at once solemn and festive: joy comes not only from trust in God's compassion but also the anticipation of renewal and fresh starts. Nearly 2,500 years ago, the prophet Nehemiah proclaimed, "Eat the rich and drink the sweet."

That sweet, rich Rosh Hashanah meal becomes more than mere rejoicing—it too is a form of prayer. The table is transformed into an altar to supplicate God, as we partake of symbolic foods embodying our wishes: honeyed and sugared treats for a sweet year; round foods for a fulfilled year, unbroken by tragedy; foods that grow in profusion at this season and those eaten in abundance, like rice, signifying hopes for fecundity, prosperity, and a wealth of merits.

Rosh Hashanah is also known as the Day of Remembrance, and eating these special dishes reminds us how we must behave. Whole or part of an animal's head (sweetbreads, tongue, etc.); an entire fish, including the head; or even a head of roasted garlic might be served, urging us to be a model of righteousness, at the head of our peers. Sweets, like challah stuffed with raisins, tell us to act in a way that would cause no sadness.

We begin dinner with a prayer for a sweet year, dipping challah (or other sweet bread) and apples into fragrant honey. Other families start with sugared pomegranates, dates, figs, or quince in rose petal syrup— or even, as at least one family with young children does, with challah and apples in chocolate sauce! Cochini Jews may have twenty fruits on the table and dip each one.

Fish, symbolizing fertility and God's blessings, is the customary first course on most menus. Rapid-growing seasonal vegetables like leeks, Swiss chard, black-eyed peas, and pumpkins—to name just a few— appear throughout the meal in major roles and supporting parts. Sumptuous main dishes follow, and usually, two (or more) sweet desserts, like a simple, fresh plum tart, a honey cake, or a noodle kugel—lush with coconut milk and caramelized pineapple—conclude the meal.

For me, no Rosh Hashanah custom captures the joy of creation, of life, like the "new fruit" ritual, when a fruit is tasted for the first time since it was last in season. We decide on a special fruit, but refrain from eating it when it arrives at our local markets in late summer or early autumn. Then, when Rosh Hashanah comes, it is as if we are tasting the fruit for the first time. Usually we cut open a pomegranate or two and spoon the seeds into little crystal bowls. Often I have not eaten this favorite fruit since last January; tasting it on Rosh Hashanah is like discovering it, participating in the brand-newness of Creation. This is the thrill expressed in the Sheheheyonu prayer, traditionally recited on Rosh Hashanah and other occasions when one experiences the pleasure of life's extraordinary moments, what Anita Diamant, author of *The Red Tent*, calls the "wow prayer."

One year, as we all held hands and recited the prayer, a tear rolled down a guest's cheek. The Sheheheyonu, he remembered, had been his late father's favorite blessing, and he had never understood why. Now, hearing it chanted again for the first time in twenty-five years, he finally understood.

Dinners on the first and second nights of the holiday (Reform Jews celebrate the first night only) are not the only times we enjoy the festive foods. Many families host special lunches after synagogue services on the first and second days. At my late mother-in-law's annual Rosh Hashanah open house, an extended bar and several buffet areas were set up throughout her sprawling Brooklyn apartment to accommodate all the family and friends who would show up at different times from various synagogues. For us, those luncheons signaled the end of the long summer, a day to reconnect, note the changes that had taken place in the past year, and make plans together for the year to come.

When I was growing up, late in the day, my family would visit relatives and close friends or entertain them in our home. This was the time to bring out sweet teatime treats like Peach Buttermilk Kugel or a mouthwatering challah bread pudding.

Sweetness and abundance are not confined to foods. Conversation is joyous—it is, in fact, forbidden to display anger. Many families develop a menu rife with food puns in the Rosh Hashanah spirit, then make a game of decoding the symbolism of the holiday dishes. And it is a mitzvah, a good deed, to invite guests, especially strangers and poor people, those, as Nehemiah said, "for whom nothing is prepared" to share the meal.

A few foods, however, are unwelcome at the Rosh Hashanah table. Nuts are not eaten by some Ashkenazi Jews because the numerical value of the Hebrew word for nuts is equal to the value of the word for sin. And nuts can cause an excess of saliva, impairing one's ability to recite prayers. Others do not eat pickles, horseradish, or other sour foods, while Moroccans avoid foods that are black, like olives and grapes—all are considered bad omens.

During the afternoon it is traditional to go to the nearest body of free-flowing water—ocean, lake, river, or in arid areas, like Israel, a well—to cast away sins, a cathartic ceremony known as *tashlikh*. Penitents, as in I. B. Singer's story on page 130, watch their sins of the past year float away into the water, tangibly expressed as the lint and crumbs shaken from pockets and handkerchiefs.

As children, we wanted to put as much distance as possible between ourselves and our iniquities. The little beach town we grew up in was an island, with both ocean and bay. For my sister and me, though, there was really no choice about where to take our transgressions. We had seen bottles, shreds of clothes, and dead horseshoe crabs tossed up by the ocean and left like offerings on the beach. We did not want our sins riding in on the waves, returned to us—or to anybody else, for that matter. In the warm slant of the Indian summer sun, we stood above the cool waters of Reynolds Channel. Our black velvet dresses had no pockets and we never carried handkerchiefs, so we peeled off our little white kid gloves, shaking out the fingers into the currents below.

Once, one of us dropped a glove. And from the dock, we watched it swim away in the roiling black waters—our accidental scapegoat, like our sins, never to return.

SUGGESTED MENUS FOR ROSH HASHANAH

*Classic Challah (flavored with cinnamon)

A selection of fresh apples and fragrant honey

A head of roasted garlic

*Leek Croquettes from Rhodes, *North African Cooked Carrot Salad

*Egyptian Ground Fish Balls with Tomato and Cumin (*Bellahat*) served with *Tomato and Sweet Pepper Sauce

*Brisket Braised in Pomegranate Juice with Onion Confit and Pomegranate Seeds, steamed basmati rice or *Syrian Pilaf

and/or

*Iranian Stuffed Chicken with Fresh Green Herbs and Golden Soup

*Egyptian Black-Eyed Peas with Cilantro (*Lubia*) or *New World *Rodanchas*

Fresh sautéed Swiss chard or spinach

*Bombay Pineapple–Coconut Milk Kugel or *Italian Carrot-Pecan Torta

Autumn fruit platter: Comice pears, champagne or Concord grapes, fresh figs drizzled with honey and mint

*Classic Challah

Pomegranates and fresh apple quarters with fragrant honey

*See index for page numbers

*Golden Gefilte Fish with Golden Horseradish

*Esau's Pottage (Red Lentil Soup)

or

*Golden Soup (with chickpeas) from previous night's *Iranian Stuffed Chicken

*Syrian Apricot-Stuffed Meat Rolls with Tart-Sweet Cherry Sauce (*Kibbe Gheraz*)

or

Fesenjan Redux (Roast Duck Breasts with Quince, Pomegranate, and Walnut Sauce)

or

*Eggplant-Stuffed Brisket Braised with Tomatoes, Saffron, and Honey

*Syrian Pilaf or steamed couscous

*Moroccan-Flavored Carrot Kugel or *Sweet Carrots with Fennel Salt or *Roasted Okra with Za'atar

Diced zucchini lightly sautéed with fresh herbs

Salad of Boston or Bibb lettuce, chopped fresh dill, mint and Italian parsley; vinaigrette of extra virgin olive oil, fresh orange, and lemon juices

*Hungarian Plum Tart or *Aunt Mary's Honey Cake

Ripe sweet melon or *Sephardi Dried Fruit and Nut Compote (*Koshaf*)

*See index for page numbers

HONEY FOR DIPPING CHALLAH AND APPLES

Traditions create the "we"-ness of families. There are traditions each family observes as Americans (we eat turkey on Thanksgiving, we watch fireworks on the Fourth of July), and there are practices followed as members of an ethnic group (as Ashkenazi Jews, we eat latkes on Hanukkah). But it is the unique traditions that each family invents for itself that make the family a "we" unlike any other.

On Rosh Hashanah many Jews dip apples and chunks of challah into honey, embodying their prayers for a sweet new year. So from her earliest days, my daughter always looked forward to the holiday, when she was actually told to indulge her Pooh-like honey-love, dunking slice upon slice of fruit and eggy bread into unmitigated sweetness.

As Alex grew older and the difference became greater and greater between carefree summer days and the more regulated ones spent in school, she no longer eagerly awaited the falling leaves or the holidays. We sought ways to ease the transition. For students, as well as for Jews, autumn is a time for beginning anew, for fresh starts. So to kindle an anticipation for school, we searched during summer vacations in France for a new notebook, in Maine for another backpack, and in Quebec for special pencils Québecois. And to make Rosh Hashanah an even

"May it be Your will, our God and God of our forebears, to renew for us a good and sweet year."

—ROSH HASHANAH PRAYER

sweeter holiday, we began scouring the markets on every trip for a different honey. Jews traditionally save a new fruit from the autumn harvest to eat on Rosh Hashanah. We had a new honey as well: creamed lavender honey one year from Provence, wild blueberry honey from Maine, chestnut honey from Italy, honey fragrant with hibiscus and frangipane from Bermuda.

Now we always bring a fragrant honey back from every trip. And that has become our own Rosh Hashanah tradition: every year we open a lovely new honey.

When we brought Alex clear across the country for her freshman year at Pomona College, we dropped off a jar of sageflower honey from Santa Barbara. "But how will you celebrate?" we asked. "What about everything else you'll need for the holidays?"

Later she told us she bought a variety of apples from the Claremont farmers' market and a challah from the village bakery. Crowded into her little dorm room, all her friends, Jews and non-Jews, dipped bread and fruit into the sageflower honey. "They all wanted a sweet new year," she said.

This year, inspired by an article on chefs who work with specialty honeys, we sprinkled fine *fleur de sel* (French sea salt) over challah glossed with acacia and tupelo honeys. Sublime as the salted caramels of Brittany, this delicate balance of sweet and salt perfectly captured our wish for a sweet year, one that was flavored with irresistible spice. It's a treat destined to become a new Rosh Hashanah tradition at our table.

There is a world of difference between ordinary supermarket honey and an artisanal product. If you absolutely can't track down a special honey for Rosh Hashanah, make your plain honey more distinctive: warm 1 cup honey in a small saucepan. Stir in sprigs of fresh thyme, rosemary, or mint; fresh sage leaves; or 2 teaspoons dried lavender. Cover and let steep for several hours, then, heating the honey first if necessary, strain it. Or beat into the honey a few drops of a flavoring extract such as strawberry, lemon, or even almond, or a spoonful of very reduced aromatic fruit juice (apple-raspberry, for example).

NORTH AFRICAN COOKED CARROT SALAD

yield: **4 SERVINGS**

The play of sweet cooked carrot and tangy dressing makes this easy traditional North African salad a favorite. I like to serve it Sephardi-style: that is, along with the appetizers, then left on the table during the rest of the meal, a welcome counterpoint to the panoply of rich Rosh Hashanah foods to follow.

FOR THE DRESSING

About 3 tablespoons best-quality extra virgin olive oil

About 1½ tablespoons fresh lemon juice

1 garlic clove, finely minced

About 1 teaspoon ground cumin, preferably freshly toasted and ground

About 1 teaspoon sweet paprika

About 1 teaspoon dried mint

About ¼ teaspoon ground cinnamon

About ¼ teaspoon ground coriander

Salt and freshly ground black pepper

Cayenne (optional)

FOR THE SALAD

1 pound sweet-tasting carrots, preferably organic and/or locally grown, scraped

Salt

2 to 3 tablespoons chopped flat-leaf parsley or cilantro

PREPARE the dressing: in a large bowl, whisk together the oil, lemon juice, garlic, cumin, paprika, mint, cinnamon, coriander, salt and pepper, and cayenne, if using, to taste.

YOU can cut the carrots into ½-inch rounds, on the diagonal—a common method—or, even better, take a few moments extra to cut them into thick matchsticks, so there is more surface area to drink in the dressing. To do this, use either the julienne blade of the food processor, a mandoline, or cut by hand, quartering the carrots lengthwise first, then slicing them into even sticks.

COOK the carrots in lightly salted boiling water until they are tender but still crisp. Drain them (the liquid would be a nice addition to the Vegetable Stock on page 34), and while they are still warm, toss them with the dressing. For best taste, let the flavors marry for at least a couple of hours.

TASTE and adjust the oil, lemon juice, or seasoning, if needed. Sprinkle with the parsley or cilantro just before serving.

LEEK CROQUETTES FROM RHODES

yield: 6 TO 8 SERVINGS

*N*icknamed the People of the Book, Jews since ancient times have thrived on inventive word play, coaxing enough meaning from words and numbers to poach old Humpty Dumpty with envy.

Rosh Hashanah, for instance, celebrates the pun in the prayers recited at the evening meal over many of the symbolic foods. On this solemn holiday, blessings in Hebrew and the many languages of the Diaspora reflect a rather humorous tickling of words. Who cannot see the twinkling in the eyes of the sages as we, in a modern English adaptation, eat beets to "beat back our foes" and dates to "date this year as one of happiness and peace?" Leek in Hebrew is kartee, *which sounds like the word* yihartu, *to cut off. So Sephardim eat leek patties to "cut off their enemies."*

The late Rachel Almeleh, a superlative New York home cook, gave me this heirloom recipe for leek-potato croquette appetizers from her native Rhodes, Greece. The croquettes are dipped in egg just before frying, so they absorb very little oil. Unusually light and delicate, they make marvelous hors d'oeuvre and cocktail nibbles.

4 medium leeks (about 1½ pounds), trimmed, washed free of sand, white and pale green parts, coarsely chopped (about 3 cups)

1 medium-large russet (baking) potato or about ½ pound other nonwaxy potatoes, such as Yukon gold, scrubbed but left unpeeled

Salt

1 slice seedless rye, semolina, light sourdough, challah, or other flavorful bread, crust discarded, bread torn into pieces (about ¾ cup)

2 tablespoons chopped fresh dill

PUT the leeks and potato in a medium saucepan with enough cold salted water to cover them by 1 inch. Bring the water to a boil, and simmer for about 40 minutes, or until the potato is tender. Drain the vegetables well. When the potato is cool enough to handle, peel it and force it through a ricer or a food mill fitted with the medium disk into a large bowl. Squeeze the leeks with your hands to extract all excess moisture. Place the leeks and the bread in a food processor, puree, and add it to the potato. Stir in the dill, salt and pepper to taste, and just enough of the beaten eggs (about 2 tablespoons) to form the mixture into 2-inch croquettes. Reserve the remaining eggs, covered and refrigerated. Cover the croquettes with plastic wrap and refrigerate for about 25 minutes.

PLACE the reserved beaten eggs in a shallow bowl near the stove. In a 10- to 12-inch heavy skillet, heat ¼ inch of oil until hot, but not smoking. Dip each croquette into the egg, letting the excess drip back into the bowl, then slip it gently into the hot oil. Fry the croquettes in batches, turning carefully once, until golden brown on both sides. Drain on paper towels.

Freshly ground black pepper

2 large eggs, beaten

Olive or canola oil, for frying

Accompaniment: lemon quarters

SERVE with the lemon quarters.

COOK'S NOTE: These are also excellent on Passover, when leeks, symbolic of springtime as well as of the food eaten by the Pharaoh's pyramid-builders, are often served. Just replace the bread with an equal amount of plain or egg matzoh soaked in chicken or beef broth or water and squeezed dry.

ESAU'S POTTAGE (RED LENTIL SOUP)

yield: 8 SERVINGS

*R*eading the story of the fraternal twins in Genesis, we are struck by Esau's impetuousness and utter lack of self-control: famished from the hunt, he sells his birthright to his brother in return for a simple pot of soup.

Or maybe Jacob, the first celebrity male Jewish cook, really had a way with red lentils. I prefer to think the latter.

I picture Jacob, gathering pungent wild onions and garlic as he tended the flocks, bringing home armloads of fragrant mint and cuminseed for Rebecca. Is that where mother and son bonded and he became her favorite—over the cooking pot? (Later we see them plotting there to deprive the elder son of his father's blessing.) A very clever cook, Jacob knew how to tantalize with gorgeous color, too: "Give me a gulp of that red stuff, that red stuff," Esau pleaded.

For thousands of years, cooks have tried to re-create the famous dish. I know Jacob never made it this way—there were no tomatoes or lemons in his tent—but this recipe has become a family staple, full of nuanced tastes and very simple to make. Sautéed vegetables and tomato provide the flavor base; no stock at all is needed. Pareve and vegan, it's perfect for meals with or without meat.

3 tablespoons olive oil

1 pound onions, coarsely chopped (4 cups)

Salt

½ cup scraped and coarsely chopped carrots

½ cup coarsely chopped celery

4 chopped garlic cloves plus 4 whole garlic cloves, peeled

3 cups red lentils, picked over carefully and rinsed well in cold water

3 canned plum tomatoes, roughly chopped

1 Turkish bay leaf

IN a very large, wide, heavy saucepan or 5- to 6-quart Dutch oven, heat 2 tablespoons of the oil over medium heat. Add the onions, salt lightly, and sauté until soft, about 15 minutes. Stir in the carrots, celery, and chopped garlic, and raise the heat to moderately high. Sauté, stirring, until the vegetables are softened and edged with gold. Add the lentils and stir to coat them with the oil. Add the tomatoes, 9 cups cold water, and the bay leaf, and bring to a boil. Lower the heat and simmer, covered, for about 45 minutes, or until the lentils are very soft. Remove the pot from the heat, and let the soup cool for 15 to 20 minutes. Remove and discard bay leaf.

PUREE the soup, in batches, in a food processor fitted with the steel blade. Or puree it in the pot, using an immersion blender.

RETURN the soup to the pot, and add the cumin and salt and pepper to taste. Simmer, stirring occasionally, for about 10 minutes.

1 tablespoon ground cumin, preferably freshly toasted and ground

Freshly ground black pepper or Aleppo pepper

1 tablespoon dried mint

About 3 tablespoons fresh lemon juice

Accompaniment: best-quality extra virgin olive oil for drizzling; lemon wedges

MEANWHILE, crush the whole garlic cloves into a paste with the mint and a little salt. Sauté the garlic paste in the remaining 1 tablespoon of oil in a small skillet over medium heat until it is just tinged with gold.

STIR the garlic paste and the lemon juice into the soup, and cook for 2 or 3 minutes to blend the flavors. Taste and adjust the seasoning.

LADLE the soup into bowls, and drizzle a thread of fine olive oil on top of each serving. Serve with lemon wedges.

COOK'S NOTE: Leftover soup is delicious, though it will thicken considerably. Just thin it with water before reheating and add a splash of fresh lemon juice before serving.

EGYPTIAN GROUND FISH BALLS WITH TOMATO AND CUMIN (*BELLAHAT*)

yield: ABOUT 8 SERVINGS

*F*avored by Egyptian Jews as a prelude to holiday and Sabbath meals, this easy-to-prepare, well-seasoned alternative to gefilte fish requires no poaching in fish stock and can be made with any white-fleshed fish. The pungent cumin that flavors bellahat tastes like today, but it is an ancient spice, sold by the Hebrews in herb markets during biblical times, and used in their soups, stews, and breads.

Over the years, my daughter and I have tweaked this family favorite, based on a version from Corinne Rossabi, an excellent home cook raised in Egypt. We no longer fry the fish balls first, but instead cook them directly in the well-seasoned tomato sauce. When summer collides headlong with fall, I prepare a sauce variation from the explosion of red, orange, and yellow at my local greenmarket (page 145).

Bellahat benefit from an extended soak in the flavorful sauce, so if possible, prepare them a day before you plan to serve them.

FOR THE FISH BALLS

1½ pounds flounder, haddock, cod, scrod, sole, hake, sea bass, snapper, grouper, or other nonoily white fish fillets, skin and stray bones discarded

½ cup matzoh meal

2 large eggs

¼ cup chopped onion

1 tablespoon minced garlic

2 teaspoons ground cumin, preferably freshly toasted and ground

About 2 teaspoons kosher salt

Cayenne

2 tablespoons finely chopped fresh parsley

MAKE the fish balls: cut the fish into 1-inch pieces. In a food processor, puree the fish with the matzoh meal, eggs, onions, garlic, cumin, salt, and cayenne until the mixture is smooth. (I usually use about ¼ teaspoon cayenne—I like this rather spicy, the traditional Egyptian way—but season to your taste.) Transfer the puree to a large bowl, stir in the parsley and the cilantro, if using, and refrigerate it, covered, for 1 hour.

WITH moistened hands, shape the mixture into 16 slightly flattened logs, using about ¼ cup for each, and transfer them as they are formed to a sheet of wax paper.

MAKE the tomato sauce: in a very large, heavy sauté pan or deep skillet, warm the garlic in 2 tablespoons olive oil until fragrant but barely colored. Add the tomatoes and their juice and salt and pepper to taste. Cook over moderately high heat for about 10 minutes, stirring occasionally, until the tomatoes break up and the sauce is thickened. Stir in the remaining 1 tablespoon olive oil and the lemon juice. Add the fish balls and simmer the mixture over low heat, covered, for 20 to 25 minutes, until the fish balls are firm and just cooked through, turning

2 tablespoons finely chopped fresh cilantro (optional)

2 to 3 teaspoons chopped garlic

3 tablespoons best-quality extra virgin olive oil

One 28-ounce can whole tomatoes with their juice, seeded, if desired, and chopped

Salt and freshly ground black pepper

Juice of 1 large lemon

Soft-leafed lettuce, for lining the platter

Optional accompaniments: chopped fresh parsley or cilantro; lemon quarters

them once or twice. Remove the skillet from the heat. Taste the sauce and adjust the seasonings. Let the bellahat cool in the sauce. If possible, cover and refrigerate for 4 or up to 48 hours before serving, turning them a couple of times in the sauce.

LINE a platter or individual plates with the lettuce leaves, arrange the bellahat on them, and spoon the sauce over the fish. Sprinkle with parsley or cilantro, and accompany with lemon quarters, if desired. Serve the fish chilled or at room temperature.

COOK'S NOTE: If you prefer a sauce with a smooth texture, puree it in the pan using an immersion blender, or transfer to a blender, food processor, or food mill. Rewarm the sauce gently before adding the fish balls to the pan.

TOMATO AND SWEET PEPPER SAUCE

yield: ENOUGH FOR ONE RECIPE BELLAHAT

*T*ry this cilantro-scented sauce when beautifully fresh tomatoes and peppers are in season. . .

2 pounds fresh plum tomatoes (if you have access to a farmers' market, look for heirloom varieties; I've particularly enjoyed a deep-flavored, juicy yellow plum tomato.)

3 tablespoons best-quality extra virgin olive oil

1½ cups chopped onion

1½ cups diced sweet red and yellow peppers (look for the long, narrow, thin-fleshed frying red peppers such as Cubanelle, or, even better, local heirloom varieties; if unavailable, substitute finely diced red or yellow bell peppers; or add a little finely chopped, thin-fleshed, mildly hot red pepper such as Hungarian wax pepper)

Salt and freshly ground black pepper

Juice of 1 lemon

2 tablespoons chopped fresh cilantro

PREPARE the tomatoes: bring a 6-quart pot of water to a boil. Add the tomatoes and cook for 60 to 90 seconds. Using tongs, transfer them one by one to a large bowl to cool slightly. Peel off the skins; they should come off quite easily. Cut off and discard the stem end of each tomato and chop the tomatoes coarsely.

HEAT 2 tablespoons of the olive oil in a 10- to 12-inch heavy sauté pan or deep skillet. Add the onions and sauté, stirring occasionally, over medium heat until softened, 5 to 7 minutes. Add the peppers, raise the heat to moderately high, and sauté, scraping and stirring the vegetables, until the peppers are soft and slightly caramelized, 7 to 8 minutes.

ADD the tomatoes and salt and pepper to taste and continue cooking, taking care to stir and scrape the bottom of the pan so the vegetables don't burn, until the tomatoes are very tender and melting. The exact time will vary depending on the juiciness of the tomatoes, but figure on 10 to 15 minutes. If you prefer a sauce with a smooth texture, puree it in the pan using an immersion blender, or transfer to a blender, food processor, or food mill to puree. Before adding the fish balls to the sauce, rewarm the sauce gently in the pan, and stir in the remaining 1 tablespoon olive oil and the lemon juice. After the fish balls are cooked, sprinkle them with the cilantro and allow them to cool in the sauce before refrigerating.

GOLDEN GEFILTE FISH WITH GOLDEN HORSERADISH

yield: **ABOUT 12 SERVINGS**

My father's mother baked whitefish smothered with chopped tomatoes, onions, and peppers, and served it cold for Sabbath meals. The only fish I remember my maternal grandmother making was canned tuna, mixed with hard-boiled eggs and onions.

So I've had to invent my own family recipe for gefilte fish—for many, the defining dish of Ashkenazi cuisine. I've eaten some very good versions at dairy restaurants, and tasted even more delicious ones in the evocative prose of Yiddish writers. I knew what I was after.

Most important is a soft, tender texture. In place of the matzoh meal filler, which might make the mixture dense, I choose bits of fresh challah, as Bella Chagall's family had done in Burning Lights, *her charming memoir of growing up in Vitebsk, Russia before she married the legendary artist.*

There's a play of flavors in the seasoning, from a jot of mellowed garlic to a tart citrus splash and the fresh, clean bite of heaps of freshly ground pepper blossoming on the tongue. And to pull all the flavors into balance, I steal a little sweetness from carrots and onions that I sauté first and then puree. These vegetables also add softness and moisture, and dab the pale fish with tiny threads of color.

But I want color that will tantalize, so like the overworked mother in Chaim Grade's novel of World War II Vilna, My Mother's Sabbath Days, *I gild the fish with golden saffron.*

When I prepare a broth for the fish, I simmer it long with sweet root vegetables and poach the fish balls short, to maximize their flavor and keep them quenelle-light. For a quick version, I dispense with the broth and bake the fish in individual custard cups in a hot-water bath; the resulting flavor and texture are a shade more delicate, if less intense.

The golden horseradish, made with cooked carrots and moistened with carrot juice for the barest suggestion of sweetness, is a beguiling, festive departure, but if you don't have time to

> "Hashed onions and soaked challa fill the fish with new blood. . . . The smell tantalizes us, tickles our noses. It brings us the first taste of Sabbath."
>
> —BELLA CHAGALL, *Burning Lights*

> " 'We also put in saffron, to make the fish yellow,' adds my mother."
>
> —CHAIM GRADE, *My Mother's Sabbath Days*

prepare it, serve the fish with the ready-made variety. Or make the classic white or beet-flavored red horseradish from the recipes on page 151.

FOR THE FISH BALLS

3 cups chopped onion

½ cup carrot, scraped and diced

2 tablespoons mild olive oil or vegetable oil, such as avocado or sunflower

1 large garlic clove, peeled

Salt and freshly ground black pepper

½ cup packed fresh challah pieces (crusts removed) or, for Passover, egg or plain matzoh, moistened with white wine or water

¼ teaspoon packed saffron threads, crushed and dissolved in 2 tablespoons hot water

3 pounds skinless fish fillets (stray bones removed), rinsed to remove any scales, patted dry, and cut into 1-inch pieces or ground by the fishmonger (see Cook's Note)

½ cup ice water

2 pinches of sugar

4 large eggs

2 tablespoons fresh lemon juice

IF STOVE-TOP POACHING IN FISH STOCK

About 3 pounds fish bones, skin, and heads

PREPARE the fish balls: in a 10-inch heavy skillet, sauté the onions and carrots in the oil over moderate heat, stirring occasionally, for about 10 minutes. Don't let the vegetables brown: you just want to soften and sweeten them. Add the garlic and season with salt and pepper lightly. Cover the pan, reduce the heat, and cook, stirring occasionally, until the carrots are soft enough to mash roughly with the back of a metal spoon, 10 to 15 minutes.

TRANSFER the vegetables and oil from the skillet to a food processor and pulse just until the ingredients are thoroughly combined. Add the challah and saffron and process until smooth. Transfer the mixture to a large wooden chopping bowl (the kind used with a crescent-shaped chopping tool, like the half-moon-shaped Jewish *hockmeisser* or crescent-shaped Italian *mezzaluna*) or a chopping board.

IF the fish is already ground, add it to the challah mixture. If fish was not purchased ground, place half of the pieces in the food processor (don't bother rinsing it out) and pulse until it is chopped medium-coarse. Add to the challah mixture. Process the remaining half of the fish in the same way, and add it to the mixture.

CHOP the ingredients, using a hand chopper with the bowl or a sharp cleaver with the board, gradually adding the ice water as you work. Continue chopping while adding 2 teaspoons salt, 1½ to 2 teaspoons pepper or to taste (the fish should be quite peppery), and the sugar. Chop in the eggs, one at a time, and the lemon juice. Keep chopping until the mixture becomes very smooth, light, and fluffy. (All this hand-chopping incorporates lots of air into the ingredients, which will make the fish balls light and delicate. Using a food processor or blender will simply puree the ingredients to liquefaction.) Refrigerate until thoroughly chilled and firm, at least 2 hours.

IF stovetop-poaching the gefilte fish, prepare the stock: rinse the fish bones, skin, and heads and place in a very large, wide, heavy saucepan. Add 2 quarts cold water and bring to a boil, skimming constantly to remove all the bitter froth and scum as they rise to the top. Continue skimming the broth while it cooks at a gentle boil for another

4 large carrots, scraped and quartered

2 large onions, peeled and quartered

2 celery stalks, including leaves, quartered

2 parsnips, peeled and quartered (they add a subtle whisper of sweetness; optional)

3 or 4 parsley sprigs

Salt and freshly ground black pepper

Sugar (optional)

IF OVEN-POACHING

1 medium carrot, scraped

Salt

Mild oil, for greasing the custard cups

Accompaniments: soft lettuce, Belgian endive, or radicchio leaves, for lining plates; Golden Horseradish (recipe follows), Classic Horseradish, White or Red (page 151), or prepared beet horseradish

Optional garnish: very finely minced flat-leaf parsley or chives

10 minutes. Add the carrots, onions, celery, parsnips, if using, parsley, and salt and pepper to taste, then reduce the heat and simmer, partially covered, for about 1 hour. Skim occasionally, as needed. Strain the broth through a fine-mesh sieve, pressing down hard on the solids with the back of a spoon to extract as much flavorful liquid as possible. Discard the solids (if you want to serve the carrots with the fish, save them and set them aside). Rinse out the saucepan and pour in the strained broth. Bring the broth to a simmer and adjust the seasonings. Add a pinch or two of sugar to remove any trace of bitterness, if needed.

WETTING your hands with cold water as necessary, form the fish mixture into ovals, using ⅓ to ½ cup of fish for each gefilte fish ball. Place the balls on one or two platters as you finish making the rest. Using a spatula, carefully lower the balls one by one into the simmering broth. Add only as many fish balls as will fit comfortably in a single layer. If they are not covered with stock, baste them with a few spoonfuls. Cover tightly and simmer over low heat, without peeking, for 30 minutes. Remove a fish ball and cut it in half to test for doneness: It should be completely cooked through, with no dark or raw spots. Cook a bit longer, as needed, but don't overcook. Remove the balls with a slotted spoon and place in a single layer in a deep dish or two. Poach any remaining balls in the same way, and transfer them to the same dish. Reduce the liquid in the pan over high heat by at least half. Pour a shallow layer of the liquid over the gefilte fish and refrigerate any remaining liquid. It should gel nicely. Refrigerate the gefilte fish for at least 6 hours, preferably overnight. To serve, arrange the chilled fish on the lettuce, surrounded by some of the fish gelatin, if desired, and any reserved carrots. Accompany with golden horseradish, classic horseradish, or prepared beet horseradish.

IF oven-poaching, boil the carrot in lightly salted water until tender. Drain.

PREHEAT the oven to 350°F. Grease the bottom and sides of twelve 1-cup custard cups. Cut the carrot into very thin slices and decoratively arrange 1, 2, or 3 slices in the center of each custard cup. Spoon the prepared fish mixture into the cups, then tap the cups sharply on the side with a butter knife to remove any trapped air bubbles and even out the mixture. Use the butter knife or the back of a spoon to smooth the tops. Cover the cups with foil. Fold a dish towel flat on the bottom of a large baking pan. Place the custard cups on the towel and pour in enough boiling or scalding-hot tap water to come halfway up the sides of the cups. Place in the oven and bake for about 30 minutes, until cooked through (they should feel solid in the center). Remove the custard cups from the hot-water bath and cool, uncovered, to room temperature. Cover the cups again with foil or wax paper and refrigerate for at least 6 hours, or preferably overnight. To serve, run a knife around the edges and unmold onto plates lined with lettuce. If desired, after inverting, dust the tops (avoiding the carrot slices in the center) with the parsley or chives. (Alternatively, before baking, you could sprinkle the custard cups with the herbs after you have added the carrot, but before spooning in the fish mixture.) Accompany with Golden Horseradish, Classic Horseradish, or prepared beet horseradish.

COOK'S NOTE: For the fish, choose an equal quantity of carp, pike, and whitefish, equal parts pike and whitefish (my preference), or your own or your fishmonger's favorite mixture. You can mix fresh and saltwater varieties, if you'd like, such as carp with halibut. Avoid very strong-flavored fish like bluefish or mackerel. For the best taste, you should have some combination of fat and lean fish. (See the chart below.)

MODERATE- TO HIGH-FAT FISH	LEAN FISH
Arctic char	cod (scrod)
buffalofish	flounder
carp	grouper
Chilean sea bass	haddock
lake or rainbow trout	hake or whiting
pompano	halibut
sablefish or black cod	ocean perch
salmon	perch (yellow)
whitefish	pike (pickerel, muskellunge)
	pollock
	red snapper
	sea bass or striped bass
	sea trout
	sole

GOLDEN HORSERADISH

yield: ABOUT 1¼ CUPS

⅓ cup scraped carrot, cut into small chunks

Enough fresh horseradish root to yield about 1 cup when grated (about 2 cups of peeled chunks)

About ¼ cup cider vinegar

About 1 teaspoon kosher salt

½ cup fresh carrot juice (see Cook's Note)

Sugar (optional)

IN a small saucepan, boil the carrots in lightly salted water until very tender. Drain and rinse with cold water until cool. Pat dry and set aside.

PLACE horseradish in a food processor fitted with the steel blade and grind until coarsely grated. With the machine on, add through the feed tube vinegar, salt, and ¼ cup of the carrot juice. Continue processing just until the horseradish is finely grated, but not reduced to a puree. Averting your face when removing the processor lid (to avoid the noxious fumes), scrape down the bowl. With the machine on, add the cooked carrots, alternating with the remaining ¼ cup carrot juice. Remembering again to avert your face, transfer the contents (including the liquid) to a bowl. Mix very well, cover tightly, and refrigerate for at least 3 hours so the flavors mingle.

STIR well and if needed, adjust the vinegar and salt before serving. The combination of the cooked carrot and carrot juice brings a delicate, vegetal sweetness to the sauce without added sugar. If you prefer a sweeter-tasting sauce, add a pinch or two of sugar.

STORE refrigerated in a tightly covered glass jar. Serve leftover sauce with beef or mix with mayonnaise for cold poultry; combined with mayonnaise or sour cream, it is a perfect foil for richly-flavored poached, smoked, or fried fish.

COOK'S NOTE: If you can not get fresh carrot juice, boil down the carrot cooking water until reduced to ¼ cup. Let it cool, then substitute it for the juice in the recipe. (Since the cooking water is thinner and not as deeply flavored as the carrot juice, using an equal quantity of it would dilute the taste of the sauce too much.)

LIKE Ginger-Beet Horseradish (page 402), golden horseradish marries well with a little freshly grated ginger. Add the ginger to taste when first grating the horseradish.

CLASSIC HORSERADISH, WHITE OR RED

yield: 1 TO 1½ CUPS

FOR WHITE (PLAIN) HORSERADISH (*CHRAIN*) Omit the carrots from the Golden Horseradish (page 150) and coarsely grind the horseradish, as described in the recipe. With the machine on, add 3 tablespoons cider vinegar or lemon juice and 1½ teaspoons kosher salt through the feed tube, and continue processing just until finely grated but not pureed. Averting your face when removing the processor lid, scrape the mixture into a clean jar or bowl. Taste and adjust salt, and add a little more vinegar, if needed, to moisten everything. While not my preference, some people like to add a bit of sugar, too. Store refrigerated in a tightly covered glass jar.

FOR RED HORSERADISH Beets (and often sugar) are added to make fiery Classic Horseradish more mellow. The more beet you add, the mellower the horseradish will taste; cooked beets (wrap in foil and roast in a 350°F oven for about 1 to 1½ hours, until tender) are sweeter than raw beets and will make a milder sauce with a softer texture, so choose according to preference. Peel a small or medium raw or cooked beet, cut it into quarters, and add it to the food processor along with the horseradish. If you want to adjust the amount of beet you're adding, grate the beet separately (either grinding it like the horseradish or using a fine shredding disk), and add small spoonfuls to the grated horseradish until you achieve a pleasing balance. Taste for salt and vinegar, and if you'd like, add a little sugar—anywhere from a pinch to 1 teaspoon. Store refrigerated in a tightly covered glass jar.

FESENJAN REDUX (ROAST DUCK BREASTS WITH QUINCE, POMEGRANATE, AND WALNUT SAUCE)

yield: 6 TO 9 SERVINGS

The jewel in the crown of khoreshes (traditional Persian saucy stews), fesenjan is a Rosh Hashanah treasure on many Iranian-Jewish tables. A blend of pomegranate and walnut giving way to an exquisite tango of tart and sweet, the sauce is served with duck—and less often, other poultry, veal, lamb, or meatballs, too—always accompanied by copious amounts of rice.

Older recipes usually call for cooking the meat in the sauce, but I prefer to roast the duck separately; the flavors taste cleaner and there's no fat to skim. Instead I add quinces to turn meltingly tender infused with the sauce, which is subtly sweetened with dates.

If you can't find duck breasts, fesenjan is also delicious served with grilled or roasted chicken thighs or whole ducklings; it can also stand up to grilled steak or roasted beef. This recipe makes quite a bit of the rich sauce, so you can dish it up Iranian-Jewish style: a generous amount of rice topped with sauce, along with a modest amount of duck. Or present it in typical American fashion to fewer guests, with more meat and less rice; freeze leftover sauce and pair it with grilled poultry or meat for a quick, celebratory meal in the future.

FOR THE DUCK BREASTS

3 to 4 pounds boneless duck breasts, skin-on (for a kosher purveyor, see Sources, page 551)

¾ teaspoon coriander seeds

1 teaspoon black peppercorns

1 tablespoon chopped garlic

Salt

Olive oil

PREPARE the duck breasts: rinse and pat them dry. Using a sharp knife, score the duck skin in a crisscross pattern, taking care to cut only through the skin and fat, avoiding the duck flesh. Grind the coriander and peppercorns in a spice grinder or coffee mill, or crush well using a mortar and pestle. Add the garlic and salt, spin or mash to a coarse puree, and rub into both sides of the duck, working some of the paste into the flesh between the score marks. Set aside while you start the sauce.

PREHEAT the oven to 300°F.

PREPARE the sauce: rinse, quarter, and peel the quinces. Using a very sharp knife, cut out the core, seeds, and any other hard bits. Cut the quinces into large chunks. Pulse the walnuts in a food processor to a mixture of fine and coarse crumbs.

IN a large heavy Dutch oven or casserole, heat the oil over medium heat until it shimmers. Add the onions and sauté, turning occasionally as

3 ripe medium quinces

2 cups walnuts, lightly toasted (see Cook's Note)

3 tablespoons olive oil

3 cups chopped onion

1 tablespoon chopped garlic

Salt and freshly ground black pepper

2 cups pure, unsweetened pomegranate juice

3 tablespoons pomegranate molasses

1 cup chicken broth, preferably homemade (see pages 62 and 70), or good-quality, low-sodium purchased

¾ cup chopped pitted dates

About 2 teaspoons fresh lemon juice

Accompaniment: freshly cooked rice

Optional garnish: fresh pomegranate seeds

they soften and then turn golden. Adjust the heat to medium-high and add the quinces. Cook until the fruit begins to speckle a deep caramel in places, lifting and tossing to avoid burning. Add the garlic, sprinkle with salt and pepper, and cook for 3 minutes to blend the flavors. Stir in the ground walnuts and briefly sauté, stirring, until their aroma arises.

STIR together the pomegranate juice and pomegranate molasses, and add along with the broth and dates. Bring the mixture to a boil, then cover and transfer to the oven, occasionally giving it a stir as it cooks. (You can simmer the sauce on top of the stove, if you prefer. I find the oven heat gentler and more even, causing less evaporation, and besides, I usually need the extra burner space on the stove.)

WHEN the sauce has been in the oven for about 45 minutes, choose a very large, heavy, ovenproof skillet (cast-iron is ideal here; if necessary, use 2 skillets or work in batches) and film it with oil. Place the skillet over medium heat until hot. Add the duck breasts, skin side down. Cook, shaking the pan occasionally or sliding a spatula under the breasts if they threaten to stick. Press down on the breasts with a spatula now and then to release more fat, and pour out the rendered fat as it accumulates; if the fat rises up to the duck flesh, its high temperature may toughen the meat. Continue cooking until the skin is well bronzed, about 10 minutes. Pour off any remaining fat from the pan, turn the duck skin side up, and put the skillet in the oven alongside the sauce. (Or, if you sautéed the duck breasts in batches or in 2 skillets, you can place all of them in one large baking pan.)

SLOW-ROAST until the duck breasts are cooked to the desired doneness, 10 to 15 minutes, or until they feel springy to the touch and a thermometer inserted horizontally into the center of a breast registers 135°F for medium-rare or 140°F for medium. Transfer the duck to a cutting board and let rest for 5 minutes.

REMOVE the sauce from the oven and place the pot over medium heat. Add the lemon juice and cook for 2 minutes to blend the flavors. Taste and adjust the lemon, salt, and pepper.

CUT the duck on the diagonal into ½-inch-thick slices. It is easiest to do this if the thick skin side is on the bottom and you cut directly into the duck flesh.

SPOON fluffy cooked rice onto a serving platter and nap with plenty of sauce and chunks of quince. Fan the duck slices decoratively on top, ladle some additional sauce over, and scatter the pomegranate seeds, if using.

COOK'S NOTE: I always taste nuts first to make sure they have not turned rancid. Once, as I started to prepare this fesenjan, I found out too late that my walnuts were stale, and had to substitute pecans. Their rich, slightly sweet edge married beautifully with the other ingredients, and even guests who find walnuts a tad too bitter for their tastes, especially children, loved the sauce. Though purists may scoff, I usually make fesenjan with pecans now.

IRANIAN STUFFED CHICKEN WITH FRESH GREEN HERBS AND GOLDEN SOUP

yield: 4 TO 8 SERVINGS, DEPENDING ON THE SIZE OF THE CHICKEN AND OTHER DISHES SERVED

You pick up strips of silky, moist poached chicken, glistening with amber broth, and wrap them in an array of fresh green herbs—mint, scallion slivers, basil, tarragon, cilantro—then pop the scented packet in your mouth. Between bites there is the stuffing—cumin-scented rice and dal-like split peas, tinted sunshine yellow with turmeric—that has been cooked to melt-in-the-mouth tenderness inside the gently simmered chicken.

Only much later do you realize that this sensory feast—unlike most from the Rosh Hashanah repertoire—is nearly fat-free, rich only in its extravagance of aromatic fragrances and brilliant gold colors.

An added bonus is the wonderful broth that comes with poaching the chicken, to be served at this meal, or saved for the second Rosh Hashanah dinner tomorrow.

The original Iranian recipe, while utterly delicious, is somewhat tricky to do, but I have come up with an easy and foolproof—though somewhat unconventional—cooking method. I precook all of the stuffing, and wrap it up in a thin piece of cotton. Then I split the bird open, slip the stuffing package inside it, and roughly truss the bird closed around it. No need to sew up the chicken and no fear that stray stuffing will seep into the broth and cloud it up. The stuffing drinks in the chicken's lovely juices, and removing it and serving it is a breeze.

Beautifully fresh herbs are essential here; some herb blossoms, if you can get them, added to the mix make for a stunning presentation.

FOR THE STUFFING

2 tablespoons extra virgin olive oil

1½ cups finely chopped onion

1½ tablespoons cumin seeds, crushed with a mortar and pestle or coarsely ground in a spice mill (for extra flavor, lightly toast the seeds until fragrant before crushing)

START the stuffing: in a wide 3-quart saucepan, warm the olive oil. Add the onions and sauté them over moderate heat, stirring occasionally, for about 10 minutes, until they are softened and just beginning to turn pale gold. Don't brown them. Add the cumin and turmeric and stir for 2 to 3 minutes, until they become very fragrant. Add the rice and split peas, and stir to coat them with the onions and oil. Add 3 cups cold water, about 1¾ teaspoons salt, and pepper to taste. Bring to a boil, then simmer, covered, over very low heat for 20 minutes. Taste and adjust the salt and pepper. Remove the pot from the heat.

½ teaspoon turmeric

1 cup basmati rice, rinsed well

½ cup yellow split peas, picked over and rinsed well

Salt and freshly ground black pepper

FOR THE CHICKEN

1 large roasting chicken, 4 to 7 pounds (neck, liver, and giblets removed and reserved for another use)

Enough fresh, cold water to cover the bird (if you use bottled water for coffee or tea, use it here)

Salt

1 large onion, peeled and cut in half

2 medium celery stalks, preferably with leaves

1 cup dried chickpeas, picked over, rinsed, and soaked overnight (optional)

Freshly ground black pepper

1 to 1½ teaspoons turmeric

TO SERVE WITH THE CHICKEN

An assortment of fresh herbs, including at least three of these: basil, mint, tarragon, cilantro, scallions

Small red radishes

Herb blossoms or other edible flowers (optional)

YOU'LL need a thin cotton cloth to enclose the stuffing. I prefer an inexpensive, large white cotton men's handkerchief (unlike other cloths, it never unravels), but a piece of clean cotton sheeting (that has been washed in unscented laundry detergent), premade muslin soup bag (sold in some kitchenware stores), or a double thickness of good-quality cheesecloth will also work well. Spoon the stuffing onto the center of the cloth and mold it into a rough oblong about 8 by 5 inches. Pull the cloth over the stuffing to enclose it completely. Twist the ends and tie them and the middle closed with kitchen string, allowing a little extra room for the stuffing to expand.

USING kitchen shears, cut through the chicken along the backbone as if butterflying it, or have the butcher do it. Remove as much loose fat as possible and rinse the chicken well with cold water. Spread the chicken open and place the bag of stuffing inside it. Fold the chicken over the stuffing to enclose it, then tie the chicken closed with a light truss. That will make it easier to turn the chicken, if needed, and to remove it from the pot. Place the chicken on the bottom of a stockpot (an 8-quart for a small bird; 10- to 12-quart size for an extra-large chicken). Add water to cover it, and about 1 teaspoon salt. Bring to a strong simmer, but don't allow the water to boil.

AS the chicken cooks, skim off all the froth and scum that rise to the surface. After the water begins to simmer gently, continue skimming for 15 to 20 minutes, until very few impurities come to the surface, then add the onion, celery, chickpeas, if using, a few grinds of pepper, and about 1 teaspoon turmeric. The water now should be a light, golden yellow (it will turn burnished gold later from the chicken juices). You may need to add up to ½ teaspoon more turmeric, especially if your chicken is large and required a lot of water to cover it. Bring the water back to a strong simmer, skimming occasionally, then partially cover the pot and reduce the heat to very low. The bubbles should be breaking slowly and silently along the surface; do not let the soup boil or the chicken will be tough. Check occasionally to make sure the chicken is completely covered with liquid. If there is not enough liquid to cover it, don't add more water—that will dilute the soup too much. Instead, turn the chicken carefully from time to time, so all sides are gently bathed in liquid during most of the cooking.

POACH the chicken for 1 to 2 hours (depending on the size of the bird), until its juices run clear when the thigh is pierced with a thin metal skewer or long-pronged fork.

WHILE the chicken is cooking, prepare the herb accompaniment: if the basil leaves are large or the stems thick, pull off the leaves and discard the stems. Trim off any hard or woody stems from the mint, and trim the cilantro and tarragon. Cut off the bearded roots and 2 to 3 inches of the dark green ends from the scallions, then sliver the scallions lengthwise. Trim the radishes and thinly slice them. Set out the herbs and the radishes decoratively in a basket lined with a pretty napkin, or on a platter. If you have any herb blossoms or other edible flowers, such as nasturtiums, violets, Johnny jump-ups, or borage flowers, intersperse them among the green herbs for a striking presentation.

TO serve the chicken, carefully transfer it to a warm serving platter. I find it easiest to do this by grabbing onto the trussing string with tongs, and holding a plate or very wide, sturdy spatula directly under the chicken with the other hand, while a second set of hands stands ready with the platter. Discard the trussing string and remove and discard the chicken skin, leaving the meat on the bones. Arrange the chicken attractively on the platter. Untie the bag and scoop out the stuffing, mounding it in the middle of the chicken. Spoon a little hot broth over everything to moisten it, and tuck a few clusters of herbs around the chicken and stuffing as garnish.

OR slice the chicken off the bone after discarding the skin, and place in warmed, shallow soup bowls. Spoon some of the stuffing around the chicken and arrange a few sprigs of herbs artfully on top. Ladle about a half cup of steaming broth over everything.

TO eat the chicken, take some herbs in hand: a strip of scallion and a couple of tarragon leaves, for instance. Then, still using your hands, pull off a small piece of chicken and roll the herbs around it. If you'd like, sprinkle with a few grains of coarse salt before popping the little packet in the mouth.

IF you have added chickpeas, taste one for tenderness after removing the chicken, and, if needed, simmer the broth a little longer until the peas are done. Discard the onion and the celery.

IF you are serving the broth and chickpeas as a prelude to or alongside the chicken, tent the chicken and stuffing with aluminum foil to keep them warm as you defat the broth. Use an inexpensive gravy separator to remove the fat or carefully spoon off as much of the clear fat layer as possible. Or scoop out the chickpeas, using a perforated ladle, and place them in a large bowl. Line a fine-mesh sieve or strainer with two to three layers of dampened paper toweling or with coffee filters, and fit the sieve over the bowl. Slowly pour the broth through the sieve into the bowl, trapping the fat in the paper towels or filters. If the broth is still fatty, repeat with clean paper towels. Wash out the pot before reheating the soup.

BECAUSE the bag of stuffing adds quite a bit of volume to the contents of the pot, necessitating more water than usual to cover the ingredients, you may need to reduce the broth somewhat to concentrate the flavors. Boil uncovered over high heat to the desired strength. Adjust the salt and pepper. Serve the broth with the chickpeas in warmed shallow bowls garnished with chopped fresh herbs and some of the poached chicken, shredded.

IF you are serving the broth at another meal, allow it to cool, *uncovered*, to room temperature, then chill in the refrigerator until the fat congeals in a layer on top. When ready to serve, spoon off the fat and discard it. Reheat the broth until piping hot. Reduce if needed and adjust the seasoning.

For Yassmine Hakim, the Jewish New Year has been almost as festive as Passover, ever since she was a child growing up in Teheran, where her huge extended family—replete with lots of mischievous, giggling cousins—gathered around her grandmother's table to eat this family heirloom, along with countless *khoreshes* (Iranian stews) and elegant rices.

Today in her New York apartment, Yassmine keeps up the celebratory level of excitement at her own Rosh Hashanah table by investing the symbolic foods, like tongue, black-eyed peas, and pomegranates, with the same degree of importance as those on the seder plate. "I scatter them around the table and offer them as hors d'oeuvre, but first, all of us, especially the children, have fun unlocking the mysteries, discussing the ritual significances of the of the different foods." After these are eaten and cleared away, a parade of main courses and rices are brought out, just as in Teheran.

BRISKET BRAISED IN POMEGRANATE JUICE WITH ONION CONFIT AND POMEGRANATE SEEDS

yield: 8 GENEROUS SERVINGS

ut open a pomegranate. Hundreds of juice sacs form a nearly perfect star, red as blood. Little wonder it is celebrated in myth and ritual by all ancient peoples—Chinese, Greeks, as well as Jews—as a symbol of fertility and abundance.

On Rosh Hashanah, Jews often eat the pomegranate, one of the miperi ha-eretz *(seven choice fruits of ancient Israel), in fulfillment of the commandment to eat a fruit not yet sampled this season. For, according to kabbalistic tradition, the pomegranate contains exactly 613 seeds, the precise number of commandments a pious Jew must follow; eating this perfect fruit on Rosh Hashanah embodies the hope that we may perform as many good deeds and righteous acts as the pomegranate has seeds.*

The pomegranate's virtues are not merely symbolic. Latest scientific research suggests it may slow the aging process and fight diseases like cancer. For the cook, it adds a tart, complex fruitiness to foods, tenderizes tough cuts, and even reduces the amount of salt needed in meat dishes. In this recipe, the juice tenderizes the brisket and invests the amethyst-tinted gravy with a haunting depth. More beautifully layered autumn colors and flavors unfold slowly: a cushion of bronze caramelized onions cooked to a jammy confit or "onion marmalade," giving way to a shower of tart-sweet pomegranate seeds. It's a glamorous showstopper, worth every minute in the kitchen.

For a discussion of pomegranate substitutions, see Cook's Note.

FOR THE BRISKET

3 tablespoons olive or canola oil

A first- or second-cut beef brisket, about 5 pounds, trimmed of excess fat, wiped with a damp paper towel, and patted dry

2 medium onions, coarsely chopped (about 2 cups)

PREPARE the brisket: heat the oil over medium-high heat in a large heavy-bottomed roasting pan, using two burners, if necessary, or in a wide 6-quart Dutch oven or flameproof casserole. Add the brisket, and brown well on both sides, about 10 minutes. Transfer the brisket to a platter and set aside.

ALTERNATIVELY, you might find it easier to sear the meat under the broiler. Just cover the broiler pan well with foil to minimize cleanup. Preheat the broiler. Place the brisket under the broiler, fat side up, and broil for 5 to 6 minutes on each side, or until nicely browned. Move the meat around as necessary, so it sears evenly. Transfer the brisket to a platter and set aside.

2 leeks, washed well and coarsely chopped (include both white and pale green parts)

6 large garlic cloves, peeled and crushed

2 large carrots, scraped and coarsely chopped

1 celery stalk celery with leaves, coarsely chopped

2 cups pomegranate juice (see Cook's Note)

2 cups chicken broth, preferably homemade (see pages 62 and 70), or good-quality, low-sodium purchased

3 fresh thyme sprigs or 2 teaspoons dried leaves

2 fresh rosemary sprigs

2 Turkish bay leaves

Salt and freshly ground black pepper

FOR THE CONFIT

3 tablespoons olive oil (or 1, if broil searing)

4 large onions (about 2½ pounds), very thinly sliced

Salt and freshly ground black pepper

¼ cup chicken broth

½ cup dry red wine

½ cup pomegranate seeds (see Cook's Note)

PREHEAT the oven to 325°F.

POUR off all but about 1 tablespoon of fat remaining in the pan (or heat 1 tablespoon of oil if you broiled the brisket), and add the onions and leeks. Cook, stirring occasionally, over medium-high heat, until the vegetables are softened, 5 to 7 minutes. Add the garlic, carrots, and celery, and continue cooking until the onions are golden, 7 to 10 minutes, stirring and scraping the pan to prevent scorching or sticking.

ADD 1 cup of the pomegranate juice and bring the mixture to a boil, scraping up the browned bits from the bottom of the pan with a wooden spoon, until the liquid is reduced by about half. Add the remaining 1 cup juice, the broth, thyme, rosemary, and bay leaves, and bring the mixture to a simmer. Season to taste with salt and pepper.

LIGHTLY salt and pepper the brisket on both sides, and add it to the pan, fat side up, spooning the vegetables all over the meat. Cover the pan tightly (use heavy-duty foil if you don't have a lid for the pan), and braise the brisket in the oven, basting every half hour, until the meat is very tender, 2½ to 3½ hours. (Turn the oven down to 300°F, if the braising liquid begins to bubble rapidly.)

THE brisket tastes best if it is allowed to rest, reabsorbing the juices lost during braising, and it's easiest to defat the gravy if you prepare the meat ahead and refrigerate it until the fat solidifies. So cool the brisket in the pan sauce, cover well with foil, and refrigerate until the fat congeals. (The gravy can be prepared by skimming the fat in the traditional way, if you prefer. If you go that route, though, do let the meat rest in the pan sauce for at least an hour.)

ABOUT an hour or so before you are ready to serve the brisket, make the confit: in a 10- to 12-inch heavy skillet, warm the oil. Add the onions, season lightly with salt and pepper, and toss to coat with the oil. Cook, tightly covered, over the lowest heat, stirring occasionally so the mixture does not burn, for 1 hour, or until the onions are very soft and pale gold in color. Add additional salt and pepper to taste, the broth, and wine. Raise the heat and boil the mixture, uncovered, stirring, until all the liquid is evaporated and the onions turn golden. Taste and adjust the seasoning (it may take quite a bit of salt), and turn off the heat. Cover the mixture and keep it warm. Stir in the pomegranate seeds just before serving.

SCRAPE off all solid fat. Remove the brisket from the pan and slice thinly across the grain.

PREPARE the gravy: bring the braising mixture to room temperature, then strain it, reserving the vegetables. Skim and discard as much fat as possible from the liquid. Puree the reserved vegetables and 1 cup of the defatted braising liquid in a food processor or a blender. Transfer the pureed mixture and the remaining braising liquid to a skillet, and reduce the gravy over high heat to the desired consistency. Taste for seasoning. Rewarm the brisket in the gravy until heated through.

SPREAD the onion confit over a serving platter and arrange the sliced brisket on top. Ladle the hot gravy over the meat and serve immediately.

COOK'S NOTE: This dish owes its distinctive character to both winy pomegranate juice and fresh, tart-sweet pomegranate seeds. Do try to get fresh pomegranates. They are usually available from the end of August through December. Look for large fruits, bulging with seeds, heavy for their size. The leathery rind should be smooth, with some sheen, not dull and dried out. Store them in the refrigerator. An easy way to remove the seeds: cut the fruit in half or lightly score the rind. Soak the fruit in a bowl of cold water for 5 minutes. Gently separate the seeds under water; the seeds will sink and the membranes float. Scoop off and discard the membranes and drain the seeds. Freeze the seeds in an airtight container for an instant burst of color and flavor in a multitude of sweet and savory dishes. One large pomegranate will give you about one cup of seeds.

You will get 2 cups pomegranate juice by squeezing 4 to 6 pomegranates (see Pomegranate-Orange Sunsets, page 192). Or, even simpler, buy bottled pure pomegranate juice at many supermarkets, health food stores, and Middle Eastern shops. Do *not* substitute pomegranate molasses for the juice.

Although the dish is not the same without pomegranates, I can suggest alternatives for a very good, if different, taste:

For the pomegranate juice, try *unsweetened* pure apple-cranberry juice, given complexity with either a couple of tablespoons of pomegranate molasses or about ¼ cup prune juice and 1 tablespoon fresh lemon juice. Taste and make adjustments according to the sweetness of the juice, until you have a good balance of tart and sweet.

And, if absolutely necessary, substitute ½ cup (about 2½ ounces) dried cranberries for the pomegranate seeds.

EGGPLANT-STUFFED BRISKET BRAISED WITH TOMATOES, SAFFRON, AND HONEY

yield: 8 GENEROUS SERVINGS

"*J*ews' food," they called eggplant in mid-nineteenth century Florence, according to Italian food historian Pellegrino Artusi in The Art of Eating Well (1891).

They were right, of course. Introduced first into Italy by the Sephardim, who had fallen in love with the meaty vegetable in Arab Spain, eggplants later came to be prized as well by Jews throughout the Balkans, Romania, and in whatever parts of Russia they would grow.

Rich and substantial, satin-skinned eggplants made ideal meat substitutes at dairy meals, and Jewish cooks lightened them with showers of fresh herbs to create refreshing appetizers and salads.

Because eggplant turns succulent and creamy to the point of butteriness when fried in oil, I find it makes an especially appealing filling for tender, but somewhat dry, brisket, so I run a velvet-luscious eggplant ribbon through the meat. A sumptuous sauce of tomatoes, saffron, honey, and cinnamon further moistens the brisket, in keeping with the exotic Middle Eastern origins of the vegetable.

FOR THE STUFFING

1 medium-large eggplant (about 1¼ pounds), peeled and cut into 1-inch cubes

Coarse kosher salt

About 3 tablespoons olive oil

1 tablespoon minced garlic

Freshly ground black pepper

FOR THE SAUCE

¼ teaspoon saffron threads

3 tablespoons olive oil

2 large onions, coarsely chopped (about 4 cups)

START the stuffing: put the eggplant in a colander and sprinkle evenly with 2 teaspoons coarse salt. Weight the eggplant down (I use a plate or bowl topped with a heavy can, like a large can of tomatoes), and let drain for about 1 hour, stirring the pieces around after 30 minutes. Rinse the eggplant with water and press it very dry with paper towels.

WHILE the eggplant is draining, prepare the sauce: dissolve the saffron threads in 1 tablespoon hot water and set aside. Heat 3 tablespoons of the oil in a large, deep, heavy skillet or sauté pan over medium-high heat. Add the onions and sauté, stirring, until they are translucent and the edges are tinged with gold, about 10 minutes. Season with salt and pepper and add the honey, vinegar, and cinnamon. Turn the heat up to high and boil the liquid in the pan, stirring, until it evaporates, about 5 minutes.

CUT each tomato into 4 or 5 pieces, and add them and their juices to the skillet. Stir in the ginger, saffron, and apricots, if using. Cook over high heat, uncovered, until most of the liquid has evaporated and the toma-

Salt

Freshly ground black pepper

¼ cup aromatic honey (choose an herb flower honey like thyme or rosemary, if possible)

2 tablespoons red wine vinegar or balsamic vinegar

¼ teaspoon ground cinnamon

One 28-ounce can Italian plum tomatoes, packed in their juice

2 peeled and finely minced teaspoons fresh ginger

3 dried apricots, diced (a tart variety especially— usually from California, not Turkey—will point up the sweet and tangy nuances; optional)

A first- or second-cut beef brisket (about 5 pounds), trimmed of excess fat, with a deep, wide pocket for stuffing (have your butcher cut along one of the short sides, extending nearly to the edge along the other three sides)

Accompaniments: steamed rice, *mamaliga* (polenta), or couscous

toes have dissolved into a thick and pulpy sauce, 10 to 15 minutes. Be sure to stir from time to time and, if necessary, turn heat down a bit so the mixture doesn't scorch or burn. Season to taste with salt and pepper and set aside.

FINISH the stuffing. Heat 3 tablespoons oil in another large heavy skillet (nonstick would work well here) over medium-high heat until hot, but not smoking. Add the eggplant in a single layer without crowding the pan, and sauté until tender and lightly browned on all sides. Work in batches, as necessary, transferring the eggplant to a platter as it is done. Add more oil as needed, but always make sure the oil is very hot before adding a new batch of eggplant—this will prevent the pieces from absorbing too much oil. When all the eggplant is browned, return it to the pan, add the garlic and cook, tossing constantly, for 2 minutes, to marry the flavors. Drain the eggplant lightly on paper towels and let cool to room temperature. Season with salt and pepper.

PREHEAT the broiler.

WIPE the brisket with a damp paper towel, and pat dry. Fill the brisket pocket with the eggplant, patting the meat to distribute the stuffing evenly. Don't overpack—save any leftover eggplant for another use (it's delicious in sandwiches). Sew the pocket closed with kitchen twine or strong cotton thread, using a large embroidery needle, as I do, or a trussing needle. (Skewers don't work as well here.) Season the brisket all over with salt and pepper and transfer it, fat side up, to a foil-lined broiler pan, about 4 inches from the heat. (I sear stuffed briskets under the broiler because there is less handling involved, so the stuffing is less likely to seep out.) Brown the top for about 5 minutes, then turn and brown the other side. Reduce the oven temperature to 325°F.

CHOOSE a baking or roasting pan or casserole just large enough to hold the brisket. Spread some of the tomato sauce over the bottom, then add the brisket, fat-side up, and top with the remaining sauce. Cover the pan tightly (use heavy-duty foil if you have no lid) and braise in the oven, basting every 30 minutes, until the meat is very tender, 2½ to 3½ hours. (When you baste, make sure that the sauce is bubbling gently. If you find it is really boiling, turn the oven down to 300°F.) Let the brisket rest in the pan sauce for at least 1 hour to reabsorb the juices released during the braising. Transfer the brisket to a cutting board.

PREPARE the gravy: skim and discard as much fat as possible from the sauce, then put it through a food mill or press through a wire-mesh sieve.

(You can also puree it in a blender, although this will result in a much denser mixture.) Reheat the gravy and, if necessary, boil it to reduce to the desired consistency. Taste and adjust the seasoning. Rewarm the brisket in the gravy over low heat.

CAREFULLY slice the brisket medium-thin across the grain at a slight diagonal, so that each slice encloses a strip of eggplant stuffing. Ladle the hot sauce over the meat and serve with rice, mamaliga, or couscous to sop up the sauce.

SYRIAN APRICOT-STUFFED MEAT ROLLS WITH TART-SWEET CHERRY SAUCE (*KIBBE GHERAZ*)

yield: 6 TO 8 SERVINGS

Syrian Jews frequently spark their festive dishes, such as stuffed grape leaves and zesty kibbe, with dried apricots, especially on Rosh Hashanah, when their deep golden color is symbolic of coins and, therefore, of good fortune.

A labor of love, kibbe are prepared by grinding rice or bulgur with lean lamb or beef to form an outer shell (a chore made infinitely easier with a food processor), which is then stuffed with a savory meat filling. This version creates a little universe of flavors. Sliced and sauced, it makes a lovely presentation: rich brown meat punctuated by orange-gold apricots and toasted pine nuts, napped with tangy pomegranate molasses or tamarind and dark, sweet purple cherries.

I prefer the tart taste of California apricots here. Rolled up with the meat filling, they provide a welcome counterpoint to the opulent flavors. If your family refrains from eating nuts on Rosh Hashanah, omit them.

I have gently adapted this from the family recipe originally given to me by Lisa Matalon, an excellent Syrian-American home cook.

FOR THE KIBBE SHELL

¾ pound (about 2 cups) long-grain white rice

1 pound extra-lean ground beef or lean ground lamb

Salt

FOR THE KIBBE FILLING

½ pound ground beef or lamb

2 tablespoons finely chopped celery (include some leaves)

1 tablespoon fruity olive oil

1½ teaspoons salt

MAKE the kibbe shell: soak the rice in several changes of warm water, drain it, and pat it dry with paper towels. Grind the rice in a food processor until it resembles meal. Add the extra-lean beef or lamb and about 1½ teaspoons salt, and puree the mixture, using the pulse motion, until very well combined. (Alternatively, have your butcher grind the meat once, then add the rice and grind again twice.)

MAKE the kibbe filling: in a large bowl, mix the ground meat, celery, oil, salt, allspice, and cinnamon until they are thoroughly blended.

NOW prepare the rolls: divide the rice-and-meat shell mixture into 4 equal parts. Repeat with the filling mixture. Place one portion of the shell mixture between two sheets of plastic wrap, and using a rolling pin (if you keep kosher and do not have a separate rolling pin for meat dishes, a wine or other smooth glass bottle will do in a pinch), roll it out into a rectangle, approximately 5 by 7 inches. Remove the top layer of plastic wrap. Cover the shell with one portion of filling. Pat the fill-

1 teaspoon ground allspice

½ teaspoon ground cinnamon

3 to 4 tablespoons pine nuts, toasted lightly (optional)

About 6 ounces dried apricots (28 to 32), preferably tart, covered with hot water and allowed to plump until soft, drained, and patted dry

2 to 4 tablespoons olive oil

FOR THE CHERRY SAUCE

1 large onion, diced (2 cups)

Salt and freshly ground black pepper

1 cup unsweetened prune juice

One 16-ounce can pitted dark sweet cherries in syrup, drained and liquid reserved

About 3 tablespoons pomegranate molasses [or even better, if you can find it, *ourt* or *temerhindi* (see page 40)]

2 to 3 tablespoons fresh lemon juice

About 1½ teaspoons sugar

Accompaniment: Syrian Pilaf (page 168) or steamed white rice

ing over the shell (or replace plastic wrap and roll it out), leaving a small border along the sides. Sprinkle the pine nuts, if using, over the filling, then follow with a flat layer of 7 or 8 apricots (the apricots should not overlap, or the kibbe will be lumpy when rolled). As you would a jelly roll, carefully roll up the kibbe, widthwise (from the short end), using the plastic wrap to help you roll. Pinch both ends together and gently press around the seam area to make sure the roll is well sealed. Keeping the roll in the plastic wrap, gently pat it smooth. Make three more rolls in the same fashion.

REFRIGERATE the kibbe for at least 15 minutes to firm them up (they will be rather soft after all that handling).

IN a 6-quart Dutch oven or heavy-bottomed deep sauté pan large enough to hold the rolls in a single layer, heat 2 tablespoons oil until hot, but not smoking. Add two of the rolls, seam side down, and fry over medium-high heat until golden. Using two spatulas or a spatula and a wooden spoon, carefully turn the rolls until they are lightly browned and gently crusted on all sides. (Don't allow a hard, dark crust to form.) Transfer them to a platter and repeat with the remaining rolls, transferring them to the platter when they are ready.

MAKE the cherry sauce: if the oil in the pan is very dark, wipe it out and add 2 tablespoons fresh oil. Otherwise, just add the onion to the oil remaining in the pan, salt and pepper lightly, and cook, stirring, over medium-high heat until soft and rich golden, 10 to 12 minutes. Stir in the prune juice, reserved cherry liquid, pomegranate molasses or *ourt*, 2 tablespoons of the lemon juice, the sugar, and salt and pepper to taste.

BRING the sauce to a boil, then lower the heat to a simmer and place all the rolls back in the pan. Spoon the pan sauce over the meat, cover the pan, and cook over low heat, basting occasionally, for 35 minutes. Add the reserved cherries and simmer for 15 minutes longer.

TRANSFER the kibbe to a platter, and if desired, reduce the sauce a bit by boiling it uncovered over high heat for a few minutes. Taste and adjust the seasoning, adding more sugar, pomegranate molasses, or lemon juice until you reach a graceful balance of tart and sweet flavors.

TO serve the kibbe, slice the rolls on the diagonal, so that each slice encloses some of the filling. Nap with the sauce. Accompany with Syrian Pilaf or plain steamed rice.

"Beckoning from the fruit baskets on the wooden stands were meaty plums and honey-sweet yellow apricots—it seemed as if onto those wooden stands and into the woven baskets of the poor women peddlers had rolled countless small suns, a treasure of golden ducats."

—CHAIM GRADE, "LAYBE-LAYZAR'S COURTYARD"

SYRIAN PILAF

To prepare this simple pilaf, Syrian Jews briefly sauté fine dried egg noodles with rice before adding the liquid. Use subtly perfumed basmati rice to heighten the distinctive nutty flavor.

3 tablespoons olive oil

²/₃ cup fine dried egg noodles

1½ cups long-grain rice, preferably basmati (about 9 ounces), rinsed in a colander in several changes of cool water, drained and patted dry

About 1 teaspoon salt

HEAT the oil over moderate heat in a heavy saucepan. Roughly crush the noodles into bite-size pieces with your hands, and add them to the oil. Cook, stirring, until they are lightly browned. Watch carefully so they don't burn. Add the rice, stir the mixture until the rice is coated with the oil, and add 3 cups water and the salt, or to taste. Bring the liquid to a boil, then cover and cook over very low heat for 18 to 20 minutes, until the liquid is absorbed. Turn off the heat. Fold two paper towels or a small kitchen towel and place on top of the rice. Replace the cover, and let the rice sit for at least 5 minutes, or until ready to serve (the rice will remain warm for about 30 minutes). Fluff the rice with a fork before serving.

COOK'S NOTE: When not serving the rice with a sauce or a saucy accompaniment, such as the kibbe or the recipe for black-eyed peas, *Lubia* (page 169), make it more flavorful. In a heavy saucepan, sauté 1 to 2 cups chopped onions in 2 tablespoons oil over moderate heat until deep gold, 10 to 15 minutes. Transfer to a bowl and reserve. Heat 2 more tablespoons oil in the saucepan, add the crushed noodles, and continue with the pilaf recipe, substituting broth for the water. When ready to serve, stir the sautéed onions into the rice and fluff with a fork. Garnish, if desired, with 3 tablespoons pine nuts, lightly sautéed in flavorful olive oil.

EGYPTIAN BLACK-EYED PEAS WITH CILANTRO (*LUBIA*)

yield: 6 TO 8 SERVINGS

lack-eyed peas probably arrived in ancient Judea from China via the Silk Route, and consuming them on Rosh Hashanah is a Middle Eastern tradition dating back to the Talmud.

For Egyptian Jews like Rachel Abboudi, who shared her family recipe with me several years ago, eating black-eyed peas symbolizes their wish for prosperity and good fortune in the coming year. In this easy-to-prepare dish, Mrs. Abboudi spikes the beans (they are related not to peas, but to the mung bean family) with tomatoes, cilantro, and garlic. I like to simmer a little of the cilantro root (or when not available, the stems) along with the beans for a different dimension and more intensified flavor of the fragrant herb.

The long-grain rice here is no afterthought, but integral to the dish: in one of those culinary mysteries, the rice's fluffy, nutty quality is needed to unlock the butteriness of the beans.

Try this too as a fine, meat-free meal, with lavish quantities of cilantro added for a wild-herbal freshness.

2 large garlic cloves, chopped

3 tablespoons olive oil

Two 10-ounce packages frozen black-eyed peas (4 cups) or 1½ cups dried black-eyed peas, picked over, rinsed, and drained (try frozen black-eyed peas, if available; they are usually more flavorful than the dried variety)

One 8-ounce can tomato sauce

2 teaspoons chopped cilantro root (or, if unavailable, chopped cilantro stems) and 3 tablespoons chopped fresh cilantro leaves, plus additional whole leaves for garnish

Salt and freshly ground black pepper

Accompaniment: Syrian Pilaf (page 168) or steamed white rice

IN a large saucepan, cook the garlic in the olive oil over gentle heat until softened and just tinged with gold, 2 to 3 minutes. Add the peas, tomato sauce, chopped cilantro root or stems, and enough fresh cold water to cover the peas by about 1 inch. Bring the mixture to a boil, and simmer, covered, over low heat. If using frozen peas, add salt and pepper to taste after cooking for 10 minutes; if using dried peas, add salt and pepper after 20 minutes. Add more water if necessary to keep the peas quite soupy: there should be enough water to form some sauce. Cook frozen peas for a total of 20 to 30 minutes, dried for 35 to 45 minutes, or until the peas are tender (exact time will depend on the age of the peas). Stir in the chopped cilantro leaves, and serve the *lubia* over the pilaf or rice, garnished with additional cilantro leaves.

NEW WORLD *RODANCHAS* (PHYLLO ROSES ON ROASTED SQUASH–PEAR PUREE)

yield: ABOUT 6 SERVINGS

*F*laky phyllo roses filled with sweet golden squash, rodanchas *are a lovely addition to Greek Rosh Hashanah and Sukkot tables. It's beauty I have admired from afar, though: rodanchas are just too sweet for me, and coaxing delicate phyllo leaves into a clever coil of a flower, too overwhelming.*

But I was intrigued by a simple technique I came across in Bon Appétit *magazine. Sheets of phyllo were scrunched into loose balls, placed atop a chicken casserole, and baked to form a crust. With its ruffly edges, the crumpled phyllo suggested, if not roses, well, avant garde rosettes.*

Instead of bland, boiled butternut squash, I decided on a fusion of roasted autumn flavors, including Bosc pear to lend a natural, caramelized sweetness and to enrich the puree, and a light dust of warm spices to add depth and balance.

An excellent accompaniment to braised and roasted meat and poultry, the result is a snap to prepare. The puree is also wonderful baked without the phyllo rosettes, for an even easier fall side dish.

Sunflower, avocado, or mild olive oil for greasing the pans, plus about 4 tablespoons for brushing phyllo

Salt and freshly ground black pepper

1 medium butternut squash, halved and peeled, seeds and strings discarded

3 Bosc pears, peeled, halved, and cored (see Cook's Note)

½ cup lightly toasted walnuts

About 1 tablespoon brown sugar

PREHEAT the oven to 425°F. Line a rimmed baking sheet with foil and generously grease it.

SALT and pepper the squash and pears, arrange them on the baking sheet, and turn to coat them well on all sides with the oil. Roast the squash and pears, core-side down, until the edges begin to brown and the flesh is very tender. The pears will probably be done after about 30 minutes; the squash may take another 30 minutes or so. Let them cool slightly. Reduce the oven temperature to 350°F.

WHILE the squash and pears are roasting, put the walnuts in a food processor fitted with the steel blade, and pulse until finely chopped. Transfer the walnuts to a large bowl. (Don't bother rinsing out the food processor.)

CUT the squash and the pears into cubes, and combine them in the food processor, along with the brown sugar, cinnamon, cloves, and ginger.

About 1 teaspoon ground cinnamon

About ¼ teaspoon ground cloves

About ¼ teaspoon ground ginger

2 large eggs, lightly beaten

About 8 sheets of phyllo (if frozen, thaw slowly in the refrigerator for 8 hours or overnight; remove the unopened package from the refrigerator about 2 hours before you begin the recipe to allow the sheets to come to room temperature)

Cinnamon sugar (2 teaspoons white or granulated light brown sugar mixed with ¼ teaspoon ground cinnamon)

Process to a smooth puree. Stir the puree into the walnuts. Taste and adjust the seasoning and sugar, if needed. Beat in the eggs.

LIGHTLY grease a 10-inch round baking dish (or a similar pan with 2- to 3-quart capacity), and spoon in the mixture.

PREPARE the rodancha crust: remove the phyllo sheets from the package and carefully unroll them on a damp kitchen towel. Cover the sheets with a large piece of plastic wrap and another damp towel to prevent them from drying out. Place a large sheet of wax paper near your work surface. Remove 1 sheet from the stack (keep the rest covered with the plastic wrap and towel), and brush it lightly but thoroughly with oil. Using both hands, carefully crumple the phyllo so it resembles a loose rosette about 3 inches in diameter. Set the rosette on wax paper. Continue making rosettes with the remaining phyllo and oil.

TOP the squash-pear puree with the rosettes and sprinkle lightly with the cinnamon sugar. Bake about 25 minutes, until the phyllo is golden and the filling is hot.

COOK'S NOTE: Fragrant pears make a difference here. With well-flavored fruit, you will only need a tablespoon of sugar; lackluster pears may require additional sweetening and seasoning.

The bottom of the phyllo rosettes tend to become soggy after resting on top of the moist filling for a long time, so these rodanchas may not taste as good reheated. To keep the rosettes crispy, do not place them on the filling until you are ready to put the dish in the oven.

You can store leftover phyllo sheets in the refrigerator, wrapped airtight, for about 5 days. Do not refreeze them.

SWEET CARROTS WITH FENNEL SALT

yield: 4 TO 6 SERVINGS

It's not just their golden orange color or sugary flesh that made carrots a tradition on Ashkenazi Rosh Hashanah menus: there's also the deep-rooted pun. "Carrots" in Yiddish is mehren; *the same word,* mehren, *in Yiddish also means "to increase." By eating carrots, we will increase in numbers as a people; our mitzvot, or good deeds, will increase; and since sliced carrots resemble gold coins, our wealth will increase, too—great expectations from a rather humble vegetable.*

Absent a sweet tooth, I quickly tire of New Year's foods sprinkled with sugar or drizzled with honey—and that's before we even get to dessert. So I bring out the carrot's natural sweetness by simmering it in reduced fresh carrot juice until even pallid-tasting specimens glow with intense carroty flavor. Then I finish with a dribble of fine oil and dust of homemade spiced salt to play against the sweetness.

FOR THE SALT

1 tablespoon fennel seeds (or substitute cumin seeds, if you prefer)

2 teaspoons coarse salt

FOR THE CARROTS

2 cups fresh carrot juice (purchased or homemade; do not use canned juice)

1 tablespoon fresh lemon juice

Salt

Pinch of ground cloves

1½ pounds carrots, preferably organic, scraped and sliced on the diagonal into medium chunks (4 cups)

Fine-quality oil, for drizzling (choose an excellent light but flavorful nut oil such as hazelnut or pistachio, or extra virgin olive oil)

MAKE the salt: spread out the fennel in a very small heavy skillet, and cook over medium heat, shaking the pan or stirring often, until very fragrant. Watch carefully to avoid burning. Or toast in a small baking dish in a 350°F oven. Combine fennel and salt in a spice grinder and grind to a fine powder. Set aside.

COMBINE the carrot juice, lemon juice, ¼ teaspoon salt, and the cloves in a wide, heavy saucepan. Bring to a boil over medium-high heat and cook until reduced to about half. Don't worry if the sauce separates: just whisk it a bit until smooth again.

ADD the carrots, cover the pot, and simmer slowly until just tender. Uncover and boil until the carrots are very tender and the liquid is reduced to a few tablespoons. Turn into a serving bowl, drizzle with a little of the oil and sprinkle with spice salt to taste. (Reserve remaining salt for another use—it's especially good on fish and lamb chops; store in an airtight container.)

ROASTED OKRA WITH ZA'ATAR

yield: ABOUT 6 SERVINGS

Slender, elegantly formed okra pods in green and deep burgundy arrive in droves at my greenmarket around August. Nicknamed "ladies' fingers"—though with their pointy tips, they are more like fingernails of some Amazonian Cruella De Vil—the quick-growing vegetable is well-loved by Middle Eastern Jews, who often serve it for the fall holidays, generally stewed slowly with meat or other vegetables and flavored with tomato. But I confess that with all the bad press about its potentially mucilaginous, seedy innards and slimy texture, okra intimidated me. I never prepared it myself.

Then when I was in Los Angeles one fall, I listened to a radio program broadcast from the fabulous Santa Monica farmers' market, featuring the pick of the day's produce. The speaker mentioned that okra is wonderful simply and quickly oven-roasted—my usual method for preparing asparagus.

Back home for Rosh Hashanah, I oven-roasted my local beauties, then dusted them with fragrant Middle Eastern za'atar. They are so easy to prepare this way. I enjoy them often now, whenever I find young and fresh ones in the market.

1½ pounds crisp, fresh, young okra pods, rinsed, stems and tips of caps trimmed without cutting into the pods

2 tablespoons extra virgin olive oil

Salt and freshly ground black pepper

Za'atar

Accompaniment: lemon quarters

PREHEAT the oven to 475°F.

ARRANGE the okra in a single layer on a large, rimmed baking sheet. Drizzle with the oil and sprinkle with salt and pepper. Shake the pan until the okra is coated with the oil on all sides. Roast, shaking the pan once or twice to turn the pods, for 12 to 15 minutes, depending on the size of the pods, until the okra is streaked golden-brown and just tender. Sprinkle generously with za'atar to taste, and serve with lemon quarters.

HUNGARIAN PLUM TART

yield: 6 TO 8 SERVINGS

*J*ews save a special fruit for the Rosh Hashanah Sheheheyonu: a blessing made over fruit savored for the first time that season. For many, the taste of Rosh Hashanah is the midnight blue prune plum that begins arriving in markets at the tail end of the summer. Carole Goldberg's mother brought the recipe for this simple but sublimely fresh prune plum tart from her native Transylvania, where her family prepared it to greet the holiday at the beginning of the last century.

Explosive with deep ripe fruit flavor and a dusting of cinnamon, it is more a cross between cobbler and crunch than a traditional tart. I have modified the original recipe slightly. Carole uses pareve margarine so she can serve the tart at a meat meal; I prefer it with the clean, sweet taste of pure butter, perfect as a tea-time treat for company with a generous dollop of ice cream. Either way, it is delicious and simple to prepare.

20 to 24 fresh prune plums, pitted and quartered, or 6 to 8 pitted black plums, cut into sixths or eighths (depending on size of plums)

¼ cup firmly packed dark brown sugar

3 tablespoons plus 1 cup unbleached all-purpose flour

1 teaspoon ground cinnamon

About 1 cup granulated sugar

1 teaspoon baking powder

¼ teaspoon salt (omit if using margarine)

1 large egg, beaten

½ teaspoon almond extract

PREHEAT the oven to 350°F.

IN a greased 13 by 9-inch baking dish, arrange the plums cut-side up in a single layer. Stir together the brown sugar, 3 tablespoons of flour, and the cinnamon in a small bowl, and sprinkle the mixture over the plums. In a large bowl, using a fork, blend together the granulated sugar (use up to 2 tablespoons less than 1 cup if you prefer, as I do, a less sweet dessert or if the plums are particularly sweet), the remaining 1 cup flour, baking powder, salt, egg, and almond extract until the mixture resembles coarse meal. Crumble it over the plums. Drizzle the melted butter or margarine over all and bake the tart in the middle of the oven for 35 to 45 minutes until the plums are tender and the topping is golden.

8 tablespoons (1 stick) unsalted butter or pareve margarine, melted, plus additional for greasing the pan

Optional accompaniment: vanilla or coffee ice cream or freshly whipped heavy cream

SERVE the tart at room temperature, accompanied by ice cream or whipped cream, if desired. It is also wonderful warm from the oven, especially with the cool contrast of the ice cream.

"In the course of the two days of Rosh Hashanah, she also eats a plum and a pear—fruits she has not tasted earlier in the season. As a child, I always marveled: where did she find the strength and patience to keep herself all summer long from sampling the fresh fruits in her own baskets, so as to be able to recite the Sheheheyonu over them on the New Year."

—CHAIM GRADE, *My Mother's Sabbath Days*

BOMBAY PINEAPPLE–COCONUT MILK KUGEL

yield: ABOUT 8 SERVINGS

*L*eaving their shoes at the portals, the Bene Israel—Indian Jews, now mostly dispersed to Britain, Canada, America, and largely to Israel—entered barefoot into beautiful synagogues illumined and perfumed by coconut oil burning in the hanging lamps.

Coconuts also provided the milk used extensively in their kosher cuisine. As a pareve substitute for dairy milk, it could be cooked with meat and employed in desserts served at meat meals without contravening the dietary injunction that prohibits mixing meat with dairy.

Inspired by armchair visits to Bombay and beguiling exhibits at local museums, I devised this pareve pudding before I met anyone from the community and fell in love with the cuisine.

It is a playful culinary pun on traditional Ashkenazi noodle kugels: coconut milk replaces the dairy variety; orzo, a pasta in rice clothing, becomes the noodles; and the pineapple and spices provide the evocative scent of the tropics.

Soft, creamy custard on the tongue, it tastes sweetly spicy and fruity, and makes a lush, elegant finish to the lavish Rosh Hashanah dinner.

One 20-ounce can pineapple rings in natural, unsweetened juice

3 tablespoons maple sugar or brown sugar

Mild oil such as avocado, canola, or almond, for greasing the pan

Salt

½ cup orzo

2 cups unsweetened coconut milk

1 cinnamon stick

½ teaspoon peeled and finely chopped fresh ginger

1 vanilla bean, split

3 large eggs

½ cup granulated sugar

PREHEAT the broiler. Drain the pineapple (use the juice for another purpose or discard it), and arrange in a single layer on a foil-lined broiler pan. Sprinkle evenly with the maple or brown sugar. Broil the pineapple on one side only until it is a rich, golden brown and the sugar has melted, 5 to 8 minutes.

LIGHTLY grease the bottom and sides of an 8-inch square baking dish with the oil. Spread the pineapple pieces (with any sugar drippings), sugared side down, in a single layer on the bottom of the pan. (If there is an extra ring or two, cut it in quarters and use it to fill in the spaces between the rings.) Set aside. Turn the oven temperature down to 350°F.

BRING 2 quarts water and 1 teaspoon of salt to a rapid boil. Add the orzo and cook, stirring occasionally, until tender. Drain well, rinse a few seconds under cool water, and drain again.

WHILE the orzo is cooking, combine the coconut milk, cinnamon, and ginger in a medium saucepan. Scrape the seeds from the vanilla bean and add along with the pod to the pan. Turn the heat to low and simmer gently for 10 to 15 minutes to infuse the milk with the fragrance of the spices. Don't allow the mixture to boil. Remove from the heat and let cool slightly.

IN a large bowl beat the eggs, granulated sugar, and a pinch of salt until thick and light. Add the coconut milk mixture, pouring it through a strainer into the bowl. Discard the spices. Add the orzo and combine well.

DISTRIBUTE the mixture evenly over the pineapple in the prepared pan. Place the pan in a larger baking pan, and add enough boiling or scalding-hot tap water to the larger pan to come halfway up the sides of the kugel pan.

BAKE for 60 to 75 minutes, or until a knife inserted in the center comes out clean. The kugel must cool to set. You can serve it right from the pan, or invert it when cool: run a knife along the edges of the pan, turn the pan upside down on a serving plate, and unmold.

SERVE the kugel chilled, but not icy cold. Or for a more exotic finale, try it slightly warm (reheat gently).

BENE ISRAEL RICE PUDDING (*KHEER*)

yield: 6 TO 8 SERVINGS

For the Bene Israel, preparing for the fall holidays in India meant cooking massive amounts of luscious sweets. Two treats—halwa (a soft confection, different from the familiar Middle Eastern sesame seed variety) for Rosh Hashanah and sweet, filled pastries to break the Yom Kippur fast—were exchanged with relatives and friends, a custom reminiscent of mishlo'ah manot, the sending of portions on Purim. Because the Bene Israel, unlike other Jews in the Diaspora, never encountered any anti-Semitism in their homeland, their friends always included Hindus and Muslims, who returned the favor, sending back treats of their own at Diwali and Ramadan.

And rice pudding—the recipe borrowed from their non-Jewish neighbors—was the highlight of a special Bene Israel harvest festival held on the third day of the new year. In fact, the holiday was known in Marathi as Khiriacha San, Holiday of Kheer. The pudding was usually made with coconut milk, so it could be enjoyed at a meat meal, but today many Bene Israel like to prepare it with dairy milk for a Rosh Hashanah tea-time treat. Florence Manglani, who grew up in Bombay and now lives in Brooklyn, is a gifted cook; her easy version is the best kheer I have ever tasted.

½ cup long-grain rice (preferably basmati)

5¾ cups whole milk

¾ cup sugar

Salt

Seeds of 2 green cardamom pods, crushed

¼ cup powdered milk

1 tablespoon rosewater

1 to 2 tablespoons coarsely chopped blanched almonds

1 to 2 tablespoons coarsely chopped unsalted pistachios

¼ cup golden seedless raisins

BRING 3 cups water to a boil in a heavy, medium saucepan. Add the rice and simmer until soft, 20 minutes. Drain and set aside.

RINSE out the pan, and in it, bring the whole milk, sugar, and a pinch of salt to a boil. Reduce the heat to moderate, and add the rice and cardamom. Cook uncovered, stirring occasionally, for 30 minutes. Continue cooking, stirring more frequently as the mixture thickens, for about 15 minutes, or until the pudding is thick enough to coat a spoon heavily. Slowly add the powdered milk, whisking well until it is completely dissolved. Stir in the rosewater, almonds, pistachios, and raisins, and remove the pan from the heat.

LET cool and serve at room temperature or chilled.

AUNT MARY'S HONEY CAKE

yield: ABOUT 10 SERVINGS

"A little schnapps" to my grandmother and great-aunt Mary meant a tiny crystal cordial glass filled with Cherry Heering. And that is the secret ingredient in Aunt Mary's honey cake recipe, passed on to me by her daughter-in-law, my cousin Judy Robinson, who now bakes a cake every year for each of her three married sons. Made of wild black cherries, the old-fashioned Danish liqueur is lightly scented with bitter almond notes derived from the cherry pits and imparts wonderful flavor to the moist cake.

For a light, more delicate honey cake, look for a floral, paler honey, such as acacia, tupelo, or lime flower, perhaps the same one you choose for your apples and challah—a metaphor for beginning and ending the year with the same sweetness. If you prefer a more traditional, robustly flavored cake, choose a darker honey, like buckwheat, and use strong coffee.

Easy to prepare, the cake can be made several days ahead; wrap well in plastic. It also freezes nicely.

3½ cups unbleached all-purpose flour

2 teaspoons baking powder

1 teaspoon baking soda

⅛ teaspoon salt

3 large eggs

1¼ cups sugar

1¼ cups canola or avocado oil, plus additional oil for greasing the pan

⅔ cup honey (8 ounces), light or dark, according to preference (see Cook's Note)

½ cup brewed coffee, cooled to room temperature

½ cup Cherry Heering

½ cup fresh orange juice

PREHEAT the oven to 325°F. Lightly grease a 13 by 9-inch glass baking dish and line it with parchment paper. (The oil will help anchor the paper in the large pan.)

WHISK together the flour, baking powder, baking soda, and salt in a medium bowl. Beat the eggs with an electric mixer in a large bowl until well-blended. Add the sugar gradually, and continue beating until thick and pale. Beat in the oil, honey, coffee, Cherry Heering, and orange juice on low speed.

GRADUALLY add the flour mixture, beating on low speed until just combined; don't overmix. Use a rubber spatula to scrape the bottom and sides of the bowl and gently fold in the nuts and raisins, if using.

TURN the batter into the prepared pan. Bake for 45 to 55 minutes, or until the cake springs back when lightly pressed and a toothpick inserted in the center comes out clean.

TRANSFER the cake to a rack to cool to room temperature. Slip a thin-bladed knife around the cake to loosen the edges, then invert the cake onto a platter. Carefully peel off the parchment paper.

SERVE with good, strong coffee (see Cook's Note) or tea.

½ to 1 cup chopped, lightly toasted nuts (walnuts, pecans, or almonds)

½ cup dark raisins (optional)

COOK'S NOTE: Before measuring the honey, measure the oil, using a glass measuring cup. Then, without rinsing the cup, measure the honey. Every bit of the honey will slide out easily.

My friend Erika Jakubovits, the elegant executive director of the Presidency of the Jewish Community of Vienna and an accomplished cook, makes an impressive cup of coffee. Her secret? In addition to using an excellent Viennese blend, Erika adds a generous pinch of salt to her freshly ground beans before brewing. Salt—integral to savories as well as to sweets—masks any bitter notes and enhances full-bodied coffee flavors. You can also add a pinch of cinnamon to the beans, as Erika does, or serve cinnamon sticks as stirrers.

PEACH BUTTERMILK KUGEL

yields: ABOUT 10 SERVINGS

With their gilded blush and sweet perfume, showy peaches dazzled the Talmudists. For decorating a sukkah, they deemed the fruit was fit to hang beside treasures like "hand-made carpets and tapestries . . . nuts, almonds . . . pomegranates and bunches of grapes, vines, oils, and fine meal." (Babylonian Talmud: Bezah 30b)

Peaches—juicy, fresh fruit in the topping and tangy dried ones dispersed throughout—bring unexpected luxury to this sleek buttermilk custard noodle pudding. A slightly more indulgent variation—creamier and sweeter—follows, as do apple and pear versions. Any would be enticing on a Rosh Hashanah afternoon. Or enjoy the kugel for breakfast, brunch, dessert, even a simple entree in a summer/fall dairy dinner.

Salt

8 ounces medium or wide flat egg noodles (not the twisted spiral kind, which won't absorb as much of the liquids and flavoring)

4 tablespoons (½ stick) unsalted butter, cut into pieces, plus additional butter or oil for greasing the pan

4 large eggs

⅓ to ½ cup pure maple syrup (use the larger amount for a dessert kugel; you may prefer to use the smaller amount if you plan to serve the kugel for breakfast or as a meal)

1 teaspoon vanilla extract

3 cups well-shaken buttermilk

6 to 7 ounces dried peaches, snipped with kitchen scissors into small pieces (1 cup)

BRING 3 quarts cold water and 1 teaspoon salt to a rapid boil in a large saucepan. Add the noodles and cook until just tender. Drain well, toss with butter, and set aside to cool. Grease a 13 by 9-inch baking dish.

IN a large bowl, beat together the eggs, maple syrup, vanilla, and a pinch of salt. Add the buttermilk and continue beating until the ingredients are smooth and thoroughly incorporated. Stir the dried peaches into the noodles (or use your fingers to toss them together and break up any clumps of dried fruit) and turn into the prepared baking dish. Pour the buttermilk mixture evenly over the noodles. Cover the pan with foil and refrigerate for at least 4 hours or, better still, overnight.

PREHEAT the oven to 325°F. Uncover and bake the pudding for 50 minutes. Meanwhile, prepare the topping: cut each peach into about 8 wedges and, if desired, toss with the almond extract, amaretto, or cassis. In a small bowl, crumble together the brown sugar, flour, butter, cinnamon, and salt with your fingers until the mixture resembles coarse meal. After the kugel has baked for 50 minutes, remove it from the oven, and arrange the peaches decoratively on top (if the peaches have thrown off a lot of liquid, drain them first). Strew the crumble mixture over the fruit and return the pan to the oven for an additional 40 to 50 minutes, until the fruit is bubbling and the kugel is golden, just pulling away from the edges of the pan, and slightly firm. (If the fruit

5 or 6 medium, ripe peaches (3 to 4 cups when cut into wedges), peeled only if the peel is thick or bitter

1 teaspoon almond extract or 2 tablespoons amaretto or cassis (optional)

About ¼ cup granulated brown sugar or packed regular brown sugar, depending on sweetness of fruit and personal preference

¼ cup unbleached all-purpose flour

2 tablespoons unsalted butter, cut into bits

¼ teaspoon ground cinnamon

⅛ teaspoon salt

you are using is somewhat firm and not particularly juicy, it will not, of course, bubble, so check that it is meltingly tender and completely cooked through.)

LET the kugel cool for at least 30 minutes until set before cutting. Serve warm (reheat if necessary), at room temperature or slightly chilled, not icy cold.

Kugel Variations

For a lighter kugel, you can omit the crumble mixture from the topping, but make sure the peaches are well drained. After arranging the peaches over the kugel, just sprinkle them with brown sugar to taste.

For a creamier, less custardy pudding, use 3 eggs and 2 cups buttermilk, and add 4 ounces of softened cream cheese. Beat the cream cheese with the eggs first, then add the maple syrup (use only ⅓ cup—you're using less of the tangy buttermilk, and the cream cheese is somewhat sweet-tasting), vanilla, salt, and buttermilk. Make sure to beat all the ingredients well, until thoroughly blended.

Later in the fall, replace the peaches with an equal amount of juicy apples with lots of character: Cortland, Grimes Golden, Ida Red, Northern Spy, Winesap. Select a mixture of three different kinds for more depth of flavor. Juicy Bartlett or Bosc pears would also be delicious. Peel and cube the fruit. Instead of the dried peaches in the filling, substitute ½ cup raisins and ½ cup stemmed dried figs, cut into small pieces (or substitute 1 cup of either). I use my hands to toss the dried fruit with the noodles: it's easier that way to break up any clumps the figs might form. Reduce the syrup to ⅓ cup (this dried fruit is sweeter). For the topping, change the flavorings to lend a whiff of the Middle East. Melt 3 tablespoons unsalted butter in a 10- to 12-inch heavy skillet. Stir in 4 to 6 table-spoons of honey or 5 to 6 packed tablespoons light or dark brown sugar (according to sweetness of fruit and personal preference), ¼ teaspoon ground cardamom, ¼ teaspoon ground cinnamon, 1 teaspoon peeled and grated fresh ginger (optional), ⅛ teaspoon salt, and 1 tablespoon fresh lemon juice. Or omit the cardamom and ginger and replace with ½ teaspoon vanilla extract and ⅛ teaspoon nutmeg, preferably freshly grated, or ground cloves. Cook for 3 minutes. Add the apples (or pears), stir well to coat them with the pan syrup, and cook, stirring for 4 minutes to meld the flavors.

Denser than peaches, the apples (or pears) will take longer to cook, so arrange the fruit decoratively over the kugel in the beginning, when first placing the kugel in the oven. Bake the kugel for 1½ to 1¾ hours, until the fruit is tender and the kugel is golden, just pulls away from the pan's edges, and feels slightly firm.

Follow the cutting and serving directions on the previous page.

SEPHARDI DRIED FRUIT AND NUT COMPOTE (*KOSHAF*)

yield: ABOUT 6 SERVINGS

I am a big fan of humble compotes made with fresh fruit or dried, especially to conclude a rich meal. Preparing this Sephardi koshaf, *a favorite of mine, is incredibly easy: just pour cold liquid over the dried fruit and let it macerate until tender. Instead of the traditional plain water or a simple syrup, I use white grape juice—a nice complement to the raisins and currants— for a light sweetening without added sugar. The flavors slowly unfold while the fruit softens and plumps up dramatically more than if it were stewed. Nuts, a welcome contrast to the sweet fruit, are softened first with boiling water to provide mellowed texture without jarring crunch.*

For the holidays, set off the koshaf *with a crown of jewel-toned pomegranate seeds.*

1 cup tart dried apricots (if only sweet ones are available, add 2 teaspoons fresh lemon juice to grape juice, or substitute an equal amount of prunes, dried peaches, nectarines, or a mixture of these fruits)

½ cup golden raisins

½ cup dried cherries or cranberries

¼ cup dried currants

2 cups unsweetened white grape juice

¼ cup shelled unsalted pistachios

¼ cup blanched almonds, halved

⅓ cup pine nuts

Optional garnish: pomegranate seeds

PUT the dried fruit in a large bowl. Pour the grape juice over the fruit, cover with foil, and set aside to macerate, unrefrigerated, for at least 4 hours, preferably overnight.

PUT the nuts in a heatproof bowl, cover with boiling water, and let them soak for about 45 minutes. Drain. Using your fingers, rub off the pistachio skins: you'll find they come off quite easily. Add the pistachios, almonds, and pine nuts to the macerating fruit at least 30 minutes before you are ready to serve the koshaf.

I prefer the compote well chilled, but many people enjoy it at room temperature. Offer the compote in a pretty glass serving bowl or in individual dessert bowls or martini glasses. For a striking presentation, garnish with ruby pomegranate seeds.

COOK'S NOTE: This is often flavored with a little orange flower or rose water, but be sure you know your audience before you add a few drops of either.

For dairy meals, serve with clouds of whipped cream, crème fraîche, or vanilla ice cream. Leftover koshaf mixed with plain yogurt makes a delicious breakfast.

OTHER SUGGESTIONS FOR ROSH HASHANAH

Either of the *Chopped Chicken Liver recipes

Any of the *Gefilte Fish recipes

*Classic Chicken Soup with *Fried Onion and Chicken Kreplach

*Pumpkin and Sweet Potato Soup with Sweet Potato Knaidlach (Matzoh Balls)

*Moroccan Fish with Chickpeas and Saffron-Lime Aioli

*Roast Turkey with Challah Stuffing, Roasted Grape and Chestnut Gravy

*Coffee-Spiced Pot Roast with Kasha Kreplach and Toasted Garlic Challah Crumbs

*Meat Tsimmes with Prunes and Carrots

Any of the *Brisket recipes

*Moroccan-Flavored Carrot Kugel

*Rhubarb-Prune Tsimmes

*Caramelized Onion and Carrot Tsimmes with Candied Ginger

*Jeweled Brown Rice

*Maple-Roasted Pears with Passion Fruit or Fresh Raspberry Sauce

*Jewish Sautéed Apple Cake

*Italian Carrot-Pecan Torta

Any of the *Sweet Noodle Kugels with autumn fruits

*Prune-Plum Custard Challah Bread Pudding

*Poppy Seed Butter Cake (Mohn Cake)

*See index for page numbers

Breaking the Yom Kippur Fast

THE FAST BEGINS BEFORE
SUNDOWN ON 10 TISHRI
(SEPTEMBER OR OCTOBER)
AND LASTS UNTIL THE
FIRST STARS APPEAR THE
FOLLOWING NIGHT

hen the first stars twinkle in the autumn sky, the piercing blast of the shofar, the ram's horn trumpet ancient as Israel, is sounded at last. Spiritually refreshed now and confident of God's compassionate judgment, Jews will break the long fast in the company of family or perhaps surrounded by friends at a potluck get-together.

On Yom Kippur, the holiest day of the calendar, Jews refrain from all food and drink, including water, denying our purely physical, animal needs to approach a resemblance to angels.

"Then my father came back to life, and in the evening he broke his fast after the Ne'ilah service."

—YEHUDA AMICHAI,
"THE TIMES MY FATHER DIED"

It is no coincidence that this solemn day occurs in the midst of the autumn bounty, just before the most exuberant of the harvest festivals, Sukkot, the Jewish Thanksgiving. In Temple times, Yom Kippur was the day the priests purified the Temple and expiated the sins of all the Israelites in anticipation of the Sukkot festivities. As Philo, the Greek Jewish historian

186

(c. 20 BCE to AD 50), explained: before Jews enjoy God's generosity when eating a meal, they always pause to utter a blessing. So on Yom Kippur, as they are about to partake of the lavish harvest they will consume in the coming year, they must stop eating entirely, to offer not just a single benediction but an entire day devoted to prayer.

The fast cleanses not only the body but the soul as well. It is not merely an act of contrition, an affirmation of sincerity; it focuses our concentration on the spiritual. And by experiencing hunger, we know suffering and are moved to genuine compassion for others. Fasting helps establish control over ourselves so that we can do better next time. The cathartic cleansing sends us back into the world with renewed vigor, refreshed with an appetite for life and the optimism that we can and will improve.

This is a time of intense self-examination, settling accounts (both financial and spiritual), and making amends. In the synagogue, we confess and ask forgiveness for sins committed against God. But equally important is seeking pardon from our fellow human beings: we must make peace with enemies and personally ask for forgiveness from friends and loved ones whom we have wronged, even unwittingly, throughout the year.

The *Haftarah* portion from Isaiah, the synagogue reading, emphasizes that fulfilling the rituals and spending the day at synagogue services is not enough. We do not find favor in God's eyes just because we have fasted: we show love for God not by starving our bodies, but by feeding the hungry; not by wearing sackcloth, but by clothing the naked. Even if the traditional rituals do not resonate with all of us, Isaiah's calls to action do.

As the fast draws to a close, excitement builds with the cathartic release that comes from starting over. At my parents' house, it was as if we had each returned from a different, faraway place, or that, for the past twenty-seven hours, we had been forbidden to use our mouths to speak as well as to eat. The solemnity of the holiday gave way before the mounting crescendo of our voices. The meal served was dairy, because it was thought to be gentle for our tender tummies, but it was anything but. The wild cacophony of our chatter was matched at the table by the loud tastes of salt and sweet—smoked and pickled fish and rich, sweet noodle puddings—to restock the bodily supplies lost during the fast.

According to tradition, the Book of Life, where our fate is inscribed on Rosh Hashanah, is closed on Yom Kippur. My neighbor Phyllis Ardman knew that her name had not been inscribed there for the coming year: the doctors had already told her that the chemotherapy had not stemmed the pancreatic cancer that was ravaging her body. But the last gathering she wanted to make—before she would become too ill to entertain—was a break-the-fast celebration at her Greenwich Village apartment. In addition to her family and friends, she invited her closest neighbors.

Like so many people I've cherished, whom I've watched go through endstage cancer, Phyllis could barely eat. But comfortably ensconced on one of the couches, dressed in her trademark exotic clothes, her long red hair flowing around her shoulders, she urged everyone to fill their plates and made introductions.

For while all of us knew Phyllis well, most of us didn't know each other, though we had nodded hello in the halls and elevators for years. Suddenly, we were all talking together, excitedly exchanging life stories.

Phyllis had not intended her guest list to be Jewish, but this being Manhattan, as it turned out everyone who wasn't Jewish had a Jewish connection: a spouse or parent, a loved one who was. And though only some of us had fasted, the delicious festive meal—catered smoked fish and salads from Russ and Daughters on the Lower East Side and home-baked desserts—tasted sacred to us all.

Phyllis was a therapist and a healer. Her break-the-fast celebration took place a few years after the events of September 11, 2001, and she knew that standing together in community, we could begin to repair a broken world. For her, that was the meaning of the Yom Kippur injunction from Deuteronomy "to choose life."

Before Phyllis died, our break-the-fasts were always intimate family meals, where we slowly came back to life. Now we end the long day with a full-scale open-house celebration.

We begin with something fresh and fruity to cleanse the palate and rev the blood sugar: winy pomegranate swizzled with orange juice or a simple instant apple ice from Iran. Following the American tradition of zesty and sweet flavors, there are a smoked whitefish salad crunchy with fennel and home-cured salmon spiced like pastrami, mellowed perhaps by a fragrant almond challah and luscious autumn blintzes. For dessert, we serve a caramelized pear noodle kugel scented with two gingers, or rich challah bread pudding—or both. And never forget a huge pot of good, strong coffee to assuage those caffeine-withdrawal headaches.

MENU SUGGESTIONS FOR BREAKING THE YOM KIPPUR FAST

*Pomegranate-Orange Sunsets

*Almond Challah, fresh bialys and bagels

*Smoked Whitefish and Fennel Salad

*Pastrami-Style Salmon or *Bernie's Lox, Eggs, and Onions

Cream cheese and assorted other cheeses

Platter of rainbow tomato slices: red, yellow, and orange

Raw, crisp red pepper rings and black olives

*Double Ginger–Caramelized Pear Noodle Kugel

or

*Prune-Plum Custard Challah Bread Pudding

or

*Turkish Silken Ground-Rice Pudding (*Sutlaj*) with *Fresh Raspberry Sauce

*Classic Walnut-Raisin Rugelach

*Iranian Rose-Apple Ice (*Poludeh*) or *Chilled Minted Cucumber Soup, served in demitasse cups

*Honeyed Quince-Apple Blintzes with Sour Cream–Date Sauce or *Roasted Pear Blintzes or *Apricot Blintzes with Toasted Pistachios and Yogurt Cream or *Apple-Cranberry Blintzes with Maple Ricotta Cream and Sugared Walnuts

*Poppy Seed Butter Cake or *Bene Israel Rice Pudding

*See index for page numbers

*Sorrel-Onion Noodle Kugel or *Spinach Cheese Squares
or *Zucchini Fritada

Salad of sliced baked beets, Boston lettuce, and fresh
chopped dill with walnut oil vinaigrette

*Old Country Cottage Cheese Cake or *Milky Way
Dreamy Cheesecake

*See index for page numbers

IRANIAN ROSE-APPLE ICE (*POLUDEH*)

yield: 6 SERVINGS

"Refresh me with apples," Solomon wrote in the "Song of Songs." Iranian Jews, too, recognize the revivifying talents of the universal fruit: they cleanse palates murky from the long fast with a light, very simple apple ice.

The added rose water provides more than mere refreshment: in some Middle Eastern temples, the shammash (sexton of the synagogue) sprinkled drops of fragrant rose water onto the congregants' hands to lift their spirits during Yom Kippur services.

Cool, clean, and delicately perfumed, Malke Anavian's Iranian family recipe makes a suave prelude to the salty, rich fish dishes at the break-the-fast table.

3 medium sweet, fragrant apples (about 1½ pounds) such as Braeburn, Gala, Jonagold, or York

5 to 6 tablespoons sugar

1 cup water (quality is important here, so if you use bottled water for coffee or tea, use it here)

1 tablespoon rose water

Finely crushed ice

PEEL the apples and grate them using the large holes of a grater or in a food processor. Transfer the apples to a bowl. Sprinkle with sugar to taste and let stand for about 30 minutes. Stir in the water and the rose water.

ARRANGE a scoop of crushed ice in each of six stemmed glasses or shallow glass bowls. Top each with a portion of the apple mixture.

COOK'S NOTE: For an especially festive presentation, serve the poludeh in hollowed out large lemon halves, garnished with unsprayed edible rose petals. And you can substitute apple juice for the water; reduce the sugar to taste.

POMEGRANATE-ORANGE SUNSETS

ephardim break the fast with several refreshing beverages: sweet "milks" made from almonds or pumpkin seeds, juices of pomegranates, apricots, watermelon, or apples. American Ashkenazi Jews traditionally drink fresh orange juice, befitting a meal at which they typically serve breakfast foods. This gorgeous juice—a mixture of pomegranate and orange—combines the best of both cultures.

Pour your guests these break-the-fast beverages in fine, clear crystal to capture the swirl of colors. Serve regular sunsets in tall tumblers or water goblets; offer frozen sunsets in stemmed cocktail glasses like frozen margaritas.

Chilled orange juice, preferably pulp-free, about 4 ounces for each serving

Ice cubes

Fresh or bottled pomegranate juice (see Cook's Note), 3 to 4 ounces for each serving

Mint leaves and/or thin slices of fresh orange, for garnish

FOR regular sunsets: pour the orange juice into tall glass tumblers or large water goblets filled with ice cubes. Gently pour in pomegranate juice to taste (I usually combine approximately half and half proportions, but exact amounts will depend on the sweetness of the juices as well as personal preference). Colors should be marbled like a vibrant sunset; if necessary, lightly mix by swirling pomegranate juice through orange juice with a cocktail stirrer or chopstick. Garnish each glass with a mint leaf and/or orange slice. Serve right away.

FOR frozen sunsets: fill an ice cube tray with pomegranate juice and freeze until completely solid. Put about 8 frozen pomegranate cubes in a blender. Add 1 cup orange juice and process until smooth. Divide between two large stemmed glasses, serve with a straw, and garnish with mint leaves and a slice of fresh orange. Serve straightaway. (If the liquid begins to separate from the frozen froth, just stir it up with a cocktail stirrer.)

COOK'S NOTE: To make fresh pomegranate juice, score just the rind of a pomegranate, as you would an orange, in quarters lengthwise. Then peel off the rind in sections carefully—it stains seriously! Scoop out the seeds and juice sacs surrounding them, breaking apart and discarding all the bitter white pith around them. Or break them apart under water (page 161). Put the seeds and the juice sacs through a food mill, or whirl in a blender—not a food processor, which would crush the seeds—for 30 seconds, and then strain. Or rub seeds and sacs against a strainer or colander. You can also put them through an electric juicer.

Just be sure to remove all of the acrid, mouth-puckering white pith. When I was pregnant with my daughter, the only thing that would settle my stomach was the terrific pomegranate punch served at Brownie's, an old vegetarian restaurant near me (now the site of the Union Square Cafe). One day, my insides in dire turmoil, I attempted to re-create the drink, throwing the entire peeled fruit, pith and all, in my juicer. I could have dyed a rug with it, but I couldn't drink it.

Three medium pomegranates will yield approximately 1 to 1½ cups juice. Fresh juice will keep for about 1 week in the refrigerator, 3 months in the freezer.

Pure, bottled juice is available in many supermarkets, specialty and health food stores, and Middle Eastern shops. Don't use pomegranate molasses for this recipe.

"Make haste, give me a cup,

Before the dawn starts to rise,

Of spiced pomegranate juice

From the perfumed hand of a girl"

—SAMUEL HA-NAGID (993–1056), "AN INVITATION"

(TRANSLATED BY DAVID GOLDSTEIN)

ALMOND CHALLAH

yield: 1 LARGE OR 1 MEDIUM CHALLAH

*T*his fragrant challah, a gift from artist and playwright Linda Rathkopf, is extra-sumptuous with sweet ground almonds, which stand in for some of the flour. A delectable accompaniment to dairy meals, it is easily made in a food processor. If you have a large capacity machine (11 cups), make the full-size loaf, a stunning bread of truly impressive proportions. The equally delicious three-quarter loaf can be prepared in the smaller 7-cup food processor. Or fashion either batter into two loaves.

I give instructions for both sizes here.

FOR THE WHOLE LOAF (1 LARGE CHALLAH)

½ cup blanched almonds (about 2¾ ounces)

½ cup sugar

2 teaspoons salt

1 cup whole milk, warmed to 100 to 110°F, plus a few additional drops as needed

2 envelopes (¼ ounce each) active dry yeast

4 large egg yolks

5 cups bread flour

16 tablespoons (2 sticks) unsalted butter, melted

FOR THE THREE-QUARTER LOAF (1 MEDIUM CHALLAH)

Scant ½ cup blanched almonds (about 2½ ounces)

6 tablespoons sugar

1½ teaspoons salt

¾ cup whole milk, warmed to 100 to 110°F, plus a few additional drops as needed

IN an 11-cup (for whole loaf) or 7-cup (for medium loaf) food processor, process the almonds with the sugar and salt until finely ground. Pour the warmed milk on top but do *not* mix. Sprinkle the yeast over the milk and allow it to dissolve and proof, 5 to 10 minutes.

ADD the egg yolks and pulse briefly. Add the flour, 1 cup at a time, pulsing briefly after each addition. With the machine on, add the melted butter, pouring it very slowly toward the end, until most of the dough forms a ball around the blade. If necessary, add a few additional drops of milk. Continue processing a few more minutes to knead the dough.

SHAPE the dough into a ball and place it in a greased bowl. Cover with greased plastic wrap. Allow the dough to rise in a warm, draft-free place until double in bulk, 3 to 4 hours.

PUNCH the dough down and divide it into two pieces, one piece containing about two thirds of the dough, the other, the remaining one third. Now divide the larger piece into three, and, using your palms, roll these pieces into three long identical ropes. Braid the ropes. An easy way to do this evenly is to start the braid in the middle, then turn it upside down and braid the other side. Turn the ends under and press down to keep them joined together. Divide the smaller piece of dough in three and braid in the same fashion.

PLACE the smaller braid on top of the first braid. Transfer to a greased baking sheet, then cover with plastic wrap. Let the loaf rise until double in bulk, 1 to 1½ hours.

1½ envelopes active dry yeast (³/₈ ounce total)

3 large egg yolks

3³/₄ cups bread flour

12 tablespoons (1½ sticks) unsalted butter, melted

Unsalted butter or oil for greasing the bowl, wrap, and baking sheet

TOPPING FOR EITHER CHALLAH

1 large egg yolk beaten with 1 teaspoon milk, for glaze

About 2 tablespoons sesame seeds, or 3 to 4 tablespoons chopped almonds

PREHEAT the oven to 350°F. Glaze the dough all over with the egg wash. Sprinkle generously all over with sesame seeds or chopped almonds. Bake 45 minutes for the large loaf, 35 minutes for the medium one, or until golden brown and the loaf sounds hollow when tapped on the bottom. Transfer to a rack and let cool.

SMOKED WHITEFISH AND FENNEL SALAD

yields ABOUT 6 SERVINGS

From a list of some long lines people endure in New York City (The New York Times, August 4, 1996):

Zabar's [the legendary New York culinary emporium that began as a humble Jewish appetizing store]: As preparations to break the Yom Kippur fast begin, the line at the lox counter has been known to wend its way out the door onto Broadway, around the block, and along West End Avenue.

Smoked and pickled fish are among the most popular break-the-fast foods for American Jews, who feel it helps the body replenish some of the essential salts lost during fasting.

The saltiness of the fish can be overbearing though, especially for stomachs reeling and tongues still furry from fasting. To temper the salt in this whitefish salad, I substitute the clean fresh taste of fennel for the traditional celery, and replace the lemon juice with slightly sweet, yet still acidic, grapefruit juice.

About 6 tablespoons sour cream

About 2 tablespoons mayonnaise

About 3 tablespoons fresh grapefruit juice

¼ teaspoon fennel seeds, finely crushed with a mortar and pestle or ground in a spice mill

1 small fennel bulb, stalks removed and reserved for another use, some of the feathery fronds chopped and set aside for garnish, if desired

1½ to 2 pounds smoked whitefish, carefully removed from the bones (about 2 cups)

2 tablespoons chopped fresh dill, plus additional for garnish

Freshly ground black pepper

Accompaniments: attractively cut fresh raw vegetables (carrots, celery, cucumbers, endive leaves, etc.); bagels, bialys, or crackers

IN a large bowl, combine the sour cream, mayonnaise, grapefruit juice, and fennel seeds. Use a vegetable peeler to trim any strings from the fennel, if necessary, then cut the bulb into small dice and add it to the bowl. Stir in the whitefish, dill, and pepper to taste. Taste and adjust the seasoning, adding more sour cream, mayonnaise, or grapefruit juice as needed. Garnish with additional chopped dill and fennel fronds, and serve with raw vegetables, toasted bagels or bialys, or crackers. For an attractive presentation, spoon the whitefish salad onto a platter and ring the perimeter with alternating slices of cucumber and lemon; if desired, punctuate with radishes, cherry tomatoes, or black olives for accent.

COOK'S NOTE: When spooned over hot latkes, this salad makes a wonderful first course in a fish meal. It is especially good on the Celery Root–Potato Latkes (page 265).

I sometimes add a little finely chopped red onion to the salad.

PASTRAMI-STYLE SALMON

yield: 10 TO 12 SERVINGS

He was receiving oxygen when I walked in.

"Did you bring them, dollek?"

"Yes, Gramp." The sick-sweet hospital smell receded before the warm, heady scents of garlic and pepper mixed with rich tobacco as I unwrapped the hot pastrami sandwich, sour pickle, and expensive cigar.

We both knew it was going to be his last meal. He was now ninety-four, and cancer of the lymphatic system coursed rapidly through his body.

Though well lubricated with fat (why bother removing it now?), the pastrami was difficult for him to swallow at this point. So he chewed slowly and deliberately, letting the aromatic meat juices trickle down his throat. Then he pulled off the oxygen tube for a few quick puffs before the nurse came in. I tamped out the cigar and put it away "for later." I kissed his bristly cheek stubble and caressed his bald pink head. "I love you, dollek."

Years later, pregnant with the daughter I named for him, I ordered one of those mile-high deli hot pastrami sandwiches, likewise moistened with quantities of the same garlic-suffused fat.

Unfortunately, I lacked his fortitude. It's been twenty-two years, and I haven't had pastrami since.

I don't miss the meat, but the seasoning is something else. I've tried a number of pastrami-style salmons, and though delicious, they wanted the heat and punch of the requisite Romanian garlic-pepper coat.

Here is my version, which avoids the need for a smoker. Simple to prepare, it costs a fraction of the commercially cured kinds. You just need to allow three or four days to cure the fish. For a break-the-fast meal, you might serve it with cream cheese and assorted breads such as bagels, bialys, and thin pumpernickel. It also makes a sophisticated starter in skinny slices garnished with lemon, capers, and chopped onion.

2 to 2½ pounds fresh center-cut salmon fillet (not salmon steak), in one piece, cleaned but skin left on

6 large, fat garlic cloves, coarsely chopped

2½ tablespoons coarse kosher salt

CUT the salmon in half, down the backbone. If desired, cut the backbone away. Try to remove as many bones as possible—a tweezer is ideal for this. Place both pieces of fish on a platter, skin-side down.

PUT the garlic, salt, paprika, and brown sugar in a food processor or blender and pulse to combine well, stopping to scrape down the bowl as necessary. Scrape out the mixture and massage it well into the flesh of both pieces of salmon.

2 tablespoons paprika, preferably smoked

2 tablespoons packed brown sugar

3 tablespoons whole black peppercorns

2 tablespoons pickling spice

Accompaniments: bagels, bialys, pumpernickel bread, or matzoh; cream cheese, lemons, capers, chopped onions, sliced tomatoes

LIGHTLY crush the peppercorns and pickling spice, either with a mortar and pestle or by placing them in a small plastic bag and hammering a couple of times with a mallet or rolling pin. Rub this seasoning onto the fish. Place one piece of fish evenly on top of the other, flesh-to-flesh, skin sides out. Place this reformed fish in a resealable plastic bag or wrap tightly with plastic wrap. Set the wrapped fish on a platter or in a pan large enough to hold it flat, and top with a large plate. Weight the plate down with a few cans or heavy bottles and refrigerate.

LET the salmon cure in the refrigerator for 3 to 4 days, removing the weights and turning the fish, still in the plastic bag or wrapper, twice a day. Remember to replace the weights after you have turned the fish.

WHEN ready to serve, scrape off and discard the marinade and spices. Pat the salmon dry, then cut it on the diagonal into very thin slices. The salmon is easiest to slice when it is very cold.

ACCOMPANY the salmon with traditional bagels and bialys, or serve with plain or egg matzoh or black pumpernickel bread spread with a thin layer of cream cheese. As a pareve presentation, garnish with lemons, capers, chopped onions, and thinly sliced dark bread. To make a terrific hors d'oeuvre, arrange a little rolled salmon slice on a cucumber round and top with a bit of minced onion and/or a few capers.

BERNIE'S LOX, EGGS, AND ONIONS

yield: **ABOUT 4 SERVINGS**

rowing up in New York, I held certain food truths to be self-evident: "Everybody knows that an appetizing store is merely a description, not a compliment." "Both bagels and bialys must be made with our local water to achieve perfect texture." "Jewish egg dishes like lox, eggs, and onions or salami and eggs are best prepared by New York delis or by those who cut their teeth eating in them."

And then I tasted my cousin Bernie Kaufman's lox, eggs, and onions.

Now, Bernie spent his early years in Chicago, then moved with his family to Los Angeles; he has never lived in New York. Yet, he makes the finest LEO—the name by which this justly famous dish is known by aficionados across the country—that I have ever eaten.

It happens that the key to Bernie's LEO seems so simple, many cooks might skip over it: he combines the caramelized onions with the beaten eggs before adding the mixture to the frying pan. But the result is incredibly creamy eggs that taste lavishly enriched with pure butter— though only a little butter is used for scrambling.

This technique is the secret to other sautéed egg-based dishes as well, including matzoh brie. Blend any sautéed ingredients you are using, such as onion or other aromatics, chopped artichokes, spinach, and so on, into the raw beaten eggs or batter before you toss it into the pan.

1 tablespoon mild olive, avocado, canola, or sunflower oil

3 to 4 tablespoons unsalted butter

3 cups diced onion

Salt and freshly ground black pepper

8 large eggs, beaten

4 to 6 ounces good deli lox or Nova Scotia, diced

Optional garnish: snipped chives and/or dill

IN a 12-inch heavy skillet, preferably nonstick, heat the oil and 1 table-spoon butter over medium heat until the butter is melted. Add the onions and sprinkle them lightly with salt and pepper. Cook for about 2 minutes, stirring, then cover the pan and turn the heat down to a gentle simmer. Cook the onions until meltingly tender and greatly reduced in volume, 25 to 30 minutes, giving them a good stir occasionally. Remove the lid, increase the heat to high to evaporate the liquids, and sauté until pale gold and just barely tinged with bronze in places. Using a wooden spoon, stir occasionally to redistribute the syrupy juices. If necessary, reduce the heat slightly if the onions begin to stick or burn. (This will take longer in a nonstick pan than in a regular one, and you'll have to stir less frequently to build up the delicious brown *fond* the onions produce.) Adjust the seasoning and transfer to a bowl to cool to room temperature.

MEANWHILE, beat the eggs in a large bowl until they are smooth and colored an even yellow with no streaks of white. Unless you are using Nova Scotia, you will probably need little, if any, salt.

RETURN the skillet to the stove and melt the remaining 2 to 3 tablespoons butter in it, swirling up the onion *fond* on the bottom of the pan using a wooden spoon. Add the lox and cook over moderate heat until it turns pinkish.

STIR the cooled onions into the beaten eggs, and pour the mixture over the lox. Cook slowly, lifting and folding the eggs as they set in soft curds. I think lox and caramelized onions are best complemented by moist, pillowy eggs; others like their scrambled eggs drier. Cook to the degree of creaminess you prefer, but remember that the eggs will continue cooking from the heat of the pan.

SERVE hot from the pan, gilding the lily if you wish, with a scatter of fresh herbs on top.

COOK'S NOTE: Since this dish must be prepared just before serving, you can speed up your break-the-fast preparations by caramelizing the onions the day before. Wrap and refrigerate until needed.

ROASTED PEAR BLINTZES

yield: ABOUT 18 BLINTZES

At the market, I look past the shiny Anjous and Bartletts, a provocative swirl of green, yellow, and fall reds nestled in tissue paper slips to the rough-skinned Boscs. I know they are a Cinderella fruit: pare away the dowdy, rusted skin, and the ivory flesh roasts up buttery soft, perfumed, and intensely sweet. Pureed, they need only a touch of sugar and spice to become a sophisticated blintz filling.

5 ripe, fragrant medium-large Bosc pears, peeled, cored, and quartered

1 tablespoon canola, avocado, or other mild oil

Ground cinnamon

Salt

About 1 tablespoon packed brown sugar

Ground cloves

Cardamom, preferably freshly ground

1 recipe Blintz Leaves (page 36)

Unsalted butter, oil, or a combination, or ghee, for frying or baking

Labneh (available in Middle Eastern and specialty stores, and some supermarkets), yogurt cream (see page 30), or sour cream

PREHEAT the oven to 425°F and line a large baking sheet with foil. Drizzle the pears with the oil, sprinkle with 2 pinches of cinnamon and a pinch of salt, and toss to coat well. Spread the pears out on the baking sheet in a single layer, cut sides down. Roast them, turning once or twice, until they are very tender and both sides are beautifully bronzed in places, 30 to 35 minutes.

LET the pears cool slightly. Combine them in a food processor with the brown sugar and a pinch each of the cinnamon, cloves, and cardamom, and puree until smooth. Taste and adjust the seasonings, if needed. Cover and refrigerate until cold, or up to 24 hours.

FILL the blintzes (see page 38), using a heaping tablespoon of filling for each of the blintz leaves, and fry or bake them. Serve right away, or prepare in advance (refrigerate them for up to 2 days or freeze them) and fry or bake them just before serving.

SERVE the blintzes piping hot, with a dollop of the *labneh*, yogurt cream, or sour cream, and lightly dusted, if desired, with a hint of cinnamon.

HONEYED QUINCE-APPLE BLINTZES WITH SOUR CREAM–DATE SAUCE

yield: 16 TO 18 BLINTZES

Fragrant quinces studded with cloves were carried to synagogue on Yom Kippur by children in Bulgaria to keep them from fainting during the long service, recalls Suzy David, in her delightful book, From the Sephardic Kosher Kitchen.

Throughout the Sephardi world, these aromatic fruits are dished up in many ways during the High Holy Days: paired with meat or poultry in stews, served in luscious compotes, or—most often—as a sugary confection known as bimbriyo in Ladino.

Once popular in the United States for making marmalade (that word derives, in fact, from the Portuguese for quince, marmelo), quinces are not always easy to find in markets today. And the hard, bitter white flesh must be coaxed with long, slow cooking, flattered with honey or sugar. Then dry and dense give way to rich and yielding, turning beautiful rose-gold along the way.

I've partnered the quinces here with apples, a frequently made match. To enjoy the blintzes at break-the-fast, prepare them a day or two ahead, or freeze them. Fry or bake just before serving.

2 ripe quinces (1 to 1½ pounds, 1¾ cups or so when diced; see Cook's Note)

1 cup unsweetened apple juice

About 2½ tablespoons fragrant honey

Pinch of salt

2 whole cloves

1 teaspoon vanilla extract

2 medium-large apples (1 to 1½ pounds, 2 cups when cut into large dice; choose juicy, sweet varieties, such as Braeburn, Golden Delicious, Jonagold, or

PREPARE the quinces: rinse them well, washing off any downy fuzz. Quarter and peel them. Using a very sharp knife, carefully cut out the core, seeds, and any other hard bits. Cut the quinces into large dice.

IN a nonreactive saucepan, combine the apple juice, honey, the salt, cloves, and vanilla and bring to a boil. Add the quinces, reduce the heat, and simmer, covered, until tender. Timing will vary: Begin checking after 10 minutes; it may take up to 25 minutes.

MEANWHILE, peel, core, and cut the apples into large dice. When the quince is tender, stir in the apples, cover, and simmer for about 5 minutes. Turn off the heat, and let the fruit cool in the pan liquid for 15 to 20 minutes.

MAKE the sauce: pour boiling water over the dates to soften them. Drain well and place in a bowl with the sour cream. Beat well with a fork, until thoroughly combined.

Melrose, to complement
the tart quinces)

½ teaspoon ground
cinnamon

1 recipe Blintz Leaves
(page 36)

Unsalted butter, oil, or a
combination, or ghee, for
frying or baking

FOR THE SOUR
CREAM–DATE SAUCE

¼ cup finely chopped
dates (snip them with
kitchen scissors, dipping
the blades into hot water)

1 cup sour cream

¼ cup sliced almonds,
lightly toasted (optional)

REMOVE the cloves from the fruit and discard. Using a slotted spoon, transfer the fruit to a bowl, leaving the cooking liquid in the pan. Boil this reserved liquid over high heat, uncovered, until reduced to about 1 tablespoon of thick, syrupy glaze. Stir the glaze into the fruit mixture. Taste, and, if needed, add a bit more honey. Stir in the cinnamon. Let the mixture cool completely (and chill it, if possible, to make it easier to use) before filling the blintzes, using a heaping tablespoon of filling for each of the blintz leaves. Fry or bake them (see pages 36–38) and serve right away, or prepare in advance (refrigerate them for up to 2 days or freeze them) and fry or bake them just before serving.

SERVE the blintzes with a dollop of the sour cream–date sauce. The toasted almond slices may seem like gilding the lily, but they add a wonderful crackle when sprinkled over the sauce.

COOK'S NOTE: Make sure the quinces are ripe. Unlike most fruits, which sweeten up nicely when stewed unripe, quinces may retain an unpleasant tannic taste, similar to unripe persimmons. Don't worry about bruises; if they are very fragrant and give slightly when pressed, they will be luscious. If you cannot find quinces, replace them with an equal amount of tart green apple such as Granny Smith, or even better, Rhode Island Greening. You'll need a little lemon juice to bring up the flavors.

APRICOT BLINTZES WITH TOASTED PISTACHIOS AND YOGURT CREAM

yield: **16 TO 18 BLINTZES**

"If you are going to be in the hospital for five days, I'll bring the sheets."

"No, Ma," I said. I had to undergo yet another procedure in my quest to become pregnant, and I was irritable.

"Sweetface, I always had the silk and lace sheets on my bed when my friends came to visit me in the hospital. And an orchid. Your father always brought me an orchid to pin to the pillowcase. I want you to have one, too."

"That was different. They were coming to visit you when you had babies. I don't need orchids for this." She stopped talking about orchids, and I continued having surgeries.

Then in November 1984, I gave birth to a big, beautiful baby girl.

My father put down the bag, redolent of hot, spicy-sweet smells from New York's Lower East Side, where they had stopped on the way to the hospital. We walked down the hall to the nursery, and I pointed out Alexandra, born with a full head of her grandmother's red hair and the ability, rare in neonatals, to cry real tears.

We walked back to my room. Halvah, pistachios, and sour apricots were crowded together on my bed tray. The starched white sheets were now covered with ecru silk trimmed on either side with rows of baroque cream-colored lace.

She smiled her radiant smile, and tears sparkled in the corners of the big, blue-gray eyes. She walked towards me, arms outstretched.

Then I saw it. The little lump of hospital pillow, swimming in lace. And firmly anchored to the top, a huge, fresh orchid, frilly white edges, vibrant magenta within.

A month later, we still had the leftovers. When friends came to bill and coo and rock Alex, I relaxed in the kitchen, rhythmically turning out these blintzes in the energized haze of euphoria and sleep deprivation peculiar to new parents. The blintzes are reminiscent of luscious palatschinken (Hungarian apricot crêpes), but the stuffing—plumped tart fruit infused with vanilla and almond—provides more nuanced flavor and texture than the traditional jam filling. I scattered the leftover toasted pistachios over the blintzes for color and a pleasant buttery crunch. Later we swirled the remains of the halvah with vanilla ice cream.

The blintzes make a wonderful break-the-fast treat.

2 cups apple-apricot juice, apple juice, apricot nectar, or other apricot- or apple-flavored juice

10 to 12 ounces dried apricots, preferably tart, cut in half or in quarters if large (about 1¾ cups)

One 2-inch piece vanilla bean, split, or ½ teaspoon vanilla extract

½ teaspoon almond extract

1 recipe Blintz Leaves (page 36)

Unsalted butter, oil, or a combination, or ghee for frying or baking

Yogurt cream (see page 30) or *labneh* (available at Middle Eastern and specialty stores), sweetened to taste, if desired, with fragrant honey

⅓ cup toasted pistachios (see page 409)

PUT the juice in a wide, heavy, nonreactive 6-quart Dutch oven or saucepan, and boil it over medium-high heat until reduced by one-third, to about 1⅓ cups. Add the apricots, vanilla, and almond extract, reduce the heat, and simmer, covered, until the apricots are very tender, about 25 minutes.

UNCOVER the pan and boil over high heat, stirring, to evaporate all remaining liquid. If you used a vanilla bean, remove it, and, if desired, dry and save it for another use or bury it in granulated sugar to flavor it. Let the apricots cool in the pan for 15 to 20 minutes, then refrigerate, covered, for another 20 minutes or up to 24 hours, if you want to fill the blintzes later.

FILL the blintz leaves with a heaping tablespoon of filling for each blintz (don't overfill), and bake or fry them (see pages 36–38).

SERVE the blintzes hot, topped with yogurt cream or labneh and a sprinkle of toasted pistachios.

PRUNE-PLUM CUSTARD CHALLAH BREAD PUDDING

yield: **8 TO 10 SERVINGS**

This warm, fragrant pudding began as a way to use up leftover holiday bread, but it is so good that I now buy an extra loaf just to make sure I have enough to prepare it for our break-the-fast. Slightly stale challah is fine; if your bread is crispish throughout, you can skip the toasting.

There is a secret here: the flavor derives not only from fresh, blue-black prune plums pumped up with their winy, dried prune cousins, but from the prune pits as well. Stone fruits—cherries, peaches, apricots, and plums—are close relatives of almonds, and their pits have a distinctive, flowery-nut taste; Europeans press an exquisite oil from prune pits and use them in pastry-making. In this pudding, I infuse the cream and milk with prune pits for a more complex almondy flavor than either almond extract or amaretto could provide.

1 cup moist prunes, unpitted

2 cups heavy cream, preferably *not* ultrapasteurized

2 cups whole milk

1 vanilla bean

One 3-inch cinnamon stick, crushed

1 small loaf challah

1½ cups Italian prune plums, pitted and quartered

½ cup packed light brown sugar

1 teaspoon ground cinnamon

4 large eggs

4 large egg yolks

½ cup granulated sugar

¼ teaspoon salt

Butter for greasing the pan

PREHEAT the oven to 250°F.

START the custard: slit open the prunes to remove the pits. Set aside the prunes (if they are not moist, plump them with very hot water to cover and let them steep). In a heavy saucepan, combine the pits with the cream, milk, vanilla (scraped seeds along with the pod), and the cinnamon stick. Bring to a simmer over low heat. Remove pan from the heat and let infuse for at least 30 minutes.

CUT the bread into thick slices and arrange in a single layer on one or two large baking sheets. Toast in the oven just until lightly colored, crisp and dry to the touch. Turn off the oven. When the bread is cool enough to handle, trim away and discard the crusts and tear or cut the bread into ½- to 1-inch cubes. You should have about 8 cups.

QUARTER the prunes (if they've been plumping in hot water, pat them dry first) and in a medium bowl, toss them with the plums, 2 tablespoons of the brown sugar, and the ground cinnamon.

TO finish the custard, whisk together the eggs, egg yolks, granulated sugar, remaining 6 tablespoons brown sugar, and salt in a large bowl. Whisk in the cooled cream mixture.

GENEROUSLY butter the bottom and sides of a 13 by 9-inch glass baking dish. Arrange the bread cubes in the prepared pan and tuck the prunes and plums among them. Pour the custard through a fine-mesh strainer evenly over the bread and fruit. Cover the pan with foil and refrigerate for at least 2 hours, occasionally pressing the bread down into the custard.

PREHEAT the oven to 350°F. Remove the foil cover and bring the pudding to room temperature. Prepare a hot-water bath: set the pan inside a larger baking pan, and pour in enough boiling or scalding-hot tap water to come halfway up the sides of the pudding pan. Place on a rack in the middle of the oven and bake for about 1 hour and 15 minutes, until the pudding is puffed and golden and a tester inserted in the center comes out clean. Remove the pan from the water bath and let the pudding cool slightly.

SERVE the pudding warm (reheat if necessary). It is wonderful topped with heavy cream or milk, whipped cream (for a real treat, add cinnamon and sugar to the cream before whipping it), vanilla ice cream, or just solo. The pudding can be made a day or two ahead, covered, and refrigerated. To reheat, bring it back to room temperature, then bake at 325°F until heated through.

DOUBLE GINGER–CARAMELIZED PEAR NOODLE KUGEL

yield: 6 TO 8 SERVINGS

*M*any of my Polish grandmother's recipes date from the time she was sent to Germany to live with an aunt and uncle after her parents died.

The German relatives forced her into a servitude out of the Brothers Grimm. Because of the extraordinary physical demands put on her body, Grandma Rebecca did not reach puberty until she arrived in America in 1911 at age 17, her passage paid for by older sister Anna.

But in Germany, she did learn to cook, and there developed an abiding passion for sweet-and-sour foods, often using gingersnaps as flavoring for dishes like carp, stuffed cabbage, and simple fruit desserts.

In this variation of one of her kugels, I combine tangy crystallized ginger with caramelized pears to mirror the sweet-and-sour gingersnap topping.

3 cups whole milk

1 thin strip lemon zest

1 cinnamon stick

1 cup fine dried egg noodles

Salt

½ cup granulated sugar

4 tablespoons (½ stick) unsalted butter, plus 2 tablespoons, softened, for topping

⅓ cup firmly packed brown sugar

1 to 2 tablespoons finely chopped crystallized ginger

2 medium-large ripe Bartlett or Bosc pears (about 1 pound), peeled and sliced about ¼ inch thick

IN a 3- to 4-quart heavy-bottomed saucepan, combine the milk, lemon zest, and cinnamon and bring to a boil over medium heat. Continue cooking over lively heat, stirring occasionally and adjusting the heat if the milk threatens to bubble over, until the mixture is reduced to a little over 2 cups. Stir in the noodles and a pinch of salt, and cook for 4 to 5 minutes. Add the granulated sugar and stir until it melts. Remove the pan from the heat and let cool to room temperature.

PREHEAT the oven to 375°F. Melt the 4 tablespoons butter in an 8- or 9-inch square baking pan in the oven (or on top of the stove if the pan is flameproof), swirling the butter around to cover the bottom and sides of the pan. Sprinkle with the brown sugar and ginger, and arrange the pears evenly on top.

IN a large bowl, beat together the sour cream, cream cheese, and ¼ teaspoon salt until smooth. Whisk in the eggs and vanilla. Remove and discard the lemon zest and cinnamon from the noodle mixture, and add the noodles to cream cheese mixture. Combine everything well. Pour the contents of the bowl over the pears. Combine the gingersnap crumbs and 2 tablespoons softened butter, and sprinkle over the top of the kugel.

1 cup sour cream
(8 ounces)

4 ounces cream cheese,
softened and cut into bits

3 large eggs, beaten

½ teaspoon vanilla
extract

About 1 cup gingersnaps,
crumbled

BAKE the kugel for about 50 minutes, until a knife inserted in the center comes out clean. (The kugel should be slightly firm.) Let cool until set. To serve, run a knife along the edges of the pan, invert the pan onto a serving plate, and unmold. Or cut and serve the kugel from the baking dish.

BEST eaten warm (reheat if necessary) or slightly chilled (not icy cold).

OTHER SUGGESTIONS FOR BREAKING THE YOM KIPPUR FAST

*Chilled Minted Cucumber Soup

Either of the *Hummus recipes

*Israeli Salad

*Apple-Cranberry Blintzes with Maple Ricotta Cream and Sugared Walnuts

Either of the *Cheese Blintz recipes

Any of the *Cheese Latke recipes

*Sorrel-Onion Noodle Kugel

*Zucchini Fritada

*Spinach Cheese Squares

Any of the *Sweet Noodle Kugels

*Bene Israel Rice Pudding

*Old-Fashioned Rice Pudding

*Turkish Silken Ground-Rice Pudding (*Sutlaj*)

*Hungarian Plum Tart

Any of the *Cheesecake recipes

*Poppy Seed Butter Cake (Mohn Cake)

*See index for page numbers

"To me it is the finest time of the year . . . The sun no longer bakes like an oven, but caresses with a heavenly softness. The woods are still green, the pines give out a pungent smell. In my yard stands the succah—the booth I have built for the holiday, covered with branches, and around me the forest looks like a huge succah designed for God Himself. Here, I think, God celebrates his Succos."

—SHOLOM ALEICHEM, "HODEL"

Sukkot

15 TISHRI (SEPTEMBER OR OCTOBER), A SEVEN-DAY FESTIVAL, IMMEDIATELY FOLLOWED BY THE FESTIVALS OF SHEMINI AZERET AND SIMCHAT TORAH

Eating a rich harvest dinner in a starry sukkah, surrounded by the smells of winy autumn fruits and fresh vegetables commingled with fragrant sprays of foliage, it is easy to feel a part of God's natural world. I remember well the sukkah we had when I was twelve: between crisp brown pears and ruby pomegranates we tied wild bayberry branches and scattered warty clusters of the powder-gray berries on the floor, suffusing the open room with their spicy scent as we scurried in and out. My brother, my sister, and I hacked tall, feather-headed reeds from sandy lots and sea dunes, spread them out on the trellised roof, and slouched them in the corners—beachy stand-ins for sheaves of corn. In the blaze of candlelight at the evening meal, I could taste the salt in the air on my sweet-stuffed cabbage. The best of camping out and eating home, it was cold but magical. And it turned out to be our last sukkah—the following year we moved a few blocks away from our house to an apartment overlooking the ocean.

The sukkah is a temporary booth made of wood, canvas, even aluminum, with a roof of leafy branches, that Jewish families construct out of doors to eat meals in during the holidays. It is symbolic on many counts, linking the festival to both its ancient agricultural origins and a deeper religious significance.

The holiday began as an exuberant feast of thanksgiving, one of the three pilgrimage festivals (the others are Passover and Shavuot) when the ancient Israelites traveled to the Temple to offer gratitude for the seasonal crops. Not only the most important harvest of the year, it was also the final one: after the fine grapes and gold-green olives were reaped and ready for pressing, and the wheat, figs, dates, and pomegranates gathered and stored, everyone was free to rejoice and give thanks, as well as to pray for the arrival of badly needed autumn rains and a plentiful harvest in the coming year.

Roofed with twisted vines and carob and olive branches, sukkot in earliest times were purely functional: makeshift little structures the vintners and farmers slept in during the harvest to protect their bounty from predators—both animal and human. When Sukkot was established as a Temple Festival, the travelers erected similar temporary booths for their sojourn in Jerusalem. Later when the holiday was linked to the Israelites' period of wandering in the wilderness, the temporary booths were given a ritual significance as well. They came to symbolize the portable shelters of the Israelites in the desert.

By the time of the Second Temple, more Jews journeyed to Jerusalem at Sukkot than at any other festival, coming to offer gratitude not just for a bountiful harvest, but for God's providential care throughout history as well. Before the Second Temple was destroyed in CE 70, they came from as far away as the western shores of the Mediterranean, from Rome and Babylon, from all the foreign lands in the ancient world where Jews had settled. Welcoming them, the city was festooned with sweet-smelling myrtles and palms, beautiful flowers and fruits. Outside the Temple, four huge golden lamps blazed, and according to the Talmud, "the illumination, like a sea of fire, lit up every courtyard of the Holy City." Priests provided music with an array of flutes, lutes, lyres, and cymbals, men paraded with glowing torches, and there was joyous singing and dancing throughout the week-long festivities. Worshipers carried floral wands, and according to Plutarch, slept beneath roofs of plaited ivy and vines.

Today, when most Jews live in urban areas and the agricultural cycle of Israel is less relevant in the Diaspora, the sukkot they construct remain evocative reminders of divine protection. At Sukkot Jews around the world recapture the jubilation of the farmer at the close of an abundant harvest, and at the same time relive the fragile, precarious life of the Israelites in the desert. For me, these bittersweet sensations are heightened as they echo in the natural world: amidst the season's bounty, the falling leaves reflect the evanescence of existence all around us.

On Sukkot mornings, in the synagogue or at home, Jews hold an *etrog* (citron) in the left hand, a *lulav* (myrtle, palm, and willow tied together) in the right hand, recite a blessing, then shake these Four Species of Plants in every direction: north, south, east, west, up, and down. Once a symbolic appeal for rain and new vegetation, the ritual has been interpreted today as a metaphoric prayer for our growth and renewal as individuals, working together to bring a flowering of peace in the world.

Not unexpectedly, vegetables and fruits, often appearing in concert together, take center stage in our menus for Sukkot: prunes enrich the caramelized onion and carrot tsimmes, and brilliant pomegranate seeds add sparkle to a pumpkin soup already lush with sweet potato matzoh balls. The traditional stuffed vegetable is well represented, including a fall-scented meat- and mushroom-stuffed cabbage. In keeping with the calendar, maple-caramelized pears sauced with passion fruit or fresh raspberries finish the rich meal.

Many Sukkot recipes are sweet. Ripe flame-gold carrots, pumpkins, and apricots are naturally sugary. Such tastes continue the wish expressed just two weeks before at Rosh Hashanah for a good and sweet year.

SHEMINI AZERET AND SIMCHAT TORAH

Opening with the solemnity, introspection, and repentance of the Days of Awe, the fall holidays conclude with the jubilant festival of Simchat Torah, a very physical rejoicing that marks ending and beginning anew the annual reading cycle of the Torah.

At the synagogue, celebrants literally embrace the Torah, kissing and dancing with the scrolls. Children joyfully wave flags impaled with bright red apples, then are blessed beneath the canopy of an unfurled *tallit* (prayer shawl). In many communities, Jews of different denominations celebrate the holiday in unison, dancing together on the streets. At home, the festive table is laden with kreplach and the finest of the Sukkot foods; lavish amounts of good wine and other strong drink are poured.

Simchat Torah feels rooted in the communal festivals of ancient Israel, but surprisingly, the holiday did not exist until the Middle Ages, when Jews universally adopted the one-year cycle for completing the Torah (the prior reading cycle was triennial).

Originally, the seven days of Sukkot were followed by another festival, Shemini Azeret, on the eighth day, when the Israelites, turning their attention to the coming year, began the prayers for rain that remain a part of the service until Passover. In the Diaspora, the second day of Shemini Azeret became the holiday of Simchat Torah; in Israel and in Reform congregations, Shemini Azeret and Simchat Torah are celebrated on the same day.

CELEBRATING SUKKOT TODAY

"Klutz-proof sukkah kits" are advertised on the Internet now and sukkah-decorating parties begin right after Yom Kippur. Once almost exclusively the province of Orthodox and some Conservative Jews, more recently the home sukkah has been reclaimed by many Reform, Reconstructionist, Jewish Renewal, and other less traditional groups as well, who relish this family-centered respite from TV and computer, set amid nature's sights and smells.

Today's vibrant communities have given birth to creative new Sukkot traditions. Friends and relatives "sukkah-hop"—admiring the pumpkins filled with autumn flowers, lace tablecloths hung on sukkah walls lit up with twinkling party lights, or ritual candles burning in scooped-out winter squashes. In a riff on progressive restaurant meals, some families share progressive sukkah dinners, enjoying an appetizer of stuffed harvest vegetables in one sukkah, a slow-braised autumn brisket in a second sukkah, and fruit-rich desserts in yet a third. Many communities invite children to visit local sukkot, where they are showered with gifts of candy and dried fruit. And at home and synagogue parties, children construct Cookie Sukkot, creating huts with graham crackers and other pastries, cemented with pastel frostings and decorated with colorful candy fruits.

Just as Jewish apartment dwellers years ago built tiny sukkot on fire escapes and tenement rooftops, contemporary urban Jews construct them on terraces, roofless balconies, co-op roof spaces, or in outdoor gardens. Those with no access to outdoor space and no nearby friends or relatives with sukkot may take their meals in the large community sukkah of their synagogue. Increasingly, many synagogues and other Jewish centers are opening their sukkot to nonmembers, the public-at-large. And, in some communities, restaurants transform their sidewalk cafes and gardens into lovely sukkot or offer lists of nearby public sukkot.

Friends and family are not the only sukkot visitors. Since the Middle Ages, traditional Jews have symbolically invited invisible guests, the *ushpizin* (Aramaic for guests), seven patriarchs of the Jewish people. Each night one of these spirits enters the sukkah, followed by the other six, each embodying a different mystical facet of God, from love to perseverance, humility to strength. Today feminists and other egalitarian Jews are re-creating the custom to include *ushpizot* (feminine of ushpizin), the prophetesses of the Talmud first mentioned by the Italian medieval kabbalist, Menachem Azarya. And some Jews are creating new rituals to welcome other illustrious souls. Rabbi Jill Hammer, of Ma'Yan: The Jewish Women's Project of the JCC of Manhattan, has invited Martin Luther King, Emma Lazarus, Vashti, and her own grandmother, in addition to the traditional male and female ushpizin, making the sukkah, as she put it, "a place to celebrate all the people who made us who we are."

Amid the glorious meals shared with special guests, we must not forget that the sukkah is a symbol of our homelessness, once-upon-a-time. We cannot truly celebrate Sukkot without thinking of those who are homeless today: the poor, the refugees, those fleeing domestic violence. In fact, the Zohar, the mystical text where the ushpizin are first explained, calls upon us to donate to the poor the portion of food and wine that we would have served to our spiritual guests if they were present corporeally.

On Sukkot, when we chose to dwell in temporary shelters, we remember those who have no choice at all.

SUKKOT

menu suggestions

*Mary's Onion Challah

*Chopped Chicken Liver from the Rue des Rosiers

or

*Chopped Chicken Liver with Caramelized Onions

*Grated Black Radish and Endive Salad in Shallot Vinaigrette

*Pumpkin and Sweet Potato Soup with Sweet Potato Knaidlach (Matzoh Balls)

*Cabbage Stuffed with Mushrooms and Meat or *Classic Sweet-and-Sour Stuffed Cabbage

*Caramelized Onion and Carrot Tsimmes with Candied Ginger

Salad of fresh tart greens

*Maple-Roasted Pears with Passion Fruit or Fresh Raspberry Sauce

or

Fresh seasonal melon splashed with a late harvest moscato or sauvignon blanc

*Tangy Russian Cabbage Soup with Pot Roast–Beet Kreplach

*Aromatic Marinated Brisket with Chestnuts and *Spiced Pomegranate Molasses Applesauce

*See index for page numbers

or *Meat Tsimmes with Prunes and Carrots

or *Iranian Grilled Chicken Thighs with Sumac

Roast potatoes

Mixed green salad

*Jewish Sautéed Apple Cake

or Fresh figs with toasted walnuts or pecans

A VEGETARIAN SUKKOT DINNER

*Pomegranate-Orange Sunsets

*Chard Stuffed with Artichokes and Rice or *Classic Hummus with Toasted Sesame-Cumin Matzohs

*Esau's Pottage (Red Lentil Soup) or *Pumpkin and Sweet Potato Soup with Sweet Potato Knaidlach (pareve version)

*Mujadderah-Filled Roasted Red Peppers in Tomato-Garlic Sauce, with *labneh,*Yogurt Cream, or sour cream

or

*Syrian Stuffed Zucchini in Tomato-Apricot Sauce (vegetarian variation)

or

*Deconstructed Kasha Varnishkes

Salad of avocado, watercress, and butterhead lettuce with oregano vinaigrette

*See index for page numbers

*Rich Noodle Pudding Baked with Fresh Plums and Nectarines (seasonal fruit topping variation)

or

*Hungarian Plum Tart with vanilla ice cream or fresh whipped cream

or

Sweet orange-fleshed melon garnished with lime and fresh mint

*See index for page numbers

LENTILS "HUMMUS-STYLE" WITH POMEGRANATE AND MINT AND TOASTED ZA'ATAR MATZOHS

yield: ABOUT 6 SERVINGS

Although hummus *actually means "chickpea," quick-cooking lentils are a delicious alternative in the garlicky spread. In this version, perfect for Sukkot or other autumn holiday meals, including Break-the-Fast, sesame tahini is replaced by other tastes from the Middle East, pomegranate and mint, which freshen the bean puree with fragrant, sweet-sour grace notes.*

The aromatic za'atar, a Middle Eastern herb blend crusting the toasted matzoh, underscores the tart, fruity flavors in the hummus.

1¼ cups brown lentils (about ½ pound)

Salt

1½ to 2 tablespoons coarsely chopped garlic, according to taste

About 6 tablespoons best-quality extra virgin olive oil

About 6 tablespoons fresh lemon juice

About 1 tablespoon pomegranate molasses

¼ cup fresh mint leaves, plus additional for garnish

Freshly ground black pepper

Optional garnish: 3 tablespoons fresh pomegranate seeds

Accompaniments: trimmed fresh raw vegetables, such as fennel, celery, carrots, red and yellow bell pepper strips, etc.; Toasted Za'atar Matzohs (recipe follows), plain matzoh, or hot pita quarters

PICK over the lentils carefully, discarding any stray objects or discolored beans, and rinse well in fresh cold water. Drain and place in a medium saucepan. Add enough cold water to cover generously and bring to a boil. Lower the heat to moderate and cook, covered, for about 30 minutes, until very soft. About 5 to 10 minutes before the cooking time has elapsed, add salt to taste.

WHILE the lentils are cooking, sauté the garlic in 2 tablespoons olive oil until just tinged with pale gold. (You only want to eliminate the raw taste.)

DRAIN the lentils, reserving about ½ cup of the cooking water, and put them in a food processor, together with the garlic and its cooking oil, 3 tablespoons fresh oil, the lemon juice, pomegranate molasses, mint leaves, and salt and pepper to taste. Process to a smooth puree. Add some of the reserved cooking water, if necessary, to achieve a soft and creamy consistency. Taste and adjust the salt, pepper, lemon juice, pomegranate molasses, and oil as needed. Spread the hummus on a large platter and drizzle with the remaining 1 tablespoon oil. Garnish with pomegranate seeds, if using, and mint leaves.

SERVE with fresh vegetables and Toasted Za'atar Matzohs or warm pita, for dipping.

TOASTED ZA'ATAR MATZOHS

yield: 4 TO 6 SERVINGS

1 tablespoon plus
2 teaspoons sesame
seeds

2 tablespoons dried
thyme

1 tablespoon plus
1 teaspoon sumac
(available at Middle
Eastern and specialty
stores)

2 teaspoons dried
oregano

½ teaspoon dried mint

Coarse salt
(start with ½ teaspoon)

Matzohs

Extra virgin olive oil

PREHEAT the oven to 400°F.

MAKE the za'atar: in a small (7-inch) ungreased heavy skillet, toast the sesame seeds over moderately high heat, stirring or shaking the pan constantly, just until they release their nutty fragrance and turn light gold. Don't allow them to brown or they'll be bitter. Remove the skillet from the heat.

TRANSFER to a mortar, add the thyme, sumac, oregano, mint, and salt, and crush coarsely with the pestle, or pulse a few times in an electric spice grinder. Or put the seasonings in a plastic bag (let the sesame seeds cool slightly first) and pound well with a mallet. A light, pleasantly salty edge will best bring out the other spices (and remember that matzohs contain no salt at all), so taste and adjust salt as needed. Brush the tops of the matzohs with olive oil, then sprinkle generously with the za'atar (I use 2½ to 3 teaspoons for each matzoh). Bake until hot and crisp. The matzoh should be very fragrant, puffed slightly, and just beginning to curl at the deep brown edges. Best served hot.

COOK'S NOTE: Some companies now package their own za'atar blends. Check the spice department of well-stocked specialty or Middle Eastern groceries. Store any leftover za'atar in a tightly closed jar. Za'atar is also delicious sprinkled on other breads: pita, lavash, nan. Brush breads lightly with oil before sprinkling with za'atar and bake until hot and fragrant.

PUMPKIN AND SWEET POTATO SOUP WITH SWEET POTATO KNAIDLACH (MATZOH BALLS)

yield: ABOUT 8 SERVINGS

"*L*et the sky rain potatoes," *Shakespeare's Falstaff cries out in quest of aphrodisiac aids. The old lecher was calling for sweet potatoes, the more common and accepted potato of the time (the word "potato" did not refer to the white tuber until around 1775, according to the Oxford English Dictionary).*

To the Jews around the globe who readily embraced the sweet potato and the other imports from the New World, pumpkins and squashes, the rapidly growing vegetables evoked not amour exactly, but abundance and fertility.

In Jewish communities from Morocco to Melbourne, these vegetables are especially prized during the fall holidays, Rosh Hashanah and Sukkot, when their sugary flesh, reflecting the many colors of the sun, symbolizes the sweetness and the seasonal plenty of an abundant harvest.

The sweet potatoes I've added to my Polish grandmother's recipe for matzoh balls (knaidlach) softly echo the pureed golden vegetables that give this soup its delicately sweet edge and velvety smoothness.

Scarlet seeds from a pomegranate hanging in your sukkah or some diced red onions add crunch, tang, and a burst of color.

FOR THE KNAIDLACH

1 large sweet potato (about 1 pound)

2 tablespoons sautéed onions (reserved from preparing the soup)

1 large egg, beaten

Nutmeg, preferably freshly grated

Salt and freshly ground black pepper

½ to ¾ cup matzoh meal

START the matzoh balls: preheat the oven to 375°F. Prick the sweet potato with a fork and bake it on a cookie sheet for 1 to 1½ hours, until tender.

MEANWHILE, make the soup: in a large saucepan or Dutch oven, cook the onion in the oil over moderate heat, stirring, until pale golden. Reserve 2 tablespoons for the matzoh balls and set aside. Add the pumpkin or other squash and sweet potato to the onions in the saucepan, and cook, stirring for about 5 minutes. Stir in 7 cups of the broth, and simmer over moderately low heat, partially covered, for 30 minutes, or until the vegetables are very tender. In a food processor or a blender, puree the soup in batches until smooth. (If you have an immersion blender, you can puree the soup right in the pot.) Return the soup to the saucepan and add salt, if needed, and plenty of black pepper. Thin the soup if you wish with some of the remaining 1 cup broth, and set it aside. (Or cover and refrigerate, if refrigerating matzoh ball batter overnight.)

2½ cups chopped onion

3 tablespoons mild olive or canola oil

1½ pounds sweet pumpkin or butternut, kabocha, hubbard, or other sweet winter squash, halved and peeled, seeds and strings discarded, flesh cut into 1-inch pieces

1 large sweet potato (about 1 pound), peeled and cut into 1-inch pieces

7 to 8 cups chicken broth, preferably homemade (see pages 62 and 70); or good-quality, low-sodium purchased

Salt and freshly ground black pepper

Optional garnish: pomegranate seeds or minced red onion

MAKE the matzoh balls: when the sweet potato is cool enough to handle, peel it. Force the sweet potato and the reserved 2 tablespoons cooked onions through a ricer or food mill fitted with the medium disk into a bowl. Stir in the egg and nutmeg, salt, and pepper to taste. Add ½ cup of the matzoh meal, or enough to make a soft dough, and refrigerate the dough, covered, for at least 1 hour or overnight. Shape the mixture into 16 walnut-size balls, transferring them as they are formed to a wax paper–lined plate.

IN a large, wide pot, bring 4 quarts water and 1 tablespoon salt to a rapid boil. Slide in the balls, one at a time. Reduce the heat to moderately low, cover the pot, and simmer the balls for about 20 minutes, until light, fluffy, and cooked through. Don't lift the lid to peek—they need all that steam to puff up.

WHEN the matzoh balls are ready, warm shallow soup bowls and heat the soup until hot. Using a skimmer or slotted spoon, transfer 2 matzoh balls to each heated bowl. Ladle the hot soup over them, and garnish each serving with a scattering of pomegranate seeds or minced onion, if desired.

Pareve Version For a pareve version, prepare the soup using well-flavored Vegetable Stock (page 34) instead of chicken broth.

TANGY RUSSIAN CABBAGE SOUP WITH POT ROAST–BEET KREPLACH

yield: 6 TO 8 SERVINGS

*L*ong ago, kreplach were more than mere ravioli: they were savory edible amulets. According to Patti Shosteck, author of A Lexicon of Jewish Cooking, Jews in seventeenth-century Germany inscribed the outside pasta with mystical incantations and messages intended to bring God's favor to them and their chaotic universe.

Kreplach continue to make magic in this recipe. Instead of raw meat simmered along with the cabbage in the soup, ready-cooked brisket or pot roast, combined with sweet beets for flavor and moistness, is enclosed in the kreplach, adding unexpected layers to the eloquent balance of tastes and textures here. And because the soup is made with beef stock, not meat, there is no fat to remove or skimming needed.

FOR THE CABBAGE SOUP

1 medium green cabbage (1½ to 2 pounds)

1 pound onions, chopped (4 cups)

3 tablespoons olive oil

Salt and freshly ground black pepper

1 small parsnip, peeled and diced (½ cup; optional)

¾ pound carrots, scraped and chopped (2 cups)

2 tablespoons finely chopped garlic

1 tablespoon peeled and minced fresh ginger

6 cups homemade Beef Stock (page 32) or good-quality, low-sodium purchased

1 cup canned Italian plum tomatoes, coarsely chopped, and their juices

START the soup: discard the tough outer leaves of the cabbage, then cut it into quarters and cut out and discard the core. Shred the cabbage coarsely or cut it into thin slices.

IN a very large, wide, heavy saucepan or 5- to 6-quart Dutch oven, sauté the onions in the olive oil over medium heat until softened, about 15 minutes. Salt and pepper lightly, then cover and simmer over low heat until very soft and sweet and almost translucent, 20 to 25 minutes. Add the parsnip, if using, the carrots, and the garlic, and raise the heat to moderately high. Sauté, stirring, until some of the vegetables are tinged dark-gold around the edges. Stir in the ginger and the cabbage, and season with salt and pepper. Continue sautéing, lifting and turning the vegetables, until the cabbage begins to soften, 7 to 10 minutes. Add the stock, tomatoes and juice, bay leaf, apricots, if using, and sauerkraut. Bring the soup to a slow boil, set the cover slightly askew, then simmer gently for 2 hours. Stir the soup occasionally.

ADD the apples, brown sugar, lemon juice, and salt and pepper to taste. If needed, adjust the lemon and sugar until you reach the perfect sweet-and-sour balance. Cook for an additional hour. Remove the bay leaf. Taste again and adjust the seasoning if needed.

1 Turkish bay leaf

2 tablespoons tart dried apricots, minced (for an added subtle sour-sweet note; optional)

1 cup sauerkraut, rinsed well

2 tart green apples, peeled and diced

About 3 tablespoons brown sugar

About 3 tablespoons fresh lemon juice

FOR THE POT ROAST-BEET KREPLACH

1 cup shredded cooked pot roast or brisket, plus 2 to 3 tablespoons gravy (if you have no leftover gravy, substitute some rich broth—that is, good broth that has been reduced by about half)

3/4 cup cooked, peeled, and very finely diced beets

3 tablespoons finely chopped fresh dill, plus additional for garnish

1 tablespoon grated onion

1 large egg yolk

Salt and freshly ground black pepper

30 to 40 wonton wrappers (have some extra in case of tearing)

Egg wash (1 or 2 large eggs as needed, each beaten with 1 teaspoon water)

WHILE the soup is simmering, prepare the kreplach: stir together all the ingredients except the wonton wrappers and egg wash, seasoning generously with salt and pepper. Refrigerate for at least 30 minutes. Fill and seal the kreplach, using 1 heaping teaspoon of filling, 1 wrapper, and egg wash for each krepl, then folding into a triangle shape. Poach the kreplach. (See page 39 for procedures.)

TO serve, place 4 or 5 cooked kreplach in each warmed shallow soup plate. Ladle in the soup along with some of the vegetables. To freshen the flavors, sprinkle with some chopped dill.

EVEN better the next day.

> " . . . Elvis ate three servings of my kreplach. He smacked his lips. 'Better than my own momma's fried chicken,' he said."
>
> —JANICE EIDUS, "ELVIS, AXEL, AND ME"

CABBAGE STUFFED WITH MUSHROOMS AND MEAT

yield: 4 TO 6 SERVINGS

Prepared with soaked matzoh instead of rice, these delicious cabbage rolls also make an elegant and filling main course at Passover. Green cabbage will work well, but I find the frilly savoy prettier and tastier.

FOR THE CABBAGE ROLLS

½ to ¾ cup flavorful dried mushrooms (about 1 ounce), preferably porcini (avoid dried shiitake here)

1 whole matzoh

1 cup chicken broth, preferably homemade (see pages 62 and 70), or good-quality, low-sodium purchased

1 head savoy or green cabbage (1½ to 2 pounds)

Salt

2 cups chopped onion

3 tablespoons olive oil

1 tablespoon plus 1 teaspoon minced garlic

Freshly ground black pepper

1 pound lean ground beef

¼ cup chopped fresh dill

3 tablespoons chopped fresh parsley

1 large egg, beaten

MAKE the cabbage rolls: put the mushrooms in a bowl, cover with very hot tap water, and let them soak, covered, for 45 minutes.

IN another bowl, crumble the matzoh into small pieces and cover with the broth. Let the matzoh steep for at least 20 minutes to drink in as much of the liquid as possible.

USING a sharp knife, carefully cut away the large outer leaves of the cabbage from the core end. Rinse, then blanch them in a large pot of boiling salted water, 4 or 5 at a time, until just soft enough to bend and fold without breaking. Drain and pat dry as they are done, and set them aside to cool. Coarsely chop the inner leaves too small to roll and set aside no more than 2 cups of them for the sauce (any remainder can be discarded or saved for another purpose).

IN a skillet, sauté the onions in 2 tablespoons of the oil over medium heat until softened and pale gold, about 10 minutes. Add 1 tablespoon of the garlic and cook for 5 to 10 minutes until the onions deepen to a rich, bronze-tinged gold. Season with salt and pepper and transfer to a large bowl. Wipe out the skillet with a paper towel.

DRAIN the mushrooms through a colander lined with a paper towel or a coffee filter, reserving the mushroom liquid for stock or gravy. Rinse the mushrooms briefly under cold water to remove any grit, dry, and chop them. In the wiped out skillet, heat the remaining 1 tablespoon oil and add the remaining 1 teaspoon garlic. Sauté for 1 to 2 minutes, then add the mushrooms and salt and pepper to taste. Cook, tossing frequently, for 2 to 3 minutes to mingle the flavors. Add the mushrooms to the onions, together with the beef, dill, parsley, and egg. Stir in the matzoh and its soaking liquid, a little at a time so it is completely absorbed. Season with salt and pepper to taste and mix everything together well (your hands are best for this).

2 tablespoons olive oil

4 or 5 large garlic cloves, peeled and lightly crushed

1 cup carrots, scraped and chopped

Salt and freshly ground black pepper

2 cups canned Italian plum tomatoes, coarsely chopped, with their juice

2 cups chicken broth, preferably homemade (see pages 62 and 70), or good-quality, low-sodium purchased

Juice of 1 lemon

Accompaniments: challah or other good bread, or mashed potatoes

PREHEAT oven to 325°F.

STUFF the cabbage leaves: place them on a work surface, curled ends up like an open palm. Cut out the hard little triangle at the base of each stem. Put about ⅓ cup of filling (depending on the size of the leaf) in the center. Fold the stem end of the leaf over the filling, then tuck in the two sides. Pull the top tightly over these folds to enclose. The cabbage rolls should be compact and rounded. Place the finished rolls seam side down as you work.

PREPARE the sauce: in a 6-quart Dutch oven or large heavy ovenproof casserole, heat the oil until hot, then add the garlic and carrots. Sauté, stirring, over moderately high heat for about 5 minutes, until the vegetables begin to turn pale gold at the edges. Add the reserved chopped cabbage, sprinkle with salt and pepper, and sauté, lifting and turning the vegetables so they don't scorch, over moderately high heat, until the cabbage is softened and very lightly browned in parts. While the vegetables are cooking, combine the tomatoes, broth, and lemon juice in a bowl and season to taste.

PLACE the cabbage rolls on top of the sautéed vegetables, keeping them seam side down. Pack them together closely, and, if necessary, make a second layer. Pour the tomato sauce evenly over the cabbage rolls, cover the pot tightly, and bring to a boil. Transfer to the oven and bake for 2 hours. Uncover and bake for an additional 30 minutes to 1 hour, until the cabbage is very tender.

YOU'LL want to sop up every drop of the lusty, deep-flavored sauce, so serve the cabbage rolls with lots of challah or other good bread or mashed potatoes.

EXCELLENT reheated and even better the second day.

SYRIAN STUFFED ZUCCHINI IN TOMATO-APRICOT SAUCE (*MAHSHI KOOSA*)

yield: 6 TO 8 SERVINGS

*P*iles of finger-size zucchini hollowed out by nimble fingers with special tools; whispered gossiping punctuated by bursts of laughter; perfumes of sautéing garlic, buttery pine nuts, and the rosewater scent of her grandmother—all this was evoked for my Syrian-Jewish friend by a single word: mahshi (Arabic for stuffed, as in stuffed vegetables). As a little girl, she couldn't wait to enter that world of mahshi, but by the time she was old enough, it had vanished.

Yet, while few people have the time today to scoop out dozens of improbably small squash, very good mahshi is still being made in Middle Eastern kitchens now using medium-size zucchini, hollowed into tubes with an apple corer and the tip of a vegetable peeler. And home cooks have updated their recipes, with fillings of leaner meats and lighter-tasting sauces.

Without fat, though, meat combined with rice makes for a rather dry stuffing, so I substitute orzo, which mimics the rice in appearance, but tastes so much moister. The subtle sweet-sour sauce gets a zingy finish here from a last-minute addition of garlic, mint, and lemon.

1/3 cup orzo

1 cup dried apricots (use the tart California variety here), diced

4 tablespoons olive oil

1/4 cup pine nuts

3 cups finely chopped onion

Salt and freshly ground black pepper

1 tablespoon plus 1 teaspoon finely chopped garlic

1 pound ground beef, lamb, or turkey (dark meat, from the thigh)

1 1/2 teaspoons ground allspice

PLACE the orzo in a small heatproof bowl and cover it with very hot tap water. Plump the apricots in another small heatproof bowl with 1 cup very hot tap water. Set the bowls aside.

IN a heavy, deep ovenproof skillet (cast-iron is ideal here) large enough to hold all the zucchini in a single layer (see Cook's Note), heat 2 tablespoons oil over moderate heat. Add the pine nuts and fry, shaking the pan frequently, until the nuts are golden, about 5 minutes. Transfer the nuts and any oil from the pan to a large bowl. Add the 2 remaining tablespoons oil to the skillet and heat until shimmering. Add the onions, salt and pepper lightly, and sauté over moderate heat, stirring, until pale gold, about 5 minutes. Add 1 tablespoon of the garlic and continue sautéing for another minute or two. The vegetables should remain lightly colored; don't let them brown. Transfer about half of the mixture to the bowl of pine nuts, leaving the remainder in the skillet. Set the skillet aside, off the heat.

½ teaspoon ground cinnamon

Generous pinch of ground cloves

6 to 8 zucchini (about 3 pounds in all)

1 cup canned tomato puree

2 tablespoons pomegranate molasses

Juice of ½ to 1 lemon

1 tablespoon brown sugar

1 tablespoon dried mint

PREHEAT the oven to 350°F.

DRAIN the orzo and add it to the vegetable–pine nut mixture. Add the meat, allspice, cinnamon, cloves, salt (figure 1½ to 2 teaspoons kosher salt), and a liberal sprinkling of pepper, and mix until thoroughly combined.

RINSE the zucchini and cut off the ends. Working from both ends, use an apple corer, supplemented, if needed, by the tip of a vegetable peeler (or a special Middle Eastern long, thin corer or vegetable reamer, if you have one) to scoop out the zucchini pulp. Carefully twist and rotate the corer to sever the pulp and withdraw it until the zucchini are hollowed out; avoid piercing the zucchini skin. Save the zucchini pulp for another dish such as soup, or sauté with garlic and dill, and serve as a vegetable (see Cook's Note).

FILL the zucchini with the meat stuffing (easiest to do using your hands), leaving a little room on either end so the stuffing won't spill out into the sauce (the orzo won't expand much more).

RETURN the skillet to the stove, add the tomato puree, apricots, and any water they have not absorbed, pomegranate molasses, brown sugar, and salt and pepper to taste, and bring to a simmer. Arrange the zucchini in a single layer in the skillet and spoon the sauce over them. Cover the skillet, slip it into the oven, and bake for 1 hour to 1 hour and 15 minutes, or until the zucchini are tender. Turn the zucchini once or twice in the sauce as they cook.

TRANSFER the zucchini to a platter. Crush the mint between your fingers and add it to the sauce, together with the remaining teaspoon of garlic and lemon juice to taste (start with the lesser amount). Simmer for 2 minutes to mingle the flavors. Taste and adjust seasonings, adding more lemon juice, if necessary, to reach a beguiling sour-sweet balance.

SPOON the sauce over the zucchini and serve.

COOK'S NOTE: If you don't have an ovenproof skillet large enough, use a regular skillet to prepare the sauce and bake the zucchini in a covered baking pan large enough to hold them snugly in one layer.

For a richer taste—and a little extra work—hollow out the zucchini first, and sauté them in a little oil before you start the stuffing.

I sometimes include the zucchini pulp in the sauce for added texture: after I scoop out the onions and garlic for the filling, I sauté the chopped and salted pulp (it is rather bland) with the onion mixture remaining in the skillet.

Vegetarian Stuffing For my cousin Adrienne, who does not eat meat, I sautéed the chopped zucchini pulp with the onions and garlic until lightly bronzed. Combined with the orzo, pine nuts, and spices, it made a delicious filling.

STUFFED VEGETABLES

Eating stuffed vegetables on Sukkot is common among Jews of many culinary traditions. Reflecting the agricultural roots of the holiday, the colorful, fat vegetables, plump to bursting with lush, savory fillings, celebrate the glorious abundance of the harvest. And on a spiritual level, the rounded, seamless parcels symbolize the continuity of the Torah, the reading of which is both finished and recommended each year on Simchat Torah, the festival immediately following Sukkot.

Here is a medley for a variety of tastes: stuffed cabbage, autumn-scented with wild mushrooms and meat; Syrian stuffed zucchini in tomato-apricot sauce; roasted red peppers filled with *mujadderah* (a mix of well-seasoned fried onions, lentils, rice, and pine nuts) in a garlic-tomato sauce; and substituting for grape leaves, fresh chard packed with rice and artichokes. And please see page 83 for a Sukkot/Simchat Torah favorite, Classic Sweet-and-Sour Stuffed Cabbage.

MUJADDERAH-FILLED ROASTED RED PEPPERS IN TOMATO-GARLIC SAUCE

yield: 8 SERVINGS

*R*oasting removes the callow edge from crisp red peppers, turning their flavor sophisticated—at once hauntingly smoky and sweet—and their texture soft and voluptuous. If I'm going to the trouble of stuffing peppers, it's roasted red ones I'm after.

For a Sukkot dinner, I wanted a vegetarian filling to equal the flavor of these peppers, one that would not make you feel there was something missing where the meat should be. Popular all over the Middle East among Jews and Arabs, mujadderah, a rice and lentil combination made scrumptious with a shower of golden fried onions, was the perfect fit. It needed only sweet toasted pine nuts for textural contrast and cilantro to lend an herby freshness.

FOR THE PEPPERS

1 cup brown lentils

Salt

4 tablespoons well-flavored extra virgin olive oil (the rich taste of the oil should shine through here)

1¼ pounds onions, thinly sliced (5 cups)

1 tablespoon finely chopped garlic

1 cup long-grain white rice

½ teaspoon ground cumin, preferably freshly toasted and ground

Freshly ground black pepper

8 large red bell peppers (choose peppers that are unblemished, sturdy, and thick-walled)

4 to 5 tablespoons pine nuts, lightly toasted

3 to 4 tablespoons chopped fresh cilantro, plus additional for garnish (optional)

PICK over the lentils carefully, discarding any stray objects or discolored beans, and rinse well in cold water. Drain, combine them in a large saucepan with 4 cups fresh cold water, and bring to a boil. Reduce the heat and simmer for 20 minutes. Add salt to taste about 5 minutes before the end of cooking. Turn off the heat, and leave the lentils in the saucepan, covered, until you are ready to add the rest of the mujadderah ingredients.

WHILE the lentils are cooking, heat 3 tablespoons of the oil in a 10- to 12-inch heavy skillet over medium-high heat. Add the onions, sprinkle with salt, and sauté, lifting and turning them occasionally, for about 15 minutes, until softened. Add the garlic, and cook another 15 minutes, or until the onions are a rich caramel color.

ADD about one third of the sautéed onion mixture to the cooked lentils, leaving the remaining onion mixture in the skillet. Stir the rice, cumin, and plenty of salt and pepper to taste into the lentils. If necessary, add more water so that everything is completely covered by about ½ inch of water. Mix the ingredients well, cover, and bring to a boil. Simmer for about 30 minutes, until the rice is tender and all the liquid is absorbed. Peek every now and then to see if more water is needed, and give the mixture a stir.

WHILE the mujadderah cooks, roast the bell peppers. It's best to do this over a gas flame, since you need to char the outsides quickly, without overcooking the tender flesh.

2 teaspoons chopped garlic

1 tablespoon olive oil

1 pound fresh plum tomatoes, peeled (see page 34 for procedure) and coarsely chopped, or about 2 cups Italian canned tomatoes, drained and coarsely chopped

Salt and freshly ground black pepper

Optional accompaniments for dairy meals: yogurt cream (see page 30) or *labneh*, seasoned perhaps with minced scallions, chives, or other fresh herbs

IF cooking over a gas flame, use a long-handled fork and spear the pepper through the stem only, making sure not to pierce through the pepper anywhere else. Roast them, like marshmallows, over the open flame. Or place the pepper on a roasting rack set over the flame. Keep turning the peppers until the skins are lightly charred on all sides.

YOU can also roast them under the broiler. Place the peppers on a foil-lined broiler rack under a preheated broiler, as close as possible to the heat source. Turn the peppers as the skins blister and blacken.

PUT the charred peppers in a paper bag and twist the bag closed, or put them in a covered bowl. Let them steam just until cool enough to handle so that they will be easier to peel. Rub the peel off with your fingers. Because these peppers are thick-walled, you can also rub off the peel with a dry paper towel, replacing the towel as it becomes saturated with the charred peel. Don't worry if you don't remove every piece of blackened skin—a few bits here and there will add to the smoky flavor. (Don't peel the peppers under water, because they will get too waterlogged.)

USING a small, sharp knife, cut out the peppers' stems and discard. Carefully pull out the seeds and membranes and discard (see Cook's Note).

PREPARE the tomato-garlic sauce: the success of this quickly made sauce depends on cooking the ingredients in a skillet, rather than a saucepan, so the watery juices evaporate before the fresh taste is lost.

IN a 9-inch heavy skillet, sauté the garlic in the oil over medium heat until fragrant and softened—don't let it color more than pale yellow. Add the tomatoes, and salt and pepper to taste, and turn the heat up to high. Cook, stirring for 6 to 10 minutes, until nicely thickened, with a still-vivid tomato taste. Adjust the seasoning.

PREHEAT the oven to 350°F.

GENEROUSLY salt and pepper the remaining sautéed onions in the skillet and cook over medium-high heat, lifting and turning, until slightly crisp in places and tinged a toasty brown. When the rice and lentils are cooked, stir these onions into them. Then stir in 3 tablespoons of the pine nuts and cilantro, if using.

SPOON some of the sauce on the bottom of a shallow baking dish just large enough to accommodate the peppers when standing upright. (Alternatively, if peppers tore and you are stuffing the pepper halves, choose a dish in which all the peppers will fit comfortably when lying flat.) Fill the peppers with the mujadderah (see Cook's Note) and sprinkle the tops with the remaining 1 to 2 tablespoons pine nuts and garnish with some additional cilantro, if desired. Arrange the peppers in the pan and spoon the remaining sauce over them. Bake for about 20 minutes, until heated through.

FOR dairy meals, accompany the peppers with rich yogurt cream or *labneh*.

COOK'S NOTE: When handling the roasted peppers, be especially gentle to avoid tearing their tender flesh. A small hole or two won't really matter with thick-walled peppers—the filling is rather dense and not likely to pour out of a little puncture. If you do rip the peppers, simply cut them all in half and lay them flat on their backs, like open palms facing you, and mound the stuffing carefully inside. You will need a larger baking pan and more sauce, though, since peppers lying flat will take up more space. Double the sauce recipe, and save any extra for another use.

The sauce is very versatile: delicious on pasta, fish, chicken, or vegetables. You can double it if you use a very large skillet. Adjust cooking time as needed to evaporate the juices and thicken the sauce. Feel free to add your favorite fresh herbs, spices, grated lemon zest, or sautéed, sliced fresh mushrooms to the sauce. Or stir in lemon or orange juice and cook over high heat until absorbed. Mellow overly acidic tomatoes with a pinch or two of sugar, if necessary, or for dairy meals, stir in a bit of sweet butter.

CHARD STUFFED WITH ARTICHOKES AND RICE

yield: ABOUT 6 SERVINGS

*F*resh grape leaves rarely come my way, and the preserved variety can be tough and tired tasting. Taking my cue from Middle Eastern cooks, I often substitute more readily available fresh green Swiss chard for the vine leaves. Served cold, traditional Sephardi recipes for meatless stuffed leaves are particularly flavorful, packed with an abundance of fresh herbs and evocative spices. I've added chips of artichoke for their velvety texture and buttery depth.

You might serve these grouped on a platter with other appetizers such as Classic Hummus (page 297) or Lentils "Hummus-Style" (page 219), strips of marinated roasted red peppers (see page 240), Chickpeas with Garlic and Barbeque Spices (page 326), or an array of crudités or composed vegetable salads, like North African Cooked Carrot Salad (page 138). These Swiss chard rolls also make excellent finger food for holiday buffets and parties.

FOR THE CHARD ROLLS

1¼ cups long-grain white rice

About 1½ pounds green Swiss chard, including stems (look for unblemished leaves, without holes or tears)

Salt

1 tablespoon finely minced garlic

2 tablespoons olive oil

1½ cups cooked fresh artichoke hearts (about 4 ½ ounces) or thawed frozen artichoke hearts, patted dry with paper towels and diced

Freshly ground black pepper

⅓ cup finely chopped fresh dill

⅓ cup finely chopped fresh mint, or 2 teaspoons dried mint

PREPARE the chard rolls: put the rice in a bowl, add enough cold water to cover by 1 inch, and let soak for 30 minutes.

RINSE the chard well, then cut the stems flush with the leaves. Set the stems aside for the sauce. In a large stockpot, bring 6 quarts water and 1 tablespoon salt to a rolling boil. Add the chard leaves and blanch until they are just pliable enough to bend and fold without breaking, 2 to 4 minutes, depending on the size of the leaves. Scoop the leaves out with a strainer or kitchen tongs and briefly shake off the cooking water or drain in a colander, and let them cool. Dry more thoroughly on kitchen towels or place them on a platter and pat dry with paper towels.

IN a medium skillet, sauté the garlic in the oil over medium heat until just pale gold, about 2 minutes. Add the artichokes and cook, stirring for 3 minutes to marry the flavors. Season with salt and pepper, then transfer the contents of the skillet to a large bowl. Drain the rice in a fine-mesh sieve, and add it to the bowl, along with the dill, mint, lemon zest, allspice, and additional salt and pepper to taste. Mix the ingredients well.

STUFF the chard: place the leaves on a work surface, shiny side down. They should be easy to roll, but with very mature leaves, you may find it necessary to cut out a hard little wedge of stem at the base. Spoon some filling (from 1 to 2 heaping teaspoons up to ¼ cup, depending on

2 teaspoons grated lemon zest

½ teaspoon ground allspice

FOR THE SAUCE
(SEE COOK'S NOTE)

Salt and freshly ground black pepper

2 tablespoons coarsely chopped garlic

⅓ cup extra virgin olive oil

about ⅓ cup fresh lemon juice

1 tablespoon dried mint

Accompaniment: lemon wedges

the size of the leaf) in the center of each leaf, near the stem end. Fold the stem end of the leaf over the filling, then fold in the two sides. Roll up the leaf, jelly-roll fashion, to form a neat little roll. The rolls should be compact, but don't roll them too tightly; you must allow a little space for the rice to expand.

PREPARE the sauce: slice the reserved chard stems into approximately 3-inch lengths, and line a 6-quart Dutch oven or large heavy saucepan with them. Place the chard rolls close together on top of the stems, seam side down, in layers if necessary. Season each layer well with salt, pepper, and some of the chopped garlic. In a small bowl, stir together 1½ cups water, the olive oil, lemon juice, and dried mint and pour evenly over the rolls. Place a heatproof plate or a pot lid just smaller than the diameter of the pan on top of the rolls and weight the plate down with several more heatproof plates.

BRING the liquid to a boil, cover the pan, and simmer the chard rolls over moderate heat, checking every once in a while to see if more liquid is needed, for about 1 hour, or until the rice tastes cooked through, the rolls are very tender, and most of the liquid is absorbed.

REMOVE the pan from the heat and uncover. The stuffed leaves will seem close to falling apart, but don't worry. They will firm up nicely as they cool, still weighted down. When they are at room temperature, remove the plates, pour off any remaining liquid, and arrange the rolls on a platter. Discard the chard stems (or nibble them for a delicious cook's perk). Taste the rolls and sprinkle with additional salt or lemon juice, if needed, then wrap well and refrigerate until cold so they will firm up further.

SEPHARDI Jews serve meatless stuffed leaves (chard, grape, and spinach) chilled or at room temperature, but not icy cold, which would obscure the delicate herbal flavor. (Meat-filled leaves, however, are served hot.) Arrange the rolls on individual appetizer plates with lemon wedges or present them as part of a platter of appetizers. Like stuffed cabbage, they are even better the next day after the flavors mingle and unfold.

COOK'S NOTE: For a tart-sweet variation, substitute 1½ cups prune juice for the water in the sauce. And instead of mint, flavor it with about 2 tablespoons pomegranate molasses and 1 or 2 tablespoons brown sugar or to taste.

GRILLED BASS WITH POMEGRANATE-MINT VINAIGRETTE

yield: 6 TO 8 SERVINGS

The soft night air smelled of fallen leaves and ocean breezes in my last childhood sukkah, and we barbecued every night the week we spent there. Though I've lived in a Manhattan apartment since my college days, I still associate Sukkot with fall foods grilled outdoors.

This year we cooked striped bass in our fireplace grill, over wood perfumed with sticks of wild fennel gathered and dried on a recent trip to Los Angeles. But if you have neither an outdoor grill nor a fireplace, this fish will still be delicious broiled or prepared with an electric grill, when lightly marinated with herbs and garlic, then drizzled with this fresh-tasting vinaigrette of lime, mint, and the subtle tang of pomegranate juice.

FOR THE MARINADE

6 garlic cloves, coarsely chopped

¼ cup fresh cilantro leaves, chopped

¼ cup fresh flat-leaf parsley leaves, chopped

⅓ cup extra virgin olive oil

1 teaspoon kosher salt

½ teaspoon freshly ground black pepper

3 pounds striped or sea bass fillets, or other firm, thick white fish, skin on

FOR THE POMEGRANATE-MINT VINAIGRETTE

1 or 2 garlic cloves, coarsely chopped

2 teaspoons dried mint

COMBINE the marinade ingredients in a large resealable plastic bag. Add the fish and rub the marinade into the sides of the fillets. Refrigerate for 30 minutes to 2 hours (since there is no citrus juice in the marinade, the fish will not turn mushy), moving the fish around in the marinade once or twice. Bring the fish to room temperature when you are ready to cook it.

PREPARE the vinaigrette: place the garlic, mint, lime and pomegranate juices in a blender and process on high speed to a coarse puree. With the machine on, slowly add the oil and continue processing for 2 minutes. Transfer the vinaigrette to a glass jar and add salt and Aleppo pepper or paprika to taste. Shake well. Adjust seasonings, adding more lime juice, if necessary. Let the flavors marry for at least 30 minutes before using. Shake the vinaigrette well before serving.

OIL a grill or broiler pan, and preheat it to medium-high. Grill or broil the fish, starting with the skin side closest to the heat source. Using two spatulas, if necessary, turn the fish after about 5 minutes. (Alternatively, grill the fish in a wire mesh fish cage and simply flip it over.) Continue grilling until the fish is just cooked through; the exact time will depend on the variety and thickness of the fish. To test the fish for doneness, insert a thin-bladed knife in the thickest part. The fish should be opaque or show a slight bit of translucence, according to your preference.

About 3 tablespoons fresh lime juice

2 tablespoons pomegranate juice (*not* pomegranate molasses)

½ cup best-quality extra virgin olive oil

Salt

Aleppo pepper or smoked paprika

Oil for grilling

Accompaniments: lime quarters; cilantro or parsley sprigs

TRANSFER the fish to a platter and drizzle with some of the vinaigrette. Garnish with the fresh herb sprigs and lime quarters and pass the remaining vinaigrette separately.

IRANIAN GRILLED CHICKEN THIGHS WITH SUMAC

yield: ABOUT 4 SERVINGS

Before there was lemon juice, there was sumac: tart, purple-red berries that grow wild all over the hills of the Middle East. Dried and ground, sumac has an alluring fruity-sour taste, more floral and less sharp than lemon, and is used anywhere lemon would provide sparkle: grilled foods, creamy soups and sauces, and salads.

In fact, it's better than citrus in the marinades that Jews from Turkey, Iran, and the Fertile Crescent favor for fish, chicken, and kebabs because it contains none of the acetic acid that can break down delicate proteins during an extended soak in a lemony bath. By the time the flesh is flavored by an acidic marinade, it might be overtenderized, even mushy.

There is no such danger with this savory sumac marinade. I remove the poultry skin so the seasoning can penetrate the meat even more, and let the chicken steep for several hours.

But all that carefully created flavor and good texture mean nothing if the bird is overcooked. Chicken breasts turn dry and tough all too easily when grilled, so I hedge my bets with thighs, likelier to remain moist and juicier, and watch carefully.

1/2 cup grated onion

5 or 6 cloves garlic, finely chopped

2 tablespoons dried oregano

1 tablespoon sumac

1 teaspoon ground cumin, preferably freshly toasted and ground

1/2 teaspoon ground cinnamon

Salt and freshly ground black pepper

1/3 cup olive oil, plus additional for greasing the rack or pan

3 pounds bone-in chicken thighs, skin, and all visible fat removed

Accompaniment: lemon quarters

PREPARE the marinade: in a small bowl, stir together the onion, garlic, oregano, sumac, cumin, cinnamon, and salt and pepper to taste. Add the olive oil and whisk until well blended. Remove 2 tablespoons of the marinade and set it aside, covered and refrigerated, until you are ready to grill.

PLACE the chicken thighs in a large, heavy resealable plastic bag, and pour the remaining marinade over them. Shake the bag until all the pieces are bathing in the marinade. Seal the bag and refrigerate for at least 3 hours, or preferably overnight, occasionally shaking the bag or moving the thighs around to ensure the marinade is evenly distributed over all surfaces of the chicken.

BRING the chicken to room temperature.

TO grill using the stovetop and oven method: preheat the oven to 350°F. Grease a large ridged cast-iron skillet or a stovetop grill. Line a shallow roasting pan or rimmed baking sheet with foil (for easy cleanup) and fit it with a rack. (If your cast-iron skillet is very large and you are able to fit all the chicken on it, you won't need the roasting pan.) Heat the skillet or stovetop grill over medium-high heat until it is sizzling. Add the chicken, in batches as necessary, and cook, turning often, until it is seared well on both sides, about 10 minutes in all. Transfer the chicken to the rack in the roasting pan (or arrange all the chicken pieces in the skillet, if they can fit in one layer). Place the pan in the oven and cook, turning once or twice, until the juices run clear when the thickest sections are pierced with a skewer or knife, 25 to 30 minutes. (This method really requires a *ridged* skillet or grill. Don't start the chicken in a regular unridged greased skillet; the marinade will burn when it hits the oil. If you have neither a ridged cast-iron skillet nor a stovetop grill, roast the chicken in a preheated 450°F oven, turning occasionally, for 35 to 40 minutes.)

TO grill outdoors or in a fireplace: grease the grill rack. Light a gas grill or prepare a fire using briquettes or hardwood. When it is moderately hot (the coals should be glowing red and covered with a moderate layer of gray ash), put the grill rack back on the grill and let it get sizzling hot. Arrange the chicken on the rack and cook, turning frequently with tongs, until the juices run clear when the thickest sections are pierced with a skewer or knife, 35 to 45 minutes in all.

BRUSH the sizzling chicken with reserved marinade and sprinkle lightly with lemon juice, fresh pepper, and salt before serving. Excellent hot, at room temperature, or cold.

COOK'S NOTE: Available in Middle Eastern markets, retail and online spice shops, and many specialty stores, sumac can vary widely in quality—one label I purchased recently from a specialty store chain had a musty, off-taste—so look for a brand you like. If you are in a store that sells spices in bulk, ask to taste before purchasing.

I use the large holes of a Microplane to grate the onion quickly.

ROMANIAN GARLICKY GROUND MEAT SAUSAGES (*CARNATZLACH*) WITH SOUR PICKLE VINAIGRETTE AND ROASTED RED PEPPERS

yield: **4 TO 5 SERVINGS**

I love pickles, though they never live up to their smell: a siren song of heady garlic, spicy peppercorns, and other enticing aromatics. Crunchy and cold, they provide refreshing respite from the dryness and density of unsauced meats, especially in sandwiches and simple grills.

Eating carnatzlach, I grew tired of alternating one bite of barbequed meat with a juicy chew of pickle, so I turned the pickle into this sauce.

This garlicky Romanian grill is wonderful anytime, but it is particularly appealing for casual Indian summer meals during the holiday. If you're cutting down on beef, well-seasoned turkey is a good substitute here.

2 to 3 tablespoons coarsely chopped garlic, or to taste

2 teaspoons sweet paprika

About 1 teaspoon salt (more if using ground turkey)

1 teaspoon dried oregano or marjoram

½ teaspoon ground allspice

¼ to ½ teaspoon freshly ground black pepper; or fresh, hot but not searing, chile (preferably Fresno or serrano, but Hungarian wax, jalapeño, or other varieties will do fine), roasted (see Cook's Note), peeled and finely chopped (be sure to use rubber gloves when preparing)

1½ pounds lean ground beef (you can substitute ground turkey—the ground thigh meat will work best—with fine

IN a food processor combine the garlic, paprika, salt, oregano or marjoram, allspice, black pepper or chile, and ¼ cup water and pulse until the garlic is chopped very fine. Add a third of the meat and process until thoroughly incorporated with the seasoning. Add another third of the meat and pulse a few times. Add the final third and continue pulsing, stopping to scrape down the bowl, if necessary, until the mixture is well combined, very soft, and almost pasty.

TRANSFER to a bowl, cover, and refrigerate for at least 4 hours or overnight so that all the vibrant flavors will meld together.

WHEN ready to cook the carnatzlach, set out a small bowl of cold water and a large platter. Moisten your hands with the water, take a small lump of the meat mixture, and roll it into a sausage 3- to 4-inches long and 1-inch wide (about the size of your middle finger, but a little wider). Place the shaped carnatzl on the platter and continue making more, wetting your hands as necessary, until all the meat is rolled. You'll have approximately 14 to 17 sausages.

PREHEAT the broiler, outdoor grill, or (my choice) a heavy ridged cast-iron skillet on top of the stove, to high temperature. (Spray rack or pan lightly with oil first, if not nonstick.) Grill or broil the sausages until beautifully browned, crusty, and cooked to desired doneness, 5 to 7 minutes per side.

TO serve, arrange some roasted red pepper strips and chopped scallions on a plate. Nestle a few carnatzlach attractively over them, and spoon results, but you may want to increase the seasoning slightly)

Oil for greasing the broiler rack or pan, if needed

Accompaniments: 2 large red bell peppers, roasted (see Cook's Note), cut into strips, and seasoned well with salt, pepper, extra virgin olive oil, and a little vinegar or lemon juice to taste; chopped scallions (both white and green parts); Sour Pickle Vinaigrette (recipe follows); half-sour or garlic dill pickles, sliced lengthwise; garlic dill tomatoes

a generous amount of sour pickle vinaigrette over everything. Garnish with pickles and garlic dill tomatoes.

COOK'S NOTE: To roast peppers, spear them with a long-handled fork, and roast like marshmallows over an open flame (a gas burner or outdoor fire). Or place the peppers on a roasting rack set directly over the flame. Keep turning the peppers until the skins are lightly charred on all sides. You can also roast them under the broiler. Place the peppers on a foil-lined rack under a preheated broiler, as close as possible to the heat source. Turn the peppers as the skins blister and blacken.

Put charred peppers in a paper bag and twist the bag closed, or put them in a covered bowl. Let them steam until cool enough to handle—this will make them easier to peel. Rub the skins off with your fingers (if preparing chiles, make sure you are wearing rubber gloves). Don't worry if you don't remove every piece of charred skin—a few bits here and there will add smoky flavor. Although this is messy and the peel will stick to your fingers, I don't recommend peeling the peppers under water, as some suggest, because it washes away the flavorful oils, making the peppers soggy and flat-tasting. Instead, dip your hands into a bowl of water every so often or wipe them on a paper towel to clean them. Pull out and discard the stem, seeds, and ribs. The peppers are ready to be used in a recipe.

SOUR PICKLE VINAIGRETTE

1 cup coarsely chopped half-sour or garlic-dill pickles

2 tablespoons liquid from pickle jar (include peppercorns and other flavorings, if desired)

3 tablespoons best-quality extra virgin olive oil

Salt and freshly ground black pepper

Fresh lemon juice

yield: 4 TO 5 SERVINGS

PLACE the pickles and pickle liquid in a blender and process at high speed until pureed. With the machine on, slowly add the oil. Continue processing another minute or two, until the mixture is smooth and emulsified. Transfer to a bowl, and add salt, pepper, and lemon juice as needed. You can serve the sauce right away, but it's best to allow the flavors to mellow for a while in the refrigerator. Stir the vinaigrette before serving.

"With several helpers, she brought platters of cold sweet-and-sour fish, stewed meat, and roasted chicken, flasks of lemonade, baskets filled with rolls and hard white pretzels, bowls of sauerkraut sprinkled with sugar, and plates filled with freshly pickled cucumbers as cold as ice."

—CHAIM GRADE, "THE REBBETZIN"

AROMATIC MARINATED BRISKET WITH CHESTNUTS

yield: ABOUT 8 SERVINGS

Back in biblical days, wily Jacob knew the value of adding chestnut to foods. After he put chestnut twigs in the water he fed to his father-in-law Laban's strongest cattle, they gave birth to spotted calves. Good news for Jacob: he had just cut a deal with Laban—all the spotted cattle in the flock now belonged to him. (The tale lives on in the beautiful spotted heirloom beans known as Jacob's Cattle.)

Today, chestnuts continue to lend their charms to many Jewish dishes. As they do for the French and the Japanese, sweet chestnuts serve as New Year's food for Jews from Transylvania, who eat them when reciting the Sheheheyonu, *a prayer for new fruits at Rosh Hashanah. At Sukkot, Hungarian Jews cook them in a special tsimmes, and I have seen several variations for a Passover haroset recipe from Padua, Italy, all calling for chestnuts.*

Here the chestnuts break up, imparting a nutty sweetness to the brisket. To build additional layers of flavor, I first stud the meat with garlic, then bathe it in a pomegranate molasses and balsamic vinegar marinade.

5 large garlic cloves, peeled

A first- or second-cut beef brisket (4 to 5 pounds), trimmed of excess fat, wiped with a damp paper towel, and patted dry

¼ cup pomegranate molasses or *temerhindi* (see page 40)

¼ cup moderately priced balsamic vinegar

12 peppercorns, crushed

2 to 5 tablespoons olive or canola oil

1½ pounds onions, chopped (6 cups)

Salt and freshly ground black pepper

8 to 10 medium carrots, scraped and quartered

CUT half the garlic into thin lengthwise slivers and set the rest aside. Make a little slit in the fat side of the brisket with the point of a small, sharp knife. Insert a garlic sliver into the slit, using your fingers and the knife tip to push it in as far as possible. In the same way, insert the remaining slivers all over the top and bottom of the brisket, spacing them as evenly as you can.

IF you have a heavy resealable plastic bag or roasting bag large enough to hold the brisket, put the meat in the bag and place it on a baking sheet. Otherwise, just put the brisket in a large nonreactive pan or bowl. Combine the pomegranate molasses or *temerhindi*, balsamic vinegar, and crushed peppercorns in a small bowl. Chop the remaining garlic and add it to the bowl. Pour the mixture over the brisket. Close the plastic bag or cover the pan with foil and marinate the meat in the refrigerator for a minimum of 2 and a maximum of 4 hours, turning the meat occasionally.

REMOVE the meat from the refrigerator and bring it to room temperature. Take out the brisket and pat it dry with paper towels. Reserve the marinade.

3 fresh thyme sprigs or
1 teaspoon dried leaves

2 cups chestnuts,
blanched and peeled
(see Cook's Note), or use
frozen or vacuum-packed,
or, less preferably, canned
or jarred (packed in
water)

Optional accompaniment:
Spiced Pomegranate
Molasses Applesauce
(page 295)

BECAUSE the brisket tends to splatter somewhat from the marinade (even if patted dry), and because it is so large, I find it easier to brown the meat under the broiler. Just cover the broiler pan well with foil to minimize cleanup. If you prefer, sear the brisket on top of the stove. I offer both methods.

METHOD one: preheat the broiler. Place the brisket under the broiler, fat side up, on a foil-lined broiler pan. Broil for 5 to 6 minutes on each side, until browned. Don't allow it to develop a hard, dark crust, which might make the meat tough or bitter. Move the meat around as necessary, so it sears evenly. Transfer the brisket to a platter and set aside.

METHOD two: heat 3 tablespoons oil over medium-high heat in a heavy-bottomed roasting pan or casserole large enough to hold the brisket snugly. Use two burners, if necessary. Add the brisket and brown well on both sides, about 10 minutes. Sear it to caramelize the meat, but don't let it develop a hard, dark crust. Transfer the brisket to a platter and set aside.

PREHEAT the oven to 325°F.

IF you browned the meat under the broiler, heat 2 tablespoons oil in a large roasting pan or casserole. If you pan-seared the meat, pour off all the fat in the pan, then heat 2 tablespoons fresh oil. Add the onions and sauté over medium-high heat until the edges are golden, about 10 minutes. Add salt and pepper to taste, turn the heat down to very low, and cook until quite softened, stirring occasionally, 15 to 20 minutes (time will vary depending on type of pan used). Add the carrots, thyme, and the reserved marinade, and bring to a simmer, scraping any browned bits from the bottom of the pan with a wooden spoon.

SALT and pepper the brisket to taste on both sides, and add it to the pan, fat side up. Spoon the vegetables over the meat. Cover tightly and place in the oven.

BRAISE the meat for 1½ hours, basting with the pan sauce and vegetables every 30 minutes. Add the chestnuts. Cover the pan again and continue cooking and basting for 1 to 2 hours or longer, until the meat is fork-tender. (When you baste, check that the liquid is bubbling gently. If it is boiling rapidly, turn the oven down to 300°F.)

REMOVE the pan from the oven and cool the meat for at least 1 hour in the braising liquid. (If possible, refrigerate the cooled brisket and other solids in the braising liquid, covered, overnight. The meat will have more time to reabsorb its cooking juices, and it will be easier to scrape off all the solid fat from the surface of the meat and braising liquid.)

WHEN ready to serve, skim off any congealed fat and bring everything to room temperature, if refrigerated. Transfer the meat, chestnuts, and carrots to a platter (reserve a couple of carrots—and some chestnut pieces, if desired—for thickening the gravy).

MAKE the gravy: remove and discard the thyme sprigs and strain the braising mixture, reserving the solids. Skim and discard as much fat as possible from the liquid. In a food processor or a blender, puree *most* of the solids, including the reserved carrots and chestnuts, with 1 cup of the defatted braising liquid. (If a completely smooth gravy is desired, puree *all* of the solids.) Put the pureed mixture, the remaining braising liquid, and any reserved solids into a clean pan, and cook until the ingredients are well combined and hot. Taste and adjust the seasoning. If the gravy is too thin, boil it down to the desired consistency over high heat.

REDUCE the heat, add the meat, the reserved carrots and chestnuts, and simmer until piping hot.

CUT the brisket into thin slices across the grain at a slight diagonal. Arrange the sliced brisket on the serving platter with the carrots and chestnuts. Spoon some of the hot sauce all over the meat and pass the rest in a sauce boat. Spiced Pomegranate Molasses Applesauce makes a smashing accompaniment.

COOK'S NOTE: Here's how to blanch and peel chestnuts. Using a sharp knife, cut an X on the flat side of the shell. If possible, pierce deeply enough to go through both the peel and the thin brown inner skin. Put the chestnuts in a big heatproof bowl or pot. Pour in enough boiling water to cover them by an inch or two, cover the bowl, and let soak for about 10 minutes. Chestnuts are easiest to peel when hot, so take them out of the water one at a time. Pull off both the shell and the papery skin. Removing the skin can be tedious; if necessary, pour more boiling water over the nuts to loosen it. They are now ready for the recipe. Cut them into bite-size chunks, or if small, leave whole.

MEAT TSIMMES WITH PRUNES AND CARROTS

yield: ABOUT 8 SERVINGS

*T*he appearance of bagels and rugelach at Christmas and Easter brunches seems proof positive that Jewish cuisine has indeed gone mainstream. But what really convinced me was a tsimmes with meat.

Meat is not unusual in the dish—the sweet vegetable and fruit stew is often either made, or paired, with brisket, flanken, or boneless beef chunks. But never with pork chops, as was the sweet potato tsimmes listed on the menu at Merge, a now-defunct restaurant in Greenwich Village.

This recipe is considerably more classic. But it is made without any added sugar or honey: carrots, prunes, and prune juice provide the sweetening, as well as a rich base for the gravy.

4 tablespoons olive oil

About 4 pounds of brisket or beef shoulder roast, trimmed of excess fat, wiped with a damp paper towel, and patted dry

Salt and freshly ground black pepper

1 pound onions, chopped (4 cups)

2 cups prune juice

2 cups chicken broth, preferably homemade (see pages 62 and 70), or good-quality, low-sodium purchased

1 cinnamon stick

1 Turkish bay leaf

6 large garlic cloves, chopped, plus 1 large garlic clove, minced

About 2 tablespoons apple cider vinegar

PREHEAT the oven to 325°F.

HEAT the oil over medium-high heat in a wide 6- to 8-quart Dutch oven or heavy flameproof casserole. Add the meat and brown it well on all sides, but don't allow it to develop a hard, dark crust, which might make the meat bitter or tough. (If necessary, cut the meat in half and brown it in batches.) Transfer the meat to a platter, salt and pepper it all over, and set it aside.

POUR off all the fat in the pot and heat 2 tablespoons fresh oil. Add the onions, salt and pepper them well, and sauté them over medium heat, lifting and tossing occasionally, until they are nicely caramelized, about 15 minutes.

ADD the prune juice, broth, cinnamon, and bay leaf, and bring to a boil, scraping up the delicious browned bits from the bottom of the pot with a wooden spoon.

REDUCE the heat to a simmer. Add the meat, fat side up, scatter the top with the chopped garlic, and spoon the pan sauce over everything. Cover tightly with foil, and place the pot lid over that.

BRAISE the meat in the oven for 2 hours, basting with the pan sauce every 30 minutes.

ADD the vinegar to the pan sauce. Scatter the carrots, potatoes, and prunes around the meat, and spoon the pan sauce over them. Cover the

10 to 12 medium carrots, scraped and quartered

10 to 12 new potatoes, scrubbed and halved

1½ cups pitted prunes, chopped

Cayenne (optional)

pot again, and continue braising and basting for 1½ to 2½ hours longer, until the meat is fork-tender. (When basting, check that the liquid is bubbling gently. If it is boiling rapidly, turn the oven down to 300°F.) Remove the pot from the oven, uncover, and let everything cool in the pan sauce for 1 hour. Refrigerate, covered, for at least 6 hours, or preferably overnight.

WHEN you are ready to reheat the tsimmes, scrape off any congealed fat from the surface. Pluck out the cinnamon and the bay leaf and discard. Transfer the cold meat to a cutting board. Spoon out enough of the prunes and carrots to equal about 1 cup, and combine the mixture with the defatted pan sauce in a food processor. Puree until smooth.

SLICE the meat thinly across the grain at a slight diagonal. Slowly reheat the meat, the potatoes, and the remaining carrots and prunes (most of the prunes will be near-dissolved) in the pureed pan sauce. Stir in the minced garlic and cook another minute or two. Taste and adjust seasoning, adding a generous dusting of black or cayenne pepper, if desired, to edge the sweetness.

ARRANGE the meat on a platter, surrounded by the potatoes, carrots, and prunes. Ladle plenty of hot pan sauce over everything, and pass additional sauce separately.

CARAMELIZED ONION AND CARROT TSIMMES WITH CANDIED GINGER

yield: **ABOUT 6 SERVINGS**

Spicy, sweet, and tangy-sour notes harmonize beautifully in this meatless vegetable-fruit melange. Serve it as a side dish or offer it as a condiment with chicken, turkey, or brisket.

3 tablespoons mild olive or canola oil

1½ pounds onions (preferably red), thinly sliced (6 cups)

Salt and freshly ground black pepper

4 or 5 medium carrots, scraped and sliced (2 cups)

1 tablespoon minced candied ginger

1 cup fresh orange juice

1 tablespoon grated orange zest

1 tablespoon fragrant honey

¼ teaspoon ground cinnamon

1 cup pitted prunes, quartered

IN a 10- to 12-inch heavy skillet, heat the oil and add the onions. Salt and pepper lightly and stir well. Cook, covered, over very low heat, stirring occasionally so the onions do not burn, for 30 to 40 minutes, until they are meltingly tender and almost transparent.

ADD the carrots, ginger, orange juice and zest, honey, cinnamon, and additional salt and pepper to taste. Raise the heat to medium-high and bring the mixture to a boil. Let it bubble for a few minutes, then reduce the heat and continue cooking, uncovered, stirring occasionally, until the carrots are tender and the onions are golden and syrupy, about 15 minutes.

ADD the prunes and simmer for 5 to 10 minutes longer, or until the prunes are quite soft. If necessary, boil for a few minutes over high heat to evaporate any liquid remaining in the pan. Adjust the seasoning. Keep the mixture warm, covered, until ready to serve.

THE tsimmes tastes best if allowed to stand for at least 10 minutes to blend the flavors (or prepare in advance and just reheat before serving.)

"Aunt Celia had red hair the color of carrot tsimmes cooked in honey and darkened with cinnamon."

—FAYE MOSKOWITZ, *And the Bridge Is Love*

MOROCCAN-FLAVORED CARROT KUGEL

yield: ABOUT 6 SERVINGS

Sweet, golden carrots are an Ashkenazi favorite not only around the fall holidays, but throughout the year as well. This light, airy pareve kugel is not at all dense and sodden like many vegetable puddings. Mint provides refreshing grace notes (I use dried here because an equivalent amount of fresh mint would compromise the mousse-like texture of this kugel.) And fresh carrot juice, either home-juiced or purchased from a greengrocer or health food store, adds a delicate sweetness to the kugel. If it is unavailable, use a light vegetable stock.

1 tablespoon olive, avocado, or canola oil, plus additional for greasing the pan

1 whole matzoh (egg matzoh works particularly well here)

1½ teaspoons dried mint

¾ teaspoon ground cumin, preferably freshly toasted and ground

½ teaspoon ground cinnamon

Salt and freshly ground black pepper

Cayenne

2 teaspoons fresh lemon juice

1 cup fresh carrot juice or Vegetable Stock (page 34)

1 teaspoon finely minced garlic

3 large eggs, separated

2 cups scraped and finely grated carrots, preferably organic

Optional garnish: fresh mint or parsley sprigs

PREHEAT the oven to 325°F. Grease an 8-inch square cake pan or other shallow 8-cup baking dish.

IN a large bowl, crumble the matzoh into small pieces. Sprinkle with the mint, cumin, cinnamon, about 1 teaspoon salt (or to taste), pepper, and a pinch of cayenne (or to taste), and the lemon juice. Combine the carrot juice or broth and garlic in a small saucepan and heat slowly until very hot. Don't let the juice boil—it may turn too bitter for this kugel. Pour over the matzoh mixture, stir, and set aside to cool.

BEAT the egg whites with a pinch of salt in a large bowl until stiff, but not dry. In another bowl, using the same beaters (no need to wash them), beat the egg yolks and 1 tablespoon oil until thick and foamy. Add the yolks and carrots to the matzoh mixture and combine well. Use a spatula to

"The feast of Sukkoth or the feast of Simhat Torah.

They looked for him everywhere.

Where is he, where is he?

It turned out that, because of the fine weather, Grandfather had climbed up on the roof, had sat down on one of the chimney pipes and was regaling himself with carrots."

—MARC CHAGALL, *My Life*

fold the whites gently into the carrot mixture. Work quickly and lightly, until thoroughly combined and no white is visible. Transfer to the baking dish.

BAKE for 40 to 50 minutes, until firm and golden brown around the edges. Let the kugel cool until set, then cut into serving pieces. Garnish with mint or parsley, if desired. Serve warm or at room temperature. This reheats well and is excellent the next day.

MAPLE-ROASTED PEARS WITH PASSION FRUIT OR FRESH RASPBERRY SAUCE

yield: 6 SERVINGS

*F*resh autumn fruit desserts—from plush apple cakes to svelte compotes—are traditional on Sukkot. For me, a light fruit dessert that is festive and satisfying without being rich makes the best coda to the multicourse meal.

In this recipe I roast maple-glazed pears to give them a buttery depth and luxurious mouth feel with no added fat. More, perhaps, than any other fruit, passion fruit—evoking puckery citrus, berries, and lush tropical fruits with unknown names—tastes of faraway places. I like to add a few spoonfuls of the exotically perfumed juice to dress up the homey pears. If you cannot find passion fruit, set the pears on a ribbon of fresh tart raspberry sauce.

Or do what I do: Serve both.

Avocado, canola, or other flavorless oil, for filming the pan

3 large, firm-ripe Bosc pears (about 1½ pounds), peeled, halved, and cored

⅓ cup pure maple syrup

½ teaspoon vanilla extract

¼ teaspoon salt

1 tablespoon fresh lemon juice

2 ripe passion fruits (2½ to 3 ounces; see Cook's Note) and/or 1 cup fresh raspberries (about 6 ounces) plus ¼ cup fresh orange juice and 3 tablespoons packed light brown sugar

PREHEAT the oven to 500°F.

VERY lightly film a 10- to 12-inch heavy ovenproof skillet with oil and set it over medium-high heat until the oil is hot and shimmery, but not smoking. Add the pears, cored side down, and cook for 2 to 3 minutes. Lift the pears with a spatula: The bottoms should be speckled or rimmed light bronze. (If not, cook for another minute or two.)

TURN the pears cored side up and transfer the pan to the oven. Roast the pears, turning them 2 or 3 times (with a spatula, not tongs), for 7 to 8 minutes, until both sides are deeply bronzed in places, and they are beginning to caramelize. Stir together the maple syrup, vanilla, and ⅛ teaspoon salt, and spoon half of the mixture over the pears. Continue roasting for 2 to 3 minutes longer, then turn the pears and coat the other side with the remaining syrup. Roast for another 2 to 3 minutes, until both sides are a rich butterscotch color, caramelized, and the pears are tender enough to pierce easily with a thin knife or skewer.

TRANSFER the pears with a slotted spoon to a glass or enamel pie plate or baking dish just large enough to hold them in a single layer. Add the lemon juice and the remaining ⅛ teaspoon salt to the syrupy juices in the pan. Cook over medium heat, stirring constantly, for a minute or two, to marry the ingredients. Spoon the mixture evenly over the pears.

IF you are using the passion fruits: Set a small fine-mesh sieve over a bowl. Cut the fruit in half. Working over the bowl to catch any drips of the precious juice, scrape all the yellow-green pulp and the seeds into the sieve. Rub the fruit through the sieve with the back of a spoon or a fork to extract every bit of the juice. Spoon the juice over the caramelized pears, tossing them gently so they are evenly coated. Cover the dish with plastic wrap and refrigerate for at least 3 hours or overnight to mingle the flavors.

IF you are using the raspberries: Put them in a blender or food processor with the orange juice and brown sugar, and puree until smooth. Strain the puree through a fine-mesh sieve to remove the seeds and store, covered, in the refrigerator until serving time. (It will keep for up to 3 days, refrigerated.)

TO serve: If you prepared the raspberry sauce, spoon it in an attractive ribbon across each of six dessert plates. Arrange a pear half over the ribbon (or in the center of the plate if you did not make the sauce), and spoon some of the syrupy juices over the pears.

COOK'S NOTE: The leathery rind on ripe passion fruits will be deeply wrinkled. Keep unripe fruit at room temperature for a few days, until the skin is wrinkled.

If you are not serving the raspberry sauce, a garnish of pomegranate seeds makes a lovely, seasonal tart-sweet finish.

OTHER SUGGESTIONS FOR SUKKOT AND SIMCHAT TORAH

*Classic Hummus with Toasted Sesame-Cumin Matzohs

Either of the *Chopped Chicken Liver recipes

Any of the *Gefilte Fish recipes

*Esau's Pottage (Red Lentil Soup)

*Classic Chicken Soup with *Fried Onion and Chicken Kreplach

*Lemon-Roasted Chicken

*Chicken Paprikash with *Nockerl* (Dumplings)

**Fesenjan* Redux (Roast Duck Breats with Quince, Pomegranate, and Walnut Sauce)

*Roast Turkey with Challah Stuffing, Roasted Grape and Chestnut Gravy

Any of the *Brisket recipes

*Classic Sweet-and-Sour Stuffed Cabbage

*Coffee-Spiced Pot Roast with Kasha Kreplach and Toasted Garlic Challah Crumbs

*Syrian Apricot Stuffed Meat Rolls

*Rhubarb-Prune Tsimmes

*Sautéed Cabbage and Garlic Noodle Kugel

*New World Rodanchas

*Cider-Baked Apples Stuffed with Halvah

*Italian Carrot-Pecan Torta

*Jewish Sautéed Apple Cake

*Aunt Mary's Honey Cake

*Hungarian Plum Tart

*See index for page numbers

"The wicks in the potatoes, our Hanukkah candles, smoked and sputtered and finally extinguished. My mother said to me, "Go wash up and we'll eat potatoes with goose fat. In honor of Hanukkah, I splurged and bought a jar of goose fat—fresh, delicious goose fat."

—SHOLOM ALEICHEM, "BENNY'S LUCK"

Hanukkah

AN EIGHT-DAY FESTIVAL
BEGINNING 25 KISLEV, (LATE
NOVEMBER OR DECEMBER)

This black and nearly moonless night will be long and chilled with winter's breath.

Against this darkness, Jews will light a candle. And at sunset every evening, they will add yet another candle, until eight days later, at Hanukkah's end, their ritual lamps, or menorahs, are ablaze with orange-gold flames.

Hanukkah, the Festival of Lights, celebrates deliverance from the darkness of religious persecution. The Syrian king from the Seleucid dynasty, Antiochus IV Epiphanes, attempting to impose Hellenistic culture over the various ethnic minorities in his empire, had outlawed all other religions. Those who practiced Judaism risked torture, even death. On 25 Kislev, 167 BCE, Antiochus defiled the Temple, polluting the altar with pagan sacrifices and desecrating the ritual objects.

The Maccabees rose in revolt. At last, they were able to recover Jerusalem. On 25 Kislev three years later, they cleansed and purified the Temple, rededicating it to God. But the single cruse of untouched oil they found was only enough to burn for one day. Instead, miraculously, the tiny amount lasted for eight days, time enough for them to sanctify a fresh supply.

Remembering these events, Jewish families kindle at least one set of lights, illumining them with a *shammash* (an extra "helper" candle). Lights are placed from right to left, like Hebrew script; the candle furthest left, representing the current night, is always lit first.

Hanukkah is a home-centered celebration, and children are encouraged to participate by lighting their own menorahs. The unique menorahs of nineteenth-century Alsace featured places for up to thirty-two lights, so many family members could light candles at the same time.

The burning menorah is a transcendent image that resonates powerfully in the dead of winter, reflecting the triumph of faith over faithlessness and hope over despair. Poignant menorahs have been fashioned from wicks of tattered clothes lit in egg shells, scooped out potato halves, and even, in a concentration camp, a shoe polish tin with a bit of machine oil.

The original oil, of course, was pure, fragrant olive oil, and that is commemorated on the table. There are crisply fried treats, both sweet and savory, especially latkes, or pancakes, made from potatoes (dished up hot and glossed with sour cream, fresh fruit sauce, or a sprinkle of sugar), or luscious cheese latkes. Unlike many other Jewish dishes, these traditional fried foods were not designed to be prepared in advance, for although Hanukkah is widely celebrated among Jews, it is a "minor festival"—meaning that Jews are not prohibited from cooking or other forms of work. The meats too are rich and fat: crackly-skinned goose or tender brisket and gravy.

After dinner the joyous mood continues with songs, games, and presents, accompanied by fresh-baked cookies and pastries, like rugelach brimming with golden caramel or sweet almond paste dotted with cranberries.

CELEBRATING EIGHT DAYS OF HANUKKAH

On the weekend that falls during the holiday—and perhaps on a couple of the other days—there may be raucous parties with a host of friends and a feast of foods or big family get-togethers. There may be the thrill of opening one or two special, lavish presents, given in lieu of, or combined with, more modest gifts for the other days of the festival.

Most of Hanukkah, though, is celebrated more simply in our homes, eating cozy meals embellished by a few of the holiday foods while burning menorahs light up the wintry night. But indelible family memories are made not only of boldface moments: each night of Hanukkah becomes special when we make it an authentically shared family experience.

While there is no religious proscription against working during Hanukkah—even for the most orthodox—as there is on some of the other holidays, there is a tradition of not engaging in work while the menorah candles are burning (usually thirty minutes to one hour). So forget the dishes, set aside the homework and the bills, turn off the TV. This is a wonderful opportunity: use this time for a special family activity, one that invites participation by all generations present.

Many families play *dreidel*, spinning a four-sided top bearing Hebrew letters that stand for "A Great Miracle Happened Here." But there is nothing sacred about dreidels, and no reason not to update tradition if your family prefers cards, chess, or board games. Our family usually sets up Trivial Pursuit for a team game, kids against adults. If we run out of time, the next night we can just pick up where we left off. A friend's family begins a thousand-piece jigsaw puzzle on the first night.

We're especially fond of storytelling of all kinds, from sharing tales rooted in our family trees to reading Hanukkah picture books that speak to all ages. Families could easily do as Isaac Bashevis Singer suggested: tell a different story each night of Hanukkah. There is a rich repertoire to explore that will engage the whole family: Jewish stories of salts and tricksters or multicultural, traditional, or contemporary tales.

Whether they are gathered around the piano or the holiday table, nothing brings the generations together like music. Devote a night or two to rousing group sings of traditional Hanukkah songs like "Rock of Ages," melodies of the Beatles, classic rock, or just old family favorites.

Or search out some of the exciting new Hanukkah music available today. When Woody Guthrie, the iconic Middle American folksinger from Oklahoma, lived on Mermaid Avenue in Coney Island, he composed a number of Hanukkah songs inspired by his mother-in-law, the Yiddish poet Aliza Greenblatt. A few years ago on Hanukkah, we went to a concert featuring Woody's son Arlo and the Klezmatics, who had recently set Woody's songs to the mournful minor keys and spirited melodies of klezmer. Songs like "Honeykey, Hanukkah Time" ("Candles are burning all over this land to light the dark road") would make wonderful additions to the family playbook.

Don't forget to highlight one night with dancing. CDs of "Hava Nagilah" for a hora are readily available, but any exuberant dancing the family enjoys will be great fun, an upbeat antidote to the winter blues.

It takes effort and planning for busy families to steal a little time together. But at the end of the holiday, you'll have eight days of cherished new memories.

Of course, you will need nourishment for all that activity. In addition to potato pancakes, experiment with recipes for other fried treats enjoyed throughout the Diaspora, like Italian-Jewish chicken cutlets or herbed spinach fritters, or try latkes inspired by other cuisines, such as scallion pancakes, reminiscent of Chinese dim sum.

Round out these foods with a salad of sliced fresh oranges, onions, and dates, or some roasted Brussels sprouts or steamed broccoli; ripe mango or pineapple, or homemade apple sauces and compotes that can be readied in advance.

End the evening with homemade cookies or a slice of creamy cheese cake.

These foods, like the uncomplicated holiday activities, are simple. But invested with a sense of family tradition, they will taste richer every year.

HANUKKAH
menu suggestions

MIDWEEK MEALS

Salad of grapefruit, avocado, and romaine, lemon-vinaigrette dressing

*Fish in Potato Latke Crust with Horseradish Cream

Steamed broccoli with butter

*Double Ginger–Caramelized Pear Noodle Kugel

or

*Almond-Paste Cranberry Rugelach

~

*Oven-Fried Smoked Salmon Croquettes

*Celery Root–Potato Latkes with Sour Cream, *Yogurt Cream, or Crème Fraîche

or

*New Mexican Sweet Potato Latkes with Lime-Sour Cream Sauce

Salad of fennel and orange slices with black olives

*Old Country Cottage Cheese Cake or *Cider-Baked Apples Stuffed with Halvah

~

Mixed green salad

*Fried Chicken Cutlets, Italian-Jewish Style

*See index for page numbers

*Wild Mushroom–Potato Kugel or roasted sweet potatoes

Broccoli rabe with garlic (see recipe for *Flanken with Tart Greens)

Fresh seasonal fruit platter: clementines, red grapes, pears, and apples

or

*Maple-Roasted Pears with Passion Fruit or Fresh Raspberry Sauce

Carry-out roast chicken or *Iranian Grilled Chicken Thighs with Sumac or *Aromatic Marinated Brisket with Chestnuts

*Jerusalem Artichoke-Parsnip Latkes or *Garlic-Rosemary Potato Latkes

Steamed spinach dressed with sesame oil, toasted sesame seeds, soy sauce, and lemon juice

Toasted hazelnuts or walnuts and a selection of flavorful apples

*Rich Beef Broth (from preparing *Flanken), served plain or with egg noodles and diced carrots

*Flanken with Tart Greens

*Crispy Shallot Latkes with Sugar Dusting or *Classic Potato Latkes or *Creamy Potato-Onion Latkes

*Fresh Applesauce or *Spiced Pomegranate Molasses Applesauce

*See index for page numbers

*Orange, Onion, and Date Salad

Fresh pineapple or papaya with lime

A LATKE PARTY

*Classic Hummus with Toasted Sesame-Cumin Matzohs

*Crispy Shallot Latkes with Sugar Dusting or *Creamy Potato-Onion Latkes

*Cheese Latkes with Fresh Persimmon Sauce or *Greek-Inspired Cheese Latkes or *Herbed Spinach Latkes with Feta-Yogurt Sauce

Sour Cream, *Yogurt Cream, *French Applesauce, *Spiced Pomegranate Molasses Applesauce

Salad of sliced blood or navel oranges, watercress, and red onions, dressed with extra virgin olive oil and orange and lemon juices

*Assorted Rugelach, *Upside-Down Caramel-Cranberry-Pecan Noodle Pudding

*Milky Way Dreamy Cheesecake

Bowl of toasted almonds and dark raisins; ripe pears

SABBATH DURING HANUKKAH

*Classic Challah

*Mediterranean Chickpea Latkes, glossed with pomegranate molasses

or

*See index for page numbers

*Scallion Latkes with Scallion Dipping Brushes

or

*My Mother's Fried Cauliflower

*Apricot- and Orange-Scented Goose with Roasted Garlic

*Sautéed Cabbage and Garlic Noodle Kugel

Salad of fresh tart greens

Fresh mango with lime juice

*See index for page numbers

LATKE LESSONS

- Latke batter should be at room temperature; cold batter will lower the oil temperature, causing the latkes to absorb too much oil. (Exceptions: cheese latkes, which may fall apart if not very cold).

- A very wet batter will produce steam. The result? Soggy, greasy latkes. If the batter has thrown off a lot of liquid, drop a measureful of batter into your hand, so you can gently squeeze out the excess moisture before slipping it into the hot oil.

- If your pan cannot be heated over high heat, heat it over the highest setting recommended by the manufacturer.

- I prefer the flavor of a fragrant, everyday olive oil (don't use extra virgin oil for latkes), and I use it whenever possible. But because olive oil has a lower smoke point than canola, it requires greater vigilance in regulating the heat. For batters that are naturally wetter or more fragile (like New Mexican Sweet Potato Latkes or Italian Apple Fritters), I choose an oil with a very high smoke point like canola.

- If you need to test the oil temperature: stand an untreated wooden chopstick in the oil. If little bubbles form around it, the oil is ready. Or flick a pinch of flour into the oil; if it sizzles, start frying.

- Between batches, scoop out any burned fragments from the pan. Every two batches or so, it may be necessary to wipe out the pan to remove burnt oil or bits and add fresh oil.

- Preparing ahead: you can keep latkes for a few hours at room temperature, in a single layer on a rack, loosely covered with a kitchen towel. Refrigerating leaves latkes sodden and lifeless. But you can freeze them for longer storage. Arrange drained, cooled latkes on a cookie sheet and slide into the freezer until solidly frozen. Store in a strong, resealable plastic bag or airtight container. To serve, reheat the latkes on a rack set on a baking sheet in a preheated 400°F oven until hot and crisp.

CLASSIC POTATO LATKES

yield: ABOUT 4 SERVINGS

The food processor ended the grater Reign of Terror that marked the Festival of Latkes. But the four-sided grater offered one advantage (aside from the bits of torn knuckles so many grandmothers swore made their latkes that much more delicious): part of the potatoes could be shredded on the coarse side, to make a crispy crust, and the rest grated rather fine, to ensure a little creamy layer within. All coarse would mean all crunch—texture without an intense potato taste—while completely fine made latkes with too much mush beneath their thin crisp coat, causing them to absorb huge amounts of oil.

The solution is simple: grate the potatoes, using the coarse shredding disk, then process about one third of them to a coarse puree. Result: crisp, crunchy, and creamy, all at once.

About 1½ pounds russet (baking) or Yukon gold potatoes, peeled and quartered

½ pound onions, peeled and quartered

1 large egg, beaten

1 tablespoon matzoh meal or unbleached all-purpose flour

About 1 teaspoon salt

About ¼ teaspoon freshly ground black pepper

½ teaspoon baking powder

Olive or canola oil, for frying

Accompaniments: apple or other fruit sauce (heavenly when freshly made; see pages 289 to 296) and/or sour cream

COARSELY shred the potatoes and the onions, using the shredding disk in a food processor. (Don't wash out the food processor—you'll be using it again right away.) Transfer the mixture to a colander or strainer and use your hands or a wooden spoon to press out as much moisture as possible.

REMOVE the shredding disk from the processor and replace with the steel blade. Return about one third of the shredded potatoes and onions to the work bowl and process, using the pulse motion, until roughly pureed. Transfer to a large bowl. Add the remaining potatoes and onions from the colander, and the egg, matzoh meal, salt, pepper, and baking powder. Mix until thoroughly combined.

IN a 10- to 12-inch heavy skillet (cast-iron is ideal), heat about ¼ inch of oil over high heat until it is hot but not smoking. Drop ¼ cup of the batter into the pan, and flatten with a spatula. Repeat with more batter, cooking no more than 4 or 5 latkes at a time; crowding the pan will give you soggy latkes.

REGULATE the heat carefully, reducing it to medium as the latkes fry until golden and crisp on the bottom, about 4 minutes. To prevent oil from splattering, use two spatulas (or a spatula and a large spoon) to turn the latkes carefully. Fry until crisp and golden on the other side.

IT'S best to flip the latkes only once, so that they don't absorb too much oil. So, before turning, lift the latkes slightly with the spatula to make sure the underside is crisp and brown.

AS the latkes are done, transfer them to paper towels or untreated brown paper bags to drain.

CONTINUE making latkes in the same manner until all the batter is used. If necessary, add more oil to the pan, but always allow the oil to get hot before frying a new batch.

SERVE straightaway, accompanied by applesauce or sour cream. If it is necessary to keep the latkes warm, place them in a single layer on a rack set on a baking sheet in a slow oven (200°F) until they are all ready to be brought to the table.

COOK'S NOTE: For *galettes à l'oignon et pomme de terre*—the addictive onion and potato pancakes sold at the Sunday organic market in Paris—follow the above recipe, but increase onion to ¾ pound, replace matzoh meal with about 2 tablespoons grated cheese (such as Parmesan), and decrease salt if necessary, according to saltiness of cheese. Before serving, sprinkle with coarse salt.

"Early in the afternoon, she would begin grating the potatoes on a vicious four-sided grater, the invention of some fiendish anti-Semite who must have seen the opportunity to maim half the Jewish population each December."

—FAYE MOSKOWITZ, *And the Bridge Is Love*

CREAMY POTATO-ONION LATKES

yield: ABOUT 4 SERVINGS

*I*t comes as no surprise that, as with other Jewish foods, there is no definitive way to make a potato latke. Most cooks use raw potatoes, but some grate boiled potatoes. And a few use a combination of both.

When made entirely of cooked potatoes, latkes, to my palate, are not latkes at all, but croquettes: they lack the requisite crunch and the deeply satisfying fried potato taste that are the hallmarks of the genus. But adding a little cooked potato to grated raw ones makes for lighter latkes, with real potato crust and soft centers (a trick employed for the Onion-Crusted Light Potato Kugel, page 113, and that Irish cooks use in their potato pancake, boxty). While this combination latke is wonderful on its own with the traditional accompaniments, its lightness makes it an excellent candidate as well for a side dish served with substantial meats and poultry.

In this recipe, I swirl savory frizzled onions into the cooked potato before combining it with the grated raw potato. The latke fries up with a thin, crackly potato crust enclosing an airy, onion-luscious mashed potato center.

1¾ to 2 pounds russet (baking) or Yukon gold potatoes, peeled

Salt

2 cups chopped onion

2 tablespoons olive oil, plus additional for frying

Freshly ground black pepper

1 large egg

1 teaspoon baking powder

Accompaniments: sour cream, yogurt cream (see page 30), or *labneh*; or a fruit sauce (pages 289 to 296)

CUT about one third of the potatoes into small chunks and boil them in a saucepan of salted water until tender. Drain and mash until very smooth (no lumps wanted here) by forcing through a food mill, ricer, or colander into a large bowl.

WHILE the potatoes are cooking, sauté the onions in 2 tablespoons oil over medium-high heat, stirring, until golden and just speckled with brown, 10 to 12 minutes. Season the still-hot onions generously with salt and pepper and stir them into the mashed potatoes. Let the mixture cool.

SHRED the remaining potatoes in a food processor fitted with the shredding disk, or grate by hand. Put the grated potatoes in a colander, rinse under cool water, then use your hands or a wooden spoon to extract as much moisture as possible.

ADD the grated potatoes to the mashed ones. Whisk in the egg, baking powder, and additional salt and pepper to taste. Mix well until thoroughly combined.

USING about ¼ cup for each latke, form the batter into small, flat patties about ½ inch thick and 3 to 3½ inches wide. Heat about ¼ inch of oil in a 10- to 12-inch heavy skillet until hot, but not smoking. Fry the latkes a few at a time: crowding the pan will make the latkes soggy.

WATCH the heat carefully, reducing it, if necessary, when the latkes are golden and crisp on the bottom. To prevent the oil from splattering, use two spatulas (or a spatula and a large spoon) to turn the latkes gently. Fry until crisp and golden on the other side. If necessary, add more oil to the pan, but wait until it is hot before adding the latkes.

IT'S best to flip the latkes only once, so that they don't absorb too much oil during the cooking. So, before turning, lift the latkes slightly with the spatula to make sure the underside is crisp and brown.

DRAIN the latkes as they are done on paper towels or untreated brown paper bags. When necessary, keep the latkes warm in a single layer on a rack set on a baking sheet in a slow oven (200°F) until they are all ready to be brought to the table. They are at their best served as soon as possible.

COOK'S NOTE: These are also delicious prepared with about 2 ounces of skinny smoked salmon slivers and 2 tablespoons minced fresh dill stirred into the batter, and fried as above. Or serve smoked salmon or Smoked Whitefish and Fennel Salad (page 196) on top of the latkes.

"They had a silver Hanukkah menorah full of the finest oil with a large shamash candle ready to kindle the other wicks. Nothing but the best. From the kitchen one could smell the heavenly aroma of freshly rendered goose fat.

'We're having latkes tonight,' Benny told me as we stood at the door, and my stomach rumbled with hunger!" —SHOLOM ALEICHEM, "BENNY'S LUCK"

CELERY ROOT–POTATO LATKES

yield: **4 TO 5 SERVINGS**

To impart an earthy, vegetal depth to latkes, try combining the potato batter with other grated root vegetables, such as beets, Jerusalem artichokes, parsley root, or parsnips. For this recipe, I add celery root, underscoring its herbaceous, nutty flavor with crushed celery seeds.

Celery root–potato latkes are excellent with most meats and poultry, and particularly good with brisket. Or serve them with sour cream, yogurt cream, or crème fraîche at a dairy meal. For a delicious appetizer or brunch dish, top these latkes with Smoked Whitefish and Fennel Salad (page 196), or some sliced smoked fish, sour cream, and dill.

1 medium-large celery root (1 to 1½ pounds, without leaves), trimmed and peeled

About 1 pound Yukon gold or russet (baking) potatoes, peeled

1 large egg, beaten

About 1 teaspoon salt

About ¼ teaspoon freshly ground black pepper

½ teaspoon baking powder

1 large garlic clove, minced

½ teaspoon celery seeds, crushed

2 tablespoons matzoh meal or unbleached all-purpose flour

Olive oil, for frying

Accompaniments: sour cream, yogurt cream (see page 30), *labneh*, or crème fraîche; or brisket or smoked fish

SHRED the celery root, using the shredding disk in a food processor. You should have about 2 cups. Transfer to a colander.

WITH the same disk, shred the potatoes. Transfer about half the potatoes to the celery root in the colander and use your hands or a wooden spoon to press out as much moisture as possible from the vegetables in the colander.

REMOVE the shredding disk from the processor and replace with the steel blade. Process the remaining potatoes, using a pulse motion, until roughly pureed. Transfer to a large bowl, add the shredded vegetables, the egg, salt and pepper to taste, the baking powder, garlic, celery seeds, and matzoh meal. Mix well until thoroughly combined.

IN a 10- to 12-inch heavy skillet (cast-iron is ideal), heat about ¼ inch of oil over high heat until hot but not smoking. Using a ¼-cup measure, drop the batter into the pan, and flatten the latkes with a spatula. Cook no more than 4 or 5 latkes at a time; crowding the pan will make the latkes soggy.

REGULATE the heat carefully, reducing it to medium as the latkes fry until golden and crisp on the bottom, about 4 minutes. To prevent the oil from splattering, use two spatulas (or a spatula and a large spoon) to turn the latkes carefully. Fry until crisp and golden on the other side.

IT'S best to flip the latkes only once, so that they don't absorb too much oil. So, before turning, lift the latkes slightly with the spatula to make sure the underside is crisp and brown.

AS the latkes are done, transfer them to paper towels or untreated brown paper bags to drain.

CONTINUE making latkes in the same manner until all the batter is used. If necessary, add more oil to the pan, but always allow the oil to get hot before frying a new batch.

IF necessary, keep the latkes warm in a single layer on a rack set on a baking sheet in a slow oven (200°F) until you have cooked a batch large enough to bring to the table. But they are at their best served as soon as possible.

CHILDRENS' DESIGNER LATKES

Children adore latkes: a platterful means a party, whether eaten at home or served as part of a school multicultural holiday presentation. To make them extra-special, buy several plastic squeeze bottles—the kind used for ketchup and mustard. Fill with sour cream and different kinds of applesauce, and let the kids use them to design faces or other fun garnishes on the latkes.

CRISPY SHALLOT LATKES WITH SUGAR DUSTING

yield: **4 SERVICES** 4 SERVINGS

*N*ot Mallomars, s'mores, or Rice Krispie Treats. My secret childhood sweet was crispy, hot potato latkes sprinkled with sugar, the way my grandmother made them. She knew that a latke's beauty is fleeting: irresistible hot, they turn charmless and sodden cold. Why rush along the process with cool toppings like sour cream and applesauce? Besides, the unlikely alliance of flavors still delights, even after all these years when former loves like her ginger-snappy stuffed cabbage and red-hot cinnamon candies no longer give me a tickle.

Instead of decreasing the onion—or eliminating it altogether—as do many Jewish cooks who serve their latkes with sugar, my grandmother laced her latkes lavishly with it. The spicy onion contrasts with the sugar, creating layers of flavor that somehow heighten the potato taste. I use shallots here because they are more deeply flavored than onions, and you need fewer to achieve an intense onion taste. Also, adding a lot of onion, which contains so much moisture, might make the latkes soggy or absorb too much oil. With shallots, the potatoes remain crispy.

Don't go overboard with the sugar—a little goes a long way. Use superfine or regular granulated, not confectioners', and sprinkle it on when the latkes are very hot so it doesn't form a powdery cloak, but really melts in. Or serve the latkes unadorned, and offer guests pretty little salt shakers filled with sugar.

You can, of course, have the latkes with the more traditional sour or yogurt cream and a fresh fruit sauce, but do try the sugar once.

1½ cups thinly sliced shallots (about 1 pound)

2 tablespoons unsalted butter or fine-quality olive oil

About 1½ pounds russet (baking) or Yukon gold potatoes, peeled

1 large egg, beaten

About ¾ teaspoon salt

About ¼ teaspoon freshly ground black pepper

½ teaspoon baking powder

IN a heavy medium saucepan, cook the shallots in the butter or olive oil over moderate heat, stirring occasionally, until they become golden and crispy, about 15 minutes. Drain on paper towels and let cool.

SHRED the potatoes, using the shredding disk in a food processor. Transfer the potatoes to a colander or strainer and use your hands or a wooden spoon to press out as much moisture as possible. (Don't bother washing out food processor.)

REMOVE the shredding disk from the processor and replace with the steel blade. Return about one third of the shredded potatoes to the food processor and roughly puree, using the pulse motion. Transfer the puree to a large bowl, add the remaining potatoes and the egg, salt and pepper

1 tablespoon matzoh meal or unbleached all-purpose flour

Olive oil, for frying

Sugar, preferably superfine, for dusting

to taste, the baking powder, and matzoh meal. Stir in the shallots. Mix until thoroughly combined.

IN a 10- to 12-inch heavy skillet (cast-iron is ideal), heat about ¼ inch of oil over high heat until hot, but not smoking. Using a ¼-cup measure, drop the latke batter into the pan and flatten the latkes with a spatula. Cook no more than 4 or 5 latkes at a time; crowding the pan will make the latkes soggy.

REGULATE the heat carefully as the latkes fry until golden and crisp on the bottom, about 4 minutes. To prevent the oil from splattering, use two spatulas (or a spatula and a large spoon) to turn the latkes carefully. Fry until crisp and golden on the other side. (Avoid turning the latkes more than once or they will absorb too much oil. Before turning, lift the latkes slightly with the spatula to make sure the underside is crisp and brown.)

TRANSFER the cooked latkes to paper towels or untreated brown paper bags to drain and sprinkle them lightly with sugar (I use a scant ½ teaspoon for each). Continue frying latkes in the same way until all the batter is used. If necessary, add more oil to the pan, but always allow the oil to get hot before frying a new batch.

IF you must, keep the latkes warm arranged in a single layer on a rack set over a baking sheet in a slow oven (200°F) until they are all ready to be brought to the table. But they are at their best served as soon as possible.

PASS additional sugar when serving (little salt shakers filled with sugar are attractive and make it less likely that a guest will dump an inedible amount of sugar on a latke), and, if desired, accompany the latkes with sour or yogurt cream (see page 30) and a fresh fruit sauce (pages 289 to 296).

GARLIC-ROSEMARY POTATO LATKES

yield: ABOUT 4 SERVINGS

*T*hese exceptionally fragrant potato pancakes require no topping or sauce as adornment. They are perfect as is, ready to accompany any roasted or grilled chicken or meat.

About 1½ pounds Yukon gold or 3 large russet (baking) potatoes, peeled

2 tablespoons coarsely chopped garlic

1 tablespoon fresh rosemary leaves

1 large egg, beaten

1 tablespoon matzoh meal or unbleached all-purpose flour

About ¾ teaspoon salt

About ¼ teaspoon freshly ground black pepper

½ teaspoon baking powder

Olive oil, for frying

Coarse salt (optional)

SHRED the potatoes, using the shredding disk in a food processor. (Don't wash out the food processor—you'll be using it again right away.) Transfer the potatoes to a colander or strainer, and use your hands or a wooden spoon to press out as much moisture as possible.

REMOVE the shredding disk from the processor and replace with the steel blade. Return about one third of the shredded potatoes to the food processor. Add the garlic and rosemary and process, using the pulse motion, until roughly pureed. Transfer the mixture to a large bowl. Add the remaining potatoes, the egg, matzoh meal, salt and pepper to taste, and the baking powder to the bowl. Mix until thoroughly combined. Let stand for 10 minutes to mingle the flavors.

IN a 10- to 12-inch heavy skillet (cast-iron is ideal), heat about ¼ inch of oil over high heat until hot, but not smoking. Drop ¼ cup of the potato latke batter into the pan and flatten with a spatula. Repeat with more batter, cooking no more than 4 or 5 latkes at a time; crowding the pan will give you soggy latkes.

REGULATE the heat carefully, reducing it to medium as the latkes fry until golden and crisp on the bottom, about 4 minutes. To prevent oil from splattering, use two spatulas (or a spatula and a large spoon) to turn the latkes carefully. Fry until crisp and golden on the other side.

IT'S best to flip the latkes only once, so that they don't absorb too much oil. So, before turning, lift the latkes slightly with the spatula to make sure the underside is crisp and brown.

AS the latkes are done, transfer them to paper towels or untreated brown paper bags to drain.

CONTINUE making latkes in the same manner until all the batter is used. If necessary, add more oil to the pan, but always allow the oil to get hot before frying a new batch.

SERVE straightaway, sprinkled with a little coarse salt, if you'd like. Or, if necessary, keep the latkes warm in a 200°F oven (arrange them in a single layer on a rack placed over an oven-proof platter or baking sheet) and serve when they are all ready to be brought to the table.

SCALLION LATKES WITH SCALLION DIPPING BRUSHES

yield: 4 SERVINGS

*N*ot even Merlin could make the magic of a potato pancake last the full eight days of the holiday, and after a while, my search for something different turns into an obsession.

These scallion latkes, reminiscent of those savory little pancakes served as dim sum, make use of ancient Chinese wisdom. The bracing, clean flavors of ginger, vinegar, and soy provide a sparkling antidote to the oily richness, as well as welcome respite from the ubiquitous sour cream or yogurt cream.

FOR THE SCALLION BRUSHES

10 to 12 thin scallions

Ice water

FOR THE DIPPING SAUCE

2 tablespoons soy sauce

2 tablespoons orange juice

1 tablespoon rice, Chinese black, or cider vinegar

2 teaspoons Asian toasted sesame oil

1 teaspoon peeled and grated fresh ginger

Chili oil (optional)

FOR THE LATKES

2 to 2½ bunches of scallions, white and light green parts, trimmed and thinly sliced (2½ cups)

2 tablespoons mild olive or canola oil, plus additional for frying

1 teaspoon peeled and minced fresh ginger

MAKE the scallion brushes: cut off and discard the roots and all but 3 inches of the green part of the scallions. Using scissors or small paring knife, cut slits about ½-inch deep into both green sections of each scallion stalk, creating a fringe. Carefully fan out the fringed edges. Place the scallions in a bowl of ice water, and refrigerate for 2 hours or until the fringed edges curl up.

PREPARE the dipping sauce: stir together all the ingredients and let the flavors mingle for at least 30 minutes.

START the latkes: in a large skillet, sauté the scallions over moderately high heat in the oil until tender and just beginning to brown at the edges. Stir in the ginger, garlic, and soy sauce, and cook, lifting and tossing, for 2 to 3 minutes. Remove with a slotted spoon and set aside to cool briefly. Make the latkes, following the directions

"Hot, plump, they glisten, the latkes, with pearls of fat, and they jump on the fire like newborn little babies when they are slapped with the hand.

We watch the cook as though she were a magician.

'Havah, the thick latke is for me, isn't it?'"

—BELLA CHAGALL, *Burning Lights*

1½ teaspoons minced garlic

1½ teaspoons soy sauce

About 1½ pounds russet (baking) or Yukon gold potatoes, peeled

½ teaspoon baking powder

1 large egg

Salt and freshly ground black pepper

2 tablespoons matzoh meal or unbleached all-purpose flour

for Crispy Shallot Latkes with Sugar Dusting on page 267, stirring in the sautéed scallions instead of the shallots. (You *will* need salt here— the soy sauce merely flavors the scallions. Putting in enough soy sauce would make the latkes too wet. Figure about 1 teaspoon of salt.)

WHEN ready to serve, pat the scallions brushes dry. Guests should use the brushes to coat each latke with dipping sauce, then top the latke with the brush.

NEW MEXICAN SWEET POTATO LATKES WITH LIME–SOUR CREAM SAUCE

yield: 4 TO 6 SERVINGS (ABOUT 15 LATKES)

Eight days before Christmas, some New Mexicans light a luminaria, a candle nestled in a paper sack, then add an additional glowing luminaria every evening until Christmas, when nine burning lights illumine the holiday darkness.

If this process of kindling flames sounds familiar, it is no coincidence. These New Mexicans are crypto-Jews: descendants of converso colonists who practiced Judaism in secret, fearing the relentless persecution of the Inquisition, whose long reach extended into the New World. Even many of those who became Catholics have kept alive their Jewish traditions to this day, lighting candles on Friday nights, abstaining from pork, observing a feast or fast of Esther, covering mirrors during the mourning period, and maintaining many other Jewish practices.

The fascinating story of these crypto-Jews is still being written. Many are rediscovering and exploring their Jewish roots, some even confirming their Jewishness through DNA testing. Some have converted to Judaism; others feel they have been Jewish all along.

Inspired by them, these sweet potato latkes glow with New Mexican spice.

FOR THE LIME–SOUR CREAM SAUCE

1 cup sour cream

⅓ cup snipped fresh chives

2 tablespoons fresh lime juice

2 teaspoons grated lime zest

FOR THE LATKES

2 pounds sweet potatoes (choose a flavorful variety such as Jewel or Garnet, if available)

Kosher salt

1 cup finely chopped onion

PREPARE the lime–sour cream sauce: stir together the sour cream, chives, and lime juice and zest in a small bowl. Let the flavors develop while you make the latkes.

MAKE the latkes: shred the sweet potatoes using the medium/fine shredding disk of a food processor. (While many recipes call for coarse grating, I find that sweet potatoes won't release as much moisture when grated that thickly and so don't bind as well with the other ingredients.) Transfer the shredded potatoes to a colander, sprinkle with about ½ teaspoon salt, and use your hands to squeeze out as much moisture as possible.

PUT the sweet potatoes in a large bowl, and add the onion, eggs, flour, salt to taste (figure 1 to 1½ teaspoons), chili powder, cumin, baking powder, and cinnamon. Mix until thoroughly combined.

IN a 10- to 12-inch heavy skillet (cast-iron is ideal), heat about ¼ inch of oil over high heat until it is hot, but not smoking. Fill a ¼-cup measure with latke batter, drop the batter into your hand so that you can squeeze

3 large eggs, beaten to blend

1/3 cup flour

2 teaspoons ground ancho chili powder

2 teaspoons ground cumin, preferably freshly toasted and ground

1 teaspoon baking powder

1/2 teaspoon ground cinnamon

Canola or sunflower oil, for frying

Optional garnish: chopped fresh cilantro

out the excess liquid, then slip it into the hot oil. Flatten the latke with a spatula. Continue making latkes in the same way, but cook no more than 4 or 5 at a time.

REGULATE the heat carefully as the latkes fry until golden and crisp on the bottom, about 4 minutes. To prevent oil from splattering, use two spatulas (or a spatula and a large spoon) to turn the latkes carefully. Fry until crisp and golden on the other side.

AVOID turning the latkes more than once or they will absorb too much oil. Before turning, lift the latkes slightly with the spatula to make sure the underside is crisp and brown.

TRANSFER the cooked latkes to paper towels or untreated brown paper bags to drain. Continue frying latkes until all the batter is used. If necessary, add more oil to the pan, but always allow the oil to get hot before frying a new batch.

SERVE the latkes right away with the lime–sour cream sauce, garnished, if you'd like, with cilantro. They are at their best eaten as soon as possible, but, if necessary, you can keep them warm, arranged in a single layer on a rack set on a baking sheet in a slow oven (200°F) until they are all ready to be brought to the table.

JERUSALEM ARTICHOKE–PARSNIP LATKES

yield: ABOUT 15 LATKES

*T*hese latkes make a superb, if unexpected, side dish for grilled or roasted chicken. On busy nights when you are on Hanukkah latke duty, pair them with a bird from your favorite carry-out shop.

The secret here is hazelnut: a few tablespoons underscore the nutty-sweet earthiness of the Jerusalem artichokes, while providing structure for the fritter. The latkes require no adornment other than a dust of fresh pepper and salt before serving—or gild the lily with some warm, freshly made applesauce.

1 pound Jerusalem artichokes, scrubbed or peeled

1 medium parsnip, peeled

¼ cup finely chopped shallots

2 large eggs, beaten to blend

3 tablespoons ground hazelnuts

1 tablespoon matzoh meal

1 teaspoon baking powder

¾ teaspoon dried thyme

Salt and freshly ground black pepper

Canola or sunflower oil, for frying

Optional accompaniment: Fresh Applesauce (page 291)

SHRED the Jerusalem artichokes and the parsnip using the medium/fine shredding disk of a food processor. (Because of their small size and knobby shape, Jerusalem artichokes are too difficult to shred by hand.) Transfer the vegetables to a colander, and use your hands to squeeze out as much moisture as possible.

PUT the vegetables in a large bowl and add the shallots, eggs, hazelnuts, matzoh meal, baking powder, thyme, and salt and pepper to taste. Mix well until thoroughly combined.

IN a 10- to 12-inch heavy skillet (cast-iron is ideal), heat about ¼ inch of oil over high heat until it is hot, but not smoking. Drop the latke batter into the pan, using ¼-cup measure, and flatten the latkes with a spatula. Cook no more than 4 or 5 latkes at a time.

REGULATE the heat carefully as the latkes fry until golden and crisp on the bottom, about 4 minutes. To prevent oil from splattering, use two spatulas (or a spatula and a large spoon) to turn the latkes carefully. Fry until crisp and golden on the other side.

AVOID turning the latkes more than once or they will absorb too much oil. Before turning, lift the latkes slightly with the spatula to make sure the underside is crisp and brown.

TRANSFER the cooked latkes to paper towels or untreated brown paper bags to drain. Continue frying latkes until all the batter is used. If necessary, add more oil to the pan, but always allow the oil to get hot before frying a new batch.

IF necessary, you can keep them warm, arranged in a single layer on a rack set on a baking sheet in a slow oven (200°F) until they are all ready to be brought to the table. Sprinkle the latkes with a light dusting of kosher or other slightly coarse salt and fresh pepper and accompany with Fresh Applesauce, if you'd like.

MEDITERRANEAN CHICKPEA LATKES

yield: 4 SERVINGS

*L*aced with rosemary and garlic, these savory latkes bring to mind the creamy-tasting fritters and crêpes made of chickpea flour in southern France and Italy, but they are fashioned instead from humble canned chickpeas. To serve with fish or vegetarian meals, stir a little crushed dried mint into labneh, sour cream, or crème fraîche, and spoon dollops on the latkes; if you'd like, drizzle squiggles of pomegranate molasses attractively on top. Or offer the latkes as an accompaniment to meat or poultry: gloss with a thin slick of pomegranate molasses or stir a few spoons of pomegranate molasses into good applesauce [or prepare Spiced Pomegranate Molasses Applesauce (page 295)], and pass along with the latkes. Either way, decorate with fresh pomegranate seeds for a glittery burst of color.

Mini chickpea latkes make marvelous hors d'oeuvre.

1½ cups cooked chickpeas (one 15-ounce can), rinsed and drained

2 teaspoons coarsely chopped garlic

1 tablespoon fresh rosemary leaves

2 tablespoons extra virgin olive oil

3 large eggs

1½ teaspoons ground cumin, preferably freshly toasted and ground

About 1 teaspoon kosher salt

½ teaspoon freshly ground black pepper

3 tablespoons unbleached all-purpose flour

½ teaspoon baking powder

Olive or canola oil, for frying

PUREE the chickpeas, garlic, and rosemary in a food processor to a coarse paste. Add the extra virgin olive oil, eggs, and 6 tablespoons water and blend until smooth. Add the cumin, salt to taste, pepper, flour, and baking powder and pulse to blend well. Transfer the batter to a large bowl.

HEAT 6 tablespoons oil in a 10- to 12-inch heavy skillet (preferably cast-iron) over medium-high heat until hot, but not smoking. Working in batches, drop the batter by heaping tablespoonfuls into the hot oil. Regulate the heat carefully as the latkes fry until golden on both sides. To prevent the oil from splattering, use two spatulas (or a spatula and a large spoon) to turn the latkes carefully. Avoid turning the latkes more than once or they will absorb too much oil. Before turning, lift the latkes slightly with the spatula to make sure the underside is crisp and brown. Drain on paper towels or untreated brown paper bags. If necessary, add more oil to the pan, but always allow the oil to get hot before frying a new batch. Serve straightaway.

HERBED SPINACH LATKES WITH FETA-YOGURT SAUCE

yield: **ABOUT 30 SMALL LATKES**

Packed with fresh herbs, these little fritters bring a beguiling whiff of springtime to wintry Hanukkah celebrations. The latkes make wonderful cocktail fare, or prepare slightly larger ones and pair with soup and a big salad for a light dinner, or fish, for a more substantial meal. The versatile piquant sauce, a variation of one I partner with mamaliga, brings sparkle to raw and cooked vegetables, lentils, and mixed green salads.

2 pounds fresh spinach, well washed, tough stems discarded, or two 10-ounce packages frozen leaf spinach, thawed

Salt

2 tablespoons unsalted butter, plus additional for frying

1 cup thinly sliced scallions (about 8), white and pale green parts only

1 teaspoon chopped garlic

Freshly ground black pepper

⅓ cup packed fresh challah or other egg bread (crusts removed), torn in pieces

½ cup snipped fresh dill leaves

½ cup packed chopped fresh mint leaves

⅓ cup chopped fresh cilantro leaves (optional)

4 large eggs, beaten to blend

IF you are using fresh spinach, cook it in a large saucepan with ¼ cup lightly salted water until tender. Cool, place in a colander, and squeeze out as much liquid as possible. If you are using frozen spinach, squeeze the thawed spinach dry. You'll be able to press out the most liquid if you do this with your hands.

IN a heavy medium skillet, melt the butter over medium heat. Add the scallions and garlic and sauté until scallions are softened, about 2 minutes. Stir in the spinach, and sauté about 3 minutes, until all liquid is evaporated. Season to taste with salt and pepper, then cool completely.

PROCESS the challah in a food processor to fine crumbs. Add the spinach mixture, dill, mint, and cilantro, if using; pulse, using on/off turns, until finely chopped. Transfer to a large bowl. Taste, adding more salt and pepper, if necessary. Mix in the eggs and baking powder.

MELT 2 tablespoons butter with 2 tablespoons oil in a 10- to 12-inch heavy skillet (preferably cast-iron) over medium heat until hot, but not smoking. Working in batches, drop the batter by heaping tablespoonfuls into the skillet, using the back of a spoon to flatten the latkes slightly. Fry until lightly browned, about 2 minutes per side. Avoid turning more than once. Using a slotted spatula, transfer the latkes to paper towels to drain.

1½ teaspoons baking powder

Mild olive, canola, or avocado oil, for frying

Feta-Yogurt Sauce (recipe follows)

FRY the remaining latkes in the same way, adding more butter and oil to the skillet as necessary, and allowing the fat to get hot before adding more batter.

SERVE with Feta-Yogurt Sauce.

FETA-YOGURT SAUCE

yield: ABOUT 2 CUPS (THIS IS MORE THAN YOU WILL NEED FOR THIS RECIPE, BUT I LIKE TO KEEP THIS USEFUL SAUCE ON HAND. IF DESIRED, JUST HALVE THE AMOUNTS CALLED FOR.)

1 cup crumbled feta (about 4 ounces)

1 cup plain yogurt (preferably whole-milk Greek-style)

⅓ cup snipped fresh chives

3 tablespoons fresh lemon juice

1 garlic clove, minced

2 teaspoons dried oregano

Freshly ground black pepper

Salt (optional)

MASH the feta in a medium bowl using a fork. Blend in the yogurt. Stir in the remaining ingredients and season to taste with pepper. Taste and add salt, if needed (the feta may be quite salty). Set aside for flavors to blend at least 2 hours before serving. (Can be made 2 days ahead. Cover and refrigerate until needed.)

CASALE MONFERRATO

We were lured by the taste of Barolo, the scent of truffles and extraordinary hazelnuts, but what we will remember most about Piedmont is the synagogue we found in Casale Monferrato. The small Jewish community in Casale, located about fifty miles east of Turin, most likely began with the refugees Ferdinand and Isabella expelled from Spain in 1492. Although there were periods of crisis and some restrictions, life under the Italian Gonzaga dukes was relatively calm for the Jews, even prosperous for some. The synagogue was built in 1595.

*B*ut when the French House of Savoy annexed the district, conditions quickly deteriorated. In 1745, Jews were crowded into a ghetto around the synagogue. Contacts between Jews and Catholics were limited, and at night they were strictly forbidden. Not until 1848 were the Jews of Piedmont granted full rights.

Now there are no longer enough Jews to make a minyan in Casale, except on the High Holidays, when Jews from other communities attend the services.

From the narrow little street, La Sinagoga degli Argenti looked like one of the apartment buildings, but inside was one of the most exquisite synagogues we have ever seen. It was late afternoon in July, and light filtered through the windows of the sanctuary highlighting for us the subtle pastels, gilded carved symbols, and gold filigree work. Our guide—who, like one we had had years ago in Venice, was not Jewish but extremely knowledgeable about the synagogue and Jewish life—pointed out the beautifully painted ceiling, a fresco of sky and clouds, whose panels announce in four Hebrew words, "This is the Gate to Heaven."

There is also an impressive museum, showcasing art and furnishings acquired from other Piedmont congregations, antique dealers, and private collections, and life-size dioramas of many of the holidays. The basement of the museum, where matzoh once was baked for all the Jews of the Monferrato region, now houses the Museum of Lights, a remarkable collection of menorahs.

The Hanukkah story of the tiny flame that produced a lasting light is the story of Jewish continuity, and the Jewish community of Casale has adopted it as its own. The museum commissions new hanukkiyot from renowned contemporary artists, Jewish and non-Jewish, who, in the museum's words, "form a bridge between the lights of the past, which must never go out, and those of the future, which must continue to be lit." One menorah is formed of two sculpted hands, the thumbs entwined to form the shamash, the flames shooting up from the fingertips; another was inspired by the notes people insert into the cracks of the Western Wall.

In the courtyard, our guide told us that for the past several years, the synagogue has invited members of all the other monotheistic faiths in the area when Hanukkah begins. Another Hanukkah story—a miracle too, perhaps—that has particular resonance for Casale.

For it would be dark, of course, when the Catholics, Muslims, Protestants, and Jews gathered to light the menorah candles here between the elegant colonnaded courtyard columns—where once upon a time any contact between Jews and Gentiles after nightfall would have been prohibited.

"Hanukkah," as Antonio Recalcati, one of the Catholic menorah artists has said, "celebrates life and light after centuries of darkness."

ITALIAN APPLE FRITTERS

yield: 6 TO 8 SERVINGS

These luscious fritters are based on a recipe from a delightful cookbook published by the Jewish community of Casale Monferrato, La Cucina della Memoria. *A word-for-word recipe appears in the classic Italian-Jewish cookbook,* La Cucina nella Tradizione Ebraica, *where its origin is attributed to Central European Jews.*

But for us, the fritters will always taste Italian.

6 medium Granny Smith apples, peeled, cored, and cut into ⅓-inch rings

6 tablespoons brown sugar

1 tablespoon vanilla extract

½ to 1 teaspoon ground cinnamon

3 large eggs, separated (at room temperature)

3 tablespoons mild olive, canola, or avocado oil

2 cups unbleached all-purpose flour

2 teaspoons baking powder

Salt

1½ cups beer

Canola oil, for frying

Confectioners' sugar, brown sugar, or maple sugar, for sprinkling

PUT the apple slices in a large resealable plastic bag and add the brown sugar, vanilla, and cinnamon (use the larger amount if you prefer a more pronounced cinnamon flavor, rather than a background note). Seal, then move the apples around in the bag until the seasonings are evenly distributed. Let the apples macerate at room temperature for about 1 hour.

IN a large bowl, beat the egg yolks with the oil until well blended. In another bowl, combine the flour, baking powder, and ½ teaspoon salt. Stir the dry ingredients into the yolks. Add the beer, a little at a time, mixing well and squooshing the batter against the bowl to break up any lumps. Stir the batter until smooth, then let it rest at room temperature for about 1 hour.

PREHEAT the oven to 200°F if you want to bring all the fritters to the table at the same time, instead of serving them right from the pan as they are done.

BEAT the egg whites with a pinch of salt until stiff but not dry, and gently fold into the batter.

IN a large, deep, heavy skillet (do not use nonstick here), heat ½ inch of canola oil over medium heat until gently sizzling (about 360°F). Dip the apple rings one at a time into the batter, making sure each is completely covered, then letting the excess drip off before slipping it carefully into the hot oil. Fry in batches, about 5 rings at a time so you don't crowd the pan, until golden brown on both sides and the apple is tender and cooked through. Use two spatulas or a spatula and a large spoon to turn them.

LINE a serving plate or ovenproof platter with crushed paper towels. Serve the fritters immediately, sprinkled with confectioners' sugar, brown sugar, or maple sugar, or, less desirably, keep warm on a rack placed over the platter in a slow oven until all the fritters are ready to be brought to the table.

GREEK-INSPIRED CHEESE LATKES

yields: ABOUT 4 SERVINGS

On Hanukkah we remember not just the courageous military exploits of the Maccabees: since the Middle Ages, it has also been the custom to commemorate the derring-do of a fearless woman.

When the ruthless Assyrian general Holofernes laid siege to the city of Bethulia, a beautiful, devout widow, Judith, devised a scheme based on what she knew best—food. Seduced by her loveliness, Holofernes invited her into his tent, where he lay under a canopy woven with purple silk, gold, and emeralds. There she fed him the salty cheese she had brought. A morsel of cheese, then a quaff of wine to slake his salty throat. And with each bite of cheese, his thirst grew ever more demanding. At last the wicked general fell into a drunken sleep, whereupon the resourceful widow grabbed a saber and beheaded him. She put the head in a bag and quietly stole out of camp.

Early the next day, the head was impaled on the city walls. Holofernes' frightened soldiers fled, leaving behind their vast plundered riches, and the siege of Bethulia was broken.

Dairy products like cheese latkes are frequently eaten on Hanukkah in memory of Judith's deed. Here the feta, an echo of her salty cheese, is offset not by wine, but the fresh tastes of green herbs and lemon.

½ pound feta cheese (a solid, unbroken chunk)

½ pound farmer cheese (a 7.5-ounce package is fine)

½ cup chopped fresh herbs, such as dill, scallions, mint, flat-leaf parsley (choose at least two kinds)

1 large egg beaten with 1 tablespoon fresh lemon juice (you may need an additional egg, so have more on hand)

KEEP both cheeses refrigerated until you are ready to start preparing the latkes, so they will be as firm as possible. Pat the cheeses dry with paper towels. Using a sharp knife, cut each cheese into 8 thin slices. If a slice crumbles as you are cutting, pat or mold it back into shape with your hands.

TAKE a slice of feta, sprinkle it with 1 tablespoon of the herbs, and cover with a slice of farmer cheese. Use your hands to form the latke into a smooth, flat patty.

DIP the latke first into the egg and then the matzoh crumbs. Continue making latkes with the remaining cheese and herbs. Refrigerate the latkes for at least 30 minutes.

HEAT ¼ inch of oil in a 10- to 12-inch heavy skillet over high heat until hot, but not smoking. Fry the latkes, in batches, if necessary, turning

1 cup matzoh crumbs (see page 24; egg matzohs work particularly well here) or matzoh meal, seasoned with freshly ground black pepper to taste and ½ teaspoon crushed dried oregano

Olive oil, for frying

Accompaniments: lemon quarters and additional chopped herbs, for garnish

once (using two spatulas or a spatula and a large spoon, to prevent splattering), until golden on both sides. These latkes must be fried quickly over high heat (or medium-high heat, if recommended by the skillet manufacturer) so the cheese does not melt.

DRAIN briefly on paper towels or other absorbent paper. Serve immediately, garnished with lemon and sprinkled with herbs.

BLACK GRAPE, GOAT CHEESE, AND NOODLE LATKES WITH FRAGRANT HONEY

yield: 4 SERVINGS

I had wandered several blocks from our Philadelphia hotel. The December sky was already purple and my toes frozen numb when I found the tiny bakery and hobbled in. Enveloped by the smells of strong coffee and a dazzling array of freshly baked focaccia, I immediately felt that all was right with the world.

The focaccia I chose was an unusual interplay of exuberant Mediterranean tastes—rosemary, goat cheese, midnight blue–black grapes and walnuts—all held in delicate balance by a final drizzle of fragrant honey.

I was so intrigued by the combination of flavors, I wanted to repeat them in another dish. I was thinking of a noodle pudding, but since it was so close to Hanukkah, I decided to update a traditional noodle latke recipe.

Honey is used here as a seasoning, not merely a sweetener. For superior results, select a honey with complex, highly aromatic notes: an herbal one, such as Greek thyme or rosemary, or musky, slightly bitter chestnut honey.

Delicious and not at all difficult to prepare, these latkes do require a bit of special attention. Since heat can make cheese soft and runny, work quickly shaping and frying the latkes to ensure that the cheese does not ooze out in the pan. Or try shaping the latkes, then chilling them again before frying.

Excellent for brunch, lunch, or as part of a dairy meal, these latkes also make a fine conclusion to a light supper.

Salt

4 ounces medium flat egg noodles (it is difficult to form these latkes with twisted spiral kind)

2 large eggs

¼ cup walnuts, lightly toasted and coarsely chopped

BRING 2 to 3 quarts water and 1 teaspoon salt to a rapid boil in a large pot. Add the noodles and cook until just tender but still firm. Meanwhile, in a large bowl, whisk together the eggs, walnuts, rosemary, and salt and pepper to taste. Drain the cooked noodles thoroughly, let them cool slightly, then combine them well with the egg mixture. Cover the bowl and refrigerate the mixture until cold and firm, about 1 hour. The noodles will have absorbed all the egg. Cut the cheese into bits and add it to the bowl, together with the grapes. Mix well.

TAKE about ⅓ cup of the mixture, making sure it includes some cheese and grape pieces, and shape it into a patty. Place it on a platter and

1 tablespoon plus
2 teaspoons finely
chopped fresh rosemary
leaves

Freshly ground black
pepper

4 ounces fresh (not aged)
goat cheese, chilled

1 cup black grapes (about
7 ounces), seeded and cut
into quarters

Unsalted butter and mild
vegetable oil such as
canola or avocado, for
frying

Fragrant honey

continue forming patties until you have used up all the batter. Handle the patties carefully—they will be somewhat fragile. If time permits, refrigerate the patties to firm them up before frying.

IN a 10- to 12-inch heavy skillet, heat 2 tablespoons each of butter and oil over high heat until hot, but not smoking. Working in batches, if necessary, add the latkes. Flatten each slightly with a spatula and fry quickly until golden brown, about 3 minutes. Turn carefully, using 2 spatulas or a spatula and a large spoon, if necessary, and brown on the other side. Avoid turning more than once. Add more butter and oil if needed to fry the rest, but be sure to let the fat get hot before adding the patties.

DRIZZLE some honey on the hot latkes and serve immediately.

CHEESE LATKES WITH FRESH PERSIMMON SAUCE

yield: 3 TO 4 SERVINGS

*C*risp potato latkes are the taste of Hanukkah for most Ashkenazi Jews. But the first latkes, according to many food historians, were probably made of cheese. Today, latkes based on sweet curd cheeses—farmer, pot, and cottage—are still popular for Hanukkah and Passover as well, for they are usually thickened with a bit of matzoh meal, not flour.

Delicate and dairy-clean tasting, this version begs for a fresh complement of bright-tasting fruit. Instead of the traditional syrup or preserves, which would overpower the natural milky sweetness, I prepare this seasonal persimmon sauce. Colored the glowing orange of menorah flames, it couldn't be fresher—or simpler. Just puree the raw pulp and season it lightly with lime and maple.

If you can't get persimmons, serve these latkes with the equally orange Intense Apricot Applesauce (page 293). Or serve both.

The latkes make a marvelous breakfast, brunch, light lunch, or snack. Or serve them as a starter or finish to a more elaborate dairy meal.

FOR THE FRESH PERSIMMON SAUCE

3 medium, dead-ripe persimmons, preferably the jelly-soft, acorn-shaped Hachiya type (see Cook's Note)

1 or 2 pinches of salt

2 to 3 teaspoons fresh lime or lemon juice

1 to 2 tablespoons pure maple syrup

FOR THE LATKES

½ pound farmer cheese (a 7.5-ounce package is fine)

2 tablespoons cream cheese

4 large eggs, separated

PREPARE the sauce: cut off and discard the leaf end of the persimmons and slice the fruits in half. To puree the fruit, scoop out the flesh and press it through a food mill or fine-mesh sieve. For less mess—with just a bit more elbow grease—puree the washed fruit unpeeled; the peels will remain trapped by the mill or sieve. Add the salt, lime or lemon juice, and maple syrup to taste. Refrigerate the sauce to marry the flavors.

MAKE the latkes: in a food processor, combine the farmer and cream cheeses, egg yolks, and vanilla and process until well blended and smooth. Add the matzoh meal, salt, and cinnamon, and process until thoroughly incorporated. Transfer the batter to a bowl. In a separate bowl, whip the egg whites until they form firm peaks. Gently fold the egg whites into the batter.

HEAT 2 tablespoons each of butter and oil in a 10- to 12-inch heavy skillet over medium heat until hot, but not smoking. Drop the batter by heaping tablespoonfuls and fry until the bottoms are golden brown, 2 to 3 minutes. Using two spatulas, turn and cook until lightly browned on the other side, 1 to 3 minutes. Remove and keep warm on a heated platter or baking sheet in a 200°F oven. Continue making latkes with the remaining batter. Add more butter and oil only if necessary, always

½ teaspoon vanilla extract

½ cup matzoh meal

¼ teaspoon salt

½ teaspoon ground cinnamon

Unsalted butter and mild vegetable oil such as canola or avocado, for frying

allowing the fat to get hot before frying more latkes. Keep an eye on the heat to make sure that the butter does not burn.

SERVE the latkes hot and pass the persimmon sauce.

COOK'S NOTE: With Hachiya persimmons, ripeness is all: the difference between mouth-puckeringly astringent and voluptuously sweet. The rounded, squat Fuyu persimmon contains no harsh tannins and is never astringent; though excellent sliced, it will not make as luscious a puree. Choose meltingly soft Hachiyas with deeply colored, unbroken skin.

Walnut-Cherry-Cheese Latkes

For a delicious, lightly sweetened variation, follow the directions above, adding ¼ teaspoon almond extract to the food processor with the cheeses, egg yolks, and vanilla. Omit the cinnamon, substitute 5 tablespoons unbleached all-purpose flour for the matzoh meal, and add 1 to 2 tablespoons granulated light brown sugar (use the lesser amount for a just slightly sweetened latke) to the food processor along with the other dry ingredients. Before folding in the beaten egg whites, add ¼ cup dried tart cherries (plumped in hot water 10 minutes, then drained) and ⅓ cup lightly toasted chopped walnuts to the batter. Serve with Chunky Cherry Applesauce.

CHUNKY CHERRY APPLESAUCE

yield: ABOUT 2 CUPS

FOR an easy-to-make sauce sweetened with cherry preserves, combine 4 Gala (or other flavorful) apples, peeled, cored, cut into ½-inch pieces (about 2 pounds) with ¼ cup unsweetened apple juice in a large, heavy saucepan. Bring to a boil, stirring occasionally. Cover, reduce heat to low, and simmer, stirring occasionally, until apples are very tender, 15 to 20 minutes. Remove from heat. Stir in 2 to 3 tablespoons cherry preserves (I prefer a sour cherry variety, but plain cherry preserves works well too). Using a potato masher or fork, mash the mixture to a chunky puree. Taste, add more preserves, if desired, and mash again. Serve warm or at room temperature. Or refrigerate until lightly chilled. Best not icy cold.

FRUIT SAUCES

Simple fruit sauces are the traditional embellishment for myriad Jewish dishes, including latkes, blintzes, and matzoh brie, and a superb accompaniment to brisket and pot roast. They are equally good on their own as dessert, with perhaps a few good cookies, or as a low-calorie lift for plain yogurt or cottage cheese. And don't forget waffles, pancakes, pound cakes, and such.

Sweetened with reduced fruit juice, not sugar, the fresh-tasting sauces here have an intense fruit flavor. After you've become familiar with these recipes, create your own favorites, capturing the season's bounty and flattering it with well-chosen spices and dried fruits.

And for another delicious fruit sauce, try the Fresh Raspberry Applesauce on page 511.

FRESH APPLESAUCE

yield: ABOUT 2 CUPS

At my Hanukkah cooking demonstrations, I've always been amazed at how humble homemade applesauce elicits the same oohs and aahs as holiday superstars like braised briskets and sizzling latkes. Made with a few varieties of good, local fruit, the simple sauce's deep apple flavor and ease of preparation are a culinary revelation to those who have never made it before. In the heat of the applesauce moment, they vow never again to buy the jarred kind.

Taste the different apples available in your markets to find your local favorites; I have noticed that some varieties are not quite the same when sampled in other parts of the country or in Europe. Using unpeeled apples is not only quicker but also adds flavor, nutrients, and a soft rosy cast to the sauce. But you'll need to peel the apples if they have been sprayed or waxed, or if you're not passing them through a food mill to mash them and trap the peels, but instead, pureeing in a food processor or mashing by hand.

About 1½ cups pure, unsweetened apple juice

1 cinnamon stick

Salt

About 2 pounds apples, unpeeled, cored, and cut into chunks (6 cups); if you want to puree the sauce in a food processor or by hand, instead of using a food mill, peel the apples (choose a mixture of at least two kinds of flavorful sweet and tangy apples to lend dimension to the sauce; avoid the bland and often mealy Red Delicious; look for fresh, local apples whenever possible)

White, brown, or maple sugar, maple syrup, or light honey (optional)

YOU'LL be reducing the juice quite a bit, so choose a 6-quart Dutch oven or wide, heavy straight-sided saucepan large enough to accommodate all of the apples generously. Pour in the juice and add the cinnamon and a generous pinch of salt. Boil uncovered, over high heat, until the liquid is reduced by about half. I've found the easiest way to determine whether the sauce (or other liquids) has reduced enough is the "story stick" method: insert a clean, heat-safe ruler or wooden chopstick into the pot before you start reducing, noting where the liquid measures on the ruler. When the liquid measures half as high, it has reduced enough.

ADD the apples, stir well to coat them with juice, and simmer, covered, until they are very tender, about 25 minutes, depending on the variety of apples. Stir them from time to time, and, if necessary, add a bit more juice to prevent them from sticking.

THE sauce should be thick and pulpy with little liquid visible. If necessary, boil it down a few minutes, uncovered. Pick out and discard the cinnamon. Put the sauce through a food mill or force it through a colander or strainer to remove the skins. Or, if you used peeled apples, process in a food processor or mash by hand until smooth or leave somewhat chunky, according to preference.

TRANSFER the sauce to a bowl. Taste and if you feel it needs sweetening, add a little sugar, maple syrup, or honey while the sauce is still very warm.

APPLESAUCE is superb at room temperature or warm from the pot with latkes, briskets, pot roasts, pancakes, or blintzes. Or serve it chilled, especially with yogurt, cottage cheese, or desserts.

COOK'S NOTE: Use this recipe as a template, varying the unsweetened juice (try cranberry- or cherry-apple), supplementing the cinnamon with a split vanilla bean, star anise, or other spices, or adding other fruits, such as quince or cranberries. A single, peeled Bosc pear added to the apples will lend a velvety finish to the sauce. Other suggestions follow.

French Applesauce
For a deliciously creamy taste, stir a tablespoon or so of unsalted butter into the finished sauce and serve while still warm with sweet latkes like the cheese latkes on page 288, pancakes, blintzes, or matzoh brie, or atop a steaming bowl of oatmeal.

INTENSE APRICOT APPLESAUCE

yield: ABOUT 2½ CUPS

*W*hen my father came home from his Saturday night gin game on Sunday morning, he would often bring lox, bagels, and bialys from The Delicacy Shop, the Jewish appetizing store in our Long Island community. When the triple "schnides" (from "schneiders"—gin rummy shutouts) were in his favor, we'd awaken to a breakfast of salmon in its many other guises—baked, pickled, and smoked Nova Scotia–style—as well as sable, whitefish, herring in sour cream sauce, scallion cream cheese, and beefsteak tomatoes.

But there would always be the Middle Eastern confection we knew as shoe leather—a sheet of dried apricot, rolled thin as onion skin, as mouth-puckering as lemonade.

Is it me or the shoe leather? Today's leather, or its many unflattering imitations, is too sweet, too thick, or too bland. I'd never make it, though—it is the kind of craving, like pistachio nuts, that demands instant gratification. When I hunger for the taste, I tuck into the tartest dried apricots I can find (in Middle Eastern or Jewish appetizing stores, these are usually the ones from California, not Turkey). If I have enough left over, I make this sauce, which is wonderful with latkes or pot roast—or just a spoon.

About ½ cup tart dried apricots (approximately 15; 2½ to 3 ounces), cut into quarters

1⅓ to 1½ cups pure, unsweetened apple juice

1 vanilla bean, split

½ teaspoon minced, peeled fresh ginger

Salt

About 2 pounds apples, unpeeled, cored, and cut into chunks (6 cups); if you want to puree the sauce in a food processor, instead of a food mill, peel the apples (choose the freshest local apples available: a mixture of sweet, spicy varieties, such as Gala and Braeburn—rather than tart Granny Smith or Rhode Island Greening—will work best in this tangy sauce)

SIMMER the apricots, 1⅓ cups apple juice, the vanilla bean, ginger, and a pinch of salt in a 6-quart Dutch oven or very wide, heavy saucepan, covered, until the apricots are very tender, about 25 minutes (it may take longer if the fruit is particularly dry). Add the apples, and continue cooking, covered, until very soft, another 25 minutes or so. Stir occasionally, and add additional juice, if required to prevent sticking. When ready, the mixture should be thick and pulpy, with no liquid visible. If necessary, boil it a few minutes, uncovered, to evaporate remaining liquid.

REMOVE the vanilla bean (if desired, rinse and dry it, so it can be reused or added to granulated sugar to flavor it). Put the fruit through a food mill. Or if you used peeled apples, puree it in a food processor to a smooth or slightly chunky consistency, as you prefer.

COVER and refrigerate until chilled. It is also lovely—and more assertive— served warm or at room temperature.

I didn't want to fall in love. I resisted the total embrace. After all, what food writer who has lived through sun-dried tomatoes would not see it as a fling?

Nevertheless, pomegranate molasses (also known as grenadine molasses and pomegranate syrup, the pomegranate essence created by slowly simmering the juice, usually with sugar and lemon until it forms a luscious, tangy syrup) shows up in several recipes in this book, making as regular appearances as wine. Which it resembles, only fruitier. Or raspberry liqueur, only tarter, and nonalcoholic.

But in the end, it has a taste all its own, a heavenly, perfectly balanced act of sweet-and-sour, floral and berry—a flavor combination particularly prized by Jews.

That is why I was not surprised when a grocer in Brooklyn's Syrian-Jewish neighborhood suggested it as a substitute for the rather difficult-to-find *temerhindi* or *ourt*, a tangy sweet-and-sour sauce made from tamarind pulp, that I needed to prepare the Syrian meat rolls, Kibbe Gheraz. "Syrian Jews from Aleppo use ourt, and the ones from Damascus cook the same dishes with pomegranate molasses."

Whether he was right or not (it is slightly tarter and more berry-tasting than *ourt*), it worked well in the kibbe, and I have been adding it ever since—to meat and chicken marinades and bastes, sauces, hummus, and even applesauce. Today it is stocked by many specialty stores and some supermarkets, as well as Middle Eastern markets. (See page 40 for more on pomegranate molasses.)

SPICED POMEGRANATE MOLASSES APPLESAUCE

yield: ABOUT 2 CUPS

ardamom and cinnamon play up the spicy notes in the pomegranate molasses here, making this a delicious complement to poultry and meats, especially briskets and pot roasts (see Aromatic Marinated Brisket with Chestnuts, page 241). It's also tempting on Mediterranean Chickpea Latkes (page 277), either plain or capped with a touch of yogurt cream (page 30) or labneh.

About 1½ cups pure, unsweetened apple juice

1 or 2 cardamom pods, lightly crushed with the side of a flat knife or kitchen mallet (use the larger amount for a more pronounced aromatic spiciness; 1 pod *will* make a difference)

1 cinnamon stick

Salt

About 2 pounds flavorful apples, unpeeled, cored, and cut into chunks (6 cups; if you are going to puree the sauce in a food processor, instead of using a food mill or strainer, peel the apples; choose a mixture of apples with sweet but complex flavors to echo the character of the sauce, such as Braeburn, Gala, and Stayman Winesap, rather than tart varieties; look for fresh, local apples if possible)

About 2 tablespoons pomegranate molasses or *ourt*

IN a 6-quart Dutch oven or wide, heavy saucepan large enough to accommodate all of the apples, combine the juice, cardamom, cinnamon, and a generous pinch of salt. Boil uncovered, over high heat, until the liquid is reduced by about half. Add the apples, mix well to coat with juice, and simmer, covered, until they are very tender, about 25 minutes depending on the variety of apples. Stir them from time to time, and, if necessary, add a bit more juice to prevent sticking.

THE sauce should be thick and pulpy with little liquid visible. If necessary, boil it down for a few minutes, uncovered. Pick out and discard the cardamom and cinnamon. Put the sauce through a food mill or force it through a colander or strainer to remove the skins. Or if you used peeled apples, process in a food processor until smooth or leave somewhat chunky, according to preference.

TRANSFER the sauce to a bowl. Stir in 2 tablespoons pomegranate molasses or *ourt* and taste. Add a little more if you want the sauce tarter. (If this is your first time using pomegranate molasses or *ourt,* you may want to start with less.)

YOU can serve the sauce chilled, but it is also excellent at room temperature or warm from the pot with briskets, pot roasts, or latkes.

COOK'S NOTE: You can use this recipe as a guide, omitting or supplementing the pomegranate molasses and spices with your own aromatic additions such as a strip of lemon, orange, or tangerine zest, a few prunes, or even peppercorns. Combine these seasonings with the juice—or try a fruitier, unsweetened juice such as cranberry- or raspberry-apple. Taste the finished sauce and adjust for sweetness.

GINGER-PEAR SAUCE

yield: ABOUT 3 CUPS

The secret ingredient in this intense fresh pear sauce is a few pureed prunes, which round out the sweet and tangy notes, adding body and a buttery finish.

It's fabulous on sweet latkes, matzoh brie and blintzes, pancakes and French toast. Or try it swirled into plain yogurt. Sweeter tooths than mine might enjoy it served alongside brisket and pot roast, or topping savory latkes.

About 1½ cups pure, unsweetened pineapple juice

1 vanilla bean, split

1 tablespoon minced candied ginger

Salt

About 3 pounds ripe, juicy pears such as Bartlett or Comice, peeled, cored, and cut into chunks (6 cups)

3 pitted prunes, quartered

Light floral honey or sugar (optional)

WE start again with a reduced fruit juice, so use a very wide, large, heavy nonreactive saucepan, such as a 5- or 6-quart Dutch oven. Put the pineapple juice, vanilla bean, ginger, and a pinch of salt in the saucepan and boil, uncovered, over high heat, until reduced to about ½ cup, about 15 minutes.

STIR in the pears and prunes, cover the pan, and simmer over low heat for 25 to 35 minutes, until the pears are very tender. Time will vary depending on the variety of pears you use. Stir from time to time, and add a little more pineapple juice, if needed, to prevent sticking.

WHEN ready, the mixture should be thick and pulpy, with very little liquid visible. Most pears are juicier than apples, so to avoid a watery sauce, evaporate almost all of the remaining liquid by boiling for a few minutes over high heat, uncovered.

REMOVE the vanilla bean (if desired, rinse and dry it, so it can be reused or added to granulated sugar to flavor it). Put the fruit through a food mill or puree in a food processor until smooth. It should not need any sweetening, but add a bit of honey or sugar if your pears are not as sweet and ripe as they might be.

THIS sauce is delicious served still warm, or cover and refrigerate until chilled. Store tightly covered in the refrigerator for 4 to 5 days.

COOK'S NOTE: This combination also makes a first-rate blintz filling. Reduce the juice, vanilla, ginger, and salt to about ⅓ cup of syrupy liquid. Sauté the pears in butter over medium-high heat. Chop the prunes fine and add to the pears along with the reduced juice. Cook until the pears are tender. Boil down any remaining liquid. Chill before filling the blintzes.

CLASSIC HUMMUS WITH TOASTED SESAME-CUMIN MATZOHS

yield: ABOUT 6 SERVINGS

On Hanukkah, I like to have a large platter of hummus and these irresistible matzohs ready for guests while I am hunkered down in the kitchen, frying up latkes.

Readers no doubt have noticed that I am no shrinking violet when it comes to garlic. But I think that most spreads—hummus included—benefit from the more rounded taste of raw garlic mellowed with some gently cooked cloves, similar to the nuanced blend of raw and sautéed onions in chopped liver or chopped eggs and onions. It takes only a few moments to color the garlic, then I toss it in through the feed tube with a couple of raw cloves until they are all finely minced, before adding the other ingredients.

I offer several suggestions here for spiffing up the dip, especially tempting served warm. The full, nutty-grain taste of whole-wheat matzoh makes a surprisingly good match for the sesame-cumin crust here, especially with generous lashings of excellent olive oil. But plain matzoh will give fine results, too.

About 5 tablespoons best-quality extra virgin olive oil

5 or 6 garlic cloves, peeled

About 6 tablespoons fresh lemon juice

¼ cup tahina

2 cups chickpeas, either freshly cooked (see page 326) or canned and rinsed; drained (discard any skins that float to the surface)

1 to 2 teaspoons ground cumin, preferably freshly toasted and ground

Salt and freshly ground black pepper

Aleppo pepper, smoked or regular paprika, or cayenne; za'atar or sumac (optional)

WARM 1 tablespoon olive oil in a small saucepan over moderate heat. Add 3 or 4 garlic cloves and cook, shaking or stirring the pan, until just tinged all over with pale gold. (You only want to eliminate the raw taste.)

WITH the machine on, drop the cooked garlic and the remaining 2 cloves of raw garlic through the feed tube of a food processor and process until very finely chopped. In a small bowl, stir together the lemon juice and tahina until smooth. Transfer to the food processor, together with the chickpeas, 5 tablespoons hot tap water, 3 tablespoons olive oil, 1 teaspoon cumin, and salt and pepper to taste. Process to a smooth puree. Taste and adjust seasonings, adding more cumin, if desired, and additional lemon juice, olive oil, or salt and pepper as needed.

SPOON the hummus onto a serving platter. Here are some attractive ways to present it. Using the back of a spoon, make an indentation in the center of the hummus and, leading out of it, some spiral- or spoke-shaped furrows; dribble a little olive oil into these indentations (especially delicious if the oil is warmed). Decorate the edges of the platter with

Optional garnishes:
chopped fresh flat-leaf
parsley, dill, mint, or
cilantro; whole cooked
chickpeas; black olives;
pine nuts lightly sautéed
in olive oil or butter

Accompaniments: trimmed
fresh raw vegetables, such
as carrots, celery, fennel,
red and yellow pepper
strips, halved cherry
tomatoes, etc.; Toasted
Sesame-Cumin Matzohs
(recipe follows) or Toasted
Za'atar Matzohs (page
220), whole-wheat or
plain matzohs, or hot pita
quarters

chopped fresh herbs, olives, or whole chickpeas. Sprinkle with any of the suggested seasoning spices and/or the sautéed pine nuts. Serve with your choice of accompaniments.

HUMMUS is sublime served warm. Spoon it into a shallow baking dish and heat in a 350°F oven until completely heated through. Add the garnishes and seasonings after removing from the oven.

COOK'S NOTE: For a New World flavor, add chopped raw or roasted finely minced jalapeño or serrano pepper or canned chipolte to the hummus instead of the other optional seasonings.

Store leftover hummus, covered, in the refrigerator, for 4 to 5 days. If it has thickened, stir in a little hot water and a bit of extra virgin olive oil to thin it out. It makes a very tasty, nourishing sandwich spread.

TOASTED SESAME-CUMIN MATZOHS

yield: 4 TO 6 SERVINGS

**2 tablespoons sesame
seeds**

2 teaspoons cumin seeds

Coarse salt

**¼ cup best-quality extra
virgin olive oil**

**About 6 whole-wheat or
plain matzohs**

PREHEAT the oven to 400°F. Prepare the sesame seeds: in a small (about 7-inch) ungreased heavy skillet, toast them over moderately high heat, stirring or shaking the pan constantly, just until they release their nutty fragrance and turn light gold. Don't allow them to brown or they'll be bitter. Immediately remove the skillet from the heat and transfer the seeds to a mortar. In the same skillet, toast the cumin seeds in the same way, just until they are very fragrant. Add them to the mortar. Let cool slightly, then add a few pinches of salt, and crush coarsely with the pestle. Or pulse a few times in an electric spice grinder, or put the seasonings in a heavy plastic bag and pound well with a mallet.

TRANSFER the spice mixture to a small bowl and stir in the olive oil. Brush the tops of the matzohs very generously with the mixture, then sprinkle with coarse salt. Bake until hot and crisp. The matzohs should be very fragrant, puffed slightly, and just beginning to curl at the deep brown edges. Best served hot.

COOK'S NOTE: Stirring the sesame and cumin mix into the oil helps to prevent the seeds from scattering every which way, though you will probably use a bit more oil with this method. But it will make the matzoh taste wonderfully rich—no bread of affliction here. For easier serving—and shatterproof eating—you may prefer to break the matzoh into large, cracker-like pieces before seasoning and heating them.

SESAME seeds naturally contain a lot of oil so they turn rancid rather quickly; store them well wrapped in the freezer.

CHOPPED CHICKEN LIVER WITH CARAMELIZED ONIONS

yield: 6 TO 9 GENEROUS APPETIZER PORTIONS

I often prepare a variation on the voluptuous Parisian chicken liver recipe (page 59) using fewer eggs. It derives its exceptional lightness—and slightly sweet taste—from a puree of caramelized onions.

4 large eggs

6 to 8 tablespoons best-quality olive oil, or 5 tablespoons olive oil plus approximately 1 to 3 tablespoons Olive Oil Schmaltz (page 27) or Poultry Schmaltz (page 28)

5 cups very thinly sliced onions, plus 1 cup coarsely chopped (about 1½ pounds total)

Salt and freshly ground black pepper

1 to 2 tablespoons balsamic vinegar or 1 tablespoon mild red wine vinegar

¼ teaspoon brown sugar (optional; use if the balsamic vinegar is rough, or with the wine vinegar)

1 pound fresh (not previously frozen) chicken livers, rinsed, fat and any green spots removed

PREHEAT the broiler.

HARD-BOIL the eggs, cool, and peel (see page 59). Cut the eggs into eighths and set aside.

IN a 10- to 12-inch heavy skillet, warm 3 tablespoons of the oil over medium heat. Add the sliced onions, salt and pepper them lightly, and sauté, lifting and turning them occasionally, until softened and translucent, about 10 minutes. Cover tightly and cook the onions over the lowest heat, stirring occasionally to prevent burning, for 40 to 45 minutes, or until meltingly tender. Uncover, add the vinegar (if the balsamic vinegar is rough or strong, use 1 tablespoon; if it is soft and mild, use 2 tablespoons) and additional salt and pepper to taste, and cook over high heat, lifting and tossing, until the moisture has evaporated and the onions are colored a rich brown, about 15 minutes. Taste to adjust seasoning: the mixture should be just slightly sweet, but well salted and peppered, and the vinegar scent should be almost gone. If necessary, add the brown sugar and additional seasoning, and continue sautéing until thoroughly incorporated. Transfer about ¾ of the mixture to a food processor, add 2 tablespoons oil, and puree.

MEANWHILE, prepare the liver: line the broiler rack with either heavy brown paper sprinkled with water, or foil. Pat the livers dry with paper towels and spread them out on the broiler rack. Sprinkle them lightly with salt, and broil about 4 inches from the flame until lightly browned on top, 3 to 4 minutes. Turn, sprinkle the other side with salt and continue broiling for another 3 to 4 minutes. Add the broiled livers to the cooked onions remaining in the skillet and sauté for a minute or two. Let cool slightly, then add to the onion puree in the food processor. Pulse on and off to chop coarsely. Add the eggs. Pulse. Add the chopped raw

Accompaniments: soft lettuce, Belgian endive or radicchio leaves; radishes, scallions, ripe tomatoes, black olives; thinly sliced rye, matzoh or other crackers, or challah; Grated Black Radish and Endive Salad in Shallot Vinaigrette (page 61)

onions, and pulse on and off until desired texture is achieved. Transfer to a large bowl, taste for seasoning, and add enough oil or schmaltz (1 to 3 tablespoons or more, if needed) to make it moist and rich. Mix well and refrigerate, covered, until thoroughly chilled.

SERVE cold on lettuce or radicchio or alternating green and red Belgian endive leaves. Or pack into small custard cups or cleaned tuna cans and invert onto frilly greens for a sophisticated presentation.

ACCOMPANY the liver with the suggested vegetables and breads. It is particularly good with grated black radish and endive salad served alongside, topped with chopped red radishes, or sprinkled with *griebenes* reserved from preparing Poultry Schmaltz (page 28).

FISH IN POTATO LATKE CRUST WITH HORSERADISH CREAM

yield: 6 TO 8 SERVINGS

*I*t's not the potato latke—or even a latke at all—that is required eating on Hanukkah. It is food fried in oil.

Each year, however, brings a new slew of picture books on Tante-something-or-other's latkes, and for many Jews, especially the children, it's hard to sever the Hanukkah-latke connection.

But crisp, fried latkes do not a meal make, though many nights they consume all my family's appetite and my kitchen time as well.

At such times, I dip fish fillets into the latke batter and serve forth a one-pan fish-and-chips, Jewish-style.

About 1½ pounds russet (baking) or Yukon gold potatoes, scrubbed or peeled, cut into chunks

1 medium onion, peeled and quartered

2 large eggs

2 large garlic cloves, coarsely chopped

1 tablespoon chopped fresh dill

1 teaspoon cider vinegar

About 1 teaspoon salt

About ¼ teaspoon freshly ground black pepper

2 tablespoons matzoh meal or unbleached all-purpose flour

Olive or canola oil, for frying

Flour, for dredging

2 pounds flounder, lemon sole, or similar white-fleshed fish fillets, wiped with a damp paper towel and patted dry (if the fillets are not small, cut them into long strips so they will be easier to batter)

Accompaniments: Horseradish Cream (recipe follows); lemon wedges

START the Horseradish Cream at least 30 minutes before serving to develop the flavors.

IN a food processor, using the medium shredding disk, shred the potatoes together with the onion. Transfer the mixture to a fine-mesh sieve or strainer and drain it well, using your hands to squeeze out all the excess moisture. (Don't wash out the processor.) Replace the shredding disk with the steel blade. Return the shredded mixture to the processor and add the eggs, garlic, dill, vinegar, salt, pepper, and matzoh meal or flour. Process to a smooth batter. Put the batter in a large bowl.

HEAT ¼ inch of oil in a 10- to 12-inch heavy skillet until hot, but not smoking. Spread some flour on a large sheet of wax paper or a plate. Dredge a fillet in the flour, covering it completely and shaking off the excess, then dip it into the latke batter, coating well on both sides. Quickly slide it into the hot oil. Repeat, frying a few pieces at a time, and making sure you do not crowd the pan. Fry until browned on both sides and cooked through (exact time will vary, depending on thickness of the fish). Drain on paper towels or untreated brown paper bags. Serve with Horseradish Cream and lemon wedges.

HORSERADISH CREAM

yield: ABOUT 1 CUP

½ cup finely diced peeled cucumber

Salt

1 cup yogurt cream (see page 30) or sour cream (plain yogurt will be too watery)

1 large garlic clove, minced and mashed to a paste with ¼ teaspoon salt

2 tablespoons chopped fresh dill

About 1 tablespoon drained bottled white horseradish

Freshly ground black pepper

SPRINKLE the cucumber with ¼ teaspoon salt. Let stand for 10 minutes. Wrap in paper towels or a kitchen towel and squeeze out as much liquid as possible. In a small bowl, combine the cucumber with the yogurt cream or sour cream, garlic, dill, and horseradish and pepper to taste. Adjust the seasoning. You can refrigerate the Horseradish Cream, but let it come to room temperature before serving.

OVEN-FRIED SMOKED SALMON CROQUETTES

yield: 3 TO 4 SERVINGS

M y mother had her own way of doing things. On New Year's Eve, the former Miss Greenwich Village of 1928 (she was disqualified when it was learned that she was only fourteen) would dust golden glitter over her red hair and Vaseline-glossed brows. No Donna Reed at home either, there she potchkehed the mundane into the marvelous. She painstakingly sewed green and bronze sequins all over our Davy Crockett T-shirts; she painted our names in Revlon's Coral Vanilla nail polish on tin lunch boxes. And when sore throats stole our appetites at breakfast, she served us steaming oatmeal with a scoop of coffee ice cream.

Her salmon croquettes too were special: humble canned salmon fishcakes given luxury treatment with slivers of buttery smoked salmon and lemon zest. I have gently reworked her recipe, replacing the matzoh meal coating with crumbs crushed from egg matzoh, which, made with apple cider, provides a slightly caramelized crunch to the crust. But other matzoh crumbs or matzoh meal will work well, too.

FOR THE CROQUETTES

One 14.75-ounce can salmon, drained, bones and skin removed, or even better, 1 pound poached fresh salmon

2 large eggs, beaten

2 tablespoons chopped fresh dill

3 tablespoons finely chopped shallots or ¼ cup finely minced onion

1 tablespoon grated lemon zest (for a wonderful contrast to the rich smoked salmon; optional)

5 to 6 ounces smoked salmon or lox, cut into fine shreds (½ to ⅔ cup)—by all means, use the less expensive "ends" if available

¼ cup matzoh meal or unbleached all-purpose flour

Salt and freshly ground black pepper

FOR THE COATING

3 tablespoons mayonnaise

2 tablespoons Dijon mustard

PREHEAT the oven to 450°F.

MAKE the croquettes: in a large bowl, flake the salmon well. Add the eggs; dill; shallots or onions; lemon zest, if using; smoked salmon or lox; and matzoh meal or flour, and combine thoroughly. Season to taste with salt (none may be needed, especially if the lox is salty) and pepper. Form the mixture into four to six hamburger-shaped patties.

PREPARE the coating: in a shallow bowl, whisk the mayonnaise, mustard, and lemon juice together. Put the crumbs or meal on a large sheet of wax paper or a plate. Using your fingers, spread each croquette on all sides with the mayonnaise. Roll each in the crumbs to coat well. To make the coating adhere better, pat it firmly on both sides of the croquettes. Refrigerate the croquettes for 15 to 20 minutes, if you have the time.

WITH the oil, generously grease a baking sheet large enough to accommodate the croquettes without touching. Heat it in the oven until the oil is sizzling. Gently shake off any excess crumbs or meal from the croquettes, then arrange them on the hot baking sheet at least ½ inch

1 tablespoon fresh lemon juice

About ½ to ¾ cup toasted matzoh crumbs, preferably made from egg matzoh, or use toasted matzoh meal (see page 24; crumbs will give you a crunchier texture)

Olive or canola oil, for oven-frying

Accompaniment: lemon wedges; Green Olive Sauce (recipe follows; optional)

apart (so they will cook crisply around the edges too). Bake until the bottoms are crisp and golden, 5 to 7 minutes. Turn and bake until golden on the other side, 3 to 4 minutes longer. Serve with lemon wedges.

COOK'S NOTE: Lush with smoked salmon, these croquettes need only a squirt of lemon, but if you really want to serve a sauce, try ½ cup mayonnaise whisked with 4 teaspoons fresh grapefruit or orange juice, 1 to 2 teaspoons capers, drained and chopped, 3 tablespoons chopped fresh dill, and 2 teaspoons minced shallots. For a lighter sauce, thin with 2 to 4 tablespoons plain yogurt. Or prepare this delicious Green Olive Sauce.

GREEN OLIVE SAUCE

yield: ABOUT ⅔ CUP

½ cup meaty, brine-cured green olives (look for olives with a deep, fruity olive oil flavor, such as Sicilian green), pitted and sliced

2 tablespoons chopped shallots

2 tablespoons fresh lemon juice

1 tablespoon Dijon mustard

1 teaspoon grated lemon zest

4 tablespoons best-quality extra virgin olive oil

Salt and freshly ground black pepper

IN a food processor or a blender, process the olives, shallots, lemon juice, mustard, and zest to a coarse puree. With the machine on, add the olive oil in a slow, steady stream through the feed tube or blender top. Season to taste with salt and pepper. Let the flavors blend together for at least ½ hour before serving.

THE sauce will keep for about 5 days, refrigerated.

COOK'S NOTE: This sauce is wonderful with other fish dishes as well, such as poached fillets or Slow-Roasted Salmon (page 404). It is also delicious diluted with a few spoonfuls of broth or mayonnaise and paired with the Veronese Rolled Turkey Loaf (Polpettone) (page 411).

FRIED CHICKEN CUTLETS, ITALIAN-JEWISH STYLE

yield: 3 TO 4 SERVINGS

*F*ried chicken lightly flavored with cinnamon is a traditional Hanukkah specialty in Italy. *Used without any sweetening, the cinnamon acts in concert here with savory garlic and lemon to produce a very fragrant, yet subtle, marinade.*

To accentuate the delicacy of the dish, I dip the chicken in egg after dusting it lightly with matzoh meal. And I fry each batch with a few pieces of celery—a trick sent in to Cook's Illustrated *magazine by one of its readers—which makes the chicken beautifully golden and more flavorful.*

¼ teaspoon ground cinnamon

4 large garlic cloves, finely chopped

3 tablespoons fresh lemon juice

1 tablespoon olive oil, plus additional for frying

Salt and freshly ground black pepper

1½ pounds skinless, boneless chicken cutlets, trimmed of fat and gristle

About 1 cup matzoh meal (use commercially ground—you'll need a very fine, powdery consistency here)

2 large eggs

2 or 3 celery stalks, including leaves, washed, dried well, and cut into 4- to 5-inch lengths

Accompaniment: lemon wedges

Optional garnish: parsley sprigs

IN a large bowl or nonreactive baking dish, whisk together the cinnamon, garlic, lemon juice, olive oil, and salt and pepper to taste. Add the chicken and toss to coat thoroughly. Cover and marinate for 2 to 3 hours in the refrigerator, turning the chicken occasionally.

SET up a work station near the stove. Spread 1 cup matzoh meal on a large sheet of wax paper or a plate and season it with 1 teaspoon salt and ⅛ teaspoon pepper, or to taste. Next to it, in a wide shallow bowl or pie pan, beat the eggs with a few drops of water until well blended and smooth.

DREDGE the cutlets well with the matzoh meal, rubbing it lightly into the chicken. Make sure each cutlet is covered all over with meal. If necessary, add more matzoh meal, remembering to add more seasoning.

HEAT about ½ cup olive oil in a 10- to 12-inch heavy skillet over medium-high heat until hot and fragrant, but not smoking. Shake a cutlet to remove all excess matzoh meal, then coat it thoroughly with the egg and slip it quickly into the hot oil. Being careful not to crowd the pan, add more chicken, dipping each piece in the egg just before placing it in the pan. Slip a few pieces of celery in between the cutlets as they fry. Using two spatulas (tongs would ruin the delicate egg coating), carefully turn the chicken when it is light golden, 2 to 3 minutes. Sauté the other side for 2 to 3 minutes longer, until cooked through. Turn the celery pieces when you turn the chicken. Transfer the cutlets to a platter lined with paper towels so they can drain. Discard the cooked celery. Keep the chicken warm in a 200°F oven until the remaining pieces are done. Continue frying any remaining chicken in batches, in the same way, adding fresh celery to the pan with each batch. Wipe out the skillet and replace the oil if some of the coating falls off and burns.

SERVE the chicken right away, accompanied by the lemon wedges and garnished, if you'd like, with fresh parsley. It really needs no sauce.

"The logs of Jerusalem were of the cinnamon tree, and when lit, their fragrance pervaded the whole of Erez Israel."

—BABYLONIAN TALMUD: SHABBAT

APRICOT- AND ORANGE-SCENTED GOOSE WITH ROASTED GARLIC

yield: ABOUT 6 TO 8 SERVINGS

ickens's Tiny Tim wasn't the only one clamoring for a fat, juicy roast goose on his holiday table. Alsatian as well as Central and Eastern European Jews who could afford a dinner of poultry to celebrate winter Sabbaths were particularly fond of goose, especially for the festive Friday night meal that fell during Hanukkah.

No golden eggs did these geese supply, but something better: streams of molten ivory schmaltz (rendered fat). Enough for delectably crisp Hanukkah potato pancakes, with plenty left over to be sealed in ritually cleansed jars for use at Passover.

Like most Sabbath foods, the succulent bird was chockablock with garlic, the ancient aromatic love potion enlisted to make sure the Friday night connubial duties would be performed.

The passion for garlic still smolders, but today a fatty bird bespeaks a déclassé cook.

There are several methods for removing most of the fat from a goose. The so-called Peking Duck technique—immersing the bird in boiling water to open its pores and then drying the skin, sometimes with a hair-dryer—reduces much of the thick fat layer. But it entails finding a pot huge enough to submerge a 10-pound bird, and worse, washing the pot clean of goose fat afterward. Not to mention the dryer.

I use a simpler method. First work your hands under the skin to pull out all the loose fat. Then douse the skin with boiling water, vinegar, and honey to melt some of the subcutaneous fat, and pierce all over so all that fat will exude. Piquant orange and apricot flavoring rubbed under the skin permeates the flesh and parries the richness.

One 10- to 12-pound goose, the neck, wingtips, and giblets removed and reserved

1 cup cider vinegar

1 tablespoon honey

1 whole head of garlic, unpeeled

START the goose: cut off and discard the tailbone. Remove all visible fat and loose skin, inside and out. Then separate the skin from the body: starting at the neck end, gently loosen the skin by sliding your hand underneath the breast and carefully working your way back to the legs. Pull out as much fat as possible from beneath the skin, paying particular attention to the fat deposits around the thighs. Discard the fat or reserve it for rendering (see page 28), as you choose. With a tweezer, pull out any quills left in the skin. Using a sharp skewer, embroidery needle, or the pointed tip of a paring knife, prick the goose all over, especially

3 to 4 tablespoons finely julienned orange or tangerine zest

6 to 8 dried apricots (preferably tart), quartered, plumped in boiling water for 15 minutes, and drained

2 tablespoons chopped fresh rosemary leaves

1 tablespoon juniper berries, crushed

1 tablespoon olive oil

Salt and freshly ground black pepper

2 cinnamon sticks

FOR THE GRAVY

1 tablespoon olive oil

The reserved neck, wingtips, and giblets

½ cup chopped shallots

½ cup scraped and chopped carrots

1½ teaspoons chopped garlic, plus 4 large garlic cloves, peeled

½ cup cider vinegar or apple brandy

1 tablespoon honey

3 cups chicken broth, preferably homemade (see pages 62 and 70), or good-quality, low-sodium purchased

1 teaspoon juniper berries, crushed

½ teaspoon peppercorns, crushed

¼ cup diced apricots (preferably tart), plumped in 1 cup boiling water until soft (this will take about 30 minutes, depending on dryness of fruit), drained, and soaking liquid reserved

where the subcutaneous fat is thickest, like around the thighs. To avoid jabbing the flesh, hold the pricking instrument almost parallel to the goose, rather than upright.

PREHEAT oven to 325°F.

PUT the goose on a rack in a deep roasting pan and set the pan in the sink. Combine 6 cups water, the vinegar, and honey in a saucepan and bring to a rolling boil. Pour half of the mixture evenly over the goose. Reheat the remaining mixture to boiling, then turn the goose and pour the boiling liquid over it. Little droplets of melted fat will begin to appear on the skin. Prick the goose again all over to encourage more of the fat to find its way out. Discard all the water in the pan and wipe the goose thoroughly inside and out with paper towels. Let it drain on the rack, uncovered, to exude more fat and air dry, as you prepare the seasonings.

SEPARATE the garlic head into cloves and discard the roughest papery outer husk, leaving the thin layer of peel intact. In a small baking dish just large enough to accommodate all the ingredients snugly, add the garlic cloves and scatter the orange or tangerine zest, apricots, rosemary, and juniper. Drizzle with the oil and sprinkle lightly with salt and pepper. Cover the dish tightly with foil and bake for 30 minutes, or until the garlic cloves are very soft. Let cool until you can handle the garlic. Leave the oven on.

SQUEEZE the garlic from the husks (discard the husks), and combine the garlic pulp and other ingredients from the baking dish in a food processor or blender. Puree until smooth.

DRY the goose again with paper towels; it should have released more fat. Spoon the roasted garlic mixture under the goose skin, pushing it all over the breast and down the drumsticks. Generously salt and pepper the goose, inside and out, rubbing the seasoning into the skin. Lightly crush the cinnamon sticks with a mallet or rolling pin and place them in the cavity. Truss if desired. (If my goose is extra-large—12 or more pounds—and its limbs, when extended, sidle over the edge of my largest roasting pan, I usually do a simple truss to make it fit more compactly.)

ROAST the goose breast side down on the rack for 1½ hours, pouring out the fat occasionally as it accumulates in the pan. Remove the goose from the oven, turn it breast side up, and prick the skin again several times. Return to the oven and roast, pouring out the fat occasionally, for another 1 to 1½ hours, until the juices of the thigh run clear when pierced with a knife and the leg meat feels soft when pressed. (These

½ cup fresh orange juice

1 teaspoon grated orange or tangerine zest

1 teaspoon chopped fresh rosemary leaves

Salt and freshly ground black pepper

are more accurate indicators than the internal temperature: a goose will often measure 170°F—well-done—long before the meat is tender yet still moist.)

REMOVE from the oven and increase the oven temperature to 400°F. Prick the goose again all over. Transfer the goose to a large rimmed baking sheet or pan with shallow sides to trap the fat. When the oven reaches 400°F, roast the goose for 15 minutes longer to turn the skin beautifully crisp and brown. Remove from the oven and let stand about 20 minutes before carving.

WHILE the goose is cooking, prepare the gravy: in a wide, heavy saucepan, heat the oil until hot, but not smoking. Add the reserved neck, wingtips, and giblets (save the liver for broiling—the cook's perk), and sauté for about 10 minutes over medium heat until golden brown. Transfer to a platter. Pour out all but 1 tablespoon of fat remaining in the saucepan, and add the shallots, carrots, and chopped garlic. Sauté, stirring, until the vegetables are tinged with brown, 8 to 10 minutes, then transfer them to the platter. Combine the vinegar or apple brandy with the honey, and use to deglaze the saucepan over moderately high heat, scraping up all the browned bits with a wooden spoon. Return everything from the platter to the saucepan. Add the broth, juniper, and peppercorns, and bring the mixture to a boil. Lower the heat and simmer slowly for about 1 hour. Strain through a fine-mesh strainer into a bowl, pressing down on the solids to extract all of their flavorful juices. Skim off any fat. Wash and dry the saucepan and return the strained stock to it. Add the whole garlic cloves, apricots and their soaking liquid, and cook the mixture over high heat until reduced by about half. Add the orange juice, zest, and rosemary, and cook for 3 to 4 minutes. Season with salt and pepper to taste. Transfer to a blender (in batches, if necessary), and emulsify until smooth. Taste for seasoning, and keep warm or reheat gently before serving.

CARVE the goose. Serve each guest a portion of the meat, topped with some of the irresistible skin. Pass the gravy.

MY MOTHER'S FRIED CAULIFLOWER

yield: 4 TO 6 SERVINGS

*M*y mother always fried up cauliflower late at night. Long ago she had decided it— or her fluffy buttermilk pancakes—was the perfect antidote to flagging appetites, so she would make a batch after she noticed one of us had eaten very little at dinner.

During school holidays or when one of us lay afflicted with some childhood bug, it was often past eleven o'clock when she carried the tray into the TV room, piled high with bronzed cauliflower nuggets and golden lemon quarters. We ate fast, lest we miss Zacherley pulling up his wife's hair or the Mummy's response when offered thirteen tanna leaves.

Because we polished it off so quickly, I always assumed it took no time to prepare. Not so. The cauliflower must be boiled until tender before being breaded and fried—necessitating another large pot to wash. I once tried to skip this step, but the whole purpose of fried foods is the contrast of the crisp and crunchy coating the soft and yielding.

I have come upon a technique though that works with fresh young cauliflower. Pour boiling water over small florets, then let them steep a while in a bowl. This not only cleans them thoroughly (farm-fresh cauliflower sometimes harbors small insects), but also eliminates the parboiling.

To coat the cauliflower, my mother usually used matzoh meal, which falls somewhere between bread crumbs and flour in terms of thickness. Because it is so bland—it lacks even salt— it must be generously seasoned. She used lots of garlic, lemon peel, and, when she had them on hand, finely minced anchovies, for a zesty nuance not readily identifiable by anchovy haters.

For perfectly fried cauliflower, I rely on two simple tricks. When possible, let the coated florets set at least fifteen minutes before frying to allow the egg dip to dry to a glue-like paste, so that the matzoh meal is less likely to fall off and burn in the oil while frying. And divide the seasoned coating mixture into two piles. After a while, dredging the egg-dipped florets in the matzoh meal renders the meal ragged with little wet eggy clumps. So when the matzoh meal is just too lumpy to coat the cauliflower, I replace it with a fresh supply.

1 medium head of cauliflower, preferably young and fresh

Salt

About 1½ cups matzoh meal

BREAK the cauliflower into small florets and put them in a large, heat-proof bowl. Sprinkle with 1 teaspoon of salt. Bring a large kettle of water to a rapid boil, and pour over the cauliflower, covering it by at least an inch. Cover the bowl, and allow the cauliflower to steep in the water for 5 to 8 minutes. Stir it around a bit so all of the pieces are sloshed by the water. If florets test fork-tender (but before they are soft

1 tablespoon dried oregano

1 tablespoon grated lemon zest

2 to 3 teaspoons pressed or very finely minced garlic

2 or 3 anchovy fillets, finely minced (optional)

Freshly ground black pepper

2 large eggs

2 tablespoons fresh lemon juice

Olive oil, for frying

Accompaniment: lemon wedges

and mushy), drain them well. If not, let them steep for a few more minutes. (Alternatively, if you have a very mature head of cauliflower, boil the florets in salted water until just tender and drain them.)

IN a bowl, stir together the matzoh meal, oregano, lemon zest, garlic, anchovies, if using, and plenty of salt and pepper. (Use the greater amounts of garlic and anchovies for a zippier taste; adjust salt to the amount of anchovies used.) Divide the mixture in two, spreading half out on a plate or sheet of wax paper and setting the other half aside. Beat the eggs well with the lemon juice in a wide, shallow bowl or pie pan.

TAKING one floret at a time, dip into the beaten egg, coating well on all sides. Let the excess egg drip back into the bowl. Dredge the florets all over with the matzoh meal mixture. When the matzoh meal mixture gets lumpy with bits of egg, discard and replace with the reserved fresh mixture. To prevent loose crumbs from falling off and burning in the hot oil, pat the coated florets firmly so the matzoh meal adheres. If possible, place them on a rack and let stand for about 15 minutes to set the coating.

HEAT ½ inch of olive oil in a 10- to 12-inch heavy skillet over medium-high heat until hot, but not smoking. Add the florets and sauté them in batches until golden brown on all sides. Drain on paper towels or brown paper bags.

SALT and pepper the cauliflower generously, like French fries, and serve with the lemon wedges. They are best hot, though they are still delicious, if somewhat greasy, at room temperature.

Anchovy-Free Parmesan Version Omit the anchovies and season the matzoh meal with about ¼ cup grated Parmesan cheese.

ORANGE, ONION, AND DATE SALAD

yield: ABOUT 4 SERVINGS

I've borrowed the Mexican technique of soaking onions in an acidic bath—here, fresh lemon juice—to tame them a little for this North African–inflected salad. A dazzling, if unusual, blend of flavors, it's an impeccable complement to a menu of latkes or other fried foods.

The salad is best served slightly chilled, so if you have time, cover the platter with plastic wrap before dressing the salad and refrigerate for about 30 minutes.

1 medium yellow or red onion, peeled, very thinly sliced, and separated into rings

⅓ cup fresh lemon juice

Salt

1½ large lemons

4 Medjool dates

4 large navel oranges, preferably Cara Caras

Lettuce leaves, for lining the platter

About 2 tablespoons best-quality extra virgin olive oil

¼ teaspoon ground cumin

⅛ teaspoon ground cinnamon

⅛ teaspoon cayenne or Aleppo pepper

PUT the onion in a medium bowl. Pour in the lemon juice and sprinkle with ¼ teaspoon salt. Toss well and let infuse for about 20 minutes.

REMOVE the lemon flesh from its rind and discard the seeds. Cut the flesh into little bite-size chunks, place in a bowl, and sprinkle with a generous pinch of salt. Cut the dates into thin slivers (easiest to do with a scissor) and combine well with the lemon pieces. Set aside for 10 minutes to mingle the flavors.

USING a sharp paring knife, slice off top and bottom ends of the oranges. Standing the fruit upright as you work, slice downward to cut off the rind and pith. Trim away the thready white membranes. Holding the fruit on its side, thinly slice the oranges crosswise, and, if desired, cut the slices in half. Arrange the orange slices on a serving platter lined with lettuce leaves. Scatter the lemon-date pieces over the oranges and top with the onion.

IN a small bowl, stir together the oil, cumin, paprika, cinnamon, cayenne or Aleppo pepper, and salt to taste. Drizzle over the salad just before serving. Taste and adjust seasoning, drizzling with more oil, if desired.

APPLE-CRANBERRY BLINTZES WITH MAPLE RICOTTA CREAM AND SUGARED WALNUTS

yield: 16 TO 18 BLINTZES

These tantalizing blintzes are an unabashed ode to the Diaspora. Apples and cranberries form the sweet and tangy filling. For the cream topping, simply sieve ricotta sweetened with maple and vanilla. Finish with a crunch of lightly sweetened toasted walnuts.

FOR THE APPLE-CRANBERRY FILLING

3 tablespoons unsalted butter

About 3½ cups flavorful apples, peeled, cored, and cut into small chunks (choose sweet varieties with lots of character, such as Gala, Braeburn, and Jonagold, which will contrast nicely with the cranberries)

⅓ to ½ cup packed brown sugar

½ teaspoon ground cinnamon

¾ cup cranberries, washed and picked over

2 tablespoons dried cranberries (optional)

Salt

FOR THE MAPLE RICOTTA CREAM

1½ cups whole-milk ricotta cheese (about 11 ounces; you can use part-skim, if desired)

MAKE the apple filling: heat the butter over medium-high heat in a large, heavy skillet until sizzling. Add the apples and sauté for about 5 minutes, lifting and turning them as they begin to turn golden. Sprinkle with ⅓ cup sugar and the cinnamon and mix well to coat the apples evenly on all sides. Add the cranberries, dried cranberries, if using, and a pinch of salt, and cook, stirring, until the cranberries have popped and the apples are very tender. Let the fruit cool in the pan, then taste and add more sugar, if necessary, depending on your preference and the sweetness of the apples.

TRANSFER the fruit to a bowl, and refrigerate, covered, for at least 20 minutes or up to 24 hours.

MEANWHILE, make the maple ricotta cream: push the ricotta through a fine-mesh sieve, rubbing with the back of a spoon. Using an egg beater or electric mixer, beat in the maple syrup, vanilla, and nutmeg, if using, until smooth and light. Cover and refrigerate to allow the flavors to marry. Rewhip briefly just before serving.

"Every place you go, act according to the custom of that place."

—LADINO PROVERB

1 tablespoon pure maple syrup

¼ teaspoon vanilla extract

⅛ teaspoon freshly grated nutmeg (optional)

FOR THE SUGARED WALNUTS

¼ cup walnuts, toasted

1 teaspoon maple or white granulated sugar

1 recipe Blintz Leaves (page 36)

Unsalted butter, canola oil, or a combination, or ghee for frying or baking

TO prepare the walnuts, coarsely chop them with the sugar.

FILL the blintz leaves, using 1 heaping tablespoon of filling per blintz (don't overfill), and bake or fry them (see pages 36–38).

SERVE the blintzes hot, topped with maple ricotta cream and sprinkled with sugared walnuts.

CARAMEL RUGELACH

yield: 32 COOKIES

I am a vanilla person: one of the few food lovers completely unseduced by chocolate's charms. Perhaps that explains why I made the match: buttery caramels with tender rugelach. It was bashert, *or meant to be; two delicious nonchocolate sweets just waiting to be introduced.*

And using purchased caramels makes these rugelach as easy to prepare as, well, the chocolate chip kind. But the sweet molten filling does tend to seep out somewhat during baking. I find that adding chopped pecans and shaping the rugelach in rectangles rather than crescents helps cut down on leakage. And when needed, I just trim away the caramel that has found its way out of the baked cookies.

See the Cook's Note for classic walnut-raisin and a sublime almond-paste-cranberry rugelach.

FOR THE PASTRY

2¼ cups unbleached all-purpose flour

¼ teaspoon salt

3 tablespoons granulated light brown sugar

8 ounces cream cheese, chilled and cut into bits

16 tablespoons (2 sticks) unsalted butter, chilled and cut into bits

¼ cup sour cream

1 teaspoon vanilla extract

FOR THE FILLING

½ cup light brown sugar, packed or granulated

1¾ to 2 cups packaged caramels (about 12 ounces), such as Kraft's, unwrapped and cut into small bits

About 1 cup pecans, lightly toasted and coarsely chopped

MAKE the pastry: in a food processor, mix the flour, salt, and brown sugar. Add the cream cheese, butter, sour cream, and vanilla, and pulse just until the mixture begins to form a ball around the blades. Do not overprocess. Transfer the dough to a work surface and knead lightly and quickly into a smooth, compact roll. (Or prepare manually: in a large bowl, quickly mix together the cream cheese, butter, sour cream, and vanilla until well blended. Gradually add the flour, salt, and sugar. Knead the mixture lightly until thoroughly combined and smooth.)

DIVIDE the dough into four equal parts. Put each piece between two sheets of wax paper and flatten into a large oblong using the palm of your hand. If necessary, refrigerate briefly until the dough is firm enough to roll.

WORK with one oblong at a time, keeping the others refrigerated. Roll the oblong between the wax paper into a 12 by 7-inch rectangle, about ⅛-inch thick. Leaving the dough in the wax paper, refrigerate for at least 4 hours or up to 2 days. Repeat with the other three rectangles.

LOOSEN the wax paper from both sides of the dough. (The paper becomes pressed into the dough with rolling and will be difficult to remove after you cut the dough, unless it has been loosened first.) Place the dough rectangle back down on a sheet of the wax paper, and sprinkle it all over with 2 tablespoons brown sugar. Now cut the rectangle in half into two 6 by 7-inch sections. Cut each section into four equal strips, giving you eight in all. Leaving a ½-inch border, place some caramel pieces and pecans over each dough strip (be generous—the more caramels, the more luscious the taste; see Cook's Note). Roll each strip up tightly, jelly-roll fashion, and place seam side down, about 1 inch apart, on a baking sheet lined with parchment. (If the dough becomes too soft to work with during the rolling or filling, place it in the freezer on a lined cookie sheet until firm again.) Refrigerate the prepared rugelach as you make more with the rest of the dough. The prepared rugelach should be refrigerated for at least 30 minutes before you bake them.

PREHEAT the oven to 375°F. Bake in the middle of the oven for about 20 minutes, until pale golden. If necessary, adjust the pans during baking so the rugelach cook evenly. Transfer the pan to a rack and let the rugelach cool completely. Remove the rugelach carefully with a thin-bladed spatula. Store the rugelach in airtight containers for up to 4 days.

COOK'S NOTE: Rugelach may be frozen, unbaked. You need not defrost before baking, but increase baking time by 5 to 7 minutes.

If your caramels are soft enough, press the pieces with your fingertips to flatten them. You'll get a smoother, tighter roll.

My good friend, Dr. Mary McLarnon, who helped me perfect these little treats, prefers them warm. She recommends gently heating them in a microwave or toaster oven. But never eat them hot: caramels, like all sugar when heated, can badly burn your mouth. She also suggests these would be delicious made with English toffee or homemade caramels.

Classic Walnut-Raisin Rugelach

Follow the filling directions for Caramel Rugelach, with these changes: stir 2 to 3 tablespoons ground cinnamon into the brown sugar. For the caramels and pecans, substitute ¾ to 1 cup dark raisins (plump them in hot water first, if they are not moist, then drain and pat dry with paper towels) and 1 cup lightly toasted walnuts, chopped. If the raisins are large, coarsely chop them with the nuts. Some people enhance this filling with apricot flavor: lightly brush the dough with apricot jam (you'll need about 1 cup) before sprinkling with sugar.

Almond Paste (Marzipan)–Cranberry Rugelach

Purchase prepared almond paste (in the baking section of most supermarkets). Grate about 6 ounces on a medium grater or cut or crumble the paste finely. Mix with 1 cup dried cranberries or coarsely chopped tart dried cherries or apricots (plump them in hot water first if they are not moist, then drain and pat dry with paper towels). Follow the filling directions for Caramel Rugelach, omitting the sprinkled sugar layer (almond paste is quite sweet).

OTHER SUGGESTIONS FOR HANUKKAH

*Tangy Russian Cabbage Soup with Pot Roast–Beet Kreplach

*Lemon Fried Chicken with Tart Salad Topping

Any of the *Brisket recipes

Either of the *Stuffed Cabbage recipes

*Roasted Eggplant-Meat Patties

Either of the *Cheese Blintzes

*Apricot Blintzes with Toasted Pistachios and Yogurt Cream

*Potato and Caramelized Onion Blintzes

*Potato-Onion Kreplach, Pot Sticker-Style

*Garlic-Mashed Potato Knishes

Any of the *Potato Kugel recipes

*Kasha Varnishkes with Fried Eggplant, Mushrooms, and Onion Marmalade

*North African Cooked Carrot Salad

*Upside-Down Caramel-Cranberry-Pecan Noodle Kugel

*Double Ginger-Caramelized Pear Noodle Kugel

*Poppy Seed Butter Cake (*Mohn* Cake)

*Rich Fudge Brownies

Any of the *Cheese Cake recipes

*Turkish Silken Ground-Rice Pudding (*Sutlaj*)

*Old-Fashioned Rice Pudding

*See index for page numbers

Purim

urim, the most joyous holiday of all, is a wild carnival of food, wine, and laughter. A time to let go in life-affirming festivities, free as possible of inhibitions, enjoying the day to the fullest.

And why not? Purim marks the period Jews were snatched from the hangman's noose at the last minute. We celebrate our physical life because we came so close to extermination.

The historical foundations of Purim as recounted in the Book of Esther have never been fully substantiated; the story itself is rife with inconsistencies. But to paraphrase Voltaire, if Purim did not exist, it would be necessary to invent it. Parallels to its central theme of genocide have been replayed throughout the Diaspora, culminating in the unspeakable: twentieth century Germany replacing ancient Persia, a thwarted Haman recast as the demonically successful Hitler. Two thousand years later, the need for Purim became even more important.

The Persian King Ahasuerus ruled an empire stretching from India to Ethiopia. His proud chief vizier, Haman, grew incensed one day when Mordecai, a Jewish courtier, refused to bow down to him. In revenge, he determined to have all the Jews in the empire annihilated. Convincing the rather wimpish king was an easy matter—Haman told him the Jews were subversive and backed up his argument with a bribe of silver talents—and the date of the genocide was set for 13 Adar. But two startling events made the king change his mind. He found out that Esther, his beautiful queen, was actually a Jew (and none other than Mordecai's adoptive daughter) when she pleaded with him to save the lives of her people. And he suddenly discovered, in the middle of an insomniac night, that he had never rewarded Mordecai for saving his life by foiling an assassination plot some time ago. So Ahasuerus ordered Haman to be hanged instead and the Jews were saved. Mordecai and Esther declared that the next day should be celebrated evermore with feasting and merrymaking.

All the stops are giddily pulled out as life turns into a lusty, riotous party. There is boisterous revelry even in the synagogue. While the Megillah, the Book of Esther, is read, children clang pots, pans and *groggers* (ear-splitting noisemakers), blotting out the name of Haman; some Eastern Jews write "Haman" on the soles of their feet and "stamp" him out. Nor is the sacred literature exempt: hilarious parodies of the Torah and Talmud are presided over by comic Purim rabbis.

Wine flows freely, adding to the jubilant mood and ensuring unrestrained rejoicing.

Disguise too offers freedom to abandon oneself. Venetian Jews, dazzled by the wild exuberance of their Gentile neighbors during Carnival (which occurs around the same time), adopted the custom of masquerading in costumes and elegant masks at the end of the fifteenth century. The tradition spread to Jewish communities around the world.

Today many children dress up for glorious carnival processions and Purim parties. In synagogues, pint-size Esthers and Jewish superheroes like the Golem and Samson vie for best costume with Batmen and Spidermen.

At home, children may trick-or-treat in costumes, or celebrate at costume parties with family and friends, whacking a Haman pinata until it explodes, showering guests with chocolates and Purim delicacies. Or a phrase from the Megillah, *"vena ha-foch,"*—meaning the opposite occurred or the tables were turned—might inspire young families to celebrate what I remember from Alex's Sesame Street years as an Opposites Day: parents and children reverse roles, everyone tries to say the opposite of what they mean, the family begins the day by dressing in pajamas and ends with breakfast instead of supper, or dessert before dinner.

But Purim celebrations today are not just for kids. There are many grownup gatherings, costumed or in fancy dress, including the elegant masked ball annually held at the Waldorf–Astoria, a fundraiser for The Jewish Museum in New York. Synagogues too sponsor costume parties for adult congregants, often centered around a special motif that changes from year to year.

Disguise and revelation also have a more profound significance in the Purim story, with Esther finally declaring herself to the king, "coming out" as a Jew. Some Jews echo this motif, choosing costumes that reflect their hidden qualities or secret dreams. And in some gay and lesbian communities, Purim parties celebrate coming out to the world as Jews who happen to be homosexual.

The Old World tradition of the Purim *Spielers* (Players), who traveled from house to house performing the Purim story and other tales, lives on in a variety of Purim shows in the community. Some synagogues sponsor jugglers, magicians, and clowns at their parties, while others host productions featuring adult or younger congregants performing contemporary theater as well as familiar Jewish plays.

On college campuses and in hip downtown clubs, today's Purim rabbi may be a stand-up comedian, deriding contemporary despots and political figures—the latest incarnation of this traditional challenger to authority.

In many countries, Purim celebrations typically included destroying symbolic Hamans. One of my favorites, described in a manual edited by the Center for Fostering Jewish Awareness, took place in Bukhara, where Purim often fell during snowy winters. The Jewish community built a large, distorted snow-Haman near the synagogue, with a beetroot mouth and a beat-up pot for a hat. After the Purim feast, they made a bonfire in front of Haman, and watched, singing, as their evil enemy melted, then disappeared.

As befits a holiday of deliverance, charity is donated: money must be given to at least two impoverished people. And the culinary highlight of the holiday begins with another gift, *mishlo'ah manot* ("sending portions"). These are platters of no less than two "portions" of baked goods, sweets or fruits, traditionally exchanged among friends and relatives.

In communities like my sister's, the two customs, contributing to charity and sending mishlo'ah manot are linked in special Purim projects. A committee devises creative, themed mishlo'ah manot baskets, filled with edible and household treats. Each family in the community pays a set price to send the gift to local relatives and friends. But instead of receiving several of the same presents from various loved ones, each family gets just one of the Purim projects, with a card listing the names of all the friends and relatives who paid to send them gifts. The money collected for the many unsent gifts—often amounting to thousands of dollars—is donated to charity.

This is the time for home-baked, bite-size hamantaschen, the traditional three-cornered cookie, prepared in generous quantity to use up all the flour before Passover. Fill them with fruits: fresh apples or a Middle East–inspired melange of dried apricots, dates, and pistachios. Or stuff buttery poppy seed hamantaschen with a raisin-walnut puree.

The Purim *seudah*—the festive meal eaten toward nightfall—is especially splendid: gefilte fish painted gold with saffron, herbed roast turkey with challah stuffing and gravy made from chestnuts and roasted grapes, or, for a dairy meal, savory prune-filled kreplach, napped with dreamy honeyed cream. Kreplach are traditional Purim treats because their hidden filling reminds us that the hand of God was concealed and echoes the themes of disguise, revelation, and surprise in the holiday story. In the midst of such lavish delicacies, we nibble on humble chickpeas, zesty in this revisionist version with garlic and barbeque spices. It is customary to serve grains and legumes because Queen Esther would not eat the unkosher meat at her husband's palace, and she contented herself at the fabulous banquets with plain peas and beans, which were said to keep her beautiful.

But there are plenty of scrumptious pastries left over from *mishlo'ah manot*. And still more wine to be drunk.

PURIM
menu suggestions

*Chickpeas with Garlic and Barbeque Spices

*Golden Gefilte Fish with Golden Horseradish

or

Rich Beef Broth (from *Flanken) with *Mishmash Kreplach (Beef, Potato, and Fried Onion Kreplach)

*Roast Turkey with Challah Stuffing, Roasted Grape and Chestnut Gravy

or

*Braised Breast of Veal Stuffed with Kasha and Mushrooms

Salad of tart greens

*Cider-Baked Apples Stuffed with Halvah

Winter fruit platter: toasted almonds and dark raisins, ripe pear, and peeled kiwi quarters

*Almond Challah

*Poached Prune Kreplach with Honeyed Cream and Pecans

*Moroccan Fish with Chickpeas and Saffron-Lime Aioli

or

*Fish Baked with Golden Onions and Tahini Sauce

*See index for page numbers

and/or

*Deconstructed Kasha Varnishkes (Kasha and Orzo with Grilled Portobello Mushrooms)

Broccoli with browned butter

*Assorted Hamantaschen: Fresh Apple; Raisin-Walnut in Poppy Seed Crust; and Apricot, Date, and Pistachio

*Poppy Seed Butter Cake *(Mohn* Cake)*

*See index for page numbers

CHICKPEAS WITH GARLIC AND BARBEQUE SPICES

yield: ABOUT 3 CUPS

A *herring tidbit in cream sauce, a stuffed grape leaf, a piece of sweet egg* kichel—*Jewish cuisine is rich in tantalizing noshes. Perhaps this is because a little snack calls for just a little* brocha *(blessing), not the full ritual benediction required before and after eating a complete meal.*

Jews have enjoyed chickpeas since biblical times. Known as arbas *or* nahit *to Ashkenazi Jews and* garvansos *to Sephardim, they are a popular snack food, eaten like popcorn, especially on Purim when they are served to mimic Queen Esther, who ate legumes and grains instead of the king's nonkosher food.*

In our house, we usually ate them boiled plain, with heaps of coarsely ground black pepper. In this recipe, I sprinkle them with a seasoning similar to a more recently beloved nosh—barbequed potato chips.

And the spiciness of this little cocktail nibble encourages one to fulfill that pleasant Purim injunction: "Drink until you can no longer differentiate between the names Mordecai and Haman."

1 cup dried chickpeas (about 1/2 pound; see Cook's Note)

1 1/2 teaspoons olive or canola oil

1 teaspoon garlic powder

1 teaspoon paprika, preferably smoked

1 teaspoon ground cumin, preferably freshly toasted and ground

1/2 teaspoon dry mustard

1/2 teaspoon cayenne, or to taste

1/2 teaspoon brown sugar

1/8 teaspoon ground cinnamon

Salt and freshly ground black pepper

PICK over the chickpeas and rinse them well in several changes of cold water. Soak them overnight in enough cold water to cover by 2 inches. Or use the quick soak method: put them in a large saucepan and add about 5 cups cold water; bring the water to a boil and simmer for 2 minutes; remove the pan from heat and let the chickpeas stand, covered, for 1 hour. Drain the chickpeas.

IN a large saucepan, bring the chickpeas to a boil with enough fresh cold water to cover by 2 inches. Lower the heat, cover, and simmer until very tender, 1 to 2 hours, depending on the age of the peas. They should be rather soft, not at all al dente, but don't overcook to mushiness. (You'll be cooking them further with the spices, and you should be able to pick them up and munch them like popcorn, dissolving in your mouth, not in your hands.) Drain well, place in a large, heavy nonstick skillet, and shake over low heat until very dry. Add the oil and toss until the chickpeas are evenly coated.

IN a small bowl, stir together the garlic, paprika, cumin, mustard, cayenne, brown sugar, cinnamon, and a generous amount of salt and pepper. Sprinkle the spice mixture over the chickpeas and cook, stirring, for about 2 minutes, to marry the flavors. Taste and adjust the seasonings as needed. These are best served warm.

COOK'S NOTE: If you must, substitute about 2½ cups canned chickpeas (rinsed and drained) for the dried ones. Dry and season them in the skillet, as instructed above. But canned chickpeas—excellent in hummus and so many other dishes—tend to be rather mushy and bland (too much flavor leaches into the canning liquid) for this recipe.

POACHED PRUNE KREPLACH WITH HONEYED CREAM AND PECANS

yield: 6 TO 8 SERVINGS

A joy at any time of year, kreplach in seventeenth century Poland and Prague were made extra special for Purim with a dough enriched with honey and spices. The opulence proliferated with lush fillings of preserves, fruit, or raisins and nuts, according to John Cooper, author of Eat and Be Satisfied.

Made with wonton wrappers, these kreplach are very simple to prepare. But they are every bit as luxurious as their seventeenth-century forebears, each taste a rich amalgam of plump prunes, sweet cream, and crunchy pecans. They make a sensational dessert or snack, or a resplendent addition to a brunch or dairy dinner.

FOR THE PRUNE KREPLACH

About 24 plump pitted prunes (it is a good idea to prepare a few extra for tasting)

Sweet red Jewish wine or red Concord grape juice to cover the prunes generously (2 to 3 cups)

1 cinnamon stick

2 whole cloves

Salt

About 48 wonton wrappers (allow a few extra in case of tearing)

Egg wash (1 or 2 large eggs as needed, each beaten with 1 teaspoon water)

COMBINE the prunes, wine, cinnamon, cloves, and a pinch of salt in a medium saucepan, and simmer over low heat, partially covered, until the prunes are very tender, about 20 minutes. Boil for a few minutes, uncovered, over high heat, stirring constantly, to evaporate any remaining liquid, watching carefully that the mixture does not burn.

DISCARD the cinnamon stick and cloves and let the prunes cool in the pan, then refrigerate them, covered, for at least 20 to 25 minutes before stuffing the kreplach.

FILL and trim the kreplach (see page 39), using one prune and two wonton wrappers for each krepl. For a festive presentation, consider using cookie cutters to make attractive shapes.

POACH the kreplach: in a large, very wide pot, bring at least 5 quarts of lightly salted water to a boil. Slip in the kreplach, one by one, being careful not to overcrowd the pot (if necessary, cook them in batches, or use two pots). Lower the temperature slightly (the kreplach might explode if the water is boiling furiously) and poach for 3 to 6 minutes, until tender (exact time will depend on the brand of wonton wrapper used). Lift the kreplach out, a few at a time, with a large skimmer, gently shaking the skimmer so the water drains back into the pot (the kreplach are too fragile to pour into a colander).

FOR THE HONEYED
CREAM

**1½ cups heavy cream,
preferably not
ultrapasteurized**

**About 2 tablespoons
fragrant honey**

1 teaspoon vanilla extract

**¼ cup pecans, toasted
and coarsely chopped**

PREPARE the sauce: put the cream, honey, and vanilla in a heavy, medium saucepan and boil over medium-high heat until reduced by about half. (If allowed to cool, reheat slowly until hot before serving.)

THIS rich dish is best enjoyed in small portions. Serve each person 3 or 4 kreplach topped with the honey cream sauce and sprinkled with the pecans.

MISHMASH KREPLACH (BEEF, POTATO, AND FRIED ONION KREPLACH)

yield: ABOUT 50 KREPLACH

They started out in three separate piles, our weekday trinity: brisket, skirt steak, or sometimes a thick meat patty (it only became a hamburger when surrounded by a roll); one hill of fluffy mashed potatoes and another of shimmering, bronzed onions. Under my grandmother's tutelage, I learned the correct way to combine them in a sublime mishmash.

First, of course, stir the onions into the potatoes, adding little spoons of gravy or meat juices to make the mixing easier. Impale the meat on your fork and bury it deep in the potato pile. Withdraw and lick it like a lollipop, flavored if necessary with copious quantities of additional gravy and judicious sprinkles of pepper—there was probably too much salt to begin with.

Years later I found out that we were not the only family that engaged in mishmashing this classic trio. In these kreplach, a paean to the combination, I fashion the same ingredients into a simple but perfect pasta package. Including mashed potatoes in a filling for pasta may seem an overload of starch. But as in my grandmother's original mishmash, smooth, rich potatoes lend a creamy sumptuousness to the golden onions and savory shards of beef, especially when encased in thin, silky kreplach like these made from wonton wrappers.

Float the kreplach in homemade beef or chicken broth. They also make an outstanding appetizer or side dish, sauced with beef gravy or topped with sautéed mushrooms. Or pat the cooked kreplach dry, then panfry them lightly in oil with sizzled onions.

2½ cups chopped onion

3 tablespoons olive oil

1 teaspoon minced fresh garlic

Salt and freshly ground black pepper

1 cup mashed potatoes (leftover is fine)

1½ cups shredded cooked beef (leftover flanken, pot roast, or brisket)

1 large egg yolk

IN a large skillet, sauté the onions in the oil over medium-high heat, lifting and tossing them frequently, until soft and golden, about 15 minutes. Add the garlic and continue sautéing until the mixture is tinged a rich caramel color in spots. (Good fried onions should be an amalgam of several degrees of doneness: from nearly clear to butter yellow to speckles of deep bronze.) Salt and pepper to taste and scrape into a large bowl. Add the mashed potatoes and the meat and combine well. Season generously to taste and stir in the egg yolk. Cover and refrigerate until cold, about 1 hour.

FILL and trim the kreplach (see page 39), using about 1 heaping teaspoon of filling per krepl, folding it into a tight triangle, and sealing with the egg wash.

About 50 wonton wrappers (allow a few extra in case of tearing)

Egg wash (1 or 2 large eggs, as needed, each beaten with 1 teaspoon water)

Accompaniments: rich homemade chicken (see pages 62 and 70) or beef broth (page 87), leftover brisket or other beef gravy, fried onions, or fried mushrooms (see Cook's Note)

POACH the kreplach. In a large, wide pot, bring at least 5 quarts of lightly salted water to a boil. Slip in the kreplach, one by one, being careful not to overcrowd the pot (if necessary, cook them in batches, or use two pots). Lower the temperature slightly (the kreplach might explode if the water is boiling furiously) and poach until tender, 3 to 6 minutes (exact time will depend on the brand of wonton wrapper used). Lift the kreplach out, a few at a time, with a large skimmer, gently shaking the skimmer so the water drains back into the pot (the kreplach are too fragile to pour into a colander).

SERVE the poached kreplach in broth, sauced with leftover brisket or pot roast gravy, or topped with fried onions or sautéed mushrooms.

COOK'S NOTE: To prepare a cloak of fried mushrooms, sauté 1 cup chopped onion and 2 teaspoons minced fresh garlic in 2 tablespoons oil over moderately high heat, stirring, until deep gold, 5 to 7 minutes; add 3 cups thinly sliced mushrooms (fresh shiitakes would be delicious, but cremini or regular button mushrooms will do very well), and cook over high heat until the mushrooms smell fragrant and release their juices; add 1 tablespoon soy sauce and 2 teaspoons fresh lemon juice, and cook for another 2 minutes; season to taste with salt and pepper; garnish, if desired, with chopped parsley, scallions, chives, or dill.

ROAST TURKEY WITH CHALLAH STUFFING, ROASTED GRAPE AND CHESTNUT GRAVY

yield: 8 TO 10 SERVINGS

*P*urim food metaphors are pretty straightforward. We eat grains and legumes because that's what Queen Esther did; in devouring pastries shaped like various parts of Haman, we swallow up our enemy; sweets are the taste of victory over forces that sought to destroy us.

But how did turkey, a bird that began in North America, become a symbol of King Ahasuerus of Persia?

His "bird brain" is one answer. While the chicken is no rocket scientist, the turkey has a reputation as a particularly foolish animal, and so is a fitting stand-in for a king who was duped by his vizier and played the fool in humiliating his first wife, Vashti, in front of his friends. Besides, Ahasuerus ruled over a kingdom that stretched mi Hodu ad Kush *(from India to Ethiopia)*, and the bird is known in Hebrew as tamegol Hodu *(Indian chicken; as yet, we eat no Purim foods associated with Ethiopia)* because it was thought to have originated in the subcontinent. (In fact, that error has been the source of controversy among some ultra-Orthodox Jews regarding the kosher status of turkey. Because not all the prohibited birds listed in Leviticus could be translated, the custom arose to eat only birds that Jews had a tradition of eating. Believing that Indian Jews had dined on the bird for centuries, the sages deemed it kosher. Of course, the only people who had a tradition of turkey dinner were the unquestionably non-Jewish Native Americans.)

For cooks, though, the problem with turkey is not its feeble brain, but its dry, rather bland flesh. In this recipe I use several techniques to produce an exceptionally moist and succulent bird—most importantly, rubbing a savory flavor paste made with challah under the skin. The bread acts like a damp sponge, continuously replenishing the meat with herby seasoning and moisture. And, separated slightly from the flesh, the skin bronzes and crisps up beautifully.

The rest of the challah loaf becomes a magnificent stuffing for the body and neck cavities. Feel free to eliminate the stuffing if you must cut down on preparation time, but I urge you to try the flavor paste: it's simple and quick and makes a real difference. (If you do omit the stuffing, decrease the final cooking hour by 2 to 3 minutes per pound.)

There's no need to prepare a giblet stock or roux for the luscious gravy: its intense flavor and thickening come from the black grapes roasted along with the bird and pureed chestnuts, mingled with the pan juices.

Enjoy this special turkey not just on Purim but Thanksgiving and the Jewish fall holidays as well.

1 small loaf challah (about 3/4 pound), to be divided for the flavor paste and stuffing

One 12- to 14-pound fresh-killed turkey

3 to 4 cups chicken broth, preferably homemade (see pages 62 and 70) or good-quality, low-sodium purchased

1 cup whole black or Concord grapes

2 tablespoons pomegranate molasses

Additional grape clusters or herb sprigs, for garnish

FOR THE FLAVOR PASTE

3/4 cup mild olive oil

1/3 cup coarsely chopped garlic (6 to 9 fat cloves)

3 tablespoons fresh lemon juice

3 tablespoons chopped fresh rosemary leaves

2 tablespoons chopped fresh thyme leaves

2 cups toasted challah cubes (from the challah loaf)

Salt and freshly ground black pepper

FOR THE STUFFING

1/3 cup mild olive oil

4 cups chopped onion

1 cup thinly sliced leeks (white and pale green parts only)

Salt and freshly ground black pepper

PREHEAT the oven to 325°F. Slice the bread and tear or cut it into 1-inch cubes. Spread the cubes out on a large, rimmed baking sheet and toast, shaking the pan occasionally, for about 25 minutes, until dry and crisp. If necessary, use two pans or work in batches. Turn off the oven for now.

MEASURE out about 2 cups packed of the toasted challah cubes for the flavor paste; put the remaining cubes into a large bowl for the stuffing.

MAKE the flavor paste: combine the oil, garlic, lemon juice, rosemary, and thyme in a food processor, and process to a coarse puree. Add the reserved 2 cups toasted challah cubes and process until smooth. Taste and add salt and pepper as needed. Transfer the flavor paste to a bowl.

PREPARE the turkey: remove the neck, wingtips, and giblets and reserve for stock or discard. Reserve the liver for chopped liver or broil later for cook's perk. Remove all visible fat. Separate the skin from the body: Starting at the neck end, gently loosen the skin by sliding your hand underneath the breast and working your way back to the thighs and drumsticks, being careful not to tear the skin. With a tweezer, pull out any quills or pinfeathers left in the turkey skin. Rinse the turkey well, inside and out, and pat it dry. Spoon half the flavor paste under the turkey skin, using your fingers to push it all over the breast and down the drumsticks. Rub all but 3 tablespoons of the remaining flavor paste inside the turkey cavity and over the surface of the bird. Set the turkey breast side down on a V-shaped rack in a roasting pan. Let the flavor paste permeate the meat while you make the stuffing. (If you want to get a headstart—and let the flavor paste perfume the turkey more deeply—slip the bird into a very large plastic bag, tie the bag securely, and refrigerate for up to 48 hours.)

PREHEAT the oven to 450°F and remove the top rack, if necessary. If you have refrigerated the seasoned turkey, bring it to room temperature.

START the stuffing: in a 12-inch heavy skillet, warm the olive oil over medium-high heat. Add the onion and leeks, sprinkle with salt and pepper, and stir to coat with the oil. Sauté, stirring, for 3 minutes. Cover, turn the heat down to low, and continue cooking, stirring occasionally, for about 30 minutes, until the vegetables are quite soft. Add the vinegar, raise the heat to high, and boil, uncovered, until the pan liquid is evaporated. Add the paprika, and sauté, stirring, for about 5 minutes, until the mixture begins to brown and the oil separates slightly from the rest of the ingredients. Transfer the mixture to the bowl of reserved

1 tablespoon plus
2 teaspoons balsamic
or sherry vinegar

1 teaspoon sweet paprika,
preferably smoked

Remaining bread cubes
from the challah loaf

2 tablespoons plus
2 teaspoons finely
chopped fresh sage

1 tablespoon plus
1 teaspoon finely chopped
fresh rosemary leaves

1 tablespoon plus
1 teaspoon finely chopped
thyme leaves

1 cup chicken broth

1 large egg, beaten

FOR THE GRAVY

1 cup coarsely chopped
shallots

2 tablespoons mild olive oil

1/4 cup coarsely chopped
garlic

Salt and freshly ground
black pepper

1 1/2 cups whole chestnuts,
cooked and peeled
(frozen, vacuum-packed,
jarred or canned are fine,
or see page 243 for
peeling raw chestnuts,
then simmer the shelled
nuts in water until tender)

3 tablespoons Marsala or
Cognac

3 cups chicken broth

1/2 cup black or Concord
grapes, halved and pitted

1 teaspoon chopped fresh
rosemary leaves

1 teaspoon chopped fresh
thyme leaves

challah cubes. Add 2 tablespoons of the sage, 1 tablespoon of the rosemary, 1 tablespoon of the thyme, and the broth, and blend well. Season to taste with salt and pepper. Add the egg and combine well.

LOOSELY pack the body and neck cavities of the turkey with the stuffing. Fasten the cavities closed: I enlist someone to help, pulling the loose skin over the neck cavity and holding the drumsticks together while I truss and tie up the bird. If you prefer, use turkey lacers or metal skewers. Don't overstuff the bird; cook any remaining stuffing later, moistened with some of the pan juices, in a greased baking dish for about 25 minutes at 350°F, until lightly browned on top and completely cooked through.

POUR 2 cups broth into the roasting pan. Roast the turkey, breast-side down on the rack, for 40 minutes. Turn the turkey breast-side up and continue roasting for 20 minutes.

REDUCE the oven to 325°F. Baste generously with pan juices. Cover the breast with foil (to slow down the cooking of this more delicate section, which otherwise would be overcooked by the time the rest of the bird is done). Add 1 cup broth to the pan. Roast 1 hour more, basting all over (including the breast beneath the foil) occasionally.

ADD the whole grapes to the roasting pan, and discard the foil covering the breast. If needed, add another cup of broth to the pan. Mix the pomegranate molasses with the remaining flavor paste and brush half of it all over the bird. Baste one more time with the pan juices, and continue roasting until the juices run clear, and a thermometer inserted in the thickest part of the thigh registers 170°F, about 1 hour longer (the temperature will rise about ten more degrees while the turkey rests). Brush with the rest of the flavor paste–pomegranate mixture once during this final roasting, but do not baste again.

ABOUT 15 minutes before the turkey has finished roasting, start the gravy base: in a large, heavy, deep skillet, sauté the shallots in the oil over medium heat for about 3 minutes. Add the garlic, sprinkle lightly with salt and pepper, and continue cooking, stirring occasionally, until softened but not browned. Add 1 cup of the chestnuts and cook for 2 minutes. Add the Marsala or Cognac, raise the heat to high, and bring to a boil, stirring to blend the flavors. When the Marsala has evaporated, turn off the heat and set aside until you have strained and defatted the pan juices.

REMOVE the turkey to a carving board. Scoop out the stuffing, place it in an oiled baking pan, and stir in the remaining stuffing herbs: 2 teaspoons sage and 1 teaspoon each rosemary and thyme. Turn the oven to 350°F. Bake the stuffing until lightly browned on top (this will eliminate any excess wetness from basting and keep the stuffing hot). Tent the bird loosely with foil and let it rest while you finish the gravy.

POUR the contents of the roasting pan (including the roasted grapes) into a fine-mesh sieve set over a large bowl. Using a wooden spoon, press down hard on the solids to extract as much liquid and flavorful grape puree as possible, making sure that any grape seeds are trapped in the sieve. Discard the solids. Remove as much fat as you can from the pan juices in the bowl.

TRANSFER the defatted pan juices to the gravy base in the skillet, and add the 3 cups broth. Cook, stirring occasionally, over medium-high heat for 15 minutes to marry the flavors. Let cool slightly, then using a slotted spoon, transfer the solids to a food processor or blender. Add some of the pan liquid and puree, in batches, if necessary, until smooth. Return the pureed mixture to the skillet and bring to a simmer. Stir in the remaining chestnuts, grapes, and herbs, and heat until piping hot. Taste and correct the seasoning. If the gravy is not as thick as you would like, raise the heat, and cook uncovered until reduced to the desired consistency.

CARVE the turkey and decorate the platter with the grape clusters and herb sprigs. Pass the stuffing and the gravy boat separately.

BRAISED BREAST OF VEAL STUFFED WITH KASHA AND MUSHROOMS

yield: 6 TO 8 SERVINGS

utty kasha, moistened with soft-fried onions and lots of dark browned mushrooms, makes a glorious filling for this spoon-tender breast of veal.

FOR THE STUFFING

½ cup dried porcini mushrooms (about 1 ounce)

4 tablespoons olive oil

2 cups chopped onion

3 cups fresh mushrooms, wiped clean, trimmed, and sliced (about ¾ pound)

Salt and freshly ground black pepper

1 tablespoon chopped garlic

1 tablespoon soy sauce

2 large eggs

1 cup kasha, preferably coarse-grind

1 cup chicken broth, preferably homemade (see pages 62 and 70), or good-quality, low-sodium purchased

¼ cup chopped fresh flat-leaf parsley

3 tablespoons chopped fresh dill

START the filling: put the porcini in a small heatproof bowl and add 1½ cups very hot water. Cover and set aside for about 45 minutes to soften. Drain the porcini through a strainer lined with paper towels or a coffee filter, reserving all the soaking liquid. Wash the porcini under cold running water to remove any remaining grit. Chop them coarsely and set aside.

WHILE the porcini are soaking, heat 2 tablespoons oil in a large heavy skillet over medium heat. Add the onions and sauté, stirring occasionally, until rich gold. Transfer the onions to a large bowl. Wipe out the skillet, add the remaining 2 tablespoons fresh oil, and place over high heat until hot, but not smoking. Add the fresh mushrooms and cook, stirring frequently, until they release some juice, 5 to 7 minutes. Sprinkle with salt and pepper, add the garlic, soy sauce, and porcini, and continue sautéing, lifting and turning often, until all the liquid has evaporated and the mushrooms are golden brown. Add the mushrooms to the onions.

MAKE the kasha: in a medium bowl, beat 1 of the eggs with a fork. Stir in the kasha and mix until each grain is thoroughly coated. Heat the broth and reserved porcini soaking liquid to simmering. In a heavy lidded skillet with high sides or a wide heavy saucepan, toast the kasha over medium heat, turning and breaking up the kasha constantly until the egg begins to dry and the grains separate, about 3 minutes. Add the simmering liquid, salt and pepper to taste, cover, and cook over very low heat until tender and all the liquid is absorbed, about 10 minutes.

ADD the kasha to the mushrooms and onions. Stir in the parsley and the dill, taste, and adjust seasoning. Cool to room temperature. Beat the remaining egg, add to the stuffing, and combine well.

PREPARE the veal: in a blender, mini food processor, or mortar and pestle, grind the garlic with the paprika, marjoram, and salt and pepper to taste, until you have a rough puree. Set aside.

6 large garlic cloves, coarsely chopped (about 2 tablespoons)

2 teaspoons sweet paprika, preferably smoked

2 teaspoons dried marjoram

Salt and freshly ground black pepper

One 5- to 6-pound veal breast (see Cook's Note)

4 tablespoons olive oil

1 cup coarsely chopped onion

1 cup scraped and coarsely chopped carrots

1 cup chicken broth

TRIM the meat of gristle and as much fat as possible. Sprinkle all over with salt and pepper, including the inside pocket. Fill the pocket with the stuffing, pushing the mixture as far in as possible, but don't over-fill—it will expand somewhat while cooking. Sew the pocket closed. (A large embroidery or trussing needle and strong cotton thread or kitchen twine work very well here. Skewering won't do the job—the stuffing is more likely to seep out into the pan gravy.)

IN a 6-quart Dutch oven or heavy flameproof casserole just large enough to hold the veal, heat 2 tablespoons of oil until hot, but not smoking. Add the veal and brown it slowly on all sides, turning carefully with wooden spoons so you don't pierce the meat. When it is nicely browned, transfer it to a platter. Wipe out the oil in the pan and heat the remaining 2 tablespoons fresh oil. Add the onions and carrots and sauté over medium-high heat until they begin to turn gold at the edges. Arrange the veal on top of the vegetables so that the fat side is up. Spread the garlic paste all over the top of the meat. Add the broth and bring to a slow bubble. Place the lid slightly askew, and braise at a slow simmer over very low heat for 2½ to 3 hours, or longer, if necessary, until the meat is very tender. Use a flame tamer (*blech*) or stack two stove burner grates if you must to keep the flame very low. Every 20 minutes or so, baste with the pan juices. If possible, turn the meat a few times; don't worry about losing the garlic paste coating—it will add wonderful flavor to the cooking juices.

TRANSFER the veal to a platter, and let it stand for 10 minutes, tented with foil to keep warm. Boil up the cooking juices for a few minutes to concentrate the flavors, taste for seasoning, then transfer to a sauce boat.

SLICE the veal about ½-inch thick, making sure that the slices enclose some of the stuffing, and cloak with some of the juices. Serve the remaining sauce separately.

COOK'S NOTE: Veal breast is a delectable but somewhat fatty cut of meat. I have my butcher bone it because it is easier to remove most of the fat that way. But leave the bones in, if you prefer—they will add flavor. Just trim most of the fat carefully. The weight listed in the recipe is before boning. In either case, have your butcher cut a large pocket for stuffing.

ROASTED EGGPLANT–MEAT PATTIES

yield: 5 TO 6 SERVINGS

*T*wice as much smoky eggplant as ground meat gives these classic Turkish fritters a delicate lushness and haunting flavor. Delicious hot or at room temperature, miniature versions make wonderful hors d'oeuvre.

Like albondigas (meatballs), another Judeo-Spanish ground meat favorite, these sautéed meat patties can be prepared with cooked spinach, leeks, celery, mashed potatoes, or carrots standing in for the eggplant.

2 pounds eggplant

1 heaping tablespoon coarsely chopped garlic

3 tablespoons packed snipped fresh dill

2 tablespoons packed chopped fresh mint

Salt and freshly ground black pepper

1½ teaspoons ground cumin, preferably freshly toasted and ground

¼ to ½ teaspoon ground allspice, according to taste

1 pound lean ground beef or lamb or ground turkey thigh meat

2 large eggs, beaten

Cream of Wheat (farina), for dredging

Olive or canola oil, for frying

Coarse salt

Accompaniment: lemon quarters

CHAR the eggplants: roast each one whole on the stove over a gas burner as you would a red pepper: impaled on a long-handled fork or set on a roasting rack placed over the flame. Turn the eggplant with tongs (carefully, to avoid piercing the flesh) until thoroughly blackened on all sides. You can finish roasting in the same way, lowering the flame slightly and turning frequently, keeping a close eye on the eggplant until it is very tender throughout. (The eggplants will probably exude some of their juices, so be prepared to sponge off the stove while they cool.)

OR after the initial charring, you may find it quicker, simpler, and less messy to place the eggplants on a foil-lined rimmed baking sheet in a preheated 450°F oven. Prick them with a fork a few times so they won't burst, and roast until tender, about 20 minutes.

(IF you don't have a gas stove, char the eggplants under the broiler, then finish roasting them in the oven.)

LET the eggplants cool until you can handle them. Peel off and discard the blackened skin and cut off the eggplant cap. Drain the eggplants well in a colander for about 30 minutes, gently pressing down on the pulp with a spoon to eliminate as much liquid as possible; otherwise the patties will be too moist to fry properly.

WITH the machine on, drop the garlic through the feed tube of a food processor and swirl until minced. Add the eggplant, dill, mint, salt (if using kosher salt, figure at least 1½ teaspoons for beef or lamb, slightly more for turkey) and pepper to taste, cumin, and allspice, and pulse until the eggplant is finely chopped. Add the meat and pulse to combine well.

TRANSFER the mixture to a large bowl, stir in about 2 tablespoons of the beaten eggs (reserving the rest), and blend well using your hands.

FORM about ⅓ cup of the mixture into a flat patty. Repeat with the remaining mixture, placing the patties in a single layer on a platter. They will be very soft and somewhat sticky, but don't worry: the farina coating will firm them up and ready them for frying. If you have the time, place the platter in the refrigerator for about 20 minutes or in the freezer for 10 minutes to firm them up a little more.

SET up a work station near the stove. Place the remaining beaten egg in a shallow bowl and spread some Cream of Wheat or farina on a sheet of wax paper or a plate.

IN a 10- to 12-inch heavy skillet, heat about ¼ inch of oil over medium-high heat until hot, but not smoking. Dust each patty on both sides with farina, patting gently to make the coating adhere, shake off any excess, and dip the patty into the egg. Slip the patty immediately into the sizzling oil. To avoid crowding the pan, fry the patties in batches, carefully turning once, until golden-brown on both sides, about 4 minutes per side. Drain on paper towels.

SPRINKLE the patties with coarse salt and serve with lemon quarters.

COOK'S NOTE: The patties can be prepared ahead and frozen, well wrapped, until needed. Thaw, then heat on a rack set on a baking sheet in a 375°F oven until hot and crisp.

DECONSTRUCTED KASHA VARNISHKES (KASHA AND ORZO WITH GRILLED PORTOBELLO MUSHROOMS)

yield: 6 SERVINGS

The bewitching aroma of sizzling, meaty mushrooms has been a powerful enchanter since ancient times. In the Babylonian Talmud, a rabbi recounts that he became so intoxicated by the captivating fragrance of a mushroom dish that his health would have been in grave danger had he not quickly been given some of the mushrooms to nibble.

This deconstructed kasha varnishkes features sliced portobellos, marinated and grilled to enhance their resemblance to meat. Instead of noodles, the pasta is orzo, cooked in broth so it is flavorful and very moist when combined with the dry, fluffy kasha.

The meat will never be missed if you serve this at a vegetarian or dairy meal, substituting vegetable stock for the chicken broth.

6 large portobello mushrooms

1 tablespoon minced garlic

1 tablespoon plus ½ teaspoon soy sauce

1 tablespoon fresh lemon juice

2 teaspoons plus 3 tablespoons olive oil

1 tablespoon chopped fresh rosemary leaves (to make the mushrooms even more meat-like; optional)

1 cup orzo

4 cups rich chicken broth, preferably homemade (see pages 62 and 70), Vegetable Stock (page 34), or good-quality, low-sodium purchased

CLEAN the mushroom caps and stems with a damp paper towel. Carefully cut the stems off flush with the caps. Trim off the woody bottom section of the stems and discard. Chop the stems coarsely and set aside. In a large resealable plastic bag, combine 2 teaspoons of the garlic, 1 tablespoon of the soy sauce, the lemon juice, 2 teaspoons of the oil, and the rosemary, if using. Add the mushroom caps, press out the air, and seal the bag. Let the caps marinate at room temperature, turning the bag over occasionally, until you are ready to broil them.

SOAK the orzo in a bowl of fresh cold water for about 5 minutes to remove some of the starch. Empty into a strainer, rinse, and drain. Bring 2 cups of the broth to a boil, stir in the orzo, and cook, covered, over low heat for 15 minutes until the orzo is tender and all the liquid is absorbed. Keep warm and covered until ready to combine ingredients.

PREHEAT the broiler.

IN a medium bowl, beat the egg with a fork. Stir in the kasha and mix until each grain is thoroughly coated. Heat the remaining 2 cups broth to simmering. In a heavy, lidded skillet with high sides or a wide, heavy saucepan, toast the kasha over medium heat, turning and breaking up

1 large egg

1 cup kasha, preferably coarse-grind

Salt and freshly ground black pepper

3 cups chopped onion (¾ pound)

Olive Oil Schmaltz (page 27), Poultry Schmaltz (page 28), butter, or margarine, if needed

Optional garnish: 2 to 3 tablespoons chopped fresh parsley

the kasha constantly until the egg begins to dry and the grains separate, about 3 minutes. Add the hot broth and salt and pepper to taste, cover, and simmer over very low heat until tender and all the liquid is absorbed, about 10 minutes. Keep covered and warm.

IN a 10-inch heavy skillet, heat 2 tablespoons of the remaining oil over medium-high heat and sauté the onions, stirring, until they are deep golden brown. Season well with salt and pepper. Transfer the onions to a large bowl. In the same skillet, sauté the reserved chopped mushroom stems and remaining 1 teaspoon garlic in the remaining 1 tablespoon oil over high heat. Cook until the mushroom edges are tinged with bronze. Sprinkle with the remaining ½ teaspoon soy sauce and pepper to taste and cook, stirring, for 1 to 2 minutes to marry the ingredients. Transfer to the bowl, keeping it covered and warm.

ARRANGE the mushroom caps on a foil-lined broiler rack, and broil them, gill-side down, about 4 inches from the heat, for about 5 minutes. Turn, baste with any juices (or spilled bits of garlic), and broil for 5 to 6 minutes, or until tender and cooked through. Transfer the mushrooms to a cutting board.

ADD the cooked orzo and kasha to the onions and mushroom stems. Combine the ingredients well and season with salt and pepper, if needed. If dry, add a little schmaltz, butter, or margarine.

TO serve, spoon some of the kasha-orzo mixture onto each plate. Slice the mushrooms on an angle and season to taste. Arrange the mushroom slices decoratively over the kasha mixture and nap with any accumulated mushroom juices. If desired, sprinkle with chopped parsley.

HAMANTASCHEN

yield: ABOUT 48 HAMANTASCHEN

As a child, I devoured butter-luscious hamantaschen by the bakery boxful. Tricornered sweet pastries enclosing open pools of jewel-toned jams—raspberry, apricot, and prune—or silver-blue poppy seeds, they are named for the arch-evil Haman. Every Purim I delighted in, consuming the wicked enemy.

My sweet tooth, I know, has grown smaller. But it seems to me that bakery hamantaschen, like bagels and muffins, have definitely grown larger. In fact, they are enormous: life-size replicas of Haman's pockets, hats, or huge, pointy ears, not the symbolic little likenesses to which the pastries have been variously ascribed. Bigger here is not better: the crusts have become drier, the fillings duller. I am bored after just a few bites.

And so I've taken to making my own miniature version. Shaping small pieces of the buttery dough was tricky—as I molded it, the warmth of my fingertips made it too soft—until I began working the dough through a sheet of plastic wrap. I am partial now to fruit fillings, studded with nuts for texture and added flavor, and three simple fresh and dried fruit recipes follow.

FOR THE PASTRY

10 tablespoons (1¼ sticks) unsalted butter, cut in pieces, plus additional for greasing the pan

½ cup sugar

1 large egg

3 tablespoons apple or fresh orange juice

½ teaspoon vanilla extract

3 cups unbleached all-purpose flour

1½ teaspoons baking powder

¼ teaspoon salt

1 recipe filling (Fresh Apple, recipe follows; Apricot, Date, and

PREPARE the pastry: in a food processor, blend the butter with the sugar. Add the egg, juice, and vanilla and pulse until smooth. Stir together the flour, baking powder, and salt, then add to the food processor. Pulse until the ingredients are combined and form a ball around the blades.

OR make the dough using an electric mixer: in a large bowl, cream the butter with the sugar until it is light and fluffy. Beat in the egg, then the juice and vanilla. Combine the remaining ingredients and mix in. Transfer to a lightly floured board and knead the mixture until all the flour is well incorporated and the dough is smooth.

DIVIDE the dough into 4 balls and wrap each well with plastic wrap. Refrigerate for at least 2 hours and up to 3 days. (The dough may also be frozen, wrapped airtight, for up to 1 month.)

PREHEAT the oven to 350°F.

WORK with one ball of dough at a time, leaving the rest wrapped and refrigerated. (If you have frozen the dough, let it thaw until it is workable.) Divide the ball into 12 pieces of equal size; when rolled between your palms into balls, they should be slightly larger than walnuts. Flat-

Pistachio (page 345); Raisin-Walnut (page 346); the filling for Almond Paste (Marzipan)–Cranberry Rugelach, (page 318); or a ready-made filling of *lekvar* or prune butter (available in the baking section of many supermarkets), plain or mixed with chopped toasted walnuts

ten the balls between sheets of plastic wrap with the palm of your hand, and pat them into even rounds about 3 inches in diameter. I find this way there is less waste, the dough won't become tough from overhandling, and it is easy for those who lack experience or skill in handling dough. Pastry mavens may prefer to roll out the dough between sheets of plastic wrap or wax paper to about ⅛-inch thickness, then cut out rounds approximately 3 inches in diameter, using a cookie cutter or the rim of a glass. Reroll the scraps and cut them out.

I'VE found that hamantaschen edges sometimes open slightly during baking if not very firmly sealed. But warm fingertips pinching the buttery dough can make it too soft to work with or result in overhandling the dough. Keeping the dough well chilled until you are ready to use it does help, but working with such small pastry rounds also means the dough will warm up rather quickly. Here's the solution: place a pastry round on a piece of plastic wrap. Spoon a heaping teaspoon of filling in the center. Working with your fingers under the plastic wrap so they don't touch the dough directly, fold up one side of the pastry, making a little rim along the filling. Then fold the two adjacent sides up and together, forming a triangle. Pinch and smooth the edges through the plastic wrap until the seams are just about invisible. The plastic wrap keeps the dough moist and pliable. You should have a little triangle of pastry, the filling exposed in the center, like a tiny, open tart. Pinch the edges together tightly at all three corners so there are no gaps for the filling to seep out.

PLACE the finished hamantaschen about 1 inch apart on lightly greased cookie sheets. (For easy clean up, you may want to line the sheets with parchment or greased foil to catch spills.) Continue making hamantaschen until you have used up all the dough and filling. Keep the unbaked hamantaschen in the refrigerator until you are ready to put them into the oven.

BAKE for 20 to 25 minutes, until pale golden. Cool on the baking sheets for about 5 minutes, then transfer to racks to cool completely (wait until they have cooled before removing them or they might crumble). Or if you don't need the baking sheets for another batch, cool them on the sheets set on racks.

"For Krochmalna, Purim was a grand carnival. The street was filled with maskers and bearers of gifts. It smelled of cinnamon, saffron and chocolate, of freshly baked cakes and all sorts of sweets and spices whose names I did not know."

—ISAAC BASHEVIS SINGER, *In My Father's Court*

FRESH APPLE HAMANTASCHEN FILLING

yields: ENOUGH FILLING FOR 48 HAMANTASCHEN

This filling makes tiny, open-faced apple-walnut tarts, fragrant with the all-American spices of an old-fashioned pandowdy and glossed with a lick of syrupy molasses.

2 tablespoons unsalted butter

About 1½ pounds sweet, flavorful apples with lots of character, peeled, cored, and diced (4 cups; try Gravenstein, Gala, Braeburn, Jonathan, and Stayman Winesap; if possible, search out local, seasonal varieties)

About 3 tablespoons packed brown sugar

1 tablespoon molasses, plus additional for glazing the filling

¾ teaspoon ground cinnamon, plus additional for sprinkling

½ teaspoon fresh lemon juice

¼ teaspoon nutmeg, preferably freshly grated

2 pinches of ground cloves

⅛ teaspoon salt

½ cup walnuts, lightly toasted and coarsely chopped

IN a 10- to 12-inch heavy skillet, melt the butter over medium-high heat until sizzling. Add the apples and sauté for about 3 minutes, lifting and turning them. Stir in the brown sugar and molasses and mix well to coat the apples evenly. Add the cinnamon, lemon juice, nutmeg, cloves, and salt, and cook over moderately high heat for 5 minutes, or until the apples are just tender. You should have no liquid left in the pan; if any remains, briefly boil rapidly over high heat to evaporate it. Taste and adjust the seasoning. You may need to add more sugar depending on your preference and the sweetness of the apples.

TRANSFER the apples to a medium-large bowl, and let cool to room temperature. Stir in the walnuts and refrigerate, covered, until cold.

WHEN you make the hamantaschen, brush the exposed filling with a bit of molasses (or just dab it on with your fingertip) and sprinkle with cinnamon.

APRICOT, DATE, AND PISTACHIO HAMANTASCHEN FILLING

yield: ENOUGH FILLING FOR 48 HAMANTASCHEN

*T*art dried apricots mellowed with lush, sugary dates and crunchy toasted pistachios—this delicious remake of the sweet bakery apricot jam fillings I grew up with brings an aura of the Middle East.

1¼ cups dried apricots (about 6 ounces), preferably tart, diced

⅔ cup dried dates (about 4 ounces), preferably a soft variety such as Medjool or Barhi, pitted and diced

5 tablespoons packed brown sugar

About ⅔ cup apricot nectar or apple juice

½ teaspoon vanilla extract

Pinch of salt

1½ teaspoons fresh lemon juice

⅓ cup pistachio nuts, lightly toasted and coarsely chopped

IN a heavy, nonreactive, 2½- to 3-quart saucepan, combine the apricots, dates, brown sugar, nectar or juice, vanilla extract, and salt. Simmer slowly, stirring occasionally, until all the fruit is very soft and the liquid is no longer visible, 10 to 15 minutes. (If the fruit is very dry, you may have to add more liquid and cook it a little longer.) Stir in the lemon juice, and cook for 3 minutes to marry the flavors. Remove from the heat, transfer to a medium bowl, and let cool. Mix in pistachios, cover, and refrigerate until cold.

POPPY SEED HAMANTASCHEN WITH RAISIN-WALNUT FILLING

yield: 48 HAMANTASCHEN

I've taken the poppy seeds from the traditional hamantaschen filling and added them instead to the tender crust. The result, which reminds me of my grandmother's delicate mohn kichel *(poppy seed butter cookies) makes a melt-in-the-mouth cushion for the rich, moist, raisin-walnut filling, my daughter's favorite.*

FOR THE RAISIN-WALNUT FILLING

½ cup packed brown sugar

2 tablespoons ground cinnamon

Pinch of salt

2 cups dark raisins (about 12 ounces)

⅔ cup apple or fresh orange juice

1 tablespoon fresh lemon juice

1 cup walnuts, lightly toasted and coarsely chopped

1 recipe Hamantaschen Pastry (page 342), made with 3 tablespoons poppy seeds added to the flour and other dry ingredients

MAKE the filling: combine the brown sugar, cinnamon, and salt in a food processor and pulse briefly to blend. Add the raisins. Pour in the juice through the feed tube, while pulsing just long enough to chop the raisins coarsely, 10 to 15 seconds.

SCRAPE the mixture into a heavy, nonreactive, 3-quart saucepan. Bring to a boil over moderately high heat, stirring to prevent burning, then lower the heat, and simmer slowly, stirring occasionally, for 7 to 8 minutes, until the mixture has thickened and almost no liquid is visible. Stir in the lemon juice, and cook for 2 to 3 more minutes to blend the flavors. Remove from the heat, transfer to a medium bowl, and let cool to room temperature. Stir in the walnuts and refrigerate, covered, until cold.

FILL, shape, and bake the hamantaschen, following the directions on page 342.

POPPY SEED BUTTER CAKE (MOHN CAKE)

yield: **ABOUT 10 SERVINGS**

*D*elicately nutty poppy seeds lend gentle crunch to this buttery bubbe cake. It's sublime just plain, but you can dress it up with a dollop of ice cream and/or fruit compote. Or serve the cake, lightly toasted, if desired, topped with sliced strawberries and freshly whipped cream.

When well wrapped, this cake freezes well.

²/₃ cup poppy seeds

1 cup evaporated milk

16 tablespoons (2 sticks) unsalted butter, plus additional for greasing the pan

1 cup granulated white sugar

¹/₃ to ¹/₂ cup granulated light brown sugar (see Cook's Note)

3 large eggs, separated

1¹/₂ teaspoons vanilla extract

2 cups unbleached all-purpose flour

2¹/₂ teaspoons baking powder

Salt

Confectioners' sugar (optional)

HAVE all ingredients at room temperature.

PREHEAT the oven to 350°F.

COMBINE the poppy seeds and milk in a small saucepan and bring to a simmer. Remove the pan from the heat and let cool to room temperature.

GENEROUSLY butter a 9- to 10-cup Bundt or fluted tube pan.

FINELY granulated sugar crystals will aerate the batter better, making the cake less likely to collapse during baking. So take 2 to 3 minutes to whirl ³/₄ cup of the white sugar together with all the brown sugar in a food processor or blender until finely ground.

IN a large bowl, beat the butter with an electric mixer on low speed until creamy. Gradually tip in the ground sugar and beat on medium-high speed until light and fluffy. Add the egg yolks, one at a time, beating on medium-low until smooth and well blended. Beat in the vanilla. If the mixture looks somewhat curdled, increase the speed to high and beat a couple of minutes until smooth.

STIR together the flour, baking powder, and ¹/₂ teaspoon salt in a medium bowl. Add one third of these dry ingredients to the butter mixture, beating on low speed. Then beat in half of the poppy seed–milk mixture, followed by another third of the dry ingredients, the rest of the milk mixture, and finally, the remaining third of the dry ingredients. Scraping the sides of the bowl as necessary, mix in each addition just enough to incorporate it into a smooth batter; overbeating can result in cake that is tough.

BEAT the egg whites with a pinch of salt in another large bowl until they form soft peaks. Gradually add the remaining ¹/₄ cup of white sugar and continue beating until stiff but not dry. Gently fold the whites into the batter.

SPOON the batter into the prepared pan and smooth the top. Bake for about 50 minutes, until golden-brown and a toothpick inserted into the center comes out clean. Let the cake cool in the pan on a rack for 10 minutes, then invert and cool completely.

IF desired, spoon a little confectioners' sugar into a small strainer and dust the cake before serving.

COOK'S NOTE: Use the lesser amount of sugar, if you prefer, as I do, a not-too-sweet tea cake; use the greater amount (and confectioners' sugar, if desired) for a sweeter dessert cake.

The top of the cake may split as it rises in the oven. Don't worry; it won't show when the cake is inverted.

Oil-rich poppy seeds can turn rancid quickly; store leftover ones in an airtight container in the freezer.

CIDER-BAKED APPLES STUFFED WITH HALVAH

yield: 6 SERVINGS

*F*rench Jews enjoyed baked apples as a coda to a fine meal at least as far back as the Middle Ages. Known even then for their *becs fins* by their coreligionists, they brought their recipes, techniques, and love of good food to the communities they immigrated to in Central and Eastern Europe, after they were expelled from their native land.

In my dressed-up rendition, halvah provides the filling, while molasses (pomegranate or regular) and reduced apple cider lend a buttery finish to the dairy-free baste. Piercing the apple peels ensures that the delicious pan juices will penetrate through to the tender apple flesh. At dairy meals, serve with a pool of heavy sweet cream, crème fraîche, or vanilla ice cream.

2 cups pure, unsweetened apple juice (do not use unfiltered juice)

3 cardamom pods, lightly crushed with the side of a knife or a kitchen mallet

Salt

2 tablespoons packed brown sugar

6 apples (Cortland, Empire, or another flavorful, sweet-tart, juicy variety that is good for baking)

⅓ cup plain or vanilla halvah

3 tablespoons chopped walnuts, lightly toasted

¼ cup light, fragrant honey

¼ teaspoon ground cinnamon

2 tablespoons mild oil (walnut, avocado, canola, or your favorite)

1 tablespoon pomegranate molasses or regular molasses

PREHEAT the oven to 375°F.

MAKE the cider baste: put the juice, cardamom, and a generous pinch of salt in a wide, heavy saucepan, bring to a boil, and cook, uncovered, over high heat until the liquid is reduced to about ½ cup. Stir in the brown sugar and cook another minute or two, until it is dissolved. Pick out and discard the cardamom.

PARE off a ½-inch strip of peel from the stem end of each apple, then pare off a thin strip around the blossom end of the apples. Starting at the stem end, use an apple corer or a sharp paring knife to cut out the core and seeds of the apples, stopping about ½ inch from the bottom.

TO ensure that the caramelly glaze reaches down into the apple flesh, using a paring knife, cut shallow lengthwise slits through the skin of the apples at 1½ inch intervals, and using a fork, lightly prick the sides of each apple in several places.

IN a medium bowl, mash the halvah. Gradually add the nuts, honey, and cinnamon, and keep mashing until well combined.

STAND the apples in an 8-inch square baking dish or other pan just large enough to hold them without touching. Place 1 teaspoon of the oil and ½ teaspoon of the molasses into the hollow center of each apple, and rub the mixture over the exposed (peeled) area of the apple. Divide the halvah mixture among the apples, pushing it down into the center and mounding the rest on top. Spoon the cider baste all over the apples.

BAKE, basting every 7 minutes or so with the pan juices, until the apples are tender enough to be pierced with a fork but not mushy, about 45 minutes, depending on the variety of apple.

SPOON the pan juices over the apples again just before serving. Good warm, at room temperature, or chilled. For nonmeat meals, accompany with cold heavy cream, crème fraîche, or vanilla ice cream.

OTHER SUGGESTIONS FOR PURIM

Either of the *Hummus recipes

*Golden Gefilte Fish with Golden Horseradish

Either of the *Chopped Chicken Liver recipes

*Tangy Russian Cabbage Soup with Pot Roast-Beet Kreplach

*Fried Onion and Chicken Kreplach

*Potato-Onion Kreplach, Pot Sticker–Style

*Moroccan Fish with Chickpeas and Saffron-Lime Aioli

*Fesenjan Redux (Roast Duck Breasts with Quince, Pomegranate, and Walnut Sauce)

*Coffee-Spiced Pot Roast with Kasha Kreplach and Toasted Garlic Challah Crumbs

*Mujadderah-Filled Roasted Red Peppers in Tomato-Garlic Sauce

*Kasha Varnishkes with Fried Eggplant, Mushrooms, and Onion Marmalade

*Jeweled Brown Rice

*Garlic-Mashed Potato Knishes

*Egyptian Black-Eyed Peas with Cilantro

Any of the *Rugelach recipes

Any of the *Macaroon recipes

*Rich Fudge Brownies

*See index for page numbers

Passover

A generous ransom paid for a much sought-after piece of broken matzoh. Horrific plagues re-created out of wine drops, and bricks from a scrumptious fruit and nut paste. So many raucous cousins, the dining table must be stretched with bridge tables until it snakes around the front door.

At every Passover seder Jews revisit magical childhood memories.

A glorious ceremonial family dinner held on the first and second nights (Israelis and Reform Jews observe one night only) of Passover, the seder brings to life the ancient Hebrews' liberation from slavery and their flight from Egypt. Nearly 80 percent of North American Jews—and many non-Jews as well—attend a seder every year, making Passover the most celebrated—and best-loved—of all the Jewish holidays.

The story of the Exodus is a universal one, a struggle for political liberation and spiritual freedom relevant to all peoples. Moses, as

God's emissary, pleaded with Pharaoh to free his people—the enslaved Hebrews who, smarting under the taskmasters' whips, were forced to build Egyptian cities. To convince the nefarious king to heed the request, God visited nine monstrous plagues on the Egyptians, ranging from boils on their skin to frogs in the water to total darkness. Still Pharaoh would not relent. Finally, God sent the worst curse of all: the death of the first-born males, and Pharaoh at last conceded. That night the Hebrews ate a hurried meal of roasted lamb and unleavened bread and fled in haste, lest he change his mind.

And that he did. Now the Hebrews stood before the Red Sea, and behind them, they could feel the hot breath of the Egyptian pursuers mingled with the desert scorch. Moses lifted his arm and miraculously the waters parted so that they could pass through to safety. When the last Hebrew reached the shore, Moses returned the waters to their natural state, drowning the Egyptians and their chargers.

It is a stirring tale, meant to be felt, not merely told, and the injunction above, to relive the Exodus personally, is taken seriously. The symbolic seder foods are used to make the narrating vivid, and because most of these foods are consumed, we actually taste the experience and ensure it will become a part of us.

The matzoh recalls not only the flat, unleavened bread quickly prepared for the flight from Egypt, it also suggests the humility of the Hebrews first as slaves, and later as grateful worshipers before God. They had become acquainted with yeasted bread in Egypt, so leavened bread (and by extension, any form of leavening), puffed and swollen as with vanity and pride, symbolized their Egyptian oppressors. Jews are prohibited not just from eating leavening (*hametz* in Hebrew) during the eight days of Passover, they must fastidiously remove every crumb of it from their homes. This is a holiday of freedom and every trace of the tyrants must be cleared away.

After the meal, a piece of matzoh stealthily hidden by the leader of the seder becomes the object of a treasure hunt for all the children. Whoever finds this *afikomen* (the word means "dessert" in Greek) will demand a ransom (contemporary requests run from cash to charitable contributions to video games), for the meal cannot be concluded until it is eaten.

The focus of the table is the special seder plate filled with other ritual foods from the Passover saga. The highly symbolic egg, eaten extensively throughout the holiday, appears on the plate either roasted or *haminado*, Sephardi-style. It speaks of many things. Primarily, it recalls the festival offerings brought to the Temple in Jerusalem, and, as a symbol of mourning, reinforces our sense of loss at the Temple's destruction. But paradoxically, it also stands for the eternal and for new life, the hope and optimism that are evoked with every spring. A roasted lamb shank bone (sometimes replaced by a chicken wing or neck or even, for vegetarians, a roasted beet) brings to mind other sacrifices at the Temple.

Salt water or vinegar gives us a taste of the tears and hard sweat of slavery, but it is tempered by the sweet vegetable we dip into it: parsley, celery, or soft lettuce, representing the renewal and growth of spring. Horseradish, arugula, romaine, or other bitter herbs sting our tongues with the harshness of slavery and oppression. And everybody's favorite is haroset, which mimics the brick and mortar the Hebrews used to build Pharaoh's cities. Variations on this fruit-and-nut theme reflect all the myriad foodstuffs available in the Diaspora. Classic Ashkenazi haroset calls for simple ingredients easy to obtain in Central and Eastern Europe: chopped apples and walnuts or almonds flavored with cinnamon and wine. Sephardis could choose from the exotic pantries of the Mediterranean. Their luscious "mortar" might blend pureed dates and wine with chopped walnuts. Coconut, pomegranate, lemon juice, pine nuts, and chestnuts are just a few possible additions.

The joy symbolized by the four cups of wine (or grape juice) each celebrant drinks during the seder is not complete: recognizing that our enemies, too, suffered during the Exodus diminishes our gladness. So, with one finger we flick out a drop of wine for each plague visited on the Egyptians. The door is opened during the service so that the Prophet Elijah, harbinger of peace and the Messianic Age, may come in to drink the cup of wine poured for him. Everyone watches this goblet closely to see if he has sipped, a sure sign of God's blessing.

Today some seders feature a special goblet, the *Kos Miryam* (Miriam's cup), created by a group of women in the 1980s. The cup is filled with water and honors Moses' sister, who provided the Israelites with water from a well that followed her throughout the wandering and dried up when she died. (For more specific details on preparing these ritual items, please see page 366, Setting the Seder Table.)

The ceremonies are spelled out in a special book called the Haggadah. To date, more than 4,000 printed (and countless hand-lettered) versions have been created; as Yosef Hayim Yerushalmi wrote in *Haggadah and History*, "it has been reprinted more often and in more places than any other Jewish classic." New editions attempt to connect the ancient struggles of our ancestors to our modern lives in passionate and meaningful ways.

This too is part of the tradition. For while "seder" means order in Hebrew, the rituals have never been set in stone. Ever since Passover became a home-centered holiday with the destruction of the Second Temple, the service has been evolving, new customs and ceremonies added over time and throughout the Diaspora.

During Talmudic times, the ancient Hebrews adopted many elements of the Greek symposium and Roman banquet. The four cups of wine owe as much to the Roman practice of drinking before, during, and after the meal as to the traditional Kiddush ceremony. Food scholar John Cooper even suggests the Greek game *kottabos*, flicking wine from a cup at a target, may have been the model for flicking wine when reciting the plagues. Greeks and Romans, reclining on couches, dined on sauces similar to haroset; the Romans often began their feasts with egg hors d'oeuvre, still the seder custom among both Ashkenazi and Sephardi Jews.

Not until the Middle Ages would the European seder plate resemble the current Ashkenazi one: rabbis then finalized the roasted shankbone and egg as appropriate substitutes for the ancient Temple sacrifices and approved the use of horseradish for bitter herbs, though as a root, it lacked the requisite bitter leaves called for in the Mishnah. And after the Crusades, expulsions, and a continuing litany of other horrors, the Middle Ages introduced the rituals associated with Elijah, because Jews desperately needed a symbol of hope and promise of redemption.

Recently, I came across the purple mimeographed words that had brought the story of the Exodus to life for me as a little girl at the close of the 1950s. My Conservative synagogue, like other Jewish congregations on Long Island, had included the old African-American spiritual, "Go Down Moses," in our Model Seder, and my Hebrew school teacher conflated the terrifying images of the nascent civil rights struggle I had been seeing on TV with our own slavery in Egypt.

It's an image that has continued to resonate for American Jews. At her 1961 seder, where the guest list included President and Mrs. John F. Kennedy, Dorothy Goldberg, wife of Secretary of Labor and later Supreme Court Justice Arthur Goldberg, noted in the margin of the family's personal Haggadah that she must remember to mention "one of the best descriptions of the Exodus is the great Negro spiritual, 'Go Down Moses.'" Today the song is considered a holiday classic, invariably found on Passover CD collections.

Of course, to some extent every family also customizes the seder to reflect the needs and desires of the participants. When I was a girl, the children all whooped through the house madly searching for the *afikomen*, while cries of "cold," "warmer," and "hot-hot" guided us to find it, finally, crumbled perhaps in the paper sleeve of a 45 rpm record like the "The Witch Doctor." Then we launched into a little night music, riotously belting out songs from *"Had Gadya"* (a lovely Hebrew allegory in the "House That Jack Built" tradition) to "Swing Low, Sweet Chariot."

As we grew older, my father wove modern parallels of oppression and liberation into the traditional Passover narrative, sparking rousing political exchanges. Particularly poignant was our seder the night Rita, a friend from Papa Doc's Haiti, joined in.

Throughout the seder, intoxicating aromas emanate from the kitchen, tweaking appetites whetted by brief tastes of the ceremonial foods. At last it is time to eat. Reclining comfortably amid pillows and soft cushions, we set to the grand feast, perhaps the most splendid of the Jewish calendar. Sweet wine, although traditional in many homes, is not mandated, and many Jews prefer to sip the excellent dry kosher-for-Passover wines available to complement the delectable food.

"Let all who are hungry come and eat," the Haggadah enjoins, and Jews make a point of inviting guests as well as extended family members to share the meal. There are rich, inventive dishes made of matzoh and the lively perfumes of early spring: fresh young fennel, asparagus, mushrooms, artichokes, and rhubarb. Slow-braised lamb and brisket, pot roast cooked with horseradish and beet juice, or gently simmered chicken with preserved lemon and olives remain moist and succulent, even when the predinner service runs late. Sumptuous desserts relying on ground nuts and eggs, instead of flour and leavening, are intensely flavored yet remarkably light.

The holiday places prohibitions on many foodstuffs. Except for specially prepared matzoh, no products made from any grain (including derivatives such as beer or grain-based vinegar) and no leavening, such as yeast, may be consumed. In addition, many Ashkenazi Jews also refrain from eating corn, legumes, and rice during Passover.

Yet, Jewish cooks had to invent a unique cuisine that would provide delicious menus not only for the seders but also throughout the eight days of the joyous holiday. Matzoh, crumbled into pieces, crushed into meal, or finely ground into matzoh cake meal, as well as ground nuts and potato starch, replaced flour and bread crumbs in cooking and baking. Generous amounts of eggs, especially the beaten whites, ensured the Passover foods would be light and fluffy. So successful were the specialties originally created to conform with the stringent demands of the holiday that many have become the most beloved of all Jewish dishes, served up year-round: featherlight matzoh balls, eggy matzoh brie, honey-drenched fritters, and special latkes, to name just a few.

The distinctive Passover foods imbue the holiday with a unique rhythm all its own. Breakfast without the quick fixes of cold cereal and bagels, or lunch with no sandwiches or pizza are more carefully planned and more leisurely eaten. The comfortable, relaxed mood that begins at the seder table with pillows and cushions remains with us through all the meals of the festival.

KOSHER FOR PASSOVER?

It all started simply enough. Following the commandments in Exodus 12:18–20 ("there shall be no leaven found in your houses . . . You shall eat nothing leavened") meant getting rid of all traces of leavening, or *hametz*, and dining on matzoh during the holiday instead of leavened bread. And there was bread, and there was unleavened bread—the first Passover.

But soon the ancient Hebrews developed more sophisticated tastes. They made bread not just from barley, wheat, and spelt but also from rye and oats. And not just bread alone: cakes, porridge, crackers, and alcoholic beverages, too.

So to avoid confusion, in the Talmud the rabbis expanded the prohibition against eating leavening to a broader ban on any of the five grains mentioned above in any form except matzoh and matzoh products. They reasoned that those grains, even when mixed with just cool water, would begin to rise naturally through contact with airborne wild yeasts (similar to sourdough starters) after a short period of time (this was later determined to be eighteen minutes). So only matzoh, prepared from start to finish in fewer than eighteen minutes, under rabbinic supervision, can be guaranteed unleavened, and, therefore, kosher for Passover. Everything else derived from those grains is hametz: flatbreads, cereals, cookies, grain-based extracts, vinegar, and alcoholic products such as beer and malt. Of course, yeast, a form of leavening, and yeast products are prohibited also.

And baking soda and baking powder? Surprisingly, that depends. Many Orthodox rabbis declare them kosher for Passover (when made with only kosher-for-Passover ingredients) because their leavening powers derive from chemicals, not from fermentation like yeast. The secret of impossibly fluffy Passover cakes and seder matzoh balls so airy they levitate above the soup is not some kabbalist cooking tip. It's just lots of kosher-for-Passover baking powder.

But if you think using leaveners—albeit, rabbinically sanctioned *chemical* ones—well, goes against the grain, so to speak, you're not alone. Many rabbis believe that with baking powder and baking soda, the holiday no longer tastes unique, and many Jewish cooks, myself included, do not use these ingredients during Passover. As Marcy Goldman, author of the excellent *A Treasury of Jewish Holiday Baking*, puts it: "My grandmothers would have had kittens! . . . . my personal feeling is that I can appreciate whipped egg whites to aerate my Passover cakes, but somehow once baking soda and baking powder are introduced, the spirit of the holiday is compromised."

KITNIYOT

While all Jews are prohibited from eating hametz during the holiday, there are other foods that are proscribed, not by commandment (*mitzvah*) but by custom (*minhag*), for various communities. The most important of these is the group of foods known as *kitniyot* (from the Hebrew, *katan*, meaning "little"), avoided by most traditional Ashkenazi Jews.

Although the Talmud specifically says that rice, millet, and other grains are kosher for Passover, during the Middle Ages, Ashkenazi rabbis worried that since flour ground from these and other grains, legumes, and seeds, or kitniyot, could resemble one of the five hametz grains from which matzoh may be prepared, people might mistakenly eat food prepared with hametz, thinking it had been made with kitniyot. And since kitniyot looks like hametz, there may be grains of hametz mixed in with kitniyot (for example, bits of barley mixed in with grains of rice). To avoid such mix-ups, these rabbis banned consumption of all kitniyot during Passover.

And that's when the *real* confusion began.

For there exists no list that everyone agrees on: There is much disagreement today among and even within the various Ashkenazi denominations as to what should be classified as kitniyot. Some dispute including certain kitniyot derivatives among the prohibited foods: for example, peanut oil has been approved by some Orthodox rabbis because it, unlike peanuts, could never be ground and mistaken for flour.

Most Conservative and many Orthodox authorities do not regard fresh string beans as kitniyot. Quinoa, a relative of spinach that looks and acts like a grain, is often not considered kitniyot, while buckwheat, related to sorrel and rhubarb and neither a grain nor a legume, is *always* considered kitniyot. And foods such as ground almonds or potato starch—both of which really do look like wheat flour and, in fact, are often substituted for it during the holiday—have never been considered kitniyot.

Some foods have been incorrectly labeled kitniyot in the past because of their names (vanilla and coffee beans) or ignorance about their true plant genus. Garlic was treated as kitniyot in several cookbooks I own dating from the 1950s, though later rabbinic authorities could find no justification for doing so. Fresh fennel is still on some kitniyot lists; while fennel seeds *might* resemble flour when ground (and, therefore, be considered kitniyot), fresh fennel could never be. Nor is it a legume: it is a member of the carrot family.

These ingredients may be considered kitniyot by some communities: alfalfa, bean, and other sprouts; anise seed; buckwheat; canola oil; caraway; chickpeas; coriander seeds; confectioners' sugar (if it contains cornstarch); corn (and derivatives such as cornstarch); cumin; flaxseed; fresh and dried beans, peas, and lentils; lecithin; millet; mustard; peanuts; poppy seeds; rice; sesame seeds; soy beans and other soy products, including soy sauce and tofu; and sunflower seeds. And the list is by no means exhaustive.

Sephardi and Mizrachi Jews usually do not avoid kitniyot, though some do not eat rice, or may go through special processes with kitniyot, such as sifting through the seeds of their Passover spices to ensure that they have not been contaminated by hametz.

Some of the recipes in this chapter call for ingredients that, while acceptable to most Sephardi and Middle Eastern Jews, may be classified as kitniyot by some Ashkenazi rabbinic authorities. (Often these ingredients are optional.) Readers must decide whether a particular food conforms to the Passover traditions observed not just by them, but equally important, by their guests as well.

HOW CAN I TELL IF SOMETHING IS KITNIYOT? Since rules of kitniyot vary, depending on one's Jewish affiliation (Orthodox, Conservative, Reform, and Reconstructionist) and level of observance, ask your rabbi or check printed or online kashrut guidelines prepared by an organization approved by your community (see "Online and Phone Order Sources and a Few Helpful Web Sites" on page 551).

If you are not affiliated, do not have family customs to guide you, but do not consider yourself part of the Sephardi or Mizrachi tradition, the criteria you follow will be an individual decision—but again, one that is mindful of the customs of those with whom you are celebrating Passover.

SO CAN SEPHARDI AND ASHKENAZI JEWS BREAK UNLEAVENED BREAD TOGETHER AT THE SAME SEDER? Kitniyot do not have the same forbidden status as hametz, so even observant Ashkenazi Jews who refrain from eating kitniyot are permitted to eat at a seder at which kitniyot foods are served to others, as long as there is no kitniyot present in the food they themselves consume. Some observant Ashkenazim will eat from plates and utensils used for kitniyot and even eat food cooked in a pot that has been used for kitniyot; others will eat from plates used for kitniyot derivatives (corn or peanut oil) but not for actual kitniyot.

In Israel, where the Ashkenazi community is not the sizable majority it is among American Jewry, the Conservative (Masorti) Movement has recently ruled that all Jews living in Israel may abandon the minhag of refraining from kitniyot. In his *responsum*, Rabbi David Golinken explained that "in light of the ingathering of Jews of all ethnic groups," observing kitniyot causes unnecessary schisms among Israel's people and inflates the importance of the insignificant (kitniyot) at the expense of the significant (hametz). Though the ruling pertains only to Conservative Jews living in Israel, it has led some American rabbis to call for a more liberal interpretation of kitniyot restrictions.

GEBROCHTS

(Yiddish for broken, referring to broken matzoh and farfel)

Some very observant Jews refrain from eating foods made with a combination of matzoh or matzoh meal and a liquid, concerned that if a little insufficiently cooked flour within the matzoh were moistened, leavening or fermentation might take place. So they avoid matzoh balls, matzoh brie, and other matzoh-based foods cooked with liquid until the eighth day of Passover.

RICH MATZOH

Made with eggs and apple juice, egg matzoh is not a "bread of affliction," but instead a *matzoh ashira* (rich matzoh). Strictly observant Jews do not eat egg matzoh on Passover, though they do consider it permissible for small children, the elderly, and the infirm.

PACKAGED PRODUCTS

Strictly observant Jews will only buy packaged goods that are certified kosher-for-Passover.

PASSOVER INGREDIENTS

Stocking a Passover pantry no longer requires a visit to communities with a large Jewish population, or schlepping from store to store in search of hard-to-find ingredients. Internet and mail order sources can provide any Passover foods you need (see Online and Phone Order Sources, page 551). But that will entail advanced planning.

So for those times when you need a substitute for a Passover product, and for Passover equivalents of hametz ingredients, here is a helpful list.

Matzoh meal: process three matzohs, broken in pieces, in a food processor fitted with the steel blade until finely ground. Yield: 1 cup

Matzoh cake meal: process matzoh meal in a mini-processor or a clean coffee grinder until it is a fine powder.

1 cup all-purpose flour: about ⅔ cup matzoh cake meal or ¾ cup potato starch.

Breadcrumb substitute: matzoh meal, homemade matzoh crumbs (page 24), ground nuts, or use a combination of ground nuts and matzoh meal.

Cornstarch: 1 tablespoon cornstarch equals about 1 tablespoon potato starch.

Confectioners' sugar: see page 462.

Vanilla extract is almost always prepared with grain alcohol, which is unkosher for Passover. Passover vanilla extract is available; unfortunately, it is often made from artificial vanilla. You can prepare your own kosher-for-Passover vanilla extract, but you'll need to start well before the holiday. To make homemade vanilla extract: split 3 plump, supple vanilla beans in half lengthwise, exposing all of the scented seeds within. Scrape the seeds gently with the tip of your knife to get their fragrance going. Put the beans into a small, clear glass jar with a tight-fitting lid and pour in 1 cup kosher-for-Passover vodka. Push the beans down into the vodka so they are completely covered with the liquid. Close the jar tightly and let it sit in a cool, dark place to infuse. The vodka will turn dark as the vanilla steeps in it, and after about two months, it will be full of vanilla flavor. Strain into a clean jar, or if you prefer, leave the extract in the original jar and simply strain out the amount you need. To remove the vanilla flecks, pour through a strainer lined with a coffee filter or paper towel.

Or substitute homemade vanilla sugar for the regular sugar called for in a recipe. To prepare it, either bury a split vanilla bean or two in a sugar canister and set aside for several weeks until fragrant or grind a split vanilla bean cut into pieces with 1 cup sugar in a blender until pulverized, then sift through a fine-mesh strainer.

You can also steep a vanilla bean in balsamic vinegar and use the vinegar for sprinkling on lightly sweetened strawberries or mango.

For an unusual, but intriguing alternative to vanilla flavoring in Passover cakes, try a small amount of dried lavender (about 2 teaspoons) or chopped fresh rosemary leaves (about 1 tablespoon), ground with 1 cup sugar.

Or substitute 2 to 3 teaspoons kosher-for-Passover liqueur for 1 teaspoon kosher-for-Passover vanilla.

Kosher-for-Passover almond extract: substitute 2 to 3 teaspoons kosher-for-Passover nut-flavored liqueur for 1 teaspoon extract. If the recipe calls for liquid, you can infuse it with prune pits (see Prune Plum Custard Challah Bread Pudding, page 206) for a wonderful, complex almondy taste.

PREPARING FOR PASSOVER

Long before the holiday, traditional Jews begin an extensive spring cleaning of every room where food may have been eaten or crumbs forgotten during the year, ridding their homes of hametz, from the stray

Cheerio buried under the toddler's toys to a chocolate-covered wafer hidden in a coat pocket.

Some year-round table- and kitchenware may be made kosher-for-Passover by scalding them in boiling water or heating them until they are red-hot. But anything that cannot be made kosher is stored away, and the special dishes, cutlery, and utensils reserved for Passover use alone are unpacked and arranged in the newly clean cabinets. We would set Great-Aunt Anna's huge white-and-gold porcelain service on the buffet, and my mother cringed every time my dad slapped a serving of sizzling matzoh brie on the eggshell-thin plates. Now it is my turn to cringe: the beautiful heirloom plates grace my cabinets.

Pasta, bread crumbs, and cereal all figure prominently in the pre-Passover meals, as the family tries to finish up their hametz before the holiday. Unopened containers of prohibited foods can be given away to shelters, churches, and social service agencies for distribution to the needy, or offered to non-Jewish friends. Or they may be sealed and stored for the duration of the holiday.

The evening before the first seder, the family goes from room to room in the final search for leavening (*bedikat hametz*). Thus, begins The Great Hametz Treasure Hunt: parents hide one or more pieces of bread, then children shine their flashlights into every nook and cranny to find the hametz. For added excitement, the parents might offer a small prize to the child who finds the most hametz. (Just be sure you remember where and how many pieces you have hidden, or you might be unpleasantly surprised during—or worse still, a month after—the holiday.)

The hametz found during the search is set aside until the morning. Then it is combined with any hametz leftover from breakfast and destroyed: usually it is burnt, but it may also be flushed down the toilet or scattered to the winds.

The house is now ready for Passover.

TIPS FOR PLANNING A SEDER MENU

THINK GREEN. Originally an agricultural holiday, Passover celebrates spring, the reawakening of the earth mirrored in the rebirth of the Jews as a free people. Even if your ancestors spent the holiday in frosty northern climes, your seder should not be a monochrome in varying shades of brown. Emphasize the flavors of the season: fresh vegetables and fruits, like asparagus, artichokes, spinach, leeks, rhubarb, and so on. Lighten heavier foods, like matzoh balls, kugels, and meat gravies with fresh herbs, local ingredients, such as ramps and wild garlic shoots, even a squirt of lemon or grated citrus zest. Include a huge salad of tender greens or a few cooked vegetable salads as a welcome antidote to a matzoh-rich meal.

FEAST OF SYMBOLS. To enrich the seder experience, weave the symbolic foods throughout the meal: matzoh in many guises, tastes of karpas greens everywhere—perhaps a salad of bitter herbs.

HORS D'OEUVRE. Guests—and cooks too—are often famished when they sit down at the table; growling bellies can make it difficult for them to enjoy the seder service. If possible, offer a nibble (and perhaps something heartier for children) before the seder begins. My sister-in-law Ellen sets out chopped liver for arriving guests. Other simple options include vegetable dips, like avocado or eggplant puree, canapes of smoked fish or tuna salad on cucumber or radish rounds, or miniature bellahat speared with toothpicks. Or serve a special, generous portion of the ceremonial foods when they are introduced during the service. For example, pass around crudités (batons of carrots, peppers, celery, florets of cauliflower) after you eat the karpas from the seder plate. Offer a few kinds of haroset or serve the more substantial Tangy Haroset Bites (page 384) at the appropriate time in the service.

PASSOVER AND OTHER RESTRICTIONS Check the dietary customs of your guests (please read Kosher for Passover? on page 357). Even Jews who eat unkosher foods throughout the year may observe special restrictions on Passover. If you are having vegetarian or vegan guests, see page 391, For Your Vegetarian Son, Your Vegan Niece, for suggestions.

STARTERS. MOST FAMILIES BEGIN WITH EGGS. Sephardim serve the roasted huevos haminados, while Ashkenazim customarily dip hard-boiled eggs in saltwater. Our family savored untraditional but wonderful chopped hard-boiled eggs and onions. Because this is such a festive meal, both Ashkenazim and Sephardim often serve two or more appetizers, in addition to the eggs (such as a fish and a soup or a separate vegetable course).

MAIN COURSES. Choose a main course that doesn't call for last-minute work, so you can join the table for the service. It should be able to withstand a good wait in the kitchen without drying out, especially if your predinner service runs long. Brisket and other slow-braised dishes are ideal.

At the seder meals, observant Ashkenazim often refrain from eating roasted meat or poultry—and some, even roasted vegetables—because they resemble the ancient burnt Passover sacrifice, forbidden after the Temple was destroyed.

For large gatherings, serve two main courses, perhaps a meat and a poultry. It's always nice to provide guests with a choice, and since many main courses can't be doubled or tripled easily, preparing two different entrees usually requires little more work.

LIGHTEN UP THE SIDE DISHES. Balance matzoh-rich foods with vegetables served in their most natural state: roasted new potatoes dusted with fresh thyme, spinach wilted in olive oil and garlic, asparagus simply roasted or lightly sprinkled with toasted matzoh crumbs and nuts.

THE SECOND NIGHT. As a child, I anticipated the second seder more eagerly than the first. My sleuthing instincts just might be sufficiently sharpened by then to snare the hidden afikomen before my brother. And my mother prepared a seductive veal chop—nearly the size of the dinner plate, crusty with well-seasoned matzoh meal that was golden-fried in olive oil and napped with lemony tomato sauce—just for me, the most finicky of the children, to lure me back to the table.

If you are making the seders both nights, you'll need to plan a second dinner as well. Some cooks decide to serve the same foods at both, perhaps fashioning some of the leftovers into delicious *minas* (matzoh pies), while others plan a different menu entirely: one that may be more casual, less traditional (families are often more willing to try new, unfamiliar recipes the second night), or more playful. A lavish dairy feast—replete with cheesy kugels and fritadas, followed by buttery desserts under drifts of whipped cream—makes for a delectable, if unusual, second seder, one sure to please most children.

TIME OUT. Hosting even a simple seder is a lot of work, and no matter how much you love to cook, there may come a time when you need some quick fixes. A few ideas: instead of gefilte fish, serve smoked fish nestled in endive or radicchio leaves (scatter with capers and stipple with horseradish mayonnaise, page 73). Or serve Slow-Roasted Salmon or cold poached halibut with Beet-Horseradish Relish, and Green Herb Oil, an herbed mayonnaise, or salsa verde. Prepare Cheater's Chicken in the Pot with Almost-Homemade Soup (page 70) or just doctor good-quality, low-sodium purchased chicken broth by simmering it with nubbins of boneless, skinless chicken breast and purchased, precut raw vegetables, then sprinkle with fresh dill. Chicken Matzoh Balls (page 395) are quickest, or simply serve the soup with seasoned matzoh (page 379), broken into croutons, if desired. Make Easy Onion-Braised Brisket (page 85) the night before the seder, and skim off the fat just before reheating. Accompany with roasted asparagus and roasted potatoes, enlivened with a grating of fresh horseradish. Finish with a crumble of fresh fruit topped with ready-made macaroons and purchased dairy-free kosher-for-Passover sorbet.

Or host a potluck seder, assembling the meal by assigning different dishes to your guests.

"The table linen is snowy white; the flowers scent the room. The karpas and the horseradish remind us of the beauty of the earth in which they grew. Grandfather's kiddush cup is old . . . but it too is beautiful, for it connects the table to three generations of seders."

—CAROL OCHS, "I WILL BE WITH YOU:

THE DIVINE PRESENCE ON PASSOVER"

SETTING THE SEDER TABLE

After the destruction of the ancient Temple, the table, according to tradition, became our altar. At no time is this truer than Passover. For Hasidim, setting the Passover table and arranging the seder plate are sacred acts.

If at all possible, do try to involve family members—especially children—in preparing the table as well as cooking the meal. They will enjoy the seder service more and participate more actively in it.

In addition to festive linens and tableware and fresh spring flowers, you will want to include most or all of the following:

- Candles: at least one pair. Kindling them signals the festival has begun. Sometimes, the hosts may set aside an area for each guest to light a candle for someone they miss: The seder service glows with their light.

- A Haggadah for each guest.

- Matzohs. Three perfect plain matzohs are separately placed in a special sectioned matzoh cover or a tray with individual compartments. Or arrange the three matzohs in the folds of a cloth napkin. Two matzohs recall the double portion of manna the Israelites gathered before the Sabbath; the third matzoh is broken in half, one piece to be eaten as the "bread of affliction" during the service, and the other used for the afikomen. The matzohs also represent the three communities of the Jewish people: Kohen (priest), Levite (assistant to the priest), and Yisraelite (all other Jews).

- Elijah's Cup. If you do not have a special ritual Elijah's Cup, use any attractive goblet, but preferably one that is larger than the wineglasses on the table. Some families begin the service with the cup filled; others ask guests to spill a little of their wine into the cup at the appropriate time in the service, symbolically making certain that everyone contributes to the redemption of the world.

- Miriam's Cup. A recent addition to many seder tables, honoring Moses' sister, this is filled with water and placed in the center, next to Elijah's Cup. You can use any nice wineglass, if you don't have a special Miriam's Cup.

- Cup of Remembrance. When my brother-in-law Larry's brother-in-law passed away suddenly, Larry initiated a ritual in remembrance. Every seder we now fill a cup for Marty, ensuring that the adored man whose presence had graced all our past seders would always remain a part of our celebrations to come.

- A glass for the four cups of wine or grape juice that each participant will drink. (If, for health reasons, a person cannot drink either wine or grape juice, you can substitute another drink.)

- Pillows or cushions. Placed on the chair of each participant (or in some families, on the seder leader's chair only), these symbols of comfort remind us that we can recline as free people.

PREPARING THE SEDER PLATE

Most of the symbolic foods (some of which are eaten, some not) are arranged on a special seder plate, *k'arah* in Hebrew. Throughout the ages, beautiful dishes have been fashioned from silver, pewter, brass, painted porcelain, and glass, with designated spaces, indented compartments, or little bowls for the ceremonial foods. If you don't have a seder plate, you can display the foods on a pretty tray or platter. Decorate the platter with fresh spring blossoms or herbs. Celebrants who are including new ritual foods will probably have to present them on

"An egg has no beginning and no end. It symbolizes eternal life. You dip the egg in a finger bowl filled with warm salt water, tears of mourning shed by Jews. You dip life into tears, then eat it."

—PATRICIA VOLK, *Stuffed*

a platter, since there may be no designated place for them on a traditional seder plate.

If you are having a lot of guests, you may want a second seder plate for the other end of a large table.

These are the traditional seder plate items.

KARPAS This is a vegetable to celebrate spring and new growth, rebirth and the beginning of new life: the sweet taste of freedom. It is usually a green vegetable, such as celery, sweet lettuce, or a spring herb like parsley or chervil. Some Sephardim choose celery leaves, if they will not be using the leaves for the maror (the same vegetable cannot be used for both karpas and maror). A few Eastern European Jews may use boiled potato, a reminder of the harsh early spring in that part of the world, making their karpas—the first of the ritual foods eaten during the service—a more substantial "snack."

If there is no room on the seder plate for enough karpas to serve all your guests, place a representative amount on the seder plate and put the remainder in a separate dish.

The karpas will be dipped in a bowl of tears—symbolic not only of the Israelites' suffering, but, some say, of God's pain when slaying the Egyptians. Ashkenazim use salted water, while many Sephardim prefer vinegar, or lemon or lime juice. The bowl may be put on the seder plate or placed alongside it.

MAROR Recalling the misery of the Israelites' slavery and oppression and the suffering that continues in our day, this bitter herb may vary from community to community, even from one family to another. Ashekenazim favor freshly ground or sliced fresh horseradish root, prepared grated horseradish, or romaine lettuce. Sephardim prefer bitter greens, choosing among endive, escarole, chicory, sorrel, arugula, dandelion, purslane, watercress, and so on, either singly or in combination. Some Sephardim choose celery leaves, which tastes sweet at first but then turns bitter in the mouth—a metaphor for the Israelites' sojourn in Egypt. And others have used wasabi, mustard greens, or, in a multicultural family, even the spicy Korean condiment kim chee.

Maror is eaten by all the participants, so if you do not have room on the seder plate for enough maror, put the additional in a separate bowl.

HAROSET This is the fruit and nut dip symbolic of the clay or mortar the Israelites used to construct the pyramids; for fun, if your haroset paste is stiff enough, sculpt it into a pyramid shape on the seder plate.

Today some hosts like to offer two or three harosets from different communities, reflecting the diversity of the Jewish people (see pages 381 to 384 for recipes and suggestions). You'll need plenty of haroset for everybody; serve the extra in a separate bowl.

HAZERET Many seder plates call for a second bitter herb in addition to the maror, to be used in the traditional Hillel sandwich: matzoh enclosing a filling of bitter herbs and haroset. This may be any of the bitter foods not used previously for maror. Plan to have enough hazeret for each guest, since it will be eaten during the service.

ZEROA (FOREARM) The roasted shankbone recalls the ancient Paschal lamb sacrifice in the Temple. It also starkly represents the protective arm of God: the Israelites marked their doorposts with blood from the lamb slaughtered on the eve of the Exodus. Seeing this sign, the Angel of Death "passed over" their homes, sparing them from God's tenth and final plague, the slaying of the firstborn males.

A lamb shank, poultry wing or neck, or, for vegetarians, a beet (mentioned in the Talmud, because beets "bleed") may be used; the zeroa is not eaten at the seder. It is roasted and scorched to simulate the burnt sacrificial offering. To prepare it, place the bone under the broiler or on a sheet of heavy-duty foil in a very hot oven until it is browned all over. Or spear it with a long-handled fork and char it over an open flame on the stove. Roast the beet, if using, on a sheet of foil, unwrapped, in a hot oven, until browned at the edges.

BEITZAH This roasted egg is symbolic of the festival sacrifice each Jew brought to the ancient Temple, as well as a complex metaphor for spring, life, mourning, and rebirth. The egg, like the shankbone, is not eaten during the regular seder service, though many Sephardim put one of the Huevos Haminados (page 386) here that all the celebrants will later eat at the beginning of the meal. Ashkenazim use a roasted hard-boiled egg. To prepare it, hard-boil an egg then wrap it, still in its shell, in heavy-duty foil, and place it in a hot oven until lightly charred. Or use tongs to hold the hard-boiled egg (again, unshelled) over an open burner flame, or place under the broiler just until lightly burnt. Whichever method you choose, be sure to hard-boil the egg first—otherwise, you'll end up with an egg explosion.

Vegans who do not use eggs can substitute spring flowers like potted crocuses and daffodils or violets.

Arrangement of the ritual foods on the seder plate varies not only according to tradition, but also from place to place; in fact, Jews in Holland may use three different plates for the ceremonial foods, while Greek Jews set the foods in a basket and Yemenites place them directly on the table. But most commonly, the seder plate is assembled as follows:

Picture the plate as a clock. The zeroa (זרוע, shankbone) is placed at 2 o'clock; haroset (חרוסת, fruit and nut paste) is at 4; if the second bitter herb (חזרת, hazeret) is used, it is set at 6 o'clock; karpas (כרפס, spring vegetable) is at 8 o'clock; and beitzah (ביצה, the egg) is put at 10. Maror (מרור, the bitter herb) may be placed at either 12 o'clock or set in the middle of the plate.

"Everyone who adds their interpretation to the story is worthy of praise," the Haggadah tells us, and many Jewish families include new, nontraditional items on the seder plate. Here are two of the most popular.

POTATO PEELS Survivors of the Holocaust and their children, recalling what a blessing it was to have a potato peel—it could mean the difference between life and death in the concentration camps—began including the peels as a symbol of the Holocaust and today's hunger and famines. For many Jews fleeing the famines of Ethiopia, potatoes—in amounts small enough for their shrunken bodies to accept—were the first food tasted when they immigrated to Israel.

ORANGE Some new seder plates are designed with a special place for an orange. Theologian Susannah Heschel, in "Orange on the Seder Plate," explains that in the original ritual she created based on a story she had read in a feminist Haggadah, she asked everyone to take a segment of a tangerine, "say the blessing over it, and eat it to symbolize our solidarity with Jewish lesbians and gay men as well as with others who are marginalized within the Jewish community [including widows, like her mother]. Since each tangerine segment has a few seeds, we added the gesture of spitting them out. . . repudiating the sin of homophobia."

Dr. Heschel's new ritual, however, was widely misrepresented in the press. I read about it in the *Village Voice* more than ten years ago, where it was incorrectly reported as an affirmation of the role of Jewish women, rooted in an exchange the theologian purportedly had with a male heckler.

Today the orange has taken on a life of its own. For some, it calls to mind Dr. Heschel's original intent. For others, it is a more general metaphor for the sweetness and fruitfulness that welcoming all people brings to the community; by spitting out the seeds, we symbolically repudiate cruelty to anyone.

PASSOVER
menu suggestions

SEDER MEALS

Matzoh

Hard-boiled eggs with salt water

*Smoked Whitefish Gefilte Fish with Lemon-Horseradish Mayonnaise

*Classic Chicken Soup with any of the *Matzoh Ball recipes

or

*Celery *Avgolemono* (Greek Egg Lemon Soup) with Chicken Matzoh Balls

*Braised Brisket with Thirty-Six Cloves of Garlic

or

*Slow-Braised Lemon Veal with Leeks

*Crackletop Potato Kugel

*Roasted Asparagus Bundles with Toasted Matzoh Crumbs

Salad of Bibb lettuce and minced fresh herbs with lemon vinaigrette

*Italian Carrot-Pecan Torta

*Coconut Jammies

Matzoh

*See index for page numbers

*Huevos Haminados

*Salmon Gefilte Fish Poached in Fennel-Wine Broth with Ginger-Beet Horseradish

or

*Slow-Roasted Salmon with Green Herb Oil and Beet-Horseradish Relish

*Chicken Soup with Asparagus and Shiitakes, Served with Roasted Fennel Matzoh Balls

*Braised Lamb with Artichokes, Lemon, and Fresh Herbs

or

*Slow-Braised Brisket with Rosemary, Shallots, and Red Wine

or

*Moroccan-Flavored Brisket with Dried Apricots and Prunes

and/or

*Chicken with Olives and Preserved Lemon

*Garlicky Swiss Chard and Mushroom Matzoh Kugel

Fresh spinach drizzled with extra virgin olive oil

*Spring Compote with *Hazelnut Macaroons

*Rich Fudge Brownies

~⌣

A Vegetarian Seder

Matzoh

*See index for page numbers

*Chopped Eggs and Onion garnished with *Grated Black Radish and Endive Salad in Shallot Vinaigrette or strips of *Roasted Red Pepper and black olives

*Artichoke Soup (prepared with vegetable broth) with Light Herbed Matzoh Balls

*Zucchini Fritada

*Wild Mushroom Potato Kugel

*Rhubarb-Prune Tsimmes

Fresh asparagus

*Salad of Bitter Herbs and Oranges

*Hungarian Chocolate-Walnut Torte with vanilla ice cream

or

*Old-Country Cottage Cheese Cake (substitute very finely crushed macaroons for cookie crumbs)

Ripe pineapple with fresh mint and floral honey served with *Toasted Cashew-Cranberry Macaroons

Matzoh

Hard-boiled eggs with salt water

*Egyptian Ground Fish Balls with Tomato and Cumin (*Bellahat*)

or

*Fish in Tomato, Rhubarb, and Blood Orange Sauce

*See index for page numbers

*Chopped Chicken Liver from the Rue des Rosiers with *Grated Black Radish and Endive Salad in Shallot Vinaigrette

*Beet-Braised Pot Roast with Horseradish and Potato Knaidlach

or

*Provençal Roasted Garlic–Braised Breast of Veal with Springtime Stuffing

or

*Easy Onion-Braised Brisket with mashed potatoes

*Chicken Mina

Mixed greens with fresh herb-lemon vinaigrette

*Spring Compote with *Toasted Almond–Coconut Macaroons

*Upside-Down Apricot-Hazelnut Torte

NON-SEDER MEALS

*Pastrami-Style Salmon on *Onion and *Dill Matzoh (see Seasoned Matzoh)

*Savory Artichoke Matzoh Brie with *Yogurt Cream

or

*Mozzarella in Matzoh Carrozza

Crisp hearts of romaine with blue cheese dressing

*See index for page numbers

Spring fruit bowl: mango, banana, and tangerine slices, moistened with fresh tangerine juice

*Honey-Ricotta Cheese Cake

~ ᴄ ᴐ

*Chopped Eggs and Onions with *Cracked Pepper and Coarse Salt Matzoh (see Seasoned Matzoh)

*Snapper Fillets in Pistachio-Matzoh Crust

Fresh asparagus or spinach

Baked potato with sour cream and dill

*Hungarian Chocolate-Walnut Torte with fresh whipped cream

~ ᴄ ᴐ

Ripe melon splashed with red wine

*Rosemary Matzoh (see Seasoned Matzoh)

*Lemon Fried Chicken with Tart Salad Topping

or

*Fried Chicken Cutlets, Italian-Jewish Style and tossed green salad

Steamed broccoli

Roasted white or sweet potatoes

Juicy, ripe apples or pears with toasted pecans

~ ᴄ ᴐ

*Garlic Matzoh (see Seasoned Matzoh) served with *Rich Beef Broth (from Flanken)

*See index for page numbers

*Flanken with Tart Greens

*Wild Mushroom–Potato Kugel

Salad of red leaf lettuce, avocado and red onion, lime-oregano vinaigrette dressing

*Mango and Sour-Cherry Macaroon Crumble

SATURDAY LUNCH

Salt and Pepper Matzoh (see Seasoned Matzoh)

*Slow-Roasted Salmon with Green Herb Oil or herbed mayonnaise

*Spinach Cheese Squares

or

*Zucchini Fritada

*Moroccan-Flavored Carrot Kugel

Salad of tart greens

*Old-Country Cottage Cheese Cake (substitute very finely crushed macaroons for cookie crumbs)

*See index for page numbers

MATZOHS

One Passover spent in Paris, I ate thick matzoh, soft and crumbly as a cookie. In shops and restaurants in both the old ghetto area in the Marais and the newer North African–Jewish neighborhood surrounding the rue des Richers in the ninth arrondissement, I came across sweet varieties as well, prepared with wine, orange flower water, and sugar, tasting like exotic tea biscuits. They were, the boxes revealed, made from a secret family recipe from Oran, Algeria.

A sweltering August morning, strolling through Venice's Gheto Novo (New Ghetto, actually older than the Gheto Vecchio, Old Ghetto, but that's another story), my husband, daughter, and I snacked on what looked like quilted pillows of intricate ivory Venetian lace. They were pane azimo, pale matzoh, soft like the ones we'd had in Paris, baked at Panificio Giovanni Volpe, which also offers, even in summer, sugar cookies, delicate macaroons, and other pane dolci, sweets made with matzoh meal.

Eating these thick, puffy matzohs, I recalled the many Italian and French Passover recipes that specified thick or thin matzoh, and understood how Italian Jews who could not bear to go without their pasta might attempt to re-create lasagne with Venetian-style matzoh.

For Eastern European Jews, though, the best matzoh is the thinnest. In Abraham Reisen's story "Matza for the Rich," the bakery workers expect a generous tip from the town's wealthy dowager for matzoh that is thin, crackly, and "comes out as if baked in the sun." Notwithstanding their plainness, when served hot and crisp, these familiar Ashkenazi matzohs can be quite tasty.

Hot is the operative word here, for hot matzoh—like hot bread—is an amalgam of wonderful toasty flavors and aromas. Watching schmura matzoh (the special matzoh handmade from wheat that is carefully watched over from the time it is harvested) being prepared by the

"When the matza came out well, she held it up on the rolling pin to show the rich lady how nice it looked."

—ABRAHAM REISEN, "MATZA FOR THE RICH"

Hasidic Lubavitcher community in Brooklyn, I was captivated by the tantalizing smells of the freshly baked matzoh. And straight from the scorching wood-fired ovens, they were a marvel: gloriously toasty and crisp.

But when I brought the box home, the matzoh had dulled to a lackluster taste—they had more flavor than the packaged variety, but

"I devoured pounds of the crisp crumbling matzohs with hunks of fresh butter and streams of honey, leaving a trail of crumbs all over the house."

—EDNA FERBER, *A Peculiar Treasure*

not much. I've learned to reheat matzohs to recrisp them as well as to recapture that fresh-from-the-oven flavor.

TO HEAT MATZOH

PREHEAT the oven to 400°F. Wet the matzoh lightly on both sides with cold water (a few spritzes from a water spray bottle is perfect for this). Toast on a rack until dry and crisp, 3 to 5 minutes.

MATZOH, so central to Passover that it is often called Hag ha-Matzot (Festival of Matzohs), is served in place of bread or crackers during the full eight days of the holiday. The plain variety contains just flour and water—no fats, salt, sugars, additives, or preservatives—so you can use them to custom-design your own crackers, seasoning them with whatever you would try on flatbreads or crackers, and enjoy them not only on Passover but also throughout the year.

SEASONED MATZOH

USE these suggestions as a guide. I'm sure you'll have many ideas of your own.

1. Sprinkle the top of dampened matzoh with coarse salt, and, if desired, freshly ground coarse pepper and/or chopped fresh rosemary or other herbs. Bake until dry and crisp.

2. Gently rub the cut side of a garlic clove or onion over the matzoh until the matzoh is slightly damp. (A couple of vertical slashes in the cut side will make the garlic or onion juices flow more easily so the matzoh won't break apart in the process.) Sprinkle or spritz with a few drops of water, dust with salt, pepper, and herbs, if desired, such as thyme, rosemary or oregano, and bake until dry and crisp.

3. Sprinkle hot matzoh with grated Parmesan, Cheddar, or other cheese, grated lemon zest, and cracked pepper. Or sprinkle the seasoning on unheated matzoh and run briefly under the broiler.

4. Brush matzoh with melted or softened butter or extra virgin olive oil. Season with salt and pepper, if desired; grated garlic or onion; and chopped fresh or dried herbs. Or steep minced garlic or onion in oil

for a while, then brush the oil on the matzoh, using sprigs of rosemary or other herbs as a brush. Bake at 400°F until hot and just beginning to brown.

5. For a sweet matzoh, brush egg matzoh with melted butter and sprinkle with brown sugar and cinnamon. Place under the broiler until the sugar melts.

FOR more on matzoh and matzoh meal, see page 23.

CLASSIC ASHKENAZI HAROSET

yield: ABOUT 2½ CUPS

You can vary the nuts, using pecans, hazelnuts, or, even better, a combination. Some people sprinkle pinches of ground ginger or cloves for a bit of spice. Straying slightly from the Eastern European roots, I sometimes include a little mashed banana, pureed dates, or even mango to create a more paste-like consistency.

1 pound apples (about 3 large, or 4 or 5 medium; choose a flavorful, eating-out-of-hand variety, such as Gala, Braeburn, or Jonagold; avoid Red Delicious, which all too often is bland and mealy), peeled, cored, and cut into eighths if large, or quarters if medium

¾ cup walnuts or almonds (best if lightly toasted)

About 1½ teaspoons ground cinnamon

About ¼ cup kosher sweet Concord grape wine or juice

COMBINE apples, nuts, and ground cinnamon in a food processor, and pulse until coarsely chopped and still chunky. Transfer to a bowl and stir in the wine or grape juice. Cover and refrigerate to let the flavors marry for a few hours or overnight. Bring to room temperature when ready to serve. Adjust the seasoning, adding more cinnamon or wine, if desired.

GRANDMA DOROTHY'S HAROSET

yield: 3½ TO 4 CUPS

*H*er haroset was sweet with snipped raisins; her fritters drizzled with honey tasted so soufflé-light, they were called "snow pancakes."

Lisa Sokoloff always knew her Grandma Dorothy's food was different. While Lisa's friends ate fluffy matzoh ball soup at their seders, her family tucked into an elixir rich with celery, carrots, chicken meat and necks, and little oniony dumplings made from whole matzoh.

But when Dorothy died, the family knew little about her heritage. Then an old article from a Brooklyn newspaper turned up, and they learned that Dorothy's grandfather, David Henry Lazarus, had emigrated from England during the Gold Rush and fought for the Union in the Civil War. When he was wounded in combat, President Lincoln shook his hand on a visit to the hospitalized troops.

The family is still working on Dorothy's story, tracking down the relatives living near London and Dublin. And part of Dorothy's story is told every Passover in the matzoh balls Lisa makes and in this simple but exceptionally delicious haroset.

She is still trying to piece together the snow pancakes.

1⅓ cups dark raisins

6 or 7 medium, flavorful apples, such as Gala or Braeburn (do not choose the ubiquitous, ironically named Red Delicious apple)

8 ounces pecans or almonds (1⅓ to 1½ cups)

½ teaspoon ground cinnamon

Sugar or honey (optional)

About ¼ cup sweet kosher wine

PLACE the raisins in a bowl and cover them with hot tap water. Set aside to soak for at least 30 minutes. Peel, core, and quarter the apples.

YOU can do all the chopping and grating in the food processor without rinsing between tasks if you follow the steps in this order. Pulse the nuts until very finely chopped and transfer them to a large bowl. Drain the raisins and pat them dry. Pulse them in the food processor until coarsely chopped (all the raisins should at least be chopped in half), and transfer them to the bowl. Remove the blade and insert the fine shredding disk. Finely shred the apples. Transfer them to the bowl.

ADD the cinnamon and mix all the ingredients well. Taste and add a little sugar or honey, if needed (if apples are sweet, you may not want added sweetening). Stir in the wine, beginning with ¼ cup and adding just enough more, if needed, to bind the ingredients together.

COVER and refrigerate until cold before serving.

DATE HAROSET

yield: ABOUT 4 CUPS

This luscious Sephardi haroset is very easy to prepare. But its simple ingredients comprise a complex metaphor of the Exodus: the dark fruit and nut paste brings to mind the mortar formed from the silt of the Nile, used to build the pyramids; the wine evokes the blood shed by the Hebrew slaves and, later, by the Egyptians during the tenth plague; and the sweetness is the taste of the Israelites' eventual freedom. In addition to these edible symbols, some Sephardim suggest the bitterness of the struggle with a few tart drops of citrus juice or vinegar, or a dusting of harsh spices, such as black pepper, cayenne, or ginger, to temper the sweetness. I like to play up the sweet-sour flavor with a squeeze of lime juice and yet another symbolic layer: a sprinkle of sea salt to recall the Red Sea crossing.

2 cups packed pitted dates (choose a soft variety such as Medjool), chopped

About ½ cup kosher sweet Concord grape wine or juice

1 teaspoon ground cinnamon

1¼ cups walnuts (best if lightly toasted)

Fresh lime or lemon juice or vinegar (optional)

Sea salt (optional)

PUT the dates in a large heatproof bowl. Pour 1½ cups boiling water over them and cover the bowl with foil. Set the dates aside to soften for about 1 hour, stirring occasionally. Scrape the mixture into a food processor and add the wine or juice and cinnamon. Working in batches, if necessary, blend to a smooth paste, adding more hot water if needed. Return the mixture to the bowl. Without rinsing the food processor, pulse the walnuts in it until they are chopped: a combination of coarse and fine will provide good texture. Stir the nuts into the date paste. Add the citrus juice or vinegar and/or the sea salt to taste, if using.

SET the haroset aside, covered and refrigerated, to let the flavors mingle until ready to use. If the mixture is too thick, stir in additional wine or juice to thin it. Adjust the seasoning. Serve at room temperature.

TANGY HAROSET BITES

yield: ABOUT 8 SERVINGS

When my daughter Alex and "goddaughter" Emily were preparing these seductive Haroset Bites for our seder in Paris, from a recipe I had devised for Food and Wine *magazine, they consumed one for every two they managed to place on the Passover platter. Luckily, I always buy way too much food. So we had plenty to assuage our hunger pangs later, when the bites provided a welcome nourishing snack at "haroset time" during the service.*

I always toast nuts for harosets. While it might seem excessive, it really does permit the slightly bitter, pure nut essence to shine through, parrying the sweet dried or fresh fruit in the paste.

1 cup walnuts

30 to 35 almonds

½ cup black raisins

½ cup dried, pitted dates (choose a soft variety like Medjool), coarsely chopped

1½ heaping tablespoons dried tart cherries or cranberries

¼ cup unsweetened purple grape juice or kosher sweet Concord wine

2 tablespoons fresh lemon juice

⅛ teaspoon ground cinnamon

30 to 35 tart dried apricots, plumped in very hot water until softened, and patted dry with paper towels

TOAST the nuts: preheat oven to 350°F. Spread the nuts out in a single layer in a baking pan and toast them, shaking the pan occasionally, until the nuts are fragrant and lightly toasted, 10 to 12 minutes. Remove from oven and let cool.

PUT the raisins, dates, and cherries or cranberries in a bowl. Stir in the grape juice or wine, lemon juice, and cinnamon. Let the fruit macerate for at least 15 minutes.

WHEN the nuts are cool, set the almonds aside and place the walnuts in a food processor. Using the steel blade, pulse on and off until the walnuts are coarsely chopped.

ADD the macerated fruit and any liquid remaining in the bowl to the food processor. Pulse on and off, until the mixture is a coarse paste. Transfer to a bowl and chill so that mixture will be easier to roll. (The haroset tastes best if flavors are allowed to mingle for several hours.)

FORM heaping teaspoons of the mixture into balls and place each on a softened apricot half. Press an almond into each ball at a jaunty angle.

EGGS

No less than twelve large brown paper bags spilled out of the kitchen for us to unpack when my father finished the Passover shopping. Every one, it seemed, contained at least one box of matzoh and a dozen eggs.

The matzoh lasted long after the eight-day holiday, when all our inventiveness had evaporated and we had thoroughly tired of eating it. But my father had to buy more eggs after just three or four days.

Eggs are indispensable for Passover cooking. Traditional favorites, like matzoh brie, knaidlach, and *bimuelos* and *bubelach* (Sephardi and Ashkenazi fritters), call for heaps of eggs to be mixed with matzoh or matzoh meal. And six to ten at a time, they are beaten into baked goods, replacing the forbidden leavening.

Symbol of life's mysteries and rebirth, they play a prominent role at the seder. There is the *beitzah* (roasted egg), on the seder plate. And most Ashkenazi Jews dip hard-boiled eggs into salt water, while the Sephardi seder favorite is huevos haminados.

HUEVOS HAMINADOS

yield: **12 EGGS**

*H*uevos haminados, also served at life-cycle events and the Sabbath or holiday midday meal, were originally cooked on top of flavorful meats and legumes in hamins, the slowly braised Sabbath stews. But when hamin is not on the menu, or pareve eggs are desired, they are prepared as in this recipe, cradled in onion skins and gently simmered overnight in the oven or on top of the stove. Spent coffee grinds, or sometimes tea leaves, are added to the roasting materials for additional flavor. My friend Leyla Schick laughingly bemoaned the current paucity of cigarette smokers among her friends because some Turkish Jews claim a smidgin of cigarette ash enhances the roasted taste.

And what is the taste of a roasted egg? Huevos haminados are somewhat similar to the hard-boiled variety, but long hours of gentle cooking give them a softer texture—tender, never rubbery—and a rich, oniony fragrance.

Forget the discarded cigarette ashes. But do remember to save all your onion peels as they accumulate from cooking chores, storing them in a large perforated plastic bag in the refrigerator until needed.

4 to 5 cups packed outer skins of onions, rinsed if dirty

12 large eggs, in the shell (make sure the shells have no cracks)

2 tablespoons coffee grounds

2 tablespoons olive oil

2 teaspoons vinegar

1 teaspoon salt

½ teaspoon black pepper

PREHEAT the oven to 200°F. Arrange half the onion skins on the bottom of a large lidded ovenproof pot or casserole. Put the eggs on top. If the eggs are tightly packed, or if you must place the eggs in two layers, use additional onion skins to cradle them. Add the coffee grounds, oil, vinegar, salt, and pepper. Cover with the remaining onion skins. Pour in 2 quarts of cold water, adding a little more if necessary to cover the eggs. Cover the pot tightly and bake in the oven overnight or for at least 8 hours or up to 12.

REMOVE the eggs and wipe them clean. Serve plain, hot, warm, or cold. Leftover eggs are easy to reheat (place them, unshelled, in a baking dish and warm in a slow oven until heated through). They are also wonderful sliced in salads (they make a terrific egg salad) or as a garnish for saucy stewed vegetables like ratatouille.

His own mother had spoiled him, her first-born son and the only child of her seven to go to college and then law school. My maternal grandmother Rebecca loved to spoil my father, too—her tall son-in-law whose blue-black hair led strangers to mistake him for her own handsome son.

"Save that piece for your father," she would admonish us. "Go, put on lipstick," she'd urge my mother. "Max will be home soon."

Ignoring her, we would strip the crackling, garlicky skin from just-roasted turkey or chicken, greedily devouring it before he arrived home. And only once can I remember my mother applying lipstick just for my father, in the candy shade of pink she wore to match the soft blush beneath her freckles. We knew when my father dished out the servings at the dinner table, the choicest morsels went first to the children, then to my mother, and he took what was left.

But if we wouldn't show him proper respect, Grandma Rebecca did. When she learned he loved chopped eggs and onions, she substituted it for the traditional Ashkenazi hard-boiled eggs dipped in salted water eaten at the beginning of the Passover meal.

I first ate eggs in salt water at a boyfriend's seder when I was seventeen. They tasted like a picnic ruined by high tide. Those who imagine I am impugning one of their favorite Passover foods might try the dish at any other time of year, without the spice of hunger to season it.

But chopped eggs and onions are delicious anytime. Spread on thin pumpernickel or egg matzoh, garnished with strips of roasted red pepper, black olives or skinny slivers of smoked salmon, it is light-years ahead of a traditional egg salad.

CHOPPED EGGS AND ONIONS

yield: 4 TO 6 SERVINGS

*M*y grandmother's chopped eggs and onions got their flavor boost from griebenes, the cracklings of fat and skin that are a by-product of making schmaltz, poultry fat. I add well-browned onions and their oil for the same effect.

For Passover, serve on soft lettuce leaves, or for a gussied-up presentation, in radicchio or alternating pale green and red Belgian endive leaves. Or pack into small custard cups or cleaned tuna cans and invert onto frilly greens. Grated Black Radish and Endive Salad in Shallot Vinaigrette (page 61) is a superb complement.

This should be rather coarse and crumbly, not at all paste-like. Using a food processor—even in pulsing motion—usually results in some overly large chunks and some paste. I find it much easier to chop this in an old-fashioned wooden chopping bowl with an inexpensive curved hand-chopper (like the half-moon-shaped Jewish hockmeisser or crescent-shaped Italian mezzaluna). It's much quicker to clean than the food processor, too.

3 to 5 tablespoons best-quality olive or avocado oil

½ cup thinly sliced onions plus ½ cup finely chopped onion

Salt and freshly ground black pepper

6 hard-boiled large eggs (see page 59), peeled and cut into eighths

Olive Oil Schmaltz (page 27) or Poultry Schmaltz (page 28) (optional)

HEAT 3 tablespoons oil in a medium skillet, and add the sliced onions. (I use sliced onion here because chopped onion can be quite watery, so it doesn't fry as well and has a tendency to burn when made in small amounts.) Sauté over medium heat, stirring occasionally, until rich golden-brown. Salt and pepper lightly and remove from the heat to cool.

SCRAPE the sautéed onion and all the oil remaining in the skillet into a wooden bowl, and chop coarsely. Add the eggs and raw onion, and continue to chop until the mixture is well blended but not pasty. Mix in salt and lots of pepper as you chop, or blend in the seasonings afterwards with a fork. (Using a spoon will make the mixture too smooth.) The mixture should hold together loosely; you will probably need to add some of the schmaltz or a bit more oil. Chill well, but remove from the refrigerator at least 15 minutes before serving.

CHICKEN SOUP WITH ASPARAGUS AND SHIITAKES, SERVED WITH ROASTED FENNEL MATZOH BALLS

yield: ABOUT 8 SERVINGS

*S*et in spring, when the earth is renewing and reassembling herself, Passover is celebrated as a sort of second New Year, reflecting the rebirth of the Jews as a free people after the Exodus from Egypt. Children start the season with new clothes, and houses are thoroughly cleaned and freshened up to make way for the new foods and special sets of dishes reserved just for Passover use.

And just as they delay until Rosh Hashanah their first tastes of the sweet new autumn fruits, so many Jews wait until Passover to savor the tender new vegetables of spring. In this delicious soup, woodsy shiitake mushrooms and early asparagus combine with delicate roasted fennel–flavored matzoh balls in a free-wheeling ode to spring.

FOR THE ROASTED FENNEL MATZOH BALLS

2 small to medium fennel bulbs (about 1 pound, weighed with 2 inches of top stalks)

2 tablespoons olive oil

¹/₂ cup chicken broth, preferably homemade (see pages 62 to 70) or good-quality, low-sodium purchased

1 tablespoon coarsely chopped garlic

Salt and freshly ground black pepper

³/₄ teaspoon chopped fresh thyme

¹/₄ teaspoon fennel seeds, ground in a spice grinder or with a mortar and pestle (optional)

2 large eggs

PREPARE the matzoh balls: preheat the oven to 400°F. Cut off the fennel stalks and reserve for another use (excellent for fish broths and stews). If there are some attractive feathery fronds, set aside about 2 tablespoons of them to garnish the soup. Quarter the bulbs and trim away the stems, the bottom hard core, and any tough parts. Choose a shallow baking pan just large enough to fit the fennel in one layer and put in 1 table-spoon of the oil. Add the fennel and toss until well coated. Roast the fennel until pale gold, about 20 minutes, then turn the fennel over and roast for 10 minutes longer. Stir in the broth, garlic, salt and pepper to taste, and ¹/₂ teaspoon of the thyme. Cover the pan with foil and cook for 35 to 45 minutes longer, or until the fennel is very soft. Remove the foil, stir, and roast for a few more minutes to evaporate most of the liq-uid. Transfer the fennel and garlic to a food processor and chop coarsely. Add the remaining ¹/₄ teaspoon of thyme, salt (it will need about 1 tea-spoon), pepper to taste, and the fennel seeds, if using. With the machine on, add the remaining 1 tablespoon oil through the feed tube.

SCRAPE the mixture into a large bowl. You need 1 cup of puree, so nosh on any extra. Whisk in the eggs, one at a time. Add the matzoh meal and stir well. If you can form a lump into a very soft walnut-size ball (the batter will become firmer when you chill it), don't add any more matzoh meal. If necessary, add just enough matzoh meal to enable you

About ½ cup plus
2 tablespoons matzoh
meal

FOR THE SOUP

7 cups homemade chicken broth (see Classic Chicken Soup, page 62 or Almost Homemade Soup, page 70)

¼ pound fresh shiitake mushrooms, stems removed and reserved for another use or discarded, caps wiped clean with a damp paper towel and thinly sliced

12 to 15 thin asparagus spears, trimmed and cut into 1-inch pieces

to do so. Refrigerate for at least 2 or up to 4 hours so the matzoh meal can drink in the liquid and seasoning.

WHEN ready to cook, bring 4 quarts water and 1 tablespoon of salt to a rapid boil in a large, wide, lidded pot. Dipping your hands into cold water, if needed, roll the batter into walnut-size balls. When all the balls are rolled and the water is boiling furiously, turn the heat down to a gentle boil. Carefully slide in the balls one at a time and cover the pot tightly.

TURN the heat down to a simmer, and cook over low heat for 30 minutes, without removing the cover. (They will cook by direct heat as well as by steam, which makes them puff and swell, and lifting the lid will allow some of that steam to escape.) Take out a dumpling and cut it in half. It should be light, fluffy and completely cooked through. If it isn't, continue cooking a few more minutes. Remove the balls gently with a skimmer or large slotted spoon—they are too fragile to pour into a colander.

WHEN the matzoh balls are almost ready, start the soup: bring the broth to a simmer in a large pot. Add the matzoh balls, the mushrooms, and asparagus and simmer for about 5 minutes, until the vegetables are tender.

USING a slotted spoon, transfer the matzoh balls to shallow soup bowls and ladle the hot soup and the vegetables over them. Garnish with the reserved chopped fennel fronds.

COOK'S NOTE: You can cook the matzoh balls up to 2 to 3 hours in advance. Drain them and cover with some broth to keep them moist before setting them aside until you are ready to reheat them.

Experiment with making matzoh balls with a puree of other vegetables, like beets, carrots, leeks, mushrooms, or shallots. Roasted vegetables absorb less moisture than boiled or steamed ones (and, therefore, require less matzoh meal, making them lighter). They are also more flavorful.

FOR YOUR VEGETARIAN SON, YOUR VEGAN NIECE

Many families need to accommodate a son returning home from college, a mother-in-law, or other diners who are vegetarian or vegan. Whenever possible, serve them foods your other guests will enjoy too, or make use of ingredients already prepped for other dishes.

Preparing a dairy seder (see suggested seder menus) or even an egg-rich one at a meat meal for a vegetarian guest is not difficult. For a pareve menu, start with Chopped Eggs and Onions or Huevos Haminados; make and serve any of the matzoh ball recipes with vegetable broth, adding extra flavor to the matzoh balls with Olive Oil Schmaltz. Latkes, kugels, and special matzoh bries, such as artichoke, can be made without meat or dairy products and work well as festive vegetarian main courses. And all of the Passover desserts are appropriate for vegetarians.

But creating food in holiday dress that is not just meat-free, but dairy and egg-free as well *and* conforms to Passover hametz and kitniyot restrictions is a real challenge. Some suggestions:

- Start with a pâté: slowly caramelize onions in oil, and set aside. Sauté sliced mushrooms and chopped carrots with garlic until deep gold. Let cool slightly, then combine all the vegetables together with toasted walnuts or almonds in a food processor, and puree until smooth. Season with salt, pepper, fresh thyme, and more oil or Olive Oil Schmaltz, if needed. Serve in endive, radicchio, or butter lettuce leaves or with matzoh.

- A plate of spinach and roasted potatoes will never pass for a main course: add complexity to vegetables with textural contrast, and layer or stuff them to make them taste more substantial.

For example, fill zucchini or cabbage with potatoes, walnuts, and mint, or make matzoh-crusty gratins of pureed cauliflower or squash. Top sautéed vegetables with a shepherd's pie layer of mashed potatoes combined with toasted nuts or sautéed herbed matzoh crumbs. Or make burgers of mushrooms, finely chopped onion, and mashed potatoes.

- Other main course suggestions: prepare dairy-free "pizzas": fashion a crust of broiled sliced eggplant or a thin layer of well-seasoned mashed potatoes, and top with roasted tomatoes and portobellos sprinkled with slivers of garlic and fresh basil. Or make "pappardelle" of very thinly sliced zucchini (use a Y-shaped vegetable peeler to cut wide strips) lightly cooked then tossed with matzoh crumbs fried crunchy in oil and garlic. Or serve pasta-like spaghetti squash with a marinara sauce or top a melange of roasted vegetables—potatoes, red peppers, carrots—with a spicy tomato sauce. Or try quinoa, the ancient Inca stand-in for grain that is not considered kitniyot by many Orthodox authorities. On the side, include either of the meat-free tsimmes recipes on pages 107 or 246.

- For dessert, serve Spring Compote (page 455) or dates, pitted and stuffed with toasted walnuts, pecans, or almonds, lightly rolled in walnut oil, then in cocoa or coconut.

SAVORY HERBED MATZOH *KLEIS* (MATZOH BALLS MADE FROM WHOLE MATZOH)

yield: ABOUT 6 SERVINGS

*H*omey dumplings have been a hallmark of German cuisine ever since the Middle Ages, and the Yiddish words, knaidl (a variant of knoedl) and kleis (which began as klosse) reveal their German ancestry. Jewish cooks in Central and Eastern Europe incorporated dumplings into their repertoire, fashioning them from bread, rolls, flour, and potatoes.

And for Passover, they made fluffy balls out of matzoh. I have found that the Alsatian, German, and Czech matzoh ball recipes, often called kleis, created from soaked pieces of whole matzoh, are frequently more imaginatively and assertively flavored than the familiar variety made of matzoh meal. And I love the way the matzoh pieces seem to inhale the seasonings far more lustily than matzoh meal does.

In my rendition, generous lacings of fresh herbs and lemon zest, along with a delicate, traditional ground-almond thickener, make for kleis that are vibrant yet gossamer-light.

6 whole plain matzohs

2 cups chicken broth, preferably homemade (see pages 62 and 70), or good-quality, low-sodium purchased

2 cups finely chopped onions

3 tablespoons mild olive oil

2 teaspoons minced garlic

2 tablespoons finely chopped fresh parsley

2 tablespoons finely snipped fresh chives

1 tablespoon finely snipped fresh dill

2 teaspoons grated lemon zest

BREAK the matzohs into small pieces in a large bowl. Heat the broth until it is very hot and pour it over the matzoh. Set aside to allow the matzoh to drink up the broth.

IN a large skillet, sauté the onion in the oil over medium heat, stirring, until soft and translucent, 7 to 10 minutes. Add the garlic and cook for 2 to 3 minutes. Stir in the parsley, chives, dill, and lemon zest. Add the soaked matzoh and cook, stirring constantly, until the mixture becomes dry and paste-like. Return it to the bowl and let cool until you can handle it.

YOUR fingers will do the best job mixing this, but if you're really averse to using them, try a potato masher, ricer, or just a heavy fork. Knead and mash the matzoh pieces until you have a fairly smooth, homogeneous mixture.

BEAT in the eggs, one at a time, and the ground almonds or matzoh meal, and season well with salt and pepper. Cover and refrigerate for at least 2 hours to allow the mixture to absorb all the seasoning and liquid.

3 large eggs

About 3 tablespoons ground blanched almonds or matzoh meal plus additional, if desired, for dredging kleis

Salt and freshly ground black pepper

1 recipe Classic Chicken Soup (page 62) or Almost Homemade Soup (page 70)

BRING 4 quarts water and 1½ tablespoons salt to a boil in a large, wide lidded pot. Place a bowl of cold water and a large platter or tray near you as you work.

NOW try rolling a little batter into a walnut- or olive-size ball. It should be somewhat sticky, but fairly easy to roll into very soft balls, with hands moistened with the cold water as needed. If the batter is too soft to roll, or the balls don't hold their shape on the platter, add just enough ground almonds or matzoh meal to achieve the right consistency. (Too much will make the kleis heavy, as will packing them too densely into a ball. A light touch is essential. Eventually you'll know quite easily when they feel just right.)

IF you'd like the kleis to look more finished, without homey, ragged edges (it's a slight tradeoff—they won't be quite as light), spread additional ground almonds or matzoh meal on a sheet of wax paper or a plate, and very lightly dredge the rolled balls in it. Put the finished balls on the platter or tray, and continue making the kleis until all the batter is used up.

WHEN all the kleis are rolled and the water is boiling furiously, turn heat down to a gentle boil. Quickly and carefully slide the balls in, one by one, nudging them in with a spoon or your finger, and cover the pot tightly. Don't crowd the pot—if necessary, prepare the kleis in two batches or use two pots. Temperature is important here: if the water is boiling with too much force, the matzoh balls may break up or disintegrate into thick sludge. If the water is not hot enough, the protein won't coagulate and the hapless balls will also fall apart. Aim to keep the water, as the French say, "smiling"—perhaps even "laughing softly," the bubbles breaking slowly and gently on the surface of the water. (You can best check the water temperature if the pot lid is glass; otherwise, listen for sounds of rapid boiling, but don't lift the lid.)

"I saw once more . . . the soup with dreamily swimming dumplings— and my soul melted like the notes of an enamoured nightingale."

—HEINRICH HEINE, *The Rabbi of Bacherach*

SIMMER over low heat for 30 to 40 minutes, without removing the lid. (They will cook by direct heat as well as by steam, which makes them puff and swell, and peeking will dissipate some of that steam.) Take out a dumpling and cut it in half. It should be tender, fluffy, and completely cooked through. If it isn't, continue cooking until the kleis tests done.

REMOVE them gently with a skimmer or large slotted spoon—they are too fragile to pour out into a colander. Add them to the soup and simmer slowly until piping hot. Ladle the kleis and steaming soup into warmed shallow bowls and serve immediately. Or cover the drained kleis with some broth and set aside until you are ready to heat them.

CELERY *AVGOLEMONO* (GREEK EGG LEMON SOUP) WITH CHICKEN MATZOH BALLS

yield: ABOUT 8 SERVINGS

*T*art and creamy egg-and-lemon is a classic combination in Sephardi repertoires all over the world. It appears as a sprightly sauce, warm or cold, napping vegetables, fish, even poached chicken, and it transforms humble chicken soup with rice into a boldface name—a favorite for pre- and post-Yom Kippur fasts and for Passover seders, when pieces of matzoh may be added.

The secret in this rendition is separating the eggs before they are whisked in: the airy beaten whites make the soup particularly light and fresh tasting. For our Passovers, I've replaced the rice with braised celery or spinach.

And since for me, it isn't a seder without matzoh balls, I've created these chicken dumplings with a nod to the Dayenu I learned about in Verona, Italy (see page 67). Because they are packed with lots of protein-rich chopped raw chicken, these matzoh balls react like meatballs when they hit the heat of the simmering liquid, firming up beautifully. There is virtually no chance of disintegration, yet they are tender and full of flavor: perfect for the formerly matzoh ball-challenged.

FOR THE CHICKEN MATZOH BALLS

2 whole egg or plain matzohs

1 cup chicken broth, preferably homemade (see pages 62 and 70) or good-quality, low-sodium purchased, plus a few extra tablespoons to moisten the cooked matzoh balls

1 pound boneless, skinless chicken breast

½ cup coarsely chopped onion

3 tablespoons snipped fresh dill

PREPARE the chicken matzoh balls: break the matzoh into small pieces in a large bowl, and pour the broth over it. Set the bowl aside, stirring now and then, while the matzoh drinks in the broth.

TRIM away all fat and sinews from the chicken and cut it into 1-inch chunks. Put the chicken in a food processor with the onions, and chop fine, using the pulse motion. Squeeze the matzoh with your hands to drain off the excess broth, and add the drained matzoh to the food processor. (Discard any remaining broth, but don't bother to rinse out the bowl.) Add the herbs, salt (figure about 1 teaspoon, but the exact amount will depend on the saltiness of your broth) and pepper to taste, and pulse until well blended.

BEAT the eggs and the oil together in the large bowl. Transfer the chicken-matzoh mixture to the bowl and combine thoroughly. Cover and refrigerate for at least 30 minutes to firm the batter and marry the flavors.

2 tablespoons chopped fresh mint

Salt and freshly ground black pepper

3 large eggs

3 tablespoons mild olive or avocado oil

FOR THE SOUP

2 tablespoons mild olive or avocado oil

2 cups diced celery

Salt and freshly ground black pepper

9 cups chicken broth, preferably homemade (see pages 62 and 70), or good-quality, low-sodium purchased

5 large eggs, separated (at room temperature)

About ⅔ cup fresh lemon juice

3 tablespoons snipped fresh dill

Thinly sliced lemon, sprigs of dill and mint, for garnish

BRING 4 quarts water and 1½ tablespoons salt to a boil in a large, wide lidded pot. Shape the batter into walnut-size balls, and place on a platter. When the water is boiling furiously, turn the heat down to a gentle boil, and slide the balls in one at a time. Alternatively, if the batter is too soft, form the balls using two spoons, pushing the batter off the spoon right into the water. You'll find that these matzoh balls are much sturdier than the regular kind, and won't fall apart as easily. And they need less room to expand, so you can fit more into the pot. Avoid overcrowding though—unless your pot is very large, you may still need to prepare them in two batches or use two pots.

WHEN the water returns to a boil, lower the heat to a simmer, partially cover the pot, and cook for about 15 minutes. Test for doneness: remove a matzoh ball and cut it in half. It should be tender, fluffy and completely cooked through. If it isn't, continue cooking for a few more minutes. Remove the matzoh balls with a skimmer or large slotted spoon to a big platter, and sprinkle them with a little broth to keep them moist as you prepare the soup.

HEAT the oil in a deep 8- to 9-inch skillet. Add the celery, sprinkle lightly with salt and pepper, and sauté for 3 minutes. Spoon over 1 cup of the broth, bring to a boil, then cover the pan tightly and braise over moderately low heat until the celery is tender. Transfer the celery and its cooking liquid to a large pot and add the rest of the broth. Cook over medium heat, stirring, until heated through. Remove the pot from heat.

IN a large bowl, using an electric mixer, beat the egg whites to soft peaks. Continue beating at low speed, while slowly adding the yolks, one at a time, and then the lemon juice. Still beating constantly, very slowly ladle 2 cups of the hot broth into the egg mixture. (Take care here: if you don't temper the eggs slowly, the mixture will curdle, and you'll wind up with egg drop soup.) Now add the egg-broth mixture back into the pot of soup. Add the chicken matzoh balls and the dill.

SLOWLY reheat, stirring constantly, until everything is piping hot. Don't let the soup approach a boil or it may curdle. Taste and adjust the seasonings. It should be very lemony and well salted.

USING a slotted spoon, transfer the chicken matzoh balls to shallow soup bowls and ladle the hot soup and celery over them. Garnish, if desired, with lemon slices and fresh herb sprigs. The flavors improve if you let the soup stand a few minutes before serving.

COOK'S NOTE: If you prefer an airy soup that is not quite as frothy, allow the soup to rest a few more minutes or simmer gently for a few extra minutes before serving.

Try flavoring the soup with some of the pale celery leaves, chopped, instead of the dill. Or boost the lemon taste with some grated lemon zest. You can substitute an equal amount of fresh fennel for the celery and proceed as above, garnishing with a few fennel fronds. Or make Spinach Avgolemono: you'll need only 8 cups broth. Omit the celery, and simply stir 2 cups fresh spinach leaves, shredded, into the broth, and simmer until wilted.

The soup is also excellent reheated, as long as you avoid high heat, and very good cold, too (when served without the matzoh balls).

ARTICHOKE SOUP WITH LIGHT HERBED MATZOH BALLS

yield: ABOUT 8 SERVINGS

When visiting food markets, I always go for the artichokes. I cannot munch on them raw, and I rarely have a kitchen on my travels where I could prepare them. Instead, I've dried big-hearted, long-stemmed beauties and graceful amethyst babies from produce stalls in California, Brittany, Provence, and Rome (the foreign-born smuggled, well wrapped and hidden beneath a pile of laundry).

At home the bouquets of fat artichokes slowly unfurl, revealing spiky fluff centers colored vivid Crayola orchid; the smaller ones spill out of purple glass bowls, alone or mingled with pomegranates, and line my dressed-up table.

So I was in artichoke heaven one warm spring evening at the height of the season in the Roman ghetto, home of the famed carciofi alla giudia (artichokes Jewish-style: the flattened whole vegetable, fried up crisp and golden-brown, then sprinkled with coarse salt). We had enjoyed a dinner at the kosher La Taverna del Ghetto featuring artichokes (in addition to the fried ones, we ate a salad of raw artichokes and a pasta topped with artichokes, bottarga, and tomatoes) and zucchini flowers (the blossoms stuffed with striped bass and fried, and tagliarini with zucchini flowers, grouper, and tomatoes). Outside the restaurant, on the ancient Via Portico d'Ottavia, the tall white flowerpots that usually sported colorful potted plants now overflowed with massive amounts of decorative artichokes, in every size and spectrum of greens and violets. At some storefronts, fabulous beasts and other dazzling topiary creations fashioned of artichokes stood guard.

Back in my own kitchen, I've logged countless hours cleaning and cooking fresh artichokes from local greengrocers and even a farmer at the Union Square Greenmarket, who occasionally coaxes them to grow in the cool clime of Pennsylvania.

But I confess I keep a box or two of frozen artichokes in my freezer. They are wonderful in savory matzoh brie, and pureed, they do very nicely in this creamy-tasting soup crowned with these exceptional featherweight matzoh balls full of herb garden flavor.

FOR THE SOUP

3 tablespoons mild olive oil

MAKE the soup: in a large nonreactive Dutch oven or lidded casserole, warm the oil. Add the leeks and the shallots, salt and pepper lightly, and sauté, stirring, over medium heat, about 7 minutes, until softened. Add

4 medium-large leeks (white and tenderest pale green parts only), washed well, patted dry, halved lengthwise and thinly sliced crosswise

3 tablespoons chopped shallots

Salt and freshly ground black pepper

2 chopped garlic cloves

Two 9- or 10-ounce packages frozen artichokes, thawed, patted dry between layers of paper towels, and cut into small pieces

7 to 8 cups chicken stock, preferably homemade (see pages 62 and 70), or good-quality, low-sodium purchased

2 to 3 tablespoons fresh lemon juice

2 teaspoons grated lemon zest

3 tablespoons coarsely chopped fresh flat-leaf parsley, plus additional for garnish

3 tablespoons snipped fresh dill, plus additional for garnish

2 tablespoons coarsely chopped fresh mint, plus additional for garnish

FOR THE MATZOH BALLS

4 large eggs, separated

2 teaspoons finely grated onion

2 tablespoons finely snipped fresh chives

3 tablespoons finely snipped fresh dill

Kosher salt and freshly ground black pepper

1 cup matzoh meal

the garlic and the artichokes, stir to coat well with the oil, and sauté over medium-high heat for 3 minutes. Add 1 cup of the broth and 2 tablespoons of the lemon juice, cover the pan, and sweat the vegetables over low heat for 10 minutes. Uncover the pan, raise the heat to high, and boil the pan liquid until it is nearly evaporated. Add 6 cups broth, salt and pepper to taste, and simmer over low heat, covered, for 20 minutes, or until the vegetables are very tender.

LET the mixture cool slightly. Working in batches, puree about half of the vegetables together with the lemon zest, parsley, dill, and mint in a food processor or blender under fairly smooth.

RETURN the puree to the pan. If desired, thin the soup with the remaining broth.

MAKE the matzoh balls: combine the yolks with the onion, chives, dill, 1½ teaspoons salt, and pepper to taste, and beat very well until thickened. In a separate bowl, using clean beaters, beat the egg whites with a pinch of salt until stiff. Gently fold the whites into the yolk mixture until well combined. Sprinkle with the matzoh meal and gently mix until completely blended in. Let rest 10 to 15 minutes.

BRING a large, wide lidded saucepan of well-salted water to a boil. Lightly form the mixture into walnut-size balls. (A light touch is essential here—perfectly formed, compact little balls will result in dense, heavier matzoh balls.) Place the balls on a platter.

SLIDE the balls one by one into the water. Avoid crowding the pot—if necessary, cook the matzoh balls in two batches. Cover the pot tightly and reduce the temperature to a slow boil. Cook without removing the cover for 20 minutes. (They need the steam to fluff up properly, and removing the cover will dissipate some of the steam, causing deflation.)

REMOVE the balls with a skimmer or a slotted spoon, draining off excess water. Place the balls in the soup or set aside, covered with a little broth, until you are ready to use them.

TO serve the soup: if the matzoh balls need warming, add them to the soup. Reheat the soup gently and adjust seasonings, adding more salt, pepper, or lemon juice as needed.

PLACE two matzoh balls in each shallow bowl, and ladle the hot soup over them. Garnish with additional fresh herbs and serve at once.

SMOKED WHITEFISH GEFILTE FISH WITH LEMON-HORSERADISH SAUCE

yield: ABOUT 24 FISH DUMPLINGS

This unusual recipe, combining smoked whitefish with a mild fillet like flounder, is from a seder meal I devised for Bon Appétit *magazine. It's much quicker to prepare than traditional gefilte fish because the delicate dumplings are steamed between cabbage leaves to keep them moist, not poached in fish broth. Leftovers can be refrigerated for a few days.*

A reader who prepared the recipe wrote: "I made these for Passover for my husband's family. They were so delicious that I made them for my family for Easter Sunday! The fishcakes are light and tasty and the horseradish sauce is to die for! I very rarely give 4 forks to a recipe but this one really deserves it—it is an excellent dish."

FOR THE FISH

Kosher salt

³⁄₄ cup scraped and thinly sliced carrots

¹⁄₄ cup matzoh meal

2 tablespoons mild olive oil

1 cup chopped onion

Freshly ground pepper

1 cup trimmed and chopped scallions, white and light green parts only (about 6 medium scallions)

4 large eggs

1 tablespoon fresh lemon juice

1¹⁄₂ pounds mild white-fleshed fish fillets (such as sole or flounder), skin and any bones removed and discarded, cut into 1-inch pieces

PREPARE the fish: bring 1 cup lightly salted water to boil in a small saucepan. Add the carrots and simmer until very tender, about 8 minutes. Drain, reserving ¹⁄₂ cup cooking water in a small bowl. Stir the matzoh meal into the reserved cooking water; let stand 10 minutes to soften and absorb liquid. Put the carrots in a food processor.

WARM the oil in a heavy medium skillet over medium-low heat. Add the onion, salt and pepper lightly, and sauté until soft and shiny, about 8 minutes. Add the scallions and stir 1 minute. Transfer the onion mixture to the food processor. Add the matzoh meal mixture and puree until everything is smooth.

USING an electric mixer, beat 3 of the eggs and the lemon juice in a large bowl until foamy and slightly thickened, about 4 minutes. Stir in the mixture from the food processor, but don't clean the processor yet.

PUT the fish fillets, smoked fish, about 1 teaspoon salt (or to taste), and about ¹⁄₄ teaspoon pepper in the food processor. Using on-off turns, chop until fine. Add the remaining egg and pulse to a coarse paste. Transfer the fish mixture to the bowl and combine thoroughly. Cover and refrigerate until very cold, at least 2 hours.

LINE a large baking sheet with waxed paper. Wetting your hands with cold water, if necessary, form the mixture into ovals, using about ¹⁄₄ cup

2 cups smoked whitefish, carefully removed from the bones of a 2 to 2¹/₂ pound fish

1 large cabbage, separated into leaves and rinsed (these are discarded before serving, so you can use slightly imperfect or dark green outer leaves)

FOR THE LEMON-HORSERADISH SAUCE

2 garlic cloves, peeled

¹/₄ cup plus 2 teaspoons prepared white horseradish

3 tablespoons fresh lemon juice

1¹/₂ cups mayonnaise

Soft lettuce, endive, or radicchio leaves, for lining the plates

for each. Place on the prepared baking sheet. Cover with waxed paper and chill while preparing the cabbage and steamer.

IN a large, wide pot with a tight-fitting lid, place a rack that stands about 2 inches high (if you don't have a vegetable steamer, a round cake rack works well; if the rack is not high enough, set it over two custard cups or empty tuna cans). Fill the pot with enough water to meet, but not cover, the bottom of the rack. Line the rack with a layer of cabbage leaves. Arrange 8 fish ovals in a single layer on the cabbage leaves; cover the fish with another layer of leaves. Bring the water in the pot to a boil. Cover the pot and steam the fish over medium heat until cooked through at center and firm to the touch, about 25 minutes. Transfer top layer of cabbage leaves to a platter. Top with the cooked fish ovals. Cover them with the bottom cabbage leaves. Steam the remaining fish ovals in additional cabbage leaves in 2 more batches, adding more water to the pot if needed. Let the cooked gefilte fish cool to room temperature. Keeping the fish covered with the cooked cabbage leaves so it will remain moist, wrap the whole platter with plastic wrap, and refrigerate until cold, at least 6 hours. (Can be prepared about 2 days ahead. Keep refrigerated.)

PREPARE the sauce: put the garlic through a press, or mince it fine, and place in a small bowl. Stir in the horseradish and lemon juice. Whisk in the mayonnaise. Season to taste with salt and pepper. Cover and set aside, refrigerated, at least 30 minutes before serving. (Can be prepared one day ahead; keep refrigerated.)

TO serve: for best flavor, serve the fish chilled, but not icy cold. Remove the fish from the cabbage leaves and arrange attractively on platters or individual plates lined with lettuce, endive, or radicchio. Accompany with lemon-horseradish sauce.

SALMON GEFILTE FISH POACHED IN FENNEL-WINE BROTH WITH GINGER-BEET HORSERADISH

yield: ABOUT 8 SERVINGS

*P*reparing gefilte fish from scratch no longer seems so daunting, with food processors and the wide availability of a variety of gleaming fresh fish fillets besides the noble triad of carp, pike, and whitefish.

Except for the broth. That still requires real commitment.

You'll need bones, of course, so you will have to befriend a fishmonger who will remember to save the trimmings. If you don't have a high-tech air filtration system, you can resign yourself to a kitchen (and perhaps living and bedrooms too) smelling for several days like old Marseilles without the charms of Panisse and Marius. Not to mention constantly skimming all that fish foam.

Which is why I sometimes prefer to use a simple but intensely flavored vegetable stock made of wine and aromatic vegetables like fennel that complement the fish beautifully.

Forget the fish jelly though: no bones, no gelatin. I don't miss it—it always seemed kind of a food oxymoron anyway. But the broth is delicious, and if enough is leftover, use it to slow-braise potatoes for an intriguing accompaniment to simple grilled or poached fish. Oded Schwartz calls the recipe "fish potatoes" in his book, In Search of Plenty: cover quartered peeled potatoes with the broth, add knobs of butter, and season with salt and pepper. Bring to a boil, then simmer slowly until most of the liquid is evaporated and the potatoes are brown and fragrant. Serve hot with sour cream.

FOR THE FENNEL-WINE BROTH

3 cups coarsely chopped onion

1 1/2 cups scraped and coarsely chopped carrots

2 tablespoons mild olive or avocado oil

1 small fennel bulb, coarsely chopped (include stalks and some of the fennel fronds)

1 parsnip, peeled and coarsely chopped (optional)

3 garlic cloves, peeled

Salt

3 cups dry white wine

PREPARE the broth: in a large, wide, heavy saucepan or 5- to 6-quart Dutch oven, sauté the onions and carrots in the oil over medium heat until the onions are softened and the carrots are tender, about 15 minutes. Using a slotted spoon, transfer about half the mixture to a food processor and let cool (you'll be using it later for the fish balls). To the saucepan, add the fennel, parsnips, if using, and the garlic. Mix well and cook over medium-high heat for 5 minutes, stirring, until the vegetables begin to wilt and soften. Add salt to taste and 1 cup of the wine, cover the pan, and let sweat gently for 10 minutes. Stir occasionally to prevent sticking. Add the remaining 2 cups wine, 5 cups water, the peppercorns, fennel seeds, if using, bay leaf, and parsley. Bring to a boil and simmer

1 teaspoon peppercorns

1 teaspoon fennel seeds, crushed (optional)

1 Turkish bay leaf

1/2 cup coarsely chopped fresh parsley leaves and stems

FOR THE FISH

1½ pounds salmon fillets, skin and any bones removed and discarded, fish cut into 1-inch pieces

1/2 pound sole, flounder or any other soft white fish fillets, skin and any bones removed and discarded, fish cut into 1-inch pieces,

2 large garlic cloves, peeled

Sautéed onion and carrot reserved from preparing the broth

2 large eggs

1 tablespoon fresh lemon juice

1½ teaspoons salt

1/8 teaspoon freshly ground black pepper

1/8 teaspoon ground cinnamon

3 tablespoons finely ground blanched almonds

FOR THE GINGER-BEET HORSERADISH

About 1 tablespoon peeled and finely grated fresh ginger

1 cup prepared beet horseradish

Soft lettuce, endive, or radicchio leaves, for lining the plates

for about 45 minutes. Taste and adjust the seasoning. If the broth seems weak, raise the heat to high and boil briefly to concentrate the flavors. Cool slightly, then strain the broth through a fine-mesh strainer, pushing down on the solids to extract all the flavorful juices. Discard the solids. Rinse out the pan and return the strained broth to it.

MAKE the fish balls: add the salmon, sole, and garlic cloves to the onions and carrots in the food processor. Chop fine, using the pulse motion, but don't puree. Put the mixture in a chopping bowl or on a chopping board. Using a hand-chopper or cleaver, work in the eggs, lemon juice, salt, pepper, and cinnamon. (Hand-chopping at this point incorporates air into the mixture, making it lighter and fluffier than pulsing in the food processor.) Stir in the ground almonds.

IT'S a good idea to do a test for seasoning. Poach a teaspoon of the fish mixture in lightly salted boiling water for a few minutes. Taste, and if needed, add additional salt and pepper. Refrigerate the fish, covered, for at least 1 and up to 4 hours. (This step makes it easier to mold and results in fluffier fish balls.)

PREPARE the ginger-beet horseradish: stir the ginger into the horseradish, adding more or less according to preference. Cover and let stand for at least 30 minutes to allow the flavors to meld.

BRING the strained broth to a gentle boil. Wetting your hands with cold water, if necessary, form the fish mixture into 16 ovals, using about ¼ cup for each. As you form them, place the ovals on a platter lined with wax paper. Carefully slip the fish ovals into the broth and reduce the heat to a simmer. If the fish is not completely covered by the broth, baste with several spoonfuls of the broth. Cover the pot, and poach the fish ovals for about 20 minutes, until an inserted toothpick tests clean and the ovals are completely cooked through at the center. Remove the pot from the heat and let the fish cool in the broth. For maximum flavor, cover and chill in the broth overnight or preferably for 24 hours.

TO serve, line platters or individual plates with lettuce, endive, or radicchio. Arrange two ovals of the chilled, drained fish attractively on top and accompany with the ginger-beet horseradish.

SLOW-ROASTED SALMON WITH GREEN HERB OIL AND BEET-HORSERADISH RELISH

yield: ABOUT 8 APPETIZER SERVINGS

This deconstructed, quick and simple stand-in for traditional gefilte fish with horseradish has all the familiar flavors but none of the heavy lifting of the original. It's a fabulous splurge with wild salmon, but high-quality farm-raised salmon substitutes nicely.

Fresh salmon is cut into serving slices and very slowly roasted, emerging melt-in-the-mouth silky and perfectly cooked throughout. Keep this in your recipe files for an effortless first course or main dish throughout the year, excellent warm or at room temperature, paired with sauces from aioli to green olive or spicy fresh tomato.

The easy herb oil brings the sweet, buttery fish to life without overwhelming it. More an accompaniment than a sauce, the flavorful relish is meant to be served in copious portions. And unlike the classic jarred beet horseradish, even children can enjoy it.

FOR THE RELISH

6 medium beets (about 1½ pounds, trimmed)

2 cups coarsely chopped red onions

About ¼ cup capers, rinsed and drained

About 3 tablespoons jarred white horseradish

3 tablespoons packed fresh flat-leaf parsley

3 tablespoons packed fresh dill

¼ cup best-quality extra virgin olive oil

About 2 tablespoons balsamic vinegar

Kosher salt and freshly ground black pepper

START the relish: preheat the oven to 350°F. Trim any greens (save and cook like spinach or chard) and the root ends from the beets. Scrub the beets well, but don't peel or dry them off. Tightly wrap each beet in foil, place on a baking sheet, and bake until tender, 1½ to 2 hours (if they are very large). Carefully remove the foil and set aside until cool enough to handle. Slip the peels off and cut the beets into large chunks.

COMBINE the beets in a food processor with the red onion, capers, horseradish, parsley, and dill, and pulse until chopped fine, but not pureed. Transfer the relish to a bowl and toss with the olive oil, vinegar, salt, and pepper. Taste and add more capers, horseradish, vinegar, or seasoning, if you like. The onion may taste somewhat sharp at first but will mellow nicely as all the flavors unfold and mingle. Cover and refrigerate for at least 1 hour before serving.

MAKE the herb oil. Combine the chives, dill, about ¾ of the oil, and a generous pinch of salt in a blender. Blend on high, stopping to stir down as needed, until roughly pureed. Remove the blender cap and with the machine on, drizzle in the remaining oil. Continue processing until you have a smooth puree. Scrape the puree into a bowl, stir in the horseradish and salt to taste. Cover and set aside to let the flavors mingle.

FOR THE HERB OIL

³/₄ cup packed snipped fresh chives

¹/₄ cup packed snipped fresh dill

¹/₂ cup grapeseed, avocado, or other flavorless oil

Salt

1 teaspoon jarred white horseradish

FOR THE SALMON

2 pounds fresh salmon fillet, skin on, any pinbones removed with a tweezer

About ¹/₄ cup extra virgin olive oil

2 teaspoons smoked paprika

Coarse salt and freshly ground black pepper

¹/₂ cup dill leaves or a mixture of dill and chives, plus additional dill leaves for garnish

PREPARE the fish: preheat the oven to 250°F. Cut the salmon crosswise into 8 equal slices and bring the fish to room temperature. Choose a shallow roasting pan large enough to accommodate the salmon slices in a single layer, and smear it with some of the oil.

COAT the fish on both sides with the oil. Stir together the paprika, salt and pepper to taste and massage into the flesh. Place the fish skin side down in the pan and scatter the herbs on top.

SLOW-ROAST the salmon. The exact cooking time will vary according to your taste and the thickness of the fish. For a seder, I prefer to serve it medium, cooked about 25 minutes: just cooked through, showing the slightest bit of translucence at the thickest part, the skin easily peeled off. Even when completely cooked through, the salmon will look rare, since it will still be brightly colored throughout. The buttery flesh will not flake as you are used to, but instead will gently separate into layers when you poke it.

TO serve, pull off and discard the salmon skin and brush away the herbs. Use a spatula to slide each salmon slice onto a plate, sprinkle with a little coarse salt, and drizzle with the herb oil. Scoop a large dollop of the relish alongside and garnish with dill leaves. Pass the remaining herb oil separately.

COOK'S NOTE: You can prepare the relish about 2 days ahead, without loss of flavor.

Leftover herb oil is wonderful stirred into mashed potatoes, soups, mayonnaise, and vinaigrettes, or stippled on fish, chicken, or vegetables.

FISH IN TOMATO, RHUBARB, AND BLOOD-ORANGE SAUCE

yield: 6 TO 8 APPETIZER OR MAIN COURSE SERVINGS

*T*omato's unexpected coupling with puckery rhubarb blossoms into a delightful marriage of flavors here. Worlds apart from the flat tomato-based sweet-and-sour foods I loathed growing up, this Sephardi fish classic sparkles with a cool, clean tang. I add just a bit of honey, relying more on caramelized onions, bright blood oranges, and the sweet heat of fresh ginger for the subtle but complex sweetening needed to tease the ingredients together seamlessly.

I steam or poach the fish separately, rather than cooking it directly in the sauce as many recipes suggest, because the liquid it exudes makes the fish too watery.

Flavored with early spring rhubarb, Greek and Turkish Jews often serve this as a fish entree at their seders. But it is equally fine as a refreshing main course, at room temperature or chilled—especially when the weather grows warm, and delicious hot as well.

Because the flavors of the sauce demand time to fully develop, this is an excellent choice for make-ahead schedules. You can prepare the sauce up to three days ahead, and cook the fish just before serving (plan on extra time for cooling/chilling the fish if you are not serving it warm). Or make the fish when you prepare the sauce, and chill it, covered with sauce, until serving.

FOR THE SAUCE

3 medium blood oranges (if not available, substitute 2 large, juicy navel oranges)

2 tablespoons olive oil

2 cups finely chopped onion

1½ teaspoons fresh ginger, peeled and finely minced

About 1 tablespoon orange blossom or other light floral honey

Salt and freshly ground black pepper

START the sauce: with a vegetable peeler, remove a long strip of zest from one of the oranges. Put it in a small saucepan with water to cover, and bring to a boil. Drain, rinse, and pat it dry. Mince the zest fine. Peel two of the blood oranges (or 1½ of the navel oranges), removing all of the bitter white pith and any seeds. Slice the oranges into chunks using a serrated knife. Set the blanched orange zest and chunks aside. (You will be using the remaining orange to garnish the finished dish.)

IN a 10-inch heavy skillet, warm the oil over moderate heat. Add the onions, and cook, stirring, for 5 minutes until they are shiny and lightly softened. Add the minced orange zest, ginger, and 1 teaspoon of the honey. Sprinkle lightly with salt and pepper. Continue cooking over low heat, stirring occasionally, until the onions are pale gold and very soft and sweet, 15 to 20 minutes.

1 pound rhubarb, ends trimmed (discard leaves; they can be toxic), tough strings removed with a vegetable peeler, and stalks cut into 1-inch pieces (4 cups)

1 cup fresh orange juice

Generous pinch of ground cinnamon

2 cups canned, peeled plum tomatoes (about 1 pound), coarsely chopped, and ½ cup of their liquid

Juice of ½ lemon

FOR THE FISH

3 pounds fish fillets or steaks (choose salmon or white-fleshed fish such as red snapper, grouper, sea bass, halibut, cod, lemon or grey sole)

If steaming the fish: mild lettuce or cabbage leaves

⅓ to ½ cup finely minced fresh mint leaves, for garnish

WHILE the onions are cooking, combine the rhubarb, ½ cup of the orange juice, the remaining 2 teaspoons of honey, the cinnamon, and a pinch of salt in a medium saucepan. Bring the mixture to a boil, then simmer, stirring occasionally, until the rhubarb is very tender, 6 to 8 minutes.

WHEN the onions are ready, add the remaining ½ cup orange juice to the skillet and boil the mixture, stirring and scraping it so it does not burn, for 3 to 4 minutes, until the liquid evaporates and the onions are deep golden. Stir in the tomatoes and their liquid, and cook over moderately high heat until they break up, about 10 minutes. Add the rhubarb mixture to the sauce, and cook over moderate heat for 5 minutes. Add the reserved orange chunks and simmer for 5 to 7 minutes, until the sauce is thickened and the flavors well blended. Season to taste with salt and pepper and some of the lemon juice. Taste again and, if needed, add additional honey or lemon juice until you reach your perfect sweet-and-sour balance.

LET the sauce cool to room temperature, then cover and refrigerate it for at least 12 hours or up to three days to blend the flavors.

TO poach the fish: in a deep, lidded skillet or sauté pan large enough to hold the fish in a single layer (if preparing several thin fillets, you will probably need to cook them in batches), bring 3 inches of water and salt and pepper to taste to a boil. Reduce the heat to a bare simmer, lower the fish into the water, and cover the pan. Poach until the fish is just cooked through, 6 to 12 minutes, depending on the variety and thickness of the fish.

TO steam the fish: in a heavy, large, wide pot, such as a 5- to 6-quart Dutch oven, add water to a depth of 1½ to 2 inches. Arrange a rack in the pan that stands at least 1 inch above the water. (If your rack's legs are not high enough, set it over 2 custard cups or empty tuna cans.) Bring the water to a boil. Line the rack with a layer of mild lettuce (iceberg or Boston, for example) or cabbage leaves, then place the fish on top in a single layer (if cooking thin fillets, you will probably have to steam the fish in batches). The leaf "bed" for the fish gentles the steam and prevents the cooked fish from falling through the rack as you lift it out. Reduce the heat to medium, cover the pot, and steam until the fish is just cooked through, 6 to 12 minutes, depending on the variety and thickness of the fish.

TO test the fish for doneness, insert a thin-bladed knife in the thickest part. The fish should be opaque or show a slight bit of translucence, according to your preference.

REMOVE the fish to paper toweling or a clean kitchen towel (unscented by detergent) to drain, then carefully transfer it to a serving platter. Peel off any skin on the fish. You can serve the fish at room temperature, chilled (but not icy cold), or warm. If not serving the fish warm, cool it to room temperature, and, if desired, cover and chill it until cold. Blot up any liquid the fish may have thrown off. Spoon a generous amount of the sauce over the fish, reserving the rest.

OR prepare the fish ahead when you make the sauce. Follow the above directions for cooking, cooling, and saucing the fish. Cover and chill the fish for at least 12 hours and up to 2 days. Serve the fish at room temperature, chilled (but not icy cold), or reheat it gently and serve it warm.

JUST before serving, blot up any additional liquid exuded by the fish. Cut the remaining orange into very thin slices. Tuck the slices around the fish and sprinkle lavishly with the chopped mint. Pass a sauce boat with the remaining sauce (heated through, if serving the fish warm).

COOK'S NOTE: The leftover sauce is also wonderful with poached or grilled chicken.

SNAPPER FILLETS IN PISTACHIO-MATZOH CRUST

yield: 4 TO 6 SERVINGS

Jacob never guessed that his gift for the "man," Pharaoh's governor, was in fact destined for none other than his own son Joseph, he of technicolor-coat fame. But he was sure it—and a double measure of money—would please.

Pistachios always taste like a treat. I find them more addictive than potato chips when eaten out of hand, and I keep a supply of the pale green nuts in the freezer to glamorize savory foods and desserts. They give more than mere crunch—pistachios have an exotic, almost flowery-sweet taste, suggesting, as Waverly Root has pointed out, a spice more than a nut. Toasted pistachio nuts give a delightful buttery finish to this matzoh crumb crust and point up the richness of the sour cream topping, so that it only needs to be lightly slathered on the fish.

Simple but delicious, this comes together very quickly.

"Take of the best fruits of the land in your vessels, and carry down the man a present, a little balm, and a little honey, spices and myrrh, pistachios and almonds."

—GENESIS 43:11

¼ cup shelled unsalted pistachios

2 tablespoons unsalted butter, plus additional butter (or oil) for greasing the pan

½ cup coarsely ground matzoh crumbs (egg matzohs are excellent for this, if you use them during Passover; see page 24) or matzoh meal

Salt and freshly ground black pepper

PREHEAT oven to 375°F. Spread the pistachios on a foil-lined baking sheet and toast until fragrant, 8 to 10 minutes, shaking the pan from time to time. Toast the matzoh crumbs or matzoh meal at the same time: melt the butter in a small baking dish in the oven; add the matzoh crumbs or meal, season with salt and pepper, and stir well. Bake, stirring occasionally, until golden, about 10 minutes.

REMOVE the pistachios from the oven and let cool slightly. Chop the nuts coarsely by hand or with a few pulses in food processor. Combine the pistachios with the toasted matzoh crumbs or meal. Raise the oven temperature to 400°F.

IN a small bowl, whisk together the sour cream, onion, lemon zest, and/ or horseradish. Lightly grease a baking pan large enough to accommo-

3 tablespoons sour cream

2 tablespoons grated onion

2 teaspoons grated lemon zest and/or—for a sassy seasoning with just a bit of heat—1½ teaspoons prepared white horseradish, drained

1¾ to 2 pounds red snapper fillets or other nonoily white-fleshed fish fillets

Accompaniment: lemon wedges

date the fish in one layer. Sprinkle the fish on both sides with salt and pepper and place in the prepared pan. Spread the sour cream mixture evenly over the fish and top with the pistachio-matzoh crumbs. Bake just until the fish is opaque throughout, 10 to 15 minutes, depending on the thickness of the fish. Serve with lemon wedges.

VERONESE ROLLED TURKEY LOAF (*POLPETTONE*)

yield: 8 TO 10 SERVINGS

*L*ike its poor relation, the Ashkenazi helzel (a goose neck filled with fat, flour, and scraps of meat), this refined loaf of boned and rolled turkey (similar to a ballotine) relies on gentle cooking within a pouch sewn of poultry skin to keep the contents moist and succulent.

A favorite for holiday meals, variations of this polpettone are found throughout the Jewish communities of Italy, some calling for additions of ground veal or pistachios, some grinding the turkey instead of cubing it. This version comes from Ester Silvana Israel of Verona, who has gathered the recipes of the city's elderly Jews. It is often featured on Passover menus, surrounded by the Italian spring trio of purple artichokes, mushrooms, and baby peas.

A wonderful alternative to turkey roasted on the bone (many Orthodox and Conservative Jews refrain from eating roast meats at the seder meals), polpettone, bathed in broth and served at room temperature, remains moist and flavorful even during the longest seder.

To make the loaf, the turkey skin is removed, sewn into a neat pouch, and stuffed with cubes of the meat. Although it looks daunting, it is time-consuming rather than difficult. The trickiest task is taking off the skin as nearly intact as possible. Turkey skin is much stronger and more elastic than chicken skin, but you must work carefully and patiently to avoid tearing it.

1 half turkey, skin intact (7 to 10 pounds)

3 or 4 eggs (use 3 if turkey is around 7 pounds, 4 if it weighs closer to 10), beaten

3 or 4 large garlic cloves, finely minced

½ teaspoon ground allspice

Salt and freshly ground black pepper

8 to 10 cups chicken broth, preferably homemade (see pages 62 and 70), or good-quality, low-sodium purchased

REMOVE and discard the clumps of fat around the neck and tail openings. Starting at the neck end, slowly work your hands under the skin, gently easing it away from the flesh. Move your hands all the way down the leg, then, using a small, sharp knife, cut the skin carefully away from the base of the leg. Now slip the skin off the leg, like pulling a sleeve over the turkey's wrist. It's very difficult to cut around the wingtip in the same way, so instead, cut a circle around the shoulder area, and slip the skin down and off the wing. You'll have a big hole there, but you'll patch it up when sewing the pouch. When you have separated all the skin from the body, gently take off whatever excess fat can be removed easily without damaging the skin. Rinse the skin inside and out and pat it dry.

THREAD a large embroidery needle with strong white cotton thread or dental floss, and using an overcast or loop stitch, sew a few stitches to close up the base of the leg, then sew up the hole left from the wing. Fold the skin in half to make a rectangle. Sew the base and outer edge

1 large onion, peeled and quartered

3 large carrots, scraped and quartered

2 celery stalks, including leaves, coarsely chopped

Optional accompaniment: Green Olive Sauce (page 305; substitute 2 teaspoons mayonnaise for the mustard), or mayonnaise diluted with some of the cooking broth

closed. You should have a neat pocket, open only at the top. (The first time I made this, I was wondering where I would get more skin: surely this would never hold all that turkey flesh. But it stretches quite a bit and is very resilient, so you will be able to fit all the meat into it quite easily.)

SET the skin aside while you cut all the meat—white and dark—from the turkey carcass and cube it. Cut away the tendons and discard. Include a small amount of turkey fat to help keep the loaf moist. Place the cubed meat in a bowl and stir in the eggs, garlic, allspice, and salt and pepper to taste.

STUFF the pouch with the meat mixture. Gently push the meat down into the pouch so you have enough room. Using the embroidery needle in an overcast stitch again, sew the top of the pouch closed. Rinse a clean, thin kitchen towel (that has been washed in unscented laundry detergent) or double layer of cheesecloth in cold water and squeeze it out. (I use inexpensive extra-large men's cotton handkerchiefs—they don't shred like cheesecloth and they can be washed and reused.) Place the pouch in the towel or cloth and roll up very tightly. Tie the cloth securely closed in several places: at both ends, in the middle, and between the middle and the ends.

PUT 8 cups of broth in a heavy saucepan large enough to accommodate the filled pouch. Add the onions, carrots, and celery and simmer for 10 minutes. Reduce the heat to a slow simmer and add the turkey pouch. If necessary, add more broth so the pouch is covered. Simmer, covered, for 1½ hours.

REMOVE the pot from the heat. Leave the turkey loaf in the pot, and weight it down with several heatproof plates or one plate with a large weight placed on top. Let cool under the weights until it reaches room temperature. Remove the weights and the cloth covering, and slice the loaf. (If it crumbles, it will still taste delicious.) Moisten each slice with several spoonfuls of the broth. Reduce some of the remaining broth over high heat and spoon over the turkey as sauce before serving. The turkey will be very flavorful, but it will need the broth to stay moist. It's a good idea to keep any leftover loaf submerged under lots of broth.

IF you want to serve the loaf warm, let it firm up at room temperature first, then reheat it slowly in the broth.

FOR a more elaborate sauce, serve with Green Olive Sauce or some mayonnaise thinned with a little broth.

COOK'S NOTE: Here is my favorite way to eat this, especially leftovers: simmer lots of chopped Swiss chard, spinach, or even broccoli rabe in some of the broth and spoon the mixture over slices of the turkey loaf arranged in a soup bowl. Then stir a little mayonnaise—or, if you have it on hand, a few spoons of pureed artichoke—into the broth to enrich the sauce. Scrumptious.

Artichoke puree is available jarred in many specialty stores or prepare your own by pureeing jarred artichoke hearts drained of oil (avoid those packed in strong marinade). Or puree cooked, frozen artichoke hearts with a little extra virgin olive oil and season to taste. Artichoke puree, also called artichoke paste, makes a superb substitute for cream or butter when you need to enrich or smooth out a meat or poultry sauce.

PASSOVER IN PARIS

I walked through the open-air market, filling my bags with the new spring garlic, brilliant vegetables, fresh-caught fish, and fragrant herbs. Preparing for Passover seders takes a long time; in our case, it was several years. And the place was Paris.

Our daughter Alex was spending her college junior year there. Since her schedule would not permit her to come home for the holiday, we decided to celebrate our seders in Paris with her.

The location would not be the only first for us: my husband Howard and I had never hosted our own seder before. For years, we have spent the first seder with my sister and her family and the second with my husband's sister's family. And while we cook for my sister's seder and contribute to the service at my sister-in-law's, we had never led one of our own.

It became a game we played every year: what would we include in our seder? We compiled booklists for creating personal seders and downloaded provocative Haggadahs from the Web. We stuffed folders with names of songs and ideas for rituals we would add.

But in the end, Passovers are made of family memories, and we were too close to our own families to enjoy seders without them. There was no way we could break with tradition and go off on our own.

Until now.

We packed the ceremonial items and rented an apartment with a good kitchen and a large dining room in an area we knew well from past visits.

I once read that a guest at a holiday table is a gift for the family because then the family looks at all the traditions, listens to the songs and the stories as if for the first time. Our service would include not only Alex, but her boyfriend, and Emily, a very close family friend also in Paris for her junior year, perhaps a few students from Alex's theater classes and relatives of stateside friends too.

We revisited and revised each section of the Hagaddah in the service we created and wove in poems, personal stories, and a profusion of songs, from "Dayenu" to "Go Down Moses" (with all song lyrics printed out), that would make the celebration not just interactive but authentically shared as well.

The day before the seder, we went to buy a brisket in the old Jewish quarter around the rue des Rosiers and came away with a renewed affection for Gallic-Jewish warmth.

As we waited for the meat in the tiny shop, M. Michel Kalifa, the Moroccan butcher, brought out wine in real wineglasses. The couple ahead of us, jewelers from the posh sixteenth arrondissement, were buying kilos of house-made cured meats for pre-seder hors d'oeuvre, and Michel insisted that we taste them, comparing the beef to the goose, and those studded with pistachios and without.

Then he placed little china plates heaped with just-cooked chicken on the tall glass display cases of meat. With surgeon's skill, he e bones in a few deft strokes. One chicken was prepared with olives, the other with both olives and preserved lemons. "Lequel préférez-vous?" he wanted to know. But we couldn't choose a favorite—both were perfectly succulent.

Michel explained that only thighs and legs, bone in, stay moist—especially important at seders when food must wait out the predinner service. "Forget the bland and dry boneless chicken breasts that most Americans use," he winked. His Moroccan chicken was the perfect complement, we decided, to our traditional Brisket Braised with Thirty-Six Cloves of Garlic.

And whether it was Paris or just the late-April date of that year's holiday, I have never cooked for a seder with such intensely flavored produce. Deeply perfumed raspberries, blood oranges, and rhubarb bursting with taste made my staple spring compote a real standout.

We began the service by blessing the children. But as the seder unfolded, we felt blessed as well.

CHICKEN WITH OLIVES AND PRESERVED LEMON

yield: 6 TO 8 SERVINGS

For us, this moist, beautifully flavored chicken will always be the taste of Passover in Paris. A recipe for preserved lemons follows, if you need to prepare your own kosher-for-Passover version; start it about one week before the holiday.

Generous pinch of saffron threads

5 or 6 large garlic cloves, coarsely chopped

About 5 tablespoons olive oil

Salt and freshly ground black pepper

1 teaspoon sweet paprika, smoked or regular

1 teaspoon ground cumin, preferably freshly toasted and ground

About 5 pounds skinless, bone-in chicken thighs and/or legs, all visible fat and gristle removed

2 cups grated onions (to make, peel, and quarter about 4 medium onions and pulse in a food processor)

2 cups chicken broth, preferably homemade (see pages 62 and 70), or good quality, low-sodium purchased

1 cup good, brine-cured olives, rinsed, pitted, and coarsely chopped (choose green olives or ripe purple-brown ones, such as Kalamatas, Gaetas, or Alphonsos)

PREPARE the marinade: crumble the saffron between your fingers into a small bowl. Stir in 2 tablespoons hot water and let soak for 10 minutes.

COMBINE the garlic, 2 tablespoons olive oil, about 1 teaspoon salt and ¾ teaspoon pepper (or to taste), the paprika, and cumin in a food processor, and pulse to chop well. Add the saffron water and process until pasty.

PLACE the chicken in a large, heavy resealable plastic bag, and spoon the marinade over. Shake the bag until all the pieces are bathing in the marinade. Seal the bag and refrigerate for at least 4 hours, or preferably overnight, occasionally shaking the bag or moving the pieces around to ensure the marinade is evenly distributed over all surfaces of the chicken.

BRING the chicken to room temperature. Preheat the oven to 300°F.

SCRAPE the marinade off the chicken and reserve it. Heat a large, wide Dutch oven or other heavy, ovenproof lidded casserole over medium-high heat. Swirl in 3 tablespoons olive oil and heat until shimmering. Add the chicken pieces (in batches, using additional oil, if necessary), and sauté until golden-brown on both sides. Transfer the chicken to a platter.

DISCARD any oil remaining in the pan. Add the onions and broth, raise the heat to high and bring to a boil, scraping up all the browned bits with a wooden spoon. Stir in the reserved marinade and reduce the heat to low. Return the chicken pieces to the pan and turn them around in the pan sauce. Fit a piece of foil over the chicken, then cover the pan tightly with the lid.

BRAISE the chicken in the oven for 45 minutes to 1 hour, until tender and cooked through, turning the pieces two or three times in the pan sauce as they braise.

The peel of 2 preserved lemons, finely chopped (recipe follows)

About 3 tablespoons fresh lemon juice

⅓ cup chopped fresh cilantro or parsley, plus additional for garnish

REMOVE the chicken to a platter and tent with foil to keep warm. Boil the pan sauce over high heat, uncovered, until reduced to about 1½ cups. Stir in the olives and preserved lemon peel, and simmer the sauce on top of the stove, stirring, for 5 minutes. Add the lemon juice, cilantro or parsley, and salt and pepper to taste, and combine well. Return the chicken to the pan and cook briefly until heated through. Taste again and adjust the seasoning or lemon juice as needed.

ARRANGE the chicken on a serving platter surrounded by the olives. Spoon the sauce generously over all and garnish with the herbs. Pass any remaining sauce separately.

PRESERVED LEMONS

yield: **6 PRESERVED LEMONS**

These lemons will take about one week to cure, so plan ahead accordingly. If at all possible, do try to find organic fruit for this recipe, since it is the peel, not the flesh of the lemon that you will be eating. Most commercially grown lemons are coated with edible-grade wax to preserve the gloss and color of the rind; be sure to scrub well to remove it. And if you even suspect that you have hangnails or tiny cuts on your fingers, it's a good idea to wear rubber gloves while working with the salt.

You'll find a slew of uses for preserved lemons, in addition to traditional North African tagines and couscous recipes. Some ideas to get you started: tuck slivers of the peel under the skin of a roasting bird or into stuffings; insert a whole preserved lemon in the cavity of roasting poultry or slip chunks inside a grilling fish; add shredded preserved lemon peel to salads composed of beans (lentils, chickpeas, and others), vegetables (such as potato, roasted eggplant, red pepper, or beet), or grains (like tabouleh); stir finely chopped preserved lemon peel into mayonnaise or sandwich spreads.

And don't discard the tart, salty juice produced during the preserving. It's excellent in vinaigrettes and fish sauces—just remember that it is quite salty, so a little goes a long way.

6 medium lemons, preferably organic

About ½ cup coarse kosher salt

1 to 1½ cups fresh lemon juice

REMOVE any stickers from the lemons and wash the fruit well. If the lemons are coated with wax, scrub it off using a vegetable brush or a new plastic abrasive (soapless) sponge.

BLANCHING the lemons will begin softening the peel, jump-starting the process. Bring a large pot of water to a rolling boil. Add the lemons and stir them around. Cover the pot and boil the fruit for 2 minutes. Drain and pat thoroughly dry.

CHOOSE a clean, dry wide-mouth glass jar with a plastic lid (metal will corrode), and sprinkle the bottom with 2 tablespoons salt.

PREPARE the lemons one at a time. Trim off any protruding tips from either end. Cut the lemons into quarters (or sixths if large) lengthwise from top to bottom end, but don't cut all the way through—the lemon quarters should still be attached on one end.

WORKING over a bowl, spread each lemon open and slather it generously inside and out with salt. Scoop up any salt that falls into the bowl and repack it onto the lemon. Close up the lemons, then pack them tightly into the jar, pushing them down hard with your hands or a wooden spoon to help release their juices.

ADD enough lemon juice to cover the lemons; if they are not completely submerged, mold may form on the top layer of the fruit.

SPRINKLE the top with about 2 tablespoons salt and close the lid tightly. Shake the jar well to dissolve the salt. Store in a cool (but unrefrigerated), dry place. Turn the jar upside down and shake vigorously everyday to redistribute the salted juice.

THE rind of the lemons should be soft and ready to use in about one week. Dribble a thin layer of oil over the lemons and store the jar in the refrigerator. When using, taste, and if very salty, rinse in cold water before adding to recipes.

THE preserved lemons will keep, refrigerated, for up to 1 year.

LEMON FRIED CHICKEN WITH TART SALAD TOPPING

yield: 4 TO 5 SERVINGS

"*W*hy on this night do we dip twice, and on other nights, we dip only once?" asks the youngest child as part of the Four Questions at the seder, seeking an explanation of the mysteries encoded in the ritual Passover meal.*

And the head of the family answers that on this night we dip bitter herbs into haroset to remind us of the mortar the Jews used to build Pharaoh's cities and the bitterness they suffered. We dip vegetables in salt water or vinegar to commemorate both the joy of spring and the tears of the Jewish slaves.

But when did we dip once? In ancient times, when the diet of the Jews comprised mainly bread—and heavy bread at that, often made from barley or other coarse grains—they dipped the bread in vinegar, onions, or bitter herbs (the maror of the seder plate) to make the leaden starch more palatable and more digestible.

Arugula was then collected wild by the poor. Purslane—a lemony-flavored, small-leafed green currently gracing mesclun salads—and cress were gathered and later cultivated by Jewish farmers. Jews dipped rough bread into the sharp greens or combined them into a sandwich. (In some Haggadahs, Ashkenazi Jews, unfamiliar with this erstwhile Mediterranean custom of dunking, have changed the question to ". . . and on other nights, we dip not at all?")

"Lo, this is the bread of affliction," the Haggadah refers to the matzoh. And after a few days of the coarse, unleavened bread in every guise imaginable, we too, like the ancients, need spring's sharp greens coursing through systems now sluggish and logy.

In this adaptation of a popular Milanese dish, we reenact the dipping one more time: the crisp, matzoh meal-coated chicken is dipped into a salad of tart greens, tomato, and onion.

FOR THE CUTLETS

2 large garlic cloves, peeled and crushed

3 tablespoons fresh lemon juice

¼ cup olive oil, for frying, plus 1 teaspoon

About 1½ teaspoons salt

About ¼ teaspoon freshly ground black pepper

PREPARE the cutlets: in a large bowl, blend together the garlic, lemon juice, 1 teaspoon olive oil, salt, and pepper. Add the chicken, toss to coat thoroughly with the mixture, and refrigerate to marinate, covered, for 1 to 2 hours. Or marinate in a resealable plastic bag. Turn the chicken occasionally in the marinade to ensure even flavoring.

BEAT the eggs well in a wide, shallow bowl or pie pan. Stir together the matzoh meal and lemon zest and spread on a large sheet of wax paper or a plate. Taking one cutlet at a time, dip it into the beaten egg, coating well on both sides. Let the excess egg drip back into the bowl. Dredge

1¾ to 2 pounds skinless, boneless chicken cutlets, trimmed of fat and gristle and pounded lightly to a uniform thickness

2 large eggs

1 cup matzoh meal, seasoned to taste with salt and pepper

1 tablespoon grated lemon zest

FOR THE SALAD

½ pound ripe tomatoes, diced (1 cup)

¾ cup finely chopped onion

2 tablespoons fine-quality extra virgin olive oil

1 tablespoon fresh lemon juice

1 teaspoon dried oregano

Salt and freshly ground black pepper

2 cups sharp salad greens (such as arugula, watercress, endive, radicchio, sorrel, flat-leaf parsley, purslane, or—preferably—a mixture of these), washed, dried, and torn into bite-size pieces

Accompaniment: lemon wedges

the cutlets on both sides in the matzoh meal mixture. To prevent loose crumbs from falling off and burning in the hot oil, pat the cutlets firmly on each side so the matzoh meal adheres, then place them on a rack and let stand for about 15 minutes to set the coating.

HEAT the ¼ cup olive oil in a 10- to 12-inch heavy sauté pan or skillet over medium-high heat until hot, but not smoking. Add the cutlets (in batches, if necessary, to avoid crowding the pan), and sauté them for about 2 minutes on each side, until golden and cooked through.

TRANSFER the cutlets as they are done to a paper towel–lined baking sheet to absorb excess oil, keeping them warm, if necessary, in a 200°F oven, until the rest are done.

PREPARE the salad: in a bowl, combine the tomato, onions, olive oil, lemon juice, oregano, and salt and pepper to taste. Add the greens and toss well.

SERVE the cutlets topped with the salad, accompanied by the lemon wedges.

COOK'S NOTE: Divide the seasoned matzoh meal in half. When the first half becomes ragged with little clumps of egg from dredging the cutlets, replace with the reserved fresh half.

BRAISED BRISKET WITH THIRTY-SIX CLOVES OF GARLIC

yield: 8 GENEROUS SERVINGS

In my take on the French classic, chicken with forty cloves of garlic becomes brisket with thirty-six cloves. All that feisty garlic turns sweet and mellow with gentle braising; when pureed, it forms a seductive gravy, which is finished with a zing of chopped raw garlic and lemon zest.

Why thirty-six cloves? Beginning with aleph, *which equals one, each letter of the Hebrew alphabet stands for a number, and so every word has a numerical value. All multiples of eighteen, the numerical value of the Hebrew word* chai, life, *are considered especially auspicious, which is why donations to charity and wedding and bar mitzvah gifts are often given in multiples of eighteen.*

About 36 fat, unpeeled garlic cloves (1²/₃ to 2 cups) or an equivalent amount of smaller cloves, plus 1 teaspoon minced garlic

3 tablespoons olive oil

A first- or second-cut beef brisket (about 5 pounds), trimmed of excess fat, wiped with a damp paper towel, and patted dry

2 tablespoons red wine vinegar

3 cups chicken broth, preferably homemade (see pages 62 and 70), or good-quality, low-sodium purchased

3 or 4 fresh thyme sprigs, or 2 teaspoons dried leaves

2 fresh rosemary sprigs, plus 1 teaspoon chopped leaves

PREHEAT the oven to 325°F.

DROP the garlic cloves into a small saucepan of boiling water for 30 seconds. Drain immediately. Peel as soon as the garlic is cool enough to handle. Set aside on paper towels to dry.

HEAT the olive oil over medium-high heat in a heavy-bottomed roasting pan or casserole large enough to accommodate the meat in one layer. Use two burners, if necessary. Add the brisket and brown well on both sides, about 10 minutes. Transfer the brisket to a platter and set aside. (Or brown the meat under the broiler: place the brisket, fat side up, on a foil-lined broiler pan under a preheated broiler. Broil for 5 to 6 minutes on each side, until browned. Don't allow it to develop a hard, dark crust, which might make the meat tough or bitter. Move the meat around as necessary, so it sears evenly.)

POUR off all but about 1 tablespoon of fat remaining in the pan and add the garlic cloves. Cook over medium heat, stirring occasionally, until the garlic edges are tinged with gold. Add the vinegar and deglaze the pan, scraping up all the browned bits from the bottom with a wooden spoon. Add the stock, thyme, and rosemary sprigs, and reduce the heat to a simmer. Salt and pepper the brisket to taste on all sides, and add it to the pan, fat side up. Spoon the garlic cloves over the meat.

Salt and freshly ground black pepper

1 teaspoon grated lemon zest

PLACE the brisket in the oven, cover (if you have no lid, use heavy-duty foil), and cook, basting every half-hour, until the meat is fork tender, 2½ to 3 hours or longer. (As the meat cooks, periodically check that the liquid is bubbling gently. If it is boiling rapidly, turn the oven down to 300°F.)

THE brisket tastes best if it is allowed to rest, reabsorbing the juices lost during braising, and it's easiest to defat the gravy if you prepare the meat ahead and refrigerate it until the fat solidifies. That is the method I use, given here, but the gravy can be prepared by skimming the fat in the traditional way, if you prefer. If you go that route though, do let the meat rest in the pan sauce for at least an hour.

COOL the brisket in the pan sauce, cover well with foil, and refrigerate until the fat congeals. Scrape off all solid fat. Remove the brisket from the pan and slice thinly across the grain.

"You could smell the brisket all over the house, it had so much garlic in it. A roast like that, with a fresh warm twist, is a delicacy from heaven."

—SHOLEM ALEICHEM, "TIT FOR TAT"

PREPARE the gravy: bring the braising mixture to room temperature, then strain it, reserving the garlic and discarding the thyme and rosemary sprigs. Skim and discard as much fat as possible from the liquid. Puree about one half of the cooked garlic with 1 cup of the defatted braising liquid in a food processor or a blender. (If you want a smooth gravy, puree all of the cooked garlic cloves.) Transfer the pureed mixture, the remaining braising liquid, and the rest of the cooked garlic to a skillet. Add the chopped rosemary, minced garlic, and lemon zest. Boil down the gravy over high heat, uncovered, to the desired consistency. Taste and adjust the seasoning. Rewarm the brisket in the gravy until heated through.

ARRANGE the sliced brisket on a serving platter. Spoon some of the hot gravy all over the meat and pass the rest in a separate sauce boat.

SLOW-BRAISED BRISKET WITH ROSEMARY, SHALLOTS, AND RED WINE

yield: 8 GENEROUS SERVINGS

*W*henever I am asked what is the best way to make a brisket, I am stumped. Sure, there are techniques I always rely on. I sear it thoroughly, then slowly oven-braise the burnished meat with aromatics. When it emerges deeply flavored and fork-tender, I let it rest a long while in the pan sauce, reabsorbing the rich juices lost during cooking, to eliminate the dryness endemic to the cut. The sauce, defatted first, is pureed, then cooked down to concentrate the luscious flavors.

But beyond that, this iconic homey Jewish meat lends itself to so many variations. Sometimes I go traditional with a savory bubbe brisket, a straightforward, rustic dish requiring no advance marinating, like Easy Onion-Braised Brisket (page 85). Other times—especially for big holiday dinners—I like to tinker the humble to the haute.

This brisket, like the Moroccan-Flavored Brisket recipe that follows it, is the latter: a pull-out-all-the-stops celebration. While it does not require much more work than many, it does entail advance planning.

Begin a day or two before the seder so the garlic-rosemary studding can infuse the meat for at least eight hours. The next day, simmer the brisket extra slowly with plenty of shallots, red wine, and tomato to develop even more profound flavors. If possible, chill it overnight in the gravy so the fat can be easily lifted off. The day of the seder all that's left to do is reheat the juicy meat in the pan sauce, enlivened with a fresh sparkle of herbs.

No, it's not bubbe cuisine. But my bubbes would have savored every bite.

FOR THE FLAVOR PASTE

6 large garlic cloves, chopped

2 tablespoons fresh rosemary leaves

1 tablespoon fresh lemon juice

1 teaspoon kosher salt

¼ teaspoon freshly ground black pepper

PREPARE the flavor paste: process the paste ingredients in a blender or mini food processor to a coarse puree. Make a slit in the fat side of the brisket with the point of a small, sharp knife. Insert a little of the paste into the slit, using your fingers and the knife tip to push it in as far as possible. In the same way, insert some of the paste all over the top, bottom, and sides of the brisket, spacing them out as evenly as you can. Rub the remaining paste into the outside of the meat. Place the brisket in a large, plastic resealable bag or wrap it tightly in plastic wrap, and refrigerate it for a minimum of 8 and up to 24 hours, so the flavorings can penetrate the meat.

A first- or second-cut beef brisket, 4 to 5 pounds, trimmed of excess fat, wiped with a damp paper towel, and patted dry

FOR THE BRAISING

2 tablespoons olive oil

3 cups coarsely chopped shallots

2 cups full-bodied dry red wine

1 or 2 canned whole plum tomatoes, seeded and coarsely chopped

8 large garlic cloves, peeled

Three 3-inch fresh rosemary sprigs, plus 1 teaspoon finely chopped leaves

Four 4-inch fresh thyme sprigs, plus 1 teaspoon leaves

3 cups Beef Stock (page 32), or good quality, low-sodium purchased

Salt and freshly ground black pepper

REMOVE the meat from the refrigerator and bring it to room temperature. Scrape off the paste and pat the meat dry with paper towels.

PREHEAT the oven to 275°F. In a Dutch oven or flameproof roasting pan large enough to hold the brisket snugly, heat the oil over medium-high heat. (If using a roasting pan, you may need to set it over two burners.) Add the brisket, and brown well on both sides (this will take about 10 minutes in all). Sear to caramelize the meat, but don't let it develop a hard, brown crust, which might make the meat tough or bitter. Transfer the brisket to a platter and set aside. (Or sear under the broiler: place the brisket fat side up, on a foil-lined broiler pan, under a preheated broiler. Broil for 5 to 6 minutes on each side, until browned. Don't allow it to develop a hard, dark crust. Move the meat around as necessary, so it sears evenly.)

POUR off all but 1 tablespoon of the oil remaining in the pan, and add the shallots. Sauté over moderately high heat, stirring, for 3 to 4 minutes. Add 1 cup of the wine, raise the heat to high, and bring to a boil, scraping up any browned bits from the bottom of the pan with a wooden spoon. Boil the mixture until the pan liquid is reduced to a glaze. Add the tomatoes, garlic, rosemary and thyme sprigs, beef stock, and the remaining wine. Boil for a few minutes, then lower the heat to a simmer.

SALT and pepper the brisket to taste on both sides, and add it to the pan, fat side up. Spoon the vegetables and pan liquid all over the meat. Cover the pan tightly (use heavy-duty foil if you don't have a lid for the roasting pan) and place in oven.

BRAISE the meat, basting with the pan sauce and vegetables every half-hour, for 3 to 3½ hours or more, until the meat is fork-tender.

REMOVE the pan from the oven and cool for 1 hour, then refrigerate, covered, overnight, in the braising liquid.

WHEN ready to serve the meat: scrape off all the solid fat from the surface of the meat and braising liquid. Transfer the brisket to a platter and cut into thin slices across the grain at a slight diagonal.

PREPARE the gravy: warm the braising liquid to room temperature. Remove thyme and rosemary sprigs and discard. In a food processor or a blender in batches, puree the pan solids with some of the braising liquid. Return this mixture to the pan and bring to a simmer. Season with salt and pepper. If the gravy is too thin, boil it down to desired consistency over high heat. Stir in the rosemary and thyme leaves.

RETURN the sliced brisket to the pan and reheat slowly, either on top of the stove or in a 325°F oven, until heated through.

ARRANGE the meat on a serving platter with some of the gravy spooned over the meat. Pass the rest of the gravy in a sauce boat at the table.

MOROCCAN-FLAVORED BRISKET WITH DRIED APRICOTS AND PRUNES

yield: 8 GENEROUS SERVINGS

*E*ach bite of this brisket embraces a concatenation of flavors. It begins with the tangy apricot paste studded directly into the meat, the more mellowed fruit of the pan sauce, then the slow-braised tender shreds of the meat itself. And it ends with a burst from gremolata-like mint, ginger, and garlic or a scatter of fresh cilantro.

But such fabulous fare requires time—though most of it unattended. The studding will more deeply flavor the meat if given several hours to penetrate. And when the brisket has finished braising, it should sit in the pan sauce overnight, so it can drink back the juices it gave up during the cooking process. Preparing the brisket in advance also simplifies defatting the gravy: the congealed fat can just be lifted off.

Of course, starting the brisket a couple of days before the seders affords you that much more time for the rest of your holiday menu.

1 tablespoon chopped garlic, plus 6 large garlic cloves, peeled

¹⁄₃ cup chopped dried apricots, plus ¹⁄₃ cup quartered (tart California apricots work best here)

3¹⁄₂ teaspoons ground cumin, preferably freshly toasted and ground

¹⁄₄ teaspoon ground cinnamon

Kosher salt and freshly ground black pepper

A first- or second-cut beef brisket, 4 to 5 pounds, trimmed of excess fat, wiped with a damp paper towel, and patted dry

3 tablespoons olive oil

4 cups chopped onion

IN a blender or mini processor, pulse the chopped garlic, chopped apricots, 1 teaspoon of the cumin, the cinnamon, 1 teaspoon salt, and ¼ teaspoon black pepper to a coarse puree. Make a slit in the fat side of the brisket with the point of a sharp knife. Insert a little of the puree into the slit, using your fingers and the knife tip to push it in as far as possible. Insert some of the puree in the same way in slits all over the top, bottom, and sides of the brisket, spacing the slits out as evenly as you can. Reserve any remaining puree. If you have time, put the brisket in a large, plastic resealable bag or wrap it tightly in plastic wrap, and refrigerate it for up to 24 hours, so the flavorings can penetrate the meat.

PREHEAT the oven to 275°F.

SCRAPE any puree that may have seeped out off the surface of the meat. Heat the oil over medium-high heat in a Dutch oven, ovenproof casserole, or flameproof roasting pan large enough to accommodate the meat snugly. (If using a roasting pan, you may need to set it over two burners.) Add the brisket and brown on all sides, about 10 minutes. Sear to caramelize the meat, but don't let it develop a hard, brown crust, which might make the meat tough or bitter. Transfer to a platter fat side up and

2 medium carrots, scraped and coarsely chopped

1 tablespoon finely chopped peeled fresh ginger

1 teaspoon ground coriander

1/8 teaspoon cayenne

1 cup dry red wine

3 cups Beef Stock (page 32) or good-quality, low-sodium purchased

2/3 cup pitted prunes, quartered

FOR THE GREMOLATA (OPTIONAL)

1/2 teaspoon finely grated peeled fresh ginger

1/2 cup chopped fresh mint

1 teaspoon pressed garlic

Pinch of ground cinnamon

Optional garnish (instead of gremolata): chopped fresh cilantro

Accompaniment: Potato-Leek Matzoh Balls (page 452) or mashed potatoes

set aside. (Or sear under the broiler: place the brisket fat side up, on a foil-lined broiler pan, under a preheated broiler. Broil for 5 to 6 minutes on each side, until nicely browned. Move the meat around as necessary, so it sears evenly.)

POUR off all but 1 tablespoon of the oil from the pan. Add the onions, and cook over medium-high heat, stirring frequently, until softened and gold. Add the whole garlic cloves, carrots, and chopped ginger, and sauté 3 minutes. Add the remaining cumin, the coriander, and cayenne, and stir 30 seconds. Add the wine and boil, stirring and scraping up any browned bits from the pan bottom, until the liquid is reduced almost to a glaze. Add the stock and bring to simmer.

SPREAD any reserved apricot mixture over the brisket, sprinkle with salt and pepper to taste, and add the meat to the pan. Cover (use heavy-duty foil if you don't have a lid) and oven-braise 3 to 4 hours, or until fork-tender, basting with pan juices every half-hour. About 30 minutes before you estimate the meat is done, stir in the quartered apricots and prunes.

COOL the brisket in the pan sauce, cover well with foil, and refrigerate overnight. Scrape off all solid fat and discard. Remove the brisket from the pan and slice thinly across the grain.

IF you are using the gremolata, combine the ingredients in a small bowl.

BRING the gravy to a boil. If it is too thin, boil down to desired consistency. (You can also thicken the gravy by pureeing some of the pan solids with a little pan liquid in a food processor or blender. Return this puree to the pan of gravy and bring to a simmer.) Season to taste with salt and pepper and stir in the gremolata, if desired.

RETURN the sliced brisket to the gravy in the pan and simmer until heated through. If you are not using the gremolata, sprinkle with the cilantro. Serve with Potato-Leek Matzoh Balls or mashed potatoes.

BEET-BRAISED POT ROAST WITH HORSERADISH AND POTATO KNAIDLACH

yield: 8 TO 10 SERVINGS

When the Purim revelries had passed, cooks in the Ukraine and northern Poland turned their attention to the long process of preparing rosl. They placed beets in earthenware crocks, covered them with fresh cold water, and let them slowly ferment, skimming the froth and foam weekly. A month later, a tangy, vegetal beet essence perfumed the shtetls, and the clear scarlet rosl was at last ready to be braised with pot roast and served as the popular Passover main course, roslfleisch.

With my cramped little kitchen and bulging closets, I've never had a place to secrete a pot of fermenting beets for more than a day or two. So I substitute a delicious fresh beet soup or even jarred borscht as the braising liquid. To replace the tart, beautifully nuanced flavor of the traditional rosl, I add a bit of sour salt and freshly grated horseradish, which throws off its clean bite when cooked and blooms with complex earthiness.

Tender, homey potato knaidlach, or dumplings, echoing the horseradish flavor, soak up the wonderful sauce the meat provides. To make them, I use prepared horseradish because the texture of freshly grated would be too coarse and woody, and the vinegar in the prepared kind preserves more of the kick, even after cooking.

FOR THE POT ROAST

Salt and freshly ground black pepper

A 3 to 4 pound boneless chuck eye roast (I've found that this produces the most succulent pot roast, but if unavailable, chuck shoulder or other boneless chuck roast will make a very good dish too), trimmed of excess fat, wiped with a damp paper towel and patted dry

3 tablespoons olive oil

1 very large onion, chopped (2 to 3 cups)

MAKE the pot roast: rub salt and pepper to taste into the meat. Heat 2 tablespoons of the oil over medium-high heat in a large Dutch oven or wide, heavy pot. Add the meat and brown it well on all sides. Transfer it to a platter.

WIPE out the pot, add the remaining 1 tablespoon oil and heat until hot, but not smoking. Add the onion and sauté over medium heat until softened and golden at the edges, about 10 minutes. Add the garlic and apples, and sauté, lifting and turning the ingredients for 5 minutes longer. Add the borscht and bay leaves and bring to a boil over high heat. Continue boiling for about 5 minutes to reduce the mixture slightly and concentrate the flavors. Turn the heat down to the lowest setting, add the meat, and spoon the vegetable-fruit mixture all over it. Cover the pot, leaving the lid slightly askew, and simmer the meat until it can be easily pierced with a fork and its juices are clear or palest rose. This

4 or 5 large garlic cloves, peeled and crushed

2 flavorful, tart-sweet apples (such as McIntosh, Northern Spy, or Cortland), peeled, cored, and cut into large dice

4 cups beet borscht, preferably homemade (see page 499), or good-quality bottled (if using bottled, strain out any pieces of cooked beet and discard or reserve for another use)

2 Turkish bay leaves

2 to 4 tablespoons freshly grated horseradish, plus additional for garnish (see Cook's Note)

Sour salt (available in Middle Eastern and European markets and specialty stores; optional)

FOR THE BEETS AND KNAIDLACH

1 pound fresh beets

6 large or 8 medium russet (baking) potatoes, (about 3 pounds) scrubbed but not peeled

2 large eggs

Salt and freshly ground black pepper

About 1½ cups matzoh meal

About ⅓ cup prepared white horseradish, drained

could be anywhere from 2 to 3 hours or more, depending on the thickness of the meat. Turn the meat every 20 minutes or so, using spoons to avoid piercing it. Make sure the liquid is gently simmering, the bubbles just barely breaking—if needed, use a flame tamer (*blech*) or stack two burner grates together to maintain a very low flame.

STIR in the horseradish, season with salt and pepper and cook 5 minutes. Transfer the meat to a platter and wrap loosely with foil. Discard the bay leaves. Strain the pan sauce, reserving the solids. Skim as much fat as possible from the liquid. Puree the reserved solids with as much of the defatted braising liquid as necessary in a blender or food processor, or use an immersion blender. Return the puree to the pot, add the rest of the defatted braising liquid, and reduce over high heat until you have reached the consistency you prefer. Taste for seasoning. I love the tangy undertone ¼ to ½ teaspoon sour salt imparts to the sauce. If you choose to add it, start with a small amount and keep tasting until you reach a beautifully subtle acid-sweet balance. And you can add a bit more horseradish, if you'd like (freshly grated and heated briefly, it is more robust and earthy than pungent). Just cook a few minutes after adding additional seasoning to marry the flavors.

WHILE the pot roast is braising, prepare the beets and knaidlach. Preheat the oven to 350°F. Trim the greens (save and cook like spinach or chard) and the root ends from the beets. Scrub the beets well, but don't peel them. Tightly wrap each beet in foil and place on a baking sheet. Bake until tender, 1½ to 2 hours (if they are very large). Carefully remove the foil and set aside until cool enough to handle. Peel and cut the beets into quarters and set aside.

MAKE the knaidlach: cover the potatoes with cold salted water, bring to a boil, and cook, partially covered, until fork-tender, 30 to 45 minutes, depending on the size and age of the potatoes. Drain the potatoes and set aside until they are cool enough to handle. Peel and mash them well (no lumps wanted here), using a ricer or food mill or by pushing through a strainer. Spread them out on a sheet of wax paper to cool to room temperature. In a large bowl, combine the potatoes with the eggs, about 2½ teaspoons salt (or to taste), and several generous grinds of pepper. Add 1½ cups matzoh meal and knead with your hands for several minutes to combine the ingredients well. Transfer the dough to a work surface, lightly dusted, if necessary, with matzoh meal. If there is too much dough to handle easily, divide it in half and knead each separately. Add a bit more matzoh meal if the dough is sticky, but avoid adding too much, which would make the knaidlach heavy. Keep kneading until the dough is smooth. Shape the dough into four balls, then divide each into smaller balls about 2 tablespoonfuls each (a standard coffee measure). Flatten the balls slightly. Place a heaping ¼ teaspoon of horseradish in the center, then pinch the edges together to enclose the filling. Reshape into a ball. Gently press the ball over the convex bowl of a teaspoon, flattening and indenting it slightly. (This will ensure that the knaidlach will cook through before the outside begins to disintegrate.) Continue stuffing and shaping the knaidlach until you have used up all the dough. (If you wish, you can refrigerate them at this point on a platter or in a baking dish, in a single layer, not touching, for 2 to 3 hours).

BRING 4 quarts water and about 1¾ tablespoons salt to a boil in a large wide pot. Cook the knaidlach in batches, so you don't crowd the pot, dropping them one at time into the boiling water. Reduce the heat to moderate, and cook, uncovered, for about 10 minutes until cooked through. The knaidlach will rise to the top, swell up, and become fluffy around the edges. To check for doneness, remove one from the pot and either taste or cut open. If knaidl is dark in the center, ascertain whether this is the horseradish filling or an uncooked part. Don't overcook the knaidlach or they will fall apart.

REMOVE the cooked knaidlach with a skimmer or large slotted spoon—they are too delicate to be poured into a colander. Place them on a platter and moisten them lightly with a little pot roast sauce or melted margarine, and tent with foil, as you prepare the remaining knaidlach. Or keep them warm in a 250°F oven.

TO serve, slice the pot roast very thin, against the grain. Surround with cooked beets and potato knaidlach. Nap everything generously with sauce. If desired, sprinkle some freshly grated horseradish over all, or offer guests some to season their food with instead of pepper. Pass additional sauce separately.

COOK'S NOTE: To grate horseradish, peel it, cut it into small chunks, and grind in a food processor. You'll avoid most of the eye-stinging volatile oils. And avert your face when opening the food processor lid for the same reason.

You may have knaidlach left over; it is difficult to decrease the recipe proportionally. They are delicious served as you would gnocchi, with tomato sauce, leftover gravy, or for non-Passover meals, toasted bread crumbs sautéed with garlic in good olive oil. To reheat, sauté the knaidlach lightly and quickly.

It's more work, but the dumplings are even more flavorful with onions added to the stuffing. Sauté chopped onion or shallots in olive oil until rich gold, season well with salt and pepper, and let cool. When inserting the horseradish, add some of the onions as well.

As with most braised meats, the pot roast benefits from a day's rest. Preparing the meat ahead not only cuts down on last-minute seder cooking, but also makes it easier to remove any fat from the gravy. Just scrape off the congealed fat while refrigerator cold.

This recipe began with a tattered French novella I read in the library. It led me to medieval towns in the south of France better known for ambrosial melons than Jewish cooking, and took me to bookstores and museums throughout Paris. It tells the story of a vanished cuisine.

I stumbled on *"les juifs du Pape"* (the Pope's Jews) while researching early French-Jewish cuisine at the New York Public library. Although the Jews were expelled from France in 1394, they were allowed to remain—with restrictions—in four small areas comprising the Comtat Venaissin under papal jurisdiction: Avignon, Carpentras, Cavaillon, and L'Isle-sur-La-Sorgue (in Hebrew, *Arba Kehilloth*).

Tantalizing snippets along the paper trail intrigued me. The French poet Frédéric Mistral, for instance, claimed that the vocabulary and enchanting folklore of the Comtat Jews had enriched the lyrical language of his native Provence. These Jews had their own Judeo-Provençal dialect, their liturgy was unique, and, by all accounts, their cuisine distinctive.

But although French Jews have written scores of cookbooks, I could find no recipes at all from this community. I was about to give up, when a fellow researcher, eyeing the books spread-eagled around me, made an offhand remark about Armand Lunel, a Comtat Jew who, he claimed, wrote evocatively about food in his fiction.

In his charming novella, *Jérusalem à Carpentras* (1937), Lunel limned with gentle humor the hot *coudoles* from the ancient Passover oven in Carpentras—matzohs so exquisite that Christians, defying the Bishop's interdiction, came banging on the gates of the Juiverie to purchase them. But it was Lunel's lavish praise for *le prin*, which he called *"le* nec plus ultra *de l'art culinaire judéo-carpentrassien,"* that convinced me. Served on Passover, this meltingly tender breast of veal, is, as he described it, the essence of spring: stuffed with a mixture of chard and spinach and a scant fistful of rice, intensely refreshing and fortifying at the same time. It sounded so delightfully contemporary, and so delicious, I had to have the recipe—or something equally enchanting from this elusive cuisine.

In Cavaillon, where a Jewish museum dedicated to the Comtat Venaissin is housed in an old matzoh bakery, I inquired about recipes or cookbooks detailing what must have been a scrumptious cuisine. None existed. In the beautiful old synagogues of Cavaillon and Carpentras, now French landmarks, I couldn't locate any members of the old Comtat community, which had been assimilated and replaced by new waves of French Jewry.

In Paris it was the same story. Even Lunel's book was out of print.

It was Passover, I was in France, and in my mind's eye, I could taste Lunel's prin. Like Proust's admirers dreaming of madeleines, I had fallen in love with a food from reading a book. But in the end, this love could only be requited through an act of imagination.

This is how I envisioned the recipe.

PROVENÇAL ROASTED GARLIC–BRAISED BREAST OF VEAL WITH SPRINGTIME STUFFING, PLUS AN ASHKENAZI VARIATION

yield: **6 TO 8 SERVINGS**

*D*on't pass by this fabulous veal because your family refrains from eating rice on Passover. When my agent Elise Goodman wanted to prepare it for her seder, we came up with a wonderful alternative mashed potato stuffing (see Cook's Note).

Veal breast is a delectable but somewhat fatty cut of meat. I have my butcher bone it because it is easier to remove most of the fat that way. But leave the bones in, if you prefer—they will add flavor. Just trim most of the fat carefully. The weight listed in the recipe is before boning. In either case, have your butcher cut a large pocket for stuffing.

Salt

1 large bunch of Swiss chard (about 1½ pounds), washed, white stems removed and reserved for another purpose, green leaves coarsely chopped (5 to 6 cups tightly packed)

1 large bunch of spinach (about 1 pound), washed, coarse stems discarded, and leaves coarsely chopped (about 5 cups tightly packed), or one 10-ounce package frozen leaf spinach, thawed

4 large garlic cloves, minced (1½ tablespoons), plus 1 whole large head, unpeeled

½ cup plus 2 teaspoons olive oil

Freshly ground black pepper

1 very large onion, finely chopped (about 2 cups)

PREPARE the stuffing: bring a large pot full of lightly salted water to a boil. Add the chard and spinach, bring the water back to a boil, and cook for 2 to 3 minutes until thoroughly wilted. Drain and squeeze out as much moisture as possible, pressing the greens against a colander with a wooden spoon. Or for a more thorough job, use your hands when the greens have cooled somewhat. Finely chop, either by hand or by pulsing in a food processor.

IN a large skillet, sauté the minced garlic in 3 tablespoons of the oil over moderate heat until pale gold, 2 to 3 minutes. Add the chard and spinach. Cook, stirring, over medium heat, until the liquid is evaporated and the garlic is thoroughly distributed, 5 to 7 minutes. The greens should be very tender. Season to taste with salt and pepper. Transfer to a large bowl and set aside.

PREHEAT the oven to 375°F.

SAUTÉ the onion in a heavy, medium saucepan over medium heat in 3 tablespoons of the oil until softened, 7 to 10 minutes. Add the rice and stir to coat the grains with the onions. In another saucepan, bring the broth to a simmer. Add the broth to the rice a few spoonfuls at a time, as if making risotto. Keep the heat medium-low, and stir, waiting until the broth is nearly absorbed before adding another spoonful. Cook the rice

1/2 cup medium- or short-grain rice, preferably arborio (medium- or short-grain is called for because you want a creamy texture, like a risotto; long-grain rice will give you fluffy, separate grains)

1 1/2 cups chicken broth, preferably homemade (see pages 62 and 70), or good-quality, low-sodium purchased

1 tablespoon plus 1 teaspoon fresh thyme leaves

2 tablespoons fresh rosemary leaves

Juice and grated zest of 1 large lemon

1 cup firmly packed fresh flat-leaf parsley leaves

1 cup firmly packed fresh mint leaves

1 large egg, beaten

One 5- to 6-pound veal breast

1 cup sauvignon blanc or other dry white wine

until just tender, 15 to 20 minutes in all. If you finish adding the broth and the rice is not yet tender, add a tablespoon or two of hot water, as needed. Season the rice with salt and pepper (taking into account the saltiness of the broth you are using), add it to the chard and spinach, and set aside to cool.

PREPARE the garlic head: break the head into single cloves and put them, unpeeled, into a small baking dish in which they fit snugly (I use a 5-inch-square porcelain ramekin). Drizzle with 2 teaspoons of the oil and 1 teaspoon of the thyme. Cover tightly (use foil if you don't have a lid), and roast for 30 to 45 minutes, until a soft puree is formed when you squeeze a clove. Avoid overcooking, which turns the garlic bitter. Squeeze the puree out by hand or run the unpeeled cloves through a food mill to trap the peels. Put the roasted garlic puree in a small bowl and add 1 tablespoon of the rosemary and the lemon juice. Stir well and set aside. Turn off the oven—you will be pan-braising the meat.

WHILE the garlic is roasting, finish the stuffing: in a food processor, pulse the remaining 1 tablespoon each of rosemary and thyme, the parsley, mint, and lemon zest until finely chopped. Add to the rice mixture. Stir in the egg until well combined.

TRIM the veal of gristle and as much fat as possible. Sprinkle salt and pepper all over, including the inside pocket. Fill the pocket with the stuffing, pushing the mixture as far in as possible, but don't overfill—it will expand somewhat while cooking. Sew the pocket closed. (A large embroidery needle and strong cotton thread or unwaxed dental floss work very well here. Or use a trussing needle and kitchen twine. I find skewering not as successful here—the stuffing is more likely to ooze out into the pan gravy.)

IN a 6-quart Dutch oven or heavy casserole just large enough to accommodate the veal, heat the remaining 2 tablespoons oil until hot, but not smoking. Add the veal and brown it slowly on all sides, turning carefully with wooden spoons so you don't pierce the meat. When it is thoroughly browned, arrange the meat so that the fat side is up. Spread the roasted garlic mixture all over the top. Add the wine and bring to a slow bubble. Place the lid slightly askew, and braise at a slow simmer over very low heat for 2 1/2 to 3 hours, or longer, if necessary, until the meat is very tender. Use a flame tamer (*blech*) or stack two stove burner grates, if you must, to keep the flame very low. Every 20 minutes or so, baste with the pan juices. If possible, turn the meat a few times; don't worry about losing the roasted garlic coating on top—it will add delicious flavor to the cooking juices.

TRANSFER the veal to a platter, and let it stand for 10 minutes, tented with foil to keep warm. Boil up the cooking juices for a few minutes to concentrate the flavors, taste for seasoning, then transfer to a sauce boat.

SLICE the veal about ½-inch thick, making sure that the slices enclose some of the filling. Nap with some of the juices. Pass remaining sauce separately.

Ashkenazi Mashed Potato Stuffing Prepare the stuffing according to the directions above, omitting rice and broth. Sauté the onion until rich gold and set aside. Simmer 3½ cups russet or Yukon gold potatoes, peeled and cubed, in cold, salted water to cover, until tender, about 15 minutes. Drain and mash the potatoes until smooth. Stir in the reserved sautéed onion (along with any oil remaining in the pan), and 1 additional tablespoon olive oil, and season to taste with salt and pepper. Add the potato mixture to the chard and spinach, set aside to cool, and continue with the recipe.

SLOW-BRAISED LEMON VEAL WITH LEEKS

yield: ABOUT 6 SERVINGS

"Even if you had supplied our needs in the desert for forty years, but did not send us manna from heaven, dayenu, it would have been enough."

The rousing seder song "Dayenu" is about gratitude, but this ninth stanza might remind us that sometimes the Israelites, like us, were anything but appreciative. "Nothing but this manna to look at," they kvetched, recalling with longing the slave food they ate: "The fish that we used to eat in Egypt, the cucumbers, the melons, the leeks, the onions, and the garlic."

Throughout the Diaspora, Jews have created rituals to concretize the story of the Exodus; Iranian and Afghani Jews seem to bring home the themes of oppression, freedom, and redemption of this excerpt by beating each other with leeks on their backs and shoulders every time they sing the refrain "dayenu" beginning with that ninth verse. A symbol of the taskmasters' whips and a potent reminder to appreciate our freedom, this fun custom, now adopted by many Ashkenazi families, too, is a highlight for adults and children alike. If leeks are too costly to provide one for each seder participant, use scallions instead.

Plentiful in the spring, fresh leeks also figure in many seder recipes. Here a hillock of them melt slowly with the braising veal to form a rich gravy. Since veal shoulder is so lean, there is no need to skim the fat: just puree the pan sauce and you're good to go.

10 fat garlic cloves, peeled

3 tablespoons packed fresh flat-leaf parsley leaves

About 6 tablespoons fresh lemon juice

Salt

One 3½-pound boneless shoulder of veal, rolled and tied

About 4 large or 6 medium leeks

4 tablespoons olive oil

PREPARE the flavor paste: process four of the garlic cloves, the parsley, 2 tablespoons lemon juice, and ½ teaspoon salt in a blender or mini food processor to a coarse puree, stopping to stir down as necessary. Make a slit in the veal with the point of a small, sharp knife. Insert a little of the paste into the slit, using your fingers and the knife tip to push it in as far as possible. In the same way, insert some of the paste all over the top, bottom, and sides of the veal, spacing them out as evenly as you can, and slip the paste in between the rolled layers of the tied meat. (If you are tying the veal yourself, spread a little paste on the boned side of the meat before you roll and tie it.) Place the veal in a large, plastic resealable bag or wrap it tightly in plastic wrap, and refrigerate it for 1 to 2 hours, so the flavorings can penetrate the meat.

REMOVE the meat from the refrigerator, bring it to room temperature, and pat it dry.

Freshly ground black pepper

Optional accompaniment: lemon quarters

WASH and thinly slice enough white and pale green parts of the leeks to make 5 cups. Dry the leeks well, using a salad spinner or patting well with paper towels.

PREHEAT the oven to 325°F.

IN a heavy flameproof lidded casserole (oval enameled cast iron is ideal) just large enough to hold the meat, heat 2 tablespoons of the oil over medium-high heat. Add the meat and brown it well on all sides. Transfer it to a platter and set aside.

WIPE out the pan, add the remaining 2 tablespoons oil and heat until hot. Add the leeks, salt generously, and stir to coat well. Cover the pan, turn heat down to low, and cook, stirring occasionally, until the leeks are tender and wilted, 15 to 20 minutes. Add the remaining 6 garlic cloves and 4 tablespoons lemon juice, and stir well. Sprinkle the veal with salt and pepper to taste on all sides. Place the veal in the pan and spoon some of the leek sauce over it. Cover tightly and oven-braise until fork-tender, about 1 hour and 45 minutes, turning every 15 to 20 minutes and basting with the leeks and pan juices. Transfer the veal to a cutting board and tent it loosely with foil.

PREPARE the leek sauce: since the veal is quite lean, there is really no need to defat the gravy. Working in batches, if necessary, puree the braising mixture, including the leeks and garlic cloves, in a blender or food processor. If desired, return the pureed sauce to the pan to rewarm and reduce it slightly over high heat, uncovered. Taste and adjust the salt and pepper. I like to add a drop or two of fresh lemon juice to the finished meat and sauce—more lemony than most diners, perhaps—so I serve the veal with lemon quarters.

CUT the veal into thin slices and arrange on a serving platter. Spoon some of the warm gravy all over the meat and pass the rest in a separate sauce boat.

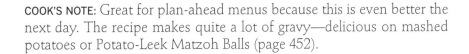

COOK'S NOTE: Great for plan-ahead menus because this is even better the next day. The recipe makes quite a lot of gravy—delicious on mashed potatoes or Potato-Leek Matzoh Balls (page 452).

BRAISED LAMB WITH ARTICHOKES, LEMON, AND FRESH HERBS

yield: 8 TO 10 SERVINGS

*R*ubbed first with wild bitter herbs, tender young lamb was roasted, often over *fragrant pomegranate wood, to mark each Passover in the Second Temple period. The Jewish historian Josephus estimated that 255,600 animals were sacrificed for the Passover celebratory feasts during the reign of Nero.*

With the destruction of the Second Temple in 70 CE, the custom lost favor as it evoked sorrowful memories of the Temple sacrifices that were no more. Eventually, Ashkenazi Orthodox and many Conservative Jews began to refrain from eating any roasted meat at the seder meals.

I have retained the ancient herb perfume in this braised lamb dish. Garlic, lemon, and artichoke build up more layers of flavor and texture—my attempt to compensate for the missing taste of roast pomegranate woodsmoke.

5 to 6 pounds bone-in lean lamb shoulder

3 to 4 tablespoons olive oil

5 cups thinly sliced onion (about 2 large onions)

10 large garlic cloves, peeled, plus 2 to 3 tablespoons finely minced garlic

Salt and freshly ground black pepper

About ½ cup fresh lemon juice

2 tablespoons chopped fresh rosemary leaves

2 teaspoons fresh thyme leaves

Shredded zest of 1 large lemon

TRIM the lamb of as much fat as possible—very tedious, but careful trimming usually eliminates the need to skim the fat from the pan later on. Cut the lamb into 1½- to 2-inch pieces, leaving the bones in (they'll add a lot of flavor). Do, however, cut the meat away from any large, unsightly bones. Pat the meat dry with paper towels.

DO the initial browning in a large heavy skillet (10- to 12-inch cast-iron is ideal). Heat 2 tablespoons oil until hot, but not smoking. Add the lamb in batches and sauté until nicely browned on all sides. Fry only a few pieces at a time; crowding the pan will steam the meat, rather than brown it. Add a little more oil to the pan only if necessary because you want to burn off as much fat as you can. Transfer the lamb as it is done to a platter.

IF there is any rendered fat remaining in the pan, wipe it out. Add 1 tablespoon fresh oil and heat until hot. Add the onions and brown over medium-high heat, lifting and turning them as they become deep gold, about 10 minutes, and scraping up any browned bits. Add the whole garlic cloves and cook for 2 minutes longer. Return the meat to the pan, season it with salt and pepper, and turn the meat over a few times to coat it well with the onions. Add ¼ cup lemon juice, 1 tablespoon rosemary, the thyme, and lemon zest, and cook for 3 minutes.

1 cup chicken broth, preferably homemade (see pages 62 and 70), or good-quality, low-sodium purchased

8 to 10 medium artichokes (see Cook's Note), or two 9- or 10-ounce packages of frozen artichokes, thawed and patted dry with paper towels

¹⁄₂ cup chopped fresh mint

TRANSFER the mixture and any scrapings from the bottom of the pan to a 6- to 8-quart Dutch oven or large, deep, flameproof casserole and add the broth. Bring to a slow bubble, cover, and reduce the heat to the barest simmer. Cook for about 1½ hours, until the meat is tender when pierced with a fork. Turn the meat frequently, basting it with the onions and pan sauce.

ADD the artichokes, and cook, covered, until they are very tender, 15 to 20 minutes. I like to continue cooking until a few of the artichoke pieces break up and melt into the sauce, but follow your preference. If there is a lot of liquid left in the pot, uncover and turn the heat up to high, evaporating enough so that the pan liquid is thick and syrupy. Stir in the mint, minced garlic, remaining 1 tablespoon rosemary, and ¼ cup lemon juice, and cook for 3 minutes to blend the flavors. Taste and adjust seasoning. There should be a pronounced lemon flavor, so add a bit more juice, if necessary. For an easier and more attractive serving, remove some of the large bones that pull away from the meat easily. Serve hot.

COOK'S NOTE: Follow this method to prepare fresh artichokes: to prevent the artichokes from discoloring, rub each surface you cut with fresh lemon. Or dip into a large bowl of cold water acidulated with the juice of a large lemon. Slice off the artichoke stem and reserve. Pull off the tough outer leaves at the bottom of the artichoke and discard. Using a serrated knife or scissors, cut off the pointy top of the leaves just above the artichoke heart or choke and discard it. With a very sharp knife, cut off and discard the remaining leaves, until you reach the palest soft leaves. Now cut the artichoke in half vertically, and pull out and discard the purple-tipped leaves in the center. With a teaspoon, scrape out all of the fuzzy choke and discard. Trim the artichoke stem and peel it. Cut the stem into bite-size chunks. Halve the heart halves again, so you have quarters. The artichoke and the stem are ready to be used in the recipe. Prepare the remaining artichokes in the same way.

This dish tastes even better the next day. To prepare it in advance while retaining an herbal freshness, hold off on the herb and lemon finish. Remove from the heat and cool 1 hour, then refrigerate, covered, overnight. Scrape off any congealed fat from the surface. Reheat gently until heated through, and proceed with the final addition of herbs, garlic, and lemon juice.

ETTY RUSSO'S LAMB MINA FROM IZMIR

yields ABOUT 6 SERVINGS

Borekas, bulemas, *and* boyos, empanadas, tapadas, *and* ojaldres—*Turkish Jews are extraordinarily fond of their savory pies and turnovers. For Passover, they make special versions using matzoh, called minas. Usually moistened matzoh squares form the top and bottom crust of a pie; in more elaborate minas, the matzoh may be layered through one or more fillings, creating a lasagne-like casserole.*

But in Izmir, southwestern Turkey, Etty Russo's lamb and chicken minas are a delectable jumble of matzoh, meat, and eggs, more akin to matzoh brie. Overlooking the turquoise waters of the Aegean Sea, sheep, poultry, vegetables, and fruit grow intensely flavorful, and the Russo minas rely on no more seasoning than garlic, pepper, and a generous dust of coarse salt. But you can brighten up more pallid foodstuffs with a few additional flavorings, if needed.

At Russo seders, this homey, easy-to-prepare lamb mina shares equal billing with the elegant roast lamb Etty serves with potatoes, fresh green beans, and peas. It makes a tasty Passover weekday supper as well.

1 tablespoon olive oil, plus additional for greasing the pan

About 2½ pounds shoulder lamb chops, well trimmed of fat and gristle

Salt and freshly ground black pepper

6 whole plain or egg matzohs

About 2 cups chicken broth, preferably homemade (see pages 62 and 70), or lightly salted water

5 large eggs

1 to 1½ tablespoons chopped fresh garlic

Coarse salt, for sprinkling

Optional garnish: chopped parsley or dill leaves

PREHEAT the oven to 350°F.

CHOOSE a heavy, deep, lidded skillet large enough to hold all the lamb snugly in a single layer. Film it with the olive oil and set it over medium-high heat until shimmering. Add the lamb, in batches, if necessary, to avoid crowding the pan, and sauté until nicely browned on both sides. Transfer the lamb as it is done to a platter and season well with salt and pepper.

DISCARD all the fat in the pan, then pour in 2 cups water to deglaze, scraping up all the browned bits with a wooden spoon. Reduce the heat to a simmer and return all the lamb to the pan. Cover tightly and cook for 25 to 30 minutes, until the lamb is tender but still juicy. Let the meat cool in the liquid, then cut it into bite-size pieces, discarding any fat and bones. Reserve the cooking liquid.

SPREAD the matzohs out on a platter or rimmed baking sheet. Moisten them with the broth or salted water and let them drink in the liquid for about 5 minutes. Break the matzohs into pieces about the size of a quarter and drain either in a colander, extracting the liquid with your hands or the back of a wooden spoon, or the traditional Turkish way, by pressing the matzoh dry between clean kitchen towels.

MEANWHILE, in another large bowl, beat the eggs until well blended. Add the drained matzohs to the eggs. Mix in the lamb and garlic and season well with salt and pepper.

GREASE the bottom and sides of a large, shallow baking pan (13 by 9-inch, 12-inch oval, or similar size). Spread the lamb-matzoh batter evenly in the pan. Measure out about 1½ cups of the reserved cooking liquid and pour it through a strainer over the batter. The lamb pieces should be covered or they may dry out, so if needed, push them down into the batter and add more of the cooking liquid. Bake uncovered for about 45 minutes, until the top is firm and golden brown.

REMOVE from the oven, cover loosely with foil, and let rest for at least 20 minutes. Sprinkle well with coarse salt and pepper, garnish with the herbs, if desired, and serve.

COOK'S NOTE: This is very good prepared a day ahead and reheated, uncovered, until hot and crusty.

Simple and flavorful as is, you can elaborate on the basic recipe, adding either fresh herbs (scallions, chives, mint, tarragon, cilantro, or rosemary) or spices like smoked paprika to the batter.

Chicken Mina Place about 1½ pounds skinless, boneless chicken thigh meat in a heavy saucepan, and add 1 tablespoon extra virgin olive oil, a generous sprinkle of salt and pepper, and cold water to cover by about an inch. Simmer slowly (don't allow the water to boil), until the chicken is barely cooked through: it should be quite juicy. Follow the lamb mina directions, substituting trimmed, bite-size pieces of the chicken for the lamb.

Can you use poached chicken left over from soup? The secret to this homey mina is very juicy, gently cooked meat. Since all of the flavor from your chicken will have gone into your soup, you'd really be left with nothing very tasty for the mina.

MOZZARELLA IN MATZOH CARROZZA

yield: 6 TO 7 APPETIZER OR LIGHT LUNCH SERVINGS

*T*his variation on the Neapolitan *mozzarella in carrozza*—*a luscious golden-fried sandwich of molten mozzarella, sauced with a blend of garlic, lemon, and anchovies—may seem unusual, but softened matzoh works remarkably well as a substitute for the fluffy, sliced white bread frequently used. The absorbent matzoh pairs beautifully with the assertive citrusy sauce.*

I especially like the subtle way the slightly sweet egg matzohs soften the saline edge of anchovies, but plain matzohs are very good, too.

The anchovies are essential here. They energize the flavors, bringing needed dimension to the dish, and when minced fine, will dissolve into the sauce virtually undetectable.

6 or 7 whole matzohs, egg or plain

Salt

About ½ pound mozzarella cheese, shredded or thinly sliced and then diced

6 to 12 fresh basil leaves, shredded (optional)

2 large eggs

Olive oil, for frying

Accompaniment: lemon quarters; fresh parsley sprigs, for garnish

FOR THE SAUCE

2 teaspoons finely minced garlic

2 teaspoons best-quality extra virgin olive oil

3 anchovy fillets, finely chopped

Juice of 1 lemon (3 to 4 tablespoons)

Freshly ground black pepper

MAKE the matzoh carrozzas: break each matzoh into 4 equal pieces. Fill a large, shallow dish or pan with well-salted water. Dip 2 matzoh quarters into the water until just softened and pliant. Place some of the cheese, and basil, if using, on one of the matzoh quarters and top with the second piece of matzoh. Pat this mozzarella sandwich into a hamburger patty shape, molding it nicely with your hands and gently squeezing out any excess water. The cheese should be completely covered by the matzoh coating. Place the finished patty on a platter to dry slightly as you continue making more, using the rest of the matzoh.

PREPARE the sauce: in a very small skillet or saucepan, cook the garlic in the oil over gentle heat until it is just tinged with gold, about 2 minutes. The garlic should remain quite soft—don't let it turn crisp or brown. Immediately add the anchovies, stirring and mashing until they have dissolved completely. Whisk in the lemon juice and pepper to taste. Cook, stirring, for 2 to 3 minutes, to blend all the flavors. Keep warm until ready to serve.

BEAT the eggs in a shallow bowl with 1 tablespoon water. Heat ¼ inch of oil in a 10- to 12-inch heavy skillet until hot, but not smoking. Just before frying, slip each patty into the egg, immersing it completely, then letting the excess egg drip back into the bowl. Slip as many egg-coated patties into the hot oil as possible without crowding the pan and fry them until crisp and golden on both sides. Avoid turning the patties more than once. Fry the remaining patties, in batches, if necessary. Drain lightly on paper towels.

ARRANGE two carrozzas on each plate and spoon some of the sauce over them. Serve with lemon quarters and fresh parsley sprigs, as garnish.

SALAD OF BITTER HERBS AND ORANGES

yield: 8 SERVINGS

Gnarled horseradish root in its native state may look positively prehistoric, but it was not the original maror, or bitter herb, of the ancients. Biblical scholars surmise that greens like chicory, dandelion, sorrel, and hyssop, which grow wild in Egypt and the Sinai Peninsula, first symbolized the bitterness of bondage at seders.

Many Jews still use bitter greens, especially romaine, not only for maror, but also for hazeret, *the other bitter herb called for on some seder plates. Why eat two different bitter herbs? According to the Mishnah, since the Bible speaks of bitter herbs in the plural, we are required to eat more than one kind.*

This salad, combining several of these bitter herbs with chunks of fresh orange, offers a lovely contrast to a lush brisket or braised lamb.

FOR THE DRESSING

⅓ cup fresh lemon juice

2 tablespoons minced shallot

1½ tablespoons chopped fresh thyme

2 teaspoons grated orange zest

1 cup extra virgin olive oil

Salt and freshly ground black pepper

FOR THE SALAD

12 to 14 cups mixed greens (choose three or more of the following: arugula, sorrel, watercress, Belgian endive, romaine, radicchio)

½ cup thinly sliced radishes

4 to 6 thinly sliced scallions (use white and pale green parts)

½ cup snipped fresh dill

2 blood or navel oranges, peeled and white pith removed, quartered lengthwise and sliced widthwise

MAKE the dressing: combine the lemon juice, shallot, thyme, and zest in a medium bowl. Gradually whisk in the oil. Season with salt and pepper.

PLACE the greens in a large bowl. Top with the radishes, scallions, and dill. Toss with enough of the dressing to coat. Add the oranges and toss again.

ROASTED ASPARAGUS BUNDLES WITH TOASTED MATZOH CRUMBS

yield: **8 SERVINGS**

When the freshest spring asparagus hits my local markets, I could eat it every day—and often do, roasting the spears to unleash their best flavors. Minutes to prepare, good hot or at room temperature, they're excellent for the quickest weekday dinner.

But for the seders, I primp them up a bit. Instead of merely snapping off the tough ends, I usually trim the lower stalks with a few shaves of the vegetable peeler and tie them with scallion ribbons into pretty bundles for easy serving. And sometimes I cloak them with savory toasted matzoh crumbs for contrasting crunch. While matzoh meal works well here, coarse crumbs home-prepared from whole matzohs really make this dish shine. If you can steal the time, it is worthwhile making a large batch (see page 24) to have on hand throughout the holiday.

FOR THE TOPPING

2 tablespoons extra virgin olive oil

1 teaspoon minced garlic

½ cup matzoh meal or coarse matzoh crumbs

Salt and freshly ground black pepper

2 tablespoons minced fresh tarragon

1 teaspoon finely grated lemon zest

FOR THE ASPARAGUS

2 or 3 scallions

2 pounds asparagus, tough ends trimmed (and peeled, if desired)

2 tablespoons extra virgin olive oil

Salt and freshly ground black pepper

2 tablespoons fresh lemon juice

PREHEAT the oven to 475°F.

MAKE the topping: heat the oil in a medium skillet over medium heat. Add the garlic and sauté 1 minute. Add the matzoh meal or crumbs, season generously with salt and pepper, and cook, stirring, until the matzoh meal is light golden brown. Remove the skillet from the heat, stir in the tarragon and lemon zest, and set aside.

CUT 8 long strips from the green part of scallions (reserve the white parts for another use, such as the Salad of Bitter Herbs). Poach the scallion strips in boiling water for 1 minute to make them pliable, then remove them and pat them dry. Divide the asparagus spears into serving size portions and use the scallion strips to tie each portion with a knot or bow into a flat bundle.

ARRANGE the asparagus bundles on a large, rimmed baking sheet. Drizzle with the oil and sprinkle with salt and pepper. Roast until tender, 10 to 12 minutes.

TRANSFER the bundles to a serving platter. Drizzle with lemon juice and dust with the toasted matzoh crumbs.

GARLICKY SWISS CHARD AND MUSHROOM MATZOH KUGEL

yield: ABOUT 8 SIDE-DISH SERVINGS

A combination of mushrooms, chard leaves' mellow, earthy edge and its succulent stems beautifully balance this eggy matzoh pudding. But this recipe will take well to other big flavors too. Try sautéed fennel or braised celery root (enhanced with crushed fennel or celery seeds), roasted garlic, or a dose of crispy fried shallots mixed with mushrooms. Prepared with diced artichoke hearts, the kugel would be especially delicious topped with toasted crushed hazelnuts. Serve the kugel cut into squares as a side dish with dinner. It also makes an excellent brunch or lunch main course.

½ cup dried wild mushrooms, preferably boletus (porcini or cèpes; shiitakes won't work well here) (about 1 ounce)

6 tablespoons olive oil, plus additional for greasing the pan

2 cups chopped onion

Salt and freshly ground black pepper

About ¼ pound fresh shiitakes or other fresh wild, exotic, or cultivated mushrooms, stems removed and reserved for another use or discarded, caps wiped clean with a damp paper towel and thinly sliced (1½ to 2 cups)

2 tablespoons finely chopped fresh garlic

SOAK the dried mushrooms in 1½ cups hot water for 30 minutes or until soft. Drain the mushrooms through a strainer lined with paper towels or a coffee filter, reserving ½ cup of the soaking liquid. Rinse the mushrooms under cold running water to eliminate any remaining grit and chop them coarsely.

IN a large, heavy, lidded skillet, heat 2 tablespoons oil over medium heat until shimmering. Add the onions and cook, lifting and tossing occasionally, until they are lightly tinged with bronze. Sprinkle with salt and pepper and transfer to a large bowl.

HEAT 2 more tablespoons oil in the pan (don't bother rinsing it out) over moderately high heat. Add the fresh mushrooms and sauté, turning occasionally, until golden at the edges. Stir in 1 tablespoon of the garlic, the dried mushrooms, and their reserved soaking liquid. Boil the mixture over high heat, stirring occasionally, until all the liquid is evaporated. Season well, then transfer to the onions.

HEAT the remaining 2 tablespoons oil in the same skillet over a medium flame. Add the remaining garlic, stir just until its heady aroma rises (about 1 minute), then add the chard stems. Cook, stirring regularly, until almost tender (anywhere from 5 to 15 minutes). Add the chard leaves (a few handfuls at a time, if necessary, until the chard shrinks in volume), season with salt and pepper, and cook, lifting and turning, until all the leaves are wilted. Cover the pan and continue cooking until

About 1½ pounds green Swiss chard, well washed but not dried, leaves separated from stems using a knife or scissors and coarsely sliced, stems trimmed and cut into ½-inch pieces

4 whole plain or egg matzohs

About 1½ cups chicken broth, preferably homemade (see pages 62 and 70) or good-quality, low-sodium purchased, or vegetable stock

6 large eggs, beaten to blend

1 tablespoon fresh thyme leaves

¼ cup fresh snipped dill (optional)

Best-quality extra virgin olive oil for drizzling

the leaves and stems are very tender, 5 to 10 minutes. Let cool in the pan, then squeeze out and discard as much liquid as possible, and add the chard leaves and stems to the onions and mushrooms.

PREHEAT the oven to 350°F.

BREAK the matzoh into small pieces and place in a large bowl. Cover with the broth and let soak about 2 minutes, stirring the matzoh around once or twice so it is evenly moistened. Drain and press out as much liquid as you can from the matzoh. Mix the matzoh and the eggs together in a large bowl and season liberally with salt and pepper. Stir in the mushroom-chard mixture, thyme, and dill, if using, and combine everything well. Let the ingredients mingle for 5 to 10 minutes.

GREASE the bottom and sides of a 13 by 9-inch heavy, shallow baking pan and put the pan in the oven until it is sizzling. Turn the batter into the pan and smooth the top. Drizzle with the extra virgin olive oil. Bake, uncovered, for 30 to 35 minutes, until the top is golden.

LET the kugel rest for about 20 minutes. If necessary, reheat before serving.

WILD MUSHROOM–POTATO KUGEL

yield: **8 TO 10 SERVINGS**

*T*he Irish potato. For most of us, the starchy tuber, like leprechauns and shamrocks, is inextricably linked to the Emerald Isle. But the potato had a profound effect as well on the Jews of Poland and Russia, where it became a staple from the mid-nineteenth century on. Without the potato, in fact, the phenomenal Jewish population explosion in Eastern Europe would never have occurred, according to the noted Jewish food historian, John Cooper.

As they decreased their reliance on bread, these Jews began eating the cheap, nutritious potato two and three times a day, breakfasting on potatoes in their jackets, eating spuds with onions or cabbage for dinner.

Potato kugel was always a treat. Although I have not found old kugel recipes calling for wild mushrooms mixed with the potatoes, the pairing makes perfect geographic, as well as gustatory, sense: boletus mushrooms (also known as porcini or cèpes) grow wild all over Poland and Russia—and Israel, too.

Here I sandwich woodsy, dried mushrooms between layers of grated raw potatoes that have been combined with savory fried onions and seasoned liberally with pepper. Baked in a hot oven, the elegant kugel emerges gloriously crusty, and full of deep, earthy perfumes.

Rinsing then squeezing the grated potatoes dry before adding them to the other ingredients concentrates the potato flavor and eliminates that watery, muddy taste that mars some kugels.

1 ounce dried wild mushrooms, preferably boletus—that is, porcini or cèpes; shiitake don't work well here (½ to ¾ cup)

¼ cup olive oil, plus additional for greasing the pan

3 cups thinly sliced onion

Salt and freshly ground black pepper

2 teaspoons chopped garlic

SOAK the mushrooms in 2 cups hot water for 30 minutes, or until soft. Drain the mushrooms through a strainer lined with paper towels or a coffee filter, reserving the soaking liquid. Wash the mushrooms under cold running water to remove any remaining grit and chop them coarsely.

HEAT the oil in a 10-inch heavy skillet over medium heat. Add the onions and sauté until crisp and light brown, about 15 minutes. Transfer to a bowl and season with salt and pepper. Combine the chopped mushrooms, garlic, and reserved mushroom soaking liquid in the same skillet (no need to wash it out). Boil the mixture over high heat, stirring occasionally, until all the liquid is evaporated. Add salt and pepper to taste and remove the skillet from the heat.

PREHEAT oven to 400°F.

6 large or 8 medium russet (baking) potatoes, peeled

4 large eggs, beaten

Best-quality extra virgin olive oil for drizzling (optional)

GRATE the potatoes, using a medium disk in a food processor (if you don't have a grating disk, use the coarse shredding disk, then replace the disk with the metal blade and pulse until the shreds are chopped). Or grate using the large holes of a hand grater. Transfer them to a colander, rinse well, then drain, using your hands to squeeze out as much liquid as possible. In a large bowl, combine the potatoes, eggs, fried onion, and plenty of salt and pepper.

GREASE the bottom and sides of a large (13 by 9-inch, or similar), shallow, heavy baking pan (preferably enameled cast-iron or metal, not glass), and place the pan in the oven until the oil is sizzling hot (this will produce a deliciously crisp crust).

TURN half the potato mixture into the pan, spread the mushrooms over it, cover with the remaining potato mixture, and smooth the top. If desired, drizzle a little extra virgin olive oil over the top. Bake uncovered for about 50 minutes, until the top is golden and crisp. Let the kugel cool until set. If necessary, reheat before serving.

CRACKLETOP POTATO KUGEL

yield: 8 TO 10 SERVINGS

*I*t practically defines crackle, tastes deeply of earthy spuds, is richly flavored with salt and oil: what could make a better crust for a kugel than the potato chip? Simply crush the chips with your hands and sprinkle lavishly over the oniony potato batter before baking.

The best-quality kosher-for-Passover chips I've found are plain, so I like to stir in some smoked paprika to mimic the barbeque-flavored ones I adore. For variety, try other seasonings or prepare toppings during the rest of the year from your favorite purchased flavored chips.

6 to 7 tablespoons olive oil

3 cups thinly sliced onion (about ¾ pound)

1 tablespoon chopped garlic

Salt and freshly ground black pepper

6 large or 8 medium russet (baking) potatoes, peeled

3 tablespoons matzoh meal

4 large eggs, beaten

Smoked sweet or hot paprika (optional)

4 to 5 ounces high-quality, kosher-for-Passover potato chips (enough to make 1½ to 2 cups when coarsely crushed by hand)

HEAT 2 tablespoons of the oil in a 10-inch heavy skillet over medium heat. Add the onions and sauté, lifting and turning occasionally, until golden brown, about 15 minutes. Add the garlic and cook until tinged pale gold, about 3 minutes. Transfer the mixture to a large bowl and season with salt and pepper.

PREHEAT the oven to 400°F.

GRATE the potatoes, using a medium grating disk in a food processor (if you don't have a grating disk, use the coarse shredding disk, then replace the disk with the metal blade and pulse until the shreds are chopped). Or grate using the large holes of a hand grater. Place the potatoes in a colander, rinse well to remove most of the starch, then drain, using your hands to squeeze out as much liquid as possible. Add the potatoes to the fried onion. Stir in the matzoh meal and 1 or 2 tablespoons oil. Season generously to taste with plenty of salt and pepper. Add the eggs and combine well.

POUR the remaining 3 tablespoons oil into a large, shallow, heavy baking pan (13 by 9-inch or similar size, preferably enameled cast-iron or metal, not glass). Thoroughly rub the oil around the bottom and sides of the pan and place in the oven until sizzling hot (this will create a crispy crust).

TRANSFER the potato mixture to the pan and smooth the top. If you are using the smoked paprika, mix it well with the crushed potato chips in a bowl. Sprinkle the potato chips evenly over the kugel.

BAKE uncovered for about 50 minutes, until the top is golden and crisp and the kugel is firm. Let the kugel rest until set, about 20 minutes.

COOK'S NOTE: Use fewer crushed chips if you prefer a thinner crust. Avoid reheating leftovers: the crust may become soggy.

VARIATIONS: For a splurge, substitute rendered Poultry Schmaltz (page 28) for some or all of the olive oil.

Add raw onion to the batter: finely chop 1 medium or large onion or grate and drain the onion along with the potatoes.

MAKE POTATO KUGEL MUFFINS: preheat well-greased muffin pans in a 375° oven. Spoon in kugel batter and bake 35 to 40 minutes for regular muffins, about 25 minutes for mini-muffins.

The variations are delicious with or without the potato chip topping. If not using the topping, drizzle with olive oil or brush generously with Poultry Schmaltz.

POTATO-LEEK MATZOH BALLS

yield: **6 TO 8 SERVINGS**

A longside the golden-fried veal chop my mother made for me for the second seder meal was a tangle of commercial Passover noodles blanketed with tomato sauce. Tangle is definitely the word here: often the noodles were a gummy mess, inalterably linked together like synapses on a circuitous route. Copious amounts of her homemade tomato sauce—so good I could eat it with a spoon, and often did—camouflaged the noodles and made believe they were Italian.

All this came back to me when I retested these potato-leek matzoh balls. I had first made them as a side dish for Moroccan-Flavored Brisket, part of a Passover menu for Bon Appétit *magazine, and my family then enjoyed a second batch with a garlicky tomato sauce, sort of Jewish gnocchi, kosher-for-Passover.*

But this time, when I pilfered a just-cooked dumpling from the platter, it was "déjà vu all over again"—and worse. Not just gummy texture, but it tasted like a ball of mushy mashed potatoes. All that work—for bad mashed potatoes? Plain old mashed were quicker and better.

I didn't have time to toss them out but let the drained potato matzoh balls sit on the platter while I finished preparing the rest of the meal.

And then I tried one again. And again. Somehow the dismal had become delicious. Now, I know that meats must rest to redistribute or reabsorb their juices; kugels and many baked goods need to firm up with time. But I never realized that some matzoh balls need a nap too, after their long hot-water bath.

So let them wait a good twenty minutes after you drain them. They will remain incredibly tender, and the well-flavored leek puree gives the dumplings a delightful buttery finish. You can rewarm them with a light coat of hot sauce or gravy or sprinkle them with a little broth, then heat in an oiled baking dish. They are very good the next day as well, especially with a good homemade tomato sauce like my mom's.

---

2 cups thinly sliced leeks (white and pale green parts only, well washed)

1½ cups chicken broth, preferably homemade (see pages 62 and 70), or good-quality, low-sodium purchased

COMBINE the leeks and broth in a heavy, medium saucepan. Bring to a boil and cook, covered, over medium heat until the leeks are very tender, about 7 minutes. Uncover, raise the heat to medium-high, and boil until the liquid is reduced by about half. Puree the mixture in a food processor or blender until smooth. Measure out 1 cup of puree, and place in a large bowl (save any leftover puree for soups or stews).

About 1¼ pounds russet (baking) potatoes, scrubbed but not peeled

Salt

2 cups matzoh meal

½ to ¾ teaspoon freshly ground black pepper

6 large eggs

⅓ cup mild olive oil, plus additional for greasing pan

Accompaniment: gravy from a brisket or flavorful homemade tomato sauce

COOK the potatoes in a medium pot of salted water until tender. Drain. Peel the potatoes when cool enough to handle, and mash them well, using a ricer or food mill, or by pushing them through a strainer. Measure out 2 cups of the mashed potatoes (save the remainder for another use or discard), add to the leek puree and combine well.

FOLD in the matzoh meal, salt (about 2 teaspoons or so, depending on saltiness of broth, but taste the batter before you add the eggs) and pepper. Beat the eggs and oil in a medium bowl until thickened and light-colored (about 8 minutes, using an electric mixer), then fold into the potato mixture. Cover and refrigerate for about 3 hours to let the flavors marry and make it easier to shape the batter.

LIGHTLY grease a large, shallow baking dish with olive oil. Bring a large, wide, lidded pot of generously salted water to a boil. Using wet hands, if necessary, form about 1 tablespoon of the cold potato mixture into a ball, and place on a platter lined with wax paper. Continue making balls with the rest of the batter. Add half the balls to the boiling water, dropping them in one at time. (Refrigerate the rest of the balls until you are ready to cook them.) Cover tightly, reduce the heat to medium, and cook, without removing the lid, for 35 to 40 minutes, until the matzoh balls are tender, fluffy, and cooked through. Remove them with a skimmer or large slotted spoon—they are too delicate to be poured into a colander—transferring them to the prepared baking dish. Add more salted water to the pot, if needed, and prepare the remaining matzoh balls in the same way. (If you are preparing the matzoh balls a few hours ahead, sprinkle them lightly with a little broth or brisket gravy to keep them moist, and set aside, unrefrigerated. They can be made up to 2 days ahead; in that case, cool them first, then cover and refrigerate.)

IF necessary, rewarm the potato-leek matzoh balls gently in an oiled baking dish, covered, until heated through. Serve as an accompaniment to brisket to catch the gravy.

COOK'S NOTE: Vary your repertoire by experimenting with other purees such as roasted garlic, porcini, or fresh herbs, using the same method.

WHAT'S FOR LUNCH?

A can of tuna and a piece of matzoh. Day two, repeat. Then for a change, hard-boiled eggs and a couple of matzohs with salt.

While opulent seder dinners inspire thoughts of freedom and joy, Passover lunches bring affliction and the bitterness of slavery more to mind. But neither bread nor pizza is necessary for a delicious lunch: the creativity of the low-carb diet gurus has certainly proven that. What is often needed, though, is some advance planning. Here are some ideas.

- My favorite brown bag lunch is last night's dinner, so I try to prepare extra servings of meatloaf, roast or fried chicken, even grilled tuna. To make "sandwiches," pack iceberg or Boston lettuce leaves, fresh herbs, such as dill or cilantro, if you'd like, maybe some cherry tomatoes, and use to make wraps of cutlets, burgers, or croquettes. Or prepare the Oven-Fried Smoked Salmon Croquettes (page 304; omitting mustard, if desired) in muffin tins.

- Prepare flavorful salads (egg or salmon with chopped olives or chicken with grapes and pecans). Mound in avocado halves, on celery or fennel stalks, in scooped out red bell peppers or cucumbers (cut cukes in half widthwise, and use an apple corer to scoop out the centers). Or bring lettuce leaves for wraps.

- Peanut butter junkies going through withdrawal because of kitniyot restrictions can try a nut butter. Lightly toast 2 cups of cashews, almonds, or hazelnuts. Let cool, then pulse in a food processor until finely ground. Add 2 tablespoons of oil (if you don't have a nut

oil, choose another mild one) and a little salt to taste, and continue processing to a puree, either smooth or chunky, as you prefer. Store tightly covered in the refrigerator (preferably upside down, so the oil will flow to the bottom, making it easier to stir when separation occurs—a good idea for peanut butter as well). Spread the nut butter on matzoh, carefully—best bet is on matzoh pieces or crackers; it's especially good on egg matzoh. Top with your favorite jam or jelly, honey, or thinly sliced bananas. Or serve on sliced apples or pears. Also delicious stuffed in pitted dates for a quick snack or dessert.

- The eggy fritadas in this book (Spinach Cheese Squares, page 108, and Zucchini Fritada, page 522) are wonderful eaten at room temperature or even cold. Prepare a batch for several lunches or make it for dinner so you will have the leftovers.

- I began making fruit and cheese lunches for my daughter, who avoided leavened bread not just for Passover but all of nursery school. To avoid monotony, try to have at least three kinds, choosing from mild, soft cheeses, like plain or flavored cream cheese or fresh goat; sliced ones such as mozzarella, Jack, or Muenster; and aged cheeses. Spread on thinly sliced pears and apples. Or serve with matzoh crackers, and include a container of cutup fruits, a bunch of grapes, or clementines.

SPRING COMPOTE

Bracing yet sweet, like the orange on some of the newest seder plates, this fresh compote features not just citrus, but rhubarb, raspberries, and prunes. Accompanied by light, homemade macaroons, it makes a perfect ending to the rich seder meal.

¾ cup sugar

1 cinnamon stick

1 vanilla bean, split

1 pound rhubarb, ends trimmed (discard leaves; they can be toxic), tough strings removed with a vegetable peeler, and stalks cut into 1-inch pieces (4 cups)

½ cup pitted prunes, halved or quartered if large

3 blood or navel oranges, or a combination, peeled, white pith and seeds removed

1 cup fresh raspberries

Optional garnish: fresh mint leaves

Optional accompaniment: Toasted Almond–Coconut Macaroons (page 456) and/or Hazelnut Macaroons (page 458)

PLACE 2 cups water and the sugar, cinnamon, and vanilla bean in a medium, nonreactive saucepan and bring to a boil. Add the rhubarb and prunes and simmer over low heat until the rhubarb is just tender, 7 to 10 minutes. Don't allow it to get too soft—it will "cook" further while macerating. Using a slotted spoon, remove the rhubarb and prunes and transfer to a large, attractive serving bowl. Slice the oranges into thin rounds (if they break apart into little sections after you slice them, that's perfectly fine), and add them, along with the raspberries, to the bowl.

BOIL the syrup remaining in the saucepan over moderately high heat until it is reduced by about half. Remove the cinnamon and vanilla bean (you can dry the vanilla and save it for another use, like burying it in a bowl of sugar to prepare vanilla sugar), and pour the hot syrup over the fruit. Stir well. Let the fruit cool to room temperature, then cover and refrigerate for several hours.

GARNISH the compote with fresh mint leaves, and serve with the macaroons, if you'd like.

TOASTED ALMOND–COCONUT MACAROONS

yield: **30 TO 35 MACAROONS**

Made of ground nuts so they are flour-free, easy-to-prepare macaroons are a Passover favorite of both Ashkenazim and Sephardim. The simple becomes seductive when the almonds are briefly toasted first, their skins left on, and drizzled with maple syrup or brown sugar.

To avoid disappointment, taste the almonds before you start the recipe to make sure they are fresh.

1¾ cups whole natural almonds (about 9 ounces)

1 tablespoon pure maple syrup or packed brown sugar, preferably dark

⅔ cup plus 1 tablespoon white or granulated light brown sugar

1 cup unsweetened shredded coconut

1 teaspoon kosher-for-Passover amaretto or ½ teaspoon kosher-for-Passover almond extract (optional)

4 large egg whites

Pinch of salt

PREHEAT the oven to 350°F. Line a baking sheet with foil. Toss the almonds with the maple syrup or brown sugar and spread them out in a single layer on the baking sheet. Toast until very fragrant, 10 to 12 minutes. Remove from the oven and let cool. Reduce the oven temperature to 325°F.

IN a food processor, grind the cooled almonds with half of the sugar, using the pulse motion, until finely ground. Combine the ground nuts, coconut, and amaretto or almond extract, if you are using it, in a large bowl.

BEAT the egg whites in another bowl with the salt until they form soft peaks. Gradually add the remaining sugar and continue beating until stiff but not dry. Gently fold the whites into the almond-coconut mixture.

LINE a cookie sheet with parchment paper. (You will probably need to use either 2 cookie sheets or work in batches.) Drop heaping table-spoons of batter on the cookie sheet about 2-inches apart. Flatten the tops slightly. Bake for about 15 minutes, until just dry to the touch and light golden with pale brown edges. Remove the sheet from the oven and transfer to a rack to cool or slide the parchment paper off.

DON'T remove the macaroons until they have cooled completely, then carefully separate them. They store well in airtight containers for at least 5 days.

Toasted Pecan–Coconut Macaroons Substitute pecans for the almonds. Be sure to use granulated light brown sugar.

Toasted Cashew–Cranberry Macaroons

Lightly toast cashews without maple syrup or brown sugar (cashews are naturally quite sweet). Follow the directions on page 456, adding 1 cup dried cranberries (plumped first in hot water if very dry or hard, then patted dry with paper towels) before folding the egg whites into the cashew-coconut mixture.

"Figs, grapes, and almonds are always beneficial, whether fresh or dried. One may eat of them as one needs."

—MAIMONIDES, *Rules For Physical Health*

HAZELNUT MACAROONS

yield: 25 TO 30 MACAROONS

These simply made macaroons are imbued with the vivid taste of hazelnuts—the toasty flavor of that transcendent Italian gelato, nocciola.

Nuts can turn rancid easily if not properly stored, so make sure yours are fresh and sweet-tasting.

2⅓ cups shelled hazelnuts (also called filberts; about 12 ounces)

1 cup plus 2 tablespoons white or granulated light brown sugar

½ teaspoon kosher-for-Passover pure almond extract, or 1 teaspoon kosher-for-Passover hazelnut-flavored liqueur, such as Frangelico, or another nut-flavored liqueur like amaretto (optional)

3 large egg whites

PREHEAT the oven to 350°F. Toast the nuts: spread them out in a single layer on a baking sheet, and roast in the oven, shaking occasionally, for about 15 minutes, until they are fragrant and most of the skins have popped. Wrap the nuts in a dish towel and let them cool slightly. Rub them vigorously against each other in the towel to remove most of the loose skins. Don't bother about the remaining skins—they'll just add to the flavor. You can turn the oven off for now.

WHEN the nuts are completely cool, grind them with the sugar in the food processor, using the pulse motion, until chopped fine. They won't be perfectly ground, and they shouldn't be. With the machine on, add the extract or liqueur, if you are using it, and the egg whites, a little at a time. Process just enough to combine the ingredients into a smooth paste. Scrape the mixture into a bowl and refrigerate, covered, for 15 to 20 minutes.

PREHEAT the oven to 325°F. Line a cookie sheet with parchment paper. (You will probably need to use either two cookie sheets or work in batches.) Drop heaping tablespoons of batter on the cookie sheet, about 2-inches apart. Smooth and flatten the tops slightly with the back of a spoon or your fingertips (the batter will be quite sticky, so you may have to dip your finger in cold water occasionally). Bake for about 15 minutes, until just dry to the touch, puffed, and beginning to color. Remove from the oven and transfer the sheet to a rack to cool or slide the parchment paper off. The macaroons will be very soft but will harden as they cool.

DON'T remove the macaroons until they have cooled completely, then carefully separate them from the parchment. They store well in airtight containers for at least 5 days.

Pistachio-Ginger Macaroons

Lightly toast 3 cups of shelled, blanched pistachios at 350°F for about 8 minutes, just until fragrant. Let them cool, then combine them in a food processor with 3 tablespoons (1½ ounces) candied ginger and 1¼ cups sugar, following the directions on page 458. Add 3 large egg whites (omit the extract) and continue with the directions. Bake for 12 to 15 minutes at 325°F. The flavor of these macaroons becomes bolder and more pronounced after a day or two.

COCONUT JAMMIES

yield: **18 TO 20 COOKIES**

J ewel-toned fillings made of jam dress up the familiar coconut macaroon. For finest results, choose a variety of tart-sweet jams—apricot, plum, sour cherry—to lend color and contrast.

2 large egg whites

¾ cup sugar

2½ cups unsweetened shredded coconut

Pinch of ground cinnamon

Pinch of salt

One or more jams of your choice

PREHEAT the oven to 325°F and line a cookie sheet with parchment paper.

BEAT the egg whites in a large bowl until frothy. Add the sugar, coconut, cinnamon, and salt. Using your hands, mix the ingredients together until they are well combined and form a moist, sticky batter.

SHAPE heaping tablespoonfuls of the batter into balls, flatten them slightly, and place on the cookie sheet about 2 inches apart. (If necessary, dampen your hands in cold water when handling the batter.) With your fingertip, make a small indentation in the center of each jammie, and fill with a dab of jam. I use the tip of a demitasse spoon or a ¼ teaspoon measure for the jam.

BAKE for about 15 minutes, until dry to the touch and golden brown around the edges. Remove the sheet from the oven, slide the parchment paper off and transfer it to a rack to cool.

AFTER the jammies have cooled completely, carefully remove them from the parchment. Store in airtight containers for up to 3 days.

COOK'S NOTE: Substitute chocolate chips for the jam fillings, for an old-fashioned Mounds Bar memory.

HUNGARIAN CHOCOLATE-WALNUT TORTE

yield: **ABOUT 10 SERVINGS**

This is a taste of prewar Hungary, from the family repertoire of my dear friend, Judy Abrams, gifted teacher and poet. Based on ground walnuts and leavened only with eggs, this light, fudge-luscious cake has not a jot of butter or flour, making it Passover-perfect for meat or dairy meals.

To conclude a meat meal, it is delectable plain or dusted fancifully with confectioners' sugar (a Passover recipe without cornstarch follows) or glazed with a simple chocolate icing.

For a dairy dish, cover the torte in swirls of lightly sweetened whipped cream or serve with scoops of vanilla ice cream on the side, accompanied by a steaming cup of strong cappuccino.

Enjoy this beautifully moist and virtually no-fail torte not just on Passover, but year round. When well wrapped (without icing), it keeps very well, tasting even better a day or two after it is made.

As with all nut pastries, be sure the walnuts you are using are very fresh-tasting.

¾ cup sugar (if using half semisweet and half sweet chocolate) or ¾ cup plus 2 tablespoons sugar (if using all semisweet chocolate)

6 ounces fine-quality chocolate, preferably half dark sweet (sometimes labeled German's Sweet Chocolate) and half semisweet, but all semisweet is also delicious; cut into small pieces

6 large eggs, separated

6 ounces shelled walnuts (1¾ to 2 cups)

3 tablespoons matzoh meal

HAVE all ingredients at room temperature.

LINE the bottom of an 8-inch square cake pan or a 9-inch springform pan with parchment or wax paper.

PREHEAT the oven to 350°F.

IN a heavy-bottomed 2- or 3-quart saucepan, combine ½ cup of the sugar and ½ cup water and bring to a boil, stirring constantly over medium heat. Continue boiling and stirring until all the grains of sugar have completely dissolved and the mixture forms a simple syrup. Remove the pan from the heat and stir in the chocolate until melted and smooth. Set aside to cool.

IN a large bowl, beat the egg yolks with an electric mixer until light and thickened, about 4 minutes. Grind the walnuts with the remaining sugar and the matzoh meal in a food processor using the pulse motion and stir into the egg yolks. Add the cooled chocolate mixture and combine thoroughly.

USING clean beaters, beat the egg whites in another bowl until they hold stiff peaks. Gradually fold the whites into the chocolate-walnut mix-

Optional accompaniments: Passover Confectioners' Sugar (recipe follows) or Chocolate Icing (page 463); heavy cream, freshly whipped to soft drifts and barely or very lightly sweetened; or vanilla ice cream

Optional garnish: walnut halves

ture, incorporating them gently but thoroughly so that no whites are visible. Pour the batter into the prepared pan and bake for 30 to 40 minutes, until puffed and almost set but still a little gooey in the center. A wooden toothpick inserted 1 inch from the edge should come out clean.

REMOVE the pan from the oven and let cool on a rack. When completely cool, unmold the cake by running a thin-bladed knife around the edges of the cake to release it from the pan (or release the springform); invert onto a platter. Peel off the parchment paper. Serve the torte at room temperature.

IF desired, lightly dust with Passover confectioners' sugar. For a lovely, simple presentation, place a doily or a stencil—handmade by you or, even better, your children—over the torte, then sprinkle with the sugar. Carefully remove the doily or stencil.

OR glaze with the chocolate icing. Lay long strips of wax paper or foil on a cake plate or serving platter and place the cake on top. Pour the glaze over the top of the cake, letting it drip down the sides. Using a spatula, evenly spread the glaze over the top and sides. Now, pull out and discard the paper or foil strips—the plate will be clean and ready for serving. If you'd like, garnish with a few walnut halves attractively placed in the center of the cake. Refrigerate the cake for about an hour to set the glaze, but bring it to room temperature before serving.

THE plain or frosted torte is heavenly with generous dollops of whipped cream or vanilla ice cream.

PASSOVER CONFECTIONERS' SUGAR

IN a blender, mini-food processor, or clean coffee grinder, whirl 1 cup minus ½ tablespoon regular granulated sugar until it is powdery. Place in a small bowl and stir in ½ teaspoon potato starch. Sift before using. (Recently commercial Passover confectioners' sugar, made without cornstarch, has appeared in some stores with large kosher-for-Passover sections. If available, by all means use it here.)

CHOCOLATE ICING

yield: SCANT 1 CUP

6 tablespoons (¾ stick) unsalted butter or margarine

6 ounces fine-quality semisweet or bittersweet chocolate, cut into small pieces

MELT the butter or margarine slowly in a heavy saucepan over very low heat. When half is melted, gradually whisk in the chocolate, stirring well as it melts. After all the chocolate has been added, stir in 2 tablespoons water and beat well until the glaze is completely smooth. Let the mixture cool about 5 minutes to thicken slightly.

RICH FUDGE BROWNIES

yield: 16 TO 20 SQUARES

"Is it done?"

"No, it's not done."

"Don't overcook it. You overcook it, it's no good. It defeats its own purpose."

Robert DeNiro, as the boxer Jake LaMotta, and his soon-to-be-ex-wife, in the film Raging Bull, *may have uttered those words about a steak. But when I'm baking chocolate—either brownies or my Passover Hungarian torte—that's pretty much the subtext when my daughter Alex begins her "I think it's ready" monologue.*

The purpose of chocolate, she has explained, is its moist fudginess. When baked to the cakey stage, it tastes not only dry but also less chocolatey.

So whether you snatch these brownies from the oven so underdone they require wet napkins for fingertips and lips, or make them just a little "rare," don't overbake them. The brownies are wonderful anytime of the year.

1 cup granulated white sugar

1 cup granulated light brown sugar

16 tablespoons (2 sticks) unsalted butter, melted and cooled, ¾ cup oil (choose avocado, walnut, or other mild, unflavored variety), or 16 tablespoons (2 sticks) unsalted kosher-for-Passover margarine, melted and cooled

4 large eggs

1 teaspoon kosher-for-Passover vanilla extract or 2 teaspoons kosher-for-Passover coffee-flavored liqueur

1 cup unsweetened cocoa powder (do not use Dutch-process cocoa)

½ cup matzoh cake meal

1½ teaspoons finely ground expresso coffee or instant expresso powder

¼ teaspoon salt (omit if using margarine)

PREHEAT oven to 350°F.

LINE an 11 by 7-inch rectangular or 9-inch square baking pan with parchment or grease it lightly.

IN a large bowl, combine the white and brown sugars with the butter, oil, or margarine. Add the eggs and vanilla extract or liqueur and beat until light and fluffy. In a separate bowl, stir together the cocoa, cake meal, coffee, and salt. Add the dry ingredients to the batter and blend until smooth.

SPOON the batter into the prepared pan. Bake about 25 minutes. Brownies should be moist. They are done when the batter is just set, the top dry to the touch, but no crust has yet formed around the edges. A toothpick inserted halfway between the center and the edges of the pan should come out just about clean; a toothpick inserted in the center will still emerge with some moist batter clinging to it. The size and material of the pan will affect cooking time, so begin checking after 20 minutes.

TRANSFER the pan to a rack and let stand until cool. Cut into squares.

ITALIAN CARROT-PECAN TORTA

yield: 8 TO 10 SERVINGS

Only distantly related to the American-style dense, spicy loaf capped with a cream cheese frosting, this light, airy cake traces its roots to the delicate carrot-almond torta that Italian Jews enjoy on Passover. I've lightly caramelized the carrots with a little brown sugar to get their sweet juices going before adding them to the batter, and I've replaced the blanched, slightly drier almonds with buttery-tasting toasted pecans to produce a moister cake with richer flavor. In fact, this torte does not taste like Passover at all and is a welcome addition to fall holiday menus, too.

Perfect unadorned, the cake dresses up with a mantle of powdered sugar, accompanied, perhaps, by a scoop of mango, pineapple, or citrus sorbet. Well-wrapped and unrefrigerated, it stays delicious for several days.

To avoid disappointment, taste the pecans first to make sure they are fresh.

1¼ cups packed scraped and finely grated carrots, preferably organic (about ½ pound)

½ cup granulated light brown sugar

1⅓ cups shelled pecans

4 large eggs, separated

Salt

½ cup granulated white sugar

3 tablespoons matzoh meal

1 teaspoon ground cinnamon

⅛ teaspoon freshly grated nutmeg

1 teaspoon kosher-for-Passover vanilla extract

1 teaspoon kosher-for-Passover almond extract

HAVE all ingredients at room temperature. Preheat the oven to 350°F.

LINE the bottom of a 10-inch round cake pan with 2-inch sides with parchment paper.

TO prepare the carrots, gently dry-fry them with some of the brown sugar: warm a large, nonstick skillet over moderate heat. Add the carrots, spreading them out evenly in the pan. Sprinkle with 2 tablespoons of the brown sugar, and cook, turning the carrots, until the sugar has melted and the carrots are glistening. Raise the heat to medium-high, and continue cooking for about 4 minutes, as the carrots begin to caramelize. Transfer the carrots to a bowl and set aside to cool.

TOAST the nuts: spread them out in a single layer in a baking dish or on a baking sheet, and roast in the oven, shaking occasionally, for about 10 minutes, until they are very fragrant. Remove from the oven and let cool. Leave the oven on.

IN a large bowl, use electric beaters to whip the egg yolks with ¼ cup brown sugar until thickened, about 5 minutes. In another large bowl, using clean beaters, whip the egg whites with a generous pinch of salt on low speed until they are foamy. Increase the speed and slowly tip

**Confectioners' sugar,
purchased or prepared
from recipe on page 462
(optional)**

in the white sugar while continuing to whip the whites until they hold stiff, glossy peaks.

GRIND the pecans in a food processor together with the remaining 2 tablespoons brown sugar, the matzoh meal, cinnamon, and nutmeg, using the pulse motion. Stir the mixture into the beaten egg yolks. Add the vanilla and almond extracts and the carrots and combine well.

GRADUALLY fold the whites into the carrot-pecan mixture, incorporating them gently but thoroughly so that no whites are visible. Pour the batter into the prepared pan and bake for about 45 minutes, or until a toothpick inserted in the center comes out clean.

REMOVE the pan from the oven and let cool on a rack. Unmold by running a thin-bladed knife around the edges of the cake to release it from the pan; invert onto a platter. Peel off the parchment paper. Serve the torta at room temperature, lightly dusted with Passover confectioners' sugar, if desired.

COOK'S NOTE: ½ cup golden raisins are a nice addition.

UPSIDE-DOWN APRICOT HAZELNUT TORTE

yield: **8 TO 10 SERVINGS**

*F*lavorful fruit makes a winning, moist crown for nut-based Passover cakes prepared without butter or other dairy ingredients. But my upside-down tortes sometimes ended up with soggy crusts. Stumped, I turned to my dear friend, Maria Springer, owner of Maja's Viennese Kitchen, a cooking school just outside of Baltimore.

A chemist by training, Maria began by analyzing the ingredients, recommending skinned nuts less oil-rich than pecans or walnuts and adding a little potato starch to the macaroon batter. She also suggested room temperature egg whites (if necessary, warm the eggs in their shells in tepid water) for the most volume. And another secret: don't spread the batter all the way to the pan edges so some of the moisture in the crust will evaporate during the baking. The result is a crust with great texture and delicious old-country flavor.

The first cake is covered with sweet-tart dried apricots. Maria's easy fresh apple topping on an almond crust follows.

FOR THE CRUST

1½ cups hazelnuts, skinned (see page 458)

⅔ cup unsweetened shredded coconut

⅔ cup plus 1 tablespoon granulated white sugar

⅓ cup potato starch

4 large egg whites

Salt

1 teaspoon kosher-for-Passover vanilla extract

HAVE all the crust ingredients at room temperature. Preheat the oven to 350°F.

ARRANGE the apricots in a single layer in a pie pan or baking dish just large enough to accommodate them. In a small bowl, stir together the apple juice, 1 tablespoon of the brown sugar, the almond extract or liqueur, and a pinch of salt, and pour over the apricots. Cover the dish tightly with foil and bake for 1 hour, or until most of the liquid is absorbed and the fruit is plump and juicy. Remove the foil and let cool slightly.

RAISE the oven temperature to 375°F.

GENEROUSLY grease the bottom and sides of a deep, ovenproof 9-inch enameled or regular cast-iron skillet. Sprinkle the remaining ⅓ cup brown sugar evenly over the bottom.

PREPARE the crust: in a food processor, pulse the hazelnuts with the coconut and ⅓ cup of the white sugar until finely ground. Add the potato starch and process briefly to combine. Transfer the mixture to a large bowl.

5 to 6 ounces dried apricots (about 1 heaping cup)

1½ cups pure, unsweetened apple juice

1 tablespoon plus ⅓ cup packed brown sugar

½ teaspoon kosher-for-Passover almond extract or 2 teaspoons kosher-for-Passover amaretto or Frangelico

Salt

Almond, walnut, or other kosher-for-Passover oil for greasing the skillet

Confectioners' sugar, purchased or prepared from recipe on page 462 (optional)

IN another large bowl, use an electric mixer on slow speed to beat the egg whites with a pinch of salt until frothy. Increase the speed and whip until they hold soft peaks. Still beating, slowly tip in the remaining white sugar. Add the vanilla extract and continue beating until the whites are glossy and stiff, but not dry. Gently fold the whites into the hazelnut-coconut mixture.

ARRANGE the apricots over the brown sugar in the skillet in concentric circles or other decorative fashion. Spoon the crust batter evenly over the apricots, but don't spread it all the way to the pan edges. Bake for about 30 minutes, until the crust is light golden and a tester inserted in the center comes out clean. Let the skillet cool on a rack for about 20 minutes.

RUN a thin-bladed knife around the edges to loosen the cake. Holding a serving plate over the skillet, turn the skillet upside-down, inverting the cake onto the plate. If any apricots remain stuck to the skillet, remove them and arrange in place on the cake.

LET the cake cool completely, then dust with confectioners' sugar, if you'd like. Serve the cake at room temperature or warm (reheat gently).

COOK'S NOTE: A little freshly grated ginger added to the apricots in place of, or along with, the almond extract is a delicious addition.

If you are preparing the cake more than a day or two ahead, hold off inverting it until a couple of hours before serving to ensure the crust remains firm.

Caramelized Apple-Almond Torte
Prepare the same crust as above, substituting 1½ cups blanched almonds for the hazelnuts.

2 cups pure, unsweetened apple juice (do not use unfiltered juice)

⅓ cup packed brown sugar

¼ cup granulated white sugar

1 teaspoon fresh lemon juice

¼ teaspoon salt

Preheat the oven to 375°F. Generously grease the bottom and sides of a deep, ovenproof 9-inch enameled or regular cast-iron skillet.

In a very wide, heavy saucepan, cook the apple juice, uncovered, over medium-high heat until reduced to about ⅓ cup. Adjust the heat to moderate, and stir in the brown and white sugars, using a wooden spoon (a metal spoon may lower the temperature too much, causing the mixture to seize and harden). Cook slowly, stirring occasionally, until all the sugar is melted and the syrup is a deep amber color. Remove from the heat and let cool slightly, then stir in the lemon juice and salt.

Almond, walnut, or other kosher-for-Passover oil for greasing the pan

5 medium-large Granny Smith apples, peeled, cored, and cut into 8 wedges each

$1/4$ teaspoon ground cinnamon

Arrange the apples in the skillet and sprinkle them with the cinnamon. Spoon the syrup over the apples (it will not matter whether you coat them perfectly evenly: the syrup will bubble up in the hot oven, generously covering all the apple pieces). Bake the apples uncovered for 20 minutes.

Spread the crust batter over the hot apples, avoiding the pan edges, and continue with the recipe above.

STRAWBERRY-RHUBARB *SHALET* (PUDDING)

yield: 6 TO 8 SERVINGS

I try to orchestrate my holiday menus to the rhythm of the seasons, and where I live, rhubarb is the first and only fruit (yes, technically a vegetable, but used as a fruit) to arrive in early spring from almost-local farms. I use it often at Passover, when its brassy flavor sounds all the right notes in the rich, multicourse dinner.

Here the tingly-tart fruit partners with strawberries in a flour-free soufflé-pudding. The simple recipe, a riff on Claudia Roden's Apple Shalet from her seminal work, The World of Jewish Food, makes a perfect airy-light conclusion to the seder. At nonmeat meals, serve the shalet with freshly whipped cream or vanilla ice cream.

4 cups rhubarb, ends trimmed (discard leaves; they can be toxic), tough strings removed with a vegetable peeler, and stalks cut into 1-inch pieces (about 1 pound)

½ cup plus 2 tablespoons packed brown sugar

½ teaspoon kosher-for-Passover vanilla extract

Salt

2 cups fresh ripe strawberries, washed, hulled, and quartered, or cut into sixths or eighths if large

Avocado, walnut, or other kosher-for-Passover oil for greasing the pan

6 large eggs, separated (at room temperature)

¼ cup granulated white sugar

PLACE the rhubarb in a bowl, sprinkle it with ½ cup of the brown sugar, and toss well. Let the rhubarb stand for 20 to 30 minutes, giving it a stir now and then to encourage release of its juices.

PUT the rhubarb and all its exuded juices in a nonreactive lidded saucepan, add the vanilla extract and ¼ teaspoon salt, and bring to a boil over medium heat, stirring occasionally. Lower the heat and simmer, covered, until the rhubarb is very tender, taking care not to let it soften to mush. Remove the pan from the heat. The rhubarb will thicken as it cools.

MEANWHILE, place the strawberries in a separate bowl, sprinkle with the remaining 2 tablespoons brown sugar, and mix well. Let the strawberries macerate as the rhubarb simmers and cools.

PREHEAT the oven to 350°F. Oil the bottom and sides of a glass or ceramic baking dish, 13 by 9 inches or the equivalent.

IN a large bowl, using electric beaters, beat the yolks until light and thickened, about 5 minutes. In a separate large bowl, using clean beaters, beat the egg whites with a pinch of salt until frothy. Gradually tip in the white sugar, while continuing to whip until the whites hold peaks stiff, but not dry. Mix the rhubarb and strawberries into the beaten yolks, then gently fold in the whites.

SPOON the batter into the prepared baking dish and bake for about 50 minutes, until the top of the pudding is uniformly puffed and golden brown.

(The top may turn light brown after only 30 minutes of baking, but you'll probably see areas of slight depression where the pudding contains more liquid. Wait until these areas puff and rise before removing the pudding from the oven.)

TRANSFER the pudding to a rack, and let it cool to room temperature. It will deflate somewhat as it cools.

REFRIGERATE until chilled, and serve either chilled or at room temperature.

MANGO- AND SOUR-CHERRY MACAROON CRUMBLE

yield: ABOUT 6 SERVINGS

*A*round Passover at our house macaroons tend to proliferate like wire coat hangers from the dry cleaners. In addition to the ones I make, there are the cakey commercial variety I purchase from my nephews, who peddle Passover sweets as a fund-raiser for their school. A lively fruit crumble is a fresh way to make use of the leftovers, and other suggestions follow this recipe (see Cook's Note).

1½ cups macaroons (homemade or commercial), crumbled

1 cup kosher-for-Passover amaretto

1 large, ripe mango, peeled, pitted, and cut into small chunks (1½ to 1¾ cups)

1 cup canned pitted sour cherries packed in water, drained

2 tablespoons dried cherries or dried cranberries

¼ teaspoon nutmeg, preferably freshly grated

¼ teaspoon ground cinnamon

½ cup almonds, lightly toasted and coarsely chopped

Pinch of salt

3 tablespoons unsalted butter or margarine, cut into bits, plus additional for greasing the pan

Optional accompaniment: vanilla ice cream or dairy-free coconut sorbet

IF the macaroons are very moist, toast them lightly on a baking sheet for 5 to 10 minutes, then let cool. Or leave them out overnight to dry until they are crumbly.

PREHEAT the oven to 375°F. In a small saucepan, reduce the amaretto to ½ cup over medium-high heat. Combine the mango, sour cherries, dried cherries or cranberries, nutmeg, and cinnamon in a bowl. Pour the hot amaretto over the fruit and stir with a wooden spoon to coat evenly. Set aside for about 30 minutes to macerate.

CHOP the macaroons coarsely by hand or in a food processor using the pulse motion. Transfer to a bowl and mix with the almonds and salt. Work in the butter with your fingers until the mixture resembles coarse crumbs.

BUTTER an 8- to 10-inch glass or ceramic pie pan or similar ovenproof dish. Spoon the fruit and accumulated juices into the prepared pan. Scatter the macaroon mixture evenly on top. Bake for 25 to 35 minutes, or until the fruit is bubbling and the topping is golden brown. Serve warm or cold, topped with vanilla ice cream or coconut sorbet, if desired.

COOK'S NOTE: Here are some other ways to use macaroons:

Old-Fashioned Biscuit Tortoni: pack softened ice cream (some suggestions: vanilla, coffee, cherry vanilla) into paper cups. Sprinkle the tops generously with crushed macaroon crumbs and press in firmly. Or fold some crushed macaroons into the softened ice cream, then top with additional crushed macaroons. Wrap tightly with plastic wrap and freeze until solid.

Italian-Style Baked Fruit: lightly sweeten pear or peach halves. (If peaches are not flavorful—they are out of season in spring—slice them with equal amounts of mango.) Combine crumbled macaroons with some butter and stuff the fruit halves with the mixture (or flatten the mixture into disks and place over the sliced fruit). Place the fruit in a baking dish, and sprinkle with toasted almonds. Add a few tablespoons of white grape juice or other sweet fruit juice or wine to the pan to keep the fruit moist and prevent it from sticking, and bake until the fruit is tender and juicy, basting occasionally with the pan liquid.

Stir crushed macaroons in fruit compotes.

Bake finely crushed macaroons until dry and use for cookie crumb crusts—especially good for cheese cake or ice cream pies.

MAKING MATZOH BRIE

You can prepare matzoh brie in several different ways, from fluffy matzoh omelets to crisp French toast–style to batter fried like pancakes. Like most breakfast food mavens, matzoh brie lovers tend to claim there is only *one* correct way to make it (theirs, of course). But I have found that personal preferences aside, different flavorings are often better-suited to one method of preparation than another: tender, delicate artichoke hearts, for example, are best savored in a matzoh brie that is light and fluffy, not thin and crisp. And I think it is easier to transform a homey, savory matzoh brie into a refined side dish or light entree when it is presented whole, like a giant frittata, at more formal meals.

All else being equal, my favorite is the combination matzoh brie, known as scrambled egg-style: a jumble of buttery crisp, well-flavored, chewy, and creamy egg-rich pieces—all in one mouthful.

When I merely want to soften the matzoh, I use cold water. Hot water leaches out the matzoh flavor. When I want a liquid like apple juice to impart flavor as well as soften, I often warm it first so it is better absorbed.

1. **For Either Fluffy or Combination (Scrambled Egg–Style) Matzoh Brie:** Soak the matzoh in cold water until soft but not mushy, and gently press out moisture with your hands, or place in a colander and press with the back of a spoon. The less liquid it holds, the more egg it will absorb and the fluffier it will be. Let the matzoh drink in the beaten eggs for about 10 minutes or longer to produce the fluffiest matzoh brie. (The egg may or may not be completely absorbed by the matzoh; it will not matter.) Use either a large, heavy, well-seasoned skillet or a nonstick one (nonstick would be preferable if the matzoh brie contains dried fruit, such as raisins or prunes). Add the matzoh mixture all at once to the hot, greased pan. Spread it out evenly, and let it cook over medium heat until it is set and golden on the bottom and around the edges. Now you have a choice.

   For attractive matzoh brie resembling a frittata: Turn the matzoh in one piece. Slip a spatula around the edges and underneath the matzoh brie to loosen it. Use the spatula to help you slide the matzoh brie out onto a platter larger than the skillet, uncooked side up. If needed, add more butter or oil to the skillet. Then, gently holding onto the edges of the matzoh brie with your fingertips, invert the platter over the skillet so that the matzoh brie drops into the skillet, uncooked side down.

Another method for flipping the matzoh brie in one piece, if your skillet is not too heavy: After you've loosened the matzoh brie, remove the skillet from the heat. Place the platter face down over the skillet. With one hand holding onto the skillet handle and the other hand placed on the center of the platter, quickly flip them over so that the matzoh brie lands on the platter, cooked side up. Return the skillet to the heat, adding more butter or oil, if needed. Wait until it's sizzling again before sliding the matzoh brie back into the skillet, still cooked side up. Cook the second side until it is lightly browned. Or, for a less-refined look, simply cut the matzoh brie into halves or quarters and then turn to brown each section. Cook until still fluffy inside or more well-done, as you prefer.

Known as **scrambled egg–style,** your alternative is matzoh brie that is homelier, but more varied in texture and taste. After the bottom is set, break the matzoh brie into sections with the spatula. Keep lifting and turning the sections as they brown until you have a superb melange of lightly crisp, chewy, moist, and fluffy pieces. Don't overcook the matzoh brie or it will be dry and hard.

2. **For Crisp, French Toast–Style Matzoh Brie:** Soak the matzoh just long enough to soften it, then gently but thoroughly press out the liquid with your hands, or place in a colander and press with the back of a spoon. For the crispest matzoh brie, moisten both sides of matzoh under the cold water tap, then dry between paper towels. Dip the matzoh into beaten eggs just until thoroughly coated: Don't let it soak. Heat a generously greased, heavy, well-seasoned, preferably cast-iron skillet, rather than a nonstick one. Add the matzoh all at once to the hot, sizzling pan, and spread it out in a thin layer. (If necessary, fry in batches: if you fry too much at once, it won't be crisp.) Fry over medium to medium-high heat until browned on the bottom. Now decide whether you want to keep the matzoh brie in one piece—it will be more attractive, certainly, but rather tricky to do, perhaps more trouble than this homey dish calls for. To keep the matzoh in one piece, try using two spatulas to carefully flip it. Or turn it like a frittata, that is, slide it out onto a platter, and then invert the platter over the skillet (see "For attractive matzoh brie resembling a frittata" on page 474). Or cook it in batches in a smaller skillet, so it will be easier to flip. If looks don't count, simply cut it in half or in quarters and turn each piece, using two spatulas.

3. **For Fried Pancake-Like Matzoh Brie:** Soak the matzoh in cold water until it is quite soft, almost falling apart. Squeeze out as much liquid as you can with your hands, or place in a colander and press with the back of a spoon. Beat the matzoh with the eggs in a large bowl until well combined. Drop the batter by heaping tablespoonfuls into the hot, greased skillet, flatten slightly with a spatula, and fry over medium to medium-high heat, flipping once, until browned on both sides.

CLASSIC MATZOH BRIE

yield: **2 TO 4 SERVINGS**

Not just for Passover. Like matzoh balls and potato latkes, matzoh brie now makes regular appearances at the table year-round.

"And then there was the great classic, matzoh brie, pieces of matzoh soaked in milk, squeezed into a delectable mess, and fried to golden curls and flakes— one of the dishes that evokes piercing darts of nostalgia in every Jewish breast and stories of childhood Passovers complete with lightly drunken uncles."

—KATE SIMON, *Bronx Primitive*

And not just for breakfast. Tony Manhattan restaurants feature entrees of fluffy matzoh brie, chockablock with smoked salmon and sautéed sweet onions, fragrant with dill, or layered with exotic wild mushrooms.

Like the best soul-satisfying starchy foods, matzoh brie is a chef's canvas, reflecting the image and nuances you choose: served like French toast, flavored with vanilla, cinnamon or almond extract and doused with maple syrup; or frittata-style, sautéed with onions, mushrooms, and sapid tender vegetables like artichokes or asparagus. In fact, I often add some soaked and drained matzoh to frittata recipes—it stretches the number of eggs used, reducing that insistent egginess that spells breakfast to so many of us.

No sweet/savory matzoh brie fault line runs through our house: though I grew up on the sweet, we thoroughly enjoy all versions. Instructions for both follow, and see the Cook's Note for a buttery caramelized onion matzoh brie, with or without smoked salmon.

4 whole plain or egg matzohs

4 or 5 large eggs (use 5 for a softer, eggier matzoh brie)

Salt

Freshly ground black pepper

3 tablespoons unsalted butter

PLEASE read "Making Matzoh Brie" and choose the preparation and cooking style you prefer. Break the matzohs, wet them with cold water, and squeeze them dry, according to the instructions, and place them in a large bowl.

BEAT the eggs until light and foamy. For sweet matzoh brie, season the eggs with ¼ teaspoon salt; for savory matzoh brie, season generously with lots of salt and pepper to taste (keep in mind how bland plain matzoh tastes). Stir the eggs into the matzoh mixture and combine well. If

Optional accompaniments:
Cinnamon Vanilla Sugar
(recipe follows), apple
or other fruit sauces
or compotes (check index
for recipes), maple syrup,
jam, honey, sour cream,
yogurt cream (see page
30), fresh (unaged) goat
or sheep's milk cheeses,
farmer cheese, or cottage
cheese

preparing either fluffy or pancake-like matzoh brie, allow the matzohs to soak in the eggs for a while.

IN a 10- to 12-inch heavy skillet (nonstick works well here), heat the butter over medium heat until it sizzles. Add the matzoh batter, either adding it in all at once, like an omelet or frittata, or dropping by heaping tablespoonfuls, like pancakes. Fry until golden brown on the bottom, then turn and fry until done to taste on the other side: either golden and fluffy or more well-done and crisp, according to preferred method. While hot, sprinkle with Cinnamon Vanilla Sugar, or serve with one or more of the other suggested accompaniments.

COOK'S NOTE: For those who crave whole grains during the holiday, try matzoh brie, savory or sweet, made from whole-wheat matzoh (available kosher-for-Passover). No, it won't summon up taste memories of McCann's old-fashioned Irish oatmeal, but it can be a wonderful comfort food when needed.

Caramelized Onion Matzoh Brie

In a large, heavy skillet, sauté 1 pound very thinly sliced onions (4 cups) in 2 tablespoons unsalted butter and 1 tablespoon mild oil until softened and golden, about 15 minutes. Salt and pepper generously, and if you want to include some smoked salmon, stir in 4 ounces, cut in slivers (you'll probably want to reduce or eliminate the salt if the salmon is salty). Raise heat, and cook, lifting and turning the onions until they are a rich gold, speckled lightly with bronze. If you'd like, add 3 to 4 tablespoons chopped fresh herbs (such as parsley or chives; include some fresh snipped dill if you've added smoked salmon), and let cool slightly. Stir the onion into the prepared matzoh brie mixture from the recipe for Classic Matzoh Brie and let stand 5 minutes, then proceed with the directions for frying. If desired, serve with yogurt cream (see page 30), sour cream, or any of the suggested cheeses.

CINNAMON-VANILLA SUGAR

yield: ½ CUP

½ cup granulated light brown or white sugar or a combination

1 teaspoon ground cinnamon

½ vanilla bean

COMBINE the sugar and cinnamon in a small bowl. Split the vanilla bean lengthwise and, using the tip of a small paring knife, scrape the seeds into the sugar. (Reserve the pod for another use or discard.) Stir well, and set aside at least 20 minutes to mingle the flavors. Store in an airtight container and shake well before using.

SAVORY ARTICHOKE MATZOH BRIE

yield: 4 SERVINGS

I usually prepare this delicious, well-seasoned version in the homey, scrambled egg–style for brunch or a casual meatless main course at lunch or dinner. But I've also brought it to the table whole like a poufy frittata, to be served in wedges as a dressy side dish. For a lovely starter, prepare this matzoh brie as individual "pancakes" (see Fried Pancake-Like Matzoh Brie, page 475), topped with smoked salmon or caviar (kosher fish roe), with or without sour cream or yogurt cream.

3 cups very thinly sliced onion

5 tablespoons olive oil, or 4 tablespoons olive oil and 1 tablespoon unsalted butter

1½ cups lightly precooked fresh or thawed frozen artichoke hearts, sliced (if using frozen, pat them dry between layers of paper towels)

½ teaspoon minced garlic (optional)

Salt and freshly ground black pepper

1 tablespoon balsamic vinegar or fine-quality red wine vinegar

4 whole plain or egg matzohs

5 large eggs

3 tablespoons finely snipped fresh dill, plus additional for garnish (also delightful and fresh-tasting with finely chopped mint leaves, added to or in place of the dill)

1 teaspoon dried oregano

IN a 10- to 12-inch heavy skillet (preferably well-seasoned cast-iron or nonstick), sauté the onions in 2 tablespoons oil over medium heat, lifting and turning them occasionally, until soft and golden at the edges, 10 to 15 minutes. Add the artichokes and garlic, if using, and continue lifting and scraping for 5 to 7 minutes, until the artichokes are cooked through and the onions are dotted with dark gold. Generously season with salt and pepper and add the vinegar. Cook for a few minutes over high heat, stirring, until the vinegar is completely evaporated and just a soft, acidic sparkle remains. Taste again for seasoning, then remove from heat and let cool to room temperature.

BREAK the matzohs into 2- or 3-inch pieces and place in a bowl. Cover with cold water and soak for 5 minutes. Meanwhile, beat the eggs in a large bowl until light and foamy. Drain the matzoh in a colander, pressing out all the water with your hands or the back of a spoon, and add to the eggs. Add the dill and oregano, and season with salt and pepper to taste. Stir in the artichokes and onions and combine thoroughly.

PLEASE read "Making Matzoh Brie" on page 474 and choose the cooking style you prefer. Wipe out the skillet thoroughly, add the remaining 3 tablespoons olive oil or 2 tablespoons oil and 1 tablespoon butter and heat until sizzling. Add the matzoh batter all at once, and cook either frittata-style (in one piece, waiting until the the entire piece is golden brown before turning, or break it into sections with the spatula to turn it) or scrambled egg–style (lifting and turning pieces as different egg-soaked matzohs begin to set). Or drop it in by heaping tablespoonfuls, like pancakes, and fry over medium heat, until golden brown on the

Optional accompaniments: yogurt cream (see page 30) or yogurt, plain or mixed with finely chopped scallions

bottom, then turn and fry until done to taste on the other side (either golden and fluffy or more well-done and crisp).

SERVE matzoh brie as soon as it is done, accompanied, if desired, by the yogurt cream or yogurt and sprinkled with additional fresh dill or mint.

CINNAMON MATZOH BRIE WITH TOASTED PECANS AND WARM VANILLA-MAPLE SYRUP

yield: 2 SERVINGS

Homey matzoh brie takes so well to flavorful additions it's easy to turn this simple breakfast treat into something special. Here I bathe the matzoh in apple juice and sweet spices before frying, then serve it with warm, vanilla-scented maple syrup to accent the crunchy pecan studding. Other suggestions for improvisations follow.

3 whole plain or egg matzohs

1/2 teaspoon ground cinnamon

About 1/8 teaspoon salt

1 cup pure, unsweetened apple juice

1/2 teaspoon kosher-for-Passover vanilla extract

3 large eggs

3 tablespoons chopped toasted pecans

2 to 3 tablespoons unsalted butter

FOR THE VANILLA-MAPLE SYRUP

1/3 cup pure maple syrup

1/2 teaspoon kosher-for-Passover vanilla extract

BREAK the matzohs into small pieces in a bowl. Sprinkle with the cinnamon and salt.

COMBINE the apple juice and vanilla in a wide saucepan, and boil over high heat until reduced to about 1/2 cup. Pour it over the matzohs and toss until all the liquid is absorbed. Beat the eggs until light and foamy and add to the matzoh mixture. Stir well and set aside for a few minutes to soak the matzohs. Stir in the pecans.

MAKE the syrup: warm the maple syrup and vanilla in a small saucepan until heated through. Keep warm until ready to serve.

PLEASE read "Making Matzoh Brie" on page 474 and choose the cooking style you prefer. In a 9- or 10-inch heavy skillet (nonstick works well here), heat the butter over medium heat until it sizzles. Add the matzoh batter, either dropping it in by heaping tablespoonfuls, like pancakes, or all at once, like an omelet or frittata. Fry until golden brown on the bottom, then turn and fry until done to taste on the other side: either golden and fluffy or more well-done and crisp.

SERVE at once, accompanied by the warm syrup.

COOK'S NOTE: This simple, sweet matzoh brie should inspire some flavor variations of your own. For soaking, use warm milk or cream flavored with 1/4 teaspoon almond extract, generous pinches of nutmeg and cloves, and honey or molasses to taste. Or dampen the matzohs instead with undiluted, thawed orange juice concentrate, then serve the matzoh brie drizzled with orange blossom honey and a sprinkle of sliced toasted almonds. And sweet matzoh brie is delicious accompanied by lightly stewed fruits such as the Fresh Raspberry Applesauce on page 511, Fresh Berried Fruit Compote, page 505, or any of the fruit sauces on pages 290 through 296.

At the Terezin concentration camp, a vibrant but surreal cultural life was played out against the horrific backdrop of starvation, disease, and death. There, children teeming with lice watched performances of the opera *Brundibar*, and elderly Jews, bodies wracked with enteritis, scavenged for potato peels before attending lectures on theology.

A holding pen where Jews—largely from Moravia and Bohemia, as well as prominent Jews from Germany, Austria, and Western Europe—were kept before being sent to death camps, Terezin, or Theresienstadt, as the Germans renamed it, was held up to the world as a Ghetto Paradise, evidence of the Fuhrer's decency to the Jews.

The cultural activity, extraordinarily prodigious because of the sheer density of talented artists and scholars imprisoned there, and feverishly intensified by the pervasive sense of mortality, was exploited by the Nazis, who trotted out the artists for a propaganda film before shipping them out to Auschwitz.

But, as Cara De Silva points out in her remarkable book, *In Memory's Kitchen*, such fierce cultural pursuits were also a form of revolt. As the Nazis tried to dehumanize them, the children produced poetry and art (later collected in a book, *I Never Saw Another Butterfly*). While the Nazis systematically blotted out their culture, the Jews of Terezin taught philosophy and circulated tens of thousands of books in a camp lending library. And they transcended their hunger by "cooking with the mouth"—talking constantly about food—and writing cookbooks. *In Memory's Kitchen*, "a memoir of life in Terezin, written in recipes," is not the only cookbook to come out of the concentration camps. According to Cara De Silva, there are five more that she knows of, and certainly others exist.

Cocooned in a warm Amtrak berth coming home from the Holocaust Museum in Washington, I read De Silva's description of one of these manuscripts, authored by Malka Zimmet, an inmate in a work subcamp of Mauthausen. She mentioned a matzoh brie with wine and prunes, and I conjured up the dish and the vanished life that had savored it. I haven't seen the recipe yet—the manuscript is in Yad Vashem, Israel's repository of Holocaust research—so I made up my own version, cooked scrambled egg-style.

MATZOH BRIE WITH PRUNES AND WINE

yield: **3 TO 4 SERVINGS**

*T*he interplay of tastes and textures—crisp, tender, and eggy matzoh pieces sandwiching tart-sweet juicy prunes—made this matzoh brie an instant hit. When my daughter was homesick during her junior year in Paris, she whipped this up with lacy French matzohs, substituting plumped, winy raisins for the prunes.

It is even better with a dollop of sour cream or yogurt, which underscores the richness of the dried fruit.

2 cups pure, unsweetened apple juice, or 1¼ cups unsweetened Concord grape juice

1½ cups pitted prunes, halved or quartered if large

1 teaspoon kosher-for-Passover vanilla extract

4 whole plain matzohs

1 teaspoon ground cinnamon

About ¼ teaspoon salt

¾ cup traditional sweet Jewish wine or Concord grape juice

4 large eggs

1½ teaspoons brown sugar

3 tablespoons unsalted butter

Accompaniments: plain yogurt, yogurt cream (page 30), or sour cream; if additional sweetening is desired, use maple syrup, preserves, or honey

PREPARE the prunes: in a wide, medium saucepan, boil the apple juice over high heat until reduced to about 1¼ cups. (If using grape juice, warm it without reducing.) Add the prunes and vanilla, and cook over medium heat until very tender, 10 to 15 minutes. You should have no more than about ¼ cup of liquid left in the pan; if needed, reduce the liquid for a few minutes over high heat.

MEANWHILE, break the matzohs into small pieces in a bowl. Sprinkle with ½ teaspoon cinnamon and the salt. Pour the wine or grape juice over the matzohs and stir until all the liquid is absorbed. Beat the eggs until light and foamy and add to the matzoh mixture. Stir well and set aside for a few minutes to soak the matzohs (the eggs will not be totally absorbed). In a small bowl, combine the remaining ½ teaspoon cinnamon and the brown sugar and set aside.

PLEASE read "Making Matzoh Brie" on page 474 and choose the cooking style you prefer. In a 10- to 12-inch heavy skillet (preferably nonstick—the sugar from the prunes will make this matzoh brie somewhat sticky) heat the butter until it sizzles. Add the matzoh and egg mixture all at once. As it begins to set and brown, break it up into largish pieces with a spatula, turning and browning them on both sides. Spoon the stewed prunes and their liquid over the cooked matzoh brie, as a topping. Or you can incorporate the prunes into the matzoh brie: when the matzoh brie is nearly browned, add the prunes and their liquid. Continue lifting and turning until all the matzoh pieces are golden brown and well combined with the prunes. If you prefer a fluffier matzoh brie, lightly fry the matzoh sections until just cooked through on all sides, adding the prunes about halfway through the cooking process.

SPRINKLE with the cinnamon sugar. Top with plain yogurt, or if you prefer something richer, yogurt cream or sour cream. It really needs no additional sweetening, but if you wish, serve it with maple syrup, preserves, or honey.

OVERNIGHT CARAMELIZED-APPLE MATZOH BRIE

yield: 4 SERVINGS

An evil apple may have done the trick for Snow White's wicked stepmother, but no apple caused Adam's downfall. Though mentioned several times in ancient Hebrew literature, the apple plays no part in Genesis. Adam and Eve sin simply by eating "fruit"—the generic kind—from the Tree of Knowledge.

Was the actual culprit the sensuous, many-seeded pomegranate? Perhaps the luscious golden apricot or the flesh-soft fig? Scholars continue to debate. While the apple was first specified as the evil fruit in Eden by Aquila Ponticus in his second century translation of the Song of Solomon from Hebrew to Greek, and later used by early translators of the Bible, it was Renaissance painters who popularized it, burnished an enticing red, to concretize our fall from grace.

The caramelized apples here certainly reek of temptation, but there's no need to lose any sleep over this matzoh brie. Prepare it the night before, then pop it in the oven the next morning while you shower and dress. It's ready when you are, for breakfast or brunch. And it's splendid too for a teatime treat.

FOR THE CARAMELIZED APPLES

4 medium-large flavorful apples (about 2 pounds; an assortment of tart and sweet, such as Winesap, Northern Spy, or Mutsu combined with Fuji, Gala, or Braeburn, works particularly well; avoid Rome apples, which will turn to mush)

3 tablespoons unsalted butter

⅓ cup pure maple syrup

½ teaspoon ground cinnamon

⅓ cup evaporated milk, half-and-half, or cream

MAKE the caramelized apples: peel, core, and cut each apple into small chunks. In a large heavy skillet, melt the butter over medium-high heat. Add the apples and cook, lifting and turning occasionally, for about 3 minutes. Add the maple syrup and cinnamon, and continue cooking until the apples are just tender, 4 to 6 minutes, depending on the variety of apples. Using a slotted spoon, transfer the apples to a bowl and set aside.

BOIL the syrup remaining in the skillet until it becomes a thick, luscious, golden caramel. Stir it frequently while it cooks, taking care that it does not burn. (Although its aroma will be tantalizing, do not taste it; the syrup is scorching hot and will badly burn your tongue.) Off the heat, very carefully add the milk, half-and-half, or cream, the lemon juice, and the salt and stir well. Return the skillet to the heat and simmer the sauce, stirring, until smooth and somewhat thickened. Return the apples to the skillet and stir until thoroughly coated with caramel sauce. Set aside to cool slightly.

2 teaspoons fresh lemon juice

¼ teaspoon salt

Unsalted butter for greasing the pan, plus 2 tablespoons, melted and cooled

4 whole plain matzohs

½ cup evaporated milk, half-and-half, or cream

4 large eggs

¾ teaspoon kosher-for-Passover vanilla extract

⅛ teaspoon salt

1 teaspoon granulated light brown or white sugar

Optional accompaniments: sour cream or yogurt cream (see page 30)

GENEROUSLY butter the bottom and sides of a large, shallow metal baking pan (approximately 13 by 9 inches, or its equivalent).

MAKE the matzoh brie: break the matzohs into small pieces and spread them evenly in the prepared pan. In a large mixing bowl, whisk together the milk, half-and-half, or cream, eggs, vanilla, salt, and sugar. Beat in the cooled, melted butter. Pour this mixture over the matzohs and let the matzohs soak up the liquid for about 15 minutes. Then smooth out the matzoh mixture, evening the top as best you can. Spread the caramelized apples—with all of their delicious sauce—evenly over the matzoh mixture. Cover the pan with foil and refrigerate overnight.

REMOVE the pan from the refrigerator and bring the dish to room temperature. Preheat the oven to 425°F. Bake, uncovered, for about 20 minutes, until thoroughly cooked and top is light golden brown. To finish off the matzoh brie, turn the broiler on and briefly brown the apple topping, rotating the pan as necessary so all sides are a rich, even brown all over.

THIS is excellent served as is, but if you'd like, accompany the matzoh brie with fresh sour cream or yogurt cream.

OTHER SUGGESTIONS FOR PASSOVER

Any of the *Gefilte Fish recipes; *Classic Horseradish, White and Red

Either of the *Chopped Chicken Liver recipes

*Egyptian Ground Fish Balls with Tomato and Cumin (*Bellahat*)

*Classic Chicken Soup with *Classic Matzoh Balls

*Cheater's Chicken in the Pot and Almost Homemade Soup

*Fried Chicken Cutlets, Italian-Jewish Style

*Lemon-Roasted Chicken, with *Rhubarb-Prune Tsimmes or *Caramelized Onion and Carrot Tsimmes with Candied Ginger

*Iranian Stuffed Chicken with Fresh Green Herbs and Golden Soup (if rice and legumes are eaten during Passover)

*Flanken with Tart Greens

*Romanian Garlicky Ground Meat Sausages (*Carnatzlach*) with Sour Pickle Vinaigrette and Roasted Red Peppers

*Cabbage Stuffed with Mushrooms and Meat

*Israeli Salad

*Orange, Onion, and Date Salad

*Zucchini Fritada

*Spinach Cheese Squares

*Bernie's Lox, Eggs, and Onions

*My Mother's Fried Cauliflower

*See index for page numbers

*Moroccan-Flavored Carrot Kugel

*Leek Croquettes from Rhodes (prepared with matzoh meal)

*Cheese Latkes with Fresh Persimmon Sauce

*Greek-Inspired Cheese Latkes

Any of the *Fresh Fruit Sauces

*Dried Fruit Compote with Fresh Pineapple, Pistachios, and Mint

*Sephardi Dried Fruit and Nut Compote (*Koshaf*)

*Old-Country Cottage Cheese Cake (Passover version)

*Honey-Ricotta Cheese Cake

*See index for page numbers

Shavuot

6 AND 7 SIVAN (MAY OR JUNE)

The symbols of Shavuot's ancient agricultural origins are sweet with the perfumes of deep spring: soft-skinned fruits and sun-warm berries, decorative branches of fresh greens and fragrant flowers. One of the three pilgrimage festivals, the holiday began as a joyous harvest celebration. Seven weeks after Passover ("Shavuot" means weeks, and the festival is sometimes known as the Feast of Weeks), the last of the barley harvest was ready to be gathered and the first fruits and new spring wheat were beginning to ripen. Together these comprised the Seven Species, the choice crops mentioned in Deuteronomy with which the ancient land was blessed: in addition to barley and wheat, dates, figs, grapes, olives, and pomegranates.

The most beautiful fruits were set in baskets fashioned sometimes of silver and gold, and carried to the Temple in long processions

490

accompanied by music and song. Grateful for the new grain they had reaped, families brought two loaves of bread made from their finest flour that season to the altar.

Later, after the Temple was destroyed, Shavuot, like Passover and Sukkot, was linked to the Exodus, acquiring a more religious significance as it came to commemorate the anniversary of the covenant made between God and Israel on Mt. Sinai, when Moses received the Ten Commandments and the Torah. If Passover celebrates the Israelites' release from slavery and their rebirth as a free people, their acceptance of God's Laws at Shavuot marks their spiritual liberation, the rebirth of their souls.

This covenant is expressed in two different metaphors. For the kabbalists, Shavuot marks the marriage of God and the Jewish people, and the Torah stands as their *ketubah*, the written wedding contract between them.

The other is the image of all Jews that ever were and that ever will be, standing together as one at Sinai. By tradition, that moment dates their conversion to Judaism: by accepting the covenant, they became Jews by choice.

And on Shavuot, we read about another convert who became a Jew by choice centuries after Sinai. This is the beautifully written Book of Ruth, like Shavuot set during the grain harvest: the story of a Moab widow whose embrace of her mother-in-law Naomi's Hebrew God parallels the Israelites' acceptance of the Torah.

CELEBRATING SHAVUOT TODAY

The word *Torah* means teaching, and many Jews stay up the entire first night of the holiday in study sessions. Reflecting the wide tent that contemporary Judaic thought and practice covers, these sessions now range from all-male groups who study traditional selections of the Torah and the Talmud to feminists focusing on issues of friendship and female bonding as exemplified in the Book of Ruth to coed *havurahs* (informal worship and study groups) who explore the personal commandments the community lives by and what it means to be a Jew today. Some of the participants bring special Shavuot foods to sustain the group as they discuss and learn throughout the night.

In the Book of Ruth, the biblical practice of gleaning—that is, leaving a portion of one's harvested fields for the poor to gather—sustained Ruth and Naomi when they came to Bethlehem penniless. In some Jewish communities, Shavuot has become a time to donate gleanings from home and wallet to those in need.

A midrash explains that as each of the Ten Commandments was given, the whole world filled with the fragrance of spices. Today on Shavuot, Jews adorn their homes and synagogues with leaves and branches, potted plants and fresh-cut flowers, just as during the Middle Ages they strewed spices and rose petals on the synagogue floor for the holiday. Iranian Jews know the holiday as Feast of the Flowers, Italians as Feast of the Roses. The sweet-smelling blossoms and greens recall the beautiful processions through Jerusalem, as well as verdant, rose-covered Mt. Sinai and the aroma of Paradise the Torah offers.

The fragrant new fruits appear in any—or every—part of the meal, from soup to dessert. Special holiday breads remind us of the Temple grain offerings.

But it is with dairy dishes that Shavuot is most closely associated. It is difficult to believe that this custom is nowhere mandated, so strong is the tradition.

One explanation, of course, is found in nature: this is the season when animals, grazing on the fresh, new pasturage, produce an abundance of milk. But there are many spiritual interpretations too, relating the holiday to the revelation on Sinai. Because Moses brought them the laws of kashrut when he descended the mountain, the Israelites were permitted hereafter to eat only meat that was kosher. By the time he returned, however, they were famished and had no time to prepare a meat meal according to ritual. So they rejoiced with festive dairy foods—including, perhaps, cheese formed from milk that had soured during their long vigil. The Torah and Israel have both been compared to milk and honey, nourishing and sweet, while the whiteness of milk and of rice—another popular Shavuot food—evokes the purity of the Laws and the Commandments. And there are still a host of other exegeses based on the numerical equivalents of various words.

Whatever the reason, dairy is a highlight of the Jewish kitchen. This is the time to savor an array of irresistible all-time Hall-of-Famers, presented here in sublime variations: from shav with salmon kreplach to a sensuous honey-ricotta cheese cake, from a richly textured cold fruit soup to luscious cheese blintzes coupled with a fresh berry compote.

SHAVUOT
menu suggestions

*Warm Shav with Salmon Kreplach or *Sorrel-Flavored Mushroom Barley Soup with buttermilk

Fresh corn-rye or pumpernickel bread with sweet butter

*Cheese Blintzes with Fresh Berried Fruit Compote

or

*Savory Cheese Blintzes

or

*Strawberry-Rhubarb Blintzes

*Yogurt Cream or sour cream

*Israeli Salad

or

Boston or Bibb lettuce salad with chopped summer herbs and light vinaigrette dressing (walnut oil with raspberry or other fruit vinegar)

*Old-Country Cottage Cheese Cake

or

*Turkish Silken Ground-Rice Pudding (*Sutlaj*)
with *Fresh Raspberry Sauce

or

*Old-Fashioned Rice Pudding

*See index for page numbers

*Almond Challah

*Grandmother's Cold Fruit Soup

*Falafel-Crusted Sole on Eggplant Puree with Cilantro-Yogurt Sauce

*Potato-Onion Kreplach, Pot Sticker–Style or *Garlic–Mashed Potato Knishes or *Potato and Caramelized Onion Blintzes with *Yogurt Cream or sour cream

Buttered garden peas with chopped mint or fresh asparagus

*Milky Way Dreamy Cheesecake

or

*Rich Noodle Pudding Baked with Fresh Plums and Nectarines

Sweet ripe melon wedges

or

*Fresh Borscht with Dilled Onion-Butter Matzoh Balls

*Fish Baked with Golden Onions and Tahina Sauce

*Zucchini Fritada

or

*Sorrel-Onion Noodle Kugel

Salad of fresh tart greens or sliced cucumbers dressed with fresh dill, coarse salt, and cider vinegar

*Roseberry-Rhubarb Gelato *Honey-Ricotta Cheese Cake

*See index for page numbers

WARM SHAV WITH SALMON KREPLACH

yield: 6 TO 8 SERVINGS

Sour pickles, tangy beets, and cabbage turned to kraut—Russian and Polish Jews have always had a taste for zoiers (sours), the acidic vegetables that nudged along the sluggish digestion of their heavy starch diets.

After a winter of stodgy stored or pickled vegetables, tart and sassy sorrel was a spring treat. Like its cousin rhubarb, the spring zoier (sorrel is also known as sour grass) was considered a blood-cleansing tonic and used principally in two soups usually served cold. The more famous, shav, was a dairy soup often enriched with eggs; the other, botvinya, combined the sorrel with spinach and chunks of fish. The beautiful green that evokes Mount Sinai, where Moses received the Ten Commandments from God, and the lavish use of milk products, made shav a Shavuot specialty.

Though I loved to munch on the refreshing, lemon-grassy sorrel leaves as a child, I couldn't abide shav. The green and cold viscosity of the egg-thick liquid put me in mind of the lower depths of a frog pond and made me gag. Then one day my mother served it warm: the slime receded, in its place a princely soup.

Years ago, reading about botvinya started me thinking about the exquisite combinations of salmon and creamy sorrel I'd eaten in the Loire Valley. Rough chunks of salmon seemed too indelicate for the shav, however, so I encased them in thin kreplach. The result is this soup.

FOR THE KREPLACH

2 scallions, thinly sliced

2 tablespoons unsalted butter

¾ pound fresh salmon, skinned, boned, and cut into chunks

1 large egg yolk

2 tablespoons snipped fresh chives

Salt and freshly ground black pepper

36 to 40 wonton wrappers (see page 39; have a few extra in case of tearing)

PREPARE the kreplach: cook the scallions in the butter in a medium skillet over moderately low heat, stirring until softened. Add the salmon and continue cooking, gently tossing the mixture, until the fish is barely cooked through, 4 to 5 minutes (it will cook further in the kreplach). Let cool slightly, then combine in a food processor with the egg yolk, chives, and salt and pepper to taste. Process the mixture pulsing until chopped fine. Transfer the filling to a bowl, and refrigerate, covered, for 1 hour, or until cold.

FILL and trim the kreplach, as described on page 39, using 1 heaping teaspoon of filling for each wonton wrapper and the egg wash to seal.

POACH the kreplach: in a large, wide pot, bring at least 5 quarts of lightly salted water to a boil. Slip in the kreplach, one by one, being careful not to overcrowd the pot (if necessary, cook them in batches, or use two pots).

Egg wash (1 or 2 large eggs, as needed, each beaten with 1 teaspoon water)

Melted butter

FOR THE SHAV

1 cup finely chopped onion

2 tablespoons unsalted butter

8 ½ cups tightly packed sorrel (14 to 16 ounces), washed, stemmed, and cut into thin strips (try rolling a few leaves together at a time and snipping them into shreds with scissors; see Cook's Note)

2 cups cold water (quality is important here, so if you use bottled water for coffee or tea, use it here)

2 cups milk or 1 cup milk and 1 cup heavy or light cream

2 tablespoons snipped fresh dill

Salt and freshly ground black pepper

2 large egg yolks

1 cup sour cream

Accompaniments: additional chopped scallions and/or dill; sour cream (optional)

Lower the temperature slightly (the kreplach might explode if the water is boiling furiously) and poach until tender, 3 to 6 minutes (exact time will depend on the brand of wonton wrapper used). Remove the kreplach a few at a time with a large skimmer, gently shaking the skimmer so the water drains back into the pot (they are too fragile to pour into a colander). Gloss the kreplach with a little melted butter and set aside.

PREPARE the shav: in a large, nonreactive saucepan or 5- to 6-quart Dutch oven, cook the onions in the butter over moderately low heat, stirring, for about 10 minutes, until very soft. Stir in 8 cups of the sorrel, turn the heat up to medium, and cook for 5 to 7 minutes, until it has melted into a puree.

ADD the water, bring the mixture to a boil, and simmer for 10 minutes. Add the milk (and cream, if you are using it), dill, and salt and pepper to taste, and heat slowly, stirring, until the soup is hot. Do not let it come to a boil.

IN a bowl, whisk the yolks with the sour cream. Slowly pour a cup of the hot soup into the egg–sour cream mixture, stirring to prevent curdling. Then gradually stir this mixture into the soup, and cook, stirring, over low heat for 3 or 4 minutes, to blend the flavors. If you prefer a more refined texture, you can puree the soup to a smooth consistency in a food processor or a blender in batches, or puree in the pot with an immersion blender. Stir in the reserved ½ cup sorrel strips.

TO serve, place 5 or 6 kreplach in each shallow soup plate and ladle the shav over them. Garnish with the chopped scallions and dill, and, if desired, a small dollop of sour cream.

COOK'S NOTE: While 5 or 6 kreplach may seem like a lot for each portion, each krepl is made with a single wrapper, not two. My guests have no trouble polishing them off.

Sorrel should be crisp and unwilted—avoid torn leaves or those with wet or soft spots; store in perforated bags in the refrigerator.

SORREL-FLAVORED MUSHROOM BARLEY SOUP

yield: ABOUT 6 SERVINGS

"*A* bread of affliction," the Passover Haggadah calls it. And the first matzoh probably was. Made of barley flour like the Hebrew breads at that time, it was dense and tooth-defying. As the lighter, more delicate wheat flour became available, baked goods made of barley flour took on an air of poverty and deprivation, gradually losing favor among Jews.*

Not so fluffy barley kernels. For soups and pilafs, where it offers a creamy, risotto-like richness, barley has remained a kitchen staple. Jewish cooks classically combine it with earthy, dried mushrooms to accent the grain's toasted nut taste.

Meaty mushrooms provide the full-bodied base for this vegetarian soup. I use tart sorrel to play up the sweet barley and dairy flavors. Add buttermilk for a fresh, light dish; rich palates will choose instead a dollop of sour cream.

¹⁄₂ cup pearl barley

About 2 ounces dried porcini mushrooms (1 to 1¹⁄₂ cups)

3 cups chopped onion

1 tablespoon unsalted butter

3 tablespoons oil

Salt and freshly ground black pepper

1 cup scraped and finely chopped carrots

2 celery stalks, including leaves, coarsely chopped, or 2 cups coarsely chopped fresh fennel

6 large garlic cloves, peeled

¹⁄₂ pound fresh shiitake mushrooms

¹⁄₂ cup dry red wine

A few fresh thyme sprigs, or ¹⁄₂ teaspoon dried leaves

THE night before, or several hours prior to starting the soup, soak the barley in 1¹⁄₂ cups cold water. (Barley soaked for 5 to 6 hours will cook in about 15 minutes in the soup. Unsoaked barley will absorb a great deal of the soup liquid while cooking, so if you don't have time to soak it, parboil it in about 3¹⁄₂ cups water for about 20 minutes, then drain and add to the soup when called for in the recipe.)

START the mushroom stock: put the porcini in a large, heatproof bowl and add 4 cups hot water. Cover and set aside for 30 to 40 minutes to soften. Drain the mushrooms through a strainer lined with paper towels or a coffee filter, reserving all the soaking liquid. Wash the mushrooms under cold water to remove any remaining grit, then chop them coarsely and set aside.

WHILE the porcini are soaking, sauté the onions in the butter and 1 tablespoon of the oil over moderately high heat in a large Dutch oven or heavy saucepan. Stir occasionally at first, then more frequently as they begin to caramelize, until they are very fragrant and colored a rich butterscotch gold, about 15 minutes. Salt and pepper lightly, then add the carrots, celery or fennel, and garlic and sauté until the vegetables are softened and dotted with gold and deep bronze, 10 to 15 minutes. Wipe the shiitakes clean with a damp paper towel. Cut off the stems flush with the caps. Slice the caps thinly and set them aside, covered with plastic wrap,

½ cup finely chopped shallots, or 1 cup chopped onion plus 2 teaspoons minced garlic

2 tablespoons soy sauce

3 cups tightly packed fresh sorrel leaves (about 6 ounces), washed well, stems removed and leaves coarsely shredded

Sour cream or buttermilk

Snipped fresh dill, for garnish

for finishing the soup. Trim off and discard the tough woody end of the stems. Slice the stems and add them to the sautéed vegetables along with the wine. Cook for 3 to 4 minutes. Add the porcini soaking liquid, thyme, and salt and pepper to taste, bring to a boil, and then simmer gently, partially covered, for about 1 hour. Strain the mixture through a wire mesh strainer into a large bowl, pressing down hard on the solids with the back of a spoon to extract as much liquid as possible. Discard the solids and set the strained mushroom stock aside.

WASH out the saucepan and dry it thoroughly. In it heat the shallots (or alternatively the onions and garlic) in the remaining 2 tablespoons of oil (or use 1 tablespoon each of butter and oil) until golden, about 5 minutes. Add the reserved sliced shiitakes and sauté over moderately high heat until they're nutty and aromatic and bronzed at the edges. Stir in the soy sauce and chopped porcini, and cook over high heat for about 3 minutes, evaporating all the liquid. Add the reserved mushroom stock. Drain the barley and add it, along with the sorrel and salt and pepper to taste. Bring to a boil and simmer for 15 to 20 minutes, until the barley is very tender. Taste and adjust seasonings.

TO serve, spoon a dollop of sour cream into each bowl, then ladle in the soup, stirring until smooth. Or gently warm some buttermilk (don't let it boil or it will curdle), and stir 3 to 4 tablespoons of it into each bowl of hot soup. When enriched with buttermilk, the soup is also delightfully refreshing served tepid, so you need not go to the trouble of heating the buttermilk on sultry days. Garnish with chopped dill.

COOK'S NOTE: The barley will literally drink up all the broth if allowed to remain in the soup. To reserve any leftover soup, be sure to separate the solids from the broth and refrigerate both individually.

FRESH BORSCHT WITH DILLED ONION-BUTTER MATZOH BALLS

yield: ABOUT 6 SERVINGS

The lovely caterer Arlette Lustyk shared the recipe for this simple, delicious soup with me in her Paris office while my husband and daughter entertained themselves poring over photographs of the giant challahs that lined the tables at her fabulous weddings and bar mitzvahs.

Madame Lustyk and her husband, Claude, recommend serving the borscht hot in winter, accompanied by klops, Polish-Jewish meatballs bursting with onions; for the summer, they combine it with crème fraîche and offer it chilled, ladled over a hot boiled potato. But it was spring when I was playing around in my kitchen and I decided to compromise. I enriched the broth with sour cream and served it warm, a supernal hot pink complement to my buttery matzoh balls.

To draw out all the fresh beet essence for the soup, the raw beets are soaked first in cold water overnight, then slow-simmered in the liquid. The resulting borscht (the catchall Yiddish name for soups containing the ubiquitous beet) is more deeply flavorful than most meatless beet broths. I find that the plain borscht, without eggs or cream, also doubles quite successfully as an easily-prepared rosl, a fermented beet juice, to be used for braising (see Beet-Braised Pot Roast, page 428).

FOR THE BORSCHT

About 2½ pounds fresh beets (weight without leaves)

7 cups cold water (quality is important here, so if you use bottled water for coffee or tea, use it here)

Salt and freshly ground black pepper

About 1 teaspoon sour salt (available in specialty stores and those that cater to European and Middle Eastern clientele)

About 2 tablespoons brown or white sugar

2 large egg yolks

A day before you plan to serve the borscht, peel the beets and slice them thinly (wear rubber gloves to avoid staining your fingers). Place them in a nonreactive stockpot and add the water. Cover the pot tightly and let it sit at room temperature overnight or up to 24 hours. Don't peek.

START the matzoh balls: in a medium skillet, sauté the onion in the butter over moderate heat until soft and golden, about 7 minutes. Salt and pepper lightly and let cool. Beat the eggs in a bowl until foamy. Add the sautéed onions (and any butter from the pan) and beat again. Whisk in the matzoh meal, baking powder, salt (about ¾ teaspoon, or to taste), and some pepper. Stir in the dill. Cover with plastic wrap and refrigerate for at least 2 hours to allow the mixture to absorb the seasonings and liquids.

WHEN ready to cook the borscht, remove the pot lid and carefully skim away all foam that has risen to the top. Add 2 teaspoons salt and pepper

FOR THE MATZOH BALLS

1 cup finely chopped onion

3 tablespoons unsalted butter

Salt and freshly ground black pepper

3 large eggs

½ cup matzoh meal

½ teaspoon baking powder

2 tablespoons finely snipped fresh dill

Optional accompaniments: sour cream, yogurt cream (see page 30), or crème fraîche; snipped fresh dill, for garnish

to taste, and cook over moderate heat for 1½ hours, vigilantly skimming off any foam and scum as it accumulates.

ABOUT 10 minutes before the borscht has finished cooking, stir in the sour salt and sugar. Season generously with salt and pepper. Adjust sour salt and sugar to a happy balance between tart and sweet.

MEANWHILE, poach the matzoh balls. In a large, wide, lidded pot, bring 3 quarts water and 1 tablespoon salt to a furious boil. Form the batter into balls the size of large walnuts. (You can also make them smaller, as you prefer.) Slip them in one at a time, then turn the heat down to a simmer. Cover the pot tightly, and don't lift the lid at all until you are ready to test them. Begin testing after 35 to 40 minutes of cooking. To test, remove a matzoh ball and cut it in half: the interior should have no raw or dark spots. They should be light, fluffy, and completely cooked through. If necessary, continue cooking until the matzoh balls test done. Remove them gently with a large slotted spoon or skimmer.

STRAIN the borscht, reserving the liquid and returning it to the pot. (If the beet slices still retain their shape and flavor, toss them with a walnut oil vinaigrette and top with goat cheese—and serve at another meal. If all the flavor has cooked out, discard the beets.)

IN a medium bowl, whisk the egg yolks until light and foamy. Ladle in about a cup of hot soup, stirring to prevent curdling. (This is "tempering" the egg yolks—adding them all at once to the hot soup would result in curdling.) Gradually stir this mixture into the soup pot, and cook, stirring over low heat, just until the ingredients are well incorporated and soup is hot and slightly thickened.

WHEN ready to serve, if the matzoh balls are no longer hot, place them in the hot soup to reheat. If needed, warm the soup gently, but do not allow it to boil or it will curdle. Put a few matzoh balls in each soup bowl and ladle the hot soup over them. If desired, add a dollop of sour cream, yogurt cream, or crème fraîche to each bowl and garnish with dill. Or pass these accompaniments separately so that guests can add their own.

"A broth of beet is beneficial for the heart and good for the eyes, and needless to say for the bowels. . . . This is only if it is left on the stove till it goes tuk, tuk."

—BABYLONIAN TALMUD: BERAKOT 39A

GRANDMOTHER'S COLD FRUIT SOUP

yield: 6 TO 8 SERVINGS

2 cups freshly brewed black tea, such as orange pekoe, Darjeeling, Earl Grey, or English Breakfast

1 cup pitted prunes, quartered

½ cup dried apricots, peaches, pears, or apples, or a mixture, cut into small pieces

2 tablespoons light floral honey, or more, as needed

1 vanilla bean, split

1 cinnamon stick

1 strip lemon zest

3 to 4 pounds mixed fresh ripe stone fruits, such as peaches, plums, nectarines, apricots, and cherries, peeled if skin is tough or blemished, pitted, and cut into chunks (3 to 4 cups)

1½ cups fresh ripe strawberries (9 to 10 ounces), rinsed, hulled, and halved, or quartered if large, or a mixture of strawberries and raspberries, plus 6 to 8 strawberry halves or 6 to 8 raspberries for garnish

2 cups unsweetened apple-cranberry juice (or a similar slightly tart fruit juice)

1 cup sour cream or yogurt cream (see page 30; plain yogurt is too watery here), plus additional for garnish

Optional garnish: 6 to 8 fresh mint leaves

To my grandmother, tiny, first-of-the-year strawberries were the luxury foods of her adopted country, meant to be savored slowly, open-faced on fresh corn-rye bread thickly spread with sweet butter and sprinkled with sugar. Not for her those seasonless behemoths whose hard white hearts you need an apple corer to remove.

Later on, as June warmed and local strawberries grew more plentiful and cheaper at her fruit market, Grandma would serve them with thick sour cream or heavy sweet cream, roll them in a blintz, and even, for special occasions like Shavuot, add them to an extravagant fruit soup.

This soup has several layers of flavor, derived from the tea, juice, and many kinds of fruit—fresh and dried—used in it. But it is the sweet melting strawberries that make it taste extraordinary.

COMBINE the tea, prunes and other dried fruit, honey, vanilla, cinnamon, and lemon zest in a large, nonreactive saucepan and bring to a boil. Lower the heat and simmer for 15 to 20 minutes, or until the fruit is very soft.

ADD the fresh fruit, berries, and apple-cranberry juice. Bring the mixture back to a boil, then simmer until all of the fresh fruit is quite soft, about 10 minutes.

LET the mixture cool somewhat, then taste, and, if necessary, stir in more honey. Remove the vanilla bean and, if desired, rinse and dry it for another use. Discard the cinnamon and lemon zest.

USING a slotted spoon, remove about half the fruit from the saucepan, and puree it in a blender or food processor. Transfer the pureed fruit to a large bowl and whisk in the sour cream or yogurt cream. Stir in the remaining fruit and liquid from the saucepan. Cover and refrigerate until thoroughly chilled, at least 4 hours or overnight.

TO serve, garnish each bowl with a dollop of sour cream or yogurt cream, a berry, and a mint leaf, if desired.

FALAFEL-CRUSTED SOLE ON EGGPLANT PUREE WITH CILANTRO-YOGURT SAUCE

yield: 6 TO 7 SERVINGS

A harmony of well-loved Israeli flavors—crunchy falafel, garlicky eggplant puree, cool yogurt with cilantro—breathes new life into same-old fried fish. To coat the fillets, I rely on packaged falafel mix; some brands are rather anemic-flavored, so I always taste a bit first, then doctor as necessary.

The versatile eggplant puree also makes a tempting dip or a dairy-free spread for challah, and the yogurt sauce is a good complement to cooked vegetables, fried eggplant, rice, and bean dishes like Mujadderah (page 230).

FOR THE EGGPLANT PUREE

2 pounds eggplant

3 garlic cloves, pressed or very finely minced

About 3 tablespoons mayonnaise

2 tablespoons extra virgin olive oil

About 2 tablespoons fresh lemon juice

1 teaspoon dried mint

Salt and freshly ground black pepper

½ cup chopped flat-leaf parsley

FOR THE CILANTRO-YOGURT SAUCE

1 cup Greek plain yogurt, *labneh*, or a mixture of ¾ cup plain yogurt, drained for about 1 hour, and ¼ cup sour cream

⅓ cup chopped fresh cilantro

MAKE the eggplant puree: an alluring smokiness is the essence of this dish, so begin by charring the eggplants. Roast each one whole on the stove over a gas burner as you would a red pepper: either impaled on a long-handled fork or set on a roasting rack placed over the flame. Turn the eggplant with tongs until it is thoroughly blackened on all sides. (Avoid piercing the eggplant with the tongs.) You can finish roasting in the same way, by lowering the flame a little and turning frequently, keeping a close eye on the eggplant until the flesh is very tender throughout. (They will probably exude some of their juices, so be prepared to sponge off the stove while the eggplants cool.)

OR, after the initial charring, you may find it quicker, simpler, and less messy to place the eggplants on a foil-lined rimmed baking sheet in a preheated 450°F oven. Prick them with a fork a few times so they won't burst, and roast until tender, about 20 minutes. Or roast the eggplants until soft on a charcoal grill.

(IF you don't have a gas stove, char the eggplants under the broiler, then finish roasting them in the oven.)

LET the eggplants cool until you can handle them. Peel off and discard the blackened skin and cut off the eggplant cap. Place the flesh in a colander for about 30 minutes to drain off any bitter juices, pressing down on the pulp with a spoon. Transfer to a food processor, add the garlic, mayonnaise, olive oil, lemon juice, mint, and salt and pepper to taste,

¼ cup snipped fresh dill

1 tablespoon finely grated onion

1 tablespoon extra virgin olive oil

1 tablespoon fresh lemon juice

1½ teaspoons finely minced or pressed garlic

Salt and freshly ground black pepper

Cayenne (optional)

FOR THE FISH

2½ to 3 pounds sole, flounder, or similar white-fleshed fish fillets (any stray bones removed with a tweezer or paring knife), wiped with a damp paper towel and patted dry

Salt and freshly ground black pepper

3 large eggs

About 2 cups packaged falafel mix

Optional additions: smoked paprika, ground cumin, coriander, cayenne

¼ cup olive or canola oil, for frying

Optional accompaniment: bottled hot sauce

and process to a smooth puree. Add the parsley and pulse a few times. Taste and adjust seasonings, adding more mayonnaise, lemon juice, or salt and pepper to taste.

PREPARE the sauce: combine the yogurt, cilantro, dill, onion, olive oil, lemon juice, garlic, salt, pepper, and optional cayenne to taste in a bowl and stir well.

MAKE the fish: sprinkle the fillets lightly with salt and pepper on both sides. Beat the eggs with 1 tablespoon water in a wide, shallow bowl or pie pan. Spread the falafel mix on a large sheet of wax paper or a plate. Taste and, if underseasoned, add smoked paprika, cumin, coriander, cayenne, and/or salt and pepper as desired. Taking one fillet at a time, dip it into the beaten egg, coating well on both sides. Let the excess egg drip back into the bowl. Dredge the fillets on both sides in the falafel mixture. To prevent loose crumbs from falling off and burning in the hot oil, pat the fillets firmly on each side so the falafel adheres, then place them on a rack and let stand for about 5 minutes to set the coating.

HEAT the oil in a 12-inch heavy sauté pan or skillet over medium-high heat until hot, but not smoking. Add the fillets (in batches, as necessary, to avoid crowding the pan), and sauté them for 1 to 3 minutes on each side, or until golden and cooked through.

TRANSFER the fillets as they are done to a paper towel–lined baking sheet to absorb excess oil, keeping them warm, if necessary, in a 200°F oven, until the rest are done.

ARRANGE each serving of fish over a puddle of eggplant puree. Top with a dollop of cilantro-yogurt sauce. Pass any remaining sauce separately, and serve with hot sauce, if desired.

COOK'S NOTE: Divide the seasoned falafel mix in half. When the first half becomes ragged with little clumps of egg from dredging the fish, replace with the reserved fresh half.

FISH BAKED WITH GOLDEN ONIONS AND TAHINA SAUCE

yield: **4 TO 6 SERVINGS**

The only time-consuming step in this easy-to-do Middle Eastern and Israeli favorite is caramelizing the onions to a deep bronze-gold. But that is the key to this recipe's success—just as it is to countless others in the Sephardi and Ashkenazi repertoire. Here the savory onions combine with creamy, slightly bitter tahina sauce and sweet, buttery pine nuts to create subtle flavor layers with every bite of fish. I sprinkle on a light dust of red Aleppo pepper or smoked paprika for a spice finish.

Tahina paste can vary greatly in quality: a couple that I have tried tasted stale or had an overly bitter aftertaste. Try a few to find a brand you like. The paste is essential for hummus, and sauces prepared from it are used for everything from dressing salads to glossing meatballs and cooked vegetables.

To add a little more complexity, some cooks grill or sauté the fish first before baking it with the sauce, but I usually use this simpler method.

3 tablespoons olive oil, plus additional for greasing the pan

8 cups thinly sliced onions (about 2 pounds)

Salt and freshly ground black pepper

½ cup tahina

⅓ cup fresh lemon juice

2 large garlic cloves, pressed or finely minced

2 pounds sole, sea bass, flounder, grouper, snapper, tilapia or similar white-fleshed fish fillets (any stray bones removed with a tweezer or paring knife), wiped with a damp paper towel and patted dry

Aleppo pepper or smoked paprika (optional)

¼ cup pine nuts, lightly toasted (or sautéed lightly in butter, if preferred)

¼ cup chopped fresh flat-leaf parsley or cilantro

Accompaniments: lemon quarters; warm pita, freshly cooked bulgur, or basmati rice (optional)

PREHEAT the oven to 350°F.

HEAT the oil in a very large heavy skillet until sizzling. Add the onions and sauté over medium-high heat, lifting and turning, until softened, about 10 minutes. Reduce the heat to medium and continue cooking until they turn a rich golden brown, about 15 minutes. Season generously with salt and pepper, cook for another minute or two, then set aside to cool slightly.

IN a medium bowl, slowly stir ¼ cup hot water into the tahina until it is absorbed. (It will start out lumpy but will soon become smooth with a little mixing.) Stir in the lemon juice, garlic, salt (about 1 teaspoon or to taste) and pepper, and mix until well incorporated.

ARRANGE the fish in a greased baking pan large enough to hold them in a single layer. Salt and pepper them lightly. Shower the fish with onions, spoon on the tahina sauce, and dust, if desired, with the Aleppo pepper or smoked paprika. Scatter the pine nuts over the sauce.

BAKE until the sauce is bubbly and the fish is cooked through.

SPRINKLE with the parsley or cilantro and serve with lemon quarters.

CHEESE BLINTZES WITH FRESH BERRIED FRUIT COMPOTE

yield: 16 TO 18 BLINTZES

A perennial favorite, creamy cheese blintzes are often arranged on Shavuot plates to resemble the Jewish Law: placed side by side, they look like the Tablets given to Moses on Mount Sinai. Or like an unfurled scroll, the Torah.

The seasonal compote here, uncooked to retain the flowery freshness of the berry trio, partners perfectly with the rich, dairy blintzes.

If you want to serve the blintzes as Tablets, arrange them atop a pool of the compote, and sprinkle five tiny parallel lines of cinnamon over each, in imitation of the Ten Commandments.

FOR THE BLINTZES

About 1 pound farmer cheese (two 7.5 ounce-packages are fine)

1/3 cup cottage cheese, preferably dry-curd (pot cheese); if unavailable, use large-curd cottage cheese

2 1/2 ounces cream cheese (about 5 tablespoons), softened

1 teaspoon vanilla extract

About 3 tablespoons sugar

2 large egg yolks

1 recipe Blintz Leaves (page 36)

Unsalted butter, oil, or a combination, or ghee, for frying or baking

YOU will have to eliminate some of the excess liquid from the cheese to avoid soggy blintzes or the need for fillers. I find a lot of liquid accumulates in the farmer cheese packaging, so after I unwrap it, I drain off the water and pat the cheese dry with paper towels. Put the drained farmer cheese in a large bowl.

IF dry-curd cottage cheese is unavailable (it is increasingly hard to find, except at some deli counters in areas with large Jewish populations), also drain the large-curd cottage cheese. This is easiest done by draining for 15 to 20 minutes through a strainer lined with a coffee filter or a layer of paper towels.

MEANWHILE, use a fork to mash the farmer cheese very well. Add the cream cheese and vanilla and blend thoroughly. Add the drained cottage cheese and the sugar and mash until smooth. Taste and add more sugar, if desired. Beat in the egg yolks, cover, and chill thoroughly. The filling will be firmer and easier to work with when cold.

PREPARE the compote: put the blueberries and 1 cup of the strawberries in a bowl, and smash them very roughly with a fork. Sprinkle with 2 tablespoons of the sugar and the cinnamon and stir well. Set aside to macerate for about 10 minutes. Puree the remaining 1 cup strawberries, 2 tablespoons sugar, and the raspberries in a blender or food processor. Force the pureed berries through a fine-mesh strainer (to trap most of the bitter seeds) into the bowl of smashed berries. Stir well, cover, and refrigerate for at least 30 minutes to meld the flavors. The flavors

FOR THE FRESH
BERRIED FRUIT
COMPOTE

**1 cup fresh ripe
blueberries (about
6 ounces), picked over
and rinsed**

**2 cups fresh ripe
strawberries (about
12 ounces), rinsed first,
then hulled**

**About 4 tablespoons
sugar**

**½ teaspoon ground
cinnamon**

**1 cup fresh ripe
raspberries (about
6 ounces)**

**Optional accompaniments:
sour cream or yogurt
cream (see page 30);
fresh mint leaves**

will continue to develop and strengthen, becoming sweeter as the sugar draws out the natural sweetness of the berry juices. Taste before serving and add more sugar, if you prefer it sweeter.

FILL and fold the blintz leaves as directed on page 38, using 1 heaping tablespoon of filling per blintz. (I find these are best when filled and folded and then chilled again, wrapped, up to 1 or 2 days before the final baking or frying. The cold cheese filling is firmer and less likely to leak out when heated.) Bake or fry as directed on page 38.

SERVE the blintzes with the fruit compote, accompanied, if you'd like, by sour cream or yogurt cream, and garnished with mint leaves.

THE blintzes are also delicious served with a fruit sauce like the Fresh Raspberry Applesauce (see page 511) or one of the dried fruit compotes (see index) instead of the berry compote.

COOK'S NOTE: Some cooks substitute packaged Chinese spring roll wrappers (made of wheat, not rice flour) for homemade blintz leaves. They would be a good, quick alternative with sturdier fillings, like cheese or potato; don't use them for delicate fruit fillings. Seal the spring roll wrappers with egg wash before frying. I find egg roll wrappers too thick for blintzes.

The compote keeps well for 3 to 4 days, refrigerated. Use leftover compote with pancakes, puddings (great with *Sutlaj*, page 529), or cheese cake.

Savory Cheese Blintzes
Omit the sugar and vanilla extract. Add salt and pepper to taste, 3 tablespoons finely chopped scallions or 2 tablespoons snipped chives, and perhaps a handful of other fresh herbs like 2 tablespoons parsley, 2 to 3 tablespoons mint or chervil, and ½ to 1 tablespoon grated lemon zest. Make the blintz leaves special by adding 2 to 3 tablespoons of snipped fresh dill to the batter.

JEWISH DAIRY DISHES

We tramped in, sandy-footed and salt-haired, a fine sweat pushing past remnant streaks of tanning lotion on our lightly baked bodies.

"We're having dairy tonight," my mother said, as she nudged us into showers before we could collapse on the sofa.

Set out on the table were fragrant berry soup, hot, fruit-filled blintzes and varenikes or oniony potato and cheese kreplach, golden mamaliga dotted with pools of melted butter and scallion flecks, trays of scarlet-edged radishes in paper-thin slices—absolutely everything slathered with a thick layer of cool, rich sour cream. Except the butter. Cold, sweet butter to spread on fat slabs of corn-rye bread, in case such ethereal fare proved too meager to fill our tummies. And before the fireflies beckoned from the falling night, there was warm, sweet cheese-filled noodle pudding with vanilla ice cream.

A dairy meal—which embraced anything from cheese blintzes to salmon croquettes—was always thought of as light, simply because no meat was served. Often lavish in butterfat and frequently followed by a rich dessert, the dairy meal was a fixture not only of Shavuot and steaming summer nights but Thursdays and preholiday evenings too, when the stomach needed rest before the next day's meat-based Sabbath or festival dinner.

Dairy recipes, whether Ashkenazi or Sephardi, are among the stars of the Jewish kitchen. They are not simply sauces or side dishes playing second fiddle to traditional main course meats or chicken. Because of the dietary regulations, when dairy products are served, no meat or poultry may be eaten. The meals are rounded out with a host of wholesome pareve foods (foods which are neither meat nor dairy): fish, grains, vegetables, and fruits.

Of course for many children—and adults—the delight of a dairy meal is its promise of dessert because all desserts, rich in cream, butter, cheese—or all three together—become possible.

POTATO AND CARAMELIZED ONION BLINTZES

yield: ABOUT 18 BLINTZES

*W*hile cheese scores as the favorite Shavuot blintz filling, savory potato perennially places a close runner-up. A combination of alliums adds complexity to this version: creamy mashed potatoes are mixed with a tangle of sweetly caramelized onions given gentle bite with grated raw ones, then rolled in pretty chive-flecked blintz leaves. For other delicious potato blintz fillings, see Potato-Onion Kreplach, Pot Sticker–Style (page 518) and Garlic Mashed Potato Knishes (page 520).

3 tablespoons mild olive, canola, or avocado oil

3 cups sliced onion, plus 2 tablespoons grated onion

Salt and freshly ground black pepper

1 pound russet (baking) potatoes or buttery potatoes such as Yukon gold, Yellow Finns, or Butterballs, scrubbed but not peeled

About 2½ tablespoons cream cheese

1 recipe Blintz Leaves (page 36), with 3 to 4 tablespoons snipped chives or dill added to the batter, if desired

Unsalted butter, oil, or a combination, or ghee for frying or baking

Accompaniment: sour cream, crème fraîche, or yogurt cream (see page 30)

HEAT the oil in a 10- to 12-inch heavy, lidded skillet over medium heat. Add the onions and salt and pepper them lightly. Cook for 2 minutes, stirring so they are thoroughly coated with oil. Cover, turn the heat down to the gentlest simmer, and cook slowly until the onions are meltingly tender, about 35 minutes. Stir from time to time to make sure the onions don't burn. When they are very soft, remove the lid, turn the heat to high, and sauté until tinged a rich bronze. Stir frequently with a wooden spoon to redistribute the syrupy juices. If necessary, turn the heat down a bit to prevent the onions from sticking and burning. Adjust the seasoning and set aside.

MEANWHILE, put the potatoes in a large saucepan, add enough well-salted water to cover by 1 inch, and bring to a boil. Partially cover and simmer for about 45 minutes, until tender when pierced with a knife tip or a thin skewer. Drain the potatoes, let them cool enough to handle, then peel.

MASH the potatoes until smooth and lump-free, using your favorite tool—a food mill, ricer, potato masher, or electric mixer (but not a blender or food processor.) Mix in the cream cheese, sautéed onion and its oil, grated raw onion, and generous amounts of salt and pepper. Taste—if not creamy enough, add a little more cream cheese and blend in well. Cool to room temperature. The blintzes will be easier to fill if the potato mixture is chilled, so, if possible, refrigerate until cold.

FILL and fold the blintz leaves as directed on page 38, using 1 heaping tablespoon of filling per blintz, and bake or fry them.

SERVE the blintzes hot, accompanied by sour cream, crème fraîche, or yogurt.

RASPBERRY-PEACH BLINTZES

yield: **16 TO 18 BLINTZES**

For very poor Jews in Eastern Europe, summer fruits from Edens like the one in Aleichem's story below were not meant for casual indulgences. The orphaned hero recalls longingly the one peach he ate years before—a Sabbath treat. The entire harvest of Menashe's beautiful pink-streaked peaches was destined for the jam pot. Other Jews reserved their precious fruits—especially berries and cherries—for juice to be drunk strictly for medicinal purposes.

Here the irresistible combination of sunny peaches and fragrant raspberries delivers summer's extravagance in a blintz.

To retain the fresh, pure fruit taste of the blintz filling, I steep the peaches and raspberries in hot, reduced, unsweetened berry juice, rather than a sugar syrup. This gentle "cooking" deepens and enriches the intrinsic flavors of not just perfect peaches, but even those that will never ripen properly to slurpy goodness. Now mingled with peach and raspberry notes, the steeping liquid is further cooked down for a refreshing unsweetened syrup to set off the blintzes.

Present the blintzes with dollops of sour cream or yogurt cream for an alluring play of flavors and textures.

> "I would tell you that the Garden of Eden is in Menashe the Doctor's orchard. . . . What fruits wouldn't you find in this orchard? Apples and pears and cherries, plums and gooseberries and currants, peaches, raspberries, rough cherries, blackberries."
>
> —SHOLOM ALEICHEM,
> "WHAT WILL BECOME OF ME"

IN a wide, heavy saucepan, bring the fruit juice, vanilla pod and its scraped seeds to a boil over medium heat, and continue cooking until the liquid is reduced to a little more than a cup. Place the peaches in a bowl and pour the boiling liquid over them. (Don't bother to wash the pan—you'll be boiling the juice in it again for the syrup.) Cover and cool to room temperature. Remove the vanilla bean (rinse and dry it, if you wish to reuse it, burying it in your granulated sugar for vanilla sugar). Stir in the raspberries.

PLACE a colander over a large bowl and drain the fruit for at least 15 minutes, reserving the juice. Taste the fruit, and, if needed, add a bit of sugar. If possible, cover and and chill thoroughly. The filling will be firmer and easier to work with when cold.

2 cups unsweetened berry-flavored fruit juice (for example, apple-raspberry, raspberry-cranberry, apple-strawberry)

One 2-inch piece of vanilla bean, split and scraped

About 2¼ cups peeled, sliced fresh peaches (5 to 7 medium)

¾ cup fresh raspberries (about 4 ounces)

Sugar, if needed

1 recipe Blintz Leaves (page 36)

Unsalted butter, mild oil, or a combination, or ghee, for frying or baking

Optional accompaniments: sour cream or yogurt cream (see page 30), Fresh Raspberry-Applesauce (recipe follows)

PREPARE the syrup: pour the reserved fruit juices into the saucepan and boil down until reduced to a maple syrup consistency.

FILL the blintz leaves, using a heaping tablespoon of filling for each blintz (do not overfill), and bake or fry them (see page 38).

SERVE the blintzes piping hot, accompanied by the syrup and, if desired, a dollop of sour cream or yogurt cream and/or fresh raspberry applesauce.

FRESH RASPBERRY APPLESAUCE

yield: ABOUT 3 CUPS

"*I*s there a blessing for a sewing machine?*" Tzeitel, Tevye's daughter, asks the rabbi in Fiddler on the Roof. "*There is a blessing for everything,*" she is assured.

In addition to the well-known prayers Jews recite when eating bread or drinking wine, there are many blessings to be uttered when relishing the beauty of the universe: seeing a rainbow, inhaling aromatic spices, and a charming one reserved for enjoying especially fragrant fruits.

That is the one for this raspberry applesauce, perfumed with the scent of fresh berries and vanilla—with a splash, perhaps, of rose water. Like exotic Indian desserts, the fragrant taste of rose water is not to everyone's liking, but my daughter and I are very fond of it, in gentle doses. Potchkehing with this sauce on a warm September day, we found that a small amount of rose water enhances the raspberry flavor and aroma. Not surprising. With shared attributes like a protective armor of thorns and sensuous perfume, the raspberry and the rose, after all, are cousins.

About 2 cups raspberry- or other berry-flavored fruit juice such as raspberry-cranberry, apple-raspberry, or apple-strawberry (use pure, unsweetened juice, not juice cocktail, if possible)

1 vanilla bean, split

Salt

About 2 pounds flavorful apples, unpeeled, cored, and cut into chunks (6 cups; sweet varieties with lots of character, such as Gravenstein, Gala, Braeburn, and Jonathan)

1 cup fresh raspberries (about 6 ounces)

Light floral honey (orange blossom would be perfect) or sugar (optional)

A few drops of rose water (optional)

YOU'LL be reducing the juice quite a bit, so choose a large Dutch oven or a very wide, heavy saucepan large enough to accommodate all of the fruit. Put in 2 cups juice, the vanilla bean, and a pinch of salt. Cook, uncovered, over high heat, until reduced to about ½ cup of thick, syrupy liquid.

ADD the apples and mix well to coat them with the juice. Cover the pan and simmer over low heat for 20 minutes. Stir from time to time, and add a little more juice, if needed, to prevent sticking.

STIR in the raspberries and cook for 5 to 10 minutes, until all of the fruit is very soft. When ready, the mixture should be thick and pulpy, with almost no liquid visible. If necessary, boil it a few minutes, uncovered, to evaporate any remaining liquid.

REMOVE the vanilla bean (if desired, rinse and dry it, so it can be reused or added to granulated sugar to flavor it). Put the sauce through the fine disk of a food mill or push the solids through a fine-mesh strainer to trap the apple skins and at least some of the raspberry seeds.

VIBRANT with raspberries, this sauce may be a bit tart for some palates, especially if the apples are somewhat tangy. If so, add a little honey or sugar to taste while the sauce is still warm. And, if desired, stir in the rose water.

COVER and refrigerate until thoroughly chilled.

STRAWBERRY-RHUBARB BLINTZES

yield: 16 TO 18 BLINTZES

The classic pie mates team up to fill a buttery blintz. The mellow tang of the sour cream or yogurt topping points up the bright flavors of the sassy fresh fruit.

Because the berries are barely cooked, look for fragrant, perfectly ripe ones to make an ambrosial blintz.

About 10 ounces rhubarb, ends trimmed (discard leaves; they can be toxic), tough strings removed with a vegetable peeler, and stalks cut into 1-inch pieces (2¼ cups)

½ cup plus 2 tablespoons packed or granulated light brown sugar

About 15 ounces fresh ripe strawberries (2½ cups), washed, hulled, and halved or quartered if large

PUT the rhubarb in a bowl and sprinkle it with the sugar. Let the fruit macerate for about 20 minutes to release its juices, stirring it every once in a while.

PUT the rhubarb and all its juices in a saucepan, and bring to a boil over medium heat. Reduce the heat and simmer until the rhubarb is very tender, being careful not to let it turn to mush.

STIR in the strawberries, remove the pan from the heat, cover, and let the fruit and its liquid cool completely. This will take at least 30 minutes.

ONCE cool, drain the fruit for 15 to 20 minutes in a colander set over a large bowl to capture the juices. Transfer the drained fruit to another bowl. If possible, cover and chill thoroughly. The filling will be firmer and easier to work with when cold.

PREPARE the syrup: in the same saucepan used for the fruit, boil down the reserved fruit juices until reduced by about one-third, or until as thick as desired. This syrup is also excellent drizzled over pancakes, waffles, ice cream, or frozen yogurt.

"At a dairy restaurant in Buenos Aires, a customer was overcome with hiccups as his waiter recounted the events of the great sour cream shortage, explaining how Gronam had declared that water was sour cream and sour cream water, single-handedly saving the Feast of Weeks from complete and total ruin."

—NATHAN ENGLANDER
"THE TUMBLERS"

1 recipe Blintz Leaves
(page 36)

Unsalted butter, mild oil,
or a combination, or ghee
for frying or baking

Accompaniment: sour
cream or yogurt cream
(see page 30)

FILL the blintz leaves with a heaping tablespoon of filling for each blintz (do not overfill) and bake or fry them (see page 38).

SERVE the blintzes piping hot, accompanied by the syrup and a dollop of sour cream or yogurt cream.

GOLDEN CHERRY-CHEESE VARENIKES

yield: 35 TO 40 VARENIKES

The ripest sour cherry popped into the mouth raw—even when deeply sugared—cannot compete with the sweet kind, dribbling dark juices down the chin, delirious as summer. Just finding a sour cherry requires real detective work. So why bother? Because when they are cooked, sour cherries are unsurpassed. It's then that their fresh, tart-acid taste leaves their sweet cousins in the dust, fleshy and flat in comparison.

Eastern European Jews relished the bright tang of sour cherries in preserves for sweetening dark Russian tea and in cold summery soups. My father's father macerated them in the fiery plum brandy slivovitz and doled out a few to his family each Friday night, a grownup Sabbath treat especially appreciated by his young sons. But they are at their best when paired with cream, like hot cherry blintzes or varenikes (fruit-filled kreplach), mellowed with sour cream, labneh, or rich yogurt cream.

Here almond extract highlights the nutty undertones of the cherries and cream cheese soaks up the flavorful juices they release. Although fresh cherries work best, canned sour cherries packed in water will do fine.

This filling would also be luscious in a blintz. Because the blintz will only be cooked a short time, however, I recommend poaching fresh sour cherries first for a few minutes in sugared water or fruit juice.

Sugar, as needed (if you have vanilla sugar, by all means, substitute it— it is lovely here)

Crystallized ginger, cut into bits (1 to 2 tablespoons)

About 1 pound sour red cherries, stemmed and pitted (about 2 cups; if you don't have a cherry pitter, a hairpin works well), or if fresh are not available, 2 cups canned sour cherries packed in water, drained

4 ounces cream cheese (1/2 cup), softened

IN a blender, process about ⅓ cup sugar with crystallized ginger to taste until the ginger is very finely minced. Add enough of the mixture to sweeten the cherries to your liking (start with about ¼ cup and keep tasting). Let macerate for at least 20 minutes. Reserve any extra ginger sugar for later. Drain the cherries of any juice they may have thrown off, saving it to flavor the sour cream or other topping you'll be serving.

MASH together the cream cheese and almond extract. Dab a little of the mixture in the center of a wonton wrapper. Set about 2 cherries on top (depending on size of cherries). Dipping your finger in the egg wash, moisten the wonton all around the filling. Fold the wonton over to make a triangle. With your fingers, press all air out around the filling then press the edges very firmly together to form a tight seal. Trim away any excess dough with a sharp knife (see page 39).

½ teaspoon almond extract

35 to 40 wonton wrappers (page 39), plus extra in case of tearing

Egg wash (1 or 2 large eggs, as needed, each beaten with 1 teaspoon water)

3 tablespoons unsalted butter, plus additional for greasing the pan

Ground cinnamon

Accompaniments: sour cream, yogurt cream (see page 30), *labneh*, or Honeyed Cream (page 328)

CONTINUE making varenikes until all the cherries are used up. Preheat oven to 400°F and butter a baking sheet generously. In a large, wide pot, bring at least 5 quarts of lightly salted water to a boil. Slip in the varenikes, one by one, being careful not to overcrowd the pot (if necessary, cook them in batches, or use two pots). Lower the temperature slightly (the varenikes might explode if the water is boiling furiously) and poach until tender, 3 to 6 minutes (exact time will depend on the brand of wonton wrapper). Meanwhile melt the butter. Remove the varenikes, a few at a time, with a large skimmer, gently shaking the skimmer so the water drains back into the pot (they are too fragile to pour into a colander). Place the varenikes on the prepared baking sheet and brush generously with the melted butter. Sprinkle to taste with cinnamon and whatever sugar you are using: the reserved ginger sugar, vanilla sugar, or plain white sugar. Bake for 15 minutes, or until golden.

STIR the reserved cherry juice into the sour cream, yogurt cream, *labneh,* or Honeyed Cream, and serve with the hot varenikes.

SORREL-ONION NOODLE KUGEL

yield: 6 TO 8 SERVINGS

They erupted in early spring, their arching dark-green curlicues and hollow stems betraying them among the lawn grasses long before their pungent waft of onion. My sister and I called these wild chives "onion grass," and we ate shafts and shafts as we foraged outside our New Jersey home for four-leaf clovers and cowering purple and yellow violets.

One day my grandfather pointed out the easily recognized arrow shape of wild sorrel, a lemony green fix to cleanse the mouth of onion and too much sun. I was hooked for life.

I find the fresh tart flavor of sorrel extraordinarily refreshing, especially with rich or stodgy foods—a sour taste, like arugula, that I adore. I no longer have access to sorrel foraged or from a garden, but I am extremely fortunate to live within blocks of the Union Square Greenmarket in Manhattan, where beautiful fresh sorrel is usually available spring, summer, and fall—not just trimmed but completely washed as well.

The intriguing medley of flavors in this suave noodle pudding—tart sorrel and sweet, caramelized onions, mellowed by cream—was inspired by Deborah Madison's opulent Sorrel-Onion Tart in The Greens Cookbook *(which was, in turn, inspired by Richard Olney's* Simple French Food.*) Serve it as a starter in a special Shavuot dinner. It also makes an elegant lunch or brunch or a fine, light summer supper.*

2 tablespoons unsalted butter

1 tablespoon canola or other mild oil, plus additional for greasing the pan

2 large onions, thinly sliced (about 1½ pounds; 6 cups)

Salt

4 cups packed sorrel, (6 to 8 ounces) stems removed, leaves cut into shreds or torn into 1-inch pieces

½ cup whole milk

4 ounces wide flat egg noodles (not the twisted spiral kind, which won't absorb as much of the flavoring)

IN a 10- to 12-inch heavy, nonreactive, lidded skillet, melt the butter in the oil. Add the onions, sprinkle with 1 teaspoon salt, and cook, covered, over moderately low heat, stirring from time to time, until the onions are almost clear and very soft, about 25 minutes. Remove the lid, turn the heat up to high, and sauté, tossing, until the onions are a rich gold, 5 to 10 minutes. Don't let the onions brown. Add the sorrel, a little at a time, and cook, stirring until completely melted down, about 5 minutes. Stir in the milk, lower the heat, and simmer until the milk is well incorporated and the sorrel becomes a puree. (Don't be alarmed when it turns an unattractive grey-green—it will taste delicious.)

PREHEAT the oven to 350°F.

BRING 2 to 3 quarts water and 1 teaspoon of salt to a rapid boil in a large pot. Add the noodles and cook until almost tender but a bit firmer than al dente. Drain, then rinse lightly under cool water. In a large bowl, whisk together the cream cheese, sour cream, and eggs until smooth.

**4 ounces cream cheese
(½ cup), softened**

1 cup sour cream

3 large eggs

**Freshly ground black
pepper**

**1 tablespoon grated
lemon zest**

**2 tablespoons grated
Parmesan cheese
(optional)**

Add the sorrel mixture and cooked noodles and combine well. Season to taste with salt and pepper.

GENEROUSLY grease a shallow 2- to 2½-quart baking dish (such as 8- or 9-inch square pan), and sprinkle the bottom with the lemon zest. Spoon in the sorrel mixture and smooth the top. Sprinkle evenly with Parmesan, if using.

BAKE for about 1 hour, until firm and golden brown on top. Remove from the oven and let rest for at least 20 minutes, until the kugel is set. Slice the kugel in the pan, or, if you prefer, run a knife around the edges and invert onto a serving plate. Serve warm (reheat if necessary).

POTATO-ONION KREPLACH, POT-STICKER STYLE

yield: **4 TO 6 SERVINGS**

Inspired by the unabashed charms of homey mashed potatoes, generations of Eastern European Jewish cooks recast them in infinite incarnations. They reappeared as chremslach (crispy fried balls) or mixed with golden onions as savory fillings for knishes, blintzes, and kreplach.

My kreplach, with a voluptuous stuffing of buttery potatoes and burnished onions, fall somewhere between boiled and fried—prepared, in other words, like Chinese pot-sticker dumplings. They make a sensational appetizer, brunch, or dairy side dish.

About 1 pound potatoes, preferably russet (baking) or Yukon gold, peeled and cut into large cubes (3 cups)

1 large garlic clove, peeled

Salt

2 cups coarsely chopped onion

3 tablespoons unsalted butter

1 tablespoon mild olive, avocado, or canola oil, plus additional for frying

2 tablespoons snipped fresh dill, plus additional for garnish

Freshly ground black pepper

24 wonton wrappers (see page 39; have some extra in case of tearing)

Flour for dusting

Accompaniments: chopped scallions and sour cream or yogurt cream (see page 30)

PUT the potatoes, garlic, and 2 teaspoons salt in a medium-large saucepan. Add 2 quarts of cold water and bring to a boil. Cook, partially covered, until the potatoes are tender, 15 to 20 minutes. Drain the potatoes, reserving about ½ cup cooking liquid. Don't wash out the saucepan.

WHILE the potatoes are cooking, in a 9- to 10-inch heavy skillet, sauté the onions in 2 tablespoons butter and 1 tablespoon oil over medium heat, lifting and tossing them, until they are speckled gold and brown, about 15 minutes.

MASH the potatoes until smooth (unlike knishes, kreplach are too small for a few homey little lumps), using your favorite tool—food mill, ricer, potato masher, or electric mixer; just don't use a blender or food processor, which would make a gluey mess. Return the potatoes to the saucepan. With the heat on very low, beat in the fried onion and all of the cooking fat, the remaining 1 tablespoon of butter, and the dill. Season well with lots of salt and pepper. If necessary, whisk in enough reserved potato water to make the mixture creamy and fluffy. Let cool, then refrigerate until cold.

HAVE a small bowl of water at hand. Place a wonton wrapper on a lightly floured surface, leaving the remaining wonton wrappers covered with a damp dish towel. Mound 1 tablespoon of filling in the center of the wrapper. Dip your finger in the water and lightly moisten the surface of the wrapper all around the filling. Now bring up the sides of the wrapper, pleating the edges as necessary, so that they completely surround the filling. The finished krepl should resemble a little open sack made of pasta, encasing the potato stuffing. The stuffing should be visible close to or at the top of the sack. Continue making more kreplach, using the remaining filling and wrappers.

HEAT ¼ inch of oil in a 10- to 12-inch heavy, lidded skillet until hot, but not smoking. Add as many filled wonton sacks as will fit comfortably without crowding the pan. As you place each sack in the skillet, lightly tamp down the bottom so that it sits flat. Cook over medium heat until the bottom surfaces of the wontons are crisp and golden, 4 to 5 minutes. Standing back to avoid being splattered, add ⅓ cup water to the pan, cover tightly, and let the wontons steam until they are fully cooked, about 2 more minutes. The sides should be springy to the touch. Remove the lid, increase the heat, and cook for another minute, until the water evaporates and the wontons are crispy again on the bottom. Cook the remaining wontons in the same way.

SERVE immediately, sprinkled with chopped scallions and dill, and accompanied by sour or yogurt cream.

"Without the potato, the Jewish Lithuanian household could not have existed. Mother was in her element with it. It was as if all her creative force bore down on that lowly tuber to transform it into one tempting magical form after another."

—DON GUSSOW, *Chaia Sonia*

GARLIC–MASHED POTATO KNISHES

yield: ABOUT 14 KNISHES

*F*at, fragrant cloves of garlic, six or seven at a time, were often sautéed whole with foods in my mother's kitchen. No one bothered to fish them out before serving—whoever unearthed the little treasures from a pile of chicken was as much to be envied as the one who landed the wishbone.

As a teenager, I was smugly pleased to read that some food savant dubbed garlic "the ketchup of the intellectuals," gratified that I had been nurtured since babyhood to stand with Camus and Huysmanns.

Readers who have noticed my lavish use of the "stinking rose" will note such love is not merely familial—it is ancestral. Stoked with Pharaoh's garlic when forced to build his pyramids, Jews loved it still when wandering in the desert and pined for it as much as for the winy, thirst-quenching pomegranates they had left behind.

In these knishes, where phyllo substitutes for the traditional pastry dough, light and fluffy garlic mashed potatoes stand in for the accustomed onion-potato filling. The garlic does not stop there, however. It is used to flavor the melted butter brushed so deliciously between each flaky phyllo layer.

10 to 12 sheets frozen phyllo, plus several extra to allow for tearing

3 large russet (baking) potatoes, or about 1½ pounds Yukon gold, peeled and cubed

Salt

12 to 16 tablespoons (1½ to 2 sticks) unsalted butter

3 to 4 heaping tablespoons finely minced garlic

About ¾ cup heavy cream, half-and-half, or whole milk

Freshly ground black pepper

1 large egg, beaten

Oil, for greasing the pan

THAW the frozen phyllo sheets slowly in the refrigerator for 8 hours or overnight. Remove the unopened package from the refrigerator about 2 hours before you begin the recipe to allow the sheets to come to room temperature.

IN a saucepan, cover the potatoes with cold, salted water and bring to a boil. Cook, partially covered, until the potatoes are tender, about 15 minutes.

WHILE the potatoes are cooking, slowly melt the butter with the garlic over low heat, stirring until the garlic just begins to color, 5 to 7 minutes. Don't allow it to cook beyond the palest blond color—it should be tender, not crunchy. Cover the pan, turn off the heat, and let the garlic sit in the warm butter so the flavors continue to mingle until the potatoes are ready.

MASH the potatoes until smooth, using your favorite tool—a food mill, ricer, potato masher, or electric mixer, but not a blender or food processor. Whisk in about 4 tablespoons of the garlic butter (use a slotted spoon to retrieve most of the minced garlic and add that too). Beat in the cream, half-and-half, or milk and season to taste with salt and pepper. The potatoes should be very smooth and light, like very thick whipped cream punctuated with bits of garlic, not dense and pasty like potato fillings you could slice with a knife. It will stiffen somewhat more when chilled. If necessary, add a bit more cream. Beat in the egg, let cool to room temperature, and refrigerate until cold.

PREHEAT the oven to 350°F. Lightly grease 2 baking sheets.

REMOVE the phyllo sheets from the package and carefully unroll them on a damp kitchen towel. Using kitchen scissors or a sharp knife, cut the stack of sheets in half, then cut these two stacks in half again, forming 4 equal stacks of rectangles (exact size will depend on brand of phyllo used). Immediately cover the cut phyllo rectangles with a large piece of plastic wrap and another damp towel to prevent them from drying out.

WORK with one phyllo rectangle at a time, keeping the rest covered with the plastic wrap and towel. Remove one rectangle from the stack and brush it lightly and quickly with the melted garlic butter so it doesn't dry out. Carefully lay another rectangle evenly on top of the first, and brush with the melted butter. Lay a third rectangle on top, brushing lightly again with butter. Spoon 1½ to 2 tablespoons of filling along the short bottom edge, leaving a 1-inch border at the sides. Fold the bottom edge toward the center so that it partially covers the filling, then fold the sides in. Roll up the knish, jelly-roll fashion, into a neat, cylindrical package. Brush the knish lightly with more melted butter over all surfaces and place seam side down on the prepared baking sheet. Keep the baking sheet lightly covered with plastic wrap as you continue making knishes with the remaining phyllo and filling, using the second baking sheet as you fill up the first. If necessary, melt some more butter and add it to the garlic butter. (You can refrigerate the knishes at this point, well wrapped, up to 1 day before baking.)

BAKE the knishes for 20 to 25 minutes, until golden brown. Serve hot or warm.

COOK'S NOTE: Prepare these in miniature for a divine cocktail nibble. Or use the filling in blintzes or kreplach.

You can store leftover phyllo sheets in the refrigerator, airtight, for about 5 days. Do not refreeze them.

ZUCCHINI FRITADA

yield: **ABOUT 8 SERVINGS**

*I*ts Ladino name reveals the fritada's origin in Sepharad *(Old Spain)*. In fact, the dish—containing vegetables, eggs, and usually cheese—was so identified with Jewish life there that a continued taste for it was a telltale sign that a professed *converso was still a Jew in his heart. As David Gitlitz and Linda Davidson point out in* A Drizzle of Honey: The Lives and Recipes of Spain's Secret Jews, *servants' testimony to the Inquisition about fritadas eaten cold on Saturdays betrayed their employers as secret Jews or* Judaizers, *as surely as did the hot Sabbath stews that were made without pork.*

Also known as almodrote as well as several other names in the Diaspora, these crustless casseroles, enriched with roasted eggplant, sautéed spinach, or zucchini, and oven-baked now, are extremely popular, especially among Jews from Greece, Turkey, and the Balkans. Warm or at room temperature, fritadas are ubiquitous at the desayuno brunch served with a host of salads after morning services on Shabbat and holidays, or as a first course at meatless Sabbath dinners.

This well-flavored zucchini version has plenty of pizzazz. A family favorite, it is especially nice for Shavuot, Break-the-Fast, and simple light suppers whenever our greenmarket overflows with either juicy emerald zucchini or the pale green Middle Eastern varieties and fragrant herbs.

If you can find the delicious zucchini blossoms—or better yet, grow them yourself—they make a stunning presentation, a bright orange starburst folded into the center of the cheesy casserole.

2 pounds zucchini, trimmed and scraped

Kosher salt

3 tablespoons olive oil, plus additional for greasing the pan

2 cups chopped onion

Freshly ground black pepper

8 ounces feta (about 2 cups), crumbled

SHRED the zucchini in a food processor or over the large holes of a hand grater. Transfer the zucchini to a colander, sprinkle with 2 teaspoons salt, and weight it down (I use a small plate or bowl topped with a heavy can) so that it can drain for at least 30 minutes. Rinse off the salt, and using your hands, squeeze out as much liquid as possible.

WHILE the zucchini is draining, heat 3 tablespoons of the oil in a heavy 12-inch skillet (preferably nonstick) over medium heat. Add the onions, salt and pepper lightly, and sauté about 10 minutes, stirring occasionally, until very soft and translucent. Add the drained zucchini, and cook, lifting and turning, about 5 minutes, until the zucchini loses its raw look. Let cool slightly.

PREHEAT oven to 350°F.

4 large eggs

1 cup packed shredded kashkaval or kasseri cheese, or a mixture of shredded Muenster and grated Parmesan

3 tablespoons matzoh meal

¼ cup fresh snipped dill

¼ cup thinly sliced scallions (white and light green parts)

3 tablespoons chopped fresh mint

6 to 8 fresh zucchini flowers, if available

MASH the feta in a large bowl. Beat in the eggs, then stir in ¾ cup of the kashkaval or kasseri (reserve about ¼ cup for the topping), the matzoh meal, dill, scallions, and mint. Add the cooked zucchini and onions. Season, if desired, with additional pepper (it will probably be well salted from the cheese), and mix well.

GENEROUSLY grease the bottom and sides of a deep 10- to 12-inch cast-iron skillet or similar size ovenproof pan, pour in the zucchini batter, and smooth the top. If you are using the zucchini flowers, arrange them decoratively. A starburst pattern (form a wide X, then make a vertical line of blossoms through its center) is especially pretty in a round pan. Sprinkle the top with the reserved cheese.

BAKE for about 50 minutes, or until the fritada is firm and golden-topped, and a tester inserted in the center comes out clean.

LET the fritada rest until set before cutting.

COOK'S NOTE: This is even better the next day or when made ahead and reheated.

If your pan is broiler-proof, you can place it under the broiler briefly until the cheese is bubbly, if desired.

SAUTÉED CHIVE MAMALIGA WITH FETA-SCALLION SAUCE

yield: 6 TO 8 SERVINGS

There are those who would deny mamaliga's place in the culinary pantheon, where it is exalted right up there with pastrami and carnatzlach in Aaron Lebedoff's nostalgic song from the Yiddish stage,"Rumania, Rumania." True, its illustrious landsmen (compatriots) resonate with more jazz—and garlic—but peasant-bred mamaliga is so deeply comforting to eat. Like its Italian cousin polenta, this velvety cornmeal porridge will happily accommodate your flavor mood of the moment, cradling savory braises, stews and grilled meats, or rich cheeses. And mamaliga, like polenta, can be served immediately after it is boiled, or baked with melting cheese, or—my favorite method—cooled, sliced, and lightly fried, as in this recipe.

I like to accentuate the corn taste by lightly toasting the meal first and by using unrefined corn oil to sauté the firm, cooked slices. For dairy meals (Romanian and Italian Jews often make it from white cornmeal on Shavuot), mamaliga is usually prepared with milk and butter and seasoned with a sharp cheese such as feta or a milder Balkan sheep's milk cheese, bryndza. I mellow the saltiness of the feta with spicy scallions and the sour tang of yogurt, a cool complement to the crunchy fried crust.

2 cups yellow or white cornmeal, preferably stone-ground

3½ cups milk

Salt

4 tablespoons (½ stick) unsalted butter, plus additional for greasing the pan and for sautéeing

¼ cup snipped fresh chives or ½ cup finely chopped scallions (white and light green parts)

Freshly ground black pepper

About 2 to 3 tablespoons oil, preferably unrefined corn oil, plus additional as needed

IN a large, wide heavy-bottomed saucepan (enameled cast-iron is ideal), toast the cornmeal slowly, stirring with a wooden spoon, until the kitchen is filled with the fragrant aroma of grilled corn and the golden color begins to deepen slightly. Watch carefully so the cornmeal doesn't burn.

REMOVE the pan from the heat, and let the cornmeal cool to room temperature. Add the milk, 3½ cups water, and 1 tablespoon salt to the cornmeal, and whisk until thoroughly combined. Simmer over moderately low heat, stirring frequently to prevent lumps from forming, until the mamaliga is very thick and pulls away from the sides of the pan, about 30 minutes. It should no longer taste raw or grainy. If necessary, cook 5 to 10 minutes longer. Stir in 3 tablespoons of the butter and the chives or scallions, and season with pepper and more salt, if needed.

TRANSFER the mamaliga to a 13 by 9-inch, lightly buttered or oiled baking dish or a baking sheet with sides. Smooth the top, let it cool, and

FOR THE FETA-SCALLION
SAUCE (SEE COOK'S
NOTE)

⅔ cup coarsely grated
feta cheese

⅓ cup yogurt cream (see
page 30) or sour cream

¼ cup finely minced
scallions

Chopped fresh fragrant
herbs, such as mint or dill
(optional)

Freshly ground black
pepper

refrigerate it, covered loosely with wax paper, until firm, about 2 hours. (It will keep in the refrigerator, tightly covered, for up to 3 days.)

MAKE the Feta-Scallion Sauce: stir all the ingredients together and adjust the seasonings. Allow the flavors to marry for at least 30 minutes.

CUT the mamaliga into thin slices or triangles in the baking pan. In a large cast-iron or nonstick skillet, heat the remaining 1 tablespoon butter and 2 tablespoons of the oil over moderately high heat until hot, but not smoking. Fry the mamaliga slices in batches, carefully turning once with 2 spatulas, until golden and crisp, 2 to 3 minutes per side. If necessary, add more oil and butter to the pan, but make sure the pan is hot before adding additional mamaliga. Serve the mamaliga topped with Feta-Scallion Sauce.

COOK'S NOTE: It's easiest to prepare mamaliga in a large batch, so I often wind up with more than I need at one time. You may want to serve half, and reserve the remainder for another meal (it will keep for about 3 days). I have, therefore, given proportions for the sauce by the cup, so you can prepare as much you need.

Prolonged heat softens firm mamaliga, as it does polenta. To avoid transforming fried slices into a runny, molten mass, keep mamaliga well chilled until you are about to fry it. The oil and butter should be hot enough to form a light crust on the mamaliga as soon as it hits the pan. Finish frying quickly; slow-cooking might melt the slices.

For a delicious breakfast or brunch, fry leftover slices as directed, top with very thin slices of Cheddar, and cover the pan just until the cheese melts. Or omit chives when initially preparing mamaliga, and serve fried leftover slices with maple syrup or honey butter. You can also bake leftover mamaliga: place in a well-buttered or oiled baking dish and drizzle with melted butter; scatter the grated or shredded cheese of your choice over the top; and bake until the mamaliga is heated through and the cheese is melted and bubbly.

RICH NOODLE PUDDING BAKED WITH FRESH PLUMS AND NECTARINES

yield: ABOUT 10 SERVINGS

*N*abokov, *in his brilliant literary study* Nikolai Gogol, *was describing the Russian notion of* poshlust *in the excerpt on the following page, but he could just as easily have been writing about the Yiddish* ongepotchkeh. *Often translated as "overdone," "gaudy," or "excessively fussy" (possibly from* potchkeh, *"to fuss with"),* ongepotchkeh *is what happens when those desperately seeking elegance collide with their own innate bad taste.*

My all-time favorite Yiddish word—just pronouncing it forces you to take a deep, round swig of life—ongepotchkeh is manifested frequently in Jewish foods. There are, of course, the extravagantly sculpted gelatin molds embedded with canned mandarin oranges and other faux-gourmet fruits. Or gefilte fish studded with sun-dried tomatoes.

But the paradigm of ongepotchkeh *is taking noodle kugel—a luxurious confection of pasta, eggs, butter, and milk or cheese or both—and then slathering it with some sweet stickiness that may have been a fruit in another life. The very lushness of a noodle pudding demands an innocent topping—not processed pie gunk filling, but the clean flavors of simple, lightly cooked fresh fruits like the subtly sweetened seasonal fruits found in American fresh fruit crisps or crumbles.*

In this version, the gentle acidity of fresh summer plums and nectarines emphasizes the sweet sumptuousness of the cheese cake—like pudding.

The trick to creating lighter, less dense noodle puddings—more pudding than noodle—is using just enough pasta for the pudding to hold its shape. And I let the kugel rest before baking for at least four hours or overnight: the noodles, bathed in the rich, sweet dairy ingredients, emerge meltingly tender and beautifully flavored.

Salt

8 ounces medium flat egg noodles (not the twisted spiral kind, which won't absorb as much of the liquids and flavoring)

8 tablespoons (1 stick) unsalted butter, cut into pieces, plus additional butter (or oil) for greasing the pan

IN a large pot, bring 3 quarts of cold water and 1 teaspoon salt to a vigorous boil. Add the noodles, and cook until just tender. Drain, stir in the butter, and let cool.

FORCE the cottage cheese through a fine-mesh strainer into a large bowl. Beat on low speed until smooth and fluffy. Add the cream cheese bit by bit, beating until it is totally incorporated. Beat in each of the following, one by one, until thoroughly combined: the milk, sour cream, eggs, maple syrup or white sugar, vanilla extract, and a pinch of salt. (I don't recommend a food processor here: it liquefies everything.)

1 cup cottage cheese

8 ounces cream cheese, cut into bits and softened

2 cups milk

¼ cup sour cream

3 large eggs

½ cup pure maple syrup or granulated white sugar

2 teaspoons vanilla extract

5 to 7 tablespoons light brown sugar, preferably the granulated variety

About 2 pounds plums and nectarines, unpeeled (unless the skins are very thick or damaged), cut into quarters or eighths if large

1 to 1½ teaspoons ground cinnamon

ADD the noodles to the bowl and stir in thoroughly. Butter the bottom and sides of a 13 by 9-inch baking pan and sprinkle with 2 to 3 tablespoons brown sugar. Pour the noodle-cheese mixture into the prepared pan. Cover the pan with foil and refrigerate for at least 4 hours or, preferably, overnight.

PREHEAT the oven to 350°F. Bring the pudding to room temperature; uncover it and bake for 45 minutes. Remove the pan from the oven and arrange the fruit decoratively on top, peel side down. Sprinkle the fruit with 3 to 4 tablespoons brown sugar (this will depend on the sweetness of the fruit—plums, especially, vary widely in sweetness—as well as your personal preference) and cinnamon to taste. Return the pudding to the oven and bake for about 30 minutes, until the fruit is bubbling and the kugel is golden. All the luscious, syrupy juices exuded by the fruit may make the top appear somewhat wet, but these juices will disappear into the kugel as it cools. It will need to cool at least 30 minutes to set before it can be cut.

SERVE warm (reheat if necessary), at room temperature, or chilled (not icy cold). Excellent for dessert, brunch, or an instant breakfast.

COOK'S NOTE: Vary the kugel with your choice of other fruits according to the season or your own favorite combinations. Some ideas: fresh figs and raspberries, cherries and apricots, strawberries and peaches. If the fruit is particularly juicy, drain before adding, and, in addition to sweetening to taste, sprinkle with one of the following toppings, as needed, to absorb some of the juice.

Cookie Crumb Topping

Crumble shortbread or gingerbread cookies. If desired, add brown sugar (light or dark) to taste.

" . . . not only the obviously trashy, but also the falsely important, the falsely beautiful, the falsely clever, the falsely attractive. . . . [L]iterary characters personifying [it] will include Polonius and the royal pair in Hamlet . . . Joyce's Marion Bloom . . . Anna Karenina's husband, Berg in *War and Peace*."

—VLADIMIR NABOKOV, *Nikolai Gogol*

Streusel Topping ¼ cup sliced almonds or ¼ cup finely chopped toasted walnuts, pecans, or skinned hazelnuts; 3 tablespoons packed light brown sugar; 2 tablespoons cold, unsalted butter, cut into bits; 2 tablespoons unbleached all-purpose flour; and a generous pinch of salt. If using almonds, put them in a bowl first and crush them with your fingers, then add the rest of the ingredients, and rub between your fingers until the mixture resembles coarse crumbs.

Graham Cracker Crumb Topping Combine ⅓ cup crushed graham crackers, 2 tablespoons packed brown sugar or white sugar, and 2 to 3 tablespoons cold, unsalted butter, cut into small pieces. Rub the ingredients between your fingers until the mixture resembles coarse crumbs.

TURKISH SILKEN GROUND-RICE PUDDING (*SUTLAJ*) WITH FRESH RASPBERRY SAUCE

yield: 6 SERVINGS

*M*ade without eggs, this velvety pudding is light and sleek, its dairy-pure sweetness nicely underscored by the sprightly raspberry sauce. I first prepared sutlaj— a standard at Turkish Shavuot, Sukkot, and desayuno meals—after hearing so many fond remembrances of it from the Turkish clients in my husband's law practice. My daughter adores puddings of every type; this rendition, my reworking of several recipes, is her all-time favorite.

Not only a smooth, refreshing summery dessert, cold sutlaj, made of cooked-down milk and ground rice, makes an excellent hot-weather breakfast, especially for finicky children. And you might try a Turkish mother's trick: write each child's initial on top of the pudding in cinnamon.

Of course, the sutlaj is also delicious served unadorned, without a sauce.

FOR THE PUDDING

1/3 cup rice flour (prepared by grinding white rice in a blender until it is powdery; you can also purchase it in many health food stores and Middle Eastern markets)

1/3 cup sugar

Pinch of salt

4 cups whole milk (*not* low-fat or skim)

1 teaspoon vanilla extract

1/2 teaspoon almond extract

Unsalted butter, for greasing the custard cups

2 tablespoons brown sugar

PREHEAT the oven to 250°F.

IN a large, heavy saucepan, combine the rice flour, sugar, and salt. Whisk in just enough milk to make a smooth paste. Turn the heat on low and, while stirring, gradually pour in the remaining milk. Although many cookbooks advise stirring slowly in one direction to avoid lumps, I find it is more important to stir thoroughly and constantly. When all the milk has been added and the mixture is smooth, raise the heat to medium and bring to a boil, stirring all the while. Now reduce the heat to low, and simmer, stirring until the sutlaj begins to thicken, about 20 minutes. Off the heat, whisk in the vanilla and almond extracts.

WHILE the sutlaj is cooking, butter the bottom and sides of six 8-ounce custard cups or ramekins. Sprinkle each cup with 1 teaspoon brown sugar and press the sugar into the buttered bottom. Pour the sutlaj into the pre- pared cups. Arrange a kitchen towel in a baking dish so it lies flat and place the custard cups on the towel (this way the cups are easier to reach, they won't jostle about, and they will cook evenly). Pour enough boiling or scalding-hot tap water into the pan to come halfway up the sides of the cups. Bake for 2 to 2½ hours, or until the tops are golden brown. Remove the custard cups from the pan. To prevent a skin from forming on the top, press a piece of plastic wrap directly onto the surface of the pudding. Let

FOR THE FRESH
RASPBERRY SAUCE

½ cup unsweetened apple
or apple-blend juice

2 tablespoons sugar

Pinch of salt

2 cups fresh ripe
raspberries (about
12 ounces)

½ teaspoon vanilla
extract or rose water

the sutlaj cool to room temperature, then cover with foil and refrigerate for at least 2 hours before serving.

MAKE the sauce: in a small, nonreactive saucepan, combine the juice, sugar, and salt and boil over high heat until reduced by about half. Stir in the raspberries and vanilla or rose water. Remove from the heat, cover, and allow to steep until it reaches room temperature, stirring every once in a while. Refrigerate until cold.

TO serve, gently slip a knife around the edges of each custard cup, place a serving plate on top of the cup, and invert. Surround the unmolded sutlaj with some of the sauce, and pass the remaining sauce separately.

COOK'S NOTE: If you want to write your child's initials on top of the sutlaj, don't unmold. (It will not show up well against the brown sugar on the bottom.) Serve the sutlaj in the cup, and pass the sauce separately.

OLD-FASHIONED RICE PUDDING

yield: 6 TO 8 SERVINGS

*L*ike matzoh ball soup, this eggy pudding is supremely comforting and the classic stuff of Jewish dairy restaurants and Greek diners alike. It also inspires nearly as much controversy about its preparation: should you add raisins or other dried fruit, sprinkle with cinnamon, nutmeg, or nothing at all? Follow personal preferences—I love it every way.

Made with prodigious amounts of whole milk, the pudding requires lots of patient stirring, lest it turn pasty instead of creamy-rich. Prepare it when you are busy in the kitchen with other time-eating chores: making soup or stew, baking, or just cleaning up after a big meal.

Unsalted butter, softened

1 cup long-grain white rice (unrinsed)

2 quarts whole milk

½ cup sugar

¼ teaspoon salt

1 cinnamon stick

1 ½ teaspoons vanilla extract

½ cup dark raisins, dried cranberries, or cherries (optional)

2 large egg yolks

Optional additions: additional whole or evaporated milk or cream to thin pudding; sliced, toasted almonds; ground cinnamon or freshly grated nutmeg

WITH long-simmering milk puddings, all too often scorched pots seem to come with the territory. To avoid hours of scouring, choose the heaviest, very large, wide saucepan you have (I use an enameled cast-iron Dutch oven). Rinse it briefly with cold water (but don't dry it), then generously smear the damp bottom with the butter. These trucs will help prevent the milk from sticking later.

COMBINE the rice, milk, sugar, salt, and cinnamon stick in the pan and bring to a boil, uncovered, over medium-high heat. Reduce the heat to moderately low and cook for about 1 hour, or until the mixture is very creamy, the rice grains swollen to form a thick porridge, like oatmeal. As the rice cooks, stir occasionally at first, then more and more frequently as the pudding thickens; this will release the rice starch and the foam created will help prevent a skin from forming. Stir in the vanilla and dried fruit, if using, and simmer 5 more minutes.

MEANWHILE, in a medium bowl, beat the yolks until well blended.

SLOWLY stir a ladleful of the hot pudding into the eggs, then add this mixture back into the remaining pudding in the pan, whisking all the time. Cook over very low heat, stirring constantly, just until the pudding begins to thicken (do not let it boil), about 3 minutes.

TRANSFER the pudding to a large serving bowl or 3-quart glass or ceramic baking dish. Press plastic wrap onto the surface of the pudding to prevent a skin, cool, then refrigerate until cold.

I like to thin the pudding with milk or cream, sprinkle with a little cinnamon or nutmeg, and/or top with the almonds for a bit of crunch.

For a short while, I actually loved going to the dentist. Though we had left Manhattan for the suburbs when I was five, we didn't change dentists for a few years. So when my appointment to have a cavity filled coincided with my father's gin game night—often the case, since he played two or three times a week in those years—I usually spent the night alone with my parents in the city while my brother and sister remained home with my grandfather.

I always wore a party dress because after my filling was securely in place, we'd go out to dinner. Then my mother and I took in a movie at one of the elegant Broadway cinema houses while my father played cards. If my hair needed cutting, we would visit Larry Matthews, an all-night beauty parlor.

Seated there on a couple of telephone books as my mousey brown hair was sheared in plain Buster Brown fashion, I watched the tall showgirls and ponies (shorter versions of the former) from the Copacabana and Latin Quarter, whose hair, in those pre-punk days, ranged from midnight blue to fuchsia.

Purple was for me, I swore. Yes, as soon as I turned sixteen.

Afterward, I'd nap in the bedroom of the apartment where the gin game was played late into the night. And I'd awake to slices of thick cream cheese cake, delivered fresh from Lindy's.

Of course, our idea of heaven changes as we get older. For one thing, I no longer want purple hair. And in cheese cakes, my tastes now run not to thick, creamy velvet, but to silk chiffon. My favorite is soft and feathery-light, less dense and less sweet. Like an old-fashioned Eastern European cheese cake, this unfussy cake is made of cottage cheese enriched with sweet butter and subtly scented with vanilla.

OLD COUNTRY COTTAGE CHEESE CAKE

yield: 10 TO 12 SERVINGS

To truly savor this cake, present it at room temperature, never cold. For a Passover version, omit the cookie crumbs and substitute blanched almonds or hazelnuts, chopped very fine with a little white or brown sugar to taste. Or use crushed Passover macaroons.

3 cups large-curd cottage cheese (24 ounces)

9 tablespoons unsalted butter, plus additional for greasing the pan

Enough plain, good quality cookies, such as Pepperidge Farm Bordeaux or a buttery shortbread, to make ½ cup crumbs when ground in a blender or food processor

⅔ cup sugar

2 teaspoons vanilla extract

¼ teaspoon salt

4 large eggs, separated

HAVE all ingredients at room temperature.

SPOON the cottage cheese into a fine-mesh strainer, and let it drain over a large bowl for about 30 minutes. Meanwhile, melt the butter over low heat, then let it come to room temperature.

MAKING the cheese cake with a hot-water bath offers some protection against cracked tops and overcooked edges. If you decide to go this route, line the bottom and sides of a 9- or 9½-inch springform pan well with heavy-duty foil to make it perfectly waterproof. Generously butter the bottom and sides of the pan. Sprinkle in the cookie crumbs and shake the pan to distribute them evenly over the bottom and sides.

PREHEAT the oven to 325°F.

USING paper towels, wipe out any liquid the cottage cheese threw off into the bowl and blot up any liquid dripping from the bottom of the strainer. With the back of a spoon, press the cheese through the strainer into the bowl. Scoop the cheese back into the strainer and sieve it again into the bowl. (Much easier the second time. All this sieving breaks up the curds more thoroughly than a mixer or food processor without liquefying the cheese and ensures a smooth, nongrainy cake.) Beat the cheese on low speed until light and fluffy. Beat in ⅓ cup of the sugar, the vanilla, and salt. Beat in the yolks, one at a time, and the melted butter.

USING clean beaters, beat the egg whites in another large bowl until they form soft peaks. Continue beating, adding the remaining ⅓ cup sugar little by little, until the whites are stiff and shiny but not dry. Gently fold ¼ of the beaten whites into the cheese mixture, incorporating them completely. Add the remaining whites, lifting and folding until they are thoroughly incorporated.

SPOON the filling into the prepared pan. If using a hot-water bath, set the pan inside a larger baking pan or ovenproof skillet, and pour in enough boiling or scalding-hot tap water to come halfway up the sides of the springform pan. Place on a rack in the middle of the oven and bake the cheese cake for about 1 hour, until puffed and lightly golden. Turn off the heat, and let the cake cool in the oven with the door open for about an hour.

REMOVE from the water bath, if used. Transfer the cake in the springform pan to a rack to cool to room temperature. Cover the room temperature cake loosely with wax paper, and refrigerate for at least 12 hours, preferably 24 hours.

FOR the finest flavor and texture, serve the cheese cake at room temperature. Leave the sides on the springform pan until ready to serve.

MILKY WAY DREAMY CHEESECAKE

yield: **ABOUT 10 SERVINGS**

"From New York? I could tell. New Yorkers are so alive—you never talk about the weather!" From the moment we sat down in her dairy restaurant, the Milky Way, ebullient Leah Adler, the consummate Jewish mother, charmed and cosseted us. She steered us to homey gems like thick, oniony potato latkes spiked with jalapeños and pillowy cheese blintzes with chunky strawberry preserves.

We told her that we had come to Los Angeles with my sister Sami and niece Arielle to pick up food for the Kiddush that would follow my daughter's bat mitzvah the next day. During her senior year at Pomona College, Alex, in between writing two theses, acting in one play and translating a second, had decided to learn Hebrew and celebrate her bat mitzvah at age 21, at the school Hillel center.

Leah was visibly touched. "You must celebrate with dessert," she insisted. Dreamy Cheesecake, it was titled on the menu, and our gracious hostess assured us it was her favorite dish at the restaurant.

It seems oxymoronic to describe it as incredibly light and rich, but that is Dreamy Cheesecake. When I asked Leah for the recipe to include in this book, she sprinted to the kitchen to copy down her chef's measurements. "It's so simple, honey. Just use it—no need to give me any credit."

Then she led us beyond the dining room to tour the photos and posters from her son Steven Spielberg's movies.

The consummate Jewish mother.

This is Dreamy Cheesecake, set in an easy graham-cracker crust.

FOR THE CRUST

1⅓ cups graham cracker crumbs (swirl crushed crackers in a food processor until finely ground)

2 tablespoons packed brown sugar

4 tablespoons (½ stick) unsalted butter, melted, plus additional for greasing the pan

HAVE all the batter ingredients at room temperature. Preheat the oven to 350°F.

PREPARE the crust: in a small bowl, mix together the graham cracker crumbs, brown sugar, and melted butter, using your fingertips or a spoon. Generously butter the bottom and sides of a 10-inch springform pan. Spoon in the crumb mixture, then shake and rotate the pan to distribute it evenly over the bottom. Using your fingertips, gently press the crumbs into the bottom and about ½ inch up the sides of the pan. Unless you're sure your springform is perfectly waterproof, wrap it tightly around the outside with foil. Place the pan in the freezer for about 15 minutes to firm up the crust.

2 cups creamy small-curd cottage cheese (16 ounces)

1½ pounds cream cheese (three 8-ounce packages)

1 cup sugar

4 large eggs

½ teaspoon vanilla extract

MAKE the batter: spoon the cottage cheese into a fine-mesh strainer placed over a bowl. Rubbing and scraping with the back of a wooden spoon or rubber scraper, press the cheese through the strainer into the bowl.

IN a large bowl, beat the cream cheese with the sugar on low speed until creamy smooth. Continuing on low speed, beat in the eggs, one at a time, the vanilla, and then the cottage cheese. Beat just until the batter is satiny smooth; don't overbeat the ingredients. Mix at low speed to prevent air bubbles (the batter should not be foamy), and remember to scrape down the bowl after each addition.

SPOON the batter into the prepared pan and bake for 50 to 60 minutes, or until the cake is set around the edges, puffed and golden, but still slightly soft and quivering in the center. Turn off the heat, and let the cheese cake cool in the oven with the door open for about an hour.

PLACE the cake on a rack and cool to room temperature. Cover the room temperature cake loosely with wax paper, and refrigerate for at least 8 hours. Release the sides of the springform before serving. Best enjoyed at room temperature or lightly chilled, not icy cold.

HONEY-RICOTTA CHEESE CAKE

yield: 10 TO 12 SERVINGS

The language of God was sweet indeed to the very young boys beginning cheder (religious elementary school). On their first day of classes, little students were presented with a slate on which the Hebrew alphabet was smeared with honey. After the teacher recited the letters, the child licked them off, tasting for the first time the sweetness of learning.

This lovely custom took place in many European communities on Shavuot, which marks the time when God gave the Torah, the written word, to the Jewish people. Dating back to at least as far as the twelfth century in France, the tradition spread to Eastern Europe, where it remained popular until the nineteenth century.

This Shavuot cheese cake, sweetened with a delicate orange blossom or acacia honey, evolved from improvisations on an ancient Roman-Jewish recipe for cassola. I sometimes perfume it lightly with a little rose water to heighten the floral notes.

The lush cake is exquisite as a solo turn with tea, or serve it as a rich finish to the Shavuot dairy lunch or dinner. It's also wonderful for dairy Passover meals.

8 ounces cream cheese, softened

¼ cup sour cream

¾ cup flavorful honey (look for a light floral one, such as orange blossom or acacia)

2 teaspoons vanilla extract or rose water

¼ teaspoon salt

5 large eggs

Scant 3 cups whole-milk ricotta cheese (24 ounces)

Unsalted butter, for greasing the pan

HAVE all ingredients at room temperature. Preheat the oven to 325°F.

IN a large bowl, beat the cream cheese with the sour cream on low speed until soft and creamy. Stir in the honey, vanilla or rose water, and salt. Beat in the eggs, one at a time (see Cook's Note). Don't overbeat the ingredients—the batter should not be foamy—and remember to scrape down the bowl after each addition.

USING a rubber spatula or the back of a spoon, push the ricotta through a fine-mesh strainer into a separate large bowl. Without washing the beaters, whip the ricotta until very light and fluffy. (This double process—sieving and whipping—will lighten the ricotta and rid it of its grainy texture.) Then, with the mixer still at low speed, slowly add the egg mixture to the ricotta, beating until just incorporated.

YOU can bake the cheese cake without a hot-water bath, but I find the gentle heat of the bath offers some insurance against cracked tops and overcooked edges. Of course, you have to make the pan perfectly waterproof, so cover the bottom and sides of a 9- or 9½-inch springform pan well with heavy-duty foil. Generously butter the bottom and sides of the pan.

"How sweet are Thy words unto my palate. Yea, sweeter than honey to my mouth!"

—PSALM 119:103

POUR the batter into the prepared pan, rotating the pan a few times to settle the batter and smooth out the bubbles. Set the pan inside a large baking pan or ovenproof skillet, and pour in enough boiling or scalding-hot tap water to come halfway up the sides of the springform pan. Place on a rack in the middle of the oven and bake for about 1 hour to 1 hour and 15 minutes, or until the cheese cake is set around the edges, but still slightly soft and quivering in the center. Turn off the heat, but leave the cheese cake in the oven for about an hour with the door open, where it will continue to cook.

TAKE the pan out of the water bath, and put it on a rack to cool to room temperature. Refrigerate the cheese cake, loosely covered with wax paper, for at least 8 hours, preferably 24 hours.

SERVE the cheese cake at room temperature or cool, but not icy cold. Leave the sides on the springform pan until ready to serve.

COOK'S NOTE: When adding several eggs to a batter one at a time, mixing in each before adding another, there's no need to stop the mixer to crack each egg. Break all the eggs at the same time into a glass measuring cup with a pouring spout. Then drop each egg into the batter as needed.

CHALLAH FRENCH TOAST STUFFED WITH MANGO, GINGER-MAPLE SYRUP

yield: 4 SERVINGS

I am a pushover for the bracing heat of fresh and candied ginger. So when I first tasted maple syrup infused with ginger, brainchild of Deep Mountain Farms in Vermont, I knew I had to devise a recipe to showcase it. This French toast, with its mango filling, plays up to the syrup's fresh, sweet bite.

Maple partners well with spicy hot flavors as I learned from tasting Deep Mountain's maple candies laced with jalapeño and ginger at New York City's Union Square Greenmarket. Later I experimented so I could replicate the syrup whenever theirs was not available.

Steeping the ginger for an hour will lend the syrup a warm glow with a bit of heat; longer infusion releases deep, spicy undertones. I like to start the syrup the night before I need it, and prepare the French toast, up to the point of frying, the night before as well.

FOR THE GINGER-MAPLE SYRUP

1 cup pure maple syrup

1 tablespoon peeled and finely chopped fresh ginger

FOR THE FRENCH TOAST

1 medium-large ripe, fragrant mango

⅛ teaspoon nutmeg, preferably freshly grated

4 large eggs

½ cup heavy cream, half-and-half, or whole milk

1 teaspoon vanilla extract

3 tablespoons pure maple syrup

¼ teaspoon salt

MAKE the syrup: combine maple syrup and ginger in a glass jar and cover tightly. Let stand at least 1 hour or as long as overnight at room temperature. Strain before using.

PREPARE the French toast: working over a bowl to catch the juices, peel the mango, then cut it into small cubes. Appearance doesn't matter here—the mango will be hidden inside the challah. Stir the nutmeg into the mango, and let the flavors mingle for a few minutes.

BEAT together the eggs, cream, half-and-half, or milk, vanilla, maple syrup, and salt in a shallow bowl until smooth.

SPREAD a slice of challah with about 1 tablespoon of cream cheese (if your challah slice is very large, you may need more cream cheese). Top with one quarter of the cubed mango, then cover with a second slice of challah. Gently pat the challah sandwich together so it is neat and compact. Repeat with remaining challah, cream cheese and mango.

PLACE the stuffed challahs in a baking dish just large enough to accommodate them in one layer (I use a glass 13 by 9-inch baking dish). Pour the egg mixture over them evenly and let soak for about 10 minutes. Using a spatula, carefully turn them and allow the other side to absorb

8 slices day-old challah, cut about ½-inch thick

4 to 8 tablespoons cream cheese (2 to 4 ounces), softened

Unsalted butter, for frying

the egg mixture for 10 minutes; at this point, you can either cover the pan with foil and refrigerate until the following morning or cook them right away.

PREHEAT the oven to 400°F.

IN a 10- to 12-inch heavy skillet, fry the stuffed challahs (two at a time, so you don't crowd the pan) in sizzling butter, until golden brown on both sides. Transfer to a baking sheet and bake for 12 to 15 minutes, until the mango is hot and bubbling.

SERVE the French toast with the syrup—even better when the syrup is warmed.

COOK'S NOTE: Fresh blueberries make a marvelous substitute for the mango.

"Fresh breezes wafted scents of tropical plants and fruits for which I had no name in Yiddish."

—ISAAC BASHEVIS SINGER, "THE IMPRESARIO"

ROSEBERRY-RHUBARB GELATO

yield: ABOUT 3½ CUPS

*T*he synagogue in Pitigliano, Italy, was bursting with roses and the sweet voices of the children's chorus filled the air. It was Shavuot, June 1938, and Edda Servi Machlin, author of the evocative cookbook-memoir, The Classic Cuisine of the Italian Jews, was celebrating her bat mitzvah in a magnificent service employing the rich Pitigliano liturgy reserved for special occasions.

Persecution of Italy's Jews had already begun, yet here, as in America, ancient Hebrew traditions were still being updated for today's Jews: the bar mitzvah, once an exclusively male coming-of-age ceremony, was revised in Italy at least as far back as the 1920s to include girls.

In her book Ms. Machlin describes the simple but exquisite refreshments served at her bat mitzvah: a glass of sweet vermouth, a piece of delicate spongecake, and homemade gelato from the hand-cranked machine of the local ice cream maker.

Reading about that Shavuot celebration of long ago moved me to devise this beautiful, deep pink gelato with intense fruit flavor and a faint fragrance of rose.

You can change the proportions of fruit here, or use all strawberries or all raspberries as you prefer. Adjust the sugar as necessary—raspberries usually require more sweetening.

About 4 ½ ounces rhubarb, ends trimmed (discard leaves; they can be toxic), tough strings removed with a vegetable peeler, and stalks cut into 1-inch pieces (1 cup)

¼ cup granulated light brown sugar and about ⅔ cup granulated white sugar, or all granulated white sugar

2 cups fresh ripe strawberries (about 12 ounces), rinsed, then hulled and quartered

IN a nonreactive bowl, toss the rhubarb with the brown sugar, if using, or ¼ cup of the white sugar, and set aside to macerate for about 20 minutes, stirring from time to time.

TRANSFER the rhubarb and all the accumulated juices to a small saucepan, and cook slowly over moderate heat, stirring occasionally, until very tender, 10 to 15 minutes. Force the rhubarb with its pan liquid through a food mill or a fine-mesh strainer into a bowl, cover, and refrigerate until cold.

COMBINE the strawberries, raspberries, and the remaining ⅔ cup sugar in a food processor or blender and pulse until the fruit is reduced to a smooth puree. Taste and adjust the sugar as needed. It should not be overly sugary, but remember that freezing will mute the sweetness somewhat. Pulse again if you add more sugar. Pass the puree through the finest disk of a food mill or a fine-mesh strainer (this will trap a good many of the raspberry seeds) into a large bowl.

About 1 cup fresh ripe raspberries (about 6 ounces)

Generous pinch of salt

½ cup heavy cream, preferably not ultrapasteurized, very cold

About 1 teaspoon rose water

STIR the chilled rhubarb and salt into the pureed berries. In a separate bowl, whip the cream until it holds soft peaks. Fold it into the fruit. For an evocative floral hint, stir in the rose water. Add a little more for a deeper suggestion, tasting as you go and mentally adjusting for the slight muting of flavors that will occur with freezing.

COVER the bowl and refrigerate for at least 3 hours, until the mixture is very cold. Place in an ice cream maker and process according to the manufacturer's instructions. If the equipment offers a choice, select the slowest freezing process, which will produce a softer consistency.

OTHER SUGGESTIONS FOR SHAVUOT

*Almond Challah

*Mary's Onion Challah

*Chilled Minted Cucumber Soup

*Grilled Bass with Pomegranate-Mint Vinaigrette

*Italian-Jewish Marinated Fried Fish (*Pesce In Saor*)

*Fish in Tomato, Rhubarb, and Blood Orange Sauce

*Slow-Roasted Salmon with Green Herb Oil

*Pastrami-Style Salmon

*Oven-Fried Smoked Salmon Croquettes

*Snapper Fillets in Pistachio-Matzoh Crust

*Apricot Blintzes with Toasted Pistachios and Yogurt Cream

Any of the *Cheese Latkes

*Herbed Spinach Latkes with Feta-Yogurt Sauce

*Spinach Cheese Squares

*Israeli Salad

*Fresh Corn Kugel

*Peach Buttermilk Kugel

*Classic Noodle Kugel

*Bene Israel Rice Pudding

Any of the *Rugelach recipes

*Poppy Seed Butter Cake (Mohn Cake)

*See index for page numbers

A GLOSSARY OF USEFUL TERMS

ADAFINA *See* Dafina.

APPETIZING STORE A Jewish institution, the appetizing store is a delicatessen specializing in foods other than meat, particularly smoked and pickled fish, barrels of pickles, dried fruit, and nuts. Many of the traditional appetizing stores expanded to purvey a cornucopia of foodstuffs. Perhaps the most famous of these is New York's Zabar's, which now sells everything from herring in sour cream sauce to fresh mesclun to fine Italian prosciutto.

ASHKENAZI, ASHKENAZIM (plural) From Hebrew *Ashkenaz*, Germany. Jews from Central and Eastern Europe and their descendants.

BAR MITZVAH Religious ceremony for a thirteen-year-old boy, after which he assumes the religious responsibilities and duties required of a Jewish man.

BAT MITZVAH Religious ceremony for a twelve- or thirteen-year-old girl, after which she assumes the religious responsibilities and duties required of a Jewish woman.

BLINTZ Very thin crêpe-like pancake rolled around a filling of cheese, fruit, vegetables, or meat, then fried or baked.

BRIT MILAH Usually referred to more simply as brit. The covenant of circumcision performed on the eighth day of a Jewish boy's life.

BUBBE (also BOBBE) Yiddish for *grandmother*.

CHALLAH (also HALLAH) A soft, eggy braided white-flour bread traditionally served on Sabbath and various holidays. For holidays, challah is often formed into special shapes like ladders, doves, circles, and so on.

CHOLENT A long-simmering Ashkenazi Sabbath stew, prepared on Friday and cooked overnight in a very slow oven, usually containing a savory combination of meat, beans, grains, vegetables, and, sometimes, a dumpling.

CHUTZPAH Unmitigated effrontery; incredible audacity.

CONVERSO A Spanish or Portuguese Jew who converted to Catholicism in the late Middle Ages to avoid persecution or expulsion; many conversos continued to practice Judaism in secret.

DAFINA From the Arabic, meaning "buried," when the dish had to be buried to remain warm for the Sabbath; also called *adafina*, *t'fina*, and the Hebrew *hamin* and Moroccan *skhena*, meaning "hot," as well as several other names. A well-seasoned, long-simmering Sephardi Sabbath stew, similar to the Ashkenazi *cholent*, prepared with a complex variety of meats, legumes, grains, vegetables, and often, eggs (*huevos haminados*) and sweet fruits like dates and apricots.

DAIRY Any food containing milk or milk products (including butter and cheese), or the dishes, utensils, tablecloths, or dish towels used in preparing, serving, and eating such foods. According to kashrut, no meat or meat products, such as chicken fat, may be cooked or eaten with dairy foods. In a kosher kitchen, one set of dishes, utensils, etc., is reserved for use exclusively with dairy foods and one exclusively for meat foods.

DAYENU A Hebrew song chanted at the Passover seder.

DAY OF ATONEMENT *See* Yom Kippur.

DAYS OF AWE The ten High Holy Days, beginning with Rosh Hashanah and ending with Yom Kippur. Also known as the Days of Penitence.

DESAYUNO Ladino for breakfast. The meal eaten by Sephardim after returning home from morning synagogue services on Sabbath and festivals.

ERETZ ISRAEL The land of Israel.

FOUR QUESTIONS As part of the Passover seder, the youngest child present asks why this night is different from all other nights of the year in four ways: Why do we eat matzoh? Why do we eat bitter herbs? Why do we dip twice? Why do we recline at the table? The leader of the seder reads the answers from the Haggadah, beginning the story of the Exodus.

FRITADA Sephardi egg-based dish, similar to a frittata.

GEFILTE FISH Literally "stuffed fish." Originally, a fish stuffed with ground fish (usually freshwater varieties like carp, pike, and whitefish); bread or matzoh meal; eggs; onions; spices, etc., then poached or baked. Today the fish mixture is usually formed into patties and poached.

HAGGADAH The story of the slavery in and the Exodus from Egypt, told at the Passover seder.

HAMANTASCH, HAMANTASCHEN (plural) Three-cornered Purim cookie, usually filled with poppy seeds, dried fruits, nuts, or apricot, prune, or raspberry preserves.

HAMETZ (also CHOMETZ) Food or drink forbidden during Passover because it is prepared from grain or leaven other than ritually prepared matzoh products made from special Passover flour.

HAMIN From the Hebrew for "hot." Long-simmering Sabbath stew (*see* cholent or dafina).

HANUKKAH (also CHANUKAH) Known also as the Feast of Dedication or the Festival of Lights, this holiday celebrates the miracle of the Temple flame that burned for eight days, and the victory of the Maccabees over the Syrians, who tried to convert the Jews to Greek polytheism. It usually falls in December.

HAROSET (also CHAROSET) One of the ritual foods on the seder plate, this paste-like mixture of fruit, nuts, wine, and spices symbolizes the mortar and bricks used to build Pharaoh's cities by the Israelites during their slavery in Egypt.

HAVDALAH The Saturday sunset ceremony that concludes the Sabbath and marks the beginning of the new week. A benediction is recited over wine, fragrant spices, and a special candle.

HELZEL Stuffed poultry neck.

HIGH HOLY DAYS (also known as THE DAYS OF AWE and DAYS OF PENITENCE) Beginning with Rosh Hashanah and ending with Yom Kippur, these ten days are marked by intense self-examination and atonement. Jews believe that God decides their fate for the coming year during this period.

HUEVOS HAMINADOS Eggs simmered with the Sabbath stew or cooked separately overnight, and served by Sephardim on Sabbath and holidays and at life-cycle celebrations.

KABBALA The highly complex and esoteric main body of Jewish mysticism.

KASHA Literally any porridge, but now refers to roasted buckwheat groats. It is available whole or ground coarse, medium, or fine in most supermarkets and health food stores.

KASHRUT Jewish dietary laws that determine what is kosher (ritually fit to eat).

KIDDUSH Blessing recited over wine, sanctifying the incoming Sabbath and other special occasions.

KNAIDL, KNAIDLACH (plural) Dumpling, usually made of matzoh meal, but sometimes of potatoes or other starches.

KNISH Pastry pocket filled with meat, cheese, kasha, or potato or other vegetables, then baked or fried.

KOSHER Ritually fit to eat according to the Jewish dietary laws.

KREPL, KREPLACH (plural) Triangular or square noodle dough, usually stuffed with meat or cheese. Like wontons or ravioli, it may be boiled and served in soup or fried and eaten as a side dish or main course.

KUGEL A baked sweet or savory pudding containing eggs, usually a starch such as noodles or potatoes, and sometimes other vegetables or fruits.

LADINO (also called JUDESMO and JUDEO-SPANISH) The vernacular language spoken by Sephardim. It is based on medieval Castilian Spanish mixed with Hebrew, Arabic, Turkish, Greek, and medieval French.

LATKE Pancake, especially the potato pancakes eaten on Hanukkah.

LOKSHEN Egg noodles.

MAH NISHTANAH (HA LILAH HA ZEH) Literally "what is the difference?" Beginning words of the Four Questions asked at the Passover seder, meaning: "why is this night different?"

MAMALIGA Romanian corn meal porridge (fine or coarse meal is used, according to preference), prepared like polenta, but served with different toppings.

MAROR Bitter herb on the seder plate, symbolizing the bitterness of slavery.

MATZOH Unleavened cracker made of flour and water, eaten instead of bread on Passover.

MATZOH MEAL Finely ground matzoh.

MENORAH Originally the seven-branched candelabrum of Temple days. Today menorah usually refers to the eight-branched (nine including the *shammash*) candelabrum lit on Hanukkah, also called a hanukkiyah.

MIDRASH A highly developed approach to interpreting the sacred texts by employing exegesis, metaphor, and parable to arrive at their deeper meaning or underlying significance; also the collection of the midrashic commentaries on the sacred texts.

MIPERI HA-ERETZ In Deuteronomy 8:8, the seven choice crops with which ancient Israel was blessed: barley, dates, figs, grapes, olives, pomegranates, and wheat.

MITZVAH, MITZVOT (plural) One of 613 commandments Jews are obligated to perform; also any good deed or kind act.

MIZRACHI JEWS Jews from the Middle East (and their descendants) whose ancestors did not originate from the Iberian peninsula and, therefore, are not true Sephardim.

NOSH Yiddish, from the German *nachen*, to eat on the sly; verb, to nosh; *nasheray, nosheray*—foods to be noshed. A snack, a tidbit, a small portion.

ONGEPOTCHKEH Excessively and unattractively decorated or fussed with to the point of tackiness.

PAREVE Neutral; refers to foods made with neither meat nor milk products, that, according to Jewish dietary laws, may be eaten with either meat or dairy foods. Examples are: fish, eggs, grains, vegetables, and fruits.

PASSOVER Also known as the Festival of Freedom, this joyous spring holiday, occurring in March or April, commemorates the Exodus of the Jews from Egypt.

PHYLLO (also FILO or FILLO) Paper-thin pastry leaves used to make both sweet and savory pastries. They are available fresh in some Greek and Arabic bakeries, and widely available frozen in supermarkets.

POTCHKEH To fuss [with] something.

PURIM The exuberant holiday in February or March that celebrates the Persian Jews' triumph over Haman's plot to exterminate them, as told in the Book of Esther.

ROSH HASHANAH The Jewish New Year; the first of the High Holy Days. The annual Day of Judgment, this solemn but joyous day usually falls in September or October.

ROSL Fermented beet juice.

SABBATH (also SHABBAT and SHABBOS) The Jewish Sabbath begins at sundown on Friday and concludes at sundown on Saturday. For observant Jews, this day of rest is a joyous interlude free not only from work but also certain tasks like cooking.

SCHMALTZ Fat. Usually refers to rendered poultry fat.

SEDER The traditional home or community ceremony, including the evening meal, of Passover.

SEDER PLATE A special plate on the table at the seder containing symbolic foods connected with Passover.

SEPHARDI, SEPHARDIM (plural) From *Sepharad*, Spain in Hebrew. Jews and their descendants, expelled at the end of the fifteenth century from Spain and Portugal, who settled in Greece, the Middle East, England, Holland, the Americas, and parts of western Europe. The term is often used to refer to all Jews not of Ashkenazi background.

SHAMMASH (also SHAMMES) The sexton of a synagogue; also the extra candle used to light the other candles on a Hanukkah menorah.

SHAV Sorrel soup.

SHAVUOT Also known as the Festival of Weeks. Commemorates the covenant made between God and Israel on Mount Sinai, when Moses received the Law (Torah). Occurring in May or June, it also celebrates the arrival of the first fruits of the summer harvest.

SHEHEHEYONU (also SHEHECHEYANU and SHEKHEYONU) Name of a prayer recited over the special, joyous, noneveryday occurrences in life, such as the first day of holidays, eating the first fruits of the season at Rosh Hashanah, etc.

SHOFAR Special ram's horn blown in the synagogue on Rosh Hashanah and Yom Kippur. It is a reminder of Abraham's sacrifice, since the ram was sacrificed in place of his son Isaac.

SHTETL Village in pre-World War II Eastern Europe where most, and in some cases all, of the inhabitants were Jewish.

SIMCHAT TORAH Immediately following Sukkot come the festivals of Shemini Azeret and Simchat Torah, when the weekly readings in the Torah are completed (with the end of Deuteronomy) and then commenced again (with the beginning of Genesis). In Israel and in Reform Congregations in the Diaspora, Simchat Torah and Shemini Azeret are celebrated on the same day.

SUKKAH (also SUCCAH), SUKKOT (plural) A booth of temporary shelter erected out of doors for Sukkot. The stars must be visible through the roof and the sukkah should be decorated, typically with fruits, vegetables, flowers, and branches from the early autumn harvest. During Sukkot the family eats in the sukkah, weather permitting.

SUKKOT (also SUCCOS) Originally an autumn harvest festival of thanksgiving, this holiday, known as the Festival of Tabernacles or Feast of Booths, commemorates the period of wandering in the Sinai Desert, when the Israelites lived in booths (sukkot). Meals are eaten in the sukkah, weather permitting.

TALMUD A massive collection of writings comprising the Mishnah (commentaries, interpretations, and reinterpretations by scholars of the Torah), and the Gemara (commentaries on and interpretations of the Mishnah). The Talmud contains not just exegeses of Holy Scripture, but reflections on a huge array of subjects, such as theology, diet, ethics, jurisprudence, mythology, philosophy, medicine, and so on. Two Talmuds exist: the Jerusalem or Palestinian Talmud (completed around the fifth century CE), in which the Gemara was the work of the scholars of the Palestinian academies; and the Babylonian Talmud (finished around the sixth century CE), whose Gemara was produced by the Babylonian academicians. The influence of the Babylonian Talmud has been far greater and is the one to which most scholars refer.

TALMUDIC TIMES Period of Jewish chronological history, from about 70 to 500 CE.

TORAH Handwritten on a parchment scroll, the Torah contains the Five Books of Moses, beginning with Creation and ending with the death of Moses: Genesis, Exodus, Leviticus, Numbers, and Deuteronomy. A portion of the Torah is read in the synagogue every morning on Sabbaths, Mondays, Thursdays, the New Moon, and festivals; completing the entire Torah cycle takes one year.

TREYF Ritually unfit to eat.

TSIMMES (also TZIMMES) A sweetened, baked or stewed mixture of vegetables and fruits. It often contains meat as well.

VARENIKES Noodle dough usually filled with fruit or meat.

VARNISHKES Noodles.

YAHRZEIT The anniversary of a person's death; close family members light special memorial yahrzeit candles on that day.

YIDDISH Almost 1,000 years old, this vernacular spoken by Ashkenazi Jews of Eastern and Central Europe mainly comprises Old German but also includes elements of Hebrew, various Slavic and other Eastern European languages, French, and English. It is written in Hebrew characters.

YOM KIPPUR The day of repentance, this is the holiest day of the Jewish calendar, marked by solemn prayer and fasting. Known also as the Day of Atonement, it is the tenth and last of the High Holy Days, occurring in September or October.

ONLINE AND PHONE ORDER SOURCES AND A FEW HELPFUL WEB SITES

FOOD SOURCES

AARON'S GOURMET EMPORIUM Rego Park, NY; telephone: 718-205-1992; www.aaronsgourmet. com. Kosher fish and broad array of kosher free-range and organic meats and poultry (including duck breasts and venison), in addition to other kosher foods.

AVIGLATT.COM Online kosher supermarket.

EKOSHERSTORE.COM Search engine for locating kosher stores.

FRESHDIRECT Telephone: 866-771-5272; www.freshdirect.com; delivery to neighborhoods in NYC and metropolitan area, including parts of NJ. Mainstream supermarket service that also offers a good selection of fresh kosher meats, poultry, and fish, as well as cheeses, wines, and other kosher grocery items.

GOURMETFOODSTORE.COM Many international kosher cheeses and other kosher specialty products, like foie gras and caviar, available.

IGOURMET.COM Large selection of kosher-certified cheeses and butters, plus several other kosher specialty items.

KALUSTYANS New York, NY; telephone: 212-685-3451; www.kalustyans.com. Israeli, Middle Eastern, and other ethnic products, including a wide array of excellent spices, condiments, grains, and legumes; some items have kosher-certification, others do not.

KOSHER.COM Online kosher supermarket; many hard-to-find items such as whole-wheat and oat matzoh meals.

KOSHERDEPOT.BIZ Manufacturer and distributor of an extensive assortment of kosher-certified products.

KOSHERGOURMETMART.COM Extraordinary source of kosher-certified products from many different vendors. Lots of unusual items, including both spelt and whole-wheat shmura matzoh, diverse kosher Asian products, and foods imported from London and Paris. They do not add surcharges; prices and shipping costs match those at the vendor Web sites.

KOSHERITALIA.COM Wide variety of Italian and French cheeses and olive oil, certified kosher under Orthodox supervision.

KOSHERMANIA.COM Specializes in kosher candies and other specialty gourmet items.

MY KOSHER MARKET North Miami Beach, FL; telephone: 877-766-2686; www.mykoshermarket.com. Specializes in kosher meats and poultry, but good selection of grocery items and kosher wines as well.

RUELAFAYETTEINC.COM Kosher French gourmet products.

SOOFER FOODS www.sadaf.com. Kosher-certified pomegranate products and other Sephardi items.

VANNS SPICES Baltimore, MD; telephone: 800-583-1693; www.vannsspices.com. Extensive selection of high-quality spices and flavoring extracts.

HELPFUL WEB SITES

KASHRUT INFORMATION

Information on keeping kosher, kosher products, consumer alerts, Passover questions, etc.; some sites will answer specific questions.

WWW.KASHRUT.COM

WWW.KASHRUT.ORG

WWW.KOSHER.CO.IL

WWW.KOSHERQUEST.ORG

OTHER INFORMATION

Jewish food, holidays, culture, history, rituals, customs, and traditions, etc.

WWW.CENTROPA.ORG A wealth of fascinating materials and discussion boards on Jewish heritage, including food, culture, oral histories, photos, travel, current events, articles, and books; originally focused on Central and Eastern Europe but now extending to Turkey and the Balkans and perhaps other Sephardi communities in the future.

WWW.CHOWHOUND.COM The kosher message board on this site is a fabulous resource not only for kosher foodies, but also for all lovers of Jewish food; enter the main site, click on Boards, then click on Kosher.

WWW.CYBER-KITCHEN.COM/rfcj Discussion board covering all aspects of Jewish food, such as recipes, holiday vegan alternatives, sourcing suppliers, and cookbook reviews.

WWW.INTERFAITHFAMILY.COM While this Internet magazine is geared to encouraging interfaith families to explore Jewish life and make Jewish choices, many of its articles and discussion boards offer insights and ideas that would enhance the holiday celebrations of all Jews.

WWW.JEWISHENCYCLOPEDIA.COM Now part of the public domain, this site contains the original contents of the *Jewish Encyclopedia*, completed more than 100 years ago; although it does not cover a significant portion of modern Jewish history, it does include much that is still relevant today; as of this writing, the Internet community may be invited to help update the encyclopedia.

WWW.JEWISHFOOD-LIST.COM Recipes and other information on holiday menus, cooking techniques, reviews, etc.

WWW.JHOM.COM Online version of *Jewish Heritage* magazine.

WWW.KOSHERTODAY.COM Online newspaper geared to food professionals, but contains an array of information including resources and new products for others interested in kosher food and wine.

WWW.SHAMASH.ORG Network for Jewish information and discussions on the Internet.

SELECTED BIBLIOGRAPHY

Most of the works previously cited at the end of each quotation and in the text are not included here.

Abrahams, Israel. *Jewish Life in the Middle Ages.* New York: Meridian Books/Jewish Publications, 1958 (reprint of 1896 edition).

Agnon, Shmuel Yosef. *Days of Awe.* New York: Schocken Books, 1948.

Anisfeld, Rabbi Sharon Cohen, Tara Mohr, and Catherine Spector, editors. *The Women's Passover Companion: Women's Reflections on the Festival of Freedom.* Woodstock, Vermont: Jewish Lights Publishing, 2003.

Ausubel, Nathan. *A Treasury of Jewish Folklore.* New York: Crown, 1948.

Baron, Salo Wittmayer. *A Social and Religious History of the Jews.* 2nd Edition. New York: Columbia University Press, 1983.

Bennett, Alan D., ed. *Journey through Judaism: The Best of Keeping Posted.* New York: UAHC Press, 1991.

Brandes, Francesca. *Veneto Itinerari ebraici: I luoghi, la storia, l'arte.* Venice: Marsilio Editori, 1995.

Chiche-Yana, Martine. *La Table Juive: Recettes et traditions de fetes.* Aix-en-Provence: Edisud, 1990.

———. *La Table Juive (Tome 2): Recettes et traditions du cycle de vie.* Aix-en-Provence: Edisud, 1994.

Cooper, John. *Eat and Be Satisfied*. Northvale, New Jersey, and London: Jason Aronson, 1993.

Dobrinsky, Herbert C. *A Treasury of Sephardic Laws and Customs*. New York: Ktav Publishing, 1986.

Encyclopedia Judaica. Jerusalem: Keter Publishing, 1978.

Encyclopedia Judaica (CD-ROM Edition). Jerusalem: Judaica Multimedia, 1997.

Gaster, Theodore. *Festivals of the Jewish Year*. New York: W. Sloane Associates, 1953.

Gitlitz, David M. and Linda Kay Davidson. *A Drizzle of Honey: The Lives and Recipes of Spain's Secret Jews*. New York: St. Martin's, 1999.

Goodman, Philip. *The Purim Anthology*. Philadelphia: Jewish Publication Society of America, 1949.

———. *The Rosh Hashanah Anthology*. Philadelphia: Jewish Publication Society of America, 1992.

The Jewish Encyclopedia. New York and London: Funk and Wagnalls, 1903.

Katz, Nathan. *Who Are the Jews of India?* Berkeley: University of California Press, 2000.

Levin, Schmarya. *Childhood in Exile*. (trans. Maurice Samuel) New York: Harcourt, Brace and Co.,1929.

Root, Waverly. *Food*. New York: Simon & Schuster, 1980.

Rosten, Leo. *The Joys of Yiddish*. New York: McGraw Hill, 1960.

Rubenstein, Jeffrey L. *The History of Sukkot in the Second Temple and Rabbinic Periods*. Atlanta, Georgia: Scholars Press, 1995.

Schauss, Hayyim. *The Jewish Festivals from Their Beginnings to Our Own Day*. Cincinnati: Union of American Hebrew Congregations, 1938.

Schwartz, Oded. *In Search of Plenty: A History of Jewish Food*. London: Kyle Cathie, 1992.

Shosteck, Patti. *A Lexicon of Jewish Cooking*. Chicago: Contemporary Books, Inc., 1979.

Tigay, Alan M. *The Jewish Traveler*. Northvale, New Jersey: Jason Aronson, 1987.

Universal Jewish Encyclopedia. New York: Universal Jewish Encyclopedia, Inc., 1939/40–43.

Waskow, Arthur I. *Seasons of Our Joy: A Handbook of Jewish Festivals*. Toronto and New York: Bantam Books, 1982.

Zborowski, Mark and Elizabeth Herzog. *Life Is with People*. New York: Schocken Books, 1978.

COOKBOOKS

There are hundreds of excellent Jewish cookbooks. The following sampling combines some particularly interesting recent titles with personal favorites, covering both familiar and less well-known cuisines.

Angel, Gilda. *Sephardic Holiday Cooking*. Mount Vernon, New York: Decalogue Books, 1986.

AvRutick, Frances R. *The Complete Passover Cookbook*. Middle Village, New York: Jonathan David Publishers, 1981.

Ascoli Vitali-Norsa, Giuliana, ed. *La cucina nella tradizione ebraica*. 2nd edition. Padua: Edizione dell'Adei Wizo, 1979.

Benbassa, Esther. *Cuisine judeo-espagnole*. Paris: Editions du Scribe, 1984.

Engle, Fannie and Gertrude Blair. *The Jewish Festival Cookbook*. New York: David McKay Company, 1954.

Fischer, Leah Loeb with Maria Polushkin Robbins. *Mama Leah's Jewish Kitchen*. New York: Macmillan, 1990.

Goldman, Marcy. *A Treasury of Jewish Holiday Baking*. New York: Doubleday, 1998.

Goodman, Hanna. *Jewish Cooking Around the World*. Philadelphia: Jewish Publication Society of America, 1973.

Greenberg, Betty D. and Althea O. Silverman. *The Jewish Home Beautiful*. New York: The National Women's League of the United Synagogues of America, 1941.

Koronyo, Viki and Sima Ovadya. *Sefarad Yemekleri*. Istanbul. Published for Society of Assistance to Old People, 1990.

Levy, Esther. *Jewish Cookery Book*. Philadelphia: W. S. Turner, 1871. [Facsimile edition published by Pholiota Press, Inc., 1982.]

Levy, Faye. *1,000 Jewish Recipes*. Foster City, California: IDG Books, 2000.

———. *Faye Levy's International Jewish Cookbook*. New York: Warner Books, 1991.

Liebman, Malvina W. *Jewish Cookery from Boston to Baghdad*. Miami: E. A. Seemann Publishing, 1975.

Machlin, Edda Servi. *The Classic Cuisine of the Italian Jews*. Croton-on-Hudson, New York: Giro Press, 1981.

———. *The Classic Cuisine of the Italian Jews II*. Croton-on-Hudson, New York: Giro Press, 1992.

Marks, Copeland. *Sephardic Cooking*. New York: Donald I. Fine, 1992.

Marks, Gil. *The World of Jewish Cooking*. New York: Simon & Schuster, 1996.

Nathan, Joan. *The Jewish Holiday Kitchen*. New York: Schocken Books, 1988.

———. *Jewish Cooking in America*. New York: Alfred A. Knopf, 1994.

Roden, Claudia. *The Book of Jewish Food*. New York: Alfred A. Knopf, 1996.

Roukhomovsky, Suzanne. *Gastronomie juive et patisserie de Russie, d'Alsace, de Roumanie et d'Orient*. Paris: Flammarion, 1968.

Sheraton, Mimi. *From My Mother's Kitchen*. New York: Harper and Row, 1979.

Stavroulakis, Nicholas. *Cookbook of the Jews of Greece*. Port Jefferson, New York: Cadmus Press, 1986.

Sternberg, Robert. *The Sephardic Kitchen*. New York: HarperCollins, 1996.

———. *Yiddish Cuisine: A Gourmet's Approach to Jewish Cooking*. Northvale, New Jersey: Jason Aronson, 1993.

INDEX